SURVIVING CANADA

SURVIVING CANADA
INDIGENOUS PEOPLES CELEBRATE 150 YEARS OF BETRAYAL

Edited by Kiera L. Ladner and Myra J. Tait

ARP Books | Winnipeg

Copyright © 2017 Kiera L. Ladner and Myra J. Tait

ARP Books (Arbeiter Ring Publishing)
205-70 Arthur Street
Winnipeg, Manitoba
Treaty 1 Territory and Historic Métis Nation Homeland
Canada R3B 1G7
arpbooks.org

Cover design by Sébastien Aubin
Interior design and layout by Relish New Brand Experience
Printed and bound in Canada by Friesens on paper made from 100% recycled post-consumer waste.
Second printing, November 2017

COPYRIGHT NOTICE
This book is fully protected under the copyright laws of Canada and all other countries of the Copyright Union and is subject to royalty.
My Country 'tis of Thy People You're Dying © Buffy Sainte-Marie

ARP Books acknowledges the generous support of the Manitoba Arts Council and the Canada Council for the Arts for our publishing program. We acknowledge the financial support of the Government of Canada through the Canada Book Fund and the Province of Manitoba through the Book Publishing Tax Credit and the Book Publisher Marketing Assistance Program of Manitoba Culture, Heritage, and Tourism.

LIBRARY AND ARCHIVES CANADA CATALOGUING IN PUBLICATION

Surviving Canada : indigenous peoples celebrate 150 years of betrayal / editors, Kiera L. Ladner, Myra Tait.

ISBN 978-1-894037-89-1 (softcover).—ISBN 978-1-927886-01-4 (epub)

1. Native peoples--Canada--Social conditions. 2. Native peoples--Canada--Government relations. 3. Canada--Race relations. 4. Native peoples--Canada. I. Ladner, Kiera L., 1971-, editor II. Tait, Myra, editor

E78.C2S915 2017   971.004'97   C2017-901212-6

Table Of Contents

Surviving Canada: Indigenous Peoples Celebrate 150 Years of Betrayal 9
    Kiera L. Ladner and Myra J. Tait

Acknowlegements 15

Nokomis and the Law in the Gift: Living Treaty Each Day 17
    Aaron Mills

Reconcile Your State of Mind 28
    Rebecca Thomas

Don't Read the Comments: The Role of Modern News Media in Bridging the Divide Between Indigenous and Non-Indigenous People in Canada 30
    Waubgeshig Rice

Canada is a Pretend Nation: REDx Talks—What I Know Now About Canada 36
    Leroy Little Bear

Anthem 43
    Erin Freeland

Inclusion is Just the Canadian Word for Assimilation: Self-Determination and the Reconciliation Paradigm in Canada 49
    Rachel Yacaaʔał George

The Path to Self-Determination 63
    Natan Obed

Can Canada Retrieve the Principles of its First Confederation? 77
    Peter H. Russell

Celebrating Canada's 150th Birthday: A Play in One Act 92
    Stephanie Irlbacher-Fox

Kapyong and Treaty One First Nations: When the Crown Can Do No Wrong 102
    Myra J. Tait

Canada, I can cite for you 150 129
    Christie Belcourt

"To Honour the Lives of Those Taken From Us": Restor(y)ing Resurgence and Survivance through Walking With Our Sisters 131
    Shalene Jobin and Tara Kappo

Lament for Confederation *149*
    Dan George

Language Rights as Aboriginal Rights: From Words to Action *151*
    Karen Drake

Canada's History Goes Beyond 150 Years *157*
    Doug Cuthand

Forgetting to Celebrate: Genocide and Social Amnesia as Foundational
    to the Canadian Settler State *159*
    David B. MacDonald

Kahwá:tsire: Canada 150 Through The Lens of Mohawk Motherhood *181*
    Kahente Horn-Miller and Waneek Horn-Miller

Canada: Portrait of a Serial Killer *193*
    Jeff Corntassel and Christine Bird

Her *210*
    Jana-Rae Yerxa

Because It's 1951: The Non-History of First Nations Female Band Suffrage
    and Leadership *215*
    Mary Jane Logan McCallum and Shelisa Klassen

My Country 'tis of Thy People You're Dying *236*
    Buffy Sainte-Marie

Reconciliation on Trial: Evaluating What Reconciliation Means in
    the Context of Aboriginal Justice *238*
    David Milward

Got Tolerance? *256*
    Felicia Sinclair

Drinking Dispossession: Shoal Lake 40, Winnipeg, and the Making of Canada *261*
    Adele Perry

Refusing Canada *274*
    Eric Ritskes

O Canada: "A country cannot be built on a living lie." *277*
    James (Sa'ke'j) Youngblood Henderson

It's Not Your Fault *290*
    Raven Davis

Unfinished Business: Bringing the Métis into Confederation *294*
    Janique Dubois and Kelly Saunders

By Any Means Necessary: Canada 150—No Reason To Celebrate
    as an Onkwehón:we Peoples *304*
    Ellen Gabriel

Canada's Three Sovereignties and the Hope of Indigenous-Led Populism *308*
    Jobb Arnold

Magic Anniversary Syndrome *332*
    Ravi de Costa

CANADA PROBLEM *344*
    Robert Jago

Building Relations: Confederation Treaties and Settler Obligations Today *351*
    Michael Asch

Let's Talk Treaty *372*
    Rob Houle

The Natives Are Restless: Indigenous Epistemic Disobedience and Thinking Ourselves Free *377*
    Hayden King and Erica Violet Lee

Letter to the Minister *386*
    Kurtis Schmitz

Encountering Memories on the Restigouche River *389*
    Fred Metallic and Amy Chamberlin

150 Years and Waiting: Will Canada Become an Honourable Nation? *398*
    Kiera L. Ladner

WE WILL HELP EACH OTHER BE GREAT AND GOOD *414*
    Louise Mandell

The Case of Invisible Racism & Disappearing Patriarchy *436*
    Helen Knott

Adopting and Implementing the United Nations Declaration on the Rights of Indigenous Peoples: Canada's Existential Crisis *440*
    Sheryl R. Lightfoot

Indigenous People Are Not the "Ghosts of History": By honouring treaties and the rights they bestow, Canada can go a long way toward restoring pride, respect, and dignity to Indigenous people *460*
    Leonard Flett with Nicole Letourneau

Editors and Contributors *463*

Surviving Canada
Indigenous Peoples Celebrate 150 Years of Betrayal

Kiera L. Ladner & Myra J. Tait

Confederation—the grand event that we are called to "celebrate" in 2017. But what, exactly, are we celebrating? Canada 150 commemorates the "founding" of Canada in 1867, being the political agreement that resulted in the union of "two founding nations"; This initial union of four provinces began the vision of creating a federal nation-state, that would eventually effect dominion over the northern part of North America.

Today, what is lacking in this myopic vision is space for a response from the peoples of this land, and moreover, a passionate response from those people who believe Canada can and must do better. In the chapters that follow, our contributors have set out a challenge. This is not a history lesson for the faint of heart, for this book is a challenge that requires a response—*your* response. Any reader expecting reminiscences from the era of the romantic "stoic Indian"—we direct you to the fiction section of your nearest bookstore. What follows is a call for Canadians to roll up their sleeves (not just the rim), consider whose land they occupy (not just sing about "our native land"), and understand that those cherished symbols of Canadian identity were embossed on to nations that were already here.

From the outset, Indigenous peoples were completely excluded from the meetings that led to the creation of Canada. As well, given that Indigenous peoples were assumed to be 'a dying race'—through eradication or assimilation by agencies such as residential schools—the only real concern of John A. MacDonald, George Brown, George-Étienne Cartier, *et al.* at the conferences in Charlottetown, Québec City, and London, England was how to implement the control and removal of Indigenous peoples from their lands, and to oversee their termination.

Truly, the only real thought Indigenous peoples were given was the small matter of which level of government—federal or provincial—would hold jurisdiction over Indigenous peoples and their lands, until, of course it was no longer relevant.

Despite considerable effort and resources directed toward the goal of emptying the land, Indigenous peoples did not die off.

In 1989, Georges Erasmus, then the Grand Chief of the Assembly of First Nations, asked this question. He participated in a committee convened by the federal government to advise on how Canada should mark both its 125th "birthday" and the 500th anniversary of the crossing of Columbus.

Erasmus used these events to question assumptions about Canada's history of injustice to Indigenous peoples.

With an impassioned, rhythmic refrain—occasionally angry—Erasmus asked the country, "What are we going to celebrate?" His answer was poignant , saying there is nothing to celebrate for Indigenous people in Canadian nationhood — unless one wants to celebrate the death of languages, an unemployment rate of 90%, a seemingly endless string of unfulfilled treaties and land negotiations, or simply the lack of basic human rights and opportunities for Indigenous peoples.[2]

Erasmus was prescient, too, noting that Canada's "French/English problem" wouldn't be *the problem* unless Indigenous peoples' concerns were taken seriously. Only a few months later, the resistance at Kanehsatà:ke—aka "The Oka Crisis"—began.

Although he believed Canada could do better and serve as an example to the world, Erasmus nonetheless concluded that, "I don't think that we have a solitary thing [to celebrate] unless we are going to do something different in the future."[3] Sadly, things are not so different today in 'Indian country', as many of the articles and stories included herein attest. The situation has actually worsened on most reserves, and for many communities, at least 50 per cent of their members live in cities, separated from their land and sometimes alienated from their culture. Thus, we find ourselves echoing Erasmus' call to action, "It's really time that the European people and their decedents, and the rest that are here—that are now Canadians—seriously begin to address the basic relationship that they have with this land and the people that were here first."[4] The Government of Canada has constructed Canada 150 as one that celebrates the 'Canadian experience' in a manner that dodges divisive political, cultural, and linguistic issues. The greatest shortcoming of this celebration of the Canadian experience and the Canadian landscape is that it seeks to render invisible Indigenous peoples and settler colonialism. Indigenous nations are not an ethnic group in the celebrated Canadian mosaic. The mere idea of the true North "strong and free," or of Canada's dominion from sea to sea to sea, only further entrenches over 150 years of dispossession and alienation. Thus this year—even more than usual—for the state, and for most Canadians, Indigenous peoples create an inconvenience by "raining on the year-long Canada parade," instead of vanishing into some distant past, while showing thanks for all they are given.

In concert with the assumed and acceptable message of 150 years of successful statehood, many educators, politicians, and organizations are participating in the celebrations, but are doing so without a sober reflection on the events of Canada's history. These invisible histories—the ones that mar Canada's cheery self-image of being a peace-loving, just, and fair people—are not simply events from the past, but are conditions that continue to shape realities for many Indigenous peoples. This volume is our attempt to render visible the indigenous experience of Confederation.

The title, *Surviving Canada: Indigenous Peoples Celebrate 150 Years of Betrayal*, was chosen to reflect the perceptions of many Indigenous peoples in Canada today. Since before Confederation, Indigenous people have continued to simultaneously survive and celebrate Canada. This is our land and it is the lifeblood of Indigenous nations; how could we not cherish these homelands? Yet, as the contributions in this volume attest, the relationships to both land and those who have "settled" Canada are marred by loss of the former and betrayal of the latter.

Thus, our vision became to produce a book that will have general appeal to community and academic audiences alike. As an anti-colonial text, we aim to challenge the normative discourse concerning the legitimacy of the Canadian state, and stimulate discussion regarding the resurgence of Indigenous Nations and rebuilding communities, both urban and 'on-reserve.' It shouldn't come as a surprise that Indigenous peoples and their allies would have something to say back to Canada about its celebrations. People have been speaking since newcomers all arrived on the coasts, lost and hungry. Unlike the popular narrative of Indigenous acquiescence, our resistance is real. Writing for a unanimous court in 2014, the Chief Justice of the Supreme Court of Canada, Beverley McLachlin, perpetuated the myth of Indigenous acquiescence: "I would note that Ontario has exercised the power to take up lands for a period of over 100 years, without any objection by the Ojibway".[5] The Supreme Court's suggestion that the Anishinaabe of Grassy Narrows have remained silent since the signing of Treaty No. 3 in 1873 resonates with insult and error. Indigenous peoples have never been silent or idle when it comes to the relationship with the Crown and settlers on our land. If it seems this way, it is perhaps because the Crown has failed to listen or simply chose to ignore Indigenous voices.

Accordingly, this work represents an attempt to educate, challenge, and inspire both settler Canadians and Indigenous people, the learned and the ignorant, and in particular, our youth. Many Indigenous nations and regions from across Canada are represented, in an attempt to make space for different perspectives. We acknowledge that some voices are missing, in part because there simply wasn't time or pages to include everyone; and in part because we truly wanted to capture a diversity of voices, including some newer ones. Others may be missing due to our oversight or because they are already fully engaged in a struggle against the state, and were unable to add one more task to their busy lives.

Whether you read from cover to cover, or simply turn to the pieces that catch your attention, you will hear over and over again the wrongs done to Indigenous peoples, and the generational trauma they continue to experience. These experiences are not only history, dredged up from the past. For many, these stories and essays speak of the ongoing reality of the loss of identity, the continued destruction of language, the generational impact of Indian Residential Schools, and overt, systemic, and systematic racism—which are within living memory, if not part of daily experience. You will notice threads of repeated themes: dispossession of land, political and judicial violence, the importance of Indigenous language and law, Canada's obsession with denial, and our hope for better days. The central message in every essay, poem, story, or visual art is that these are not "Indian" problems—these problems belong to Canada. This book is a call to all Canadians to do better.

This call to do better has inspired us to bring this collection together. We need to be mindful of past and present, and to build something for future generations. For us, Canada 150 represents an opportunity to share some stories of this land and of the peoples from this land. It is also an opportunity for all peoples to come to terms with what it means to live together on the Indigenous lands we call Canada. To live together in a way that honours the treaties, and to figure out a way to live together in a manner that is mutually agreeable and mutually beneficial for all. Thus, as one reads this book we hope that people will keep in mind Erasmus' call to action and what it means for them, for their community and for Canada. We ask that as you read, consider how your own individual acts of decolonization, transformative and meaningful reconciliation and resistance can make Canada better.. We all have something to do.

Shortly after being elected Mayor of Calgary, Naheed Nenshi challenged Calgarians to do "Three Things for Calgary".[6] His asked each citizen to think about three things that would make their street, neighbourhood, or city better, and then, simply, do those things. Mayor Nenshi said if every Calgarian accepted the challenge there would be "more than 3 million actions making Calgary an even better city. Amazing."[7]

Mayor Nenshi has reissued his challenge. This time he asked each Canadian to think about three things they could do for Canada, to make Canada a better nation.[8] Inspired by that, the 3 Things for Canada campaign was launched. It asks for acts of community service, large or small. Just imagine if every Canadian took up that challenge with an action that supports the concerns and ideals expressed in an essay, an article, or a story in this book. Imagine the improvement that could be made in the lives of Indigenous peoples and in transforming the relationship between Canada and Indigenous nations.

As Thomas King said in his 2003 Massey Lecture, "Don't say in years to come that you would have lived your life differently if only you had heard this story. You've heard it now."[9]

1. CBC Digital Archives, 1989, "Georges Erasmus: Nothing to Celebrate", online: www.cbc.ca/archives/entry/georges-erasmus-nothing-to-celebrate.
2. CBC Digital Archives, 1989, "Georges Erasmus: Nothing to Celebrate", online: www.cbc.ca/archives/entry/georges-erasmus-nothing-to-celebrate.
3. CBC Digital Archives, 1989, "Georges Erasmus: Nothing to Celebrate", online: www.cbc.ca/archives/entry/georges-erasmus-nothing-to-celebrate.
4. CBC Digital Archives, 1989, "Georges Erasmus: Nothing to Celebrate", online: www.cbc.ca/archives/entry/georges-erasmus-nothing-to-celebrate.
5. *Grassy Narrows First Nation v Ontario (Natural Resources)*, [2014] 2 SCR 48, para 40.
6. City of Calgary, 2017, "3 things for Calgary", online: www.3thingsforcalgary.ca.
7. City of Calgary, 2017, "3 things for Calgary", online: www.3thingsforcalgary.ca.
8. http://www.threethingsforcanada.ca
9. CBC Radio Ideas, 2003, "The 2003 CBC Massey Lectures, "The Truth about Stories: A Native Narrative"", www.cbc.ca/radio/ideas/the-2003-cbc-massey-lectures-the-truth-about-stories-a-native-narrative-1.2946870.

Acknowledgements

Several years ago, Myra and I were discussing what we might do to commemorate Canada 150. I recall her suggesting that we host a conference or a series of events through Mamawipawin—the research space that we run at the University of Manitoba. Whilst I agreed wholeheartedly, my commitment was anything but stellar. Had it not been for Myra's vision, persistence and commitment to this project, it would not exist. After numerous conversations and several bottles of wine, we settled on a book—in large part because we had not heard of any Indigenous-based initiatives responding to Canada 150, and we were already growing weary of the celebratory talk that was sweeping the nation. By the time we got down to work we had about 14 months before the projected release date. Surprisingly, this wasn't a problem, due to the amazing people at ARP Books, and the fantastic group of scholars, activists, artists, youth and community leaders who became involved. Despite the short timeframe, the response to our initial call-out in March 2016 was tremendous. So many people seemed to share Myra's vision and enthusiasm.

It has been our privilege to read such passionate and articulate work. Thank you to every contributor—you've poured heart and soul into your work, and it shows. Our contributors are academics, artists, politicians, activists, and "ordinary people" who have been supporting the resistance that has continued uninterrupted, since settlers first began to overstep their place. We are encouraged by the compassion and commitment of our allies, who rather than replacing Indigenous voices, continue to uphold our people and concerns, and speak back to their own peers. We see such potential for this volume to be read and enjoyed by those who are truly brave and free, and to provide an accessible and meaningful perspective to young learners of all ages and curious allies who want to do better. As the former Canada Research Chair in Indigenous Politics and Governance, Kiera extends special thanks to the CRC Program, which provided support for the production of this book. We further wish to acknowledge Todd Besant of ARP Books, our ever-patient executive editor, without whom this book would not have happened, and the staff and editorial collective at ARP—especially Esyllt Jones. Thank you to Meagan Cloutier for your assistance.

To all of our readers, thank you for daring to envision Canada as a better place for all. We welcome your feedback and inquiries by email to: Mamawipawin@gmail.com.

thank you	oujannamiik	háw'aa
ᑭᓇᓈᐢᑯᒥᑎᐣ (kinanâskomitin)	masi cho	merci
miigwech	ish nish	maarsii
ᐅᔭᓇᐃᓂ (ouyanainni)	hai, hai	wela'lioq

Nokomis and the Law in the Gift
Living Treaty Each Day

Aaron Mills

As I thought about what I might contribute to a volume reflecting on Canada's 150th anniversary, my mind turned to the many conversations I've had with *nokomis*[1], Bessie Mainville. On August 19, 2013, I was sitting in my usual seat at her kitchen table. Nokomis shared teachings about the importance of *Anishinaabemowin* (the Anishinaabe language) in understanding Anishinaabe law, and our clan system. After discussing such topics, we reflected generally on our time together. Although our efforts are rewarding and fun, they can also be very hard work. There are lots of good reasons for this, but chief among them is how nokomis is unfairly taxed by having to express herself in English, her second language, owing to my fairly basic understanding of Anishinaabemowin. This being the case, I wanted to better understand what her commitment to sharing with me is all about.

The first thing she said was, "I can honestly say that's the purpose of my visits with you. We need to come up with . . . I want them (settler people) to understand a way of life."[2] This statement draws together two commitments that have proven deep-rooted. The first regards nokomis's teaching that Anishinaabe law exists as a way of life.[3] A few moments later, she added, "I guess what I really want to pay attention to is how the government broke our law of living."[4]

Sitting in the same two seats on a similar day the following summer, nokomis said about our elders that "when they say 'a way of life,'" these are *laws*, and she heavily emphasized this last word.[5] About a year later, from the other end of my phone, nokomis once more expressed that "when we talk about the ways, those are our laws. Those are the laws, we just don't call them that."[6]

The second commitment I hear expressed in that first statement is the importance of sharing our lifeway and the kind of law it generates with settler society, so that we might be better understood and thus, ultimately, so that we can all have a better relationship. Nokomis has often reiterated this desire. In one of her most direct formulations, she said that she wants our law explained to the "lawkeepers of the Canadian government," because "they need to know how we feel and how important it is that we get along well."[7]

I've had the benefit of many influences and gifted teachers throughout my journey learning Anishinaabe law, but nokomis has had by far the greatest impact on me, and I've deeply internalized both of her commitments in my own understanding. It's fair to say they do significant work in driving my doctoral project. It sure didn't happen immediately though. It took me two years to understand that when nokomis is explaining responsibilities associated with different kinds of relationships, or when she's explaining ceremonies we do at different points in an individual's or in a community's life, she's explaining our law.

Wrapping my mind around the notion of law as a particular way of living (not to mention struggling to appreciate the logic that animates such a view!) hasn't been an easy thing.[8] But living it has often proved much harder still.

As mentioned, I've had many other Anishinaabe law teachers, some for many years. For a long time I felt considerable strain in my relationship with one of them.[9] He has quite a traditional approach to teaching, and since we aren't family, this meant that our relationship was slow to build, as of course was his willingness to share. But I visited often, and as years rolled by he shared a great deal about many things. Then one fall, things started to change. It was unmistakeable. Both the tone and subject of our conversations transformed and I felt lost. I grieved the shifting connection and at times found the new relationship extremely difficult. I tried my best with each visit, which often meant spending quite a bit of time preparing myself. A year into this, something was said one afternoon, something that shared much more and travelled further than bare words intended. At once I realized what had happened and why my teacher's attitude had changed so much, and I struggled not to cry in front of him. I wanted to hold him and I was so shamed by my former anger.

I hadn't done anything wrong that resulted in the changed relationship, and yet I was still the problem. My teacher's needs had changed and I'd failed to notice. His new needs called for different gifts: I had new responsibilities and I'd been failing to meet them. Now, instead of learning our law in the way I'd grown accustomed, I was being called on much more directly, to live it. Today, the tone and subjects of our conversations remain roughly the same, but this no longer oppresses me. Now as I make the drive out to my teacher's home, I'm free. I have the window down, the music up, and all the patience in the world.

Here's another story about the living of Anishinaabe law being much harder than the understanding of it. Last weekend I participated in a walk for Missing and Murdered Indigenous Women in Fort Frances, five minutes from my reserve. When I showed up, my chief gave me the responsibility of being our community's flag carrier. This meant that I walked at the front with the other flag carriers, just behind the drum. I had an excellent view of the police officer driving the lead car, and also of the two officers on foot, directing traffic impacted by our march. On multiple occasions, we marchers were forced to a standstill as one of the police officers allowed a truck to squeak through, before its access was blocked off. By the fourth time this had happened I'd moved from surprised, to irritated, to angry. The whole *point* was to be present for those who are not; to be seen and noticed, and that means that others *should* be inconvenienced. It's not asking too much for them to be held up long enough to notice. To me, the police privileging the momentary inconvenience of local traffic over the uninterrupted march was an instance of the very colonialism we were marching against. I was livid. As he neared, I was about to direct one officer to do his job and to communicate to the others to do so too, but he suddenly turned and was then farther than I could communicate without yelling, and I didn't want to yell. So I let it go.

Am I ever glad I let it go.

When we'd returned to our starting point and finished the walk, all the chiefs and elders present (all of them Anishinaabe) made a point of shaking the hands of each police officer, and I heard several of them thanking the police for having done a good job.

Clearly, I still have work to do.

If it's this hard for me, I can imagine that conducting oneself in accordance with an Indigenous legal order must be overwhelming for most settlers. But I don't see how we can have a good relationship until settlers understand and live within Indigenous systems of law. Why should the system of law of only settler society govern our relationship? How can such a reality possibly be justified? It's not like Indigenous peoples are a minority group who've established a presence here post-Confederation and are now asking Canada to allow us the practice of our own systems of law, against the expectations of the masses. We were already here living within our own constitutional orders and the systems of law they sustain. Much to the contrary, it seems to me that Canada must articulate how it's sovereignty can be justified against the reality of already-existing Indigenous constitutional orders that exhausted all of the jurisdictional space on Turtle Island.[15]

Until this has happened, I suggest that Canada has no option but to acknowledge *settler supremacy* as a foundational constitutional principle.[11]

I know there are many Canadians for whom settler supremacy is a good enough justification for Canadian sovereignty, and more personally, for their individual belonging to a political community. None of them are reading this.

I also know that there are many Canadians who yearn to belong without having to predicate their belonging on violence, who care deeply about Indigenous oppression, who care deeply about the disgusting material inequality the Canadian political status quo not only accepts but actively maintains, who are moved to action and do their best, or who are moved to action but don't know how to get started. The rest of my remarks are offered to you.

A common and easily accomplished suggestion nowadays for settlers wanting to be accountable is to make space for Indigenous voices in almost all that you do. There's a whole politics built up around this idea that ranges from protocols of territorial and treaty acknowledgment, to practices of allying and supporting, centring Indigenous presence, understanding one's status as a colonial beneficiary, and simply ensuring that one always speaks with, never for. In attending so dutifully to unequal power relations that we all need to be conscious of, this politics has generally done a lot of good. But I also think that for the kind of relationship nokomis and I have in mind, simply making space for Indigenous voices is woefully inadequate. Beyond making space for our voices, I want you to live as if what we say matters. As discomforting and perhaps overwhelming as this reality may be, the fact that our political communities, and thus our systems of law, were here before Canada matters not only for how we live our lives but also for how you live yours.

So long as your home is on colonized Indigenous lands (and there's nowhere on Turtle Island where this isn't the case), I want you to respect—and that means live by—Indigenous legalities as they exist within Indigenous constitutional orders. I'm not expecting that you already know how to do this, and even as you learn, I'm not expecting you'll get it right. Given where our relationship is at, what your government has decided not to teach you about it—and has not expected from you within it—your total lack of understanding of our law is the very thing to be expected. I want you to want to learn, to care passionately, and to risk the vulnerability necessary in trying your hardest. I want you to persist even though some of us will judge and sneer, because after 150 years (and in light of the Truth and Reconciliation Commission's Final Report[12]), you've accepted responsibility for understanding where the hurt that causes such behaviours comes from, and you account for that knowledge as you endure these negative experiences. I want you to pursue an understanding of the law of the Indigenous peoples whose territory you now call home as if not only your legitimacy but also your life depended on it, because for many Indigenous persons, it does. I want you to have no expectations of your government to do even a minute's worth of any of this for you; I want you to take up responsibility for our relationship personally. I want you to have a hunger so great to learn who we are and how our law works that Indigenous communities are buoyed by it. Given Canada's 150 years of failure, I want to see what we can do together without giving Canada (in the sense of its institutions and processes of government) any role at all: I want to see how you choose to exercise and organize the power-in-people you've always had, to build a home on our lands, through our law, in a good way.

Finally, if you do want to, and indeed will, pursue this transformative change in our relationship, I want—again, without expecting—for the Indigenous peoples who pre-existed and who survive despite Canada to support you in your learning. Because although this learning is your responsibility, you'll need help. I hope that despite the rage, hopelessness, and indifference that attend 150 years of the formal settler supremacy you've tolerated until now, Indigenous peoples choose not to give up on you. If you're willing to exert this much effort, I hope we'll step up and honour it. All of this taken together, I want us to be treaty people: treaty is how your presence can be legitimized within our Indigenous systems of law, and all of us can lead healthy lives and enjoy belonging that doesn't depend on violence.[13]

I certainly realize that my hopes will not be well received by all. There will be settlers who reject this view, saying, "that's an awful lot of want," perceiving it as a gross imposition. Despite the irony of settlers reacting to the idea of a gross imposition, such a perspective makes the error of presuming the legitimacy of settler autonomy, when this is the very thing not just cast in doubt but outright rejected (that is, it is their autonomy that settlers holding this view feel is imposed upon). In other words, you can't feel slighted by my desire to have you live within the law of the Indigenous peoples, whose territory you call home, if even you can't tell me why your own legal order should stand at all, much less stand alone.

Similarly, there will be Indigenous peoples who reject this vision. Some will reject the notion of treaty, but I think a misapprehension as to what I mean by "treaty" is a full answer to this complaint. I, too, reject the notion of treaty-as-contract (significantly, in which land and jurisdictional cessions are said to be made)—but I have yet to encounter a Turtle Island Indigenous people who don't engage with other Indigenous peoples through particular relational frameworks worked out between them. This is my understanding, that treaty is a relationship.

Others will reject this vision on the grounds that it gives settlers too easy an out. There must be a firm accounting made for all that has been taken from us, and for all that we've suffered. First, I worry that the strict restitution approach invokes the anti-relational logic represented by treaty-as-contract, and thus for remedy invokes the legality of our colonizer. But more practically, I think that if one understands the magnitude of the implications flowing from a relationship in which settler peoples live under Indigenous law, the claim of "easy out" is simply wrong. While redistribution of land and material welfare might not occur *as ends in themselves*, they would nonetheless *necessarily* follow from our relationship as treaty partners, and moreover—and this is the critical bit—we won't have to bargain for this result. Under a treaty-as-relationship constitutional arrangement, settlers will *want* to do so. Since our connection isn't a contract, neither of us is looking to get as much as possible from the other side, while giving as little as possible ourselves. Relationships aren't zero-sum. On the contrary, we hold each other up. Now, why do we do so? Not so long ago, nokomis said to me, "we need to be friends with the non-natives and the non-natives need to be friends with us, because we need one another to live our lives."[14]

There's a lot said in that statement. There's a powerful word in Anishinaabemowin that grounds this vision of treaty and this entire discussion: *miinigowiziwin*. Anishinaabe elders from Manitoba say, "[m]iinigowiziwin covers all of the gifts given by Creator. This includes land, culture, language, values, teachings and history,"[15] and "[t]he First Nations in Manitoba have a unique understanding of the world that is based on the concept of giftedness—*miinigoowiziwin*. Our people know that an individual is in the right place, in the right time, for the right reason, and that he or she is gifted with purpose. You are taught how to use these gifts by the Creator over time."[16] Nokomis adds that miinigowiziwin means, "we have been given all the gifts that we need for life."[17] In fact, when I ask nokomis about Anishinaabe law and she replies that it's *a way of life*, she explains herself through sharing one or two of the gifts we were given. A few examples from over the years include teachings on the gift of dreams and visions, clans, different drums, myriad ceremonies, legends, our language, medicine power to heal, and being an effective speaker. It's why sometimes she opens our meetings with her pipe.

But there's a wrinkle. As individuals, none of us has all of the gifts necessary for a good life, *minobimaadiziwin*; each of us depends on the gifts of others.

This is true not just of the sacred gifts like those mentioned above, which regard Anishinaabe *inaadiziwin*—our way of life—but also of the more mundane gifts the average day calls upon: sacrifice, care, labour, knowledge, skills, and abilities, in which some of us are much more proficient than others. Therefore it's *necessary*, for creation to continue, that different kinds of beings (including different human societies) vary as much as we do. Without our differences, we'd all have the same gifts to offer and thus we'd all have unmet need: none of us would be free. *Gete-Anishinaabe* Ken Courchene says: "look at how we sat in a circle. All differently. We got to sit in this way. Everyone is different and yet equal. And we always had that belief, that difference is not to segregate someone is higher or lower. To acknowledge the will and the way of the Creator that we're not all made the same way, there were differences."[18] Treaty is a relationship in which distinct peoples manifest this understanding as a political community of political communities. We commit to supporting each other by sharing our gifts to help meet the other's needs, and to have our own needs supported by their gifts, too. Because the needs of all members of the relationship change through time, we need to meet often to check in with one another and to make adjustments in how we relate; we call this renewal. The same dynamic group of Manitoba elders concisely connects this view of treaty back to the problem of settler supremacy:

> The Anishinaabeg Elders have a specific term for the Treaty relationship—*Waakoodiwin*. It speaks to the way the Treaty had brought together the Anishinaabeg and the Crown. The term is interpreted as follows: we Anishinaabeg had plenty to offer and we were willing to share with you. However, the Newcomers have feasted at our table for so long they have forgotten whose home this truly is.[19]

In this paper, I'm adding my voice to those who've been asking you to remember. I've acknowledged my appreciation for the deep challenge this presents. In addition to the conceptual challenges, there are the immediate practical ones. I don't pretend to have obvious answers for you. All I know is to live these teachings in my own life, as best I can, knowing I'll make mistakes. Fortunately, when I've made mistakes, the gifts of others have made it right or have helped me to, and I learned. So long as I understood that it was my work, I've never wanted for helpers. If you're willing to learn and to practise the Indigenous law governing the territory you live within, and thus to live as a treaty person, you'll make everyone in that territory stronger.

I'd be remiss if I failed to offer a caveat, although I hope you'll find it unnecessary. In expressing my hope that you'll take up Indigenous law in your life, I'm not inviting you to participate in our ceremonies (and certainly not to perform them!); to visit our sacred sites; to wear, repurpose, or reproduce our sacred things; or to participate in any other form of cultural appropriation. Such behaviours don't just fail to approximate our law; they violate it. If you accept the responsibility I'm urging you to pick up, you have to be yourself. That, too, is part of Anishinaabe law as I understand it. What I'm hoping for is that you'll learn how to create and to sustain healthy relationships in the territory of your home, and to understand that you're connected to and thus always in relationship with everybody there, including all those non-humans who fly, walk, crawl, swim, reach, and rumble. This asks you to do much more than simply make space for our voices.

That's the gist of what I've come to understand. But I wanted to know what nokomis thinks about settler-Indigenous relationships today, and how they might be improved. So I asked her.

I began by explaining what I was hoping to hear about. Nokomis thinks awhile. When she speaks, she gives me a word: *windamaagoozi*. She explains its meaning: That Creator picks certain individuals to receive powerful dreams (or visions, if awake), and that these dreams confer vitally important knowledge. These dreams guide the actions of their recipients, and she connects this belief to an imagined moment of first encounter between settlers and Anishinaabeg. She shares her belief that we responded with openness and care, because that's what came to us through vision, and in those days dream knowledge was firmly respected.[20] She also shares, however, that it would have been quite challenging for the elders who spoke on our behalf, because getting to the point where everyone supported the position would have been a challenge. It would have taken some time, and people would have moved very carefully in taking up the opposition.[21]

She then shared a dream with me, by way of explaining why she believes so resolutely in the power, significance, and guidance of dreams. Since we both knew I'd be writing about this for the purpose of this essay, I asked if I could articulate back to her what I'd understood. She said yes, and when I did so, she smiled and said I got it.

But this was only half of the answer to my question. The discussion around the role dream-guidance played in orienting Anishinaabeg to settlers is part of a larger relational framework. She introduces the word *wichitowin*, which she explains means "helping one another," something she says was often discussed when she was young.[22]

I seize upon this to ask my burning question about the other side (although I took it as no accident that her reply was focused solely on us): "Noko, if our relationship is about helping one another, what about today? What about the settler people? Do they help us?" Nokomis giggled at the enormity of the question her grandson placed before her. Then seeing I was serious, she explained she wasn't laughing *at* me and proceeded with her reply. She, too, used to be angry with settlers. She shared a family story about tuberculosis in the '30s and '40s, and how it took both of her parents away.

But, "as time went on I changed," she said, "just by listening and being busy taking care of my family. But I guess a big part of it is knowing about God. We all come from him. And little by little, I changed about the white people and the government. I just realized it's much more important to be positive than negative. It took time; I didn't always act like a kind person."[23] As I listened, I imagined what she might have said to me had I shouted at the police officers during the march. Probably just smile and give me a story showing a better way.

"But what do we do about the fact that they mistreat us? That they act like they own all the land? That they act like their law controls us? That our communities are struggling because of this? How do we stop that?"

"Keep doing what I'm doing," she said. "Just be being the way I am."[24] Yes indeed: living her law. There's an obvious tension here to my mind, but I think it's one she anticipates. Before I can ask about it, she says, "I liked talking to older people; I liked asking them questions about what we did, a long time ago. When I was very young."[25] I agree with her message. I know it's hard to approach our elders, because many of us are disconnected from them and don't know how to approach respectfully, and also because some of them aren't always kind to us for not already knowing who we are. But I think if we really want to develop the gifts we carry, these aren't reasons to walk away for good.

At last I dropped it all on her, asking whether settlers needed to go home. As an aside, that certainly isn't my view, but I wanted to learn from what nokomis would say to this.

Nokomis smiled one of those great big ear-to-ear smiles. "No," she said. "We're being the gift of sharing. I don't think you should ask them to go home. We just learn to live with them. They help us and we help them."[26]

And if I've been listening carefully enough, I should add, "and for those who don't share their gifts, we show them how to."

1. "Nokomis" is *anishinaabemowin* for "my grandmother."
2. Mainville, Bessie (August 19, 2013) Teachings at the home of Bessie and Elmer Mainville, Couchiching First Nation.

3. Mainville, Bessie, "Traditional Native Culture and Spirituality: A Way of Life That Governs Us," *Indigenous Law Journal* 1 8(1) (2010).
4. Mainville, August 19, 2013.
5. Mainville, Bessie (June 17, 2014) Teachings at the home of Bessie and Elmer Mainville, Couchiching First Nation.
6. Mainville, Bessie (June 14, 2015) Teachings at the home of Bessie and Elmer Mainville, Couchiching First Nation .
7. Mainville, June 17, 2014.
8. I don't unpack that logic here, but I've begun to do so in Aaron Mills (2016), "The Lifeworlds of Law: On Revitalizing Indigenous Legal Orders Today," 61:4 McGill LJ. 847.
9. The teacher is a *gete-Anishinaabe*, which is a respectful term for old man, and is often rendered in English as "elder." I'm not keen on that translation though.
10. For further thoughts and an accessible genealogical account of an idea very similar to this one, see the insightful and inspiringly honest remarks of Justice LaForme in LaForme, Harry S., (nd) "Resetting the Aboriginal Canadian Relationship: Musings on Reconciliation, " Ontario Bar Association: www.oba.org/en/pdf/sec_news_abo_may13_laforme.pdf
11. In *Reference Re Secession of Quebec* 2 SCR 217 (1998), the Supreme Court of Canada acknowledged the presence of "underlying constitutional principles," which "inform and sustain the constitutional text: they are the vital unstated assumptions upon which the text is based" [Ibid., at para. 49]. The Court then recognized that at least four such constitutional principles, "federalism, democracy, constitutionalism and the rule of law, and respect for minority rights," are "defining" and "foundational" [Ibid..], and stated that they "dictate major elements of the architecture of the Constitution itself and are as such its lifeblood" [Ibid., at para. 51]. I'm suggesting that settler supremacy stands among them as a fifth equiprimordial constitutional principle.
12. Truth and Reconciliation Commission of Canada (2015), *Final Report of the Truth and Reconciliation Commission of Canada*, Vols. 1-6, Montréal: McGill-Queen's University Press.
13. I've endeavoured to offer an account of this vision of treaty in Aaron Mills, "What is a Treaty? On Contract and Mutual Aid" in John Borrows & Michael Coyle, eds. (forthcoming), *The Right(s) Relationship: Reimagining the Implementation of Historical Treaties*, Toronto: University of Toronto Press. While it doesn't specify treaty as an Indigenous constitutional form, I also suggest readers wanting to better understand the idea of treaty-as-relationship (instead of the treaty-as-contract vision both the Crown and the Supreme Court of Canada offer), may be interested in this wonderful paper: Erik Anderson (2013), "The Treaty Annuity as Livelihood Assistance and Relationship Renewal" in *Aboriginal Policy Research: A History of Treaties and Policies*, vol. 7, Toronto: Thompson Educational Publishing, Inc. Ch. 5: www.apr.thompsonbooks.com/?q=content/volume-7
14. Mainville, Bessie (January 19,) Teachings at the home of Bessie and Elmer Mainville, Couchiching First Nation.
15. Pratt, Doris, Harry Bone, & The Treaty and Dakota Elders of Manitoba (2014), *Untuwe Pi Kin He—Who We Are: Treaty Elders' Teachings Volume I*, 2nd ed., Winnipeg: Treaty Relations Commission of Manitoba & Assembly of Manitoba Chiefs Secretariat, at 27.
16. Ibid., at 41.
17. Mainville, Bessie (October 25, 2015) Teachings at the home of Bessie and Elmer Mainville, Couchiching First Nation.
18. Pratt, Bone, & The Treaty and Dakota Elders of Manitoba 2014, *Volume I*, p. 31.
19. Hyslop, Joe, et al. (2015), *Dtantu Balai Betl Nahidei, Our Relations to the Newcomers: Treaty Elders' Teachings Volume 3*, Winnipeg: Treaty Relations Commission of Manitoba & Assembly of Manitoba Chiefs Secretariat, at 131.

20. Mainville, Bessie (October 16, 2016) Teachings at the home of Bessie and Elmer Mainville, Couchiching First Nation.
21. Ibid.
22. Ibid.
23. Ibid.
24. Mainville, Bessie (September 20, 2016) Teachings at the home of Bessie and Elmer Mainville, Couchiching First Nation.
25. Ibid.
26. Ibid.

Reconcile Your State of Mind

Rebecca Thomas

As a Nation we have missed our mark by one hell of a mile.
For the history that defiled my father's culture when he was just a child,
To the society that exoticizes our braided hairstyles,
To the public that buries their heads in the sand piles
Whose finger pointing reviles our Chiefs and beliefs can breathe easy
Because as of 2015,
We are reconciled.

Which means, we're no longer judged and a Dakota child won't be sent
    home for the fact that he
smudged because he found his brother cold when touched.
And there is no grudge against the fact that sometimes I get tax-free gas.
But only in pre-approved, monitored amounts,
I wouldn't want to be brash with the spending of my government-given cash.

We have accepted the norm of more Natives in prison,
Unable to forgive them for the traumas they've suffered,
Content to maintain a buffer between reality and comfort.
Our biased history spun to finally deal with the Indigenous conundrum.

And we have come to terms with the panic in my father's eyes
When he reads the apology of lies,
Taking time to exorcize the demons that swirl in his soul,
The one that was saved and placed into the whole left by the loss of his language.
But at least he's got $3000.00 in education credits to sandwich his time in lieu
Between now and years he spent in residential school.
Dad I have been practicing. Kesulul.

I'm sorry if this reference is so tensile,
I'm working my way through the stages of grief,
Still caught in denial that I nearly forgot! We are reconciled.
The highway of tears? Girl, that was so last year.
No need to fear that you'll be snatched or attacked, because it's a fact.
We are reconciled.

Now may I be so bold as to make a suggestion?
Instead of a budget and a timeline for reconciliation,
How about an accurate portrayal of history in our nations education?
Bring back the National Aboriginal Health Organization?
Institute classes for language reclamation?
Question why there are so many Aboriginals in incarceration?
Or at least develop a strategy for suicide prevention because we kill ourselves
    up to eleven times more often,
And if we had one, Dakota kids wouldn't have to see their little brothers in coffins.
And to soften the line in the sand we all tend to draw,
And eliminate common words like redskin and squaw.
I've washed my hands so many times that they're raw,
but I can't shake the frustration that we are still referred to as "Indians"
    under the law.

Worry not.
Take off my shoes.
No need to walk that mile.
Because Canada has spent enough money,
Checked all the right boxes,
All of our accounts have been compiled,
Our "perks" and "benefits" beguiled.
Congratulations, Canada,
You have finally reconciled this nation's state of mind
So that in the face of our suffering.
You will always turn a blind eye.

Don't Read the Comments
The Role of Modern News Media in Bridging the Divide Between Indigenous and Non-Indigenous People in Canada

Waubgeshig Rice

Coming closer to the day's deadline, my fingers tapped steadily on the keyboard as I assembled words into lines on the screen in front of me. The script for my story, which would air on that evening's television news, was nearly complete and ready for vetting.

Out of the corner of my eye, I noticed my colleague sit down at her desk to my right. I took my hands away from the keyboard and turned to look at her. She wiped tears from her eyes with the back of one hand, clutching a sheet of paper in the other. I didn't need to ask her how that meeting went.

"Are you okay?" I asked. She shook her head no. She inhaled deeply through her nose as she handed me the paper. "It's horrible, Waub," she said. "The things they're writing about us are just horrible."

I looked down at the printout and saw lists of words in different columns. They were crude, vulgar, and offensive: squaw, redskin, chug, injun, and so on. It wasn't clear to me how they were arranged, but their intent was all the same. My work friend sniffled again before explaining. "These are the ones they flag, before they do anything," she said.

It was late winter 2009, and we were working as TV reporters at CBC in Winnipeg. Earlier that year, an Indigenous political organization had called out CBC for letting racist comments fester on its website following the tragic story of a house fire in a southern Manitoba First Nation in which children were killed. One comment said something about the house being prone to fire because it was saturated with alcohol, alluding to a home full of stereotypically drunk Indians. Other comments were just as hurtful and ignorant. Indigenous leaders were fed up with what they saw as a forum for hatred in the comments sections of CBC news articles, and even called a news conference to address the matter.

We Indigenous staff at CBC had raised the issue of racist comments repeatedly in the lead-up to this public expression of frustration. We'd had meetings with management about how to control the racism that so freely proliferated at the bottom of web articles. We were often told that web logistics made it difficult to monitor everything, and even when that happened, that work had to be outsourced.

My Nehiyaw co-worker was returning that day from another of those meetings that I couldn't attend because of my deadline. The printout of slurs was to show what those third-party monitors looked for when deleting racist comments. It did little to convince any of us that the problem was coming under control.

Fast-forward to November 2015, and CBC decided to close comments on Indigenous-related stories altogether. As web traffic climbed in the social media age, so too did racism in the comments sections. It simply became too much to bear for the CBC itself, its journalists, and most importantly, its readers.

I was very proud of my employer for taking such a pronounced and public stand against racism. When the dust settled, I felt thrilled and relieved, but also defeated; we finally found a solution to eliminating explicit racism on our pages, but that was only because racism became simply too much to resolve.

That was by no means my first glimpse into the prejudice and malice that mainstream media in Canada has helped perpetuate, both directly and indirectly. And as negative attitudes toward Indigenous people simmer throughout this country, I expect similar encounters to continue. If anything, racism is bubbling to the surface more and more today due to the influence of all kinds of media. It's a perfect storm that I've seen brewing my whole life.

I realized from a young age that, for the most part, mainstream Canadian media didn't properly reflect my community or experiences. It sustained the divide between Indigenous and non-Indigenous people by often pitting them against each other. It was a de facto extension of the country's education system, which failed generations of Canadians by not teaching them the true history of the original people of the land.

These realities became even clearer once I began my career as a journalist. As Canada now celebrates its 150th anniversary amidst great fanfare promoted by the mainstream media, among others, it is now even more incumbent on those news organizations to make a genuine effort to rightly include Indigenous people in their newsrooms, and for their journalistic output to honestly portray a narrative of cultural inclusion.

One of my earliest memories of seeing "Indians" on the news was during the resistance at Oka, Québec in 1990. I was eleven years old, and already knew more about what was going on there with the Mohawks through my parents and my community, rather than what was on TV or in the newspaper. Our Anishinaabe community of Wasauksing First Nation was hundreds of kilometres away, but their stand resonated deeply with us.

The uprising of the Mohawks at Oka was a defining moment that united Indigenous peoples across Turtle Island. I was inspired by the pride and resolve to protect lands and rights that seemed to flourish everywhere. We marched in solidarity with the people of Kanesatake; there seemed to be a buzz unlike anything I had ever experienced before.

But what unfolded at Oka was shown in mainstream Canadian media in a much different light. In intros and headlines, national broadcasters and newspapers used words like "crisis" and "outlaws" instead of "resistance" and "defenders." The news portrayed the Mohawks as unlawful troublemakers—obstacles to Canadian settler desires. They were getting in the way of a golf course. It was in stark contrast to what we saw: a community standing up for its land and culture after centuries of interference and outright theft by European, and eventually Canadian authorities.

It was a trend that I saw continue throughout my teen years. In high school, Indigenous issues and experiences were by and large absent from curricula. Fellow students and teachers knew very little, if anything, about the Anishinaabe communities that surrounded them in that part of central Ontario. Wasauksing is only a ten-minute drive from the town of Parry Sound, but for a long time it seemed a distant land altogether.

For generations, people who attended school in town didn't learn much about their Indigenous neighbours. By the late 1990s, as I was finishing high school, there wasn't even a unit on residential schools in my Canadian history class. I reminded the teacher, and at the last minute he devoted part of a lesson to what's widely regarded now as one of the most crucial parts of this country's story.

From a community perspective, news media wasn't making up for what the education system failed to do. While the town newspaper occasionally covered our powwow and other cultural events, mainstream outlets from cities like Sudbury, Barrie, and Toronto only came to our reserve in times of crisis, tragedy, or controversy.

The only time I remember seeing our community make the bigger papers and TV news during my teen years was when my grandmother and aunts occupied the band office, after chief and council overspent funds allocated for education, plunging the administration into third-party management. Predictably, the coverage that followed focused on the tired narrative of another Indian band blowing taxpayers' money.

As a result, I had difficulty believing Canadian media was there to serve me, and I never imagined that there would ever be a place for me in a newsroom. At the time, I was unaware of the brilliant Indigenous journalists who were already blazing trails within different news organizations. Despite that, I was guided to journalism thanks to writing and storytelling opportunities that came at the right time. Mentoring journalists opened my eyes to the possibility of changing the story of this country, by allowing Indigenous people and communities to speak their truths.

I knew change would be slow. That became clear when I began the journalism program at Ryerson University, where there was only one other Indigenous student in a class of 120. I learned that the general shortfall of Indigenous students trended at journalism schools across Canada, and continues today. The obvious result is poor representation in contemporary newsrooms and in many of the stories produced by non-Indigenous journalists.

At the core of that problem is lack of awareness and understanding. Because many don't know much about Indigenous communities or the real history of Canada, non-Indigenous reporters are uncomfortable reaching out to people in those communities and properly sharing their stories with other Canadians. That barrier is a direct result of Canada's assimilative and oppressive measures to erase Indigenous culture, and it's sustained by the unwillingness of media to provide meaningful coverage. If reporters don't learn, then readers, listeners, and viewers will never learn.

And the fallback reportage that has plagued news organizations' treatment of Indigenous peoples is parachute journalism. That's when media outlets—usually based in cities—only send crews to reserves when there's a tragedy or a controversy that fits the stereotypical bill of Indian problems. They stay only long enough to gather what they need to file a story on time, then leave. Traditionally, there've rarely been additional stories filed for context or background, given the tragedy or crisis. So Canadians just come to believe that reserves are rife with problems, with no understanding as to why.

So the call from communities has long been to simply counter those tragic reports with positive ones. They often plead with mainstream media outlets to spend more time in First Nations, to present the realities of day-to-day life there—to show that bad things don't always happen. It's a straightforward request that doesn't require much additional investment from news management, and humanizing First Nations people fairly is an effective solution in combatting the racism that flourishes off-reserve.

Now, more and more news outlets are heeding that call. They're seeing the value in properly portraying the Indigenous people of this land, who are the fastest-growing demographic in Canada. Indigenous communities are also more and more connected, consuming and sharing online media to an astounding degree.

During my time at CBC—a little more than a decade—the national public broadcaster has undertaken a variety of journalistic initiatives to do just that. I've been involved in a number of special projects to provide that crucial context and start a better conversation about what it means to be Indigenous in Canada. I've considered it a huge honour to have contributed to shows and initiatives like *ReVision Quest*, *8th Fire*, and now CBC Indigenous, which has a committed staff to provide that space for real Indigenous journalism.

That said, everyone can always do better, and the best way to accomplish genuine journalism about Indigenous issues is to employ more Indigenous journalists. Currently, many Canadian newsrooms have a few. But many more have none. As stories from those newsrooms are increasingly focused on this country's commitment to so-called reconciliation with Indigenous people, that is simply unacceptable.

Now, after 150 years of Canada, the onus is on its educators and storytellers in journalism to step up to help erase racism. After allowing animosity and prejudice to flourish, there is a real opportunity to take the lead in rephrasing this country's story. Genuine awareness and understanding would be the ultimate cause for celebration, and the best way to accomplish that is by advancing Indigenous voices, both in newsrooms and in the stories journalists cover.

Therefore, Canadian news media outlets should become truly inclusive to reflect the people who inhabited this land before this country came to be. Every newsroom needs Indigenous staff. After ignoring Indigenous voices and pushing them into the periphery over the course of Canadian history, mainstream journalism is now playing catch-up. It cannot accomplish genuine reflection without employing Indigenous storytellers. News media organizations have to make this a priority in order to be truly viable.

As this happens, journalists and newsroom management need to make an effort to better understand the Indigenous communities they cover. This requires outreach at the grassroots level; getting involved in community initiatives that foster a better relationship between news organizations and Indigenous people even before stories happen. All the while, accessing and studying resources like the Truth and Reconciliation Commission's Calls to Action will help reporters bolster their core knowledge of Indigenous communities and their histories.

Once this is accomplished, online news articles and forums may one day become practical sites for constructive discourse. Hateful and ignorant commentary will be squeezed out. With good information trickling down to readers, listeners, and viewers, negative biases and prejudice will eventually dissipate. When the Canadian news media in all its forms better reflects Indigenous communities, the country as a whole will benefit.

Canada is a Pretend Nation
REDx Talks—What I Know Now About Canada

Leroy Little Bear

What follows is the presentation given at the inaugural session of the Redx Talks on October 10, 2015 in Calgary. It has been updated for this volume.

Having gone back and forth across the country, many times, I have come to the conclusion that what I know about Canada is that it is a "Pretend Nation." And let me tell you why. In order to do that, and in order to really understand, we have to engage in a little bit of history. And it's very apropos at this time, especially in terms of Canada's 150th anniversary. We're going to be hearing people talk about what Canada is all about. Well, a definition of a nation is that a nation is a group of people, or a society with a common culture, history, customs, language, traditions, art, and religion. A nation is a sovereign entity. A nation comes from the word *nación* in Latin, which means a set of people. That's what the word's really all about.

Now, sometimes there's confusion about what a nation is. Sometimes it's confused with the notion of a state. A state is a political and judicial entity occupying a patch or territory of land. States get together, like the original thirteen colonies, to make a nation. States have political, legislative, and judicial powers deriving from the nation. States generally are very regional in nature. Today, because of that confusion, it seems that nation and state have been combined to describe a nation in the international community.

Now, in order to understand this notion about nation and people and where things are today, how they came to be, let's engage in a little bit of historical discussion. I'm going to use England as my example, because it seems to me that most of what Canada is or claims to be comes from England. In England, the first people were of what you would call Iberian stock. They came, combined, and mixed with Celtic people in what is now known as Great Britain.

However, there must have been something very special about that island we know as Great Britain. Why? Because a whole bunch of other nations and societies came along and took over England. In other words, there was a succession of takeovers: by the Romans, the Picts and the Scots from the north, the Anglo-Saxons and Jutes, and the Norseman. The last major takeover of England was by the Normans: William the Conqueror in 1066. Though the name suggests otherwise, William the Conqueror wasn't much of a conqueror. Recall England was made up out of a whole bunch of little tribal kingdoms, and they were always at war and battling with each other. Also recall that these people, the kings and queens, and "all the king's horses and all the king's men" (remember Humpty Dumpty?), would intermarry. So it was from one of those intermarriages that a call went out to William the Conqueror that basically said, "You know, we've been fighting amongst each other for too long." And so, "William, can you come over and bring about some order?" And that's how William the Conqueror came to England.

And William succeeded in bringing about some order regarding fights had over the land. Remember the feudal system, and new ways of dealing with the land, and so on? But the important takeaway from those successive takeovers is that today, England is just a mixture of traditions and cultures. England is all about cultural borrowing. In other words, all those successive takeovers have resulted in there being nothing Indigenous in what we refer to as England. What was Indigenous was all wiped out. So, what constitutes English culture—if we could say English culture—today? It's simply a mixture of all those other cultures, traditions, practices, and so on, from successive takeovers.

For me, one of the primary "tests," if you could put it that way, for something being Indigenous, for a people being Indigenous to a territory, is religion. What's the official religion of England, of Great Britain, today? Of course, it's the Church of England. Of course, it's Christianity. The Indigenous religion should have been about Druidism. But you never hear about the Druids in England today. What you hear about is Christianity. But Christianity comes from way over there, from the Middle East. That's what's being used as a foundational base today. That's the reason why we can look at England as a mixture of things, and a nation that's based on cultural borrowings.

The implications and ramifications of all those takeovers is inconsistency. The British are famous for, "If this doesn't work, if Roman ways don't work, let's try some other way." And so, there's never any cultural consistency. In other words, we will change into "whatever appropriate costumes" for the occasion. I always think about, but can never remember, a comic figure that had a trunk beside it that said "Costumes for All Occasions." And, depending on the situation, he would put on the appropriate costume. Today, a good example of this is the whole notion of treaty. Remember making Treaty Seven? In the 1870s, the treaty costume was the appropriate costume. But, do you think Canada wants to wear the treaty costume today? No. The costume today is the *Indian Act*. That's one of those results I am referring to as inconsistency. But if you can hold those thoughts, let's go back a little bit.

Somewhere in the fourth century, around 350 AD, there was a development that took place in the Middle East, in what we refer to as the Holy Land. The Muslims had taken it over (and it's still happening). I think it was St. Ambrose or St. Augustine who was having a sleepless night because he was worried about holding a conflicting belief. The reason he was worried about this was because of one of the Ten Commandments, which says, "Thou shall not kill." But thinking to himself he basically says, "But we have to do something about those Muslims over there." And so, at three o'clock in the morning or so, he takes out his iPad and writes a note to himself that says, "It is not a sin to conduct holy wars against infidels"—meaning non-Christians. That was the justification for moving against those infidels, the Muslims. But that was just a note to himself.

A few hundred years later, in the mid eleventh century, the Pope of the day, Pope Urban the Second, discovered the iPad. Coincidentally, he was sent an invitation by the Byzantine Empire, who was worrying about the same thing. They said, "Can you guys come and help us. We need to save the Holy Land." And the Pope agreed. To rally and to have people come and volunteer to fight against the Muslims, he gave them one-way tickets to heaven. He basically said that I guarantee you, you will get into heaven if you come and fight in this Holy War. Guess what? Those one-way tickets were interpreted, unfortunately, as a free for all to commit atrocities against so-called "infidels." Consequently, that's when the crusades began. So the Holy Wars, Muslims refer to them as Jihads . . . they're still going on: the hunt for terrorists, which is very similar to the McCarthy era of the late '40s and early '50s, when the USA was hunting communists among its own citizens. So the whole "crusade" or "holy war" notion is still very much with us.

In the twelfth century, the Pope opened up a new office called the Inquisition. The Inquisitions were not much different from what's going on today, hunting down terrorists, except it was heretics who the church thought threatened its beliefs, rules, and power. The Office of the Inquisition was renamed the Holy Office,

[Margin notes top: "Inquisitions → hunting terrorists today (diff but same) → continuity → colonealism today Canada is a Pretend Nation"]

which acted as a court of appeal for those being brought to trial by the church. In 1965, that office was renamed the Congregation for the Doctrine of the Faith. But the important thing to remember is, it was still the same office, it just changed its name. As a result, a whole bunch of Inquisitions were started under the office of the Inquisition. For instance, in 1478 just before Columbus came to America, was the Spanish Inquisition. And you will recall the Pope, in his visit to the Americas, had canonized a saint: Junípero Serra. Junípero Serra was responsible for a lot of atrocities against Native people, especially in the state of California.

With this history, you can begin to see the mindset of the Europeans and Columbus, especially the Spanish Catholics. You know, you could almost say they were constantly searching out non-Christians, infidels. When they came over to the Americas and discovered the Indians, you could see them scratching their heads and saying, "Oh no, not again. More infidels?" So much so that the Spanish had this practice called *requerimento*. They would bring their public announcement systems, if they had PAs, out into the jungle, and they would make public announcements for all the Indians to come and surrender to them. And if the Indians didn't comply, it was reason enough to go hunt and kill them. So you can imagine what the Church and Columbus were thinking, and all of those that followed them, when they came across more infidels and non-Christians. They had no qualms about committing atrocities on the Indians.

Now let's hold that thought while I point out something else. At this time, other historic developments were taking place, such as the rivalry between England and Spain. This, you will recall, developed because Henry VIII had decided to break away from the Catholic Church and start the Church of England. As a result, there was this rivalry between the Spanish Catholics and the newly formed Church of England. The English people knew about the Americas. They knew because people would "text" them a little bit about it. But they were a little bit cheap—they must have been hitting hard times economically. Maybe their oil ran out. They, in essence, said, "It's too expensive to go all the way over there. How about if we go over to Ireland? It's right next door. Let's go colonize it." Then eventually they came to the Americas, after having had a colonization practice run with the Irish.

When it came to North America, remember those successive takeovers? Well, they started to come up with justifications for them. Remember the inconsistencies? They started to come up with a whole bunch of theories. *Terra nullius*. Infidels. Discovery. And so on. Those were their justifications for laying claim to North America; to Indian territory.

[Margin note bottom: "justifications"]

Now, in the sixteenth century, there was another important development happening. This was a movement largely against the Church and the divine rule of kings. Again, Humpty Dumpty: "All the king's horses and all the king's men." Because the Church and the monarchs were the holders of the knowledge, they were the ones who had the libraries. They were the ones who wrote the books. The commoners didn't have that much access. And so, the commoners eventually started saying, "We don't have to read all those books. We can come to know anything and everything just through pure reason." That is what's known as the Enlightenment. I prefer to call it "the Age of Reason." The Age of Reason was really kind of a paradigmatic, philosophical movement against the Church and the monarchs. "We don't have to read all those books. We can reason things out." It's just like today's students say, "I don't have to go to the library. I don't have to sit in the library. I can ask Siri."

The Age of Reason was about rationalism. A belief that you can come to know and arrive at the truth strictly through reason, as opposed to faith, reliance on the path, intuition, and metaphysics. Now the Church saw this coming and they jumped on the bandwagon, bringing about the notion of deism. And deism says, "We can come to know anything and everything from God's gift of reason. In the same time period was science, as we know it today. Newtonian science was just coming into its own; the whole notion of reason was brought about. So the Age of Reason says, "God made an orderly universe, and it's good and it's beautiful." Einstein, my favourite scientist, said, "God does not play dice with the universe." Walter Cronkite, "And that's the way it is." Those are examples of notions of rationalism.

The Age of Reason attempted to subject everything and anything to rationalism. It did away with the subjective, dealt only with the objective. It did away with emotions and feelings. Ideas such as the separation of church and state came into existence. Mysticisms, miracles, spirituality, and anything similar were frowned upon by scientists and by people adhering to this Age of Reason. Measurement and hence, the role of mathematics, came into being. There was no room for anything that could not be measured, for anything that cannot be measured is not science. In other words, you can't measure feelings. Nor is there room for subjectivity.

The Age of Reason was in full bloom at the time of North American colonization. This is the reason why the traditional knowledge of North American Indians was simply pushed aside—because that traditional knowledge included notions of spirituality. It was about "all my relations." And we are talking all relations, not just human relations. We are talking about those bears out there, those trees out there, those rocks out there. We are talking about the Earth. Those are all our relations. But see, that you couldn't measure. So they were totally discounted and pushed aside.

So let's go back to the beginning of our talk, where we defined nation. Let's add another layer. Every society, in one way or another, lays claim to a territory. And within that territory, a culture arises as a result of the mutual relationship between the ecological base and humans. It's not a one-way street. It's not just humans. It's not like in *Genesis*, where it is said that everything was made for the benefit of man. But in the Native way of thinking, it was that symbiosis that developed between the land, the environment, and ecological aspects. It was about that relationship. A culture consists of paradigms, concepts of values, and customs. Paradigms are those foundational bases we use in our everyday decisions, for our behaviours, our beliefs, and our relationships. That's what defines a nation. So every society, through its mutual relationship with the land, develops icons, images, paradigms, religions, and so on. All these act as repositories for the knowledge that develops as a result of the mutual relationship with the totality of the environment. In turn, they are embodied by the people through stories, beliefs, and metaphysics. They establish an identity.

So when we look at Canada, it is not much different than a multi-billionaire whose wealth is strictly on paper. It is not connected to the land. It's like a person originally from San Francisco or Seattle, who then lived in Calgary for fifty or sixty years, and somebody asks, "Where are you from?" After fifty or sixty years of living in Calgary, the person answers, "I'm from San Francisco." Identity is being drawn from elsewhere. So it seems to me that if Canada were to be a true nation, it's going to have to embody the knowledge that has always been here. It's going to have to acknowledge its Aboriginal roots. Canada may have a constitution. Canada may have a government. Canada may have a legal system. But, just like that multi-billionaire whose wealth exists entirely on paper, all the above are simply a paper existence—not substantive in any sense. It doesn't arise from a mutual relationship with the totality of the ecology of the territory.

The only way Canada, as we've said, will become a true nation is by embodying the Indigenous roots of the territory it claims. Thousands of generations of Native Americans (for example, Blackfoot people) have existed on the back of what we call Turtle Island. They have developed and embodied icons, images, and symbols. And, those have become embodied in their customs, traditions, values, and beliefs. They are embodied in our stories, in our songs, in our ceremonies. They have become part of that relationship with the land. That's what you can refer to as being Indigenous. Until that embodiment comes about for Canada, it will continue to have an identity problem. Until that embodiment comes about, Canada will continue to be a pretend nation. Canada will continue to be a nation that exists only on paper.

You can also look at it from a slightly different perspective, that of a constitutional point of view. What is a constitution? A constitution is a document that spells out basic principles detailing how a society, how a nation, is to run its affairs. How it's going to set up its government, its legal system, its justice system, and the powers that this office and that office are going to have. That's what a constitution is about. A constitution is also a sovereign statement to everybody else in the world. We are serving notice to other nations that we are also a nation, and we are to be reckoned with. A constitution can also be looked at as a statement to our own people that says, collectively, this is how we, internally, are going to run the show.

Now, the Canadian Constitution and other conventions that make up the Canadian Constitution are all administrative in nature. If you look through the documents from 1867 to 1982, all those thirty-some pieces that today make up the Canadian Constitution, they are all administrative in nature. They say nothing about who are as Canadians or what Canada is all about. There is nothing in those documents about how they are connected to the land. This is why John Ralston Saul observes that Canadian identity comes from Europe, and in some cases maybe from the United States. If Canadian identity is being drawn from elsewhere, does that mean that Canadians, deep down, still consider themselves foreigners? And continue to consider themselves as visitors? If this is the case, Canadians really do have an identity problem. Paraphrasing Dan George's 1967 "Lament for Confederation," O Canada, you claim to be 150 years old, and you still don't know who you are? So my message, just like Ralston Saul's, just like Dan George's, is: Canada, look at yourself in the mirror, and ask yourself, "Who am I really?"

Anthem

Erin Freeland

Oh Canada, name we were trained to call you. We sing you into being with empty anthems. I used to sing so proud. I used to stand on a chair and sing so loud they let me do it in front of the whole school assembly. True North Strong and Free!

They let children lead the lie.

Then I saw.

In the woods. In my homes. In the shacks beside the lake with no water where we would bring firewood for Margaret. I started to see you, Canada, and I learned that what they taught us we were and what we are was so many lies. So many lies that I stopped singing. I ripped off that righteous patch I had sown so carefully on my backpack. When I started to listen to all the lies I had learned to repeat, it made me sick. Now I know that purging is healing. Undoing all these lies inside is ceremony. Because if I let reconciliation become just another lie, then I keep breeding zombies instead of warriors. Then we will have condoned all the things we know are not all right. And to condone that which is wrong is evil.

My people came, from Ireland, France, England, Ukraine, landless. We came to settle on you. On Ojibwe, Migmaw, Saulteaux, Cree, and Algonquin lands. We came to Nepisiguit, before the Wabanaki Confederacy. Ignorant of the prophecies. Knowledgeable of prices.

Fed on the stories of the great emptiness, waiting to be fertilized with farms and god. My people showed up hungry.

My people showed up knowing dispossession, loss, patriarchy, colonization. My people knew these things and came. My people knew these things and sowed them into your flesh, picks, roads, rail, mine, dick, bible, shrine.

Closing and opening at the same time.

Our ceremonies are so confusing.

My Baba's Canada was an acre garden tended by hand and hoe, clearing back boreal forest and boulders to grow cabbage in wooden barrels so there would be sauerkraut all winter. Her days read: diabetic child, seizure, biting onto wooden spoon, dirt floor, drunken husband. She could not read.

Don't forget we brought the drunks.

We cleared the land with a place to expand Europe, to make it new again. New York. New Caledonia. Nullius New. We knew that if you have land you have power. Some church logs tell me what my family did. Ouvrier. Spinster. Bûcheron. Labourer. I don't know how they acted, what they said. I can only ask as far as my great- grandparents. Everything else I didn't hear in a story; I learned it on ancestry.ca. Cracked pictures and sliver memories. For settlers, the Internet is our wampum, this electric highway where we try to find ourselves. I'm trying to find myself in you, Canada. I'm trying to distil what my people have sown, trying to digest the genocide, the taking, the renaming and remaking.

I'm trying to understand where I've been on you, what I've done to you. I'm trying to make it real, all those things we say you are, of peace and justice, true and free. I want that to be real, Canada. See, I want to believe in you. To believe in what we are behind the lies. What we can be. But as I grey, I slow down. I breathe. Hunter or hunted? Have I been tricked by your fancy words? Your shiny raven nationalism selling me things? I was taught that I was born in Canada, of Canada. This land is your land, this land is my land . . . but I've learned I was born in Denendeh. A nation that pre-dates even the twinkle in Britain's eye of what they thought lay under the snow.

Denendeh, I know your soft places, hiding cranberries; where I can lie down in your welcome and eat and eat. I know where the sweet water comes out of cracks in the mountains, and I know where the caribou used to run through those mountain valleys and how good fresh ribs taste on the fire when our hands are still bloody from the hunt. I know how sacred you are, and I am so tired of the continual dishonouring; I'm so tired of them stealing the good parts of you, showing you off, then raping you after the lights have gone off and everyone has left the birthday party. I'm tired of the patriarchy and the pipelines. I don't just want to be unsettled; I want to be reborn. With just the good parts. I'm wearing the past on my heart, I have to honour everything bad my ancestors did as a lesson, scars to tell the story of the time we did not know and the times we forgot.

This country is a procession of wounds.

My mother was born in Churchill, Manitoba, her friends the relocated Sayisi Dene and Inuit. Tagged and rowed into pre-made homes. No names, just numbers. Dog tags around their necks. Clogging the bathtub drain with seal guts because Indian Affairs architects didn't design homes for Inuit; they designed homes to try to change Inuit into white people.

My parents are settlers, our family spread across many houses. I have siblings by marriage and blood who belong to nations that pre-exist my own. Dene Nation, Tlicho Nation. Chipewyan, Cree. My daughter asks me "Why is Auntie Aven-Lee (who is brown) ten times more likely to get missing and murdered than Aunty Alex (who is white)?" My daughter was eight. We talk a lot about colonization and why things are the way they are, and how they should and could be. She says, "If I was the mayor of Oka, I would just say, 'You can't build a golf course on a graveyard.'"

See, justice is a very simple thing for children.

They can feel it in their gut. It is visceral. We grow up in this country and our schools teach us how great this "Canada" is and how lucky we are to live in this great nation, and how our diversity is so integral to this beautiful mosaic. But I could feel the discord when Tlicho language class was out back behind the school, in an old trailer with a wood boiler, because this kind of learning was after class, was extra-curricular, was not integral. I became so confused, so ashamed of you,

Canada. Why did we tell ourselves so many lies? Why are my people so good at forgetting? Why don't my people tell stories like their stories? Where are my stories to think with? I realize I will have to practice again to be human. I have to start telling stories and living teachings—you can't be one thing and say you are another, Canada. You taught me this. You can't paddle a river, or hunt and pretend. There is doing, and there is talking. Talk is cheap, Canada, and I know that your lessons are deep. Canada. This is your given name. I feel you where something before Canada, before we labelled you as such.

I see it in my son's eyes when he watches the geese migrating back to us. The first geese of spring flew overhead just after you where born, son, and each year they are coming earlier, leaving later, so much open water everywhere. Where we expect them to be they are not, where the stories tell us they are they are no longer. We have done so much to change you. Even the stories that used to feed us are leading us to places that don't make sense.

What are my ceremonies? Baptism, prom, losing my virginity, marriage, divorce. Bankruptcy.

All the white ladies are crying. They are so uncomfortable that we might question why they, with their degrees and six-figure jobs, might not be as well positioned as an elder to be in charge of Aboriginal language. And this makes us so uncomfortable, to even ask. Why am I here and not someone else? Why not someone Indigenous? Every Canadian needs to ask this question. Why you?

Reconcile this, Canada.

Knowing where you come from matters. Knowing why our country is the way it is matters.

Who is this Canada that says she is so many things that she is not? Strong and Free but only for some?

All of these comfortable lies and comfortable lives.

Gently remove all the things you have been called that are not you, clean these wounds upon your rugged perfection, tear off these pipeline extensions, these dams, and all the other violence we laid upon you calling it "progress."

See how pretty you look now/ See how good you feel now

No one who has lain with you can deny your power. My face is buried in the moss and you absorb all our sobs and stupidly just keep giving and giving.

Reconciliation is not for cowards. I try reconciling myself with what all the before messes have done, might have done, for sure did.
When I can reconcile with myself then I can begin.

Like a mother, you are staying with us, feeding us, offering us drink, holding the deep and sacred hope that one day we will remember what it is to love the land. That we will reconcile the fundamental loss we carry with us, the burden of capitalism, of colonization, that trains us that we are to be exploited and in turn exploit the land. This cycle of undoing, of abuse, on bodies of women and water, women and water. I can no longer be settler, I can only be unsettled.

Canada, I know you are all what we dream you to be and more. It is blasphemy and disrespect, these lies we tell ourselves about who you are and how we treat you and each other upon you.

"Canada" is a baby, but Dé is forever.

I am not Canadian, but I am working so that one day I can be proud that we were brave enough as humans to grow up and begin to listen to our children and to the land. To the deep truths that never waver. Where there is leadership beyond ego, and treaties that are about relationships and all the beautiful things we can become together.

Canada is just a fragment of us, the land before and after: we are she, we are all together. Canada just a tessera in this cosmic mosaic of sacred places. 150 years from now, 10,000 years from now, what will that story be? I know we are so beautiful.

I know we are so sacred. Every day, braiding, being so that this place can be free of our lies and we can be free of our fear. Reconciliation is not for cowards; no, reconciliation is for bankers. What we want is beyond reconciliation. What we want is Reciprocity. What we want is Revolution. We are teaching our children so they know the truth. We are teaching our children to remember. We are teaching our children while we de-school our selves. This is a time of great unlearning. Beyond the fear, beyond Canada, are places were we live in love.

Who is the Queen and who gave her sovereignty over us?
    You are the Queen, child, and only you can decide who and what is sovereignty to you.

That is the difference between consent and consultation.

If we can unlearn the deepest lie we tell our selves, the state does not fall apart, rather the state of things falls together.

Inclusion is Just the Canadian Word for Assimilation
Self-Determination and the Reconciliation Paradigm in Canada

Rachel Yacaaʔat George

When the clock ticked over from 2016 to 2017, Canada began its sesquicentennial, the celebration of its 150th birthday. But what exactly are we celebrating? For some this means the celebration of 150 years since Confederation, and a moment to take pride in the supposed brighter aspects of Canadian history, such as the Canadian *Charter of Rights and Freedoms*, and an international reputation as a defender of human rights—however flawed those perceptions may be. For Indigenous peoples, this year marks 150-plus years of resistance against an ongoing colonial assault. It is a reminder of our strength, our resilience, and the vitality of our nations. It is a moment to recognize our resistance and resurgence, as well as the work that still needs to be done. While some will praise the positive aspects of Canadian history, there is a marked opportunity to draw continued attention to the true history of this country, to shift the dialogue, and to force a re-imagining of the relationship between Indigenous nations and Canadians.

For generations, Indigenous peoples in Canada have found their identities forcefully defined by, and within the context of, the Canadian state. The denial of our sovereignty, disregard for treaties, and the continued subjugation that Indigenous peoples face has sought to alienate us from our ways of being and knowing. In the wake of the sesquicentennial and the emerging reconciliation paradigm, which advances state building under the guise of "justice" and "renewed relationships," we continue to assert our Indigeneity against new and re-generated forms of assimilation and erasure. The reconciliation discourse has been built upon feigned redress, in conjunction with drawing new attention to, and developing deeper understanding of, what it means to be self-determining.

Yet what the state suggests is "reconciliation," and the expression of our self-determination, is an unambiguous inclusion in the capitalist structure of Canadian society—an inclusion that is nothing more than thinly veiled assimilation, drawing us further into the colonial system and subjugation to the will and assumed sovereignty of the Canadian state. Our self-determination within this context is defined by the politics of state recognition, which seeks to reconcile our assertions of nationhood with settler-state sovereignty. This is done through the "accommodation of identity claims in some form of renewed legal and political relationship with the Canadian state,"[1] but in no way embodies inherent self-determination. As the country contemplates the past 150 years, resurgence and true expressions of self-determination, as described and asserted by Indigenous nations, are critical to constructing a just nation-to-nation relationship with the Canadian state, and to envisioning our futurity.

Colonialism has not faded into the past, despite attempts by the Canadian state to convince its citizens of the veracity of this statement. The continued and lasting impacts of engagement with the colonial system are harboured within Indigenous peoples today. Until we break the shackles of colonialism in their entirety, we will continue to feel the effects. As Taiaiake Alfred notes: "colonialism is best conceptualized as an irresistible outcome of a multigenerational and multifaceted processes of forced dispossession and attempted acculturation—a disconnection from land, culture, and community—that has resulted in political chaos and social discord within First Nations communities and the collective dependency of First Nations upon the state."[2]

Yet within and beyond this understanding of colonialism is the ever-present reality of Indigenous struggle, strength, and resilience. In the face of genocide, our resilience is unmistakable; we were not supposed to be here. Although the tactics have shifted, the state remains intent on our destruction and suppression as it strives to create its own legitimacy. Jeff Corntassel and Cheryl Bryce note it most eloquently, stating: "being Indigenous today means engaging in a struggle to reclaim and regenerate one's relational, place-based existence by challenging the ongoing, destructive forces of colonization."[3]

Conflicting Conceptualizations of Self-Determination

Over the past few decades, self-determination has become a popular buzzword and rallying cry for Indigenous activists' entry into human rights regimes. The utility of this word has been springboarded by decolonization movements in the wake of World War II. Although the UN Special Committee on Decolonization has not listed Indigenous nations in Canada or the United States as "Non-Self-Governing Territories,"[4] and thus decolonization does not apply, self-determination and decolonization continue to have a pressing and persistent applicability to Indigenous communities. The utilization of self-determination as it relates to Indigenous nations has been further bolstered by its inclusion in the United Nations Declaration on the Rights of Indigenous Peoples (UNDRIP):

> *Article 3*
> Indigenous peoples have the right to self-determination. By virtue of that right they freely determine their political status and freely pursue economic, social and cultural development.
>
> *Article 4*
> Indigenous peoples, in exercising their right to self-determination, have the right to autonomy or self-government in matters relating to their internal and local affairs, as well as ways and means for financing their autonomous functions.[5]

While UNDRIP represents an integral starting point for the envisioning of new relationships between the settler-state and Indigenous communities, it also represents the conflation of self-determination with self-government, two concepts that, while linked, are not synonymous. The document imposes specific restrictions on the understandings of self-determination that emphasize self-government, while negating explicit reference to the importance of our land and water-base. As a stand-alone, Article 3 is an eloquent representation of the intent of self-determination. However, as noted by Charmaine White Face, Article 4 is particularly "limiting and dangerous to the self-determination of Indigenous Nations because of the words *internal and local affairs*, which are not explained or elaborated from an Indigenous perspective."[6] This vague phrasing leaves room for states to impose their own meanings, which further limit Indigenous peoples; an imposition that often negates the centrality of our territories. Further, the version of self-determination explicitly expressed in Article 46[7]—and contrary to the understanding of self-determination as it is applicable to all other peoples—strips away the self-determining autonomy of Indigenous communities in order to ensure the maintenance of the territorial integrity of colonial states around the world.

Similar to the limiting articles within UNDRIP, the political discourse in Canada has tended to structure self-determination as interchangeable with terms like "self-government" and "sovereignty." The domestication of self-determination by the Canadian state has confined Indigenous nations to the borders of Canada, thereby denying international agency and amputating Indigenous peoples from relatives across colonial borders. These terms only scratch the surface of what is truly meant when Indigenous communities describe their inherent rights and responsibilities. More often than not, these terms neglect a true reflection of all aspects of our responsibilities, which include the importance of ties to our territories for our existence as Indigenous peoples. This is evident in various action plans put forth by the Federal Government that advance restrictive concepts of self-government. While many definitions of self-determination fail to fully encapsulate the rights and responsibilities Indigenous peoples have, the understanding that seems to be the most encompassing comes from community members themselves, and is well articulated by Corntassel and Bryce: "Self-determination . . . entails unconditional freedom to live one's relational, place-based existence and practice healthy relationships."[8] This relationality goes far beyond the interpersonal understanding held by Canadians; it is held within our teachings. For the Nuu-chah-nulth people, a central teaching and worldview is *hishuk ish tsawalk*, which translates to "everything is one." We are taught about our unity, interconnectivity, and relationship to all of creation. When we understand our positionality to all of creation, our self-determination not only encompasses our relationship to it, but also our responsibilities, our rights, and our governance. A freedom to live our relational, place-based existence and practice healthy relationships embodies our nationhood.

Despite the passing of UNDRIP in 2007, the struggle to restore self-determination is a present reality for Indigenous peoples in Canada. Roderic Pitty suggests that this stems from "the refusal by states to renegotiate their political relationships with Indigenous peoples based on the distinct status accorded to those peoples in the Declaration."[9] While there may be truth to this assessment, it does not get at the heart of the refusal to honour Indigenous self-determination, which lays in the fact that Canada views Indigenous self-determination as being in direct conflict with its sovereignty because of claims to land and waters. In an effort to resolve this conflict, Canada has redefined self-determination as self-government, while eliminating Indigenous claims to their territories. This redefinition is evident in policies such as the British Columbia Treaty Process and the *Nisga'a*

Final Agreement, which are based on the extinguishment of rights and title, as well as other half-hearted implementations of free prior informed consent that hold Canadian authority as the fundamental reference. Despite this incontestable infringement on genuine self-determination, the Canadian government heralds these policies as an embodiment of its commitment to respecting Indigenous rights and implementing UNDRIP.[10] Further, the path to self-determination has become intermingled with the newly emerging reconciliation paradigm in Canada in such a way that it distorts the true understanding of self-determination as the unconditional freedom to live our place-based existence and practice healthy relationships.

The Movement for Redress

Similar to other countries across the globe, Canada has been engaged in a period of heightened performative morality over the last few decades as it seeks to contend with state-sanctioned violence. Although these redress mechanisms are most notably utilized in a transition to democracy,[11] they can and do exist where no such transition has occurred. Culminating in apologies, action plans, compensation payments, and truth and reconciliation commissions, these measures are touted as facilitating justice. However, when applied in colonial contexts, settler states seek to advance the colonial project by manipulating the idea of justice in order to quell the discontent of Indigenous nations. These mechanisms frame colonialism as an entity of the past, while simultaneously denying the present and lived experiences of coloniality that Indigenous peoples contend with daily. As Glen Coulthard notes: "'reconciliation politics' converge with a slightly older 'politics of recognition,' advocating the institutional recognition and accommodation of Indigenous cultural difference as an important means of reconciling the colonial relationship between Indigenous peoples and the state."[12] This method of reconciliation and recognition serves as a settler move to innocence[13] in which Canadians are not required to make substantial structural change, or to question their continued benefit in the colonial project.

Reconciliation, as developed in the context of international mechanisms of redress, has come to denote a regeneration of broken relationships. The concept hinges on an idea that parties were once whole, experienced a rift, and need to be made whole again. In this context, reconciliation is at its core a state-building project that seeks to eliminate the difference forcing groups apart. Through the application of justice, these projects seek connection, and not separation, to orient their work.[14] Advanced within the framework of transitional justice, reconciliation has sought to bring communities previously fraught with violence back into a collective oneness as a state by providing closure through "justice." However, by privileging national unity, reconciliation actively silences marginal voices that do not subscribe to the nation-state mentality. This is extremely problematic for Indigenous communities who do not see themselves within the settler state but as self-determining nations. Further, it becomes especially challenging to restore a relationship to a wholeness that never existed between Indigenous nations and the state. The central focus on state building advances the destruction of Indigenous nations in an effort to eliminate what is viewed as the difference that caused the broken relationship. In effect, reconciliation in colonial contexts denotes a more capacious inclusion in the nation-state framework while negating Indigenous nationhood.

Among the various redress mechanisms implemented by settler states, truth and reconciliation commissions were initially appealing to Indigenous peoples in their claim to provide validation and voice to the destruction of colonial policies. Despite the apparent responsivity to Indigenous demands for redress, the Truth and Reconciliation Commission of Canada (TRC) was confined by a limited mandate that identified injury as a single colonial policy—residential schools—and failed to address the restitution of stolen lands. This, along with the other reconciliation initiatives implemented in Canada, is a deliberate tactic designed to allow the government and dominant (settler) society to nullify future claims for redress, while simultaneously assuaging any settler and state responsibility and guilt for past abuses. As Andrew Woolford notes, this framing in effect "transfers the legitimate justice demands of Indigenous peoples into tidy boxes of repair, removing them as a challenge to the legitimacy of the settler colonial nation."[15]

While there is power in giving voice to our experiences, truth and reconciliation commissions addressing colonial violence engage with truth in extremely problematic ways. Alfred and Corntassel note that there is danger in allowing colonialism to become the only narrative of Indigenous lives.[16] The sole focus of these commissions on injustice casts Indigenous peoples as victims, whose experiences are strictly held in relation to colonialism. Not only does this constructed narrative erase the resiliency and resurgence of our communities, but also it holds settler power as the fundamental reference and assumption,[17] thereby dissolving our agency. In these forums, our victimization is the truth that is sought. That victimization becomes a spectacle for settler consumption, structured to allow settlers to progress quickly through guilt and shame. The emphasis on closure constructs truth as an entity of the past and allows settlers to distance themselves, thereby occupying a space of absolution. Further, the victim-centred nature of this commission effectively creates the appearance that "the TRC will rely upon the survivors to do the work to be reconciled or perhaps reintegrated (or 'conciled'/integrated) into Canadian society,"[18] while settlers bear witness. It is this disassociation that shifts culpability and crafts the truth and reconciliation commission as a "'politics of distraction,' yet another exercise of 'affirmative repair' or 'settler magic' aimed at staving off demands for the restitution of stolen lands,"[19] and addressing various other forms of dispossession. This performativity structures the discourse of reconciliation and negates any fundamental change to the colonial relationship.

The TRC's explicit examination of previous policy has crafted Indigenous experiences with colonial violence within the confines of the past. While the Commission admittedly did draw attention to the continued linkages to current experiences, it remains an understated narrative that escapes many Canadians who bear witness to the TRC process. Rosemary Nagy and Emily Gillespie noted that during the Québec National Event in Montréal, "despite ample opportunity to do so, there was simply no reporting on reconciliation in terms of land, treaty, gender and the Two Row Wampum, which were addressed in a series of panels organized by the local Kanien'kehaka people over the course of the event."[20]

These topics relating to our self-determination are silenced in an effort to remove any challenge to the legitimacy of the settler colonial nation. This selective reporting has been representative of virtually all media coverage of the TRC across the country. Shaping reconciliation in this way allows for Canadians to believe that once the issues outlined by the commission are addressed and, hopefully, rectified, the colonial process is over and everyone can move on. This is not the case. Struggles for stolen land are ongoing, Indigenous children continue to be found in state care at disproportionate rates, colonial violence continues and can be seen in the high numbers of missing and murdered Indigenous women and girls, and self-determination is continually ignored and infringed upon.

Given reconciliation's goals of national unity and legitimacy, which reduces Indigenous self-determination to cultural rights devoid of connection to our land and waters, and strips us of political agency, we must regard its calls for cultural revitalization with caution. With the same watchful eye that we consider how an apologizer benefits from the apology, we must reflect on what states that embrace cultural revitalization stand to gain from this project. For example, in the TRC's Calls to Action, Indigenous language is viewed as "a fundamental and valued element of *Canadian culture and society*."[21] This articulation aims to disassociate indigeneity from Indigenous nations, and encapsulate it within Canadian society as a part of the nation-state identity. In this context, the revitalization of Indigenous languages becomes an inclusion into multiculturalism. This inclusion in the national policy of multiculturalism seeks to emphasize equality by fashioning a universal immigrant status[22] while erasing Indigenous nationhood. Inclusion does not embody decolonization or self-determination, but is an extension of assimilative colonial policy.

The rhetoric of inclusion is also prevalent in municipal affirmations of reconciliation. Following the TRC's National Events, a number of cities have issued proclamations of a "year of reconciliation." Among these are Vancouver, Toronto, Edmonton, Calgary, and most recently Winnipeg. In these declarations, officials committed to various initiatives including "creating more opportunities for Aboriginal cultural events."[23] The emphasis on cultural accommodation seeks to create a new political relationship with the Canadian state while drawing attention away from genuine assertions of self-determination. Canadians engaged in this framework truly believe that: "We are committed to supporting the fulfillment of the vision of Aboriginal peoples, to building a fairer and more just country . . . We will work, each in our own way, and together, towards achieving the goal of reconciliation and, in the end, *a much stronger, more inclusive Canada*."[24]

By revising Indigenous peoples' vision to live freely as self-determining nations, into a state-building project of inclusion within the settler-state framework, the reconciliation paradigm advances the continuation of the colonial relationship under the guise of justice. These projects of social inclusion are not reflective of self-determination but instead subject Indigenous communities to continued colonial policy. They seek to divest Indigeneity from Indigenous communities, consuming it as Canada's multicultural identity, and effectively extinguishing Indigenous nationhood. What is needed is not more social inclusion for Indigenous peoples within settler society, but true decolonization and self-determination; this is a relationship that honours "unconditional freedom to live one's relational, place-based existence and practice healthy relationships."[25] Reconciliation as advanced by the state is nothing but pretty window dressing for the new and more insidious manifestation of assimilation: social inclusion.

Of further divergence from self-determination, reconciliation's conceptualization of justice as embodied in interpersonal relationships inherently undermines

Indigenous worldviews. By constructing our relationality as solely tied to human connection, the reconciliation discourse undermines *hishuk ish tsawalk*—the Nuu-chah-nulth view of the interconnectivity of all of creation. This compartmentalization of our relationships allows for an emphasis on a Western view of land, waters, and nature as outside of society, and frames its primary purpose as resource extraction and capitalistic development. This strategic colonial framing is expressed in the TRC's sole dealing with Indigenous peoples' relationships with their territories: "sustainable reconciliation on the land involves *realizing the economic potential of Indigenous communities* in a fair, just, and equitable manner that respects their right to self-determination."[26] Hidden under the guise of benefitting Indigenous communities through economic prosperity, this framing privileges the destruction of the land for capitalistic gain.

With the Canadian understanding of self-determination, which holds colonial authority as the fundamental assumption, the above structuring of reconciliation allows for the denial of inherent Indigenous self-determination when it is in conflict with colonial desires. It denies the self-determining authority of Indigenous communities to refuse engagement with the continued disruption of our individual and community relationships with the natural world for the purposes of economic benefit and resource extraction. Take for example the approval of the Kinder Morgan Trans Mountain Pipeline in November 2016. Despite numerous Indigenous objections, the Canadian government approved the pipeline under the assertion of benefit to all Canadians. "Consultation" with Indigenous communities is viewed as not only fulfilling Canada's commitment to UNDRIP but also its commitment to respecting Indigenous self-determination. Structuring reconciliation within the scope and bounds of capitalistic exploitation reconstructs self-determination to be tenable with Canadian assumed authority, furthers primitive accumulation ("the violent transformation of noncapitalist forms of life into capitalist ones"[27]), and seeks to deny our grounded normativity.[28] In this way, what is suggested to be "reconciliation" is an unambiguous inclusion in the economic structure of Canadian society, and inclusion is nothing more than thinly veiled assimilation deeper into the colonial system.

Resurgence vs. Reconciliation

Alongside the emerging reconciliation discourse and continued attempts by the Canadian government to redefine self-determination, Indigenous nations have been actively engaged in resurgence. In contrast to reconciliation, resurgence is inherently based on action. To counter the politics of distraction evident in the reconciliation discourse, decolonization and self-determination demand strategies centred on action via the recovery of Indigenous homelands, and the regeneration of cultures and community.[29] Resurgence calls on Indigenous communities to draw themselves away from seeking legitimacy and recognition from the settler colonial state, and to focus instead on asserting our self-determination. As Sheryl Lightfoot notes in her discussion on global Indigenous diplomacy and politics, when we engage from a place grounded in our ontologies we alter relationships with state actors.[30] Moreover, when we understand that our relationships have a basis in treaty,[31] we inherently foreground action through the renewal of our responsibilities. Rooted in our relationships to all of creation, resurgent practices are fundamentally at odds with settler-state reconciliation practices, which seek to construct our indigeneity as a part of a multicultural identity and divorce us from our relationships to the land, all under the auspices of justice for colonial abuses.

Resurgence actively works toward decolonization through the regeneration of Indigenous practices and relationships. Intent on untangling ourselves from the colonial framework, decolonization foregrounds freedom, fundamentally altering relationships between the colonial state, settlers, and Indigenous peoples. These practices affirm our self-determination, and force settlers to engage with our communities on a nation-to-nation basis. Resurgence centres the (re)imagination and (re)creation of diverse Indigenous worldviews and practices, as well as the (re)establishment of healthy relationships.[32] These projects actively engage with, protect, and regenerate Indigenous knowledge that holds our nationhood at its core. When we centre and engage with our traditions, we turn away from seeking legitimacy and accommodation through the structures complicit in ongoing violence, and focus instead on the relationships that form the basis of who we are as Indigenous nations and communities.[33] For Nuu-chah-nulth peoples, this means (re)centring *hishuk ish tsawalk*. When we understand this teaching, we necessitate a consciousness that all of creation is interconnected and in relation. This calls on us as Nuu-chah-nulth people to consider our responsibilities and how we enact *iisaak*—respect. As Indigenous peoples, our understandings of *iisaak* are inherently tied to the reciprocal relationship we hold with all of creation. This is a fundamentally different understanding than the one held by settlers who structure respect compartmentally. Resurgent practices envision our futurity by regenerating Indigenous teachings, and continually renewing our relationships and responsibilities to all of creation.

Further, when we advance decolonization as the goal, we alter the terms of engagement with Canadians and actively assert our self-determination—the freedom to live our relational, place-based existence, and to practice healthy relationships. Contrary to the reconciliatory process that does not force change in colonial power dynamics, alliances that are built as Indigenous nations assert our self-determination shift the power relations to develop a common future[34] that affirms Indigenous nationhood. The process is inherently unsettling as it shakes Canadian privilege and comfort, which has ultimately gone unquestioned. Decolonization "cannot be motivated by an effort to maintain as much comfort or privilege as possible."[35] For settlers, decolonization means deconstructing central national myths, such as the "peacemaker,"[36] that instil notions of benevolence while silencing Indigenous experiences. These are myths that should be actively deconstructed as Canada contemplates its past 150 years and seeks to envision its future. This process transforms the relationships we hold with settlers, and allows for the continued creation of Indigenous futurity. It is a transformation outside the capacity of reconciliation projects that seek to regenerate assimilation under the guise of justice.

Envisioning Our Futurity

As we reflect on the past 150-plus years of Indigenous resistance and resilience, and strive to envision a new relationship with the Canadian state, we must reject the current framing of reconciliation as a pathway to justice and decolonization. At its core, reconciliation is a state-building project that seeks to silence Indigenous nationhood and expressions of our inherent self-determination. By envisioning repair as renewed interpersonal relationships, reconciliation contradicts and alienates Indigenous worldviews grounded in our interconnectivity, relation, and responsibility to all of creation. Even where the repair of relationships is advanced, it is premised on the inclusion of Indigenous peoples into the folds of settler society as equal immigrants in a multicultural nation-state. To engage with reconciliation projects that strive to alter how we contextualize and understand our relationships is to live amputated from who we are as Indigenous peoples.

In light of this new regeneration of assimilation, which relies heavily on the politics of representation and recognition, the necessity of genuine self-determination and decolonization remains an even more pressing reality for Indigenous peoples in ensuring our survival as distinct and strong nations. Our self-determination as nations means confronting existing colonial institutions, structures, and policies that attempt to displace us from our lands, waters, and relationships.[37] As Corntassel notes, decolonization operates on multiple levels, and necessitates moving from an awareness of being in struggle to actively engaging in everyday acts of resurgence.[38] These acts of resurgence are grounded in the (re)centring of our ways of being and knowing, and the creative envisioning of our futurity outside of the grasps of colonial forces. They seek to inherently change power dynamics by privileging our worldviews, held in our relationality. As elder gkisedtanamoogk asserts: it "has been an incredibly long and continuous fight for our right to *Be* as we wish to be," and "there is no reason for [us] to become something other than our selves. Our life and place on this Earth is the intention of... the Great Creator."[39]

When the clock ticked over to 2017, we came to a crossroads. As the country engages in reflection and celebration of its history, it is a pivotal moment to draw continued attention to the history of ongoing colonization. This is the moment to shift the dialogue and to genuinely envision a new relationship. For Indigenous peoples, we cannot allow the state to define our identity, or to subsume it into a multicultural Canadian identity that seeks to erase us as distinct nations. We must continue to engage in everyday acts of resurgence that continue to breathe life into our communities, and take self-determination into our own hands. It is about asserting our rights, and practicing healthy relationships with all of creation. Until we fully commit to this as nations, we will become trapped in the web of inclusion and submission to the settler state.

1. Coulthard, Glen (2014), *Red Skin, White Masks*. Minnesota: University of Minnesota Press, p. 3.
2. Alfred, Taiaiake (2009), "Colonialism and State Dependency," *Journal of Aboriginal Health* 5.2, p. 52.
3. Corntassel, Jeff and Cheryl Bryce (2012), "Practicing Sustainable Self-Determination: Indigenous Approaches to Cultural Restoration and Revitalization," *The Brown Journal of World Affairs* 18.2, p. 152.
4. United Nations Special Committee on Decolonization (2016). "Non-Self-Governing Territories," www.un.org/en/decolonization/nonselfgovterritories.shtml
5. United Nations General Assembly (2007), *United Nations Declaration on the Rights of Indigenous Peoples: resolution adopted by the General Assembly*, A/RES/61/295, 4-5.
6. Charmaine White Face (2013), *Indigenous Nations' Rights in the Balance: An Analysis of the Declaration on the Rights of Indigenous Peoples*. Minnesota: Living Justice Press, p. 41.
7. The wording within this article explicitly states that "Nothing in this Declaration may be interpreted as implying for any State, people, group or person any right to engage in any activity or to perform any act contrary to the Charter of the United Nations or construes as authorizing or encouraging any action which would dismember or impair, totally or in part, the territorial integrity or political unity of sovereign and independent States." This negates any real discussion of independence and self-determination as it has been applicable to all

The Path to Self-Determination

Natan Obed

(This keynote address was presented at the Inuit Studies Conference, St. John's, NL, on October 8, 2016.)

Nakummek, Gary. Thank you so much.

Unusaakut. Good afternoon, everyone.

As I've been introduced, I'm Natan Obed, President of Inuit Tapiriit Kanatami.

I know that I'm speaking before a supportive and enthusiastic crowd. It's great. Usually I don't have that luxury, so I'll try to make it count today. I also want to recognize the people who aren't in this room, and also the people who are listening and watching on webcast, and people hopefully from across Inuit Nunangat.

I want to talk today about the path to self-determination, and it's a path that we take every single day as Inuit. If I look around the room, and since I've been here this morning, I've seen a host of people that I've shared this path with, Inuit and non-Inuit alike. I've worked on Inuit issues now for fifteen years, and over that course of time we have seen some significant changes and we should be proud of them, but there still is much work to be done. And the more that we get into the work, the more that we realize sometimes we're not thinking about these things the right way. We're thinking in an incomplete set of circumstances that lead us to the problems that we're trying to solve. So I'll start today with talking a bit about cultural appropriation.

Alethea Arnaquq-Baril made a Facebook post about five or six days ago about Kate Middleton, who was wearing ulu earrings during her trip to Canada, and those ulu earrings weren't made by an Inuk artist. And she talked about cultural appropriation and why this was something we should consider, as Canadians or as artists or as business people, and the context of what it means to not own something that is yours, that is a symbol of your culture and society. Now, if there are patent lawyers in the room, I would imagine that you're immediately thinking, "Well under Canadian Law this isn't an individual's item to own." You would immediately start thinking about the reasons why Inuit can't say that we have any right to be able to exclusively make things that look like ulus. But you have to unpack this; you have to think about where we started.

If you think about the beginning of the land claims movement, Inuit had to understand that the land we had lived on and occupied since time immemorial wasn't actually ours. That the title that we had to it, that was tenuous at best, was something called "Aboriginal title." It's not fee simple in the way that you think of, perhaps if you own a home and you own land, the way you think of that. And that we have had to explain our land use and occupancy to the Government of Canada just to be able to sit down and talk about a negotiation that would lead then to land claims. So we were told that the land that was ours was actually not ours. And then you talk about, say, the minerals that are under our lands, or any of the natural resources that are under our lands, and those aren't ours either. And why? Because sub-surface is different from surface. And I understand the Canadian constructs that govern us—the legislation, the Supreme Court rulings, the way in which the Canadian government has articulated this issue to the Inuit. But again, we see mining companies, we see natural resource developers who come into our land, and we negotiate with them for Impact Benefit Agreements; we may get shared royalties with the province or territory in which we live. We may get business opportunities if we meet the criteria that are set out as being fair. But it comes back to the same issue: what we thought was ours isn't actually ours. And the fact that people can come onto our lands, take from our lands, and leave us still a marginalized people and largely in poverty, while the wealth generated from those lands goes to private corporations and to the rest of Canada.

And then we have education. Actually this one hits home for just about everyone here in this room: That the way in which we educate our children, and the way in which we imagine them to be productive members of our society, was deemed irrelevant. That we were told we were doing it the wrong way. And that especially in the 1950s and '60s, this idea that Inuit needed to be put in residential schools, and needed to be indoctrinated into a western construct and not keep their language, and not keep their cultural ties and their ties to their parents as a prerequisite for them to be rehabilitated into, quote-unquote, "a good Canadian citizen." The effects of that still resonate today.

So then we have an education system where the way that we educate our children is wrong, and you have to educate your children in a southern Canadian way. And then we get into governance, and we get into the mobilization of Indigenous people in Canada, and the creation of Inuit Tapiriit Kanatami in 1971, and the driving force of Inuit representation organizations in settling land claims. And restructuring the Canadian map . . . And that's exciting, but here we are in 2016, and when we say Indigenous peoples and Inuit need to have a participatory role in the way that the government conducts its business, which is supported by the Constitution, by the UN Declaration of the Rights of Indigenous People, we're shown again and again that that request and that reality aren't taken seriously. So even the place that we play in Canada, the governance model that we've created, how we've self-determined to the world to say this is who we are, can be overrun by a government bureaucrat who decides that they don't necessarily like Inuit Tapiriit Kanatami's position on things, so perhaps they will bring in another Inuk who will represent the Inuit voice. It could be something as innocuous as cross-cultural training, or it could be something as large as consultation on particular program reviews.

The fact remains that there is still a basic lack of respect for Inuit and the way in which we are trying to self-determine to the world. So let's bring it back to the earrings. That somehow no matter where we go, no matter what we do, we're being told that who we are is secondary to who others want us to be, and our place in Canada is largely dictated by rules that we didn't create and governments that see us more as adversaries than as equals—or partners. This is an example of how it then mushrooms out into the rest of society, where others take our cultural imagery and repurpose it, and use it as their own, on their own terms, and describe to the world, in a different way, who we are, what we look like, how we dress, what items we use for daily life. And I think that is at the heart of a lot of this frustration.

And so here we are today, talking about self-determination across a number of different crosscutting issues. But I'll start a little bit with governance. I've already mentioned it. Inuit Tapiriit Kanatami is a democratic institution. It doesn't need to exist. We only play a role because the four Inuit land claim regions have given us that role. The four presidents of our land claim organizations—the Nunatsiavut Government, Makivik Corporation, Nunavut Tunngavik Inc., and the Inuvialuit Regional Corporation—are our board of directors, and they elect the president of the organization and direct the organization's mandate and work. So it is a true expression of democracy—Inuit democracy. From every single one of you in this room who is a beneficiary of one of our four land claims, you get to elect your president, or your chair, as in the Inuvialuit Regional Corporation. And then those presidents, in thinking about your interests, elect a national and international leader to represent Canadian Inuit.

I don't have the power to do the things that I'm doing or say the things that I'm saying by myself. I didn't go and create a platform and a mandate for myself, and then through lobbying and public support get to where I am today. I am an agent of Inuit Tapiriit Kanatami. I'm an agent of the board. I'm saying what they want me to say. My power comes from the regions. And I think that's really powerful because not all Indigenous peoples have that luxury in Canada, of being united enough to have a national president. This is really important because all the different constructs that we'll talk about today—the United Nations Declaration on the Rights of Indigenous peoples, the over-arching relationship between the Government of Canada and Inuit—all of that is predicated on that counterpoint, that the Inuit counterpoint for the Government of Canada is Inuit Tapiriit Kanatami. And *we* have decided that. And that's an exciting thing. It's a step on the path to self-determination.

I want to talk a little bit about dreams and who gets to have them. I recently watched a Stephen Hawking movie—*The Theory of Everything*, I think is its name—and it's interesting to me that a lot of his life's work, somebody who is renowned as one of the smartest people alive, was actually wrong and has been debunked, and he has moved on to different constructs around black holes. Why that's interesting to me is that entire societies believed what he had to say, entire groups of academics. It was so powerful and meant so much to them, and it made so much sense, that they followed that line of thinking for some time.

Now how that equates to us here today is: Who gets to decide what's best for us? If you think about education, and how our children go to school and what curriculum they use, what language they speak, whose bright idea is it? Is it just a century-and-a-half of principles that have been developed over time by Canada and thrust upon Inuit as if we could benefit from them the same way somebody in suburban Ontario could?

Also, the ideas of who we are in relation to Canada. When we dream of our place within Canada, I don't think I need a lawyer to do that. I don't think Inuit need lawyers to do that. Now, the legal construct is what we live in, and our ability to interact with legislation and policy is imperative to our success as advocates for Inuit at ITK. But if you get down to the central tenant, the central questions, and you dream about a universe, you dream about the way the universe fits, and if you think about it as an Inuit universe you go back to this idea of Aboriginal title, or back to the idea that limitations on funding are the only things holding us back from achieving social equity. Then you're able to expand your thinking about what's possible.

There's a Health Accord being negotiated right now between the Federal Government and provinces and territories. Why couldn't there be an Inuit Health Accord that puts the necessary funding forward to address some of our massive needs, especially in relation to mental health? It's entirely possible, but why would we not think that way? Because the Federal Government has already decided what the priorities are. They've already entered into discussions with provinces and territories, with service delivery agents, about how the federal ideas would then be implemented in provinces and territories.

We also think about our policy space. What space do we occupy as Inuit? We'd like to say we occupy an Inuit Nunangat space. Thirty-five percent of Canada's landmass, 50 percent of its coastline—the foundation for Arctic sovereignty. That's the space we say we occupy. But the Federal Government often thinks of this space as "northern equals territorial," and other Inuit regions fall outside of a lot of those policy discussions. So even the ability to dream of the way in which the country works on Arctic issues is something we don't have the right to control. But that doesn't mean that can't happen.

People in a dominant society can convince entire groups of people to believe in bad and incorrect ideas, which happens all the time. So the idea that what grounds us to our current realities is infallible—I reject that. The idea that we can't build a better pedagogy for education, I believe we can. Shouldn't it be based on what we want our Inuit children to become? Should we not be talking to academic institutions about what it means for the Inuit reality when Alberta-based curricula is the standard because of the entrance requirements for colleges and universities, when so few of our students can go to those universities or colleges anyways without years of struggle to get through? The purpose of all of this, the purpose of the Inuit movement, land claims and otherwise, can grow, and it can occupy larger spaces than we've already occupied. And that's why I said that in my speech last year in Cambridge Bay, when I was in the election process. I think that with all of the assets we have today, the fact that there are so many Inuit that are educated, or that are knowledgeable and have wisdom, who are willing to work on causes that we have been working on for 40 or 50 years, there is no reason to think that we cannot make as big a difference today and tomorrow as our parents did in creating land claims and representational organizations.

I have a picture on my phone that I'm going to show the Prime Minister—it's of my father standing in what looks to be a parliamentary room, but standing with Pierre Trudeau alongside a couple of other Inuit leaders as well. I want to show the Prime Minster this picture and talk about what it means, to both of us, to be legacies. Our parents worked on these issues and now we're working on them. But I also want to talk about how little has changed from what we said and the inclusion that we want to have, and how it shouldn't be another generation of photo opportunities and platitudes that replace real action. With that in mind, I want to transition into a discussion about what our priorities are at ITK and how they relate to self-determination.

Earlier this year, we passed our strategic plan for 2016 to 2019, which will guide our organization for the next three years. We have seven objectives within our strategic plan. The first is in relation to suicide prevention. We released the National Inuit Suicide Prevention Strategy this summer, in July, and in it we want to change the way Inuit and the rest of Canada think about our interaction with suicide and suicide prevention. Canada was transfixed this spring on Attawapiskat and other Indigenous suicide stories. There was even an emergency debate in the House of Commons, which talked about the need for action. But a lot of the discussion was based on a couple of different things. First, an individual perspective on what is a public health policy issue. For some reason, in this field, an individual perspective can replace a public policy best practice. The other thing that I noticed is that the answers seem to lie with those most affected, and the issues are focused around the time that people are in crisis. The country wants to think about this issue as relating to Indigenous youth, and they want to talk about this through the lens of suicide attempts and completions. And I don't think that we deal with any of our public health policy issues like that, and the World Health Organization says that suicide is a largely preventable public health crisis.

In Québec, there is a strategy that has lowered the rate of youth suicide by over half during the last twelve years. It's possible. We know that we come from a low-suicide reality. Elevated rates of suicide only started happening in the 1970s. We were empowered by this data, this evidence, so we set out to create an evidence-based Inuit-specific suicide prevention strategy that's globally informed. And the outputs of it—and this is when it comes to self-determination—is the idea that we won't get where we need to go without social equity. Housing, education, and healthcare are the key foundations of social equity. We have 40 percent overcrowding rates for housing, our education attainment rates are approximately 30 percent for high school graduation, and we have 250 times the tuberculosis rates of all other Canadians who were born in Canada—we have a long way to go on social equity. So it goes from this society, where we have huge challenges that then spur on negative consequences at community and family levels. We know that we have historical trauma; we know we haven't had the ability to heal from all those things that happened to us in the 1950s and '60s, and that now have been cast upon subsequent generations of Inuit. These things are not ethereal; they are practical understandings of these concepts.

There is an inability for the Canadian public, or the government, to accept that there is cause and effect, and that even before we talk about mental health services or providing specific care to all those who are in need, we must first focus on the transformative societal shift that needs to take place to ensure that we are not creating risk factors for suicide. If you live in Inuit Nunangat, you and your children are at a higher risk for suicide. And it doesn't matter how many protective factors you have, or how successful you are, or how strong your personal mental health is. The fact that we are encompassing entire populations with risk factors that then spill into society means that no matter who you are, you are affected. You know somebody who's died by suicide. You have been put in situations where there's been crisis. You or your family members have been abused; 50 percent of Inuit women in a health survey reported being sexually abused in childhood. That is a reality and it's unacceptable, and we need to change it. So all of these different things come together to create a National Inuit Suicide Prevention Strategy. We did this together. It wasn't a couple of people at ITK who created this document. The Alianait Inuit Mental Wellness subcommittee, the Mental Health Commission of Canada, Health Canada—especially with support from their First Nations Inuit Health Branch—and the board of ITK, and the National Inuit Committee on Health, of which there are members here today, all worked on this together. It is our statement to Canada, and once again we're saying, "This is what we want."

And what's interesting then, in this time of reconciliation and self-determination, is: How is Canada going to perceive that? How are the academics in this room, whose field is mental health, going to perceive it? Are you going to pick it apart? Are you going to say it's not really what Inuit want? Or perhaps part of it's good, but the rest of it could be improved. Or will you accept that Inuit have said to Canada, this is what we need, and work with us to achieve that goal through the way in which we decided to move toward it. That is the way in which everyone, all Canadians, can play a role in self-determination for Inuit. By accepting that we have things to say, and we do so in a way that respects our people and also respects human knowledge.

We talked about housing. Housing is ITK's second priority. I also want to think about self-determination in housing. For most of Canada, the idea of housing is that there exists a private housing market, a rental market, and social housing. People usually float between the three in their lifetime. Perhaps during university you're in a dorm, so you're in an assisted rental situation. Those markets and that structure came to be over the course of the history of Canada. But housing in Inuit Nunangat, and the infrastructure in Inuit Nunangat, came about in fits and starts and weren't ever meant to be long-term solutions. We're not a people that had private housing markets before contact and before core settlement into our communities. So the idea that now we'd be able to figure it out in 20, or 30, or 40 years is really a hindrance to the work that needs to be done. We still don't have a sustainable housing model. In parts of Inuit Nunangat, we have private home ownership. The majority of our people live in social housing without a true sustainable transition into any other form of housing. So the task in front of us today is to understand that there is a massive need, 40 percent overcrowding as I've mentioned, but that there is also a question on the floor that hasn't been answered. And you can get into as much discussion as you want about the cool new innovative designs for housing, but that still doesn't get us to a sustainable housing solution—it is a component of it.

The idea for Southern Canada is that you build equity through your home. It is an essential building block for your own personal worth, and then is something that you pass on and accumulates wealth over time. That is the model. So for Inuit, what is the model? How do we create a sustainable housing structure? Next week there will be an Inuit Housing Summit and we'll be talking about these issues, but these are academic questions as well. Perhaps there are solutions we haven't thought of yet; perhaps there are partnerships to be had. But the idea on self-determination in housing is not just that we need a lot of money and need to keep building the same sort of structures and the same governance models that we already have. It is to reimagine what is possible and then to try to go ahead and achieve it. It's the same thing for infrastructure. You think about who built the infrastructure in Inuit Nunangat. A lot of it was built by the US Military. They proved in the late '40s and early '50s that you can build long-term sustainable infrastructure in the Arctic, yet we still don't have that second wave filling in for that first wave, which was dominated by Cold War considerations and a government that isn't our own. So all those Distant Early Warning sites that we pass when we fly on our trips, or the airstrips that we probably fly on every time we go to the Arctic in Goose Bay or Iqaluit. Who do you think built those? And what does that say about our place within Canada? That we don't have a second phase of build in Canada built upon the sustainability of our communities and our society, instead of the interests of sovereignty and the Cold War.

The third objective in our strategic plan is reconciliation, and this is an interesting one. The government of Canada has made it their priority to talk about reconciliation, and has done very unilateral things in this process. We think of the name change on day one from Aboriginal Affairs and Northern Development to Indigenous and Northern Affairs Canada. We didn't work with the government to change that name. There is no letter you can find from three Indigenous groups in Canada that says, "We request the Government of Canada start using the term Indigenous instead of Aboriginal." Just think about that point. It shows the transparency of where we are today rather than the communicated space that the Federal Government wants to have with us. Is it one of empathy, sympathy, working together, partnership, and renewed relationship? I believe that's possible. I believe we'll get there. But reconciliation isn't easy and it isn't done by changing terms to fit your political angle.

Reconciliation is not just something that you do today that you didn't do yesterday. It's premised on action. So the Missing and Murdered Indigenous Women and Girls Inquiry, or the Truth and Reconciliation Commission's 94 Calls to Action, or the United Nations Declaration on the Rights of Indigenous Peoples—their acceptance and implementation are two different things. Accepting that they exist and saying that they're important allows for the Canadian government, and Canadians to think that we're actually doing something, when we aren't until we have implementation plans and actions associated with each one of those things, which are created from the ground up with Indigenous people. And that's where reconciliation breaks down.

Everyone wants in on reconciliation today, but often on non-Indigenous terms. You don't want true partnerships; you just want to be branded with that term, to feel good about the fact that you're doing something for us, with us. My central take on reconciliation is that it's not as easy as it looks. And it should be hard. When you think about the residential school existence and the entirety of the residential school structure, you should then juxtapose that with other cultural genocides that have happened across the world. They think about the lack of change in the way that we talk about our history, and the individuals within our history, based on what we know now about the true intent of residential schools. And the fact that there were whistle blowers in the 1920s, there were people who spoke out against the treatment of Indigenous people, and there was action and there were actual people in charge of implementing these racist policies that killed thousands of children. And yet our history books don't change to reflect the enormity of that atrocity. No individuals have to bear the brunt of that history. That somehow, within Indigenous peoples, it still remains a society issue. That was a different time; the societal norms were different.

I would hope that if I did anything like what happened, that if I was responsible for anything like what happened to those children in residential schools, that history would not treat me kindly, and that the good deeds I've done today would be recast into the reality of the actions that I let happen. And I would hope that we all would think that of ourselves. That the things that we do today, some of them may seem wrong in the future, like "Oh I really shouldn't have supported that particular program," or "those socks look awful on me." You have these things you regret in the future, but then there are objective truths, and the truths that we discover over time, that many researchers in this room have helped uncover. And that's when we have to think differently about the past and about the people that we lift up, and the people that we still consider to be heroes. And the new place that we have to then reconcile with. So I hope that reconciliation does include a change in the way people think about those past actions, because the world has accepted nothing less in other places where genocide has happened, and it should be the same here in Canada.

Number four is in relation to education. It's interesting that reconciliation and education, in our strategy, come together. I've already talked a little bit about not accepting the present when it comes to education. I've given this example before. Just think about this: I have a nine-year-old, Panigusiq, and a seven-year-old, Jushua. They were lucky enough to be able to go to daycare in Inuktitut. That isn't a reality that all Inuit children have. They can go to school in Inuktitut from kindergarten to grade four, but there is nowhere in Canada that I can move where my child can then continue to go to school, in his first language, beyond grade four. And the first day of school last year—this is when my eldest was going into grade three, and this was before I became ITK President—he asked me, "Ataata, can we move somewhere where I can still go to school in Inuktitut?" And to think that I would have to go to Greenland to make that happen makes no sense. Sixty percent of all Inuit in Canada, no matter how much language loss we have, still say that Inuktitut is our mother tongue. The fact that we cannot create a bilingual education system is our failing, and it's failing our children. It isn't the failing of the Federal Government or a province or territory by itself. It is what our parents and our grandparents wanted for us. And it's something that we have to do more to achieve. So the construct of why we have education and what is K-12 education for? Reconsider this. What do our communities want our children to do? What skills and abilities do we want them to have by the time they're eighteen? And if you empower the local communities to answer those questions, and create curriculums that satisfy those questions with answers that empower our society and communities, then we'll have real success. Not only in our K-12 system but also in our early childhood development, and also then going on to post-secondary. The world's leading post-secondary institutions, the students who go to them, don't come from our reality.

There are a myriad of ways to get the skills necessary to compete in the global environment and to get the best quality education. Often we have not thought beyond the things that service delivery agents can provide. Teacher accreditation: Is there any magic in a four-year BA? That's not to put anyone down who has taken one and is a wonderful teacher. But it was only in the 1970s that many who were taught in Canada were taught by teachers who went to normal school for a year, and then were taught on the job in a sort of apprentice-style manner, becoming amazing teachers who generated the children who went through those systems and now lead those societies. But somehow we're stuck saying we don't have a enough teachers, we don't have enough teachers who speak Inuktut, and we don't know how to get from here to there without massive influxes of cash to teach the same way that we're already teaching, when there are other ways to do it.

I'm going off-script I think, from ITK's positions, at the moment, but I'm doing that for a purpose. I am putting this to the room. This is an academic setting; we're in a university, what do you do in post-secondary? What do you do in all higher education? You contemplate questions and you try to find answers that move our society forward. So this is what I'm trying to do today.

Number five of seven is the environment. Last week I was on *Power & Politics*, and I hopefully was heard by more than just my social media following. I talked about reconciliation and climate change being just as close a fit as the economy and climate change. Minister McKenna, the Prime Minister, many different jurisdictions have talked about the need to link climate change and the economy. Whatever you think of that concept, you should also be thinking of the concept of reconciliation and climate change. Isn't this one of the foundational tenants of the differences between non-Indigenous Canadians and Indigenous Canadians? The way that we treat the environment. The way that we look at the natural world. The love that we have for the species that live within our environment. The fact that we consider ourselves a part of our environment, and that we do not dominate or control it. If Canadians cannot understand these concepts and don't accept them then we will have a response to the Paris Declaration, the framework for action in Canada, that focuses on an economic reality that all Canadians are concerned about. The idea that they would also be concerned about our health and our wellbeing, and our wish to ensure that our environment stays intact, those are new concepts. So I would say that would be a reconciliation moment, if the Government of Canada, and provinces and territories, and all Canadians, would just accept that the way in which we interact with our environment and the way in which climate change will affect us is foundationally and fundamentally different than the way it will affect them. It isn't about gas going up another ten cents. It isn't about not being able to skate on the Rideau Canal for two more weeks during the year. This is about the entirety of our society staying intact. And I don't think, today, there is a great enough appreciation for that.

Number six is in relation to research. This is something that we talked about this morning. We had panellists from across Inuit Nunangat talking about what activities we're undertaking in relation to self-determination in research. But at the national level, and at our level, we still don't have the ability to partner and participate in research. There are no Inuit on governing councils and tri-councils in any one of the agencies. We can be excluded from the room because of a credentials argument, even though we do have credentialed people. There are Inuit in all sorts of fields, and so I would never say there is no Inuk that isn't a Masters or a PhD, because there probably is. But the idea that we don't have a right to be in the room when the tri-councils are an agency of government and have little control from ministers responsible for allocating funds and then providing hierarchal strategic direction is offensive. It's okay for them to bend their own rules to suit their governance model, but when it comes to us it's a hard and fast reality. That "No, No. We couldn't do that. We couldn't provide Inuit representation at the highest levels of CIHR or NSERC," because that isn't how it works.

But somehow a minister is able to completely change the direction of the way in which these organizations run and function. This is the challenge that we face.

It's a combination of knowledge, and shared purpose, but also respect. So there is a shared purpose. We want the best for our research. We have a multitude of research questions that we need answered. We don't even know the ideation rates for suicide in our regions. In the creation of our Inuit Suicide Prevention Strategy, we had to go and dig through coroner data to even get the rates of Inuit-specific suicides in each one of our regions. We had to do that ourselves. We have basic gaps in knowledge. We also have a basic lack of respect for our people in the governance model that then dictates how monies are spent and who gets them. And these are things that need to change. It's part of this dream that we all, I think, have to have about self-determination. The constructs you have about who's in and who's out has to change. The idea that we are excluded from rooms because we aren't the foremost expert that has been selected by a panel to take one space out of fifteen, versus we have knowledge that no matter how smart you are in a non-Indigenous setting you will never have because you will never know the Inuit reality as Inuit know it. That is the fundamental shift I hope we can all see. And that is the self-determination in regards to research at the national level that I hope we can usher in, in this new era of Inuit-to-Crown and nation-to-nation.

The last point on self-determination is in relation to health and wellbeing, and Inuit get tired of hearing about the gaps in outcomes. Actually, our rates drive researchers to us. There are very few places in the world where you can have research findings that attract a national interest . . . Because they are so bad, and there are such broad discrepancies between the Inuit-specific reality and the Canadian reality. And so these are questions that need to be answered, but it goes beyond that. We have a better understanding now of our health condition. We understand what we need to do to try and solve it. The question is: How can we work in partnership with governments to create the solutions that we know are necessary? I think that we'll look back on this time as, hopefully, the end of inaction.

I'm a huge fan of Cindy Blackstock and the work that she does for the First Nations Child and Family Caring Society of Canada and for all Indigenous children. And if you think about that, the specific things that organization is uncovering about the basic inequity between what is spent on Indigenous children versus what is spent on non-Indigenous children in one particular point in our health and social services spectrum, I think that you would imagine that if we had one hundred Cindy Blackstocks there would be one hundred different examples that are equally as powerful. And so that is the challenge of our time as well: to create social equity in health and our social reality that allows for us to move forward and take advantage of self-determination in a way that our ancestors did, in a way that we know that we can, moving forward.

I appreciate your attention here today. I hope we can work together moving forward. And I also thank all of you who have done amazing work in this room, on behalf, with, and for Inuit. Nakummek.

Can Canada Retrieve the Principles of its First Confederation?

Peter H. Russell

It is well known that Aboriginal peoples did not take part in the 1867 Confederation. Much less known by non-Aboriginal Canadians is another confederal event that took place a century before that most celebrated Confederation of Britain's North American colonies. At Niagara, in 1764, the British Crown entered into a confederation-like agreement with Indigenous nations. The principles underlying that agreement provide a much more promising basis for just and mutually beneficial constitutional arrangements with Canada's Aboriginal peoples than anything contained in the *British North America Act, 1867*.

My purpose in this essay is fourfold: first, to explain why Confederation in 1867 was an inappropriate basis for constitutional agreements with Aboriginal Peoples; second, to show why the Treaty of Niagara in 1764 is more promising; third, to recount how the principles underlying that treaty, for more than two centuries, were subverted; and finally, to consider how those principles might animate Canada's constitutional relationships with First Nations, Inuit Peoples, and the Métis Nation, now and in the future.

In her magisterial history of Canada's "founding peoples," Olive Dickason records that when the Confederation of British North American colonies was agreed to in 1867, Indigenous peoples were not consulted: "the question of their partnership was not even raised."[1] She adds that no one thought of consulting or even informing the Inuit when the Privy Council issued a proclamation in 1880 transferring Britain's Arctic territories to the Dominion.

But even if through some miracle of enlightenment the suggestion had been made to invite representatives of Indigenous peoples to the Confederation talks in the 1860s, it is highly doubtful that such an invitation would have been taken up. For more than two centuries, nations native to North America had been regulating their relations with imperial powers and settler governments by means of treaty-like agreements. There was nothing like that on offer at Charlottetown or Québec City in 1864. Later on, proponents of provincial rights would talk about Confederation as a compact or treaty among the founding provinces, but that rhetorical treaty has nothing in common with the treaties that First Nations had been making with the Crown before Confederation, and would continue to make after Confederation. From the Indigenous perspective, treaty-making was the appropriate way of establishing formal relationships with the authorities of incoming settlers, not hanging around watching white men join their colonies together in a federal union.

If any Indian representatives had been given observer status in the Confederation conferences, they would have been no more impressed than their descendants were a century later when offered the chance to listen in on the talks Canada's first ministers were having on revisiting Confederation. At Charlottetown in September 1864, they would not have heard a word about Aboriginal peoples. A month later, in the first week of the conference at Québec City, members of the Fathers of Confederation's families took a carriage ride to visit the Wendat settlement at Lorette, up the St. Lawrence from Québec City, and meet its old chief, Ondialerethe (Simon Romain).[2] You can be sure that the women and children and chaperones on this tour did not visit the Wendat chief to talk about the constitution. This was a tourism outing.

It was not until the final week of the Québec conference that the delegates passed a resolution on the powers to be given to the federation's new central parliament, which included the following statement:

> It shall be competent for the general legislature to pass laws respecting
> 1) Indians

In the final text of the BNA Act, this becomes the 24th of the 29 "matters" Section 91 assigns exclusively to the Parliament of Canada, and is worded: "Indians, and Lands reserved for the Indians."[3]

Section 91(24) is the only mention of Aboriginal peoples in Canada's founding Constitution. It treats "Indians" not as people, let alone partners in Confederation, but as a subject matter of federal legislation. The addition of "Lands reserved for the Indians" reflects the practice of reserving small parcels of land for the exclusive use of Indians, either through what British and colonial authorities regarded as land session treaties or administrative fiat. Section 91(24) makes it clear that the Indians living on these reserves, and the reserve lands themselves, were entirely subject to the legislative authority of the Parliament of Canada. It is doubtful that any Indigenous person on the territory claimed by Canada and Britain would have agreed with such a provision.

The Fathers of Confederation's assumption of having control over Aboriginal peoples and their lands was a far cry from the relationship between the Crown's representatives and First Nation leaders that was the basis of the covenant entered into at Niagara in 1764. Back then, Indigenous leaders met with representatives of the British Crown on terms of rough equality in political and military terms. Between 1764 and Confederation, much had changed materially and ideologically.

After repulsing the American invasion of Canada with Aboriginal help, the British made peace with the United States, but in the 1814 Treaty of Ghent dropped its support for an independent Indian buffer state to block American expansion. Britain had used its support for an Indian buffer state to induce First Nations to fight on its side.[4] The end of the war brought a flood of Loyalists and British settlers, drastically reversing the ratio of Indigenous people to settlers—a demographic revolution that was tragically accelerated by Indigenous vulnerability to European disease. In the 1830s, Britain relinquished Aboriginal policy to settler control. Indigenous peoples had no positive place in the self-governing polities the colonists were building in pre-Confederation Canada. They were a problem, not a political partner. The English-speaking settler vision of the fate of Indigenous peoples was captured in the Province of Canada's *Gradual Civilization Act*, introduced by Attorney General of Canada East John A. Macdonald in 1857. Indians would be confined to reserves safely away from "civilized society," until one by one their men passed morals examinations entitling them and their families to live off reserve, enter civilized society, and no longer be Indians.[5] Is it any wonder that John A. and company did not consult with Indians about their plan for a Canadian federation?

As Macdonald, Canada's first prime minister, went to work on expanding Canada westward, he could not ignore the Métis Nation. In 1869, after securing Britain's agreement to Canada's purchase of the Hudson's Bay Company's interests in Rupert's Land, Macdonald was confronted by a Provisional Government in the Red River area of Assiniboia. This government was led by Louis Riel, the leading spokesman of the Métis Nation, descendants of families formed by French and Scottish fathers and Saulteaux, Cree, and Assiniboine mothers who, through decades of pressing their rights in the fur trade and participating in the Buffalo hunt on the western plains, had developed a strong sense of national identity. Though very much the largest and most powerful component of the Red River settlement, the Métis reached out to the English-speaking community so that it had parity representation on the Council of the Provisional Government. Macdonald had the good sense to recognize that the Provisional Government was effectively filling a governmental vacuum. He postponed the purchase of Rupert's Land, withdrew the mandate of his cabinet colleague William McDougall—whom he had sent to be lieutenant governor of the new territory—and sent Donald Smith, the Hudson's Bay Company's Chief Factor, to Red River to pave the way for a peaceful union of the territory with Canada.

In the winter of 1870, a 40-person convention, with equal representation from the Métis and English-settler communities, drew up a List of Rights that would be the settlement's conditions for joining Canada as its fifth province. The list included the people's right to elect their own legislature, that their government be bilingual, that concerns about land title be tackled, that treaties be negotiated with the several tribes of Indians in the territory, and that the new province have fair representation in the Canadian Parliament.[6] A negotiating team (that did not include Riel) went to Ottawa in March 1870 and was able to get many of the demands of the Red River community written into the *Manitoba Act*, creating the Province of Manitoba. Though the province, in its first iteration, was postage stamp in size, confined to the Lake Winnipeg river basin, 1.4 million acres was set aside for the children of the Métis families settled in river lots along the Red and Assiniboine rivers. Delay in giving effect to this provision of the *Manitoba Act*, a delay that was found, much later, by the Supreme Court of Canada to have breached the honour of the Crown,[7] cheated the Métis from having a block of land in Manitoba that could have been their nation's homeland.[8] Even though the creation of Manitoba had a tragic outcome for the Métis Nation and its leader, Riel, who was driven into exile, in process it came close to providing an Indigenous people with a democratic path to joining Confederation.

What I refer to as the first Confederation, at Niagara in 1764, was not of course an agreement on the terms of joining Canada. In function, it was the making of a peace treaty defining the terms on which Indigenous nations would be willing to share territory with people subject to the authority of the British government.

In May 1763, war had broken out between Britain and a confederacy of

Indigenous North American nations, led by Odawa Chief Pontiac. The uprising occurred when rumours were confirmed that France and Spain had ceded all of Canada and Louisiana east of the Mississippi to Great Britain. Indigenous leaders were outraged by the apparent disregard on the part of Britain for the fact that the land in the territory referred to in their peace treaty belonged to the Aboriginal nations. Added to this was deep distrust of the British and their colonists. Nations that had enjoyed a reasonably harmonious and beneficial alliance with the French were concerned that Britain would push its policy of mass settlement into Indian territory west of the Allegheny Mountains.

The Pontiac uprising gathered strength as the oratory of the Delaware Prophet Neolin summoned Indigenous peoples to make a final stand against the seemingly unending encroachments of European nations. In six weeks, Indian nations, including the Chippewa, Delaware, Kickapoo, Mingo, Miami, Neutral, Odawa, Potawatomi, Seneca, and Wyandot had taken all the forts in the northwest that the British had taken over from the French, and had Niagara, Detroit, and Fort Pitt under siege. Raiding parties attacked settler communities along the frontiers, killing 600 Pennsylvanians. An American historian compares the shock and terror of these attacks to Pearl Harbor.[9]

At this point, Britain had to make a policy decision. Its North American Commander-in-Chief, Jeffrey Amherst, pushed for responding militarily to the Pontiac uprising. That would have required reinforcing its army in America. At the end of an exhausting seven years world war with France and Spain, pursuing a war with the Indians would have been a tough sell in the British Parliament. The alternative was the policy of peace and negotiation favoured by Sir William Johnson, the king's special envoy to the northern Indian nations. The king and his advisers chose Johnson's policy. In the fall of 1763, Amherst returned to England and Johnson's policy was incorporated in the final six paragraphs of a proclamation issued by King George III on October 7, 1763.[10]

Most of the Royal Proclamation provided governments for the colonies Britain had taken over from France and Spain: East and West Florida, Granada, and Québec. In its concluding six paragraphs, addressed to "the several Nations or Tribes of Indians with whom We are connected," the British sovereign did not purport to impose a system of government on the Indian nations. He recognized them as independent political societies, whose friendship his government wished to secure. King George III apologized for the "great Frauds and Abuses [that] have been committed in purchasing Lands of the Indians." Here he was referring to the practice of his settler subjects purchasing land from Indians, who had no authority to sell it. The King promised "to prevent such irregularities for the future" by ordering that "no Private person presume to make such purchases." Settlement would be permitted only on lands purchased by the Crown from Indians "at some public meeting or Assembly" of the Indian people. He also ordered the removal of any of his subjects who had settled on lands that had not been ceded to or purchased by the Crown.

The recognition of the Indian nations' political independence and ownership of their land pointed in the right direction for an agreement. However, in places the Royal Proclamation used language that was and is unacceptable to Indians. At one point, it speaks of the lands and territories outside Québec, or the territory granted to the Hudson's Bay Company, as being reserved for the Indians "under our Sovereignty, Protection, and Dominion." The Indigenous nations might accept a British claim to sovereignty aimed at excluding other European powers from having dealings with them, but not a claim aimed at exercising sovereignty over them. Why should they? They had governed themselves for centuries and had certainly not been conquered by Great Britain. Moreover, the implication that somehow Britain had acquired ownership of their land, but was now being decent enough to reserve it for them, was arrogant and utterly unacceptable to the Indian nations. The references to the British acquiring land for settlement though sale or cession made land agreements sound like real estate transactions—a far cry from how Indigenous peoples envisaged sharing their country with the newcomers.

The Royal Proclamation of 1763 could not serve as a peace treaty with First Nations. Besides its unacceptable language, it was issued unilaterally by the British monarch, thousands of miles away from the territory of the Indigenous nations. With that in mind, Sir William Johnson persuaded leaders of the Algonquin and Nipissing nations to send messengers with copies of the Royal Proclamation and various wampums to nations around and west of the Great Lakes, inviting them to meet with him at Niagara in the summer to consider the terms of peace Britain was offering.[11] For many Indigenous communities, Johnson's invitation was problematic. Generally, they distrusted the British, and were upset by the abandonment of gift giving and departures from established fur-trading protocols. Nonetheless, many nations decided to send envoys. In July 1764, canoes began arriving at Niagara. They came from all directions bearing sachems, warriors, and chiefs of at least 24 nations. One historian describes the meeting as the most widely representative gathering of North American Indian nations ever assembled.[12]

The atmosphere at Niagara in July 1764 was tense. Many of the Indian leaders who camped on the west side of the Niagara River were wary of the British. Some had met Sir William Johnson at Fort Detroit three years earlier, when he tried to assure them that they had nothing to fear from Britain's defeat of France—that they could coexist with Britain in *le pays d'en haut* (the great stretch of North America around the Great Lakes over to the Mississippi) as well as they had with the French. But under General Amherst's command, and against William Johnson's urgings, British officials curtailed gift giving and cut off the supply of ammunition to trading posts. Settlers continued to stream in to unceded land along the Ohio River and its watershed. For his part, Johnson was furious that nations he thought were coming to accept friendship with the Crown had instead taken up arms against Britain and its colonists. In his account of Aboriginal-Crown relations, Bruce Munro emphasizes that the Covenant Chain forged at Niagara in the summer of 1764 took place in an environment of "war, intrigue, hard-edged and often illicit trading practices, and an array of related conflicts."[13]

The opening days of the meeting were taken up with diplomatic exchanges and negotiations between Johnson, representing the Crown, and individual nations. These involved exchanges of prisoners and of wampum belts. Johnson came loaded with gifts that facilitated a process of reconciliation. But he was very rough on the Seneca, the westernmost and most pro-French of the Iroquois nations, bullying them into giving up land on both sides of the Niagara River. On July 29, Johnson left Fort Niagara on the east side of the Niagara, where Haudenosaunee leaders already aligned with Great Britain were encamped, to meet several thousand encamped in "Indian territory" on the west side of the river near what is now the town of Niagara-on-the-Lake. There he delivered a long oration, and concluded the treaty with the Indian nations with the presentation of a Covenant Chain belt, and in exchange received a Two Row Wampum.[14]

The Covenant Chain showed figures representing 24 nations linking arms with the Crown. The Two Row Wampum drew on many years of First Nations diplomacy with Dutch and British representatives. A leading Native American scholar, Robert A. Williams, explains that on the Two Row Wampum, "the two rows will symbolize two paths or two vessels, travelling down the same river together. One, a birch bark canoe, will be for the Indian people, their laws, their customs, and other ways. The other, a ship, will be for the white people and their laws, their customs, and their ways. We shall each travel the river, side by side, but in our own boat. Neither of us will try to steer the other vessel."[15]

That Sir William Johnson chose to make peace with Indigenous peoples through their diplomatic protocols shows his understanding of their law and practice. But the downside of this choice of instruments is that the government and people he spoke for did not share his understanding. For the political leaders and officials to whom he was accountable, the written word of a legal text was sacrosanct. This meant that while the Treaty of Niagara did bring about a cessation of hostilities between Indigenous nations and Great Britain, it did not produce an agreement on the principles upon which Great Britain and the Indigenous nations could peacefully coexist in the same territory.

Two principles were essential conditions of peaceful coexistence for the Indigenous leaders, who gathered at Niagara in 1764. The first was their political independence. They were not British subjects—Johnson insisted on this point. He remonstrated with Amherst's officers, who ignored it in their dealings with Aboriginal people. Writing to a British officer, he said, "You may be assured that none of the Six Nations or Western Indians ever declared themselves *subjects*, or will ever consider themselves in that light, while they have any men or open country to retreat to . . . The very idea of subjection would fill them with horror."[16] The Indian nations' willingness to share the British monarch with the British people, as has frequently been pointed out, marked a family relationship, not a political relationship of subordination. The Indigenous peoples of North America may have sensed that the European powers might have greater numbers and military strength, but that did not for them translate into an obligation to accept European rule. The Pontiac uprising indicated that, whatever the odds, they would fight to the death for their liberty. The whole point of the ship and the canoe taking parallel paths on the Two Row Wampum was, and is, to insist on the political equality of the peoples they represent.

The second principle was sharing the land. That is the point of showing the ship and canoe proceeding along a shared river. The Indian nations were willing to admit newcomers on to their lands and waters in ways that are mutually beneficial. Working out how to do that would require ongoing agreements, not once-and-for-all land deals in which the newcomers take most of the territory for themselves, leaving the original owners with small reserves. Indigenous peoples, then and now, did not accept that the newcomers' government had somehow acquired a sovereign power to have the final say of what could be done on Aboriginal-owned land. Though Sir William Johnson recognized Aboriginal ownership of land, and endorsed the policy of keeping settlers off Indian lands until proper treaties were made with the Crown, as a loyal servant of the Crown he most likely accepted the underlying British legal doctrine, evident in the 1763 Royal Proclamation, that Great Britain somehow had acquired an underlying sovereign right over the land owned by the nations and tribes that she had never conquered, but with whom she was connected.

So our first Confederation at Niagara in 1764, like our second in 1867, had some ambiguity—a lack of full agreement on first principles. In both cases, the "s" word, sovereignty, is the root of different understandings. In 1867, Macdonald and his Anglo colleagues did not share with their French Canadian colleagues a common understanding that sovereignty is divided in a federal Canada, between the provinces and the central government. At Niagara, a century earlier, Johnson and the government he represented harboured a belief in an underlying Crown sovereignty, not over the Indigenous people but over their land and resources—a belief that was not shared by Indigenous peoples. While the underlying disagreement, latent in the 1867 Confederation, was resolved fairly quickly through political action of the provinces and decisions of the courts, the gulf between British and settler governments, and their Indigenous allies and neighbours, quickly widened as the former came to exercise their superior power. It will take over two centuries for conditions to change sufficiently to make it possible for Canada's relationship with Indigenous peoples to be rebuilt on the principles depicted in the instruments of the Treaty of Niagara.

The two centuries I refer to are roughly from the early nineteenth century to the late twentieth century. During that long period, British and Canadian settlers pursued a policy of domination aimed at the disappearance of Indigenous peoples. That was the game plan written into John A. Macdonald's 1857 *Gradual Civilization Act*. After Confederation, that plan was pursued with vigour by Canada, her provinces, and her territories. The *Indian Act* imposed a totalitarian regime on First Nations, dispossessed and shattered by treaties and policy into tiny reserve communities, ruled by agents of the Canadian government. The Métis Nation, cheated out of its homeland by government delay in implementing the terms on which it had agreed to join Canada, was militarily crushed. Police rule was imposed on the Inuit People, once Ottawa got around to exercising the sovereignty over their land that Britain purported to transfer to Canada.

As with all of the projects of European imperialism, the policy of assimilation was framed as having a positive moral purpose, grounded in the Europeans' sense of their own superiority—to save the Aboriginal peoples from themselves by making those who were capable as much as possible like the Europeans, in belief, culture, and technology.

This long period of colonial domination cannot just be blotted out of our shared history. Indigenous and non-Indigenous Canadians cannot move forward together in a relationship based on consent and mutual respect unless there is some understanding among non-Indigenous people of what was fundamentally wrong with that relationship during the colonial period. There is no hope for "reconciliation" if the prevailing attitude among Canadians is "too bad we didn't get the job done. We wouldn't have an Aboriginal problem if those peoples had just disappeared by blending in with us." The recently concluded Truth and Reconciliation Commission of Canada is an important step in getting to a shared understanding of the practical and moral failings of the period of colonial domination.

The period of settler colonialism has not only been long, it has also been transformative. For Aboriginal peoples, there is no going back to the circumstances of 1764. Then they were free peoples, and the dominant peoples in most of the territory that we now call Canada. Now they are nations or peoples within a larger federal nation-state, constituting a small minority of the total population. The kind of decolonization that occurred in the Third World—the exodus of the colonizers—is not an option for what George Manuel called the Fourth World, the colonized Indigenous peoples within the First World.[17] The settlers, as Chief Justice Antonio Lamer famously said, are "here to stay."[18] The transformation has entailed much more than a change in the material circumstances of Aboriginal Peoples. Through education, much of it brutally and insensitively imposed, Aboriginal Peoples in Canada have learned how to advance their interests in the political space of the Canadian majority. Political lobbying, court actions, use of mass media, civil disobedience, and participation in the institutions of the dominant society have replaced warfare as the means of asserting their rights.

Change on the settler side has also been much more than material. The ideological change most relevant for the relationship with Aboriginal peoples is a decline in racism. This change came relatively recently and is by no means complete. A lack of respect for Aboriginal Peoples and the assumption that their only viable future was to give up their historic identities and treaty rights, and become just ordinary, garden variety Canadians, was alive and well among Canada's governing elites as recently as 1969, when Pierre Trudeau and Jean Chrétien put forward their White Paper in 1969.[19] Much has changed since then. Aboriginal peoples—First Nations, Inuit, and Métis—have succeeded in having their rights, including treaty rights, recognized in Canada's Constitution. The country's highest court has rendered fairly liberal interpretations of those rights. Progress has been made toward self-government, particularly for three of the four main Inuit communities. A formal apology for the dreadful harm done to Aboriginal peoples through the residential school program has been made in the federal Parliament. The apology led to the Truth and Reconciliation Commission of Canada, which has recommended an extensive program of further reforms, including meeting Canada's international obligations set out in the United Nations Declaration on the Rights of Indigenous Peoples. The most recently elected Federal Government is committed to implementing the TRC recommendations.

The question now is: Can the principles on which the Indian nations made treaty with the Crown in 1764 be retrieved as the foundation for re-building a relationship today that could amount to Canada's third Confederation? This will require federal, provincial, and territorial governments, and the electorates to whom they are accountable, to emulate Sir William Johnson and respect treaty-making as the appropriate constitutional instrument for reforming relations with Indigenous peoples. Further, it will require First Nations to recover their capacity for confederal political action that transcends local loyalties.

The first principle agreed to by the Crown and First Nations at Niagara in 1764 was the political independence of Indigenous peoples. Since the frustrating first ministers constitutional conferences of the mid-1980s, we have come a long way in recognizing Aboriginal peoples inherent right to self-government. Federal, provincial, and territorial governments agreed to including that right in the Charlottetown Accord, albeit with the caveat that the right must be exercised within Canada.[20] Although the Charlottetown Accord was defeated in the October 1992 referendum, the Aboriginal sections of the accord were not a cause of that defeat. A further step toward decolonization came in 2012, when Canada agreed to commit to the United Nations Declaration on the Rights of Indigenous peoples. In doing so, its governments accepted that, according to Article 3 of the Declaration, Indigenous peoples in Canada have "the right to self-determination," and more specifically, "the right to maintain and strengthen their distinct political, legal, economic, social and cultural institutions," as stated in Article 5.[21] The Declaration's only mention of sovereignty is in its final clause, Article 46, which stipulates that nothing in the Declaration is to impair "the territorial integrity or political unity of sovereign and independent States." This kind of sovereignty is what member states of the United Nations insist upon in their dealings with one another. It is not a claim to govern Indigenous peoples or nations within their territories; otherwise it would negate Articles 3 and 5.

The Supreme Court of Canada, in some of its most progressive decisions on Aboriginal rights, continues to adhere to the common law doctrine that the "radical" title and sovereignty of the Crown underlie the recognition of Aboriginal rights. At the very end of *Delgamuukw v. British Columbia*, Chief Justice Lamer wrote that "the basic purpose" of recognizing Aboriginal rights in Section 35 of the *Constitution Act, 1982*, is "the reconciliation of the pre-existence of aboriginal societies with the sovereignty of the Crown."[22] More recently in *Tsilhqot'in Nation v. British Columbia*, Chief Justice McLaughlin, writing for the court, softened Lamer's dictum by saying that the reconciliation to be achieved through Section 35 is "between the group and broader society."[23] But, the court still retains the position that on land, where Native title is recognized under Canadian law, the Government of Canada (perhaps also provincial governments) could justifiably impose its will with respect to developments on that land, for a "compelling and substantial objective."[24] The threshold for imposing non-Indigenous government policy on land recognized to be under Aboriginal ownership has been raised since *Delgamuukw*, but the belief in the justice of asserting Crown sovereignty over an Aboriginal nation or people and its land is still there.

Canada can and must outgrow the imperial premises embedded in common law recognition of Native title. For the Government of Canada to insist on having an overriding veto power on lands that are recognized as Aboriginal is to say that Aboriginal Peoples cannot be trusted to do the right thing with their land. Such a lack of trust is incompatible with retrieving the kind of relationship Sir William Johnson and Aboriginal leaders were tying to establish at Niagara in 1764. If Aboriginal leaders accept the caveat in Article 46 of the UN Declaration securing Canada's territorial integrity, and in addition the authority of Canada's courts to settle claims regarding the boundaries of their ancestral lands, that should be enough.

The practical obstacles to retrieving Indigenous peoples right to govern their societies and their lands are likely to be greater than legal or ideological issues. Canada's colonialist policy fractured many of the historic Indigenous nations into small reserve communities that cannot take on the responsibility of delivering the governmental services that Aboriginal people need and expect today. Putting governmentally viable Indigenous societies together again can only be done by Aboriginal peoples themselves. Many are doing that through the formation of tribal, treaty, and regional councils, and the rebuilding of historic confederacies in various parts of the country.

The other practical issue is adequately resourcing Aboriginal polities. First Nation leaders were wise not to accept the Harper government's proposal to hand over responsibility for education to them without a commitment to provide adequate funding. Aboriginal self-government will not be advanced by deliberate underfunding. Part of the necessary funding can come from revenues derived from the economic use of their lands. For treaty peoples, the lands must encompass all the so-called surrendered lands, not just the postage-stamp reserves.

Here we see how the principle of political autonomy is intertwined with that other principle incorporated in the wampums at Niagara—sharing the country's bounty. A productive homeland is essential for Aboriginal peoples for both material and spiritual reasons. The Supreme Court's decision in *Tsilhquot'n* provides a foundation for First Nations that have not entered into treaties to secure effective economic access to their ancestral lands. The same possibility is open to First Nations that are party to historic treaties, through a process of treaty renovation aimed at applying treaties in a manner portrayed by the Two Row Wampum— sharing this country in a respectful and mutually beneficial way. The four major Inuit communities in the country have largely done that, although they continue to encounter difficulty in getting Canada to keep its promises. A homeland for the Métis Nation will most likely be a linkage of lands on which Métis settlements exist in various provinces and the NWT. The sharing of the bounty of these homelands will often be effected through private sector partnerships. Canadian capitalists and business-page columnists will have to accept that worthwhile economic development need not always meet the standard for profit maximization.

I believe that the ingredients are in place for building a third Confederation that includes Canada's Aboriginal peoples, based on principles that all Canadians can share—principles that were present, in embryo, at Niagara in 1764. Of course, this third Confederation must be realized through the institutions and practices of the day—one of which is federalism. It was federalism that made Confederation in 1867 acceptable to leaders of French Canada and the majority of French Canadians. It did this by establishing a province in which French Canadians would be a majority, with sufficient power to protect and enhance the key components of their distinct culture. I am not suggesting an Aboriginal province. Aboriginal Canada is far too diverse in its allegiances and practices for that. But the basic federal principle of combining self-rule with shared rule does mark the path along which Aboriginal Peoples relations with Canada are evolving. Self-rule for First Nations, the Métis Nation, and the Inuit must be accompanied by participation in the institutions of federal, provincial, and territorial government. That has been happening on a personal basis, with members of Aboriginal communities participating in growing numbers in parliament and legislative assemblies, the public service, and the courts. Whether this is enough to ensure that Aboriginal interests and perspectives are adequately expressed in governing the country—the shared river in the wampum belts—remains to be seen. The idea of a Canadian Aboriginal Parliament along the lines of the Sami parliaments in Scandinavian countries was recommended by the Royal Commission on Aboriginal Peoples.[25] An Aboriginal Parliament would be a third house of Parliament whose main function would be to provide advice to the House of Commons and the Senate on legislation and policy issues relating to Aboriginal peoples. Aboriginal peoples have never shown much interest in such an institution. Given the frustration they continue to experience in communicating with the Government of Canada, it may be time that they gave this proposal a closer look.

As for process, I am very doubtful about the possibility or desirability of a big, magic moment, in which a comprehensive agreement is reached with all of Canada's Aboriginal peoples, one that could amount to a third Confederation. As I understand the process at Niagara in 1764, it was mainly a matter of each nation making peace and exchanging wampums with the Crown—not a once-and-forever agreement but a relationship to be periodically reviewed and renewed.

The federal, provincial, and territorial governments (that have taken over from George III) might issue a proclamation similar to King George's, setting out their commitments in reforming relations with Aboriginal Peoples. Many, perhaps all, of their commitments cover matters contained in the Truth and Reconciliation Commission's recommendations and the UN Declaration. It would help for these commitments, especially those relating to land and self-government, to be set out in some detail with some timelines and an accountability process attached.

Canada 150 will be an occasion for First Nations, the Métis Nation, and the Inuit Peoples to test the willingness of Canadian governments to honour their commitments. So far, the new Trudeau government has dealt only with the relatively easy stuff. If it can show an appetite for dealing with the hard stuff—land and self-government—that was on the table at the first Confederation in 1764, a third Confederation might get under way.

1. Dickason, Olive Patricia (1992), *Canada's First Nations: A History of Founding Peoples from Earliest Times*. Toronto: McClelland & Stewart, p. 256.
2. Moore, Christopher (2015), *Three Weeks in Quebec City*, Toronto: Allen Lane, pp. 176-8.
3. *Constitution Act, 1867*, s. 91 (24).
4. Allen, Robert S. (1996), *His Majesty's Indian Allies: British Indian Policy in Defence of Canada, 1774-1815*, Toronto: Dundurn.
5. Canadian Royal Commission (1996), *Royal Commission on Aboriginal Peoples*, Ottawa: Canada Communications Group, Vol. I, p. 145.
6. Siggins, Maggie (1994), *Riel: A Life of Revolution*, Toronto: Harper Collins, pp. 150-1.
7. Manitoba Métis Federation Inc. v. Canada, 1 SCR 623 (2013).
8. Chartrand, Paul L.A.H. (1991), "Aboriginal Rights: The Dispossession of the Métis," 29 *Osgoode Hall Law Journal*, pp. 463-482.
9. Flexner, James Thomas (1959), *Mohawk Baronet: A Biography of Sir William Johnson*, Syacuse: Syracuse University Press, p. 256.
10. The Royal Proclamation of 1763 is the first document in *Canada 125: Constitutions 1763-1982*, Ottawa: Canada Communication, 1992.
11. Borrows, John (1998), "Wampum at Niagara, the Royal Proclamation, Canadian Legal History and Self-Government," *Aboriginal and Treaty Rights in Canada*, ed. Michael Asch, Vancouver: UBC Press, pp. 173-207.
12. Braider, Donald (1972), *The Niagara*, New York City: Henry Holt & Company.
13. Quoted in Tidridge, Nathan (2015), *The Queen at the Council Fire: The Treaty of Niagara, Reconciliation, and the Dignified Crown in Canada*, Toronto: Dundurn, p. 65.
14. For a description of these instruments, see Tidridge, Nathan, ibid., pp. 60-66.
15. Quoted in Borrows, John, "Wampum at Niagara," p. 162.
16. Stone, William L. (1865), *The Life and Times of Sir William Johnson bart*, Albany, NY: Munsell, Vol. 2, p. 228.
17. Manuel, George and Michael Posluns (1974), *The Fourth World: An Indian Reality*, Toronto: Collier-Macmillan.
18. Delgamuukw v. British Columbia, 3 SCR 1010 at paragraph 186 (1997).
19. Weaver, Sally (1981), *Making Canadian Indian Policy: The Hidden Agenda, 1968-70*, Toronto: University of Toronto Press.
20. *Consensus Report on the Constitution. Charlottetown, August 28, 1992*, section 41, in Russell, Peter H. (1993), *Constitutional Odyssey: Can Canadians Become a Sovereign People?* Toronto: University of Toronto Press, 2nd edition.
21. The UN Declaration is available online, and is Appendix 1 in Henderson, James (Sake'j) Youngblood (2008), *Indigenous Diplomacy and the Rights of Peoples: Achieving UN Recognition*, Saskatoon: Purich.
22. *Delgamuukw*, 3 SCR 1010, at paragraph 186.
23. Tsilqhquot'n Nation v. British Columbia, 2 S.C.R. 257, at paragraph 23 (2014).
24. Ibid., at paragraph 67.
25. *Report of the Royal Commission on Aboriginal Peoples* (1996), Vol. 2, Part One, Ottawa: Canadian Communication Group, pp. 377-8.

Celebrating Canada's 150th Birthday
A Play in One Act

Stephanie Irlbacher-Fox

Curtain Opens

Pierre Landbridge, on the set of the CBC show One on One. *In sober suit and tie, Order of Canada pin on his lapel, he contemplates the camera. Parliament buildings are in the background, and Canadian flags.*

LANDBRIDGE: (*In a deep, sincere voice*) At this age, one expects Canada to be in a position to dole out advice.
  On this, your 150th birthday, what advice do you have? What would you have done differently? What has it taught you about how you want to live now?

A RAVEN *enters, squawks, and turns to the camera, which follows it. Glinting in its beak is a quarter. The camera focuses in on the caribou head side of the coin. The* RAVEN *squawks a harsh "Tuktu!" and the camera follows it as the shining disc falls, rolls a few feet toward a sewer drain, and comes to rest in the mud beside a discarded yet pristine Starbucks cup with a black marker-ed "Wab" scrawled inside a heart near its rim.*

RAVEN: (*Squawking dialogue, cocks its head to mirror* LANDBRIDGE, *and stares into the camera.*) How much time do you have left?
  Are you the same Canada that was born 150 years ago?
  Or are you a newcomer, freshly inhabiting the role?

The camera pans back to LANDBRIDGE. *The camera angle widens, revealing a video screen beside him, a montage of aerial shots of Canadian Wilderness.*

LANDBRIDGE: This is the first of a seven-part series asking Canada for its advice and lessons learned over the past 150 years on a variety of questions. Tonight, we ask Canada for its understanding and advice about its relationship with Indigenous peoples. Specifically, we speak with two Canadians from different perspectives, experiences, and walks of life.

The camera pans out to reveal a panel on the video screen that now dwarfs LANDBRIDGE. *Seated in a line facing the camera are a tall, elegant, white, middle-aged male and a striking middle-aged white woman with large eyeglasses. Both are neatly dressed, coiffed, and made up. The camera zooms back in to a close-up on* LANDBRIDGE.

LANDBRIDGE: I had the opportunity to speak with these two Canadians one-on-one. Before we get to our panel discussion, let's take a look at highlights of some of our conversations.

The camera switches to another montage of aerial shots of various resource-based industries: a farm scene, fishing trawlers, oil sands, pipelines . . . Upbeat, wholesome music plays, marred for a moment by the sound of a raven squawking, then brief scuffling noises before it is suddenly silenced.

The camera switches to LANDBRIDGE *in a dark, wood-panelled office with expensive furnishings, its windows revealing an exclusive view from a top-floor office in Toronto. A sterling silver tea service on an antique table foregrounds a 4' x 6' brightly painted original Norval Morrisseau painting, which hangs above the pristine desk of the middle-aged male panel member, reclining in a leather executive chair.*

LANDBRIDGE: Mr. Street, thank you for welcoming us to your 40th-floor office here in downtown Toronto. It's a beautiful summer day in June of 2016. Your perspective is shaped by decades of laudable personal and business philanthropy, something that has been a strong tradition in your family for ten generations; indeed, your family and its charitable organization are as old as the country itself. In your lifetime, your family's philanthropic focus has turned to Indigenous peoples. Tell us, what advice do you think Canada would have to give us about its relationship with Indigenous peoples after 150 years?

MR. STREET's *expensive smile is brief before his face becomes pensive, thoughtful.*

MR. STREET: (*He speaks carefully and deliberately.*) This is an important question, Peter. And my thoughts have been shaped greatly by discussions with my Indigenous friends, such as former National Chiefs of the Assembly of First Nations, Indigenous authors, and also non-Indigenous friends who have themselves taken a keen interest in Indigenous peoples and issues—among them a philosopher who has recently written on the comeback of Indigenous peoples in Canada, and a former Prime Minister, now active in Indigenous philanthropy himself.

It seems to me that Indigenous peoples have come forward in the last few years and have so courageously shared their experiences with us. And as Canadians we have discovered how harmful some government policies were toward Indigenous peoples, and I think the business community and certainly those of us involved in philanthropy have seen that we now have a better understanding of Indigenous peoples. And that we have reached a time in history where their young people and leaders have made us listen to what they have to say, and that they want partnerships, particularly to help themselves out of poverty and to join in the promise of Canada. Because as the Canadian philosopher John Ralston Saul says, we really are a Métis country.

LANDBRIDGE: (*Attentive, nods gravely*) So one lesson then from our history, is perhaps about listening, and working together to address the problems they face—that we face together as a country, we are Métis in the sense that we all have a stake in this?

MR. STREET *listens intently, then nods vigorously, body turned square to face* LANDBRIDGE. *His palms are clasped and index fingers steepled beneath his chin.*

MR. STREET: Yes, actively listening and taking those views, and helping to frame them in terms of action: How do we move forward? What are the tools that we can offer as partners—because we need to be cognizant that we need not offer specific or limiting solutions, but instead, support solutions within communities. And every community or nation is different and will want to move forward in ways that build on their unique strengths.

So as philanthropists, and as business people, we need to think about how we move forward together. And appreciating that terrible things happened to Indigenous individuals, these were terrible things—for example with the residential schools—and now we need to keep our eyes on the horizon, and work with the potential these communities have, particularly with their youth. So for example, our foundation has set up scholarships for high school graduates to university and professional programs.

LANDBRIDGE: And you also support early childhood programs—

MR. STREET: (*Smiles and nods*) Yes that's right, we support on-reserve programs for pre-kindergarten, an extremely under-served program area on many reserves and rural areas of Canada.

LANDBRIDGE: So why Indigenous peoples? Why is Canadian philanthropy taking this focus? Why now?

MR. STREET: Indigenous youth are the fastest-growing population in Canada. They represent a huge economic resource to their own communities, and to this country. The people who are going to help to shift the relationship dynamic in this country are the young, educated Indigenous men and women who will work with their communities, work with industry, work with governments and, and . . . work with each other, to create better partnerships and innovative solutions. We need to invest in them, and those of us who have the means to do so need to contribute according to our abilities . . . because it is in our own interests as well, as Canadians. As stewards of our economy and society. Many Canadians think Indigenous peoples are a net drain on this country, but in reality they are an untapped resource.

LANDBRIDGE: So, supporting the potential of Indigenous youth, an untapped resource, is key to Canada's future social and economic wellbeing. That's solid advice.

MR. STREET *leans forward, Rolex flashing in the sunlight as he reaches forward to shake hands with* LANDBRIDGE. *He smiles benevolently.*

MR. STREET: We need to meet the challenge of the future head on. Thank you.

The screen fades to a montage of poverty and protest images: infamous shots of young children sniffing gas in Davis Inlet, interior shots of flooded houses in Attawapiskat, flashes of video clips of the Oka Crisis, Gustafsen Lake protests, and more recent protests in BC over oil pipelines. The camera pans out to reveal LANDBRIDGE *standing beside the screen as the images continue.*

LANDBRIDGE: We now turn to my discussion with university professor of Indigenous Studies and self-styled activist known as Professor Ally. Her academic publications include several books and journal papers about Indigenous issues, and in addition to her academic work, she has spent 20 years working with small Indigenous communities negotiating treaties; we spoke with her on location at Cambridge University in England, where she was attending a scholarly conference.

The scene changes, showing LANDBRIDGE *sitting across from* PROFESSOR ALLY *at a small wrought iron café table on a manicured lawn beside a river, with looming vine-covered gothic buildings in the background. Songbirds chirp musically, marred by a short, unexpected squawk of a raven, making both jump with surprise. They laugh suddenly, self-consciously; the microphone picks up a faint, quiet curse from* LANDBRIDGE, *who clears his throat and smiles into the camera.*

LANDBRIDGE: I am here today at Cambridge University, in England, with Professor Ally, to discuss what Canada's advice would be to us about Canada's relationship with its Indigenous peoples. Good morning, Professor.

PROFESSOR ALLY *smiles and leans forward to shake* LANDBRIDGE's *hand, gravel crunching against her shoes as the ground takes her weight.*

PROFESSOR ALLY: Thank you, Peter. And I should start by mentioning: Indigenous peoples are not Canada's, though it is not unusual for them to be described in possessive terms—a deplorably common error, and one that betrays a condescending and troublingly subconscious attitude toward Indigenous peoples.

LANDBRIDGE *grimace-smiles, and graciously nods assent.*

> "Indigenous peoples are not Canada's"

PROFESSOR ALLY: And it is thematically on point, with respect to the lessons learned, that Canada would have to contemplate before doling out advice. Settler condescension has been one of the main pillars of Canada's approach to its relationship with Indigenous peoples.

From the earliest days of the settler-colonial influx, where Indigenous peoples were physically removed from their lands and homes to make way for the fur trade, farms, mines, forestry, or settlements—this fundamental assumption of settler superiority, and consequent condescension, has shaped both government policy toward Indigenous peoples and the social relations arising between Indigenous and non-Indigenous Canadians.

LANDBRIDGE *frowns and clears his throat. He rests his chin on the knuckles of his right hand, and gestures with his left.*

> settler condescension

LANDBRIDGE: So what are the lessons that Canada needs to contemplate?

PROFESSOR ALLY: (*Pushes her glasses farther up on her face, earnestly gestures with both hands, palms out.*) We can consider specifics, such as residential schools, which involved the massive theft of children from their families and subsequent substandard education and institutional abuses; starvation experiments; forced relocations; illegal dispossessions of lands; segregated and sub-standard hospitals and health care; massive mismanagement of oil royalties or other income of Indian bands that were never set aside for their use but instead were treated as general government revenues . . . there is long list.

Or, we can consider the principles that underpinned such actions. So we would look at specific policies, laws and conventions, or practices that enshrined principles resulting in specific and ongoing events.

And we would also want to consider: those principles, of which there were many, were all predicated on the goals that Canada wanted to achieve in relation to Indigenous peoples. They tell us that a relationship, in the sense of creating and honouring a shared inter-subjectivity predicated on mutual respect, or even transactional mutual interests, was never in the cards. Canada did not want a relationship—and some would argue that, based on the evidence, it still does not want a relationship—but instead wants to realize its own interests *at the expense of* Indigenous peoples.

LANDBRIDGE: (*Leans forward intently, brow furrowed.*) So what are those interests? What are those goals that Canada had, which, in your view, meant that there really never was—and maybe never can be—a relationship, providing Canada continues to pursue those interests or goals?

PROFESSOR ALLY: (*Laughs bitterly.*) What I have witnessed and have been told is that it is all about the land, for Canada. Every single policy is about removing Indigenous peoples out of their lands. And for Indigenous cultures, land is life. Languages and cultures are built around the land, the experience of being on the land. Social relations are rooted in and mediated by the experience of being connected to the land: sharing of meat, berries; co-existence with and dependence on animals for survival; and human interdependence and shared experiences. Wellness is dependent on that relationship with the land. It is the well that feeds identity, the soul, and the body.

Canada's policies also have a focus on solidifying disconnection from the land by emphasizing access and primary value of opportunities that further alienate Indigenous peoples, particularly children and youth, from their lands. So for example, schooling in Indigenous communities with a thriving Indigenous language will only be in English or French. There are scholarships for formal western education, but few opportunities for land-based users to be supported, or for educational institutions to incorporate land-based learning as a pedagogical approach. And then of course there are legal and regulatory regimes and rules around land uses that give primacy to exploitative resource industries, or capitalist economies over Indigenous land-based economies.

LANDBRIDGE: (*Frowns and leans forward.*) So you would disagree with Mr. Street's Canada, that the scholarships and pre-schools are not the investments his philanthropy should benefit? That instead the focus should be on language programs or hunting skills?

PROFESSOR ALLY: (*Frowns, considers for a moment.*) I think most people would agree that where there is a need, philanthropy could contribute to solutions: philanthropy is always welcome. And, having watched the conversation with you and Mr. Street, I was struck by how some approaches to addressing Indigenous peoples priorities are devoid of knowledge or acknowledgement of the purpose of Canada's actions being primarily to sever the relationship between Indigenous peoples and their lands—physically, culturally, psychologically.

[handwritten: if Indigenous people get ahead then it's a loss for everyone else]

Mr. Street's view strikes me as a profoundly capitalist analysis of the situation, and therefore a superficial one, in that such an analysis leads to a limited understanding of the context and therefore of the outcomes of Canada's policy choices as a government, and outcomes of settler colonialism institutionally, socially, and politically. And I don't think Mr. Street wants to understand or admit to a deeper analysis, because Indigenous peoples relationships with the land, their need for actual land in a way and to an extent that provides them with opportunities to literally exist as Indigenous, is at odds with a Canadian economy that needs Indigenous peoples to be severed from their lands.

LANDBRIDGE *shifts in his seat, uncomfortable, seemingly unsettled.*

LANDBRIDGE: So, are you then proposing that the Canadian economy needs to be re-oriented to make things better for Indigenous peoples? And what about the rest of us who rely on that economy?

PROFESSOR ALLY *purses her lips, squares her shoulders, and places her hands on the table, as though bracing herself.* [handwritten: zero-sum game]

PROFESSOR ALLY: That sounds like an overwhelming proposal, doesn't it? And I am always struck how immediate reactions seem to see this as a zero-sum game: if Indigenous peoples get ahead, it is a direct loss for the rest of society. That is fiction.

We need to go back to principles. There is not just one way to live on the land; there is not just one way to build a mine; there is not just one source of energy that can power a home, or a factory, or a pulp mill. Yes, we will need to reorient the economy. However, we need to start doing that anyway—because of climate change, because of technology. Economic reorientation has already begun. [handwritten: economic reorientation]

But to start with, reaching that larger goal of reorientation might start with specific measures, such as a national Indigenous Guardians program, employing land-based knowledge holders to engage in environmental monitoring and protection, that could be funded through royalties from renewable and non-renewable resource extraction, considering our royalty regimes in Canada are extremely low in comparison to other countries.

And in addition to economic measures, Canada needs to consider engaging in negotiations over lands, governance authorities, and resources based on principles seeking a shared reality that demonstrates that Indigenous peoples interests are valued and shape the outcomes. This may not be easy, since Indigenous peoples interests are not homogenous but, as Mr. Street mentioned, vary between communities and nations.

LANDBRIDGE: (*Shifts uncomfortably in his seat.*) So your advice for Canada after 150 years of getting this wrong: Rethink the basics? Revise the principles on which 150-year-old Canada approaches a relationship with Indigenous peoples?

PROFESSOR ALLY: (*Smiles.*) And on which its economy is based. (*She winks;* LANDBRIDGE *reddens slightly.*) And reorienting its principles—economic or otherwise—in doing so. Take the advice of Mr. Street: listen first and support; don't prescribe. At 150, I think Canada sees itself as a mature adult, and knows that it needs to try something substantively different to see different outcomes.

The sound is muted and music begins to play as the camera angle widens on the two continuing to chat, then fades back to the studio, where LANDBRIDGE *is standing with the two panellists, the three of them chatting amiably. As the music fades out, he notices the camera and breaks off the conversation, turning his shoulders to it as it pans in for a close up.*

LANDBRIDGE: We are here in the studio now with Mr. Street and Professor Ally, and only have time for a couple of quick questions. Mr. Street, let's start with you: What's your final impression of the advice Canada should give?

The camera shifts to a close up of MR. STREET, *dressed in an elegant black suit and deep yellow tie. He smiles.*

MR. STREET: It is clear, Peter, that we need to build on the many strengths and positive potentials that exist in every Indigenous community and nation, and we need to do it in a way that supports their priorities and decisions. Education will raise people out of poverty.

LANDBRIDGE: (*Nods, and gestures to Professor Ally.*) And you, Professor Ally? Any last thoughts?

PROFESSOR ALLY: Peter, yes, I was wondering why three middle class white people are here discussing this issue. Did you ask Indigenous panellists onto this show? Or were you specifically looking for settler Canadians to speak to settlers?

LANDBRIDGE: (*Shifts his weight, perplexed.*) You didn't seem to mind coming on the show when you were asked . . .

A faint smile appears on the face of MR. STREET. PROFESSOR ALLY's *face colours a deep red.* LANDBRIDGE *turns to* MR. STREET.

LANDBRIDGE: Mr. Street, what's your take on this?

MR. STREET: (*Coolly.*) Well, Peter, the foundation's board certainly has Indigenous members; however, I am the spokesperson. And yes, of course, the panel should have been broadened had your various considerations allowed it.

Upbeat music begins to play, muting the conversation's end as the camera pans out. The three begin chatting again as the credits roll. LANDBRIDGE leans across to shake hands first with PROFESSOR ALLY, then MR. STREET. As MR. STREET reaches across to take LANDBRIDGE's offered hand, a small black feather falls from his sleeve, almost imperceptibly, as at the same time his Rolex glints in the studio lights, momentarily blinding Landbridge. Both men laugh at the unexpected shared surprise, clearly relieved.

CURTAIN

Kapyong and Treaty One First Nations
When the Crown Can Do No Wrong

Myra J. Tait[1]

Treaties: "So What's the Big Deal?"

Throughout Canada's history, as we were most recently reminded in the Truth and Reconciliation Commission's Final Report, the Crown—first the British and now Canadian—has in so many ways utterly failed Aboriginal peoples. Nowhere does this failure show through more than in the Crown's failure to uphold its treaties with First Nations as solemn agreements. From the outset, these legal documents were intended to be the foundation that governs the relationship between the Crown and Indigenous peoples of Turtle Island, and have since been constitutionally recognized as such. The ultimate purpose, the Court tell us, of this constitutional recognition, is reconciliation. The Final Report of the TRC took pause to remind Canadians:

> In 1996, the *Report of the Royal Commission on Aboriginal Peoples* urged Canadians to begin a national process of reconciliation that would have set the country on a bold new path, fundamentally changing the very foundations of Canada's relationship with Aboriginal peoples ... In 2015, as the Truth and Reconciliation Commission of Canada wraps up its work, the country has a rare second chance to seize a lost opportunity for reconciliation.[2]

As a nation poised to celebrate and reflect on its 150 years since confederacy, we are again reminded of the need for reconciliation, and its increasingly urgent necessity. Racial tensions, environmental crises, and widespread unrest continue to gain momentum, adding to the gross impoverishment and marginalization of Aboriginal peoples. As a nation, Canada can no longer afford to turn a blind eye to its own history, continuing to ignore its solemn obligations. Among Canada's myriad conflicts with First Nations peoples is the legal battle over Kapyong, an abandoned military base in the City of Winnipeg. As a prime example of the Crown's *modus operandi*, the dispute over the Kapyong land parcel depicts the long-overdue necessity of treaty implementation, which would facilitate urban reserves as a legitimate means of economic development for First Nations people, and the red herring objections about tax fairness.

But let's back the story up for just a moment: the beginning of this appalling epic reaches back to 1871, a time of great upheaval for First Nations peoples due to the huge geographic expansion of settlers looking for a better life in the unspoiled expanses of the newly formed Canadian state. Those who came to settle, predominantly from England and France, were accommodated through Treaties with the original nations, not conquest. Grounded in the belief that Indigenous peoples were vulnerable to the "great Frauds and Abuses" of colonists, King George III issued the Royal Proclamation of 1763, a law that governed treaty-making and continues to be recognized by Canadian law. Simply, Aboriginal land could only be acquired through fair negotiations, accompanied by compensation. Some suggest that the land designated as Indian Reserves (along with a bundle of less-observable benefits like education and healthcare—being less than the universal benefits enjoyed by all Canadians, a five-dollar annuity for each Indian,[3] and some very limited tax provisions) constitutes full and fair payment for all of the territory and resources claimed by the Crown on behalf of Canada. Even if one were to accept this position, in the case of Treaty 1, the Crown has never—ever—fully met its side of the bargain. Despite reliance on its own estimates of First Nations band populations to determine the per capita land allowance promised in Treaty 1, the Crown failed to honour its own agreements. The promise of a per capita land allotment in Treaty 1 is where the Kapyong saga begins.

In the heart of the nation sits the City of Winnipeg, Manitoba, which the Treaty Relations Commission of Manitoba identifies as one of the "communities sharing the obligations and benefits of"[4] Treaty 1. Beginning in 1871, Treaty 1 promised a new direction—a new kind of relationship between Her Majesty the Queen (Victoria) and Her government, and the "Chippewa and Swampy Cree Indians of Manitoba" (more correctly, the Anishinaabe and Nehiyaw peoples). The Numbered Treaties, as they have come to be called, reached further than the "peace and friendship" treaties of earlier years, and defined a means to peacefully share land and resources with the anticipated droves of European settlers. While the Crown continues to describe these treaties as "simple land cession treaties," even the most cursory reading of the text of Treaty 1 reveals a vision for an enduring and mutually beneficial relationship. The gains for new settlers were obvious: vast tracks of arable land; abundant supplies of lumber, water, wild game, and fish; and a new life without threat of conflict. In return, Treaty 1 nations agreed to continue in their traditional ways—including their legal, political, and cultural practices—but moreover, they expected to participate in a rapidly changing economy. The Crown promised (at the very least) to ensure access to traditional hunting and fishing grounds, farming implements, and livestock for each community with a view to promote agriculture, and annuities that, at the time of signing, far exceeded the mere *symbolic* five-dollar payments of today. The 1871 land allotment, based on a very flawed process undertaken by the Crown's Indian Agent, set out the amount of land to be "reserved" for the exclusive and perpetual use by Treaty 1 nations—an amount that, in 2017, has yet to be fulfilled by the Crown.

Although in 2009 Treaty 1 nations resorted to litigation to hold the Crown accountable for decisions pertaining to Kapyong, the Crown was already keenly aware of its failures—and likely had been since the signing of Treaty 1. Treaty implementation has been problematic (at least for the Crown) since the ink dried on their supposedly impeccable documents. In simplest terms, requiring little or no interpretation, this Treaty required that the Crown set aside 160 acres per family of five (or in that proportion) for the exclusive use of each "band," as the Crown called them. The fact that Treaty 1 First Nations were short changed has been admitted many times by the Crown, the Court, and parliament alike. Yet, the debt remains outstanding, the effects of which continue to perpetuate fresh injustices upon First Nations peoples. Sadly, Treaty 1 nations are not unique in this position, and government has been stymied as how best to maintain the appearance of honour, while continually deferring meaningful action to pay its debt.

As early as 1884, "Indians contended that they had signed the 'numbered treaties' of the 1870s to allow the 'whiteman' to 'borrow,' not 'buy,' their lands, and Government had not fulfilled its treaty obligations … In answer to this charge, Deputy Superintendent-General Vankoughnet stated in December 1884 that the Indians had:

> … no good reason for serious complaint", that they were "most generously treated by the government far beyond any expectation they could have entertained under the most liberal interpretation" of the treaties. The Department had not fulfilled some treaty promises by

1885; however, it was not due to any oversight or corruption, but the view that some bands had not sufficiently advance to take full advantage of the promised tools, livestock and schools.⁵

The Crown's skewed view of its own impeachable honour, combined with its go-to myths of white superiority, undermined the importance of the Treaties and maligned the capacity of Indigenous peoples to act with integrity.

Having placed the bulk of Crown land in the hands of provincial governments at the time of Confederation, the Crown complicated the means by which it would meet its outstanding treaty obligations. However, in 1930, the Crown reiterated its pledge to fulfil its side of the Treaty by adding Section 11 to the Constitution, in order to enable Canada to fulfil its obligations under the treaties. Although these jurisdictional barriers were eliminated from the apparent conflict of Provincial ownership of lands and resources, the Crown never prioritized fulfilling its outstanding treaty obligations. In 1947, a Special Joint Committee of the Senate and House of Commons recommended the creation of an Indian specific claims commission, to assess Crown breaches of the Treaties and settle proven claims. The call for an independent claims commission also came from Diefenbaker (while in opposition) in 1950; in 1961, a Joint Committee of the Senate and House called for the establishment of a formal commission. However, in 1965, legislation introduced to establish a commission died on the order paper. It was not until 1973 that a specific claims policy was established, but the process attracted heavy criticism in 1979 in an "unpublished report prepared for Canada [citing] 'conflicting duties' in the Federal Government's involvement in claims settlement and [recommended the establishment of] an impartial, independent body."⁶

The Federal Government's failure to honour its debts to Treaty nations dragged on, and the issue was addressed in the Penner Report of 1983, as well as the House of Commons Standing Committee on Aboriginal Affairs in 1990, both calling for the creation of an independent quasi-judicial tribunal to assess Crown breaches of the Treaties. Finally, in 1991—more than a century late—"Canada took concrete steps to remedy its breach of Treaty No. 1,"⁷ and the Indian Specific Claims Commission (ISCC) was established. The ISCC was rife with shortcomings, which were pointed out by the Royal Commission on Aboriginal Peoples (1996), a task force on the specific claims process, and by virtue of the introduction of the *Specific Claims Resolution Act* (SCRA). Although the SCRA received royal assent and became law in 2003, First Nations overwhelmingly rejected it, objecting to, among other things, the government's arbitrary cap of 7 million dollars on all settlements. The SCRA was accordingly repealed in 2008.

Prior to the 1982 constitutional changes to protect the legality of Treaties, and despite the fact that the Crown afforded itself the power to make unilateral changes to treaty terms before this change, Crown breaches of Treaty agreements were never in question. In what could only be considered an act of cowardice, the Crown amended the *Indian Act* to effectively bar all legal action by Aboriginal peoples, thereby removing any opportunity for First Nations to demand redress. Amendments in 1882 "revised the seventy-eighth clause of the 1880 Act which permitted Indians to sue for *debts or to compel performance of obligations contracted with them* . . . to curtail 'Indian fondness for petty litigation.'"[8] In other words, an Indian had no access to the courts, except as an accused in criminal proceedings or as a defendant in a civil trial. This legislation remained in place until 1951. Unsurprisingly, the Crown's take it-or leave approach to settlement during this time was less than successful. The Numbered Treaties (and others, stemming from the authority of the Royal Proclamation of 1763) together with Canada's modern treaties form the only legitimate basis for Canada's existence as a nation, and unless the Crown is prepared to live by those agreements, Canada lacks all credibility as a free nation.

Treaties and the Highest Law—"Talking with Forked Tongues"

In 1982, there was hope that the Crown truly intended to reset its relationship with Aboriginal peoples when Schedule 1 of the *Constitution Act, 1982* was added, to affirm (among other things) the legally binding nature of the treaties and the resultant obligations upon the Crown. The recognition and affirmation of "existing aboriginal and treaty rights"[9] in Section 35, and the non-abrogation clause of Section 25, set the stage for resolution and reconciliation. Moreover, this provided a firm legal foundation on which First Nations could now press their claims, preferably through negotiation—or so it seemed.

In 2006, the Government of Manitoba supported the Federal Government's initiative to create legal mechanisms to deal with per capita land debts arising from Crown breaches of the Numbered Treaties, through a Treaty Land Entitlement (TLE) review process. This process led Treaty 1 First Nations, along with a total of 29 Manitoba First Nations who collectively were owed 1.423 million acres,[10] to have their claims validated by the Crown. In 2007, a Government of Manitoba news release recognized the TLE settlement process as a priority, and committed to "expediting the provincial work on the long-standing Treaty Land Entitlement Framework (TLE) Agreement including completing the transfer to Canada of 1.2 million acres originally identified as TLE land within the next four years."[11] This mandate was also highlighted in the 2007 Manitoba Speech from the Throne, wherein the Government declared that settlement was an "economic necessity for First Nations [... pointing to the need to ...] support a long-overdue major acceleration of TLE claims through a more decisive settlement process."[12]

By 2011, the Province claimed it was making "substantial progress in meeting its obligations under treaty land entitlements,"[13] which it deemed "to be a provincial priority and can be an important component in the future economic development plans of First Nations."[14] Similarly, Indian and Northern Affairs Canada (INAC) published their policy directive "Specific Claims: Justice at Last," wherein the Minister outlined a comprehensive action plan:

> Canada's New Government plans ... to accelerate the resolution of specific claims in order to provide justice for First Nation claimants and certainty for government, industry and all Canadians. After years of debate, we are taking a new, decisive approach to restore confidence in the integrity and effectiveness of the process to resolve specific claims ...
>
> The Government of Canada has a policy in place to resolve these claims *through negotiations rather than through the courts*. To honour its obligations and right these past wrongs, Canada negotiates settlements that provide justice to First Nation claimants as well as fairness and certainty for all Canadians. Negotiation is always better than confrontation in securing peaceful settlements that respect the interests of all parties.[15]

However, neither legal force nor moral imperative appears to have generated any sense of urgency for the Crown to resolve remaining claims through good faith bargaining. In February 2015, INAC estimated that Treaty 1 First Nations were still owed over 236,000 hectares (583,000 acres) of land.[16] Worse, "In the last two years [2014 and 2015], only a 0.046-hectare plot has been converted to reserve land."[17] Continuing this trend, a mere 4.21 acres of urban land (necessary for the establishment of urban reserves) was added in all of 2016,[18] drawing into question the Crown's commitment to Treaty implementation as a means of economic development.

After nearly a century and a half of Euro-Canadian immigration, facilitated by Canadian property law to "crystalize" private ownership, the means to rectify the Crown's debt have become increasingly complex. It would seem to have been better for all concerned if the Crown had made genuine efforts to honour its Treaty obligations from the outset. Through the TLE process, however, all doubt as to what was owned, to whom, and now, most importantly, how land would be transferred to First Nations ownership, was resolved. The basic structure of these agreements was for the Crown to set aside funds—that is, financial compensation for its breaches of the Treaty terms, which could be used by the respective aggrieved First Nations, for future purchases of "surplus" Crown land.[19] Canada agreed "that it would 'in good faith, use [its] best efforts to fulfil the terms' of the agreement and to act on a timely basis."[20] Having met the burden of proof to support their claims before the ISCC, First Nations negotiated TLE agreements, thereby creating legal mechanisms by which the Crown is to fulfill its Treaty obligations.

Treaty 1 First Nations have waited 146 years—so far—for the Crown to follow through on its obligations. Nevertheless, in continued defiance of the terms of Treaty 1, as well as the explicit terms of the TLE agreements, when the Kapyong land became available, the Crown moved to divest itself of the surplus land, without consideration of or consultation with Treaty 1 First Nations. The transfer of the resident Canadian Forces troops to a new permanent home was announced in April 2001, which according to Treasury Board guidelines, resulted in the land being designated "surplus" Crown land. Just weeks after the Kapyong announcement, in July 2001, the Treasury Board invented new rules, and "divided surplus property disposal into two categories: routine and strategic. All property falls into the first category unless it has an especially high market value or is 'sensitive'—in which case it becomes 'strategic.'"[21] This effectively removed the land from consideration in any TLE agreement.

Since treaty rights are constitutionally protected by literally the highest law of the land, Treaty 1 nations claimed that the Crown's unilateral decision to remove the surplus land, without considering the legal interests of Treaty 1 nations, was unlawful. The TLE agreements in essence created a first-right-of-refusal for recipient First Nations to consider the purchase of surplus—but not strategic—Crown land, in order to satisfy their original entitlements under Treaty 1.[22] The surplus Kapyong land was exactly the type of opportunity that would, and indeed did, attract the interest of Treaty 1 nations. The Crown ignored their explicit expression of interest, and rather than uphold the terms of the TLEs—the intent of which was to implement the terms of the 1871 Treaty—and with disregard for its constitutional duty to consult First Nations on Crown actions that may negatively impact treaty rights, the Crown made plans that excluded possibility of First Nations acquiring the land through the TLE process.

As a result, the affected First Nations[23] initiated court action, seeking a declaration that the Crown was required to consult with them before excluding the parcel from their TLE settlements. In the words of Federal Court Justice Campbell, "if the standard for meaningful consultation ... is not met ... the chain of legal dispute will not be broken, and disruption to the aspirations of Canada and the Applicant First Nations will continue."[24] Since first filing an application for judicial review in January 2008, this legal contest has involved *seven* related hearings,[25] two of which were before the Federal Court of Appeal—after being heard twice at the Federal court level, all on the same question. At every stage, the Crown has resorted to litigation, yet failed to make its case that it had the power to act unilaterally and continued to ignore its obligations.

In his 2009 decision, Campbell, J affirmed that "Canada's decision to act on the Treasury Board Directive [to remove Kapyong from the 'surplus' listing] is unlawful and a failure to maintain the honour of the Crown."[26] He noted that the record "establishes that from the beginning to the end of the decision-making with respect to the lands, it is clear that Canada had no intention to grant the First Nations any meaningful consultation."[27] Highlighted in this decision was also the importance of Treaty implementation as a means to reconciliation:

> The Treaty Commissioner for Saskatchewan sees Treaty implementation as part of a process of reconciliation. The Commissioner's following comment, cited by the Applicant First Nations, is a helpful observation in understanding the importance of a non-litigious engagement between Aboriginal People and government when making decisions which directly affect Aboriginal Treaty rights:
>
>> In law, as both the Haida and Mikisew cases emphasize, reconciliation is a "process," and that process does not end with the making of a treaty. The process carries on through the implementation of that treaty and is guided by a duty of honourable dealing. The very nature of the treaties is to establish mutual rights and obligations.[28]

In what has become the Crown's standard for dealing with Aboriginal peoples, and despite the clear duty upon the Crown to consult, the Government responded by filing an appeal. This response flies in the face of the rhetoric promising Aboriginal peoples that their constitutionally entrenched rights will be respected, the Crown's preference for negotiation over litigation, and the Crown's stated goals to correct its century-old breaches of the treaties through the TLE processes.

Thus, the matter proceeded to the Federal Court of Appeal, where Appeal Court Justice Marc Nadon, writing for a unanimous court, deemed the reasons for the original order "rife with uncertainty and contradiction [and are] inadequate. They do not grapple with and attempt to resolve the difficult legal issues and the confusing evidentiary record that were before him."[29] Nadon, JA found, among other things, that the decision left Canada "in the position of being ordered to consult, but being unsure with whom it must consult."[30] He found that Campbell, J "failed to adequately distinguish between the different circumstances of the respondents,"[31] and "it was an error on the Judge's part to fail to seriously consider Canada's alternative argument that its duty to consult had been fulfilled."[32] Finding "the Judge failed to seize the substance of the critical issues before him,"[33] Nadon, JA ordered that the matter be referred back to the Federal Court, shot the messenger and explicitly excluded Campbell, J as a potential adjudicator, and, despite his many criticisms aimed almost exclusively at the trial judge, awarded costs to the Crown. Before sending the matter back to the Federal Court for retrial, Nadon, JA also implicated Brokenhead First Nation as an author of its own misfortune, by failing to exercise the alternative dispute resolution mechanism in its TLE agreement instead of pursuing their interests in the Court.[34] Shortly after releasing what seems to be a particularly nasty decision—one that fell just short of absolving the Crown of all wrongdoing—Appeal Court Justice Nadon, JA was appointed by former Prime Minister Harper to the Supreme Court of Canada, albeit unsuccessfully.[35]

Carefully working through the concerns raised by Nadon, JA in December 2012, Federal Court Justice Roger T. Hughes released his comprehensive, 47-page decision concerning the Crown's duty to consult the affected First Nations. In his reasons, Hughes adopted verbatim nearly half of the Campbell, J (Federal Court) decision, and added substantial detail to *affirm* the original finding that "Canada has failed to fulfil the scope of its duty to consult with the Applicants."[36] On this point, Hughes was unequivocal: Canada, despite conceding it has a duty to consult,[37] "[e]ven at a minimal level . . . did not fulfil its obligations."[38] Further, the "matter is more egregious in the 2006 to 2007 period. Canada simply ignored correspondence written by and on behalf of the Applicants,"[39] wrote Justice Hughes.

The legal challenge to the Crown's decisions regarding this land indeed "has an unhappy history,"[40] as Justice Hughes termed it. To make his point, his order contained a request for submissions on costs, which was a signal to the Crown that the Court was displeased with the course of litigation. In 2013, a separate hearing was held as to costs, wherein Hughes determined appropriate costs based largely on the belligerent behaviour of the Crown: "Had that concession [regarding the *prima facia* duty of the Crown to consult] been made earlier, substantial effort and evidence could have been saved. The respondents failed to make full and candid disclosure of the documents relating to the decision at issue. This made the argument and decision difficult."[41] Clearly, the warning issued by Justice Hughes in his original decision went unheeded. Quoting the Crown's oral argument at length, Hughes noted this belligerence, wherein Crown counsel boasted,

> if we can't reach an agreement [through consultation] or we can't reach accommodation, well, we'll then just proceed to sell the property to the Canada Lands Company. We'll do whatever it is that we had to do. If my learned friends have an objection at that point to our transferring the property because the consultation in their opinion was not thorough enough or satisfactory, it's open to them to bring the matter back to the Court for review.[42]

This "unhappy history" of Crown-Aboriginal relations is not unique, and sadly demonstrates the Canadian government's vacuous interpretation of what it means to act in accordance with the "Honour of the Crown." Despite being defined by the Court and constitutionally entrenched, it would seem that the Crown's duty to consult with Aboriginal peoples is only meaningful where persistence and very deep pockets support the legal challenge necessary to force the Crown to submit to its own law. When called to account for the lack of substantive action to address breaching the treaty relationship, the Crown continues to be both insolent and dishonourable. Unsurprisingly, the Crown again appealed the new Federal Court decision.

The long-awaited (second) Federal Court of Appeal decision on Kapyong was released in August 2015, seventeen months after hearing it for the second time in early 2014, and more than fourteen years after the initial announcement that the Kapyong base was to be vacated. This highly valued parcel of land in the City of

Winnipeg is one that holds great potential for First Nations economic development, but moreover, is an opportunity for the Crown to fulfill, at least in part, its outstanding obligations to Treaty 1 nations. In adjudicating the Kapyong question, the Federal Court of Appeal put it this way: "For over a century, Canada had broken a treaty promise to provide certain Aboriginal bands with lands. And to remedy the broken promise, Canada entered into certain agreement with some of the bands, including four of the respondent bands, to facilitate their acquisition of lands."[43]

The remedy sought in the Kapyong cases had always been a petition for the court to issue a declaration that the Crown owed a duty to consult with Treaty 1 nations before selling the Kapyong land to other buyers, and an order to restrain the Crown from selling the land through the Canada Lands Company, which would make any future negotiations on the land irrelevant. At every level, the Court agreed that the Crown had, and continues to have, a duty to consult Treaty 1 nations on the Kapyong land sale. The Crown eventually conceded on the first point, although it argued that it had met that duty. The Federal Court of Appeal disagreed with the Crown, defined sixteen specific points[44] on which the Crown failed to consult, but the Court was nevertheless gentle and generous in its reproach:

> [117] In my view, the treaty land entitlement agreements, seen in their proper historical context, reveal a genuine, *bona fide* desire, intention and commitment on the part of Canada—consistent with its obligations of honourable conduct, reconciliation and fair dealing with Aboriginal peoples—to engage in a process to rectify Canada's broken promise in Treaty No. 1 over time.
>
> [133] In doing this, we must ensure that we are not applying too exacting a standard . . . Even in healthy relationships where there is mutual trust and ample communication over simple issues, there can be isolated innocent omissions, misunderstandings, accidents and mistakes.
>
> [137] Examining the record myself, I see no particular *animus* on the part of Canada. Instead, fairly read, the record shows a repeated lack of understanding on the part of Canada about the nature and scope of the duty to consult in the particularly unusual circumstances of this case . . . As these reasons suggest, it should have altered its

course. But that sort of inertia is not enough to warrant the use of the term "egregious."[45]

Despite over a hundred years of legal inertia, if not out right aggression toward First Nations, the court credits the Crown with being honourable, and any mistakes were simply that, innocent mistakes. This is not incidental to the well-being of Aboriginal peoples. The fact that Treaty implementation and economic development are so closely tied, and there exists a desperate and chronic need for economic opportunities for First Nations, recognized as a "priority" by government after government, one has to wonder if the Crown can ever do wrong? To add to the injustice—and remember, this decision was a "win" for Treaty 1 First Nations—the Court said this:

> [147] Although we must show deference to remedial choices made by the Federal Court, in my view there was no basis in principle or on the facts of this case for the Federal Court to make the restraining order and the supervision order. Thus, I would set aside paragraph 4 of the judgment of the Federal Court.
>
> [148] First, the restraining order. In my view, on this evidentiary record, it cannot be sustained. *One cannot say that Canada will not obey the letter and spirit of this Court's decision.* For many years leading up to the judgment of the Federal Court, Canada was free to transfer the Barracks property to the Canada Lands Company but did not. *There is no reason to think that Canada will now act unfairly or unilaterally concerning the Barracks property.* Further, as a result of these reasons, Canada is now well-aware of its obligations, and there is no evidence to suggest that it will not govern itself accordingly.[46]

The Court thus removed the orders issued by the Federal Court, and required nothing more than simply trusting that the Crown to do the right thing. After 146 years of failing to act, this should give rise to some reason to think that the Honour of the Crown is nothing more than a legal fiction. The Kapyong decisions again denied First Nations any justice, and this by a nation that claims a common law history founded on the Rule of Law. Having faced legal contest after legal contest, and forcing First Nations to invest scarce resources in what appears to be a vain attempt to hold the Crown accountable, Treaty 1 First Nations are no closer to receiving what they are due. The Federal Court of Appeal put it very simply:

"The Aboriginal bands fulfilled their side of the bargain under Treaty No. 1. But Canada did not. It never fulfilled the per capita provision. It broke the solemn promise it had made."[47] Nevertheless, it refused to hold the Crown to its word and facilitate reconciliation. The obvious repercussion of such an impotent decision is that without land, economic opportunities will continue to be scare for First Nations peoples. Treaty implementation, and indeed a renewed relationship with First Nations, requires that the Crown begin to speak with truth, not double-talk.

Economic Development and Urban Reserves: "Hey, You Indian . . . Get a Job"

The Crown's belligerent reticence to fully implement the 1871 Treaty 1 per capita land allocation is apparent in the Kapyong court decisions, the result of which are clearly adverse to the economic interests of those First Nations. "Breaches of government duties have had the effect of depriving First Nations of access to land and resources that they desperately need to sustain themselves and struggle toward prosperity and have been among the principal causes of poverty and lack of opportunity in First Nations communities."[48] The economic potential of the barracks land remains considerable, given that it is situated in the City of Winnipeg, proximal to two affluent neighbourhoods, and is already zoned for commercial development. This may be among the reasons why the Federal Government chose to restrict how the land would be disposed. Despite the fact that this parcel of land appears to fit the criteria that would enable the Crown to make some progress on meeting its Treaty obligations, as detailed in TLE agreements and now affirmed by the Federal Court of Appeal (discussed above), the Barracks remain a vacant lot.

The Crown's rational for the decision to change the designation of the Kapyong land from surplus to strategic was to "optimize the financial and community value of strategic government surplus properties through effective planning, including rezoning and site servicing for property development, so as to achieve the highest and best use of the land."[49] This designation has since been successfully applied to convert other abandoned military urban sites into premier "legacy" neighbourhoods in Edmonton, Calgary, and Chilliwack. Clearly, the Government of Canada envisioned this "highest" and "best" use of the land should necessarily exclude ownership and development by First Nations. Despite the rhetoric about the importance of economic development for First Nations, the Crown appears to be determined to prevent an urban reserve in Winnipeg on the former Kapyong Barracks land.

Urban reserves are considered by many to be one of the most promising avenues to prosperity for First Nations peoples, and are at least notionally promoted by government. For example, in 2008, Aboriginal Affairs and Northern Development Canada (as it was called at the time) released a "Backgrounder" policy statement on urban reserves. This statement set out the challenges to First Nations economic participation as something removed from the historic reality of Crown mistreatment. Urban reserves are promoted as innovative opportunities for First Nations to overcome their unfortunate happenstance of history: "Many First Nations in Canada are located in rural areas, far from the cities and towns where most wealth and jobs are created. This geographic remoteness can sometimes pose challenges for First Nations trying to increase their economic self-sufficiency. Urban reserves are one of the most successful ways to address this problem."[50]

Is there any question as to why First Nations continue in a state of perpetual poverty? *Zemblanity*,[51] meaning an "unpleasant *unsurprise*," is the perfect word to explain the economic and social conditions of many on—and off—reserve First Nations peoples. The systematic exclusion of economic opportunity, largely through restrictions imposed by the *Indian Act*, the deliberate placement of many reserves on unproductive land, or, conversely, their removal from areas that offered abundant natural resources, the deleterious and lasting effects of Indian Residential Schools that destroyed education advancement potential of several generations, and commonplace racism—just to name a few barriers to success—are obvious precursors of the "challenges" now faced by First Nations. These conditions would be tragic enough if they simply happened like the weather; sadly, however, the whole of the enterprise was crafted and maintained by the Canadian Government.

Kapyong could have been, and perhaps may yet be, the crown jewel of Treaty 1 First Nations economic enterprises. At this point, however, it is difficult to imagine how this can come about. Even if they are able to purchase the land, they must also seek the approval of the Federal Government to convert the land to "reserve" status. This involves a long and complex process. "Of 1,275 ATR [Additions To Reserves] projects started between 2005 and 2012, 88.9% were for legal obligations; 10.9% were for community additions; and 0.2% were for new reserves/other (Standing Senate Committee on Aboriginal Peoples, 2012). Therefore, only small numbers of applications have fallen in the category for 'new' urban reserves."[52]

> Reserve creation often stems from Canada's legal obligation to settle and implement outstanding land claims. The majority of urban reserves are created as a result of specific claim and Treaty Land Entitlement settlements, which provide First Nations with cash payments that may be used to purchase land. As with any private individual or corporation, First Nations have the right to buy land from a willing seller. Once acquired, they also have the option of asking the federal government to transfer their land to reserve status, whether the property is located in an urban or rural setting.
>
> Approval of reserve status is not automatic. In order to get land designated as a reserve, federal policies require that a step-by-step approach be taken to address the concerns of everyone involved, including municipalities and environmental authorities. The Department's Additions to Reserves/New Reserves Policy requires environmental site assessments prior to any land acquisition by the federal government. This serves to protect both Canada and First Nations from adverse impacts.[53]

Adding to this already complex problem is the impact of widespread public opposition to an urban reserve in this area. Whether through misunderstanding or wilful ignorance—especially among an apparently highly educated population—the lack of accountability of the Crown for its disregard for its treaty promises is perpetuated. In September 2014, Probe Research asked Winnipeggers to respond to this question: "The division between aboriginal and non-aboriginal citizens is a serious issue in our city?" and reported "that most (in fact, over 75 percent of) *Winnipeggers* believe there is a deep racial gulf between Aboriginal and non-Aboriginal citizens—and this this is indeed a serious problem for the city."[54]

For whatever reasons, many citizens have voiced their objection to the possibility of an urban reserve at Kapyong, with some assuming it is yet again a demand for a handout made by Aboriginal people. Nothing could be further from the truth. Clearly, by the Crown's own admission, and again most recently the Court's confirmation, it is the Crown that insists on the "free lunch," to use the language of the Canadian Taxpayers Federation.[55] While Aboriginal people continue to experience poverty and disadvantage like no other group in Canada, the Crown has resisted at every turn allowing Treaty 1 nations the opportunity to *purchase*, at fair market value, the Kapyong parcel for development as an economic centre. Public comments from individuals identifying themselves as residents of the Tuxedo and River Heights neighbourhood range from overtly racist to mildly sympathetic, but not enthusiastic by any measure.

Although an urban reserve would involve commercial development, community opposition is not even made on these grounds. Since the Kapyong dispute began in 2003, several major businesses have already capitalized on the economic potential of the area, and the City of Winnipeg has facilitated this through the development of roadways to accommodate consumer traffic. This area now includes a 400,000 square foot Ikea store and a Cabela's (hunting and fishing) retail superstore. Future development includes the 400,000 square foot Seasons of Tuxedo retail-shopping complex, and an Outlet Collection cluster of retail stores. All of this development nicely compliments the existing Costco Wholesale, a mere 3.4 kilometres away.

Promotional material from developers of the Seasons of Tuxedo location boasts that the "trade area average household income is 60% higher than the Canadian average and is located in Winnipeg's most affluent community. 30% of the population has university degree [sic] making this the most educated community in the city."[56] The development is expected to draw from a "Regional Retail Trade Area [of] 2.3 Million"[57] people, including all of Manitoba, parts of Saskatchewan and Ontario, and extending south past Fargo, North Dakota. In light of the staggering economic potential for commercial development in this area, it becomes all the more alarming that while Treaty 1 First Nations have been occupied in courts of law, attempting to force the Crown to take its treaty obligations seriously, private developers have jumped in to scoop up the opportunity. Meanwhile, the Kapyong Barracks site sits unused and is rapidly deteriorating. Estimates of the cost to government to maintain the empty site, not to mention the cost of litigation to fend off First Nations attempts to purchase the property, run in the tens of millions of dollars. Instead of facilitating reconciliation through honouring its treaty obligations, the Crown continues to reinforce social and economic marginalization of First Nations peoples.

Why has the Federal Government of Canada chosen to sabotage the economic future of Treaty 1 First Nations at Kapyong? As has been demonstrated time and again, urban development can and does facilitate the aspirations of Indigenous Nations for economic prosperity, while simultaneously contributing to the mainstream economy. In light of this fact, how can this resistance be explained? For some, the answer is extremely simple.

The justification myth goes something like this: What were once Indigenous lands are now settler lands by virtue of the Doctrine of Discovery. Since the settler society has a more noble purpose for the land and natural resources of Turtle Island, it is they who must benefit from the exploitation of them. Treaties with First Nations became the means to "legally" remove the land from them, and them from the land. Those who were dispossessed but survived are now assumed to be part of the larger nation, thus no special benefits should flow their way. Non-Indigenous interests, both business and personal, should not be disadvantaged today, particularly as the result of archaic promises dating back to the 1800s. The treaties, whether adhered to or not, constitute fair, full, and final compensation for their lands. Adherence to this myth has allowed the Crown to have its cake (the claim of acting honourably) and eat it too (exploit the land without accountability). This right to have it both ways is called "sovereignty."

Courts continue to uphold this underlying claim of indisputable, indivisible Crown sovereignty, propped up by this historical justification myth. Peter Russell explains this myth as "legal magic" stemming from "a belief in the inherent inferiority of the Aboriginal peoples as peoples . . . [and] the bed-rock presumption of imperial rule."[58] This "historically validated arrangement," as Paul McHugh terms it, has infused the courts' understanding of treaties, such that "the sovereignty of the Crown-in-Parliament was put beyond any historical explanation."[59] This perspective has hobbled the Crown's ability to consider the true spirit and intent of historical treaties with Indigenous peoples. As Michael Asch points out, for Canadians, "Treaties, then, and not the constitution, are our charter of rights."[60] The inability of the courts, and indeed Parliament, to recognize the sovereign basis of treaty agreements, relegates them to an inferior rendition of their original intent, forcing them to become increasingly creative in justifying the lack of implementation and honour accorded them. What is missed in this perspective is that treaties create a perpetual relationship between equals. Asch states, "while these [treaty] commitments were laid out, they were merely a tangible expression of a larger commitment to ensure that [First Nations] would benefit, not suffer, economically as a consequence of settlement."[61] While the courts are determining "who is in charge" in jurisdictional squabbles between the provincial and federal Crowns, First Nations peoples are looking to treaties as a means of partnership with them.

Asch urges the Canadian state to step up to the challenge and apply its own constitutional interpretive framework to treaties. By doing so, he argues, treaties can assume their proper legal importance:

> If we take the view that [the Crown] lied, the treaties become worthless pieces of paper and we are back to square one. But if we take the view that we meant what we said, they become transformative, for through them, we become permanent partners sharing the land, not thieves stealing it, people who are here to stay not because we had the power to impose our will but because we forged a permanent, unbreakable partnership with those who were already here when we came.[62]

This transformative potential, accepting that settlers meant what they said, then has great implications for the future prosperity of Indigenous Nations. It is clear that self-determination and economic prosperity are inseparably linked. Given the resistance that Indigenous communities face when attempting to take hold of the prosperity envisioned in the treaties, it is incumbent upon the Crown to will itself to act honourably.

It is important to understand that Treaties are not simply about hunting and fishing rights—most of which have (incidentally) been established through criminal proceedings. Although economic opportunities in remote areas have always existed—the billions of dollars extracted or generated from Aboriginal lands and waters testifies to this fact—Treaty Indians in particular have been historically shut out of sharing in the prosperity. Now, with a growing urban Aboriginal population, treaty implementation also affects the nearly 50 percent of Status Indians who reside in urban centres like Winnipeg. The challenges for First Nations peoples to finding meaningful employment in urban centres are many: prejudice and stereotypes held by potential employers, general racism (which is alive and well), poor educational outcomes, and lack of opportunity are obvious barriers. Even where individual Indians are successful, as many are, it is on an individual basis only. When considering Treaty implementation as a means to economic development vis-à-vis urban reserves, opportunities for First Nation bands/communities become possible. The bottom line here is simple: urban reserves have the potential to create the economic activity necessary to employ whole communities. Ironically, it is often those who oppose the development of urban reserves who are quick to demand that Indians get jobs and become contributing members of society. Perhaps this enthusiasm would be better directed at the Crown to uphold its treaty obligations, so Indians can get on with business … literally.

Taxation and Indians: "That's Not Fair!"

Public opposition to urban reserves frequently coalesces around the fact that the *Indian Act* contains certain tax provisions for Status Indians on reserves. There remains a persistent myth, despite living in the so-called information age, that all Indians are tax-exempt. While there is a grain of truth to this, it is far from the whole truth. Amid blatantly racist commentary from Winnipeggers and other "concerned" parties who opposed the acquisition of the Kapyong land by Treaty 1 nations, are objections to the special tax status that some Registered Indians can claim. The most contentious of these provisions include the potential for tax-free employment earnings, sales tax exemptions on retail purchases, and businesses that are exempt from paying property taxes. It is this seemingly "unfair" tax treatment within an urban reserve—also termed an "economic zone" that so often draws the scorn and protest of non-Indigenous peoples.

One particularly loud voice is the Frontier Centre for Public Policy (FCPP). Published in the *Winnipeg Free Press* as an "analysis," the policy think tank urged Treaty 1 nations to "reconsider their position." The article, written by FCPP research associate Joseph Quesnel, stated:

> First Nations frequently convert lands they acquire in urban areas into "urban reserves" because of the tax-exemption status attached to the land, which they often view as its primary value . . .
>
> Manny Jules, chief commissioner of the First Nations Tax Commission, told the Standing Senate Committee on Aboriginal Peoples that, "the problem with additions to reserve is that they make formerly productive lands unproductive by converting valuable fee-simple land into Indian reserves. Reserve lands are generally about one-tenth as productive as other lands in Canada. They are subject to systems of governance and land tenure that make it very difficult to do business or attract investment." . . .
>
> But, as discussed above, if they convert it to a reserve, they lose substantial value. Commissioner Jules, in his address, stated that in a future First Nations Property Ownership Act, indigenous communities should maintain full economic value and obtain jurisdiction over their lands.[63]

Representing the views of the FCPP, Quesnel argues for the rejection of urban reserves in favour of individual, fee-simple ownership. However, this reasoning is flawed and contradictory. Quesnel points to Jules's report, wherein Jules argues for the dismantling of all reserves—urban and otherwise, ignoring the fact that the establishment of reserves is an explicit term in all of the Numbered Treaties. Further, Jules (and by reference Quesnel and the FCPP) offers no rationale for the apparent sudden "unproductivity" of converted land, yet advocates for a better "Additions to Reserve" process. Considering the vast potential of the Kapyong neighbourhood in Winnipeg—already being developed by others—this is simply not true. In fact, it is precisely because of the high value of the development potential that Treaty 1 nations have expressed interest in purchasing it.

This view suggests that the best, and perhaps only, solution to economic challenges for First Nations is to completely dismantle reserves and communal First Nation ownership of land, and to fully assimilate into Canadian mainstream economy and society. This recommendation ignores both the solemnity and constitutional importance of the Treaties, and disrespects the unique place that First Nations occupy in this nation. Assimilation is antithetical to a Treaty relationship. The logical and legal alternative[64] to a treaty relationship is that the nation-state of Canada, being incapable of fulfilling its side of the bargain, return to the respective Treaty nations the land and wealth acquired through the treaties.

Concerns over tax implications, while holding some benefits for certain businesses and individuals (not unlike the many exclusions and exceptions written into Canada's *Income Tax Act*, for corporations, families with children, or those making donations to political parties, just to name a few), should not obscure the importance of the potential for economic development. Advocates of fair taxation, including the Director at the Centre for Aboriginal Policy Change (of the Canadian Taxpayers Federation), are clearly misinformed about the history of this nation and its taxation policies, and give credence to miscreants by ignoring the larger picture. This is the position of the Canadian Taxpayers Federation (CTF):

> Urban reserves create two problems. Unfair competition is the first. True, Native bands negotiate an agreement with municipalities to pay fees for services—such as sidewalk and road maintenance—in lieu of the regular property taxes. However, in addition to sidewalk and road maintenance property taxes pay for civic development projects, which the Native bands would be exempt from paying. Native Canadians working on urban reserves do not pay income tax, so businesses can pay lower wages without the workers losing any take-home pay. Furthermore, a Native-owned business would not have to pay

> taxes for goods and supplies delivered to their shop located on reserve land. Native-owned businesses, Native workers and businesses operating in partnership with urban reserves have a clear and unreasonable advantage over the competition. This unfair competitive advantage may in fact cause existing Winnipeg businesses to become bankrupt. Obviously, the tax breaks would help a Native-owned business operating on an urban reserve. But most of us realize there is no such thing as a free lunch, someone has to pay the bill.[65]

There are several obvious problems with this position. First, the issue of fairness is a red herring. It is absurd that CTF is crying for fairness when the whole Kapyong debacle is due to a century-long breach of the Crown, and one that could have been remedied long ago, or at least in part through this land sale. Second, the CTF wrongly characterizes the beneficiaries of tax benefits as "natives." The *Indian Act*—the legislation that sets out the tax provisions in this case—applies singularly to "Status Indians," as defined by the *Indian Act*. "Native" is not synonymous with "Indian"; the provisions do not apply to Inuit peoples, Métis peoples, and most importantly, to non-status "Indian"—all of whom make up a category more appropriately labelled Aboriginal or Indigenous peoples. The group to whom this provision applies is very small relative to the *larger* population of Aboriginal peoples, and extremely small relative to the larger Canadian population. Even for this extremely small sector of "registered status Indians," only a few meet the restrictive tests set out by the Court to be recognized as tax exempt on employment income. To decry how "Natives" have overwhelming advantages is nothing short of ridiculous. If there was a free lunch to be had, I'd suggest it is the progeny of wealthy, powerful families (and their enterprises) of Winnipeg, who have received the fiscal advantages of racist and sexist policies of yesteryear, who will undoubtedly pass along in turn this advantage to their kin. While laws and policies affecting Aboriginal Peoples have been somewhat reformed, including the *Indian Act*, the advantages that were handed to white settlers since 1867 (and surely, long before Canada's Confederation), continue to be held by an elite sector. There has indeed been over a hundred years of free lunches, but they were never served on the tables of Aboriginal peoples.

> It is very important Native Canadians enter the mainstream of Canada's economy. Viable business ventures are one way to achieve this. In a free market system, all players must be on an equal footing.

> Unfair competitive advantages, such as tax breaks, disrupt the system by off-loading the tax burden to other citizens and businesses.[66]

Understanding the true issues, both historic and legal, in a dispute like Kapyong goes a long way toward reconciliation. Holding steadfastly to racist, erroneous information, perhaps even with the intent to misinform Canadians about urban reserves, is divisive and destructive. In many ways, Kapyong serves to highlight how Aboriginal peoples in what is now Canada have lived in a post-truth era since 1867.

The key issue to consider here, however, is the larger picture of fairness. Viewed simply through a lens of taxation—a principle of which is for horizontal and vertical fairness, the real issue is one of treaty implementation. It is the Crown that continues to proclaim its own honour—and nowhere more than in its dealing with Aboriginal peoples—while it champions the Rule of Law and extolls the virtues of peace, order, and good governance. Except, it seems, when it comes to its foundational relationship with the First Peoples of Turtle Island. At issue then is this: Is it *fair* to renege on treaties, systematically dispossess and demoralize its First Nations peoples, and then feign concern for their economic and social well-being? Are the perceived advantages of Section 87 of the *Indian Act* provisions that are "given" to First Nations peoples really about taxation? How then, in the face of legislation—namely the *Indian Act* and Crown agreements such as the TLEs, Constitutional Law Sections 25 and 35, and Court decisions—especially those dealing specifically with Kapyong—can the Crown continue to impede the resolution of the Kapyong matter on the basis of a claim of unfairness? It is this larger context to which Canadians must pay attention.

Accounts of the Crown's dealings with Aboriginal peoples in what is now Canada have been, and continue to be, shaped and reshaped to reinforce the grand project of colonization. The historic rationale, official or otherwise, for Canada's Indian policy found expression in the *Indian Act*, Indian Residential Schools, and other law and policy regimes aimed solely at the assimilation of First Nations peoples. Over time, the net effect of this ill-fated project has been the accumulation of an inaccurate and often denigrating record of Aboriginal peoples, a deep well from which lawmakers and policy advisors continue to draw. This perspective has contributed more than any other single factor to the continued uncertainty for the original rationale, and indeed endurance, of the tax provisions of the *Indian Act*. This apparent legal uncertainty has served to undermine Treaty terms, and in turn left the public at large with, at best, only a vague understanding of the tax provisions available to Registered and Status Indians.

Nevertheless, it is also apparent that the archetype of the poor Indian continues to echo through jurisprudence, such as in *Recalma v. The Queen* (1998); despite being overturned by subsequent law, the aversion to the wealthy Indian continues to influence both jurists and the general public. Even the slightest hint that Indians (and indeed all Aboriginal Peoples) might rise up and manage their own affairs in their own way makes most Canadians nervous. Hence, the "protect, civilize, assimilate" goals of Indian policy continue to linger, resulting in more Aboriginal peoples being marginalized, excluded from traditional territory, family connections, cultural ties, opportunities for economic participation, and ultimately human dignity, in greater numbers than at any other time in Canadian history. The Court's narrow interpretation of the *Indian Act* tax provisions is but one indicia of where the Court has lost sight of the foundational nature of the Treaty relationship.

This special legal status is now understood to have formed the foundation of Canadian Indian law and policy, albeit one that has been marred by prejudice and ruthless colonial ambition, but nevertheless is a relationship that began with treaties. Jurisprudence since 1982 indicates that the Court has raised expectations for its own consideration of the treaties, giving recognition to the fact that Aboriginal peoples have their own perspectives, and which the Court suggests are equally legitimate and requiring accommodation. This proposition, one that has consistently been held by Aboriginal Peoples, gained traction in 1984 with the *Guerin v. The Queen*[67] decision, and continues to resonate in subsequent jurisprudence.[68] While having due regard for Aboriginal perspectives remains to be fully explored by the courts, Indigenous scholarship and Aboriginal perspectives of the treaties and the rights protected by those special agreements have much to contribute to understanding the historic basis for the *Indian Act* tax provision. The intrinsic connection between Aboriginal peoples and their traditional territories, and the rights that flow from that relationship, is slowly becoming apparent to jurists and legislators alike. Legal scholar John Borrows put it this way:

> Even in parts of the country where treaties were signed, Indigenous peoples experience broad denials of their freedom and autonomy to land, governance, and other vital resources... Canada has not only done a poor job in reflecting Indigenous peoples within its constitutional

order, it has greatly harmed their social, economic, and spiritual relations and practices throughout most of its history. As Chief Justice McLachlin observed, Canada committed cultural genocide in relation to Aboriginal peoples. Colonialism is not only a historic fact of Canadian life—it is a present distressing reality.[69]

The last words on the Kapyong matter from the 2015 Federal Court of Appeal were thus:

> Finally, it is to be hoped that whatever rancour, bitterness and mistrust among the parties may have existed in the past, the parties will now proceed to engage in constructive, respectful consultations concerning the Barracks property for the benefit of all.[70]

Recall, however, that the Federal Court of Appeal refused to issue any order or directive for the Crown, and justified this position by assuming the Crown's sense of honour is to be relied upon: "There is no reason to think that Canada will now act unfairly or unilaterally concerning the Barracks property. Further, as a result of these reasons, Canada is now well-aware of its obligations, and there is no evidence to suggest that it will not govern itself accordingly."[71] And so we are back where we started, with a call for reconciliation. Treaty 1 nations have done their part; it's now time for the Crown to step up and act with honour.

1. Acknowledgments: This paper was presented in part at *Unsettling Conversations, Unmasking Racisms*, on October 18, 2014 in Edmonton, Alberta, and at the International Studies Association Annual Convention on February 18, 2015 in New Orleans, Louisiana. Research was funded in part by SSHRC (Insight) and UManitoba GETS. I also wish to thank Berens River FN (PSSSP) for financial support, and Kiera Ladner for her collaboration on this paper.
2. Truth and Reconciliation Commission of Canada (2015), *Honouring the Truth, Reconciling for the Future: Summary of the Final Report of the Truth and Reconciliation Commission of Canada*, Winnipeg: p. 7.
3. The term "Indian" is used in its legal sense, as defined by the *Indian Act*, s 2(1) and s 6, and differentiates those to whom the *Indian Act* applies—namely "Indians"—from other Aboriginal peoples, including Inuit, Métis, and other non-registered persons of Aboriginal descent. The Court has made clear distinction as to the applicability of the *Indian Act* in *Reference whether "Indians" includes" Eskimo*" SCR 104 [*Re Eskimo*] (1939), and *Daniels v. Canada (Indian Affairs and Northern Development)* SCC 12 (2016).
4. "Treaty No. 1," Treaty Relations Commission of Manitoba: www.trcm.ca/treaties/treaties-in-manitoba/treaty-no-1/
5. Leslie, John, Ron Maguire, and Robert G. Moore (1978), *The Historical Development of the Indian Act*, Ottawa: Treaties and Historical Research Centre, Research Branch Corporate Policy, Indian and Northern Affairs Canada, p. 80, notes removed.

6. Minister of Public Works and Government Services Canada, Minister of Indian Affairs and Northern Development (2007), "Specific Claims: Justice at Last," p. 6.
7. Canada v. Long Plain First Nation FCA 177, para 15 (2015).
8. Leslie, Maguire, & Moore ,1978, pp. 80-81 (emphasis added).
9. *The Constitution Act, 1982, Schedule B to the Canada Act 1982 (UK)*, (1982), c 11, ss 25 & 35.
10. "Province makes Good Progress on Meeting Treaty Land Entitlement Obligations: Robinson," (2011) Province of Manitoba: www.news.gov.mb.ca/news/?item=11913
11. "Province Targets Four-Year Completion Time Frame for First Nations land Settlements," (2007) Province of Manitoba: www.news.gov.mb.ca/news/index.html?item=1871&posted=2007-06-28
12. Manitoba, (2007) Speech from the Throne, 1st Sess, 39th Leg Ass, June 6, 2007 (John Harvard).
13. Province of Manitoba, 2011.
14. Ibid.
15. Minister of Public Works and Government Services Canada, Minister of Indian Affairs and Northern Development (2007), "Specific Claims: Justice at Last", p. 1 (emphasis added).
16. Crown debt to Manitoba First Nations exceeds 1.14 million hectares (2.8 million acres). First Nations in other provinces have made similar successful claims for Crown breaches of their corresponding Treaties. See: Indigenous and Northern Affairs Canada, (nd) "Treaty Land Entitlement," : www.aadnc-aandc.gc.ca/eng/1100100034822/1100100034823
17. Welch, Mary Agnes (2015), "After Supreme Court ruling: a clash of claims between Métis, First Nations," Winnipeg: *Winnipeg Free Press*: www.winnipegfreepress.com/local/clash-of-claims-on-metis-first-nations-291943961.html
18. Indigenous and Northern Affairs Canada, (2017) "Approved Additions to Reserve Proposals,": www.aadnc-aandc.gc.ca/eng/1466532960405/1466533062058
19. The Government of Canada defines surplus real property as: "Real property that is no longer required in support of a department's programs." Government of Canada, (nd), "Policy on Management of Real Property," online: tbs-sct.gc.ca/pol/doc-eng.aspx?id=12042#appA.) It should be noted that land purchases also include the potential to purchase "other land," being real property held in fee simple (private land), if there is a willing seller.
20. *Long Plain First Nation*, FCA 177, para 26 (2015).
21. Canada v. Brokenhead First Nation, FCA 148, para 13 (2011).
22. The TLE Framework is not unique to Manitoba, and can be exercised by First Nations (Treaty Nations) across Canada, where claimants have successfully proven that the Crown breached its obligations in any of the Numbered Treaties.
23. Canada has recognized only five claimants, all of which have outstanding TLE claims: Long Plain FN, Swan Lake FN, Roseau River Anishinaabe FN, Brokenhead Ojibway Nation, and under a separate agreement, Peguis FN. On October 7, 2011, Brokenhead FN filed a notice of discontinuance, removing itself as a party to the joint application.
24. Brokenhead First Nation v. Canada , FC 982, para 38 (2009).
25. *Brokenhead First Nations*, FC 982 (2009); Canada v. Brokenhead First Nation, FCA 148 (2011); Long Plain First Nation v. Canada, FC 1474 (2012); Long Plain First Nation v. Canada, FC 86 (2013); Peguis First Nation v. Canada (Attorney General), FC 276 (2013); Peguis First Nation v. Canada (Attorney General), FCA 7 (2014); *Long Plain First Nation*, FCA 177 (2015).
26. *Brokenhead First Nation*, FC 982, para 37 (2009).
27. Ibid., para 28.
28. Ibid., FC 982, para 12.
29. HMTQ v. Brokenhead, (2011) FCA 148, paras 34 and 50 (2011).

30. Ibid., para 38.
31. Ibid., para 40.
32. Ibid., para 48.
33. Ibid., para 51.
34. Ibid., para 45. These sentiments were echoed in the Federal Court of Appeal decision, *HMTQ v. Long Plain First Nation*, FCA 177, paragraph 139 (2015): "As is often the case when relationships become dysfunctional, fault can be found on both sides." Also see paragraphs 158 and 159 of this same decision, wherein the Court opines on the "reciprocal duty on aboriginal peoples."
35. In *Reference re Supreme Court Act, ss 5 and 6* SCC 21 (2014), Nadon's appointment was found to be unconstitutional, and was deemed to have never taken effect.
36. Long Plain First Nation v. HMTQ, FC 1474, para 80 (2012).
37. Ibid., para 66.
38. Ibid., para 78.
39. Ibid., para 69.
40. Ibid., para 4.
41. Long Plain First Nation v. HMTQ , FC 86, para 7 (2013).
42. *Brokenhead First Nation*, FC 982, para 38 (2009).
43. *Long Plain First Nation*, FCA 177, para 9 (2015).
44. Ibid., para 134
45. Ibid., paras 117, 133, and 137.
46. Ibid., paras 147 and 148 (emphasis added).
47. Ibid., para 13.
48. Alan Pratt Professional Corporation (2004), "Validating Claims Under the *Specific Claims Resolution Act* (And Beyond!)," p. 4.
49. Ircha, Michael C. and Robert Young, eds. (2013), *Federal Property Policy in Canadian Municipalities*, Montréal: McGill-Queen's University Press, p. 19.
50. Aboriginal Affairs and Northern Development Canada, (2008) "Backgrounder—Urban reserves: A Quiet Success Story," Aboriginal Affairs and Northern Development Canada: www.aadnc-aandc.gc.ca/eng/1100100016331/1100100016332
51. A term Wikipedia claims was coined by William Boyd to describe "making unhappy, unlucky and expected discoveries occurring by design," as an antonym of "serendipity." Source: Wikipedia: "Serendipity," last modified on January 27, 2017: www.en.wikipedia.org/wiki/Serendipity
52. Poholka, Holli (2006), *First Nation Successes: Developing Urban Reserves in Canada*, Masters in Urban Planning Thesis, Kingston: Queen's University, p. 17.
53. Aboriginal Affairs and Northern Development Canada: www.aadnc-aandc.gc.ca/eng/1100100016331/1100100016332
54. Probe Research (2014) "Winnipeg is a Divided City, Citizens Say," www.probe-research.com/documents/141003%20Aboriginal%20Relations%20Release.pdf
55. Fiss, Tanis and Adrienne Batra, Canadian Taxpayers Federation, (2005) "Urban Reserve—Coming to a City Near You," www.caledoniawakeupcall.com/CTF/050916ctf.html
56. Forester Projects & Harvard Developments Inc. (nd) "Seasons," www.seasonswinnipeg.ca/leasing
57. Ibid.
58. Russell, Peter (2005), *Recognizing Aboriginal Title: The Mabo Case and Indigenous Resistance to English-Settler Colonialism*, Toronto: University of Toronto Press, p. 31.

59. McHugh, Paul (2000), "Sovereignty this Century—Maori and the Common law Constitution," *Victoria: University of Wellington Law Review*, 16; 31:1.
60. Asch, Michael (2014), *On Being Here to Stay: Treaties and Aboriginal Rights in Canada*, Toronto: University of Toronto Press, p. 99.
61. Ibid., p. 94.
62. Ibid., p. 99.
63. Quesnel, Joseph, (2017) "Consider all options for Kapyong Barrack site," *Winnipeg Free Press*, www.winnipegfreepress.com/opinion/analysis/consider-all-options-for-kapyong-barracks-site-412855663.html
64. This is a basic principle of equity in English (and by import, now Canadian) trust law, when a fiduciary fails to fulfill its obligations. For example, see Guerin v. The Queen, 2 SCR 335, p. 361 (1984). Concerning the Crown breach of its fiduciary duties to Guerin and others, Justice Wilson of the Supreme Court of Canada, citing established jurisprudence, stated: "The cases to which I have referred demonstrate that the obligation to make restitution, which courts of equity have from very early times imposed on defaulting trustees and other fiduciaries, is of a more absolute nature than the common-law obligation to pay damages for tort or breach of contract . . . The form of relief is couched in terms appropriate to require the defaulting trustee to restore to the estate the assets of which he deprived it."
65. Fiss & Batra, 2005.
66. Ibid.
67. Guerin v. The Queen, 2 SCR 335 (1984).
68. The Supreme Court continues to retreat from this position. In Mitchell v. Peguis Indian Band, 2 SCR 85 (1990), a tax case, the Court denied the possibility that the "aboriginal perspective" could ever "alter the basic structure of Sovereign-Indian relations [nor are] aboriginal peoples . . . outside the sovereignty of the Crown" (p 109). In Tsihqot'in Nation v. British Columbia, SCC 44 (2014), the Court diminishes the utility of the "Aboriginal perspective" when considering Aboriginal practices, but instead as an understanding of practices needing to be "approached from both the common law and Aboriginal perspectives" (at para 49) and qualified by "the perspective of the broader public" (at para 81).
69. Borrows, John (2016), *Freedom & Indigenous Constitutionalism*, Toronto: University of Toronto Press, p. 107 (notes removed).
70. *Long Plain First Nation* , FCA 177, para 163 (2015).
71. Ibid., para 148.

Canada, I can cite for you 150

Christie Belcourt

Canada,
I can cite for you 150
Lists of the dead
150 languages no longer spoken
150 rivers poisoned
150 Indigenous children taken into care last month
150 Indigenous communities without water
150 grieving in a hotel in Winnipeg
150 times a million lies
told to our faces to steal our lands.

Canada,
I can cite for you 150
Forms of resistance
150 battles to the death
150 water warriors walking
150 naming ceremonies
150 ways we shake the ground with dance and song
150 tattooed expressions of sovereignty
150 times 2 million days faces were painted
with earth of this land.

Canada,
I can cite for you 150
Summers coming of resurgence
150 thousand babies birthed in ceremonies
150 thousand status cards burned

150 thousand youth marching for water
150 thousand children with braids and feathers in their hair
150 thousand Indigenous words being spoken without English
150 summers coming
of Mother Earth calling out to our hearts
150 summers coming
where you too, will finally come to understand
the power and spirit of these lands and waters
as our ancestors have known and have been trying to tell you for 500 years.

#WaterIsLife #LandIsSacred #Canada150?

"To Honour the Lives of Those Taken From Us"

Restor(y)ing Resurgence and Survivance through Walking With Our Sisters

Shalene Jobin and Tara Kappo

Preface

I know grief.
In the never-ending pain of your absence,
The unanswered questions,
The longing for what was,
and should still be,
The life taken from us.
I know grief.

And in the grief,
With the grief,
through the grief,
Using beads, needles, thread,
Bone, stone, birchbark,
Plastic, paper, paint,
Bright fabric and powerful medicines,
Songs, tears, and laughter,
Guided by respect, gentleness, humility,
My memories, shining and shaded,
Gathered with prayers,
Become a memorial to you.

And I know love.
I think of you, niwâhkômâkan (my relative).

You are missing from our lives,
We miss you in our lives,
But we remember you,
And we honour you,
And we know love.

ᐊᓐᑭ ᑲᐱᒍᑦᑦ'

Introduction

For over 150 decades, Indigenous peoples have been nations on Turtle Island. In 150 years of Canadian Confederation, Indigenous peoples have witnessed the exploitation of our lands and bodies.[1] Indigenous women, girls, Two-Spirited persons, and residential school children have been especially affected by the heteronormative patriarchy embedded in Canadian colonialism. As an anniversary of mourning, loss, and continued colonization approaches, we counter Canada's acts of colonial remembering with accounts of Indigenous honouring. This chapter is not about Canada's shameful treatment of Indigenous women, girls, Two-Spirited persons and residential school children; rather, we draw attention to *Walking With Our Sisters* (WWOS) as a beautiful story of strength, resilience, and resurgence of grassroots responses to honour and centre Indigenous lives.

Reflecting the spirit of WWOS, this chapter is a collaborative work that brings together ideas from the authors' different perspectives. Tara Kappo draws from her experience as a contributing artist, local organizer, and community helper with the WWOS National Collective; while Shalene Jobin, who has been involved as a volunteer and supporter since the first memorial installation in Edmonton, Alberta, provides another perspective on connection and involvement in WWOS. In the first part of this chapter, we present an overview of WWOS. In the second part, reflecting on our understanding of WWOS and acknowledging similar contributions emerging in academic literature,[2] we seek to add to the growing narrative around WWOS by drawing from our personal experiences and presenting what we consider to be powerful lessons from the work of WWOS. Altogether then, from our own experiences and reflections, we share our view of this profound memorial ceremony, which we believe powerfully and profoundly expresses survivance and resurgence.

Walking With Our Sisters

Walking With Our Sisters emerged from a place of compassion that follows the foundational and crucial work and advocacy of families that has gone on for decades. We recognize that "[f]or over 30 years, family members, advocates, and organizations have been working to raise awareness of missing and murdered Indigenous women."[3] WWOS is a response from a loving and creative collective heart. Specifically, and as described on the WWOS website, it is a collective action

"to honour the lives of missing and murdered Indigenous Women of Canada and the United States; to acknowledge the grief and torment families of these women continue to suffer; and to raise awareness of this issue and create opportunity for broad community-based dialogue on the issue."[4]

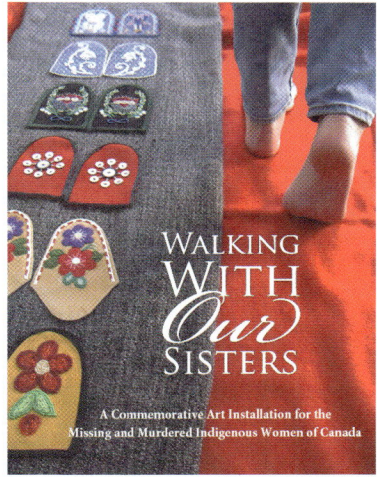

Promotional poster depicting the original concept of *WWOS*.
WWW.WALKINGWITHOURSISTERS.CA

Although we now understand WWOS as a memorial ceremony, it was initially described as a commemorative art installation. As explained on the WWOS website, "In June of 2012, a general call was issued on Facebook for people to create moccasin tops. The initial goal was to collect 600 pairs, one for each of the women in the Sisters in Spirit database."[5] Métis artist and grassroots leader Christi Belcourt made the call and people responded. The vamps were to represent the unfinished lives of Indigenous women. The vision behind the call was to create an art installation that placed the vamps along pathways on the floor beside which people could follow in parallel. In this way, participants could walk alongside—with—the women represented by the vamps.

As recounted on the WWOS website, "the public response far exceeded . . . expectations"[6] One year later, by July of 2013, over 1,600 "vamps meticulously handmade and donated by individuals from across North America and beyond"[7] had been received.

Google Map showing locations (red pins) from which vamps originated.
WWW.WALKINGWITHOURSISTERS.CA

This unexpected response signalled that an incredible movement was underway. As Stephanie Anderson beautifully describes:

> Many of the vamps were stitched by family members and friends in memory of a lost loved one—a mother, a sister, a grandmother, a daughter, a friend—while others were made as a show of solidarity and support, a call for awareness, a form of political alignment and protest, and an urge to action. Whatever the motivation, each set represents a personal resolve not to remain voiceless or complacent, to pick up a needle and thread and create a visible, tangible representation of that which cannot be adequately expressed in words . . . This gesture itself—the response to a call, the acceptance of personal responsibility and the determination to act—is an integral component of the final installation, one which is experienced viscerally through contemplation of the time, labor, and love that was invested in each crafted piece.[8]

Although it started as a way of honouring missing and murdered Indigenous women, through its journey WWOS also came to acknowledge missing and murdered Indigenous girls and Two-Spirited/trans people, as well as children who were taken through the Indian residential school system. Alongside this expanded focus was a transformation from understanding the memorial as an art installation to understanding the memorial as a ceremony. As preparations for the inaugural "installation" in Edmonton took shape, the centrality of a ceremonial ethic emerged more clearly. Having sought advice and direction from Elder Maria Campbell, the memorial was gently yet insistently grounded in ceremonial protocol. It became evident early on that the language of "art installation" or "project" failed to express or describe our actions properly. As we moved toward the first memorial, we came to understand we were preparing for ceremony, and our language began to shift accordingly. The items donated for WWOS—including the vamps, songs, medicines, and eagle staffs—might have initially been referred to as a "collection" but our preparations led us to understand this instead as "the bundle." We also came to understand, and speak of, our installation as a "lodge" in which we were preparing to hold ceremony.

Vamps dedicated to the memories of Cecile Moostoos and her daughter Philomene Moostoos (of the Sturgeon Lake Cree Nation) made and contributed by Tara Kappo.

Initially, as was shared on the *WWOS* Facebook group page (and later included on the *WWOS* website), the vamps were made "to create something that built upon the love and traditions of my family in remembrance, love and respect for our sisters. It was the medicine I wanted to share, the love and healing this work represents to me." As an example of one of the incredible stories of *WWOS*, the vamps were dedicated by Moostoos family members to the memories of their mother and sister. PHOTO COURTESY OF TARA KAPPO

There is a multitude of ways to understand the material and spiritual significance of this; a key one is that the bundle is a collection of items—the physical and non-physical—that are integral to many Indigenous ceremonies. Another key understanding is that in Indigenous worldviews, a bundle is actionable; it has its own agency. We can see this in the ways in which many people describe having been touched by WWOS and moved to gift items, time, and love. The recognition of agency also contributes to an understanding of the bundle as a type of living being with whom we have a relationship; this helps restore and maintain a practice of relationality consistent with Indigenous worldviews that extends beyond us, to those who are no longer with us and to non-human beings.

WWOS is an honouring of Indigenous women, girls, Two-Spirited persons, and residential school children that also produces a stand against violence and a stand *with* Indigenous women, girls, Two-Spirited persons, and residential school children in the physical and in the metaphysical. Dakota scholar Kim TallBear explains how Indigenous peoples emphasize the "... complex forms of relatedness of peoples and non-humans in particular places," where "... [I]ndigenous peoples consider identity to be the product of a co-constitution of human and non-human communities."[9] TallBear talks passionately about this extension of relationality: "[W]e may not all have the same relations with those who move without bodies amongst us, but it is impossible to live in a tribal community and not live within a world where these spirit persons do things. For us, materiality is part of gaining us, not the other way around."[10] When they went missing or were murdered, our relatives were often alone, but in the creation of the moccasin vamps, the bundle, and the lodge, the sisters stand together, and we stand with them.

The lodge being prepared for the 2015 ceremony in Red Deer, Alberta. Pictured are the vamps made by members of Vancouver's Downtown Eastside (DTES) community; these are laid first in recognition of DTES's longstanding grassroots leadership and advocacy for MMIW. Also visible are other items of the bundle that have been gifted at various locations on the journey.
PHOTO COURTESY OF TARA KAPPO.

The bundle and the lodge form a ceremonial space intended to be loving, welcoming, and safe. In this lodge we walk with our sisters, girls, Two-Spirited persons, residential school children, and each other. In each community where the bundle visits, the lodge is raised, and our ceremony is held, we connect to each other in love, respect, and compassion, to honour the lives of those taken from us.

In the lodge, through the complete experience of the ceremony, we see people connecting on a heart level. This can be profoundly transformative for all who experience it. Notably, where non-Indigenous people are able to experience this type of heart-level connection, the harmful systemic beliefs embedded in Canadian society can be bypassed and, once connected back to the intellectual, effect a changed perception of Indigenous peoples. Stephanie Anderson explains:

> Brought together in physical space . . . the installation has an impact which surpasses its constituent parts, arousing an overwhelming sense of the quantity and scale of the tragedies they represent. The metaphorical sense of walking, in solidarity, compassion, and resolve with the lost women, is here intensified by the bodily investment required to navigate through the memorial. As noted by some visitors, the empty footprints seem almost to constitute the absent bodies which might have filled them, offering, for some, the humbling and intensely emotional experience of walking among the spirits of those lost.[11]

The profoundly affective experience for the people who join in the ceremony can, and should be, connected directly to the way WWOS is governed. Remaining mindful that we are called together to honour our loved ones, it was most fitting

Part of the lodge being set up for the 2015 ceremony in Yellowknife, NT, incorporating elements important to the Indigenous peoples of the area, with the children's vamps placed in the heart of the lodge. PHOTO COURTESY OF TARA KAPPO.

to turn to the wisdom of our grandmothers to guide us to, and through, the most appropriate forms for our honouring work. This emerged as a grassroots-governing framework that guides our collective response and helps us ensure we uphold good relationships. This is expressed through four principles that guide the process, and is maintained by the guidance of the Elders who are part of the national collective, as well as the Elders and spiritual advisors who guide the territorial specificities in each community in which the lodge is situated. The four principles that provide a foundation for the governing process are:

1. Humility. All who attend this ceremony are equal and all are welcome. We remain grounded in humility as helpers by remembering that this work is not about us, but about honouring the women, girls, and Two-Spirited people, and supporting their grieving loved ones.
2. Protocol. We hold that traditional protocols must be followed throughout our work from start to finish. These protocols help us to ensure we approach our ceremony and each other in very respectful ways.
3. Love. At all times, we must take a gentle approach and treat all who come to the ceremony with patience, kindness, and loving care.
4. Volunteerism. We are all volunteers. In ceremony, we bring our selves and our willingness to participate, and we ask for nothing in return.

This expression of compassion and love from so many people reflects another very important feature of WWOS: how it enacts a community-based ethic—a reliving of place-based relationality—while simultaneously reconnecting with Indigenous peoples across Turtle Island (and beyond). Thousands of people have chosen to become involved and volunteer. To give a sense of what this community actually looks like, right now there are over 21,000 members in the Facebook group. That group, however, does not represent everybody who has been involved and continues to get involved with this project. There are many more people who are not present at all on social media.[12] As of the end of 2016, the bundle, or the ceremony, has travelled to sixteen communities across Canada and one in the United States. The bundle will continue travelling until 2019, when the collective will hold its final ceremony in Batoche, Saskatchewan.

These connections began with an initial call-out and are carried on through the beading circles and the remembering of loved ones to the organizing and the public memorial. Stephanie Anderson explains:

> [I]t is not uncommon for those who engage in this type of handwork to note its strong connection to the related experiences of storytelling, thinking, mourning, healing, the showing of care, the passing of memory, and the expression of agency . . . [M]any participants in WWOS . . . recount the process of making their vamps as an intensely emotional one. For some—for those who have not experienced loss personally—this reflection has been an empathetic one. Some contributors recount spending their making-time trying "to imagine losing a loved one," or . . . engaging in conversations about the social and political issues underlying the frequency of violence against Aboriginal women. The repetitive motions of making offer time for contemplation and reflection, or for the communal sharing of stories, song, and skill. Through such activities, knowledge, mourning, and healing can be gained through intimate, embodied and experiential modes of transmission. They can facilitate an enhanced sense of connectedness, and thus responsibility and solidarity.[13]

Often, the families and friends of missing and murdered Indigenous women, girls, Two-Spirited people, and residential school children have been denied a chance for public grieving or memorial for their loved one(s); WWOS is an opportunity for the families to come and grieve collectively. This reconnecting in the physical and in the metaphysical is a special part of the WWOS story.

Learning from our Sisters

Storytelling and Restor(y)ing

The histories of our peoples on Turtle Island speak to stories of traversing the landscape, diverse Indigenous nations meeting in sacred places— *pêhonânak*, in the Nêhiyawêwin language—for ceremonies, for activism, for mourning, for diplomacy, for trade, for celebration, and to share stories.[14] Qwul'sih'yah'maht (Robina Thomas) is a Coast Salish woman and associate professor of social work at the University of Victoria. She describes storytelling as both a historic and contemporary pedagogy (teaching method) for resisting colonialism—a pedagogy in which the student must learn to listen, not simply hear. Qwul'sih'yah'maht explains that Indigenous storytelling practices share crucial teachings and produce counter-stories that provide ways of resisting the often negative, officially documented story of our peoples told from the perspective of the Canadian state.[15] Tracy Bear, a Cree scholar and WWOS national collective member, explains how the ceremonial elements of WWOS—"founded in elements of accountability, memorialization, protocol, stories, relationships, kinship circles, reciprocity, and responsibility"—can be seen as a type of transformative theory.[16] Cora Voyageur, a Dene woman and sociologist, co-edited the book *Restorying Indigenous Leadership* with Laura Brearley and Brian Calliou. Restorying is described as a dynamic type of storytelling that uses the past, present, and future to revisit our power and beauty as held within stories in order to educate and heal.[17]

Beading circles emerged in a number of locations in response to the call for vamps. Here, a beading circle held at the University of Alberta (2013).
IMAGE FROM WWW.WALKINGWITHOURSISTERS.CA

Each pair of vamps is a story—or perhaps a collection of stories—intended to honour and remember loved ones. For example, as reported in the Whitehorse *Hub*, Kim Beaulieu made a special pair of moccasin uppers to honour her niece-by-marriage, Leah MacDonald, and Leah's mother. Leah MacDonald shared how her mother's story came full circle by being included in this commemoration.

"She died when MacDonald was 10, in Edmonton where she worked as a nurse. While her death was ruled a suicide at the time, MacDonald knew then, and remains convinced, her mother was murdered . . . 'This is probably the most touching thing ever,' MacDonald said of the treatment of her mother's story. 'The exhibit is starting out in Edmonton, and as that's where my mother was murdered, it's really empowering.'"[18]

Through the process of making and displaying the vamps, as well as through the news article, Leah's mother's passing was restor(y)ed, countering the explanation of suicide and Leah's description of the original police report on her mother's death as "really dismissive and condescending."[19] Kim Beaulieu's counter-story reflects the family's understanding of the events as a murder and also shifts the focus through a visual narrative, representing Leah through the outstretched hand and Leah's late mother as the dove, which speaks of considerable love and kindness.

Walking With Our Sisters takes another step

Online charity auction raises awareness for missing and murdered aboriginal women

SARAH LADIK
reporter@hayriverhub.com

When Kim Beaulieu first heard of the Walking With Our Sisters project – in which women sew uppers to contribute to what will become a travelling exhibit in honour of missing and murdered aboriginal women and girls across Canada – she thought it was a nice idea, but that she didn't really have the time to participate.

These uppers Kim Beaulieu made were a last-minute addition to the Walking With Our Sisters collection. The dove represents her niece Leah MacDonald's mother and the outstretched hand Leah herself.

"I didn't want to submit uppers just because," she said. "But the idea slowly grew on me. Then I thought of my nephew's wife, whose mother was murdered, but it was ruled a suicide, and I just knew."

Beaulieu made the decision to make a special pair of uppers to tell the story of her niece-by-marriage, Leah MacDonald, at the beginning of July. With some creative postmarking, she got them completed and sent to the project co-ordinators by the July 15 deadline.

Walking With Our Sisters grew fast. The original goal was to garner about 600 pairs of uppers to represent the more than 600 women and girls believed to have been victims of foul play or who simply remain unaccounted for in Canada. Organizers received more than 1,000 pairs.

With costs for the travelling installation increasing as a result, the Auction for Action was created to help crowdsource funding for the exhibit. The online auction – nothing more formal than a Facebook group in which members post photos of items on the block and place bids – grew from zero to 2,600 members in a week and had raised more than $15,000 as of Aug. 11. Along with Walking With Our Sisters, the sales and donations from the 20-day auction will go to Families of Sisters in Spirit and Tears4Justice, sister groups sharing the goal of raising awareness for violence against aboriginal women.

"They wanted uppers, not completed slippers, to represent the lives of those ladies that were also incomplete," Beaulieu said. "And what better way to honour these women's lives?"

Leah MacDonald said she felt her mother's story had come full circle with its inclusion in the project. She died when MacDonald was 10, in Edmonton where she worked as a nurse. While her death was ruled a suicide at the time, MacDonald knew then, and remains convinced, her mother was murdered.

"I got a hold of the police report when I was 31 or 32," said MacDonald, now mother to three children of her own. "It was one page and just felt really dismissive and condescending."

After many years of working with detectives in Edmonton, MacDonald said the situation has undoubtedly improved for aboriginal women in that city and that police officers are far less likely to write off their deaths and disappearances than when she was young.

"This is probably the most touching thing ever," MacDonald said of the treatment of her mother's story. "The exhibit is starting out in Edmonton, as that's where my mother was murdered, it's really empowering. This sort of awareness just snowballs and it's time this issue was brought to light."

MacDonald and Beaulieu plan to travel to Alberta together for the exhibit's opening, but are both still in the process of deciding who else will make the trip.

MacDonald would like to bring her children and have them experience a part of their own history she glossed over for many years, while Beaulieu hopes to bring a few

Leah MacDonald, left, and her aunt-by-marriage Kim Beaulieu agree many people can benefit from the Walking With Our Sisters project and hope to see it tour as widely as possible.

of her new clients.

"I was just starting in this position when the Walking With Our Sisters project started rolling," she said of her new job as co-ordinator of victim services on the Hay River Reserve. "It all just fits together. I think (seeing the exhibit) could really have an impact on some of these women who have been harmed by crime. It could show them they're not alone and maybe give them some insight."

The bundle is restor(y)ing the landscape of Turtle Island, re-engaging our relationships by hosting communities in places to which the lodge is invited and along the highways that connect these gathering places (the collective's members drive the bundle to the location of each lodge). Often the violence enacted against our relations occurred on these highways (such as the Highway of Tears); social movements like WWOS and others are re-taking and restoring these landscapes. Jacqueline Carriere volunteered at the Yellowknife memorial. She explains that "[e]ach set of [moccasin] uppers represents a missing or murdered woman, and the incomplete moccasins represent an incomplete life . . . [A]s I was going through, I was walking with these women . . . I was walking so that they wouldn't be alone, and I thought of how they died alone." She explains how the vamps show ongoing care through the messages of "still looking," "love you," and "miss you."[20] While our relatives endured this violence when they were physically alone,

the bundle is a material demonstration of community—of physical and non-physical beings, being together—travelling the highways of Turtle Island, and in *pêhonânak* (gathering places) where the lodge is held. It is Indigenous peoples together, speaking and enacting solidarity, survivance, and resurgence.

Similar to the dynamic nature of storytelling, there is a multitude of ways in which the stories are shared, and a multitude of senses engaged through the memorial. There are stories shared through words attached to the backs of the vamps, stories shared orally, stories shared through songs, stories of medicines that fill the air with their healing aromas, stories shared through the ceremony, and stories shared through the visual commemoration. Anishinaabe/Ashkenazi scholar Jill Carter argues: "The first task in this post-TRC period of designing, dramaturging, and erecting our memorials is, I believe, to speak to and for our own through aesthetic principles and narrative structures that resist that oppositional binary of 'victim' versus 'oppressor' around which the mythology of 'Canada' is structured."[21] Carter points to WWOS as an example of how "[o]ur artists are claiming space—physical, virtual, and the spaces of the imaginary—and they are reconfiguring these spaces in most ingenious ways, filling them with life, good wishes, blessing, and expectation."[22] Describing the experience of the ceremony, she observes:

> The magnitude of loss—of lives lost, of women absent—is staggering. Rows and rows of unfinished shoes cover the floor. The sheer numbers overwhelm. While the weight is palpable, however, it does not paralyze. Audiences do not follow a trail of discarded shoes, shoes

that have been wrenched from their wearers. These shoes are new. Awaiting their wearers, they are material evidence—but not of hatred, violation, or violence. Crafted with love, they bespeak the hope that some of these wearers will return to claim their gift: some of these vamps could become moccasins someday to be worn by the woman or girl whose interrupted journey they chronicle here. Like a name, these vamps carry the expectations of their makers, and they carry blessings and best wishes. Their every stitch sings with the hope that "my girl" will encounter and exercise virtue and kindness throughout her journey. Creative energy fills this space—the love and life of a People.[23]

The commemoration is a restor(y)ing, a counter narrative to the one depicted most often in news, police reports, and legal proceedings, and murmured among many seemingly good-hearted Canadians. It is a story we have heard countless times and in countless versions over the 150 years since Canadian Confederation. Anishinaabe scholar Gerald Vizenor explains that when we re-tell our own stories, we can bear witness to generations of "ongoing cultural survivance," in order to "create spaces of synthesis and renewal."[24]

Survivance and Resurgence

We see WWOS as a grassroots collective that provides a practical example of the theoretical work of Indigenous scholars on survivance and resurgence. Regarding survivance, we see the concept by Vizenor as instructive to WWOS. He explains that while survival is simply a reaction or response, we can shift this focus to "writing about the stories of tragic wisdom in survivance . . . the strength and imagination . . . the survival of these communities."[25] Vizenor makes a call to Indigenous readers: "This is survivance; we must reject victimization and victimry, or not be the object of Western interpretations as a victim. That only perpetuates dominance and objectivism."[26] In this vein, we focus on the strength and resilience of Indigenous peoples and collective responses to ongoing acts of colonial violence, such as the example of WWOS. By telling our own stories to bear witness to acts of survivance, Cayuga/Mohawk-Hungarian author Emerance Baker draws on Vizenor to explain how we are moving "in the face of overwhelming cultural genocide to create spaces of synthesis and renewal. The making and telling of our stories teach us to do more than react to and survive in this world; they bring us ways to heal ourselves, our families, and our communities."[27] Survivance involves acts of resisting "marginalizing, colonial narratives and policies so [I]ndigenous knowledge and lifeways may come into the present with new life and commitment to that survival."[28] Although WWOS is a living memorial to those stolen or missing, the framing has shifted—the centre involves honouring our loved ones, not reifying a colonial gaze of victimry that only perpetuates the violence against Indigenous women, girls, Two-Spirited persons, and residential school children.

Survivance, with its roots in survival, may seem an incorrect concept when honouring murdered Indigenous peoples, but it is in this very incongruity that the strength of collective Indigenous responses like WWOS becomes clear. Typically, in mainstream media and settler-societies like Canada, the reporting of a stolen or killed sister elicits a reification of the colonial gaze of victimry, one that only serves to perpetuate violence against Indigenous women, girls, and Two-Spirited persons. As Jill Carter argues, "We cannot control the actions of our neighbors. Nor can we entrust our healing to a foreign government now that so many have laid bare their throats. But we can commit ourselves to and devise the interventions that will carry us from survival to survivance."[29] In the teachings embedded in WWOS, the embodiment of Indigenous peoples standing together in the physical, and through the vamps, the living memorial of those stolen or missing is a gaze that moves away from Western understandings of Indigenous victimhood toward, instead, centring on love and strength. This shift enacts Indigenous resurgence.

Collectively, WWOS is creating one unified voice to honour the people we love and miss, to honour their families, to call attention to the issue of missing and murdered Indigenous women, girls, and Two-Spirited people, and to remember the children taken through the residential school system. Cherokee scholar Jeff Corntassel writes that Indigenous people today are "struggling to reclaim and regenerate . . . relational, place-based existence by challenging the ongoing, destructive forces of colonization. Whether through ceremony or through other ways that Indigenous peoples (re)connect to the natural world, processes of resurgence are often contentious and reflect the spiritual, cultural, economic, social and political scope of the struggle."[30] In many Indigenous nations, such as that of the Nêhiyawak, there exist special societies who play integral roles to the wellbeing of the nation. This includes the collective role of Crier.[31] The role of the Crier in society has historical significance and we can see the principles behind this being enacted in the present. The aspects of the philosophy underpinning criers include standing up to injustices and advocating from a place of love, kindness, honesty, and strength.[32] Another role of the collective of the Crier is to communicate to people what is happening and what the needs of the people are—a type of call-and-response.

There are different enactments of Indigenous governance in the various elements of this social movement. There is the national collective. The bundle only goes to where it is invited by a community. Therefore, communities—place-based communities—are the ones who host the bundle. There is also the extension of Indigenous governance in networked spaces, for example the governance of social media and how this is enacted on Facebook and other sites. Among the really interesting phenomena here is the demonstration of true engagement with people through the call-and-response activism offered by tools like Facebook.

Indigenous resurgence literature also discusses the connection between funding dollars and Indigenous movements. Leanne Simpson, a Nishnaabekwe scholar and artist, sees the importance of confronting the funding mentality in Indigenous communities, as she believes that "it is time to admit that colonizing governments and private corporations are not going to fund our decolonization."[33] The original decision by the people involved in WWOS was not to accept government funding and not to accept industry funding, but the question remained of how to enable the construction of a memorial and its movement to each community. Crowd-sourced fundraising has been a really exciting feature of this Indigenous resurgence movement. In a call-and-response fashion, artists, writers, and other community members have voluntarily donated items through a Facebook page, and other community members bid on and pay for these items. This provides the financial resources needed to move the bundle from place to place, and also provides a platform from which to explore innovative Indigenous funding models based on ethical ideals and practices.

Another interesting element of WWOS relates to the rebuilding of relationships. With Indigenous peoples codified, first for First Nations in the *Indian Act* and then for Aboriginal peoples in Section 35, and the continuation of state policies based on Indigenous peoples extinction and elimination, state-funded Indigenous nationhood has often been based on a logic of scarcity that can be enacted as sites of exclusion. Many of our missing and murdered relatives have experienced exclusion: in Canadian society and sometimes in Indigenous societies as well. When not within the nation-state's capitalist logics of scarcity that often binds government funding arrangements, Indigenous grassroots activism such as WWOS is framed by logics of place-based inclusion and relationality. Jeff Corntassel argues

Indigenous peoples need to shift from focusing solely on our rights to focusing on our responsibilities.[34] In the social movement visible through WWOS—which extends across Turtle Island and is always hosted by a place-based community incorporating their local protocols—people are focusing on commemorating by coming together. Collectively we are acknowledging relationships and speaking against violence. Crucially, we are also breaking down those boundaries that are historically based and are fundamental to a long-standing colonial logic of divide and conquer that we, as Indigenous peoples, have sometimes internalized and lived out. Indigenous social movements like WWOS are re-engaging with kinship relationships that are not exclusive and also with place-based relationships that are not based on rejection, and reimagining how we relate on territory together.

Conclusion

In this chapter, we focussed on the strength and resilience of Indigenous peoples and collective responses to ongoing acts of colonial violence as embodied by, for example, the resilience demonstrated by the families and supporters of WWOS. There are many visual representations of violence against women, and Indigenous women specifically, and correspondingly the accumulated impact of these representations on Indigenous women and society. In the spirit of survivance, and through a call-and-response, the collective of contributors in this book are re-framing the nation-state's "celebration" of 150 years of Canadian Confederation. By disrupting this discourse of patriotism founded on dispossession, exploitation, and heteronormative patriarchy, we offer a re-framing centred on Indigenous stories of resurgence. This is also our collective response to disrupt the state's call out to reify a settler-colonial "his-story" of Canadian splendour through their Canada at 150 commemorations. Our restor(y)ing of the Canadian landscape is a way to support each other and those Canadians who may be listening, that our peoples have always had stories of these places—stories to heal, to thrive, and to survive.

WWOS is a commemorative ceremony that honours the lives of the women, girls, Two-Spirited persons, and residential school children who have been taken from us. In each territory, the lodge is created as something unique, although the bundle remains constant. At a material level, through this collective honouring, the unanticipated gifts generated include a visual counter-story that disrupts violent narratives and thus serves as an alternative response to the colonial violence experienced by too many of our loved ones. It includes the creation of an alternative grounded in the collective vision and gifts of over 1,000 creators and continually growing. It is an intellectual, physical, emotional, and spiritual experience that results in a shared space where we can stand against the violence and walk with missing and murdered Indigenous women, girls, Two-Spirited people, and residential school children.

WWOS embodies an alternative way of connecting to human relations, passed-on relations, and with non-human beings. It is restoring and restorying. These honourings are all grounded in place, while re-engaging in inter-nation relationships across territories. Turtle Island is the home of Indigenous women, girls, Two-Spirited persons, residential school children, and Indigenous nations:

we remember, we honour, we love.

1. Native Youth Sexual Health Network: www.nativeyouthsexualhealth.com/environmentalviolenceandreproductivejustice.html
2. For example, see Anderson, Stephanie G. (2016), "Stitching through Silence: Walking With Our Sisters, Honoring the Missing and Murdered Aboriginal Women in Canada," *TEXTILE* 14(1), pp. 84-97, doi:10.1080/14759756.2016.1142765; Bear, Tracy (2014), "Commentary: Walking With Our Sisters: An Art Installation Centered in Ceremony," *aboriginal policy studies* 3(1-2), pp. 223-30, doi: http://dx.doi.org/10.5663/aps.v2i1-2.21708; Recollet, Karyn (2015), "Glyphing Decolonial Love through Urban Flash Mobbing and *Walking with our Sisters*," *Curriculum Inquiry* 45(1), pp. 129-45, doi: 10.1080/03636784.2014.995060; and http://walkingwithoursisters.ca/news/print-coverage/ for links to numerous articles on WWOS.
3. Walking With Our Sisters: www.walkingwithoursisters.ca
4. Ibid.: www.walkingwithoursisters.ca/about/the-project/
5. Ibid.
6. Anderson, 2016, p. 88.
7. Ibid.
8. Ibid.
9. TallBear, Kim (forthcoming), "Beyond the Life/Not-Life Binary: A Feminist-Indigenous Reading of Cryopreservation, Interspecies Thinking, and the New Materialisms," Cambridge: MIT Press, pp. 179-202, at 185.
10. Tallbear, Kim (2016), "Making Love and Relations Beyond Settler Sexuality," the 2016 Annual Valentine's Day with Feminism Lecture, Department of Women's and Gender Studies, Faculty of Arts, University of Alberta, Edmonton.
11. Anderson, 2016, p. 89.
12. At the time of writing this article, the (remarkably active) Facebook page has 21,084 members and rising, constituting an active, supportive community of followers who share stories, opinions and experiences (Walking with Our Sisters): www.facebook.com/groups/walkingwithoursisters/photos/). Anderson, 2016, p. 90.
13. Anderson, 2016, p. 91.
14. Jobin, Shalene (2013), "Cree Peoplehood, International Trade, and Diplomacy," *Revue Générale de Droit* 43(2), pp. 599-636.

15. Thomas, Robina Anne (2005), "Honouring the Oral Traditions of My Ancestors Through Storytelling," eds. Leslie Brown and Susan Strega, *Research as Resistance: Critical, Indigenous, and Anti-oppressive Approaches*, Toronto: Canadian Scholars' Press, pp. 237-254.
16. Bear, 223.
17. Voyageur, Cora, Laura Brearly, and Brian Calliou (2015), *Restorying Indigenous Leadership: Wise Practices in Community Development*, second edition, Banff, Alberta: Banff Centre Press (page numbers?).
18. Ladik, S., "Walking With Our Sisters Takes Another Step," *Hub* (Hay River, NT), August 14, 2013, p. 6.
19. Ibid.
20. Ladik, S., "Walking With Our Sisters Draws Emotional Responses," *Hub* (Hay River, NT), January 25, 2015, p. 1.
21. Carter, Jill (2015), "Discarding Sympathy, Disrupting Catharsis: The Mortification of Indigenous Flesh as Survivance-Intervention," *Theatre Journal* 67(3), pp. 413-432, at 421.
22. Ibid.
23. Ibid., p. 422.
24. Gerald, Vizenor (1994), 53, cited in Baker, E. (2005), "Loving Indianess: Native Women's Storytelling as Survivance," *Atlantis: Critical Studies in Gender, Culture & Social Justice*, Halifax: Mount Saint Vincent University, 29(2), pp. 111-121, at 111.
25. Isernhagen, H. (1999), *Momaday, Vizenor, Armstrong: Conversations on American Indian Writing*, Norman: University of Oklahoma Press, p. 129.
26. Ibid.
27. Baker, 2005, p. 111.
28. King, L., R. Gubele, and J. Rain Anderson (2014), *Survivance, Sovereignty, and Story: Teaching American Indian Rhetorics*, Logan: Utah State University Press, p. 7.
29. Carter, 2015, p. 429.
30. Corntassel, Jeff (2012), "Re-envisioning Resurgence: Indigenous Pathways to Decolonization and Sustainable Self-Determination," *Decolonization: Indigeneity, Education & Society*, Toronto: University of Toronto (OISE), 1(1), pp. 86-101, at 88.
31. Makokis, Leona (2009), *Leadership Teachings from Cree Elders: A Grounded Theory Study*, Köln: Lambert Academic Publishing, p. 74.
32. Jobin, Shalene (2005), "Guiding Philosophy and Governance Model of Bent Arrow Traditional Healing Society," A Community Governance Project Report submitted in partial fulfillment of the requirements for the degree of Master of Arts in Indigenous Governance, Victoria: University of Victoria, pp. 48-9.
33. Simpson, Leanne (2008), "Our Elder Brothers: The Lifeblood of Resurgence," ed. L. Simpson, *Lighting the with Fire*, Winnipeg: Arbeiter Ring Publishing, pp. 73-88, cited in Corntassel, (2012), p. 97.
34. Specifically he writes: "[t]his shift means rejecting the performativity of a rights discourse geared toward state affirmation and recognition, and embracing a daily existence conditioned by place-based cultural practices. How one engages in daily processes of truth-telling and resistance to colonial encroachments is just as important as the overall outcome of these struggles to reclaim, restore, and regenerate homeland relationships" Ibid, p. 89.

Lament for Confederation

Dan George

How long have I known you, Oh Canada? A hundred years? Yes, a hundred years. And many, many seelanum more. And today, when you celebrate your hundred years, Oh Canada, I am sad for all the Indian people throughout the land.

For I have known you when your forests were mine; when they gave me my meat and my clothing. I have known you in your streams and rivers where your fish flashed and danced in the sun, where the waters said "come, come and eat of my abundance." I have known you in the freedom of the winds. And my spirit, like the winds, once roamed your good lands.

But in the long hundred years since the white man came, I have seen my freedom disappear like the salmon going mysteriously out to sea. The white man's strange customs, which I could not understand, pressed down upon me until I could no longer breathe.

When I fought to protect my land and my home, I was called a savage. When I neither understood nor welcomed his way of life, I was called lazy. When I tried to rule my people, I was stripped of my authority.

My nation was ignored in your history textbooks—they were little more important in the history of Canada than the buffalo that ranged the plains. I was ridiculed in your plays and motion pictures, and when I drank your fire-water, I got drunk—very, very drunk. And I forgot.

Oh Canada, how can I celebrate with you this Centenary, this hundred years? Shall I thank you for the reserves that are left to me of my beautiful forests? For the canned fish of my rivers? For the loss of my pride and authority, even among my own people? For the lack of my will to fight back? No! I must forget what's past and gone.

Oh God in heaven! Give me back the courage of the olden chiefs. Let me wrestle with my surroundings. Let me again, as in the days of old, dominate my environment. Let me humbly accept this new culture and through it rise up and go on.

Oh God! Like the thunderbird of old I shall rise again out of the sea; I shall grab the instruments of the white man's success—his education, his skills—and with these new tools I shall build my race into the proudest segment of your society.

Before I follow the great chiefs who have gone before us, Oh Canada, I shall see these things come to pass. I shall see our young braves and our chiefs sitting in the houses of law and government, ruling and being ruled by the knowledge and freedoms of our great land.

So shall we shatter the barriers of our isolation. So shall the next hundred years be the greatest in the proud history of our tribes and nations.

—See more at: http://www.ammsa.com/content/chief-dan-george-footprints #sthash.RFR74IEz.dpuf

Language Rights as Aboriginal Rights
From Words to Action[1]

Karen Drake

Canada's 150th anniversary, coming as it does on the heels of the Truth and Reconciliation Commission of Canada's *Final Report*, offers an opportunity to advance reconciliation between Indigenous and non-Indigenous peoples. The revitalization of Indigenous languages must be a component of the reconciliation project. The Truth and Reconciliation Commission documents the ongoing decline of Indigenous languages in Canada and concludes that, "all Aboriginal languages spoken in Canada are considered vulnerable to extinction."[2] The fundamental purpose of Section 35(1) of the *Constitution Act, 1982*—which provides constitutional protection to Aboriginal and treaty rights—is reconciliation. This chapter argues that Section 35(1), when understood in the light of the Truth and Reconciliation Commission's findings, protects a right to publicly funded immersion education in Indigenous languages.

Section 35(1) of the *Constitution Act, 1982*, states: "The existing aboriginal and treaty rights of the aboriginal peoples of Canada are hereby recognized and affirmed." In other words, Section 35(1) establishes that Aboriginal rights and treaty rights have constitutional protection; both legislation and judge-made law that are inconsistent with Aboriginal rights or treaty rights are of no force or effect to the extent of the inconsistency,[3] unless the government can demonstrate that its infringement of Aboriginal or treaty rights satisfies certain requirements established by the courts.[4]

Are Aboriginal language rights protected by Section 35(1)? Although Canadian courts have not explicitly addressed this question, some lawyers and scholars argue that the answer is: yes. For example, David Leitch and Lorena Fontaine have been working toward launching a constitutional challenge, arguing that under Section 35(1) the Federal Government has not only a negative obligation not to stifle Aboriginal languages, but also a positive obligation to provide the resources needed to revitalize those languages.[5]

The latter claim is the most challenging, while the former is more straightforward. The analysis of both types of claims begins by applying the requirements, or test, for establishing a Section 35(1) Aboriginal right. Although this test has ballooned into a labyrinth of steps, sub-steps, and sub-sub-steps,[6] the core of the test has remained relatively constant since the Supreme Court of Canada's decision in *R v. Van der Peet*: "in order to be an aboriginal right an activity must be an element of a practice, custom or tradition integral to the distinctive culture of the aboriginal group claiming the right."[7] Many argue that Indigenous languages easily meet this test. As Leitch puts it, "there is no more distinguishing feature of most cultures than their languages."[8] The reason is the inherent connection between language and culture.[9] As Marie Battiste and James Sákéj Youngblood Henderson recognize, language is not merely a tool for communication.[10] A language structures and embodies a culture's worldview, including its particular ontology, epistemology, logic, and values.[11] Battiste and Henderson explain that this "is the power of 'newspeak' of George Orwell's *Nineteen Eighty-Four*, the idea that if people have only one language available to them, then their range of thought will be accordingly contained."[12] Indigenous languages are no different in this regard; Indigenous languages structure Indigenous philosophies,[13] which include Indigenous ontologies, epistemologies, logics, and values. For this reason, Battiste and Henderson critique the "illusion of benign translatability."[14] Translating Indigenous concepts into western languages, which embed western worldviews, often corrupts the meaning of the Indigenous term at issue.[15] Accordingly, Indigenous languages are integral to Indigenous cultures and thus arguably satisfy the *R v. Van der Peet* Aboriginal rights test.

An additional nuance can be added to this argument. When interpreting and applying the *R v. Van der Peet* Aboriginal rights test, courts have concluded that the practices, customs, and traditions protected by Section 35(1) include Indigenous laws, understood as Indigenous peoples own laws as opposed to Canadian or international law as they affect Indigenous peoples.[16] As Aaron Mills explains, an Indigenous language such as Anishinaabemowin discloses an Anishinaabe worldview—or as he puts it, lifeworld—which in turn underlies Anishinaabeg laws.[17] To even begin to comprehend Indigenous laws, one must first comprehend the lifeworld of the Indigenous nation in question.[18] Thus insofar as Indigenous languages structure Indigenous worldviews, they also structure Indigenous laws, including laws pertaining to the natural world, such as our responsibilities in our relationships with land.[19] As Leanne Simpson explains with respect to Nishnaabeg laws: "There are many good ways to be Nishnaabe, but those ways are constructed and exist within our knowledge and our language."[20] Basil Johnston illustrates this point when he explains that within Anishinaabemowin, the wolf, the bear, and the caribou are our elder brothers, not beasts, objects, or resources.[21] In other words, within an Anishinaabe ontology, animals are not categorized as property as they are within a western ontology and western law. Instead, animals are our relations. This different ontology gives rise to different laws. Because animals are our relations, we have certain responsibilities to them that we must fulfill, and we are not entitled to treat them as property. Thus, at least some Indigenous languages meet the *R v. Van der Peet* test by being integral to their respective cultures not merely insofar as they reflect the fundamental worldviews of those cultures, but also insofar as they reflect the Indigenous laws that are included within the practices, customs, and traditions protected by Section 35(1).

The analysis thus far may support a negative right to be free from government laws prohibiting Aboriginal peoples from speaking Aboriginal languages.[22] But the real issue is the revitalization of Indigenous languages. As Leitch asks: Do Indigenous peoples "have the right to educate their children in their own languages at public expense"?[23] In other words, do governments have a positive obligation to provide Indigenous peoples with immersion education in Indigenous languages?[24] Commentators have answered this question in the affirmative by appealing to the Supreme Court's jurisprudence on Canada's official languages.[25] According to the majority in R v. Beaulac, "[l]anguage rights are not negative rights, or passive rights; they can only be enjoyed if the means are provided."[26]

An additional argument in support of a positive language right can be deduced from the Section 35(1) jurisprudence. The Supreme Court has emphasized that the purpose of Section 35(1) is to promote reconciliation between Aboriginal peoples and non-Aboriginal people in Canada.[27] Section 35(1) should be applied and interpreted in the light of this purpose.[28] After spending six years gathering over 6,750 statements from residential school survivors and others,[29] the Truth and Reconciliation Commission of Canada concluded that reconciliation requires the preservation and revitalization of Aboriginal languages,[30] and issued numerous Calls to Action on the topic, one of which states: "The federal government has a responsibility to provide sufficient funds for Aboriginal-language revitalization and preservation."[31] Language figures prominently in the Commission's analysis because the very purpose of the residential school system was the destruction of Indigenous cultures and languages for the sake of assimilating Indigenous peoples into non-Indigenous culture.[32] Children were prohibited from speaking Indigenous languages both inside and outside the classroom.[33] As Leitch notes, no "other cultural group in Canada has been subject to a state-sponsored attempt to eradicate its language."[34] Thus, the case for a positive obligation on governments in this context is compelling. The Federal Government took active steps to destroy Indigenous languages, and so reconciliation requires that it take active steps to revitalize those languages.[35]

Hopefully Leitch and Fontaine will not need to pursue court action,[36] as the Liberal Party of Canada promised to implement all 94 of the Commission's Calls to Action,[37] and despite some apparent waffling,[38] the Federal Government claims to support all articles of the United Nations Declaration on the Rights of Indigenous Peoples (UNDRIP) "without reservation."[39] Article 13 of UNDRIP states that "Indigenous peoples have the right to revitalize ... and transmit to future generations their ... languages" and that "[s]tates shall take effective measures to ensure that this right is protected." In June 2016, Prime Minister Justin Trudeau said he looks forward to discussing the idea of recognizing Indigenous languages as Canada's official languages, alongside French and English.[40] More recently, the Prime Minister announced that "the federal government would be proposing a Canadian Indigenous Languages Act," but did not provide details about the proposed legislation.[41] Whether such an Act will contribute to reconciliation depends precisely on these details. Merely granting official status to Indigenous languages is not sufficient. As Betty Harnum argues, the *Official Languages Act* of the Northwest Territories grants official status to nine Indigenous languages in addition to English and French.[42] And yet, Indigenous languages in the Northwest Territories are still "declining at an alarming rate."[43] Although the *Official Languages Act* grants the right to use those languages designated as official within certain government institutions, it does not obligate governments to fund immersion education in the nine designated Indigenous languages.

Publicly funded immersion education is necessary in order to truly revitalize Indigenous languages, as called for by the Truth and Reconciliation Commission. The many shortcomings of Canada's current ad hoc approach to Indigenous language education have been comprehensively documented.[44] As Christi Belcourt concludes, based on her experience as a founder of the Onaman Collective, which organizes Anishnaabemowin immersion weekends, "A couple of hours a week is not enough to produce language speakers ... We need full-immersion programs."[45]

An *Indigenous Languages Act* sounds promising, but it is time to move from words to action.

1. An earlier version of this chapter was posted on the website of the National Observatory on Language Rights on July 25, 2016: www.odl.openum.ca/en/language-rights-as-aboriginal-rights-from-words-to-action/
2. The Truth and Reconciliation Commission of Canada (2015), "Canada's Residential Schools: The Legacy," *The Final Report of the Truth and Reconciliation Commission of Canada*, Vol. 5 Montréal and Kingston: McGill-Queen's University Press, p. 112.
3. *Constitution Act, 1982*, being Schedule B to the *Canada Act 1982* (UK), 1982, c 11, s 52(1).
4. R v. Sparrow , 1 S.C.R. 1075 (1990).
5. Luksic, Nicola and Tom Howell, "Constitutional challenge looks to revive aboriginal languages", *CBC News: Aboriginal*, April 10, 2016: www.cbc.ca/news/aboriginal/aboriginal-language-constitution-1.3525982; "Do First Nations have a right to Indigenous Language Schools," *CBC Radio*, www.majorlaw.app.box.com/s/j5njlltrw9b3pucucec32ndsnj4j8qt5.
6. For the most recent articulation of the "integral to a distinctive culture test," see Lax Kw'alaams Indian Band v. Canada (Attorney General), 3 S.C.R. 353 (2011).
7. R v. Van der Peet, 2 S.C.R. 507, para. 46 (1996).
8. Leitch, David (2006), "Canada's Native Languages: The Right of First Nations to Educate Their Children in Their Own Languages." *Constitutional Forum constitutionnel* Vol. 15, No. 3: 107. Similarly, the *Huffington Post Canada* reports that Prime Minister Justin Trudeau recently acknowledged that Indigenous languages "are at the core of indigenous culture and identity": Puxley, Chinta, "Trudeau: Restoring Indigenous Languages 'Essential' To Preventing Suicides," *HuffPost Politics: Canada*, June 3, 2016: www.huffingtonpost.ca/2016/06/03/restoring-indigenous-languages-key-to-preventing-suicides-prime-minister_n_10283048.html
9. The Truth and Reconciliation Commission of Canada, Vol. 5., p. 113; Poliquin, Gabriel (2012), "Protection d'une Vitalité Fragile: Les Droits Linguistiques Autochtones en Vertu de l'Article 35," *McGill Law Journal* Vol. 58, pp. 579-580.
10. Battiste, Marie and James (Sa'ke'j) Youngblood Henderson (2000), *Protecting Indigenous Knowledge and Heritage: A Global Challenge*, Saskatoon: Purich Publishing Ltd., p. 84.
11. Ibid., p. 73.
12. Ibid., p. 81.
13. Battiste, Marie (2013), *Decolonizing Education: Nourishing the Learning Spirit*, Saskatoon: Purich Publishing Ltd., p.146; Simpson, Leanne (2011), *Dancing on Our Turtle's Back: Stories of Nishnaabeg Re-Creation, Resurgence and a New Emergence*, Winnipeg: Arbeiter Ring Publishing, pp. 49, 53.
14. Battiste and Henderson, 2000, p. 80.
15. Henderson, James (Sa'ke'j) Youngblood (2006), *First Nations Jurisprudence and Aboriginal Rights: Defining the Just Society*, Saskatoon: Native Law Centre, p. 120.
16. *Sparrow*, para. 1112; *Van der Peet*, para. 40; Delgamuukw v. British Columbia, 3 S.C.R. 1010, para. 147-148 (1997); Tsilhqot'in Nation v. British Columbia, 2 S.C.R. 257, para. 34-35, 41 (2014); Borrows, John (2010), *Canada's Indigenous Constitution*, Toronto: University of Toronto Press, p. 11.
17. Mills, Aaron (2016), "The Lifeworlds of Law: On Revitalizing Indigenous Legal Orders Today," *McGill Law Journal* Vol. 61, No. 4, p. 852.
18. Ibid., p. 872.
19. Henderson, James (Sa'ke'j) Youngblood, Marjorie L. Benson, and Isobel M. Findlay (2000), *Aboriginal Tenure in the Constitution of Canada*, Scarborough: Carswell Thomson Professional Publishing, p. 405.

20. Simpson, 2011, p. 53.
21. Johnston, Basil (1990), "One Generation from Extinction," *Native Writers and Canadian Writing*, ed. W.H. New, Vancouver: UBC Press, p. 10.
22. Poliquin, 2012, p. 583, 592; Leitch, 2006, p. 116.
23. Leitch, 2006, p. 107-108.
24. "Right to Indigenous Language Schools," *CBC Radio*.
25. Leitch, 2006, p. 116; Poliquin, 2012, p. 589.
26. R v. Beaulac, 1 S.C.R. 768, para. 20 (1999).
27. *Van der Peet*, para. 31; *Delgamuukw*, para. 186; Haida Nation v. British Columbia (Minister of Forests), 3 S.C.R. 511, para. 20 (2004); Mikisew Cree First Nation v. Canada (Minister of Canadian Heritage), 3 S.C.R. 388, para. 1 (2005); *Tsilhqot'in Nation*, 2 S.C.R. 257, para. 17.
28. *Van der Peet*, para 21. See also Poliquin, p. 589, arguing that Section 35(1) has a remedial purpose that supports an argument in favour of a positive right to language under Section 35(1).
29. Truth and Reconciliation Commission of Canada, (2015), *Honouring the Truth, Reconciling for the Future: Summary of the Final Report of the Truth and Reconciliation Commission of Canada*, Montréal and Kingston: McGill-Queen's University Press, p. 25: www.trc.ca/websites/trcinstitution/File/2015/Findings/Exec_Summary_2015_05_31_web_0.pdf
30. The Truth and Reconciliation Commission of Canada, Vol. 5, p. 105.
31. The Truth and Reconciliation Commission of Canada, (2015), *Calls to Action*, #14: www.trc.ca/websites/trcinstitution/File/2015/Findings/Calls_to_Action_English2.pdf. See also Calls to Action #10 and #13.
32. The Truth and Reconciliation Commission of Canada, Vol. 5, p. 103.
33. Ibid.
34. Leitch, 2006, p. 5.
35. The Truth and Reconciliation Commission of Canada, Vol. 5, p. 121.
36. Luksic and Howell, 2016, "Constitutional challenge."
37. Liberal Party of Canada, "Truth and Reconciliation," last modified December 2015: www.liberal.ca/realchange/truth-and-reconciliation-2/
38. Kirkup, Kristy, "Government supports Indigenous declaration without reservation: Wilson-Raybould", *CBC News: Aboriginal*, July 20, 2016: www.cbc.ca/news/aboriginal/government-supports-undrip-without-reservation-1.3687315, reporting that federal Justice Minister Jody Wilson-Raybould stated at the 2016 annual meeting of the Assembly of First Nations that "'simplistic approaches' like adopting the *United Nations Declaration on the Rights of Indigenous Peoples* into Canadian law are 'unworkable.'"
39. Ibid.
40. Puxley, 2016, "Trudeau: Restoring Indigenous Languages."
41. Harnum, Betty, "Justin Trudeau's proposed Indigenous languages act will need teeth to succeed," *CBC News: North*, December 16, 2016: www.cbc.ca/news/canada/north/betty-harnum-indigenous-languages-act-1.3897121.
42. Ibid.
43. Ibid.
44. Everett-Green, Robert, "Trudeau promises aboriginal language bill, but activists say whole system needs overhaul," *Globe and Mail*, December 29, 2016; www.theglobeandmail.com/news/national/trudeau-promises-aboriginal-language-bill-but-the-whole-system-needs-an-overhaul/article33444970/.
45. Ibid.

Canada's History Goes Beyond 150 Years

Doug Cuthand[1]

It's 2017 and Canada is turning 150 years old. In the last several years I have been to Rome, India, and Central America. In each place, 150 years is like last week. Anyway, here we are, the new kid on the block, still in short pants comparatively speaking.

But Canada is a lot older than we might think. The Canadian Shield, which makes up half of the country, is the oldest rock in North America and much of the world. Deep Bay, on the southern end of Reindeer Lake, was formed by a meteor impact 100 million years ago—40 million years before the death of the dinosaurs.

More recently, the glaciers melted about 10,000 years ago, and the first humans moved in. Wanuskewin Heritage Park records human habitation going back 6,000 years.

In fact all across Canada, as the glaciers receded, human habitation followed. Indigenous people can rightfully claim to be the first Canadians, since dry land didn't even exist before we moved in.

In 1670, the company of adventurers got a Royal Charter to trade within all the rivers that flowed into the Hudson Bay. They had no idea how much land this was. In any event, it wasn't until the late 1700s that they actually ventured inland. The local Indigenous peoples told them of fierce tribes and said they would be better off if they stayed put. Meanwhile, the Cree were trading with Hudson's Bay Company goods and selling furs to the Bay.

When the fur trade finally got started in earnest, they found a vast infrastructure of canoe routes, portages, and villages located all across the northern part of the country. To call them explorers is a misnomer. They were guided into this land that was new to them.

At this point the First Nations held status as economic partners within the newly developing country of Canada, but this was about to change as the new country grew.

In 1867, Canada became a dominion, or an independent nation within the sphere of the British Commonwealth. The country consisted of Upper and Lower Canada, the Maritime Provinces, and British Columbia. In the middle was a vast territory called the North West Territories. British Columbia signed on with the provision that a railway be built to link it with the eastern provinces.

In order to build the railway, the government had to gain title to the North West Territories. This meant that under the terms of the Royal Proclamation of 1763, they had to make treaty with the Indigenous nations.

The negotiations for the treaties were a land grab in typical British fashion. The terms included many promises, including economic, social, and political rights, none of which they intended to keep. In the 1870s, the British Empire was in full bloom and it was the practice of the British to say one thing and do another. Canada was not really an independent nation; it was still run by British imperialists who thought they had a God-given right to say and do whatever was necessary to get the job done.

They had to hurry because the United States was looking northward, and its vision of America and manifest destiny included gobbling up much of Canada. When the chiefs signed the treaties, they received a British flag and a treaty medal with Queen Victoria's image on one side. The Chiefs were to wear the treaty medal when they were on official business, and the flag was to be flown above the Chief's lodge to indicate his band had made peace with the Crown. In this manner the Americans were informed that the British flag was planted on the Prairies and they could not violate their sovereignty. Dreams of American manifest destiny spreading north of the 49th parallel died with the treaty negotiations. The treaties also cemented the 49th parallel as the legitimate border between the two nations.

This year we celebrate Canada's 150th year, but in reality a lot of history preceded it. So let's not look back at the last 150 years in isolation; instead, it's time that the first founding nation became a full party to this new country.

1. Previously published on January 7, 2017 in the *Saskatoon Star Phoenix*.

Forgetting to Celebrate
Genocide and Social Amnesia as Foundational to the Canadian Settler State[1]

David B MacDonald

> "'And it's as good as if it never happened,'... at a crucial passage in *Faust*, is uttered by the devil in order to reveal his innermost principle, the destruction of memory. The murdered are to be cheated out of a single remaining thing that our powerlessness can offer them: remembrance."
> —THEODORE ADORNO, *The Meaning of Working Through the Past* (1959)

To truly celebrate the 150th anniversary of Confederation, we may ironically have to forget many things about how the country was created. This chapter addresses how both the commission and the forgetting of multiple genocides of the Indigenous peoples of Turtle Island have been foundational to the Canadian settler state. I review here what genocide means in international law, how understandings of genocide might be decolonized (by expanding western conceptions of groups beyond humans and how groups are targeted), and how genocide relates to the Indian Residential Schools. Many settlers display a high level of historical amnesia, especially when it comes to the history and legacies of colonization. Amnesia is at work when settlers lament that they are tired of providing "handouts," and ask why Indigenous peoples cannot simply "move on" with them as a united people in the Canadian settler state. Such simplistic views are dangerous and counterproductive, as well as being disrespectful. Such views promote European-style liberal democracy as the only legitimate form of government, while seeing Indigenous governance and identity as cultural artifacts and non-viable models for exercising self-determination.

Some non-Indigenous people of colour are contributing to this volume and I am one of those few. My mother is Indian, from Trinidad, descended from many generations of indentured labourers who were brought in at the height of the sugar cane industry. But whatever my skin tone, it's clear that settlers like me, to paraphrase this volume's title, are surviving Canada, because Canada has been established for our survival, which is paralleled by the disappearance of Indigenous peoples as political actors. Yes, it's true that people like me were not envisaged in the *British North America Acts*, were purposefully barred from entry into the dominion,[2] and were also denied a legal relationship with Indigenous peoples. As Robinder Sehdev has argued: "people of colour have been written out of, perhaps forgotten in, the treaty relationship between the Crown and Aboriginal nations."[3] At the same time, people of colour have benefited far more from the colonial system than Indigenous peoples, and so we occupy at times a sort of middle ground, understanding both many of the privileges and some of the negative aspects of living in Canada.

What Do We Mean by Genocide?

In my work involving Indian Residential Schools, I have often heard survivors use the term genocide to describe the IRS system. The creator of the term, the Polish Jewish lawyer Raphael Lemkin, defined it in 1944 as "a coordinated plan of different actions aiming at the destruction of the essential foundations of the life of national groups, with the aim of annihilating the groups themselves."[4] Yet, he was clear that genocide was about far more than killing, and could imply other acts also designed to bring about the "disintegration of the political and social institutions, of culture, language, national feelings, religion, and the economic existence of national groups, and the destruction of personal security, liberty, health, dignity . . ."[5] Lemkin's understanding included forms of colonization, the theft of Indigenous land, and attempts to destroy Indigenous peoples, cultures, languages, spiritualities, and relationships.

Through Lemkin's tireless efforts, by 1948 the United Nations, then only a few years old, passed the Genocide Convention, whose second Article defines genocide as follows:

> any of the following acts committed with intent to destroy, in whole or in part, a national, ethnical, racial or religious group, as such:
> (a) Killing members of the group;
> (b) Causing serious bodily or mental harm to members of the group;

(c) Deliberately inflicting on the group conditions of life calculated to bring about its physical destruction in whole or in part;
(d) Imposing measures intended to prevent births within the group;
(e) Forcibly transferring children of the group to another group.[6]

When we think of genocide in Canada, there are numerous historical instances that might come to mind. Early examples of genocide have been exposed by Mi'kmaq historian Daniel Paul, who has focused on genocide in the Atlantic provinces during the eighteenth century related to starvation, the forced spread of disease, and bounties placed by British colonial leaders on Indigenous scalps.[7] James Daschuk's *Clearing the Plains* recently made the case for genocide, arguing that the Federal Government deliberately starved Plains Indigenous peoples during the late nineteenth century. Particularly implicated was Canada's first Prime Minister, John A. Macdonald, whose plan "to starve uncooperative Indians onto reserves and into submission might have been cruel," Daschuk argues, "but it certainly was effective."[8]

Of course, more recent discussions of genocide relate to the network of Indian Residential Schools, established and run by the Federal Government, with the enthusiastic collaboration of the four mainline Christian churches. These operated from the 1880s to 1970s, with the last of the schools closing only in 1996.[9] Such institutions were designed to aggressively assimilate Indigenous children into an emerging settler society, while destroying Indigenous identities and laying the basis for the wholesale theft of land for settler colonization.[10] At least 150,000 children passed through 125 schools. The long-term intergenerational legacies of the system are well known to most Indigenous peoples and to many settlers.

Indigenous cultures were destroyed and personal lives shattered. At the same time, children were given few skills to help them cope in a structurally racist, white settler society. As Jan Hare and Jean Barman put it: "The Department of Indian Affairs was ensuring the inability of Aboriginal Peoples to compete socially or intellectually with their white neighbours, while also attempting to remove any traces of their culture that would ensure their survival within their own communities."[11] The Indian Residential School Survivors Society outlined the scope of the problem some years ago:

> First Nation communities experience higher rates of violence: physical, domestic abuse (3x higher than mainstream society); sexual abuse: rape, incest, etc. (4-6x higher); lack of family and community cohesion;

suicide (6x higher); addictions: drugs, alcohol, food; health problems: diabetes (3x higher), heart disease, obesity; poverty; unemployment; illiteracy; high school dropout (63 percent do not graduate); despair; hopelessness; and more.¹²

In 2007, as a result of widespread litigation on the part of survivors against the Federal Government and the four Christian denominations that ran the schools, the Indian Residential Schools Settlement Agreement (IRSSA) was signed between legal representatives of survivors and government and church plaintiffs. In addition to creating a financial compensation system for survivors, another goal was to create a permanent record of the schools and the stories of survivors through a Truth and Reconciliation Commission (TRC), funded from a portion of the settlements awarded to survivors. Its six-year mandate, from 2009 to the end of 2015, included seven national events and many more regional ones. The TRC completed its mandate in 2015, compiling a final report of over two million words, and notably argued that the IRS system was culturally genocidal in its intentions and practices. Based on a wealth of archival evidence and testimony, the TRC concluded:

> For over a century, the central goals of Canada's Aboriginal policy were to eliminate Aboriginal governments; ignore Aboriginal rights; terminate the Treaties; and, through a process of assimilation, cause Aboriginal peoples to cease to exist as distinct legal, social, cultural, religious, and racial entities in Canada. The establishment and operation of residential schools were a central element of this policy, which can best be described as "cultural genocide."¹³

The term "cultural genocide" was invoked in 2013 by former Prime Minister Paul Martin, and again in mid-2015 by Supreme Court Chief Justice Beverly McLaughlin.¹⁴ The Commission clearly describes a deliberate process on the part of the Federal Government and the four mainline churches to "destroy the political and social institutions of the targeted group," through seizing land, and forcibly transferring and restricting the movement of Indigenous peoples. This process, the TRC concluded, was bolstered by banning Indigenous languages, persecuting spiritual leaders, and forbidding their practices, while confiscating items of spiritual, cultural, and historical significance. The end goal, the TRC argued, was to disrupt families, "to prevent the transmission of cultural values and identity from one generation to the next."¹⁵ The report then laid out a detailed factual and historical study over the course of several thousand pages, beginning with the advent of European colonialism in the Americas, and ending with 94 detailed Calls to Action, and more sub-recommendations for what reconciliation should look like in practice.

Cultural genocide is an academic term, which potentially had some legal teeth in the 1947 draft of the UN Genocide Convention. It was, however, removed during debates and negotiations between UN member states, including Canada. We might define it, following David Nersessian, as actions that extend "beyond attacks upon the physical and/or biological elements of a group and seeks to eliminate its wider institutions."¹⁶

Why only cultural genocide? What about the UN Convention, which has legal ramifications in international law? Since the 1970s, academics and activists have been using the word genocide, and deploying the UN definition to guide them. Roland Chrisjohn and Sheri Young,¹⁷ Dean Neu and Richard Therrien,¹⁸ and Agnes Grant, all used the Convention in their analyses of the IRS system.¹⁹ Yet, the TRC, under its mandate, could not conclude that the state had committed UN-defined genocide. Under the settlement agreement that created the TRC, the commissioners were prohibited from finding the Federal Government or the churches guilty of anything that was actually illegal in domestic law. The TRC was forbidden from holding formal hearings, public inquiries, or conducting formal legal processes; they could not subpoena witnesses, nor compel anyone to attend or participate. They could not name the names of suspected perpetrators, and could not prosecute or provide amnesty to anyone.²⁰ It's not for me to question the agreement or the mandate, and indeed, one could argue that the focus on truth over western forms of criminal justice may have helped make the experience of truth telling less traumatic for survivors.

However, while the TRC was limited by its mandate, genocide scholars like me are less constrained in our ability to explore how the UN Convention might apply, and I have done so in several publications. The founders of the system, I have argued, intended to "destroy, in whole or in part, an identifiable group of persons."²¹ I have tended to focus my research on forcible transfer, namely Article 2(e) of the UN Genocide Convention,²² and have highlighted legislation, for example, such as the 1920 amendment to the *Indian Act*, which made school attendance compulsory for all Indigenous children aged seven to fifteen. This meant in practice that a large proportion of Indigenous children were forced to attend residential schools located at a considerable distance from their homes, as day schools near or on reserves were sparse.²³ In terms of implementation, the *Indian Act* allowed settler officials to kidnap children; Section 119 empowered a truant officer to "take into custody a child whom he believes on reasonable grounds to be absent from school contrary to this Act and may convey the child to school, using as much force as the circumstances require."²⁴ The vulnerable children of colonized peoples were thus confronted with the full power of the settler state and its enforcement mechanisms.

Equally important in understanding forcible transfer, beyond legislation and the physical act of kidnapping children and delivering them to the schools, was the deployment of a very high level of coercion once the children were at these institutions. This was designed to destroy their previous identities through continually abusive and traumatic treatment.²⁵ The TRC has concluded: "Not only was abuse prevalent at schools throughout the country, but, for a large percentage of former students, it was also extremely violent, intrusive, and harmful."²⁶ Children's identities were broken down through replacing personal names with numbers, cutting hair, stealing personal possessions, forcing children to wear uniforms, and suppressing language, spiritual practices, and worldviews. Much of this took place, as we know, in an environment marked by extreme violence, sadistic cruelty, traumatic abuse, rape, and continual humiliation and degradation.²⁷ The system created legacies of intergenerational trauma, as some families experienced five or six generations of their children being forced to attend these schools.²⁸

What if parents sought to resist? The larger political climate was one where traditional governance and spiritual practices were outlawed.²⁹ An illegal, albeit Crown-endorsed pass system, which went contrary to the treaties, prohibited Indigenous peoples from travelling from their reserve without the written consent of the Indian agent or employer.³⁰ In 1927, an amendment to the *Indian Act* made it illegal for Indigenous peoples to hire lawyers in pursuit of land claims or other matters. To this, we can add the Sixties Scoop and the forcible transfer of Indigenous children away from their families, and their adoption by white families in Canada and the United States.³¹ The TRC's final report and the establishment of a National Centre for Truth and Reconciliation are only the beginning steps of a very long journey to uncover the full scope of the genocidal activities of the state. It should be noted here that the TRC had to go to court several times before the Federal Government and some of the churches would release their documents.

As genocide scholars, activists, and many others, we will continue to find more examples of genocide as we go along, and the death toll will expand. Alongside more evidence, we are also pushing beyond the confines of how genocide is defined in western law, to take into account some Indigenous understandings and lived practices of group identity, with other Indigenous nations, with plants, animals, rocks, rivers, and everything around us. The scope for understanding a large range of multiple genocides thus progresses. For example, Tasha Hubbard's work on buffalo genocide pushes beyond the traditional boundaries of "groupness" in western genocide studies, promoting a decolonizing term, which would apply an "Indigenous epistemological framework" to include buffalo as fellow members of the group who were under attack by perpetrators of genocide. Given the close history of Cree Peoples with the buffalo, this accurately reflects how group identity can be defined beyond the human. Hubbard thus speaks to the strong interrelated nature of plains peoples' lives with buffalo, while refuting Eurocentric notions of human dominance and primacy.[32]

Moving beyond a restrictive western understanding of group identity, Matt Wildcat promotes viewing genocide not simply as the targeting of individual groups *per se* but also as a process of destroying the "webs of relationships and kinship" between groups of Indigenous peoples. The destruction of these "inter-Indigenous bonds," he observes, was a strategy of the settler state to weaken Indigenous identities and resistance to colonial expansion, yet it does not form part of the UNGC.[33] Such work by the next generation of Indigenous genocide scholars challenges a European human-centric focus on tightly defined human-only communities, who live and operate largely decontextualized from the world around them, but of which they are an interdependent part.

The Parasitical State

The German biologist Heinz Mehlhorn has observed in his work on the interactions of parasites and hosts: "It is in the interest of parasites to avoid to kill their hosts, since their death would endanger their own individual existence and would block any chance to become transmitted to other hosts."[34] As such, were we to analogize, a successfully functioning parasitical relationship will not seek to entirely eliminate Indigenous peoples, but will seek to destroy their ability to resist the implementation of a permanent exploitative system. Mehlhorn suggests, however, that in the early phase, "initial contacts of parasites with new host introduce much higher adverse effects than long-lasting contacts which lead to a balance of host-parasite relationships."[35] To extend the analogy, violence and death accompany the early stages of colonialism, tapering off as Indigenous peoples and institutions are weakened. This is a balance designed to benefit the parasite at the expense of the host, and the literature presents us with a useful dual definition of host: one who unknowingly or unwillingly supports the survival of a permanent, unwelcome guest, a parasitical guest whose continued presence continually weakens and reduces the life chances and opportunities of the host.

As we confront the 150-year history of the political experiment that is Canada, we might reflect on a growing body of scholarship that questions the nature of the unwritten but assumed social contracts that founded western states—contracts which are at their root parasitical. Carole Pateman's *Sexual Contract* (1988), together with the work of V. Spike Petersen (1999) and Cynthia Enloe (2014), suggests that state and social institutions have been established to benefit men, to the detriment of women.[36] In his exploration of what he called the "racial contract," Charles Mills applied a similar logic to looking at white people and the establishment of a state system that exploited Black, Brown, Indigenous, and other peoples as part of a global project of white domination.[37] Taiaiake Alfred, Glen Coulthard, Audra Simpson, Jeff Corntassel, Vine Deloria, Marie Battiste, and many others have highlighted the ways in which the settler state system has been designed to exploit Indigenous lands and Indigenous peoples.[38]

Such work describes a state system based not only on the marginalization and exploitation of some people, but on a fundamentally parasitical relationship at the heart of the western state: that the state was created expressly for white people to exploit everyone else. Martin Luther King Jr. argued during the civil rights era in the 1960s that there was a fundamental tragedy at work in the foundation of the United States. While the Constitution guaranteed equality for all, African Americans had been systematically excluded from the benefits of US citizenship. While the legitimacy of the American system of government was not in question for King, its inability to distribute justice equally led to the enslavement and disenfranchisement of African Americans. Yet, the inability of the government to deliver equality did not invalidate the basis of the social order, he observed somewhat optimistically.[39] By contrast, Mills and others have asserted that the political system was never designed for equality and indeed could never work that way. The state was always constructed on the basis that some peoples (namely white men), and some groups (namely Indigenous peoples and people of

[Margin note top: State constructed so that some groups would always be in a state of exploitation]

colour, particularly African Americans) would be in a permanent state of exploitation.[40] They would be the hosts on which the parasitical state would feed, and only in this way would the state be successful.

[Margin note: State = parasite; Exploited group = host]

What was true within the domestic confines of the state was also true at the international level. Marilyn Lake and Henry Reynolds have described a global colour line, established by transnational British parasitical actors, expanding a colonial project designed to starve the hosts in order to engorge the parasitical empire. "Whiteness," they argue, should be understood as a "transnational form of racial identification," which created "whitemen's countries and their strategies of exclusion, deportation and segregation." By making Canada a white man's country, the state was created as a vehicle for ensuring white comfort and prosperity, while internally displacing Indigenous peoples and keeping non-white people outside the state's boundaries.[41] Many of these actors saw themselves as imperial subjects, defined by race, class, and gender, with their actual national identity as largely incidental to their being Anglo-Saxon.

Until 1947, lest we forget, there were no Canadians, only British subjects by various degrees, and others. Canada existed in a form from 1867, but there were never any "Canadians." Settlers were not really settlers until 70 years ago; they were technically imperial migrants who followed the same laws, served the same sovereign, and more often than not, spoke the same language and worshipped the same god. As Duncan Bell describes, imperial subjects worked to fashion a transnational system, to "reconfigure the spatial ordering of world politics to secure 'Anglo-Saxon' dominance in perpetuity." As Bell puts it: "All those born in territories ruled over by the monarch were classified as 'British subjects'," although there were clear divisions between "'civilised' and 'uncivilised' populations" based on race.[42]

For Canada's founders like John A. Macdonald, the core of Canadian identity was "British subjecthood," as Belshaw recalls, observing that: "In Macdonald's day and age, being part of the biggest imperial chain on the planet was something to boast about, and he was counting on other Canadians to feel the same way when he uttered this statement."[43] Indeed, in the nineteenth century an imperial identity was attractive in connecting British subjects to a transnational empire that both created and sustained their identity. This leads to many questions as to with whom or what exactly Indigenous peoples were signing treaties. At the time these signatories would have represented a racially white but transnational imperial crown, and were not representative of a stable nation-state in the ways we might understand it today.

[Margin note bottom: → State relies on these groups to survive]

Early Canada qualifies as what some theorists have called a "herrenvolk democracy," a western-based political system that is founded on the principle of establishing some racial groups as dominant over others, and in which the policy features both the "*demos* and the other." *Demos*, in this case, refers to those who are seen to be citizens and who have the right to have their views represented in Parliament. They get to vote in elections, stand for Parliament, and make the laws that everyone must follow. The others, by contrast, have no political power.[44] Canada has also been dubbed an "ethnic democracy," based on the privileging of British people and British norms in English Canada and French in Québec.[45] But it is designed to do more than that; it creates a system of dominance and control, and certain types of group identity, which are then frozen into law.

Forgetting as Celebrating

When we look at Canada's upcoming birthday, what are we celebrating or lamenting exactly? The BNA Act in 1867 created the Dominion of Canada, comprised of the "Provinces of Canada, Nova Scotia, and New Brunswick." The Act specified, "Canada shall be divided into Four Provinces, named Ontario, Québec, Nova Scotia, and New Brunswick." Presaging racial contract theorists and historians of transnational imperialism, the Act was clear that "such a Union would conduce to the Welfare of the Provinces and promote the Interests of the British Empire." And this was essentially the case. Indigenous peoples were not mentioned here; they were largely an irrelevance to this political project.[46] Canada was created as if Indigenous peoples did not matter.

What does genocide look like from the point of view of a state that has perpetrated it? It looks a lot like deliberately forgetting. As Greg Stanton has argued in his ten-part typology of genocide, the final stage of genocide is denial—because if genocide is successful, all that remains is to clean up afterwards and pretend that nothing bad actually happened. As he puts it, perpetrators "deny that they committed any crimes, and often blame what happened on the victims."[47] In 1822, Ernest Renan famously observed: "the essential element of a nation is that all its individuals must have many things in common but it must also have forgotten many things." More recently, Stanley Cohen has noted how societies deliberately forget uncomfortable knowledge, which then becomes a series of "open secrets," known by everyone but not discussed. This becomes "social amnesia."[48] Debra Thompson prefers the term "aphasia," which, unlike amnesia, indicates a deliberate attempt to forget and highlights the purposefulness of the evasion as "a calculated forgetting, an obstruction of discourse, language and speech." At the same time, aphasia can be seen as a constant process that continues into the future, and she notes: "the reality of racial aphasia links our racist pasts to the still racist present, perhaps connected by collective silences as much as by the persistence of oppression, domination and inequality."[49]

What's fascinating about the settler preoccupation with forgetting and celebrating is how, even as evidence was actively being collected about the crimes of colonization—including widespread accusations of genocide—the settler public and the more educated classes appear to have taken little interest. As the TRC went throughout the country listening to Survivors, holding national and regional events, and collecting testimonies of what occurred, the Canadian state and society continued to engage in a project of overt denial that anything really wrong had occurred.

In its analysis of the BNA Act, the Canada History Project called it "A Country by Consent,"[50] suggesting a consensual framework for the creation of the state. Where were Indigenous peoples when the state was formed? Seemingly their consent was not required, because it was not designed to be a state that would represent Indigenous interests. Indeed as they have put it, "natives" (as they choose to describe Indigenous peoples) faced hard times with the advent of European settlement:

> European contact brought a lot of drastic and irreversible changes to the native [sic] world. The Beothuk became completely extinct very early and we know little about them. Others diminished more slowly and their culture and languages have almost been lost. Along with their loss of culture came a loss of pride which combined with some cruel and insensitive treatment by successive white governments to put the remaining native peoples into a state of poverty and despair.[51]

Much of this is delivered in the passive voice, as if there was something natural or historically inevitable about settler state actions against Indigenous peoples and in pursuit of land. Many historians of Indigenous genocide have noted the frequent use by settlers of terms like "vanishing."[52] The romantic ideal of vanishing or "melting away" suggests that the disappearance of Indigenous peoples, while sad, was really no one's fault. One might abstractly blame historical inevitability and a Darwinian belief in evolution and "progress."[53]

More recently, Indigenous peoples have been made to vanish in the ways the history of the nation is told. For example, in Citizenship and Immigration Canada's *Discover Canada* publication, we see a settler state largely devoid of Indigenous presence. This occurs at a number of levels. First, at the level of how the state should be personified, we have the British monarch, who stands in for the country and its people, and so: "Canada is personified by the Sovereign just as the Sovereign is personified by Canada."[54]

Second, the state's history and the history of immigration is the history of Canada: "Canada has welcomed generations of newcomers to our shores to help us build a free, law-abiding and prosperous society. For 400 years, settlers and immigrants have contributed to the diversity and richness of our country, which is built on a proud history and a strong identity."[55] Within this particular historical framework, Indigenous peoples are part of the nation as *first immigrants*, whose ancestors "are believed to have migrated from Asia many thousands of years ago."[56]

However, it's clear that Europeans are central to Canada's identity: "Canadian society today stems largely from the English-speaking and French-speaking Christian civilizations that were brought here from Europe by settlers."[57] In this way, settlement can, overall, be seen as positive. Before colonization: "Warfare was common among Aboriginal groups as they competed for land, resources and prestige." Presumably, colonization put an end to these destructive relationships. Of course, there were some negative aspects to settlement, since "Large numbers of Aboriginals died of European diseases to which they lacked immunity." Fortunately, however, "Aboriginals and Europeans formed strong economic, religious and military bonds in the first 200 years of coexistence which laid the foundations of Canada."[58]

So what symbols and images underwrite the country? In all cases, the nation is defined by European elements. First, we have the British monarch, followed by English law, "an 800-year old tradition of ordered liberty, which dates back to the signing of Magna Carta in 1215 . . ."[59] Followed by this is the "Canadian Crown," then the Canadian flag, with its red and white hailing from the "colours of France and England since the Middle Ages." Not even the maple leaf has Indigenous roots, since it is a symbol chosen by Europeans, having been "adopted as a symbol by French Canadians in the 1700s, hav[ing] appeared on Canadian uniforms and insignia since the 1850s . . ." The Canadian Coat of Arms "contain symbols of England, France, Scotland and Ireland as well as red maple leaves." Finally, the two official languages are "important symbols of identity." The guide concludes:

"English speakers (Anglophones) and French speakers (Francophones) have lived together in partnership and creative tension for more than 300 years."[60]

The guide demonstrates rather well the sort of studied exclusion we as a state promote when welcoming newcomers to Canada; it also epitomizes the larger problems of strategic forgetting that are at the centre of the settler colonial project. There is not, for example, any "partnership" or "creative tension" worth mentioning between settlers and Indigenous peoples. The purpose of this guide was to assist newcomers in their integration into the mainstream of settler life, which often includes ignoring—or if recognizing, then decontextualizing Indigenous civilizations. Everything worth knowing about the country, we are told, comes from Europeans. Esyllt Jones and Adele Perry in their *People's Citizenship Guide* observed some time ago that the citizenship test reflected a "nationalistic, militaristic, and racist view of Canada and its history," equally asserting that "Confederation marked the end of Canada's history as a British colony, but the beginning of its career as a colonizing force."[61]

Another illustration of how Indigenous peoples have been made to vanish is provided by Rudyard Griffith's 2008 book *101 Things Canadians Should Know About Canada*. Sponsored by the Harper government and the Dominion Institute (also known for their glorification of John A. Macdonald), none of the 101 "things" pertain to Indigenous peoples or their contributions. This project was based on an online survey of over 3,000 adult respondents, including "522 educators who deal with subject areas related to social sciences, history, geography, civics, music, art or culture, as well as 274 members of the Order of Canada." The survey identified five categories of what it meant to be Canadian: "People, Places, Events, Accomplishments, and Symbols." The top ten in these five categories featured no Indigenous peoples, events, landmarks, or symbols. When it came to people who defined Canada, the survey revealed, "Canadians say Pierre Elliott Trudeau is the most defining person in Canadian history, followed by Wayne Gretzky and Terry Fox. Celine Dion is fourth, while Sir John A. Macdonald rounds out the top five." The exception was "Louis Riel and the 1885 Rebellion" under the Events category, which placed eighth in Manitoba/Saskatchewan but failed to rank in any other province.[62] Ultimately, this glaring omission of Indigenous peoples was identified, and they were unceremoniously tacked on in 102nd place in a special little section at the end.

These are examples from the Harper era, yet in the era after the release of the TRC Final Report and the media discussion of cultural genocide, the election of the Trudeau government and its promises about UNDRIP, the TRC recommendations, and the promise of a national inquiry for missing and murdered Indigenous women and girls, there remains still a deep ignorance and amnesia amongst settler peoples. In June 2016, the Ottawa-based public policy firm Environics released a survey based on telephone discussions with 2001 non-Indigenous respondents.[63] The survey sought to gauge settler knowledge and impressions of Indigenous peoples and issues, and in particular the Indian Residential Schools and the work and recommendations of the TRC.

The survey revealed widespread ignorance about Indigenous peoples and their experiences in the IRS system. Based on their findings, and through my own analysis and calculations: 72 percent of respondents claimed to know nothing about survivor abuse, and 88 percent knew nothing about language and culture loss.[64] Overall, only 2.6 percent of respondents connected the term cultural genocide with the IRS system, an amazingly low total given the level of media coverage.[65] There were further revelations in store. Respondents failed to see Indigenous peoples as possessing a unique legal and historical status predating Canada. When asked in general terms about what makes Canada unique, 43 percent of respondents proffered "multiculturalism and diversity," with "land and geography" a distant second (17 percent), followed by "freedom and democratic system" at 14 percent, and the "'nice,' 'friendly,' 'humble'" nature of the populace at 11 percent. Indigenous peoples came in at 2 percent.[66] Added to a low level of recognition, respondents also had difficulty seeing any links between settler prosperity and Indigenous marginalization. Only 33 percent agreed with the statement: "Mainstream Canadian society today benefits from ongoing discrimination against Aboriginal peoples," versus 71 percent who disagreed.[67] The larger point is that most of us settlers know little and will probably not be exposed to enough information about the IRS system and the wider colonial context to develop an informed understanding of the parasitical nature of the Canadian political experiment.

Yet, settler amnesia/aphasia about Indigenous genocide in Canada doesn't translate into genocide amnesia in general. There is a politics of deflection involved here by which we willingly recognize genocides when settlers in their former countries were the victims, the perpetrators were foreign governments, and Canada acted as a haven for the survivors. Thus we recognize five genocides: the Armenian genocide, the Ukrainian famine (the Holodomor), the Holocaust, Rwanda, and the Srebrenica massacre, but we have taken no steps to recognise the IRS system as genocide.[68] Michael Rothberg has called this "competitive memory," where some genocides are deliberately commemorated and made to be part of the national narrative, in part to turn the public's attention away from genocides actually perpetrated by the state.[69]

Of course, these genocides are worthy of recognition and commemoration. The Holocaust is often divided into narrow and broad variants, the narrow referring to the six million Jews who were killed as a result of a deliberate Nazi policy of extermination; the broad version encompasses the large number of other German victims including Roma and Sinti, Slavic populations, and many others. The total number of Nazi victims is approximately 50 million in Europe, including the horrific death tolls in the Soviet Union.[70] Commonly accepted ranges for other genocides of the twentieth century are roughly 1.5 million for the Armenian genocide, 3.9 million for the Ukrainian famine genocide, 800,000 to 900,000 for the Rwandan genocide, and between 7,000 and 8,000 Bosnian Moslem men and boys in Srebrenica.[71]

However, we must also be clear that Indigenous peoples died in high numbers with the onset of western colonization due to starvation (a result of the decimation of food like the bison), disease (smallpox, malaria, whooping cough, tuberculosis), and other conditions.[72] Indeed, of the two million Indigenous people estimated to have been living in what is now Canada at the end of the fifteenth century, by the end of the nineteenth century that population had been reduced by 95 percent, leaving about 100,000 to 125,000 Indigenous people remaining.[73] In the IRS system itself, the TRC reports an overall death toll of 3,201 children from 1867 to 2000, although due to financial and time constraints the TRC was not able to complete its investigations, so the actual death toll may be significantly higher.[74]

The lack of recognition has ramifications for how IRS history is being represented. For example, the Canadian Museum for Human Rights features displays on the IRS, but generally avoids the genocide question in Canada. As put by genocide scholar Dirk Moses, "In a Darwinist zero-sum game, the highlighting of the one group's genocide is experienced as obscuring another's."[75]

The politics of deflection are obvious when federal and provincial legislatures recognize other genocides, casting perpetrator regimes as the antithesis of provincial or national societies. Thus, when the Saskatchewan legislature passed an act commemorating the Holodomor genocide of the 1930s, it argued, "the people of Saskatchewan prize democratic freedoms, human rights and the Rule of Law, appreciate the values of compassion and honesty and cherish the multicultural vibrancy of the province."[76] Similarly, when the federal Parliament approved a national Holodomor memorial day, it opined: "Canadians cherish democracy, defend human rights, and value the diversity and multicultural nature of Canadian society."[77] In promoting Armenian Genocide Memorial Day, the Québec legislature averred: "Quebecers have always rejected intolerance and ethnic exclusion."[78] Arguably, recognizing federal complicity in genocide against Indigenous peoples in state-run schools would hardly promote the same sort of positive narratives; indeed it would do the reverse.

In a comparative perspective, when confronted with their history of genocide against Aboriginal and Torres Strait Islander people in Australia, many settlers chose to deny that genocide occurred, or even that the colonization of Australia had a negative impact on Aboriginal peoples. In assessing the violence of colonization and its legacies, Prime Minister John Howard, who navigated the settler state through these discussions in the 1990s, condemned those who highlighted an Australian genocide as promoting a "black armband history," to make the balance sheet of Australian history appear overwhelmingly negative when in fact the reverse was true.[79] Many on the left responded by accusing the Howard government of donning a "white blindfold."[80]

I have always hoped that Canadian settlers would be better than the Australians about this issue—that when the time came to discuss genocide, we would be able to call a spade a spade, and talk frankly and openly about these issues. This has not occurred. Most settlers don't seem to care, and those that do are not interested in believing. Howard always argued that while there were some negative aspects of Australian history, the historical balance sheet was always positive. Therefore, no one could realistically suggest that Australian crimes were so bad that it might have been better if Australia had not existed at all. Sussex-born, Oxford-trained historian Charlotte Gray recently produced a birthday book, *The Promise of Canada*, in which she echoes some aspects of these earlier Australian debates, particularly regarding our historical balance sheet: "I realized that, for all its faults and challenges, this country is an extraordinary success story." Gray, who has been in Canada for four decades, has produced a richly illustrated panegyric, an ideal Christmas present for many settlers curling up by their gas fire while the snow falls; indeed, this may be its intended market. As such, having the balance sheet shift to extraordinary success is to be expected. Most countries relish such works, along the lines of, "well, we have made a few mistakes but overall it's been a rollicking success."

Conclusion

> "I'm feeling that the train is slowly moving. But we still have a ways to go before we can get it up to any kind of speed. And we have a long distance to go once we get to that speed."
>
> —SENATOR MURRAY SINCLAIR in *Maclean's* (2016)[81]

While it's tempting, especially when confronting the power of the state, to see it as homogenous, powerful, and permanent, another way of viewing the state is to understand it as a collection of people and institutions, always moving, always doing things, always engaging in activities that may promote or marginalize Indigenous interests. The political theorist David Campbell has emphasized that:

> [S]tates are never finished as entities; the tension between the demands of identity and the practices that constitute it can never be fully resolved, because the performative nature of identity can never be fully revealed. This paradox inherent to their being renders states in permanent need of reproduction: with no ontological status apart from the many and varied practices that constitute their reality, states are (and have to be) always in a process of becoming.[82]

The argument here (and admittedly some of Campbell's language is opaque) is that societies are evolving and changing all the time, which means there are always windows of opportunity for bringing about change, for refusing to accept the status quo; there are always sites of resistance to make thing better. Those of us who work on genocide can see the merits of challenging the dominant Canadian narrative of a peaceful and apologetic country. By pushing for the state and settlers to recognize that genocide happened here, we may oblige the state to change the way it does business, and the way it presents itself to the world.

In 2016, Maeengan Linklater and Robert Falcon-Ouellette, Liberal MP for Winnipeg Centre, prepared a private member's bill to create an Indian residential school commemoration day for June 2 every year. The bill, however, asks for more than a memorial day; it also seeks official Federal Government recognition that genocide—UN-defined genocide—was perpetrated in the IRS system.[83] At the time of writing, it is difficult to predict whether Falcon-Ouellette's bill will pass, and if it does, what form it will take. He is after all a Liberal MP, a member of the government led by a man who has pledged to create new nation-to-nation relationships with Indigenous peoples. Justin Trudeau's legacy so far seems rather half-hearted, with pipeline approvals and a reluctance to incorporate UNDRIP into domestic law, mixed with positives such as a national inquiry into missing and murdered Indigenous women and girls, and a pledge to renew Indigenous languages.

For me, the genocide recognition bill is a real litmus test of the government's commitment to whatever it sees as reconciliation. That term "reconciliation" is contested, and I agree that we will not see reconciliation in our lifetime. The TRC did its job against extremely difficult odds, by bringing as much truth to light as its mandate, its time, and its funding would allow. Now that we have started on the journey toward collectively engaging with that truth, we need to recognize that genocide was foundational to the creation of Canada. Hopefully, the 150th anniversary can be a time to more openly discuss and commemorate genocide, and to seek a fairer, more balanced approach to engaging with the past. A discussion of IRS genocide may also help create the climate for a broader discussion of the genocidal tendencies of colonialism, in line with the work of recent Indigenous genocide scholars.

1. The research and writing of this chapter is made possible by SSHRCC Insight Grant 430201. My thanks to Brian Budd, Kiera Ladner, Myra Tait, Andrew Woolford, and Paulette Regan.
2. Bhatia, Amar (2013), *We Are All Here to Stay? Indigeneity, Migration, and "Decolonizing" the Treaty Right to Be Here*, Windsor Yearbook of Access to Justice, 13(2), pp. 39-64.
3. Sehdev, Robinder Kaur (2012), *People of Colour in Treaty*, in *Speaking My Truth: Reflections on Reconciliation and Residential School*, eds. Shelagh Rogers, Mike DeGagne, and Jonathan Dewar, Ottawa: Aboriginal Healing Foundation, p. 272.
4. Lemkin, Raphael (1944), *Axis Rule in Occupied Europe: Laws of Occupation—Analysis of Government—Proposals for Redress*, Washington: Carnegie Endowment for International Peace, p. 79.
5. Ibid. pp. 27-28.
6. For a full text of the Convention see OHCHR-UNOG Online: www.unhchr.ch/htm>l>/menu3/b/p_genoci.htm (Accessed 10 October, 2005).
7. Paul, Daniel (2006), *First Nations History: We Were Not the Savages Third Edition*, Winnipeg: Fernwood Publishing.
8. Daschuk, James (2013), *Clearing the Plains: Disease, Politics of Starvation and the Loss of Aboriginal Life*, Regina, SK: Regina University Press, pp. 127-28.
9. Haig-Brown, Celia (1988), *Resistance and Renewal: Surviving the Indian Residential School*, Vancouver: Arsenal Pulp, pp. 31-32.
10. Milloy, John (1999), *A National Crime: The Canadian Government and the Residential School System, 1879 to 1986*, Winnipeg: University of Manitoba Press; Miller, James R. (2004), *Reflections on Native-Newcomer Relations*, Toronto: University of Toronto Press, p. 84.
11. Barman, Jean and Jan Hare (2000), *Aboriginal Education: Is There a Way Ahead?*, in *Visions of the Heart: Canadian Aboriginal Issues*, ed. David Long and Olive Dickason, Toronto: Harcourt Brace Canada, pp. 336-37.

12. Indian Residential Schools Settlement Agreement (2006) as discussed in MacDonald, David (2007), *First Nations, Residential Schools, and the Americanization of the Holocaust: Rewriting Indigenous History in the United States and Canada*, Canadian Journal of Political Science, 40(04), p. 1002.
13. Truth and Reconciliation Commission of Canada (2015), *Canada's Residential Schools: The History, Part 1 Origins to 1939*, Montréal/Kingston: McGill-Queen's University Press, pp. 3-4.
14. Paul Martin Accuses Residential Schools of "Cultural Genocide," CBC News, April 26, 2013: www.cbc.ca/m/touch/politics/story/1.1335199; Fine, Sean, "Chief Justice says Canada Attempted 'Cultural Genocide' on Aboriginals," *Globe and Mail*, May 28, 2015: www.theglobeandmail.com/news/national/chief-justice-says-canada-attempted-cultural-genocide-on-aboriginals/article24688854/
15. Truth and Reconciliation Commission of Canada, pp. 3-4
16. Nersessian, David (2005), *Rethinking Cultural Genocide Under International Law*, Human Rights Dialogue: "Cultural Rights," 2(12), pp. 7-8.
17. Chrisjohn, Roland D., Sherri L. Young, and Michael Maraun (1997), *The Circle Game: Shadows and Substance in the Indian Residential School Experience in Canada*, New Brunswick: Theytus, p. 17.
18. Neu, Dean E. and Richard Therrien (2003), *Accounting for Genocide: Canada's Bureaucratic Assault on Aboriginal People*, Halifax: Fernwood Publishing, pp. 11-13.
19. Grant, Agnes (1996), *No End of Grief: Indian Residential Schools in Canada*, Winnipeg: Pemmican Publications, p. 24.
20. Truth and Reconciliation Commission of Canada, *Our Mandate: Schedule N of the Indian Residential Schools Settlement Agreement*: www.trc.ca/websites/trcinstitution/index.php?p=7
21. MacDonald, David (2014), "Genocide in the Indian Residential Schools: Canadian History through the Lens of the UN Genocide Convention," in *American Colonial Genocide in Indigenous North*, eds. Andrew Woolford, Jeff Benvenuto, and Alexander Laban Hinton, Durham: Duke University Press, pp. 465-93.
22. Quoted from MacDonald, David and Graham Hudson (2012), *Contextualizing Aboriginal Residential Schools in Canada: How International and Domestic Law Can Help Us Interpret Genocide Claims*, Canadian Journal of Political Science, 45(2), pp. 597-613.
23. Remembering the Children, 2008: www.rememberingthechildren.ca/
24. *Backgrounder—Changes to the Indian Act Affecting Indian Residential Schools*, Aboriginal Affairs and Northern Development Canada, 2010: www.aadnc-aandc.gc.ca/eng/1100100015573
25. Assembly of First Nations (1994), *Breaking the Silence*. Ottawa: Assembly of First Nations, pp. 3-4.
26. Truth and Reconciliation Commission of Canada, pp. 400-05.
27. Milloy, 1999, chapters 5, 6, and 7; Miller, 2004, chapter 11.
28. Charles, Grant and Mike DeGagné (2013), *Student-to-Student Abuse in the Indian Residential Schools in Canada*, Child and Youth Services, 34(4), pp. 343-359.
29. Furniss, Elizabeth (1999), *The Burden of History: Colonialism and the Frontier Myth in a Rural Canadian Community*, Vancouver: UBC Press, p. 24.
30. Carter, Sarah (1999), *Aboriginal People and Colonizers to 1900*, Toronto: University of Toronto Press, pp. 162-163.
31. Carreiro, Donna. *Indigenous children for sale: The Money Behind the Sixties Scoop*, CBC News, September 28, 2016: www.cbc.ca/news/canada/manitoba/sixties-scoop-americans-paid-thousands-indigenous-children-1.3781622
32. Hubbard, Tasha (2014), *Kill, Skin, and Sell: Buffalo Genocide*, in *Colonial Genocide in Indigenous North America*, eds. Andrew Woolford, Jeff Benvenuto, and Alexander Laban Hinton,

Durham: Duke University Press, pp. 294-295. For a discussion in general of Indigenous and animal lives see Nadasdy, Paul (2016), *First Nations, Citizenship, and Animals, or Why Northern Indigenous People Might Not Want To Live In Zoopolis*, Canadian Journal of Political Science, 49(1), pp. 1-20.
33. Wildcat, Matthew (2015), *Fearing Social and Cultural Death: Genocide and Elimination in Settler Colonial Canada—an Indigenous Perspective*, Journal of Genocide Research, 17(4), pp. 391-409.
34. Melhorn, Heinz, ed. (2015), *Manipulations by Parasites and Viruses*, Switzerland: Springer International Publishing, chapters 2 and 4.
35. Ibid.
36. Pateman, Carol (1988), *The Sexual Contract*, Stanford: Stanford University Press; Enloe, Cythia (2014), *Bananas, Beaches and Bases: Making Feminist sense of International Politics, Completely Revised and Updated*, Berkeley: University of California Press; Peterson, V. Spike (1999), *Sexing Political Identities/Nationalism as Heterosexism*, International Feminist Journal of Politics 1(1), pp. 34-65.
37. Mills, Charles (1997), *The Racial Contract*, Cornell: Cornell University Press.
38. Alfred, Taiaiake and Jeff Corntassel (2005), *Being Indigenous: Resurgences against Contemporary Colonialism*, Government and Opposition: An International Journal of Comparative Politics, 40(4), pp. 597-614; Coulthard, Glen (2007), *Subjects of Empire: Indigenous Peoples and the "Politics of Recognition" in Canada*, Contemporary Political Theory, 6, pp. 437-60; Wolfe, Patrick (2006), *Settler Colonialism and the Elimination of the Native*, Journal of Genocide Research, 8(4), pp. 387-409; Simpson, Audra (2014), *Mohawk Interruptus: Political Life Across the Borders of Settler States*, Durham: Duke University Press.
39. King, Martin Luther Jr., *I Have a Dream*, August 28, 1963: www.archives.gov/press/exhibits/dream-speech.pdf (accessed 15 July, 2016).
40. Mills, 1997.
41. Lake, Marilyn and Henry Reynolds (2008), *Drawing the Global Colour Line: White Men's Countries and the International Challenge of Racial Equality*, Cambridge: Cambridge University Press, pp. 3-4.
42. Bell, Duncan (2014), *Beyond the Sovereign State: Isopolitan Citizenship, Race and Anglo-American Union*, Political Studies, 62, pp. 418-34.
43. Belshaw, John Douglas (2014), *Canadian History: Post-Confederation*, Thompson Rivers University, pp. 727-27.
44. Warren, Mark E. (1999), *Democracy and Trust*, Cambridge: Cambridge University Press, pp. 10-11.
45. Smooha, Sammy (2001), *The Model of Ethnic Democracy*, ECMI Working Paper #13, Flensburg, Germany: European Centre for Minority Issues, p. 20.
46. Government of Canada. *British North America Act, 1867—Enactment Number 1*: www.justice.gc.ca/eng/rp-pr/csj-sjc/constitution/lawreg-loireg/p1t11.html.
47. Stanton, Gregory (2016), *The Ten Stages of Genocide*, Genocide Watch: www.genocidewatch.net/genocide-2/8-stages-of-genocide/
48. Buckley-Zistel, Suzanne (2006), *Remembering to Forget: Chosen Amnesia as a Strategy for Local Coexistence in Post-Genocide Rwanda*, Africa, 76(2), pp. 132-34.
49. Thompson, Debra (2013), *Through, Against and Beyond the Racial State: The Transnational Stratum of Race*, Cambridge Review of International Affairs, 26(1), pp. 133-151.
50. *A Country by Consent*, Canadian History Project: www.canadahistoryproject.ca/1867/1867-12-bna-act.html
51. *Native Peoples: Introduction*, Canadian History Project: www.canadahistoryproject.ca/1500/index.html

52. Barkan, Elazar (2003), *Genocides of Indigenous Peoples: Rhetoric of Human Rights* in *The Specter of Genocide: Mass Murder in Historical Perspective*, eds. R. Gallately and B. Kiernan, Cambridge: Cambridge University Press, p. 117.
53. Wilson, James (1998), *The Earth Shall Weep: A History of Native America*, New York: Atlantic Monthly, xxii-xxiii; p. 45; Dippie, Brian (1982), *The Vanishing American: White Attitudes and U.S. Indian Policy*, Middleton: Wesleyan University Press.
54. Citizenship and Immigration Canada (2012), *Discover Canada: The Rights and Responsibilities of Citizenship*: www.cic.gc.ca/english/pdf/pub/discover.pdf
55. Ibid., p. 2.
56. Ibid., p. 10.
57. Ibid., p. 12.
58. Ibid., p. 14.
59. Ibid., p. 8.
60. Ibid., pp. 38-39.
61. Jones, Esyllt and Adele Perry (2011), *People's Citizenship Guide: A Response to Conservative Canada*, Winnipeg: ARP Books, pp. 5, 24.
62. IPSOS Reid (2008), *Canadians Choose the People, Places, Events, Accomplishments and Symbols that Define Canada*, Toronto: The Dominion Institute: www.historicacanada.ca/sites/default/files/PDF/polls/canada101_part1_en.pdf.
63. Environics, *Canadian Public Opinion on Aboriginal Peoples*, p. 2.
64. Ibid., p. 12.
65. Ibid., p. 31.
66. Ibid., p. 9.
67. Ibid., p. 28.
68. Moses, A. Dirk (2012), *The Canadian Museum for Human Rights: The "Uniqueness of the Holocaust" and the Question of Genocide*, Journal of Genocide Research, 14(2), pp. 215-38.
69. Rothberg, Michael (2009), *Multidirectional Memory: Remembering the Holocaust in the Age of Decolonization*, Stanford: Stanford University Press.
70. Young, James E. (2002), *Germany's Holocaust Memorial Problem—And Mine*, The Public Historian, 24(4), p. 80; Moshman, David (2001), *Conceptual Constraints on Thinking About Genocide*, Journal of Genocide Research, 3(3), p. 433.
71. Jones, Adam (2011), *Genocide: A Comprehensive Introduction*, 2nd Edition, London: Routledge, pp. 150, 180, 194, 323, 327.
72. Carter, 1999, pp. 37-39, 100.
73. Saul, John Ralston (2008), *A Fair Country: Telling Truths About Canada*, Toronto: Penguin Canada, pp. 22-23.
74. Truth and Reconciliation Commission of Canada, pp. 95-96.
75. Moses, 2012, p. 22.
76. Government of Saskatchewan (2008), *Ukrainian Famine and Genocide (Holodomor) Memorial Day Act*, The Statutes of Saskatchewan: www.qp.gov.sk.ca/documents/English/Statutes/Statutes/U0-1.pdf
77. Ibid.
78. Government of Québec (2003), *An Act to Proclaim Armenian Genocide Memorial Day*: www2.publicationsduquebec.gouv.qc.ca/dynamicSearch/telecharge.php?type=5&file=2003C10A.PDF
79. MacIntyre, Stuart, Anna Clark, and Sir Anthony Mason (2004), *The History Wars*, Melbourne: Melbourne University Publishing, p. 3.

80. MacIntyre, Clark, and Mason, p. 131; see also Brantlinger, Patrick (2004), *"Black Armband" versus "White Blindfold" History in Australia: A Review Essay*, Victorian Studies, 46(4), pp. 655-74.
81. Macdonald, Nancy, *Sen. Murray Sinclair on Truth and Reconciliation's Progress*, Maclean's, June 1, 2016: www.macleans.ca/news/canada/sen-murray-sinclair-on-the-progress-of-truth-and-reconciliation/
82. Campbell, David (1998), *Writing Security: United States Foreign Policy and the Politics of Identity*, Minneapolis/Manchester: University of Minnesota Press/Manchester University Press.
83. See my discussion in Farber, Bernie, David MacDonald, and Joseph Boyden, "How Canada Can Take Responsibility for its Genocidal Past," *Globe and Mail*, October 31, 2016: www.theglobeandmail.com/opinion/how-canada-can-take-responsibility-for-its-genocidal-past/article32576667/

Kahwá:tsire
Canada 150 Through The Lens of Mohawk Motherhood

Kahente Horn-Miller & Waneek Miller

Wat'kanonwerahton sewakwekon (Greetings to all of you),

This is a conversation between two sisters. Two Mohawk sisters who are also mothers. As mothers, we are the central fire of our families—*kahwá:tsire*. This dialogue came about as we stood in a kitchen one morning passing a baby between us and drinking coffee. Waneek had just had her youngest daughter and we were thinking and talking about what it meant to be Mohawk. As many mothers do, we were discussing our hopes and fears about the world our children were inheriting. We talked about our own upbringing, and about life's experiences that shaped us. As mothers, we were evaluating and tossing back and forth the kinds of worldly lessons we had to pass on to this new little one.

My name, Kahente, means "she walks ahead." I am Kanien'kehá:ka (Mohawk), a mother, an auntie, a sister, an academic, a writer, and sometimes a performer. If we are thinking about where the root of this piece took shape, Oka was my own point of awakening. The point where I took a look at the world around me with awareness. I can say that the journey I've been on since then has been a hard one. It has forced me to look at who I am; examine the roots of pain in my family and community, and the anger in myself. My education became a way for me to understand myself better, and turn the anger I felt at the time of Oka into a positive tool for change. I see my role in the future we are discussing as being a bridge builder, both in the work I do in the classroom and with my own daughters. Doing what I love required me to leave my home community and work in a large city. I no longer live among my community of Kahnawà:ke. In doing so, I've come to understand the struggle in maintaining a sense of who you are in the city. I am lucky to live around the corner from my sister, Waneek. We have coffee moments like these often. I also like to think we've replicated the rez in the city.

My name is Waneek. I am a mother, partner, sister, auntie, and daughter. I am Indigenous, and a Mohawk Olympian. At the 2000 Sydney Olympics I was very proud to showcase what our people are capable of on the world stage. But first I had to decolonize my identity. I had to get to know myself and my potential in direct contrast to what society and my own people thought was possible for me as an Indigenous woman. I worked harder than I ever thought possible to achieve my dream of being on the world stage, an elite athlete. It was my and my family's achievement. No one can ever say this opportunity was handed to me because I was Indigenous. Achieving my dream has given me a lot of confidence. It has become a building block for much of what I have done since then and plan to do in the future. I have a strong desire to create more of these opportunities for our people because of what I have experienced. I always remain rooted in family and a very important teaching, from my mother long ago—that before I was Mohawk I was a human being, and that I must always seek to find common humanity with others.

This is a discussion about living as a Mohawk, about what it means to live with intent. It is about our personal perspectives on reconciliation and is reflective of a much larger conversation that the women of our family have each time we gather. There are four sisters, many adopted sisters, loads of grandchildren—mostly females. Our 76-year-old mother, Kahentinetha, is the feisty matriarch of this bunch. Anyone who knows her can attest to her will to be present in the world. As such, it is a window into our family and the kinds of conversations we have, as women, mothers, aunties, and sisters. In these conversations there exists a wide range of emotions, from happiness and laughter to outright battles. This is the way of our family: each of us has our own strong mind and will. We discuss, we argue and then we seek a common ground. We don't claim to speak on anyone's behalf but our own. We grew up with the idea that everyone finds their voice at some time, and that when you do, you have a responsibility to share it. So this conversation is two sisters sharing our voices.

We grew up with a mother who had us believe we always had the power to do something. This is what living with intent is all about. "You have two hands to work," she'd say. "Well, use them. You have a mind to think," she'd say. "Well, use it, find a way, find a solution." Our mother taught us to be self-reliant. Too often we've only had each other to rely on, and our mother at our backs. This gave us the confidence to take on whatever was in our path. We learned to look at the world in a very practical way through this kind of teaching. And to take action.

In our family, we think about these things a lot. We can't help it. When we are out in the world we are always asked about our upbringing. We were asked as children, "Did you know your mother was an Indian princess? Are you going to be feminist like your mother?" What do you do when confronted with such questions? Growing up with a mother who is such a vibrant figure in Canadian history means that her legacy is part of us. This is impossible to avoid. It's like a mirror is put up to our faces and we are asked, Who are you? Who are you as a Mohawk? Who are you in the context of Canada? What will be your legacy? This continues to happen. Growing up like this makes us reflect on the kinds of things our mother has passed down, and ultimately, what we are passing to our own children.

So it is appropriate then that we respond to Canada's 150th birthday. As we have lived out our experiences and become mothers ourselves, we have thought deeply about what kind of legacy we are handing to our children. Why do we do what we do? we asked ourselves. What motivates us as Mohawk women? As we thought about this, and Canada 150, we started talking about what is happening globally and how it will affect our children. Conversations in our family have the habit of going from the local to the global and back. It makes for some very rich discussions and dialogue. This is what we have to share with you.

Through the Lens of Motherhood

WANEEK: We were raised with the understanding that, within our culture, motherhood is celebrated for many reasons. It is meant to be a transition period for a woman, from looking inward to looking outward, and forward, for the sake of our children.

When children choose us to be their mothers, it is a great honour. An honour that carries much fear and anxiety, as well as hope and love. As a new mother, all I ever wanted to do was create the most perfect, safe, and loving environment. It is our instinctual drive to want to protect our children from all we fear. Our fear as mothers stems from our own experiences. Whether extreme, overt forms of colonialism like the Oka crisis or more subtle forms like institutional racism, oppression, and subsequent lateral violence and identity politics, we fear for the future of our children.

It is times like these when we stand together talking and holding and cuddling the newest member of our family. We look in her face and see the most pure form of love—*konnorónhkwatshera*—and we see hope. We know we must dig into our own spirits to find that within ourselves to mirror back. The warrior in us knows that we cannot leave it to anyone else to make the change we want to see in her world.

Where will we find that power to make change? Like our Haudenosaunee ancestors who brought us the Great Law, we understand that the basis of this future is to seek peace. That is hard at a time when there is so much imbalance. Our ceremonies and teachings are guides to finding that balance.

We must use our own minds and spirits, and the inspiration given to us from our children, to use those guides to seek a new peace within the country they call Canada.

KAHENTE: I think in the same way you do. It's almost insulting to think about Canada's 150th birthday and the state of our own communities. What do we have to celebrate? Our communities are in disarray. Our people are suffering. We are struggling to hang on to what we have left.

I tend to step back in these moments and, like you, reflect on what it means to be a mother. I am a mother first, before an academic or a writer or anything else. I draw on what I have learned through 23 years of motherhood. But what is that? I ask in this moment. My awareness of the larger world began with Oka. It was my personal awakening as a Mohawk. Then my first daughter, a few years later, opened my eyes further to me as a woman. I always promised her that I would try to make this a better place. It is her and my other daughters that have motivated me through so much school and beyond. Eighteen years of it in fact.

I think about that teaching—that our children choose us and not the other way around. So all these beautiful children we have, including this little one we are holding here, have chosen us. How fortunate are we? So very fortunate. I like to think they looked down from Sky World and said, Yup, there she is! That one's mine. But what does that mean? What kind of responsibility does that put upon us as women? If the perspective we are coming from is as Mohawk mothers, what do we have to contribute to this discussion?

Through our abilities as progenitors we have a deep connection to the natural world. We are reminded of this fact every 28 days. But what does this have to do with Canada? I like to think that having children means I am confronting colonialism head on. I don't need to stand at the frontlines or block bridges like Mom did. By the very fact that I have four daughters with Mohawk names and an awareness of their identity as Mohawk or Kanien'kehá:ka they are part of that ongoing fight against what Canada has wrought on our people. Take that Canada 150! You got four more women who know the history, have a voice, and are going to share it.

Really though, I am a humanist at heart. I like to see us all as human beings first and not races. This is what I teach my children. I think this is one thing that our mother has taught us, to see the humanity in the world. Not to say she is not without her contradictions. But above all what I have taken away from what she has taught us is her love of humanity. She never lets us forget to live life to the fullest.

What Does Reconciliation Mean?

KAHENTE: Reconciliation can be looked at, in very basic terms, as a way to describe the breaking of a relationship and its re-establishment through conciliatory practices. When I think about reconciliation, I think about how we might use Haudenosaunee philosophical grounding to bring this idea further. I think our ancestors were practicing reconciliation for many generations, way before the term ever achieved cachet through the Truth and Reconciliation Commission.

I think, what are some of the underlying philosophical principles that come out of our culture that we might use to describe a Haudenosaunee conception of reconciliation? When we think of reconciliation, we think of it in action terms. Our language is verb based and denotes continued action. That said, reconciliation then is a movement forward and begins with the individual.

WANEEK: It is my understanding that our ancestors practiced reconciliation when they formed the Great Peace. They had to reconcile and come to one mind at a time when much damage and killing was being done to one another. They were inspired to find a way to reconcile by the konnorónhkwatshera—the love they had for their children. They identified that as being the most powerful energy in the world, and what should be the basis for all actions and decisions beginning with the individual, then the couple, then the family, onto the clan, and then finally the nation.

We can find inspiration in their actions. They understood the seven generations concept, and that you must keep looking forward to what is possible and living a life based on konnorónhkwatshera and intent to make it so.

What is Living with Intent?

KAHENTE: Our mother raised us to be independent in spirit, thought, and act. To think through all aspects of a situation before making a decision. To critically engage with what is before us. To question everything. This is also part of reconciliation and living with intent.

This kind of thinking about reconciliation doesn't come out of the current dominant narrative, where we are limited by thinking in terms of what is reconciliation within the context of Canada 150. Rather, what kind of thinking we are doing on this issue comes out of our own Indigenous tradition and practice. Our Haudenosaunee traditions are about the building and renewal of relationships.

WANEEK: We have ceremonies that are about this, too. About building relationships. But we have strayed far from this kind of thinking. You know, in our own community, the dominant talk isn't about the need to rebuild families, the community. There seems to be a deep-rooted fear and pain, and that leads to an urge to exclude those that are perceived as not belonging. This is what people are talking about.

KAHENTE: We are supposed to be a people who were all about discussion and dialogue. We had the ability to resolve conflicts between large groups of people by the words we said, the ceremonies we did, the physical touching of each other that brought balance back. I am talking about the At The Woods' Edge ceremony. It brought balance into the minds of the people as they entered back into our communities. This was so important. It seems like we lived with intent—an intent to be balanced and in peace.

WANEEK: I think if we are considering Canada 150, and what this country needs in order to move forward with intent, we need to renew our treaty relationships. We need to dust them off and renew the terms of the relationships with each other. Not only between Indigenous peoples and Canada but also between Indigenous nations.

What is the Lesson as we Head Toward Canada 150?

WANEEK: We must put the children at the centre of this country. What kind of world do we want to create for them? Re-discovering the act of treaty making on all levels of Canadian consciousness, and celebrating and reinvigorating that relationship each year.

Our past is riddled with so much damage, killing, and genocide. As Haudenosaunee, we need to continue to look forward. This will take reconciliation within our selves, and an incredible amount of trust. We have the inspiration of our ancestors who did just that in a time of great upheaval. It wasn't easy and there were people who did awful things. But we don't need to look at the people sitting across from us as reincarnations of those men of the past, but for who they are now.

A great Condolence needs to be done to wipe away those tears to see the truth, clear out our ears to hear the truth, and a drink of the purest waters to be able to wash away the pain we carry in our throats, so we are able to speak the truth.[1]

When I am asked, "How can you do this work after what happened to you during Oka?" I respond that before all this I am a mother and an auntie. I am inspired by my nieces, nephews, and now my children, who are a daily reminder of the obligation I have to keep alive that Great Peace within myself. I see my work in spreading that Great Peace far and wide.

KAHENTE: I think too that our people have a lot to teach others about respect and what it means to find balance. I always go back to the Seventh Generation philosophy, which is at its base about accountability, a deep accountability. I tell my students, imagine living with a sense of accountability not only to yourself but to the coming faces, the next seven generations. It makes one think very hard about the long-term outcomes, before you act or speak. It structures your life in a way that is very different from the individuality that we learn from the dominant society.

I like to imagine a world where societal constructs are built upon the idea of building relationships between people. So that the education system we put in place is meant to foster relationships between people, or the business structures we put in place are about bringing people together. It would make for a very different reality. It would force us to act differently toward each other. This is my dream. The question is: How can Canada entertain this kind of thinking and philosophy? It seems daunting.

WANEEK: I think we have the possibility for great things as a country. Deep down I feel like I want to be part of something bigger. A reserve, is that it for me? No, I don't think so. We have so much strength to offer. Being a part of the Olympic team was powerful. Seeing us work together impacted how I feel about multiculturalism. My twelve teammates and I all had different strengths, we had different passions, prayed different, but used them all to get to the same objective. I was valued for what I could do, not my skin colour. I liked how I could empower the whole team with who I was and the people I come from. It wasn't perfect, but it made me believe that there could be something bigger. Perhaps that is my path for understanding. I really think we need to strive for something bigger, something new. However, we cannot make the mistake of thinking that we are to go back to a time when things were perfect, like there is a template we can follow. Make no mistake: we are trying to create a kind of society that has never existed.

When I realized that I might be part of something bigger, I knew I could find the power to sit across from people that have wronged me. Last year, I spoke to the Department of Defence. I knew there were going to be soldiers and generals attending who had been at Oka. At first I didn't want to speak to them. I never wanted to have anything to do with them again. In the days leading up to this talk, my anxiety built. I was trying to figure out what I was going to say, and my mind kept taking me back to 26 years ago. I don't often let my mind think too deeply about what happened during Oka. Of course I can speak about the bigger event and what happened, but the details, the personal events, those are what bring back memories and so much more.

You know, I wasn't a major player or spokesperson during the Oka Crisis. But, I know what we witnessed was powerful. Our sister, Kaniehti:io, and I had the unique viewpoint of two young girls witnessing history in the making. As the day of the speech drew near, I did something I don't let happen very often—I let my memory flow back to those hot summer days.

Oh man, it was like I could feel the humidity on my skin; hear the sounds of the race riots and helicopters thundering in my ears. I remembered the feeling of the cool metal of an AK-47 on my nervous fingertips, and the whispered instructions of how to dismantle and clean it. I could even see the faces of the soldiers peering out from behind their guns and armoured personnel carriers. That sick, anxious, scared feeling came back, the one I carried in my stomach all summer and for a very long time after.

Why would I do this? Let myself go back there and feed the anxiety I have lived with for 26 years? Well, I wanted those feelings, that spirit, to infuse themselves into my words, and I wanted to slip them into their mouths like a pill so they could feel all of "IT" in their blood and their bones. I wanted them to understand what outright aggressive warfare and oppression felt like for a fourteen-year-old girl.

You know that, for many nights, I re-lived, thought, and formulated courage only to wake having lost it? The morning of the speech, I almost called to cancel. But then I looked across the table at my children, watched the peaceful way they smiled, weightless and free to banter and bug each other, without a care in the world.

It was then I was reminded of my promise to them: to be the change I wanted to see in their world. I felt this overwhelming need to guard this peacefulness, and to fight to make their world better so they never have to go through what I did. That fierce feeling grew like a fire as I sat there watching. It grew so big, it seemed to burn away my all my fears, and it gave me a sense of courage I had never known. You know that kind of courage only your children can give you, well it was that—that gave me the strength and the peace I needed to get in my car and head down the Department of Defence. I almost threw up the whole way there and the entire time I was speaking, but I did it.

I know I walked away a better person for it. I cannot be sure, but perhaps they will remember my words. Maybe they even felt my emotions. What I hope for most is, next time they head out on a battlefield, they will not just see faceless enemy combatants but rather people—perhaps even a fourteen-year-old girl with hopes and dreams.

I don't know what it all means, but maybe I am making a small change, and at the same time perhaps helping to find my balance. But I do know after doing this speech I feel like I am a more powerful person, and a more peaceful person. I really want a society with this kind of inner peace.

Surviving for Canada?

KAHENTE: I have recently been inundated with Canada 150 everywhere I turn. It forces me to ask myself if I am going to participate in the festivities. I don't know. Perhaps not. And, as I have come to find out, giving a face of incredulity when asked doesn't do much to explain my reasoning. But it's hard to make faces or stay aloof and maintain a position based on the knowledge I have of colonial history. I mean, how do you explain to my ten- and six-year-old daughters why they shouldn't be carried along in the tidal wave of Canada 150? I think if I can get them to understand, then I can explain it to anyone. That said, I imagine I am going to be explaining myself a number of times over the next while. Really though, it's around us at every turn, and it's hard to ignore.

WANEEK: I have to say, I too am as conflicted as ever on the whole celebration. Much like when I competed for Canada at the Olympics, I could see the political issues and debates of playing for a country that had done so much to hurt me. However, I have travelled so much and met so many Indigenous and non-Indigenous people who I call friends and family. Those are the people I played for at the Olympics. They were the ones I wanted to be proud of me. It is these people I will always hold my hand out to and say, "Let us learn from the last 150 years. Let us never forget what has happened, but for our children's sake, we must look forward together. Dream together. Work harder than we ever thought possible to create a country that in another 150 years our descendants can honestly celebrate."

KAHENTE: Okay, you are perhaps a bit more open-minded than me. With what we have been witnessing in our own community of Kahnawà:ke and the identity dilemma. It shows me that our people have been left to survive the destructive wake that colonialism has left within our communities. Is the dysfunction in the colonial policies we are forced to adhere to something to celebrate? Especially when the celebration is couched in the idea of reconciliation.

As we talk, I am becoming somewhat critical of that term here, as we think about Canada 150, contrary to what I said earlier. In thinking further, we have conciliation as our foundation, not reconciliation. If reconciliation is based on the idea that there was peace before the break, we know that's not the case. Conciliation then is what our people are all about. We know that the Haudenosaunee Confederacy was founded on this idea of bringing warring nations together. Our Great Law, ceremonies, and philosophy are about conciliation. This term speaks to me. It guides me as I think about Canada 150. I think there is even a Kanien'keha word to describe it. I just have to think on it some more. I'll ask Mom.

But really, in thinking about Canada's birthday, show me a future based on the recognition of the harms done to Indigenous peoples and the active mending of our relationship and we're talking! It's all about moving forward from here. Imagine if we organized a mass condolence! Brought people together in our common humanity to share in the process of cleansing the eyes, ears, and throat so that true dialogue could begin. Whoa! Maybe that's what the Truth and Reconciliation Commission was about, that first step of condolence. A cleansing the eyes and ears of Canada. It's something I'm thinking about.

WANEEK: I think that perhaps focusing on trauma as the foundation for a way forward isn't healthy. It shouldn't be the fuel with which we are inspired. But I agree we cannot forget. I think that we need to find a way to heal and perhaps a

Condolence Ceremony is the way. But like Mom always said, "Sorry is just a word, unless it is backed up by actions." The mending of hundreds of years of hurt and pain isn't going to happen overnight, or even one generation. It will take generations. We need to start somewhere. Where is that? Is it today? Do we mark this birthday as the real beginning of Canada?

KAHENTE: I don't know. Maybe we can mark it as the start of that healing process. I am not sure what Canada's future looks like. Indigenous peoples are speaking out and acting up. The future could either be painful or filled with dialogue, discussion, action, and hope. I would like people to start talking to one another. Social media is making us so distant from each other. It's so easy to hurt from across the Internet. We can hide behind our keyboards and shoot flaming arrows of lateral violence at each other. It hurts! I think we need to spend more time around the kitchen table talking to each other. I've started inviting people into my home to do beadwork, share food, and talk to each other face to face. I think this is what builds strong community. It's my contribution to a collective future based on looking each other in the eyes, recognizing our common humanity, listening intently with open and kind ears, and speaking with good words. This is what we do around my table and you can see the beauty that comes out in the things we create.

WANEEK: I know that this is going to sound like a cliché, but I have to say that trust is built one day at time. I always look back to my water polo days. See, my teammates and I were as different as different could be. But as a team, you don't want thirteen women exactly the same. Collectively our differences made us a strong team. We had a joint objective and a game plan but needed our individual strengths to achieve that objective. As a team, we learned not to fear each other for our differences but to celebrate them as part of our team's character. We had a toughness that no other team could break.

So, thinking about that, we need to see Canada as a team that requires the uniqueness and creativity of each of our citizens to make the country stronger. I believe that our team objective is the Great Peace—all we need is a game-plan.

Conclusion

And so it shall be said. This is what they say in the longhouse at the conclusion of a speech act. It is meant to put finality to the talk that has taken place. It rounds out the discussion and acknowledges that people have come and shared a part of themselves for the betterment of the collective. This is what consensus is all about. Facing each other, looking each other in the eye and acknowledging our common humanity and desire for a better future for the next generation.

As sisters, we have shared a part of ourselves, and the teachings that have been passed down in our family. We built on the legacy our mother has put to us. Coming from a place of violence and direct action of the 1960s, we have gone a step further and brought forth the teachings that she fought hard to protect and reinvigorate by her political activism. We see the world a bit differently, perhaps not with so much anger and animosity but the possibilities for change, balance, and ultimately peace.

This is what we think Canada's next 150 years could be about. We can begin by listening to each other and acknowledging our common humanity. By working to find common ground, to begin building a new foundation for Canada. We know no one is going anywhere and we are all inhabitants of the Great Turtle Island. The question remains: How do we begin? Well, from the perspectives of two Mohawk mothers, we look forward while being inspired by our ancestors. It must begin with Konnorónhkwatshera and seeking the Great Peace, and of course be inspired by the love we all have for our children.

Skennen sewakwekon thok nikon (Be peaceful, we've come to a close).
KAHENTE AND WANEEK

1. The Condolence Ceremony is about transforming a loss into strength, about bringing minds imbalanced after a death back into balance. It is about bringing comfort and strength to the family that is in morning. Translated to the everyday, condolence is also about opening the eyes so that one is aware and sees clearly what is before them. It is about opening the ears so that one listens carefully and with respect to others. It is also about clearing the throat so that when one speaks, they speak with clarity and kindness. The ceremony and philosophical underpinnings creates a situation of respect, deep listening, and dialogue necessary in our times.

Canada: Portrait of a Serial Killer[1]

Jeff Corntassel and Christine Bird

Canada is a serial killer. This truth has been staring you in the face for more than the last 150 years. Most people think of serial killers as men, and sometimes women as accomplices. However, in this chapter we will reveal the extent to which Canada has carried out a murderous assault on Indigenous peoples. We will also reveal the extent to which Canada uses various state apparatuses, such as legal and political systems, to target and victimize Indigenous peoples. We will also discuss how Canadians uphold and support this methodical and murderous assault on Indigenous lands and bodies.

Investigators of serial killers often look to the killer's childhood for evidence or signs of pathology. Canada's violent beginnings are manifestations of an emerging serial killer, evidenced by the slaughter of the buffalo,[2] militarized massacres of Indigenous peoples, biological warfare (with the distribution of smallpox blankets and the transportation of Spanish influenza via Indigenous waterways), and through the introduction of invasive species (plants, animals etc.).[3] Over time, Canada's methods became more devious and duplicitous, systematically importing and creating bodies to carry out mass murder that include but are not limited to: the church, the military, the North-West Mounted Police (later the Royal Canadian Mounted Police), the government, and settlers.

Indigenous phrases for settlers provide some insights into the mentality of a serial killer back when Canada was first becoming a country. Mohawk scholar Taiaiake Alfred reminds us that the word "Canada" is derived from a Kanien'kehaka term, *Kanatiens*, which means, "they sit in our village."[4] A contemporary translation of this term would be "squatter." There are many other Indigenous words for settlers or non-Indigenous people that shed light on the pathological violence that undergirds the state. In Anishinaabemowin, "white" people were often referred to as *Chimookamonnug*,[5] which can be translated as "big knife," referring to the bayonet in their (European's) guns that they used to kill our people.[6] Similarly, another word that the Anishinaabe used to refer to the white man was *Zhimaaganish*, which can be translated as a jack, solider, or policeman.[7] This is telling because the military and the police (RCMP) are often the tool of choice for Canada as a serial killer. What these words tell us is that our Indigenous languages carry deeper insights and meanings into our contemporary struggles and challenges as nations and peoples.

Since its assertion of statehood, Canada's systematic approach to the murder of Indigenous peoples have included the state's laws and policies, political and governing bodies, and education systems that have implanted themselves in the minds, bodies, and consciousness of Indigenous peoples and Canadians. Embedded within these systems are narratives and practices that serve to:

a. Uphold Canada's paternalistic policies that continue to result in the death of Indigenous women, remove their reproductive abilities, and restrict Indigenous motherhood, thereby reducing their biological threat to Canada;

b. Attempt to eliminate Indigenous Two Spirit and queer peoples as a means to alter and subjugate Indigenous identity and communities;

c. Physically, emotionally, mentally, and spiritually remove Indigenous men via death and incarceration, thereby divesting them of their ability to protect Indigenous communities; and

d. Carry out the mass murder and dispossession of Indigenous children as a means to threaten Indigenous futurity.

Indigenous peoples' existence and survival in Canada is evidence of their ongoing resistance to Canada's plan to physically and legally erase Indigenous peoples from their land, and to publicly and legally dispose of Indigenous peoples.

While thinking of different ways to convey Indigenous perspectives of Canada's 150th anniversary, we were listening to reporters Connie Walker and Marnie Luke's powerful CBC News podcast entitled *Who Killed Alberta Williams?* It examines the unsolved 1989 murder of a 24-year-old Indigenous woman from Gitanyow Band of the Gitxsan First Nation.[8] In episode eight of the podcast, Walker discusses the formation of Project E-PANA, a Task Force created in 2005 to determine whether a serial killer or killers have been responsible for eighteen of the unsolved murders of Indigenous women on Highway 16, or the "Highway of Tears" as it has come to be known, between 1969-2006. As Walker points out, "... in 11 years, the taskforce has only made one arrest, in one case. And no one's been convicted yet."[9] These sobering statistics only led to more questions for us: How did some cases end up on E-PANA's list of eighteen over others? And how active are the investigations in the over 1,000 additional cases of murdered and missing Indigenous women?[10]

It quickly became clear to us that E-PANA has been focusing on the wrong suspects as serial killers all along. A standard definition of a serial killer describes "someone who commits more than three murders over a period that spans more than one month. For the most part, serial killers commit murder for some sort of psychological benefit."[11] Based on the preceding definition, Canada, accompanied by its accomplices, can be named as prime suspects in the murders of Indigenous peoples. Canada clearly far exceeds this threshold of "more than three" murders when it comes to Indigenous peoples, having taken place during the 150-year span of Canada's existence. Additionally, the primary psychological benefit Canada derives from these systematic killings is to perceive their illegal presence on Indigenous lands and waters as legitimate. In short, these psychological benefits are derived from the erasure of Indigenous peoples from the landscape so that Canadian sovereignty is perceived as lawful and authentic.[12] As Kahnawake Mohawk scholar Audra Simpson aptly notes, "Canada requires the death and so called 'disappearance' of Indigenous women in order to secure its sovereignty."[13]

In the following sections, we begin by examining how the state-centric system enables and facilitates the serial killing of Indigenous peoples under the guise of state building and sovereignty. Here we draw on Andrew Woolford's "ontology of destruction" when describing serial killing as a function of genocide; that is, we examine serial killing and ultimately genocide "from the perspective of how destruction is experienced and made sense of by targeted collectivities who define their worlds within culturally specific meaning systems."[14] Additionally, we will look at ways that the state attempts to cover up the evidence, and ways that Canada and its citizens attempt to hide their complicity in the ongoing genocide of Indigenous peoples. We conclude with some strategies that Canadians can take to embrace the hard truths of Canada as a serial killer, and assist in the dismantling of state systems that uphold these homicidal tendencies and result in the ongoing violence and death of Indigenous peoples.

The Making of A Serial Killer

States like Canada are founded on legal fictions such as the Doctrine of Discovery and all the predatory assumptions that went with it, including the belief that Indigenous peoples were sub-human and therefore legitimate targets for a serial killer. The establishment of Canada as a country required the military and police to impose the illusion of law and order, while drawing on the church to justify the violent dispossession of Indigenous peoples. The police and the church combined forces to violently remove Indigenous children from their homes, unjustly disrupting Indigenous cultures, languages, families, and ways of life.[15] The state wielded Christianity in its efforts to terminate Two Spirit and queer populations. Ultimately the state "serves the interests of what is understood now as 'straightness' or heterosexuality and patriarchy, the rule by men."[16] Consequently, Canada seeks to eliminate extended family and kinship structures, as well as relationships with the natural world, and replace them with nuclear family units. These religious weapons also gutted Indigenous governance structures and attempted to erase Indigenous peoples from the land, altering our relationships with each other and to all of creation. In using the church as a weapon, Canada effectively created the conditions of vulnerability required for the mass murder that would be practiced in state-sanctioned Residential Schools.

Canada's sovereignty is rooted in the state's claim to have the exclusive authority to forcefully intervene in all activities within its borders.[17] This monopoly on the state's use of violence is triggered any time Indigenous peoples challenge the legitimacy of the state's authority over them. States operate in violent ways by "claiming jurisdiction over Indigenous bodies [and lands], facilitated through the construction of Indigenous political activities as criminal."[18] While the self-determining authority of Indigenous peoples emanates from their relationships to the land, water, and the natural world, the state's assertion of sovereignty is rooted in violence and forms of "lawfare," which is a strategy of using law to reinforce state legitimacy.

This creation of an all-encompassing governing principle grounded in violence and lawfare lays the groundwork for a serial killer to operate freely within the state. According to Sherene Razack, "The discovered enter into the arrangements of European legal regimes forever subordinate, awaiting improvement, and invitation always deferred, to join the nation-state."[19] This subordination created the perfect conditions for a serial killer to operate, and to initiate regimes that regulate and target Indigenous peoples' bodies and lands.[20] Canada's plan to "kill the Indian in the child" was carried out by Canadian law and policy, Indian Agents, the church, and the RCMP. Canada made it illegal for Indigenous parents to resist the removal of their children for the Residential School system. In response to Indigenous parents' resistance to their children's removal, the state also implemented the pass system, which was designed to monitor and regulate Indigenous peoples movement, effectively preventing them from locating and reclaiming their children. Any Indigenous person "caught" off the reserve without a pass would be charged and imprisoned. Such legislation also made it legal for Canada as well as Canadians to lawfully participate in the criminalization, incarceration, and murder of Indigenous peoples.

According to the FBI's National Center for the Analysis of Violent Crime Behavioural Analysis Unit, "much of the general public's knowledge concerning serial murder is a product of Hollywood productions."[21] This is the "politics of distraction"[22] that the state manufactures and sells to an eager citizenry. Storylines are created to heighten the interest of audiences, rather than to accurately portray serial murder. Canada's politics of distraction attempts to divert our attention from the perpetrator(s) while focusing on the performances of reconciliation orchestrated by the state. Consider the fact that between 1867 and 2000, 3,200 children were murdered in residential schools.[23] State discourse is careful to use language like "children who died" to conceal Canada's malevolent desire to "cause Aboriginal people to cease to exist."[24] This is a well-known element of Canada's genocidal Indian Policy to "kill the Indian in the child."[25] According to the TRC, 1,150 children "died" before 1940.[26] The numbers identified in "official government reports" do not include the murder of children who were buried in unmarked and mass graves. The numbers game that Canadians often see is also a distraction, preventing Canadians from realizing that each number represents someone's child. That aspect of humanity becomes lost within the apparatus of Canada's distractive tools. Consistent with a serial killer, many of Canada's child victims remain unidentified to this day. Sadly, Canada's killing spree did not end with the residential school system or the final report of the Truth and Reconciliation Commission (TRC), nor was it limited to Indigenous children.

Alfred and Corntassel refer to the shape-shifting nature of colonialism, where "the instruments of domination are evolving and inventing new methods to erase Indigenous histories and senses of place."[27] As a serial killer, Canada continually shifts its target and time frame. To further support Canada's objective of the destruction of Indigenous families, it supplemented the Residential School system with the forced removal and adoption of Indigenous children through the Sixties Scoop.[28] Children were literally scooped from their homes and communities without the knowledge or consent of families and communities.[29] Consistent with Canada's assimilation policy, the Sixties Scoop supported the dispossession of Indigenous children, effectively severing their ties to family, community, and identity. Canada not only moved the bodies of Indigenous children, but simultaneously implemented policies relating to child welfare, creating various Child Welfare Acts. In doing so, the state effectively shifted the focus away from removal and dispossession to the state regulation of Indigenous children through the Ministry of Child and Family Development. According to Gitksan scholar Cindy Blackstock, "the number of First Nations children in care outside their own homes today is three times the number of children in residential schools at the height of their operation."[30] These policies make Indigenous children even more vulnerable to Canada's homicidal tendencies as they are carried out on multiple levels that include Canadians, government policy, law, and even Aboriginal organizations and politicians that are funded and mandated to carry out Canada's homicidal plans. As Simpson reminds us, it is not just state structures (for example, the Ministry of Children and Family Development) and agents (such as the RCMP) that engage in serial killing: "States do not always have to kill; its citizens can do that for it."[31]

Most serial killers have very defined geographic areas of operation. Residential schools were sites of mass murder; however, today metropolitan cities such as Vancouver, Edmonton, Winnipeg, and Toronto have become the main geographical areas for the murder of Indigenous women and girls, Two Spirit, and queer. A report completed by the Royal Canadian Mounted Police stated that 1,017 women and girls identified as Indigenous were murdered between 1980 and 2012.[32] In its statistics on homicide, the RCMP report only includes cases where the original investigating police force has concluded that a murder has taken place. The report explicitly does not include unexplained and suspicious deaths.[33] What is even more disturbing is realizing that *Missing and Murdered Aboriginal Women: A National Operational Overview*,[34] conducted by the RCMP in 2014, is basically an internal investigation.

If Canadians are able to navigate the bureaucratic chain of evidence that the state has worked so long to hide, they might realize that the reason the RCMP were created in the first place was to remove children from their homes, keep parents from finding their children and remove Indigenous peoples from their land. When examining colonial narratives and foundational myths, Canadians might find that the murders of Indigenous women and girls, Two Spirit, and queer, have been consistent throughout the last 150 years of the state's presence on Indigenous lands. The RCMP's documentation of Canada's murders only became an issue when the increasing number of Indigenous women, Two Spirit, and queer, was brought to the attention of the Canadian public; earlier deaths just weren't documented.

It is well known that serial killers take trophies of their victims. The trophies in this case are right in front of us: the news, social media, government policies, law, and state forums, such as the Royal Commission on Aboriginal People (RCAP), the Aboriginal Justice Inquiry of Manitoba, the TRC, and more recently, the National Inquiry into Murdered and Missing Indigenous Women. These forums have provided Indigenous peoples with an opportunity to provide evidence of Canada's homicidal actions; however, these forums ultimately tend to clear Canada and Canadians of culpability for the murder of Indigenous peoples. Consequently, inquiries and forums continue to endorse Canada's promotion of the "peacemaker" myth, avert Canada's criminal and moral liability, and promote narratives of suffering that only serve to reaffirm Canada's sovereignty over Indigenous peoples. Canada's violence against Indigenous peoples is intrinsically linked to Indigenous lands, as attempts to erase Indigenous peoples are interrelated with the destruction of Indigenous lands and waterways. Consequently, as Mohawk scholar Taiaiake Alfred states, "First Nations today are characterized as entrenched dependencies, in physical, psychological and financial terms, on the very people and institutions that have caused the near erasure of our existence and who have come to dominate us."[35]

What Canadians fail to see is the evidence. Consistent with the profile of a serial killer, Canada has created and managed to uphold a very complex system of distractions that many Canadians have come to uncritically support in the last 150 years. These distractions include racism and cultural stereotypes; colonial narratives[36] and binaries;[37] policy and law; and more recently, colonial discourse, all aimed at creating confusion amongst Canadians regarding their status on Indigenous lands and their role in the mass murder of Indigenous people. The trophies that Canada has accumulated, such as the TRC and RCAP, provide further clues about the violent underpinnings of the state.

Cover-Ups & Complicity

The attempt to continually erase Indigenous peoples occurs because we are still being viewed as sub-human, as financial burdens, and ultimately as embarrassing to Canada's narcissistic "peacemaker" identity. Canada has utilized a politics of distraction to hide its political and judicial policies, and agents that violently target Indigenous bodies and lands. As Paulette Regan points out, "The peacemaker myth lies at the heart of the settler problem; it informs, however unconsciously, the everyday attitudes and actions of contemporary politicians, policy makers, lawyers, and negotiators, and it remains an archetype of settler benevolence, fairness, and innocence in the Canadian public mind."[38] Canada's narcissistic peacemaker narratives endorse the violence in Canada's social organization, heteronormativity, patriarchy, and privilege that is still being taught, upheld, and promoted in public education systems such as universities, as well as media and government institutions.

According to Sherene Razack, "When inquests and inquiries instruct us in the pathologies of Indigenous peoples, states provide themselves with alibis not only for inaction but also for crimes of overt violence."[39] Canada is especially adept at covering up its mass murders by channelling Indigenous demands for justice into state-driven investigative forums. For example, when seeking redress for the genocidal legacy of residential schools, Indigenous people brought their claims of abuse, violence, and mass murder to the Canadian Justice System through state mechanisms, such as the Residential Schools Class Action Litigation,[40] which led to the Common Experience Payment (CEP),[41] and eventually Canada's Apology.[42] Canada soon realized that no amount of money as restitution or public apologies could cover the tracks of the Canadian serial killer. Canada responded to Indigenous calls for justice with the TRC, which diverted attention away from the perpetrators of the crimes and kept Canadians pre-occupied for several years while Canada planned its next mass murder.

Prior to the TRC, the RCAP[43] was Canada's heavily militarized response to resistance by the Kanien'kehaka community of Kanesatake (and later Kahnawake, Akwesasne) regarding the expansion of the Oka golf course over Kanien'kehaka burial grounds. The Oka Crisis revealed Canada's commitment to maintaining state legitimacy via the threat of violence. This was a 78-day standoff between 2,000 SQ police, 4,500 heavily armed soldiers equipped with tanks, and the town of Oka versus an estimated 300 Mohawks.[44] Instead of addressing Canada's lethal desire for Indigenous lands, the state responded by enlisting one of its many distractive tools, a Royal Commission, which examined the relationship between Canada and Indigenous peoples. Instead of addressing the violence directed at Indigenous peoples by Canada and Canadians, the state effectively offset its culpability by promoting a benevolent narrative of "renewed relationships." The utilization of this commission further entrenched Canada's pattern for investigating the very violence and destruction against Indigenous peoples that it is implicated in.

Canada's use of state forums, such as the Aboriginal Justice Inquiry of Manitoba, are structured to re-direct attention away from state mechanisms and re-focus on specific injustices and wrong doings. For example, the Aboriginal Justice Inquiry was a response to the 1988 wrongful shooting of J.J. Harper by Winnipeg City Police, the sixteen-year cover-up of the 1971 violent death of Helen Betty Osborne,[45] and the "overrepresentation" of Indigenous peoples in the criminal justice system. These are very specific and individual cases that were designed to absolve Canada of any systemic wrongdoing. Instead, what came to light in each investigation is that Canadians play a very specific role in supporting Canada's violent regime. In the case of Helen Betty Osborne, the entire community and RCMP in The Pas, Manitoba knew who her four killers were but never said anything. After sixteen years, when a criminal investigation was finally initiated, only one of the four were actually charged and convicted with her death.[46] In the case of the 1988 murder of J.J. Harper by a Winnipeg City Police Officer, it was later revealed through an independent investigation that the police officer shot J.J. Harper because he fit the profile of a suspect they had been chasing. The Aboriginal Justice Inquiry was completed in 1999 and since then has basically disappeared from the consciousness of Canadians. Why? Because Canada creates the very forums investigating its own criminal acts. Drawing on the politics of distraction, it redirects investigations away from state mechanisms and focuses on criminalizing Indigenous peoples themselves.

Indigenous peoples' calls for an unbiased and independent investigation into the missing and murdered Indigenous women and girls, Two-Spirited, and queer peoples were met by Prime Minister Stephen Harper's statement: "it isn't really high on our radar, to be honest . . ."[47] It's been documented that between 1980 and 2012,[48] 1,017 Indigenous women and girls, including Two Spirit and queer peoples, were murdered. When it became obvious that it wasn't a priority for the state to investigate or address this fact, the Native Women's Association of Canada (NWAC) and the Feminist Alliance for International Action (FAFIA) appealed to the Inter-American Commission of Human Rights (IACHR) to investigate. The IACHR released their report in February of 2015 documenting how "the police have failed to adequately prevent and protect Indigenous women and girls from killings, disappearances and extreme forms of violence, and have failed to diligently and promptly investigate these acts."[49] Similarly, Human Rights Watch (HRW), a prominent global organization documenting human rights violations worldwide,[50] released an examination of the abusive policing and failure to protect Indigenous women and girls in northern British Columbia.[51] In an in-depth critical analysis of how Indigenous girls' violent encounters with the police are intertwined with the politics of territorial seizure characteristic of settler colonies, as well as the maintenance of settler sovereignty, Jaskiran K. Dhillon states:

> "In cities and towns across Canada, Indigenous girls are being hunted, harassed, and criminalized by local law enforcement agents and the Royal Canadian Mounted Police. These normalized outbreaks of state control, often punctuated by the use of deadly force, are not isolated incidents in an otherwise just and fair social order. Rather . . . they are reflective of Indigenous girls' daily realities embedded within an *ongoing* settler colonial social context that includes the strategic (historic) invention of the criminal justice system to police (quite literally) the borderlands of possession and dispossession."[52]

It is not surprising that Canada responded to the IACHR report and the HRW report by implementing a National Inquiry into Murdered and Missing Indigenous Women. This inquiry represents another patterned response by Canada to divert attention away from the mass murders of women and girls, Two-Spirited, and queer, while providing a political veneer of justice and human rights.

What becomes obvious is that the RCMP only serves to legitimize their own systemic position as a tool for Canada's genocidal desires. This is not only evident in the lack of concern for and commitment to investigating and holding Canadians accountable for gendered violence against Indigenous women and girls, Two-Spirited, and queer,[53] but also evident in the treatment and death of Indigenous men. Much like the National Inquiry into MMIW, the RCMP also investigated their role in the "starlight tours" that usually took place in Saskatoon, Saskatchewan, between twelve and three in the early morning hours.[54] There have been only 76 "reported" cases to the RCMP of First Nations men being dropped off outside city limits and two deaths despite the 250 cases filed with First Nation leaders regarding these starlight tours.[55] Police corruption and abuse of power were determined to be crucial factors in the death of seventeen-year-old Neil Stonechild, following the Stonechild Inquiry in 2003.[56] While two constables were fired following the inquiry, they were never found criminally responsible for Stonechild's death.

Thirteen years after the Stonechild Inquiry, not far from Saskatoon, a white farmer named Gerald Stanley shot 22-year-old Colten Boushie[57] when he and his friends from the Red Pheasant reserve pulled into the farmer's yard with a flat tire. RCMP issued a biased and prejudicial news release[58] stating that the people in the vehicle were under investigation for theft and had been taken into custody.[59] The events that followed can only be described as shocking and appalling. The RCMP's treatment of Colten Boushie's family compared to the treatment of Gerald Stanley's family stand in stark contrast. The RCMP's initial statement regarding theft fuelled racialized harassment and violence, but also veiled the fact that a white man was able to take the law into his own hands, based on an assumption, and kill another human being. The fact that a 22-year-old Indigenous man's life had been taken was disregarded. Instead, the RCMP were more concerned with whether or not theft had anything to do with the killing, ignoring the fact that local farmers felt they had a right to carry and use firearms.[60] This is a clear example of how Canadians' sense of justice is tied to their privilege, which is essentially premised upon the dehumanization of Indigenous peoples.

While investigating Canada's relationship with Indigenous peoples and nations, and in his role as UN Special Rapporteur on the Rights of Indigenous Peoples, James Anaya observed the following:

> Canada faces a continuing crisis when it comes to the situation of indigenous peoples of the country. The well-being gap between aboriginal and non-aboriginal people in Canada has not narrowed over the last several years, treaty and aboriginals claims remain persistently unresolved, indigenous women and girls remain vulnerable to abuse, and overall there appear to be high levels of distrust among indigenous peoples toward government at both the federal and provincial levels.[61]

What Anaya misses in his observation is that the high levels of distrust do not just exist between Indigenous peoples and government. They also exist between Indigenous peoples and Canadians. Through their participation in societal structures, Canadian citizens have too often been complicit in legitimating

Canada's assumed sovereign authority and ongoing violence against Indigenous peoples. Despite Canada's self-imposed image of benevolence, some Canadians, and people from other countries across the globe, are starting to see Canada and Canadians for what they truly are: violent offenders of Indigenous peoples' bodies and lands. This was made obvious during the Idle No More movement when people from across the world responded via social media with their support for Indigenous land defenders and communities seeking to exert their self-determining authority. Despite Anaya's warnings, Canada nonetheless remains at large as a serial killer targeting Indigenous women, men, children, Two-Spirited, and queer, as well as lands and waterways. Until citizens see through the politics of distraction by exposing the endless trail of cover-ups via inquiries and commissions, acknowledging their complicity in state violence, and beginning the difficult process of decolonizing their relationships, the killings will only continue.

The Verdict

It is beyond the scope of this paper to identify every single documented and undocumented death of Indigenous peoples. The purpose of this investigation is to take a step back and focus on what is not often said: that Canada has carried out the mass murder of Indigenous peoples and the destruction of Indigenous lands and waterways with Canadians as accomplices, and neither have ever been held accountable. In Indigenous minds and memory, and in line with the logic of the ontology of destruction, the systematic violence and murder of Indigenous peoples has spanned 500-plus years. However, for Canadians, who have been distracted by cover-ups and complicity, the veneer of the benevolent peacemaker narrative has only begun to be challenged. From the beginning of the colonial onslaught, Indigenous people have responded and continually resisted having their ways of life, their cultures, languages, and relationships to the land assaulted in every possible way. Indigenous peoples continue to resist victimization and have overcome overwhelming atrocities at the hands of Canada. In fact, Canada places the onus of responsibility on Indigenous peoples to respond in respectful and strong ways to the violence and serial murders of our people. Every time Canada has offered an apology for murdering Indigenous people, it has been Indigenous peoples who are put in the position of conditionally accepting an apology, participating in the colonial discourse of inquiries and commissions, and taking responsibility for the violence and death of their own people.

As complicit citizens trained by the state, settler Canadians have consciously and unconsciously participated in the legitimation of the state and the murder of Indigenous peoples. Canada's sesquicentennial celebration should mark a new turn toward truth-telling and change. Canadians can do this by letting go of the racism and ignorance that stand in the way of accepting that, as human beings, it is wrong to justify and support the killing of another human being, regardless of colour. Canadians must accept responsibility for their ignorance, whether unintentional or wilful, by exposing the violent underpinning of the narcissistic and pathological Canadian state. If Canadians don't change, Canada's killing spree will continue.

Fundamental to truth-telling is the acknowledgement that Canadians live on stolen Indigenous lands. What Canadians are not aware of, because of the silences in Canadian history, is the fact that Indigenous people were often dispossessed from their lands, via policies of genocide and violence, in order to accommodate settlement by their ancestors. Canadians must support the return of Indigenous lands to Indigenous peoples. Canadians need to see that the modern day land claims process is inherently flawed because it is also a tool of distraction employed by Canada. This distraction is what has allowed the Canadian government to legally rape and murder the land and water for profit. This is most evident in the Alberta Tar Sands, but exists throughout Canada. Canada's arsenal is evident in the pipelines that continue to carry death to the land, waters, and our non-human relatives. Pipelines are the bloodlines of a serial killer. Canadians must wake up and realize that it's no longer just Indigenous lands that Canada is destroying; it is "Canadian" land, and waters, too. Canada's serial killings have become increasingly careless, and its frantic desire for Indigenous land and waters has placed Canadians and their futurity at risk. Canadians have a responsibility to protect Indigenous lands and waters for their future generations. As human beings, we need water to survive, not oil.

Finally, Canadians must refuse to participate in the ongoing violence and murder of Indigenous people. RCMP members, lawyers, court clerks, educators, politicians, farmers, and everyday Canadians must recognize how they are implicated in ongoing gendered violence, racism, and the destruction of the land and waters. Contrary to what Canadians have been led to believe through Canada's narratives, law, and history, Indigenous peoples are not the problem. Indigenous peoples have a problem with the serial killer we call Canada, and the Canadians who support and uphold the ongoing colonial assaults. It is time that Canadians begin to identify, question, and deconstruct Canada's lethal, destructive, and distractive tools that have endorsed the mass murder of Indigenous peoples, and take full responsibility for their shared history by honouring Indigenous self-determination and nationhood.

1. This article is dedicated to the late Alberta Williams and all of the missing and murdered Indigenous Peoples who have been taken from their communities, families, and homelands. We acknowledge the insightful and critical feedback on earlier drafts of this chapter from the editors of this volume as well as Heidi Kiiwetinepinesiik Stark, Corey Snelgrove, Rachel George, Jana-Rae Yerxa, Sarah Boivin, John Carlson, and Jessica Tessier. Any mistakes are our own.
2. For more details on this aspect of Canadian history, see Tasha Hubbard's documentary film *Buffalo Calling* (2014).
3. See for example, Daschuk, James William (2013), *Clearing the Plains: Disease, Politics of Starvation, and the Loss of Aboriginal Life*. Regina: University of Regina Press.
4. Corntassel, Jeff, Chaw-win-is, and T'lakwadzi (2009), "Indigenous Storytelling, Truth-telling, and Community Approaches to Reconciliation," *English Studies in Canada*, 35(1), pp. 137-159.
5. Ningewance, Patricia (1993), *Survival Ojibwe: learning conversational Ojibwe in thirty lessons*, Winnipeg: Maazinaate Press.
6. In conversation with Midewin elder and cultural teacher Dan Thomas (2017).
7. Ibid.
8. Williams, Connie and Marnie Luke (2016), "Who Killed Alberta Williams?" *CBC News*: www.cbc.ca/missingandmurdered/podcast
9. Ibid. Available at: http://www.cbc.ca/missingandmurdered/podcast/ep7transcript
10. The 2014 Royal Canadian Mounted Police (RCMP) report on *Missing and Murdered Indigenous Women* identified 1,181 missing and murdered Indigenous women and girls in Canada between 1970-present. However, these figures continue to increase and, beyond the numbers, the systematic violence against Indigenous women's bodies continues. Lavell-Harvard, D. Memee, and Jennifer Brant, eds. (2016) "Introduction: Forever Loved", *Forever Loved: Exposing the Hidden Crisis of Missing and Murdered Indigenous Women and Girls in Canada*. Ontario: Demeter Press, pp. 1-13.
11. "Serial killer," *The Free Dictionary*. Available at: www.medical-dictionary.thefreedictionary.com/serial+killer
12. Stark, Heidi (2016), "Criminal Empire: the Making of the Savage in a Lawless Land," *Theory and Event*, 19(4): pp. 1-20.
13. Simpson, Audra (2016), "The State is a Man: Theresa Spence, Loretta Saunders and the Gender of Settler Sovereignty," *Theory and Event*, 19(4). Available at: www.muse.jhu.edu/article/633280#f1-text
14. Woolford, Andrew (2009), "Ontological Destruction: Genocide and Canadian Aboriginal Peoples," *Genocide Studies and Prevention: An International Journal*, Vol. 4(1), Article 6. Available at: www.scholarcommons.usf.edu/gsp/vol4/iss1/6
15. Kirmayer, Laurence and Gail Valaskakis (2009), *Healing Traditions: The Mental Health of Aboriginal Peoples in Canada*, Vancouver: UBC Press.
16. Simpson, 2016: www.muse.jhu.edu/article/633280#f1-text
17. Corntassel, Jeff (2012), "Living in a Longer Now: Moving Beyond the State-Centric System," *For Indigenous Minds Only: A Decolonization Handbook*, eds. Waziyatawin and Michael Yellow Bird, Santa Fe: SAR Press. pp. 85-98.

18. Stark, 2016, p. 20.
19. Razack, Sherene (2015), *Dying from Improvement: Inquests and Inquiries into Indigenous Deaths in Custody*. Toronto: University of Toronto Press, p. 12.
20. Wolfe, Patrick (2006), "Settler Colonialism and the Elimination of the Native," *Journal of Genocide Research*, 8 (4), pp. 387-409.
21. Federal Bureau of Investigation Report on "Serial Murder: Multi-Disciplinary Perspectives for Investigators." Available at: www.fbi.gov/stats-services/publications/serial-murder
22. Smith, Hingangaroa G. (2000), "Protecting and respecting Indigenous knowledge," *Reclaiming Indigenous Voice and Vision*, ed. M. Battiste, Vancouver: UBC Press, pp. 209-224.
23. Truth and Reconciliation Commission of Canada. *What we have Learned: Principles of Truth and Reconciliation*: www.myrobust.com/websites/trcinstitution/File/Reports/Principles_English_Web.pdf
24. Ibid.
25. "The Residential Schools System" University of British Columbia, Indigenous Foundations. arts.ubc.ca: www.indigenousfoundations.arts.ubc.ca/home/government-policy/the-residential-school-system.html
26. "Aboriginal children at residential schools often buried in unmarked graves, report reveals," *CTV News*, December 15, 2015: www.ctvnews.ca/canada/aboriginal-children-at-residential-schools-often-buried-in-unmarked-graves-report-reveals-1.2701373
27. Alfred, Taiaiake and Jeff Corntassel (2005), "Being Indigenous: Resurgences Against Contemporary Colonialism," *Government and Opposition*, 40: pp. 597-614.
28. "Sixties Scoop: The Sixties Scoop & Aboriginal Child Welfare," University of British Columbia, Indigenous Foundations.arts.ubc.ca: www.indigenousfoundations.arts.ubc.ca/home/government-policy/sixties-scoop.html
29. Dr. Raven Sinclair, "The 60's Scoop," Origins Canada: Supporting those separated by adoption: www.originscanada.org/aboriginal-resources/the-stolen-generation/
30. There is a current estimate of 27,000 First Nations children in care today. Blackstock, Cindy (2008), "Reconciliation Means Not Saying Sorry Twice: Lessons from Child Welfare in Canada," *From Truth to Reconciliation Transforming the Legacy of Residential Schools*, eds. Marlene Brant Castellano, Linda Archibald, and Mike DeGagné, Ottawa: Aboriginal Healing Foundation, pp. 163-175. Available at: www.speakingmytruth.ca/downloads/AHFvol1/11_Blackstock.pdf
31. Simpson, 2016: www.muse.jhu.edu/article/633280#f1-text
32. "Missing and Murdered Indigenous Women and Girls: Understanding the numbers," Amnesty International: www.amnesty.ca/blog/missing-and-murdered-indigenous-women-and-girls-understanding-the-numbers
33. Ibid.
34. "Missing and Murdered Indigenous Women and Girls," RCMP: www.rcmp-grc.gc.ca/aboriginal-autochtone/mmaw-fada-eng.htm
35. Alfred, Taiaiake (2009), "Colonialism and State Dependency," *Journal of Aboriginal Health*, 5(2), pp. 42-60.
36. Irlbacher-Fox, Stephanie (2009), *Finding Daasha: Self-government, Social Suffering and Aboriginal Policy in Canada*, Vancouver: UBC Press.
37. Memmi, Albert (2013), *The Colonizer and the Colonized*. NY: Routlege Pubishers.
38. Regan, Paulette (2010), *Unsettling the Settler Within: Indian Residential Schools, Truth Telling, and Reconciliation in Canada*, Vancouver: UBC Press. P. 87.
39. Razack, Sherene (2015), *Dying from Improvement: Inquests and Inquiries into Indigenous Deaths in Custody*, Toronto: University of Toronto Press, p. 5.

40. Residential Schools Settlement: Official Court Notice: www.residentialschoolsettlement.ca/english_index.html
41. Indigenous and Northern Affairs Canada, *Common Experience Payments*: www.aadnc-aandc.gc.ca/eng/1100100015594/1100100015595
42. *Statement of Apology to former students of the Indian Residential Schools*, Indigenous and Northern Affairs Canada: www.aadnc-aandc.gc.ca/eng/1100100015644/1100100015649
43. *Renewing the relationship: Key Documents*, Indigenous and Northern Affairs Canada: www.aadnc-aandc.gc.ca/eng/1307458586498/1307458751962; Corntassel, Chaw-win-is, and T'lakwadzi, "Indigenous Storytelling," pp. 141-142.
44. *The Oka Crisis*, Warrior Publications: www.warriorpublications.wordpress.com/?s=oka+crisis
45. Report of the Aboriginal Justice Inquiry: Aboriginal Justice Implementation Commission November 1999: www.ajic.mb.ca/volume.html
46. The Death of Helen Betty Osborne: The Aboriginal Justice Implementation Commission: http://www.ajic.mb.ca/volumeII/chapter1.html
47. "Murdered and missing aboriginal women deserve inquiry, rights group says," *CBC News Politics*, January 12, 2015: www.cbc.ca/news/politics/murdered-and-missing-aboriginal-women-deserve-inquiry-rights-group-says-1.2897707
48. Amnesty International: www.amnesty.ca/blog/missing-and-murdered-indigenous-women-and-girls-understanding-the-numbers
49. Laboucan-Massimo, Melina and Christa Big Canoe, "Missing and murdered: What it will take for Indigenous women to feel safe?" *CBC News Indigenous*, March 18, 2015: www.cbc.ca/news/indigenous/missing-and-murdered-what-it-will-take-for-indigenous-women-to-feel-safe-1.2977136
50. *CBC News Politics*: www.cbc.ca/news/politics/murdered-and-missing-aboriginal-women-deserve-inquiry-rights-group-says-1.2897707
51. "Those that take us away: Abusive Policing and Failures in Protection of Indigenous Women and Girls in Northern British Columbia, Canada," www.hrw.org/report/2013/02/13/those-who-take-us-away/abusive-policing-and-failures-protection-indigenous-women
52. Dhillon, Jaskiran K. (2015), "Indigenous girls and the violence of settler colonial policing," *Decolonization: Indigeneity, Education & Society* Vol. 4(2), pp. 1-31.
53. Kuokkanen, Rauna (2015), "Gendered Violence and Politics in Indigenous Communities," *International Feminist Journal of Politics*, 17:2, pp. 271-288.
54. "Starlight Tours Synthesis and Commentary," Police Evidence: Articles and Commentary on Deviance and Accountability in Policing: www.policedeviance.wordpress.com/category/starlight-tours/
55. Ibid.
56. "Ten Years Later: the Neil Stonechild Inquiry's effect on Saskatoon," *CTV News* Saskatchewan, October 24, 2014: www.saskatoon.ctvnews.ca/ten-years-later-the-neil-stonechild-inquiry-s-affect-on-saskatoon-1.2070628
57. "The night Colten Boushie died: What family and police files say about his last day, and what came after," *Globe and Mail*: www.theglobeandmail.com/news/national/colten-boushie/article32451940/
58. "RCMP accused of victim blaming after fatal shooting of First Nations man Colten Boushie," Inquisitor: News worth sharing, August 14, 2016: www.inquisitr.com/3418798/rcmp-accused-of-victim-blaming-after-fatal-shooting-of-first-nations-man-colten-boushie/
59. "'Our peoples are not equal': First Nations say RCMP 'blamed the victim' of fatal on-farm shooting," *National Post*, August 14, 2016. www.news.nationalpost.com/news/canada/our-peoples-are-not-equal-first-nations-say-rcmp-blamed-the-victim-of-fatal-on-farm-shooting

60. "Why one Saskatchewan man says farmers need firearms," CBC Radio: www.cbc.ca/radio/outintheopen/what-does-colten-boushie-say-about-us-1.3923927/why-one-saskatchewan-man-says-farmers-need-firearms-1.3923963
61. Anaya, James S. (2014), *The Situation of Indigenous Peoples in Canada*, United Nations General Assembly: www.unsr.jamesanaya.org/country-reports/the-situation-of-indigenous-peoples-in-canada.

Her

Jana-Rae Yerxa

Author's Note: The ongoing colonial violence that disproportionately affects Indigenous women in Canada is not accidental. Canada, in its current form, remains a settler colonial state that requires this violence in order to survive. With Canada's upcoming 150th anniversary, it is imperative that we ask ourselves: If we are celebrating, what exactly are we celebrating?

Sometimes all you know is that something feels terribly wrong despite the world trying to convince you otherwise. You don't know what you need in those moments other than for things to stop. But how do you make things stop? What if you can't? How do you not only survive, but keep living?

The Rolling Stones have a famous song that goes, "You can't always get what you want / But if you try sometimes well you might find / You get what you need." Recently, in those moments when I desperately want things to stop but can't despite my best efforts, is when I began to see Her.

The lyrics remind me of Her because I imagine all the neat and tidy ways I had hoped for things to play out in those moments. Neat and tidy is code-speak for "easy," but we both know there is nothing easy about living in this colonial world while being an Indigenous woman. Or at least, we should know that by now. So back to my neat and tidy imaginings. In my mind, it usually went something like this: I would build what I thought was at least somewhat of a meaningful relationship; or if this was a new encounter I would still engage. Respectfully, of course, like my grandparents taught me. My grandpa always says, "Be strong. Not hard." I try to remember his advice in the face of adversity. So I speak up. I listen. I do my best to make sense. I include facts to accommodate a logical argument. A sound, logical argument, supported with facts, which make sense, should be enough to shut things down when things are not making sense, right? Wrong.

Unfortunately, that is not how this world works—especially for this Anishinaabe Kwe. Anyways, rather than things stopping all neat and tidy, as I had hoped for, I got Her instead, like Mick Jagger sang about.

She would come at the most unexpected times. At first I was scared to tell anyone about Her because, quite honestly, I didn't know what to think of Her myself. But I will tell you about my encounters and see what you make of it.

I remember the first time I saw Her, the memory still fresh, ever impaled into me. I was sitting in a crowd of white. Not the plain Gap-plaid-shirt-wearing kind of white. No. This crowd was fancy, elite white. The kind of white that could have had guest starring roles in *The Devil Wears Prada*, that would have made Meryl Streep proud. As colonialism often sets the stage, there was a white man talking confidently at the front of the room . . . again. This time, the white man was speaking about global humanitarian efforts regarding black and brown bodies. Women's bodies, specifically.

Oh, white, c'mon. How come you think you are so knowledgeable about everything and everyone, yet often times remain clueless about yourself?

I digress. The white man at the podium was speaking about the sexual violence black and brown women were enduring on a global scale. He, as well the rest of us, was gathered on the traditional lands of the Wendat people. Throughout his discussion on sexual violence against racialized women, he made no mention of the violence that we, as Indigenous women, experience right here in our homelands. Which he is still living on. Homelands that we are still living on despite white's various attempts to change this. No mention of the thousands of Indigenous women, girls, and Two Spirit people that continue to be murdered and go missing in this country. None. Zero. Zilch. His focus, and probably the majority of the room's focus, was on the atrocities happening far, far away in lands many of us have never been to. Atrocities committed by other black and brown bodies to other black and brown women. You know, atrocities they can easily detach from. How convenient.

Maybe this is why She appeared.

She wasn't happy with this set up. The lies. The façade of care, and extended only to atrocities happening in some faraway place. The erasure of Her and Her loved ones. The normalization of violence that colonialism demands we endure, as if our lives do not matter.

Okay, maybe unhappy is an understatement.

What I understand now, but didn't then, was that She was there to disrupt this façade with her presence.

Her body came swinging down from the beams. Knocking the white man off centre stage. She hung there. Her body unsettled, which unsettled everyone else's, including my own. I still get shivers when I think about that day. Her long black hair flowed due to the speed at which She dropped. She dangled back and forth, then stabilized above the platform where the white man once stood.

It took me a while before I realized She was hanging by a noose around her neck. Yet, She was not dead. No, not at all.

Am I the only one in the room who realizes She is performing? Art imitating life?!

I could tell She was enjoying Her performance. So was I. She carried with Her an important message.

The crowd, at this point, were no longer enjoying themselves. Their calm, smiling demeanours replaced with horror. Chaos blanketed the banquet hall. The table I was sitting at, once filled with smiling faces, had been replaced with panicked people who'd begun to flee. They wore disgust on their faces while they covered their mouths, pointing to the stage where She was hanging. It was like they wanted assurance from one another that they were seeing correctly and at the same time, intrinsically, silently communicating a collective response. They were shocked by the vulgarity of what appeared to them to be a dead Indian woman's body, hanging centre stage. As gasps and screams filled the room, I wondered to myself, calmly, oddly enough, why everyone was shocked by the presence of what appeared to be a dead Indian woman's body.

This is what their society demands in order to exist. Indigenous death.

This was the point She was trying to get across while they were all dressed up, congratulating one another, gathering to sympathize with violence happening someplace else, ignoring the violence taking place right here, underneath their noses.

Some left, running out so they did not have to look at Her. Others tended to the white man She'd knocked off the stage with Her body. Yet no one went to Her.

She did not care. She knew exactly what She was doing. What She was there for. What her message was. "Colonizers, colonialism kills!" Her body screamed. A message my own body knows all too well. A reminder that comes in the form of anxiety and exhaustion.

Even in that room, although the smiles and fancy clothes attempted to mask the violence, colonialism still kills. This She knows . . .

The next thing I recall was being confused. She was gone. I didn't know why She had left or where She went. The white man, unfortunately, was back at centre stage. Things had calmed down tremendously following the flurry of Her entrance, but I don't know how. Fancy, elite whites were back to their smiling selves while giving their humanitarian a standing ovation. I was just relieved that I no longer had to listen to him.

Yes, that was the first time I had seen Her. It was a while before the next visit.

Again I found myself in a room full of white. I was in a familiar, frustrating setting where we, Indigenous women, were the subject matter. *Ignorant, misinformed opinions masquerading as truth*, I was thinking. Before She arrived, I'd had a lengthy internal dialogue that lasted a matter of seconds. My own well-versed script: *Do I speak up? Do I have the energy? Is it worth it? Am I wasting my time? What will happen if I let them walk away uninterrupted?*

So I spoke up. I spoke back. I spoke hard. No one listened. Not more than they listened to themselves anyways. *Not the first time*, I thought, followed by my coping mechanism: "it's not a big deal."

All of a sudden, there She was. But this time She was right next to me. Her body, like before, flowed back and forth; the noose was still around Her neck. She was laughing. Perhaps at how silly they all were. Or maybe She was laughing at me. Or maybe all of us. Them, thinking they know us and what we need. Me, lying to myself that it doesn't hurt.

No one else knew She was there, which was okay because I was no longer engaged in the discussion with white. White didn't notice that I had checked out of our conversation, either. It was obviously a conversation neither of us wanted to engage in. I was fixated on Her. When Her body settled from swinging, She began twirling her thumbs like She was bored of this tired routine.

I got Her message. Colonialism is a big deal, and despite the constant violence it brings our way, in various forms, we are not what happens to us. We are so much more. She reminded me to trust myself even when I think I am the only one in the room. But this time, I am not. She is with me.

She stopped twirling her thumbs and looked up at me. A playful look. A comforting look. "Let's get out of here," She winked. She knew I understood the reason for Her visit.

But how She knew I needed Her is something I still wonder. *Is She me? Am I Her?*

She scares me, but I do not scare Her. I admire her clarity. Her bravery. Her humour. Her transparency. Her tenacity. Especially Her presence. She helps me escape by providing me with relief in much-needed moments.

She is my saving grace.

I wonder when I will see Her again. Will she be wearing a noose? Will white pay attention to Her beyond their own shock? And if they do, what, if anything at all, will they do? In the meantime, I'm glad She came and made it all stop in Her own way. I hope She keeps coming.

Because It's 1951
The Non-History of First Nations Female Band Suffrage and Leadership[1]

Mary Jane Logan McCallum and Shelisa Klassen

Introduction

In the last few years, many historians in Canada, ourselves included, have been strongly encouraged to reflect on 150 years of the Canadian nation-state, and 100 years of women's suffrage in Canada. In doing so, one cannot help but be struck by the absence of public celebrations and commemorations honouring the history of Indigenous women, in formal positions in band and other governments. In fact, it is difficult to find any discussion at all on the history of Indigenous women voting in Canada. What little does exist focuses on white suffragists' imperialist exclusion of Indigenous women—from their campaign and studies of Indigenous women's absence and underrepresentation at polls and in elected positions to their "new" presence as of late.[2] There is some work that discusses Indigenous women's roles in family and community governance and politics; however, it fails to take into consideration change over time and the very specific historical context of band governance in the twentieth century. Unlike general women's suffrage in Canada, First Nations women's right to vote has not been the subject of frequent and lengthy public debate, or the result of sustained collective effort to "win" the vote. In fact, many of the first women nominated to run in the band elections of the early 1950s were surprised when they found out they could. Thus, it seems that for Indigenous women, the exclusion from and extension of suffrage is neither a key frame of historical inquiry nor a central field of activity in which Indigenous women's social and political roles have been defined and challenged. But this is not the end of the story.

As Joyce Green and others have argued, key to the story of Indigenous women's politics is the *Indian Act*.[3] The *Act* represents a consolidation of laws and policies that define and apply to First Nations people in Canada. It regulates many important aspects of our lives, from birth to death. Imbedded in the *Indian Act* are nineteenth-century Victorian and imperialist aspirations for control over Indigenous lands and people. Gender—and more specifically the subordination of Indian women in law—is key to the *Act*; even though the *Act* has been amended many times since 1876, this remains true. For example, the *Indian Act* defined what an "Indian" was, and this is important because it set out the guidelines in terms of eligibility for treaty rights, participation in government, and access to land and resources; the Act defined Indian in decidedly exclusionary patrilineal terms.

The *Indian Act* defined a system of Indian governance that abolished traditional governing forms and replaced them with a male-only elective system with limited powers, and which operated largely under the control of the local Indian agent. Further, it outlined a set of wide-ranging regulations, disabilities, and penalties that applied to Indians. For example, sections of the *Indian Act* deemed traditional ceremonies illegal, banned consumption of liquor, dealt with agriculture and mining, the management of Indian funds, and the surrender of Indian land. The *Indian Act* also described a process of enfranchisement, or the means by which Indians could relinquish their rights and become voting Canadian citizens. Those who wanted to become full Canadian citizens had to renounce Indian status and would receive a part of the reserve as private property. The process involved separating Indian land into allotments, and severing band members from communities. Until 1960, the *Indian Act* allowed only First Nations people to join the national community as enfranchised, assimilated individuals.

Perhaps it is not surprising then that the *Indian Act* plays a vital part of the story of First Nations women's band franchise. As part of the 1951 *Indian Act* revisions, the band governance system was altered to allow First Nations women, who were 21 or older, to run for positions of chief and counsellor, and to vote in band elections. Women's initial exclusion from the *Indian Act* band system was articulated first in the *Gradual Enfranchisement Act* of 1869,[4] and carried through to the *Indian Act* of 1876:

> Councils and Chiefs:
> 61. At the election of a chief or chiefs . . . those entitled to vote at the council or meeting thereof shall be the male members of the band of the full age of twenty-one years.[5]

In the 1951 version of the *Indian Act*, the word "male" was simply dropped from the text. As Cora Voyageur notes in her study of women chiefs, the amendment "did not specifically mention the inclusion of women in reserve politics, but did not exclude them either. The 1951 amended legislation read as follows: Section 76 (1) A member of a band who is of the full age of twenty-one years and is ordinarily resident on the reserve is qualified to vote for a person nominated to be chief of the band, and . . . vote for persons nominated as councillors."[6]

By simply removing the word male, the doors were opened to a generation of women leaders. In March 1953, a report by the Department of Citizenship and Immigration on its Indian Affairs Branch proclaimed "Indian women played an increasingly active role in band affairs, 21 having been elected to the office of chief or councillor since the new Act came into operation in September 1951."[7] In 1958, feminist Florence Bird remarked that the rate of women's elections to formal leadership positions in bands surpassed that of other jurisdictions.[8] In 1960, 66 women councillors and seven women chiefs held office under the elective system. An additional eight women held office under the band custom system, which approximated the elected system but allowed for bands to choose their chiefs and councillors according to their own custom, rather than follow the rule that allowed for only one chief per band and one councillor for every 100 members.[9] Thus, immediately following the extension of the band franchise to women, women were elected as chiefs and councillors. This inspires closer examination of the 1951 changes and the immediate aftermath, including the representation of early women band leaders in Canada.

In this essay, we hope to complicate women's historical narrative of suffrage in Canada by exploring the circumstances surrounding the extension of the band franchise to women. We use Canadian media as a key resource—what few stories covered this shift to political participation. We found that from 1951 to 1961, reporting on Indigenous women chiefs was brief, unsophisticated, and lacked an understanding of the context of band politics. This is perhaps not surprising, as the newspapers we consulted (with the exception of the *Indian News* and the *Indian Record*) were not written with a First Nations audience in mind—or even a mixed audience.[10] Moreover, it is also not surprising that, as a racialized minority, Indigenous women politicians continue to be misrepresented in media.[11] What we were most struck by, however, was the real lack of attention to the important changes to the *Indian Act* in 1951, and the subsequent inclusion of First Nations women as band election voters and candidates.

The significant numbers of women who were ready and prepared to take on formal band leadership positions demonstrated the failure of the *Indian Act*, which was intended to impose a patriarchal system of band governance. Women were not intended to be equal participants in band governance, and so we expected that this change would have sparked some discussion. This "failure" of the original intent of the *Indian Act* was not officially acknowledged or discussed in any of the newspapers, and instead we can read these stories as important evidence of resistance against the *Indian Act*, and of survival. The women chiefs, although they do not seem to be engaged in suffrage movements prior to 1951, immediately seized the opportunity for leadership, and continued the work many of them were already doing informally within their communities.

First Nations Women and Voting in Canada: Why 1951?

Studies about First Nations people and voting in Canada have tended to approach the topic using deficit models, and to focus on federal and provincial elections; for example: Why *won't* First Nations people vote in federal or provincial elections? Why are there not more First Nations people in leadership roles as MPs, MPPs, and MLAs? How can they be encouraged to vote and to take leadership roles in this vacuum of Canadian politics? Often these questions are framed as a sort of salve to a serious problem of Canadian democracy. As explained by Anna Hunter, the "lack of representation of Aboriginal Peoples in formal political processes signifies such a high degree of political alienation that it threatens the legitimacy of the Canadian democratic system."[12] Responses to these questions have varied, but tend to focus on two main factors. First, some First Nations people, like Pamela Palmater, choose not to vote because it flies in the face of Indigenous sovereignty, jurisdiction, and right of self-determination.[13] Rather, they strive to deal with the Federal Government as equals, on a nation-to-nation basis, and see their primary relation being with the federal Crown as opposed to the provinces. Second, First Nations have a long history with the "conditional franchise," as outlined in the enfranchisement clauses of the *Indian Act*. As mentioned, the condition of franchise was the forfeiting of legal status as First Nations, treaty rights, and band membership. Voting was historically associated with a policy of assimilation, and legal and cultural termination, and this remained a serious concern for First Nations people even after 1960, when First Nations women and men were granted the unconditional franchise to vote in Canadian elections.

While such questions abound regarding First Nations and their history of voting in federal and provincial elections, there is relative silence about the band franchise and its gendered history. Most discussions of First Nations women and the band franchise merely mention the shift in 1951 without exploring what led up to it. Our search for some clues to the question of why the franchise was opened to women in 1951 led to some fairly confusing answers. One unnamed "official" at Indian Affairs suggested that this new authority "had its beginning in 1945 . . . when the Federal Government first granted the Indians family allowance cheques which were made payable to the women. Over the objections of the men, the Government held firm."[14] This seems a bit of a stretch. Community women's organizations like the Homemakers' Clubs already played roles in elections, including counting ballots and working on elections. Women may also have performed roles in voting, perhaps even heavily influencing a husband's, son's, or brother's ballot. There is certainly evidence that women also wrote letters of complaint about particular band leaders, and sometimes even petitioned for their removal.[15]

If this was the case in some places, it clearly went against the intentions of the *Indian Act* governance system, which, like the legislation itself, clearly gendered Indians as male. Moreover, the *Indian Act* was patriarchal and saw status as inherited and passed on by men alone. Children and women, in parentage and marriage, took the identity of the dominant, determining male. "By the stroke of a pen," Winona Stevenson and Ann McGrath argued, "Indian women and their children could be denied their birth right as tribal members depending on whom they married."[16] Thus, Indian women "marrying-out" lost their status, and non-Indigenous women who married an Indian man gained status, reserve residence, and rights, and so too did their children. Demographically and culturally, the loss of many Native women and their children, grandchildren, and great grandchildren, who are no longer counted as Indian, is incalculable, and many argue that it is tantamount to genocide. On Canada's 150th year, let's consider what this has meant for Indigenous survival.[17]

The Act thus imposed the idea that, like Europeans, First Nations women and their children should be subject to their fathers and husbands. The 1951 version of the *Indian Act* was even more stringent, making women who married non-status men completely separate from the band, by legally removing their band membership and treaty rights. This European system of patrilineage seriously undermined the matrilineal-descent rule of many First Nations that were organized socially and politically by female heads of families. Clan membership, roles, and responsibilities were traditionally inherited from mothers, and thus the governance provisions in the *Indian Act* seriously disrupted traditional kinship systems, matrilineal descent patterns, and matrilocal residency patterns. In light of this, the band franchise is intimately connected to what Martin Cannon calls the "major event" in First Nations history—when paternity became the "ordinary way of doing things."[18] Navajo historian Jennifer Denetdale argues that in this context, tribal leadership comes to seem appropriately, even "traditionally" male; consequently, women are discouraged from equal political participation in reserve government.[19]

While it does not seem like there was a distinct criticism of gender discrimination in the *Indian Act* before 1951, there was increased interest on the part of the Federal Government in revisiting it, due in part to the growing population of First Nations (rather than the predicted decline), and the "robust Indigenous participation in the war effort and increased attention to human rights globally."[20] In 1946, Prime Minister William Lyon Mackenzie King called for a Special Joint Committee to examine the *Indian Act*, and to propose changes to the Act and its administration.[21] Enfranchisement—or full citizenship rights (including voting)—was a matter of special interest for the joint committee, and committee members returned often to the question of whether First Nations "wanted the vote." It is unclear whether the committee had a sustained interest in voting rights for women in band elections, although it appears to be one of the questions asked as part of an early survey undertaken by the Committee in 1946. Women's right to vote in band elections appeared only sporadically within the minutes of the committee, and so it is very hard to tell if that committee had a hand in the amendment. What is clear is that once the legislation was changed, women were immediately elected into leadership positions in some communities, which suggests that it was a change people were ready for.

While the 1951 amendment happened without much publicity, First Nations women immediately became formally active in the political leadership of their communities. We were surprised that, even in the first years of the band franchise when, theoretically, the band electorate doubled, First Nations women's desire for political participation and the efforts to achieve it are rarely mentioned. Like Liberal Prime Minister Justin Trudeau's glib justification for forming a gender-balanced cabinet after his election ("Because it's 2015"), it seems women's band suffrage was something whose time had come—simply because it was 1951.

Women's Band Suffrage—Upbeat and Back Page

Canadian newspapers did not reflect much on the formal introduction of women's suffrage to First Nations band governance; when they did cover it, women's voting rights were buried in the "real" story, which was the introduction of an amended *Indian Act*. For example, on January 2, 1952, the *Lethbridge Herald* ran a short article about the changes to how chiefs and councillors would be chosen. This article included comment by G.H. Gooderham, the regional supervisor of Indian agencies, that "under the proposed new system a chief's term will last for two years rather than for the remainder of his life. Women will also be allowed to vote if the suggested change is approved."[22] The remainder of the article discussed how younger, educated men wanted to take leadership away from the older generation to keep with the changing times. Women were not mentioned again, and every reference to chiefs or leadership used masculine pronouns. While women were expected to be voters, it appeared that no one expected that they would ever run for leadership.

Over the next two years, even with the appearance of a significant number of women in roles as formal band politicians, women involved in band elections make only brief appearances in mainstream newspapers.[23] Later, in the 1950s, more of these stories were covered in Canadian newspapers, albeit briefly and peripherally. For example, in 1959, the *Ottawa Journal* published a short paragraph headed simply "Women Chiefs," under a column called "Side Lights," beside an article entitled "Canadians are Salad Conscious," and above "Short bits from Hansard." The column reads, "Two more Indian bands have elected women as their chiefs—another sign that more women are playing an effective part in community life . . . Fifty-eight women are also councillors, a major step forward considering Indian women were not even allowed to vote before 1951."[24] Articles on women chiefs frequently (but not always) appeared in back pages, or on the "woman's page," where stories deemed to be of interest to women appeared. For example, an article on Chief Elsie Knott entitled "Has Special Recipe For Taking Care of Husbands," appeared on the Women's World page of the *Lethbridge Herald* in June 1959, beside the daily recipe and a tome about "manners." The article read, "Mrs. Elsie Knott, 36, stern ruler of about 500 persons, has a special recipe for taking care of husbands. 'Some husbands are entirely spoiled by mishandling,' she advises, 'and so are not tender and good. Some women keep them constantly in hot water, others put them in a stew or keep them in a pickle . . . no husband will be tender

"Has Special Recipe For Taking Care of Husbands," *Lethbridge Herald*, 11 June 1959, p 18.

managed this way, but they are delicious when properly treated.'" This is followed by, "Men Approve: And according to the men of Curve lake, Mrs. Knott is as fine a chief and a cook as they have ever had." "Elsie is a good chief," one of the reserve men says. "She really keeps us in line. Like a woman she's always changing something, but it's always for the better."[25]

In striking contrast, at around the same time, a photo of Chief Elsie Knott in a headdress appeared at the top of page one of the *Medicine Hat News*, under the title "Indian Ruler." It was given the following description: "Mrs. Elsie Knott, 36-year-old chief of the Curve Lake Ojibway Reserve 23 miles from Peterborough, Ont., is a busy lady. She arises at 3:30 am each day to handle her many duties— which include a full-time job, a family of three, head of the reserve's Sunday School and chief of the tribe. Her job, though, keeps her feeling young, she says and she enjoys every minute of it."[26]

Part of what makes this piece so striking is that it sits between three international news stories, and on the front page of the paper. The only other image on the page was of striking ironworkers in Vancouver. It seems that, at least in

"Indian Ruler," *Medicine Hat News*, June 24, 1959, p 1.

this paper, Knott's leadership was a going interest, even as far away as Medicine Hat and Lethbridge.

Where there was media coverage about women chiefs, the story was often premised on their being the "first." These articles usually are insufferably upbeat and positive, and inevitably never mention gender and racial discrimination, or the political, social, and economic inequalities women faced on reserves, and in Canada at large. Media analysts have shown that "unusualness" is a common frame for stories about Native people,[27] and in this context, "firsts" seem to point to the prior, supposed backwardness of Indigenous communities, and that women's leadership was a matter of these communities modernizing. Indigenous traditions of female autonomy and leadership, of course, are effectively erased; in only one article did we read a reference to histories of First Nations women leadership.

Ironically, there were actually a number of claims to being the first woman Chief, as a result of the significant number of women elected in the years 1952 to 1954. Elsie Knott from Curve Lake First Nation, Arletta Silver from Chippewa of the Thames First Nation, Grace Vickers from the Kitkatla Band in British Columbia, Gwen O'Soup from the Key Band near Norquay in Saskatchewan, and Jessie Lumm from the Hazelton Band in the Babine Agency in British Columbia, were all hailed as such in local media. Chief Elsie Knott and Chief Arletta Silver tend to be recognized as the first women chiefs in Canada; however, articles were not consistent on this, and local, regional, and provincially specific titles were contested and corrected on several occasions. For example, the *Indian Record* reported a false claim in the early 1950s: "Along with Mrs. Helen Hunt of Fort Rupert, near Port Hardy, Mrs. Grace Vickers of Kitkatla were elected prior to Chief Gwen O'Soup, who had a prior claim to being 'the first woman in Canada to be elected chief of an Indian tribe.'"[28]

"Chief Miss": First Nations Women, Gender, and Band Governance in Canadian Media

Using newspapers to tell the story of elected women chiefs can present some problems, as Mark Cronlund Anderson and Carmen L. Robertson point out in *Seeing Red: A History of Natives in Canadian Newspapers*. They write, "[n]ewspapers in Canada have long imagined Aboriginal women within the stereotypical binary of the Indian princess/Indian 'squaw,'" and this binary extended beyond newspapers and into popular culture, such as books and film.[29] Woman chiefs, as elected leaders in a role perceived as traditionally male, were presented in newspapers in distinctly gendered and racialized ways as "modern" Indian women. The information the newspapers chose to include about each of the women demonstrates an effort to place them into gendered categories similar to the "Indian princess." Anderson and Robertson write that the "princess image evokes a hopeful yearning for assimilation," and "the passivity of the princess renders a malleable construct not just unthreatening but sexually attractive as a paternalistic and patriarchal construction."[30] A closer examination of newspaper articles about women chiefs demonstrates that their physical appearance and familial status were frequently the focus of articles, establishing them in connection with their fathers, husbands, and children.

Articles about women chiefs in Canadian newspapers often tended to portray women chiefs in terms of their adoption of a "modern way of life." These Indian "new women"[31] were described in terms of conventional notions of beauty; their educational background and employment experience were usually mentioned, and their familiarity with the world outside the reserve was often stressed. Their work on reserves was usually depicted by their involvement with school boards, homemaker associations, and church groups, and was described in a way that implied cooperation with and approval of the local Indian agent. This type of coverage fully established these women as cooperative, even conforming, and as well-meaning family women trying to improve social and economic conditions in their communities.[32]

This does not mean that these women chiefs did not protest or assert themselves. In fact, they often ran their own businesses and started organizations to give their communities more autonomy and make them less reliant on the government, as in the case of Chief Flora Tabobondung of Parry Island First Nation, who opened and managed "Canada's first Indian marina" several years after becoming chief.[33] Likewise, they also protested against the government and inequality, as demonstrated by Chief Theresa Gadwa of Kehewin First Nation, who joined band members in protest when a baby died after being refused treatment at the nearby hospital. Chief Gadwa is quoted as saying, "We are human beings, not dogs."[34] However, both of these incidents occurred in the years after the first women were elected, and the initial coverage of their elections, where it existed, described them in much more passive terms.

Women chiefs were reported as having various levels of experience before becoming chiefs, and it was also recorded if, and how many, men they defeated. Gwen O'Soup was the youngest to be elected in 1954 at only 25 years old. The *Indian News* praised her as the "first woman to be elected head of any band in the three prairie provinces."[35] The newspaper also reported that "Mrs. O'Soup [...] has five children [and] always has taken a keen interest in band affairs."[36] The newspaper also mentioned that she started a Homemakers' Club as one of her first acts in office. In reporting this election, the *Winnipeg Free Press* wrote, "For the first time in Saskatchewan and possibly in Canada, a woman has been elected chief of an Indian reserve." The writer noted Chief O'Soup was "fairly young and very smart," and had defeated "three men."[37]

The history of Indian Homemakers' Clubs is a complicated one. The clubs originated in Saskatchewan in 1937, the brainchild of Dr. Thomas Robertson, Inspector of Indian Agencies for that province.[38] While initially the clubs began as organized sewing circles intended to further the interest in running appropriately "domestic" households, it did not take long for these meetings to turn political. Aroha Harris and Mary Jane Logan McCallum write that:

> Club and League women recognized and even respected state expectations, yet reworked state goals to make their own. They creatively navigated the tensions that existed between state expectations and the women's aspirations for themselves, their families and communities. They used the organizations to enter the public sphere and engage with what they saw as the most important and relevant Indigenous political and community issues of the mid-twentieth century.[39]

While the "federal mandate for the Clubs was to further the goals of assimilation, integration, and citizenship," the members regularly used their meetings to discuss policies and ways to improve their communities, as well as to preserve and pass on traditional skills.[40] While all the labour (including charity drives, organizing guest speakers, and community events) was voluntary, and the clubs were separate from the Department of Indian Affairs, "the Welfare and Training Service Branch collected information about them and recorded it alongside other branch activities."[41] With this increasingly political focus of the clubs in the postwar years, it is unsurprising that so many of the first generation of women chiefs had a history of running Indian Homemakers' Clubs, or quickly set them up after taking office. These women-centred spaces, though not officially political, often acted as informal local governments, administering financial aid as well as offering educational training, such as home nursing and first aid courses. The clubs also provided services such as home visitations for those who were sick, raising funds for teams and music bands, and caring for reserve cemeteries.[42] Essentially, prior to the *Indian Act* amendments in 1951 (and continuing after), Indian Homemakers' Clubs facilitated women's involvement in community governance, despite their limited opportunities for any official action.

Arletta Silver had a different path to becoming chief, as she was unexpectedly elected Chief of the Chippewa of the Thames First Nation during a 1952 by-election after her husband, Clarence Silver, had become too ill to carry on in the position. The *Lethbridge Herald* covered Silver's election with the claim that she was the "only woman Indian chief." After "edging out her male opponent" at the by-election, she planned to run again the following year. The paper presented the news of the election in gendered and racialized terms, writing that "the Chippewa tribe will put on election war-paint," and that "Chief Arletta Silver runs the tribal councils like a homemakers [sic] club, keeps the boys down to business and has well-defined views about most things." Silver's previous involvement as the supervisor of four Homemakers' Clubs was also included. In this article, once again surprise was expressed that women would participate so fully in politics. The article read, "When the Canadian government gave the Indian women their franchise under the revised Indian Act, such whole-hearted acceptance of the vote and the power to sit on Indian councils wasn't expected."[43] It would be almost 70 years before another woman would be elected chief at Chippewa of the Thames.[44]

Grace Vickers represents a different side of the women who were elected chiefs. Vickers was elected the chief of the Kitkatla Band at the age of 36, a white woman who "became a member of the band when she married Mr. Arthur Vickers." According to the *Indian News*, Vickers moved to the community after graduating from Three Hills Bible College in Alberta, and became a teacher at the Kitkatla Day School. She worked in the community in various roles both before and after her marriage, and the newspaper reported, "her husband is, like all this band, a salmon fisherman. They have four children." Her efficient leadership was credited for the success of many band programs, and when she was elected in 1952, "she was the sole choice of her people."[45] There was no further discussion about this seemingly rare occasion of a woman who had married into Indian status becoming chief; in fact, Vickers was not alone in this circumstance. Mrs. Genevieve Mussell, another "white woman" elected chief of an Indian band, was named Chief of the Skwah Band at Chilliwack Landing by acclamation in 1959. "I am native by marriage," she explained to the *Vancouver Province* reporter. Initially when she got married, she found herself with different rights and restrictions than she had prior to marriage, because "[w]hen she married William Mussell in 1937, her life was to be governed by the Indian Act." The "38-year-old mother of six" hoped to "give" her husband's people "some incentive to help themselves . . . [and] do something to help them lose their feeling of inferiority, so they can get ahead."[46]

Of course, Grace Vickers and Genevieve Mussell were not the only women to "become" Indian, as defined in the *Indian Act*, by marriage to an Indian man. In fact, this was, until 1985, legislated that wives of Indians who were not already legal Indians themselves became Indian by law through marriage. These women therefore became subject to restrictions of the *Indian Act*, which did not apply to them prior to their marriage or to other women in Canada. In a 1951 *MacLean's* article, Anne Rosemary Paudash, an English war bride who immigrated to Canada and "married an Indian" from Rice Lake, commented:

> I soon found out that I not only couldn't drink [alcohol], I couldn't vote—all because I'd married a Treaty Indian; that is, an Indian who remained on a reservation and accepted the privileges of the Indian Act. The first time I got ready to go out and vote [in a Canadian election] I was told by my new friends on the reserve that I couldn't. I threatened to do everything but call out the British Navy. But it didn't do any good. The only vote I have is for the chief and councillors of our band, whom the Indians elect every three years.

Paudash knew that it was possible for her husband to enfranchise, and thus become "an ordinary Canadian citizen." She tried to get her husband, a welder with Canadian General Electric in Peterborough, to do it instead of doing everything "the hard way," but as this would "mean he would have to leave the reserve and . . . give up the home he had inherited from his parents and leave the place of his birth,"[47] he refused.

Elsie Knott's background and road to leadership is far more typical of this first generation of women chiefs. She had grown up in the community, and was involved in Sunday schools and drove the reserve school bus. She was in charge of the local Cubs, Scouts, and Guide groups, and had three teenage children. Her husband was a band councillor, both before she was elected chief and afterwards.[48] Elsie Knott was credited as "Canada's only woman Indian chief" in an article in the *Indian News*, from October 1958. At the time, she was serving her third term as chief, and the article stated that she was "one of 70 women who are serving on band councils, indicative of the changing positions of women in Indian society."[49] She was first elected in 1954, at the age of 33.[50] The *Indian News* also briefly mentioned that the Norway House Band had elected five women to its twelve-member council, which was "a record so far among Indian reserves."[51]

The *Indian News* ran an issue in December 1960 in which the front page featured the headline "Indian Women of Today." The majority of the stories were centred on the achievements of women. Naturally, this included a discussion of women engaged in formal politics, as well as in paid labour[52] and voluntary community programs such as Homemakers' Clubs, health committees, and school boards. The section about women chiefs presented short profiles of ten of the eleven chiefs in office at the time; the 66 women serving as band councillors were mentioned, but not by name.[53] These profiles outlined the educational background of the women chiefs, as well as their volunteer involvement and their family life. Notably, the women were are not referred to by their title, as "chief," but rather as "Mrs. _____." A December issue of the *Globe and Mail* covered the twelve women chiefs in office at the very end of the year. Of these, six were in BC bands and four were from Ontario.

Chief Jessie Watts, like many other women chiefs, was not the first chief in her family. Her father had also been chief of the Opetchesaht Band in British Columbia. Her profile also said, "under the former tribal system of election, her grandmother led the band."[54] A different article, published in the *Ottawa Journal*, stated that she was the "attractive 34-year-old daughter and sister of chiefs."[55] For

Chief Jessie Watts, the role of chief was part of her family heritage for both men and women, as her brother, father, and grandmother had all previously held that position under the tribal system of election.[56]

The majority of even the shortest news pieces that discuss women chiefs of the period take time and space to discuss their roles as wives and mothers, as well as their community involvement. In these instances, we are reminded that women at this time were often defined by their men, and rated by their own and their men's achievements in endeavours perceived as non-Indigenous. Women chiefs' marital status was also mentioned. For example, Chief Louise Underwood (called "Chief Miss"), elected by the Cowichan Indian Band in 1960, was introduced as the "first unmarried woman elected chief of a B.C. band."[57] Chief Amelia Wani, from the Gull Bay Band, was also an exception to the norm, as she never married or had children of her own. However, to establish her maternal side, the article mentioned that, "Miss Wani looks after her home, takes care of her aged mother and a child who is not a member of her family."[58] Her election, Wani stated, "came as a big surprise."

> I went to the superintendent's place to collect my treaty money—I didn't even know an election was on. Some of the people wanted me to stand for councillor, but there were too many already nominated.
>
> Then somebody asked if I would stand for chief. We never had a woman chief before and I wasn't too sure about that. But then I said it would be okay with me.
>
> Well, I guess all the women voted for me because I won by one vote. There were five men standing for chief too.[59]

At the same time, in several articles, the reporter wanted to know, "how do the men react to having a woman as the band's 'head man'?" Sam King, a councillor serving with Wani, replied:

> When we held that election it was the first time we knew that a woman could be a chief. We had three men chiefs before that, so some of us thought it would be a good idea to nominate Amelia.
>
> There were a few complaints among the men when she was elected. But she's doing a real good job for a woman. She doesn't go ahead and do things on her own—she talks to the other people and gets advice.[60]

We are reminded here that the media and non-Indigenous people aren't the only ones with narrow assumptions about the roles and abilities of women. Other articles also wanted to hear what Indian Affairs had to say; in this case, too, DIA officials agreed that women chiefs and councillors "compare very favourably with the men."[61]

The Band Franchise and Canadian Women's History

The nation's 150th anniversary is an interesting time to think about First Nations women's history and politics in Canada. This is especially so because so much of our oppression and resistance has been articulated as connected to the Canadian state and its legal, social, economic, and ideological marginalization of Indigenous women. Recent developments, including the National Inquiry into Missing and Murdered Indigenous Women, the celebrated Idle No More movement of resistance and voice led by women, and ongoing criticisms of gender discrimination in the *Indian Act*, manifest deep dissatisfaction with the ways our nation-state has treated Indigenous women. While Canadians are learning more and more about the myriad ways Indigenous women have been legally and illegally prevented from full participation in political, economic, social, and cultural life, this comes as no surprise to others who live this marginalization daily.

Within this context, it has been difficult to interpret the history of First Nations women's band suffrage. Perhaps this is because within a broader context of Indigenous women's history in Canada, the shift toward making a voice for Indigenous women in politics is contradictory. The 1951 version of the *Indian Act*, in many respects, was a lot like the original 1876 version,[62] and was in fact much stricter about the removal and disenfranchisement of Indigenous women who married non-status Indians. In this context of loss then, studying First Nations women who thrived, took on new roles, and were acknowledged leaders in their community is vital. These stories teach us a little of what it has been to survive the white patriarchal state.

We provide below a list of women chiefs in Canada between 1951 and 1961, their approximate dates of first election to office, and the name of their band at the time, based on our research of the newspaper and other records. This list is incomplete; however, we include it here as neither Indian Affairs nor the Assembly of First Nations tracks data on gender equity in band leadership. By including this list, we honour these women.

> Chief Arletta Silver, Chippewa of the Thames, ON, 1952
> Chief Grace Vickers, Kitkatla Band, BC, 1952

Chief Elsie Knott, Mud Lake Band, ON, 1954
Chief Gwen O'Soup, Key Band, SK, 1954
Chief Jessie Lumm, Hazelton Band, BC, 1954
Chief Florence Tabodondung, Perry Island Band, ON, 1959
Chief Genevieve Mussell, Skwah Band, BC, 1959
Chief Jessie Watts, Opetchesaht Band, Reserve, BC, 1959
Chief Anna Whiteduck, Golden Lake Band, ON, 1959
Chief Louise Underwood, Cowichan, BC, 1960
Chief Mary Pius, Fort George Band, BC, 1960
Chief Gravelle, Tobacco Plains Band, BC, 1960
Chief Amelia Wani, Gull Bay, ON, 1960
Chief Mary Bernard, Lennox Island, PEI, 1960
Chief Alphonsine Lafond, Muskeg Lake Reserve, SK, 1960
Chief Gertrude Guerin Musqueam Band, BC, 1961

1. We thank Jill McConkey for her editorial work in the preparation of this paper. We also received support from the University of Winnipeg Joint Masters Program in History Research Assistance Funds.
2. The recent 2015 election, with its women-led campaigns to "rock the Indigenous vote," and the subsequent celebration of the election of seventeen representatives (ten Indigenous MPs and, in Manitoba, seven MLAs), one third of whom are women (six), was depicted as a watershed moment for Indigenous women in politics. For an excellent bibliography on women and suffrage, see Magnolia Pauker "Suffrage Campaigns and Enfranchisement With Special Reference to Canada: Extended Bibliography," for Veronica Strong-Boag at www.womensuffrage.org. Lianne Leddy's work on the Franchise is an important intervention: "Indigenous Women and the Franchise," in *The Canadian Encyclopedia*, online at www.thecanadianencyclopedia.ca/en/article/indigenous-women-and-the-franchise/.
3. See for example, Green, Joyce (2001), "Canaries in the Mines of Citizenship: Indian Women in Canada," *Canadian Journal of Political Science*, 34(4), pp. 715-738; Wheeler, Winona (1999), "Colonialism and First Nations Women," *Scratching the Surface: Canadian Anti-Racist Feminist Thought*, eds. Enakshi Dua and Angela Roberts, Toronto: Women's Press, pp. 49-80; Barker, Joanne (2006), "Gender, Sovereignty, and the Discourse of Rights in Native Women's Activism," *Meridians: Feminism, Race, Transnationalism* 2006, 7(1), pp. 127-161; and Eberts, Mary (2014), "Knowing and Unknowing: Settler Reflections on Missing and Murdered Indigenous Women," *Saskatchewan Law Review*, 77(1), pp. 69-104.
4. Canada, Cap VI *An Act for the gradual enfranchisement of Indians, the better management of Indian Affairs, and to extend the provision of the Act 31st Victoria*, Chapter 42, SC 1869, c 42, June 1869, section 10, Indigenous and Northern Affairs (INAC): www.aadnc-aandc.gc.ca/DAM/DAM-INTER-HQ/STAGING/texte-text/a69c6_1100100010205_eng.pdf
5. Canada (2014), Chapter 18 *An Act to amend and consolidate the laws respecting Indians*, SC 1876, c 18, April 1876 as cited in Smith, Kevin, *Strange Visitors: documents in Indigenous-Settler Relations in Canada from 1876*, Toronto: University of Toronto Press, pp. 10-13. Women were also formally barred from voting on land surrenders in the 1876 Act; surrenders to the Crown

were to be assented to by "a majority of the male members of the band of the full age of twenty-one years ... [who] resides on or near and is interested in the reserve in question."

6. Voyageur, Cora (2008), *Firekeepers of the Twenty-First Century: First Nations Women Chiefs*, Montréal: McGill-Queen's University Press, pp. 4-5.

7. Department of Indian Affairs (1953), *Annual Report*, p. 40.

8. In 1958, feminist Florence Bird wrote, "Indian women have, after all, a much better record than the rest of us when it comes to holding political office." She remarked that two Indian women had been elected chief, "which is the equivalent of being a mayor or reeve. And no fewer than 68 Indian women serve on band councils which is about the same as being an alderman." She calculated that 70 Indian women held public office out of about "156,000 Indians." Bird held this out as a pattern which "the rest of us should follow." "By embarrassing contrast," she wrote, "out of more than sixteen million other Canadians, last year, there were only 10 women mayors, nine reeves and about 90 councillors and aldermen." Bird accounted for this difference by explaining that many First Nations were matriarchal. Moreover, "in recent years Indian women went into politics because they had a personal contribution to make." Bird also thanked Homemakers' Clubs, which "lead Indian women from an interest in the family to a wider interest in the community. They wanted to do something about housing, social welfare, schools, poverty—things which concern women with a conscience." Bird mentions nothing about the inability of First Nations women to vote in band elections even up to seven years prior, or their inability to vote federally. Francis, Anne, "One Woman's View," *Ottawa Journal*, May 17, 1958, p. 19. Using a conglomerate of online sources, rough current figures for female participation in formal politics are: 18 percent of chiefs are female and 26 percent of provincially and federally elected officials are female. Information on gender equity among First Nations leadership is not collected or shared by Indian Affairs or the Assembly of First Nations.

9. Department of Indian Affairs (1960), *Annual Report*, p. 46. A total of 357 bands that year used the elective system, while 200 were under band custom governance.

10. For the purposes of this chapter, we searched the *Globe and Mail* and two newspaper databases—newspapers.com and newspaperarchives.com—for content on Indigenous women, band elections, and chiefs and councillors, between the years 1951 and 1971. We also searched the database of the *Indian News* available at the WinnSpace Repository at the University of Winnipeg website: winnSpace.uwinnipeg.ca/handle/10680/451; and the *Indian Missionary Record* (aka the *Indian Record*) available at Archives and Special Collections of Algoma University at www.archives.algomau.ca/main/.

11. See for example, Iserhienrhien, Abigail Iguosatiele (2014), "Gender, Race and the media Representation of Women in the Canadian 41st Parliament: A Critical Discourse Analysis," MA Thesis, Saskatoon: University of Saskatchewan.

12. Hunter, Anna (2007), "Exploring the Issues of Aboriginal Representation in Federal Elections," *Electoral Insight*, 5(3): 27 as cited in Kiera Ladner and Michael McCrossan, "The Electoral Participation of Aboriginal People," Elections Canada Working Paper Series on Electoral Participation and outreach Practices, Ottawa: p. 23.

13. A significant conversation about voting took place during the 2015 election at the University of Winnipeg Weweni Lecture Series. Pamela Palmater was challenged by Robert Innes, who argued that those in favour of voting have articulated two considerations: first, Indigenous people are of significant numbers in many ridings to make a difference in electoral outcomes; second, they have a significant stake in many of the outcomes of the elections. Gazan, Leah, Rob Innes, and Pamela Palmater,

"Should Indigenous People Vote in Canada's Federal Election?" Weweni Indigenous Scholars Speaker Series, University of Winnipeg, October 22, 2015: www.youtube.com/watch?v=PuS9H-m2PLo&list=PL_2Kjr9FLZXO-8AW1bODGImRcNjkyp4Zj.

14. "Women Chiefs Head Twelve Indian Bands," *Globe and Mail*, December 30, 1960: p. 11.
15. For example, the Department of Indian Affairs reported in 1952 that "Homemakers' Clubs, eighteen in number, continued to play an active role in the social betterment of many reserves, with members showing an increased interest in band affairs and in many cases taking an active interest in council elections." Department of Indian Affairs (1952), *Annual Report*, p. 49. Cannon, Martin J. (2006) writes about the absence of discussion of Indigenous women's agency in adjusting to their formal exclusion from formal band politics: "[i]t is peculiar that the literature has focused so exclusively on the once esteemed status of women in historical political organization while remaining virtually silent about the agency that Indigenous women have exercised over time," in "An Act to Amend the Indian Act (1985) and the Accommodation of Sex Discriminatory Policy," *Canadian Review of Social Policy*, 56, pp. 48 and 56.
16. McGrath, Ann and Winona Stevenson (1996), "Gender, Race, and Policy: Aboriginal Women and the State in Canada and Australia," *Labour/Le Travail*, 38, pp. 37-53.
17. Wolfe, Patrick (2006), "Settler Colonialism and the elimination of the Native," *Journal of Genocide Research*, 8(4), pp. 387-409. For a critical deconstruction of the national history in Canada, see Perry, Adele (2016), "Homes and Native Lands: Settler Colonialism, National Frames and the Remaking of History," *How Empire Shaped Us*, eds. Antoinette Burton and Dane Kennedy, London: Bloomsbury Publishing.
18. Cannon, pp. 49-50. See also, Kirk, Sylvia Van (2002), "From 'Marrying-in' to 'Marrying-Out': Changing Patterns of Aboriginal/Non-Aboriginal Marriage in Colonial Canada," *Frontiers: A Journal of Women Studies*, 23(3), pp. 1-11; and Lawrence, Bonita (2004), *"Real" Indians and Others: Mixed-Blood Urban Native Peoples and Indigenous Nationhood*, Vancouver: UBC Press.
19. Denetdale, Jennifer Nez (2006), "Chairmen, Presidents, and Princesses: The Navajo Nation, Gender and the Politics of Tradition," *Wicazo Sa Review*, 21(1), pp. 9-28.
20. Smith, 2014, p. 231.
21. Ibid., p. 23.
22. "Indians To Decide How Chiefs And Councillors To Be Chosen," *Lethbridge Herald*, January 2, 1952, p. 5.
23. The *Indian News*, however, a newspaper published by the Indian Affairs Branch of the Canadian government, did cover this moment in its pages, and this is an important source of information about women elected to band leadership from 1952 on.
24. "Women Chiefs Head Twelve," *Ottawa Journal*, July 17, 1959, p. 6.
25. "Has Special Recipe for Taking Care of Husbands," *Lethbridge Herald*, June 11, 1959, p. 18.
26. "Indian Ruler," *Medicine Hat News*, June 24, 1959, p. 1.
27. See Freeman, Barbara M. (2001), *The Satellite Sex: The Media and Women's Issues In English Canada, 1966-1971*, Waterloo: Wilfrid Laurier University Press; and Weston, Mary Ann (1996), *Native Americans in the News: Images of Indians in the Twentieth Century Press*, Westport: Greenwood Press.
28. "Frown On Claim," *The Indian Missionary Record*, February 1955, XVIII(2), p. 5.
29. Anderson, Mark Cronlund and Carmen L. Robertson (2011), *Seeing Red: A History of Natives in Canadian Newspapers*, Winnipeg: University of Manitoba Press, p. 193.
30. Anderson and Robertson, 2011, p. 193.
31. Freeman, 2001, p. 190.

32. For example, when Chief Wani was elected, she was described as "a jolly woman in her 30s." Williams, Tom, "Indian Women Speak Up," *Winnipeg Free Press*, June 15, 1961, p. 15. When Chief "Mrs Gertrude Guerin" was elected at Musqueam, she was described as a "43-year old grandmother, housewife and vice president of Southlands elementary school." The first woman to be elected chief at Musqueam, she was described as having "a friendly manner, cheery smile and bouncing energy," and thus "well suited for the job requiring a crying shoulder for the personal problems of the villagers and a knowledge of business administration." "First Woman Elected Chief, Indian Reserve," *Lethbridge Herald*, April 4, 1961, p. 14.
33. Williams, Ken, "Indians operate Georgian Bay marinas," *Indian News*, December 1978, 19(8), p. 5.
34. "Death of Indian baby draws Kehewin protest," *Indian News*, March 1974, 16(10), p. 1.
35. *Indian News*, April 1955.
36. "First Woman Plains Chief," *Indian News*, April 1955, 1(3), p. 7.
37. "Woman Heads Indians For the First Time," *Winnipeg Free Press*, December 16, 1954, p. 7.
38. Harris, Aroha and Mary Jane Logan McCallum (2012), "'Assaulting the Ears of Government': The Indian Homemakers' Clubs and the Maori Women's Welfare League in Their Formative Years," *Indigenous Women and Work: From Labor to Activism*, ed. Carol Williams, Champaign: University of Illinois Press, p. 226.
39. Ibid.
40. Ibid., p. 227.
41. Ibid., p. 229.
42. Ibid., p. 228.
43. "Only Woman Indian Chief," *Lethbridge Herald*, May 2, 1953, p. 1.
44. Honyust/Yenatlio, Shirley, "Chief profile: Leslee White-Eye, Chippewa of the Thames First Nation," *Anishinabek News*, September 1, 2015. In that election, there were only women in the running for the position of chief. See *Anishinabek News*: www.anishinabeknews.ca/2015/09/01/chief-profile-leslee-white-eye-chippewas-of-the-thames-first-nation/.
45. "Women show growing interest in band affairs, hold numerous council posts," *Indian News*, January 1955, 1(2), p. 5.
46. "Native By Marriage: White Woman Elected Chief of Indian Band," *Vancouver Province* article reprinted in the *Indian Record*, XXII: May 5, 1959, p. 3.
47. Paudash, Anne Rosemary, "I Married An Indian," *MacLean's*, December 1951, p. 27.
48. "Women show growing interest," 5. See also, From Cora Voyageur and others' research, we know more about Knott than any other of the early women chiefs. Voyageur, pp. 26-44. See also Sarah DeCarlo, Dir., "Elsie Knott," Final Fire Production in Association with Girls Action Foundation, online: www.youtube.com/watch?v=N3giLrZIbCo and a beautiful dedication in Knott's honour by Petten, Cheryl, "Footprints: Elsie Knott," *Windspeaker*, March 1, 2006.
49. "Elect Mrs. Knott Third Time As Chief Now 70 Women Serve Band Councils," *Indian News*, October 1958, 3(2), p. 4.
50. "Elected Indian Chief," *Lethbridge Herald*, July 8, 1954, p. 16.
51. "Elect Mrs. Knott," *Indian News*, p. 4.
52. There was no salary for chiefs, but there was an annuity for chiefs that ranged from $25-175. The total paid annuities for the year 1953, the year Knott was elected, was $4,375. Department of Indian Affairs (1953), *Annual Report*, p. 56.
53. "Indian Women of Today," *Indian News*, December 1960, 4(3), pp. 6-7.
54. Ibid., p. 7.

55. "Woman Chief," *Ottawa Journal*, April 3, 1959, p. 30.
56. "Women Chiefs Head Twelve," p. 11.
57. "Chief Miss," *Brandon Daily Sun*, December 7, 1960, p. 7.
58. "Indian Women of Today," *Indian News*, December 1960, p. 6.
59. Williams, Tom, "Indian Women Speak Up," *Winnipeg Free Press*, June 15, 1961, p. 15.
60. Ibid.
61. "Women Chiefs," p. 11.
62. *Final Report of the Royal Commission on Aboriginal Peoples*, Vol. 1: Looking Forward, Looking Back, pp. 310-1 available online at the Library and Archives Canada: www.collectionscanada.gc.ca/webarchives/20071115053257/www.ainc-inac.gc.ca/ch/rcap/sg/sgmm_e.html.

My Country 'tis of Thy People You're Dying

© Buffy Sainte-Marie

(Punctuation guides the singer or reader.)
Now that your big eyes are finally opened.
Now that you're wondering, "How must they feel? "
Meaning them that you've chased across Canada's movie screens;
Now that you're wondering, "How can it be real? "
that the ones you've called colorful, noble and proud
in your school propaganda,
They starve in their splendor.
You ask for our comment, I simply will render:
My country 'tis of thy people you're dying.

Now that the longhouses "breed superstition"
you force us to send our children away
to your schools where they're taught to despise their traditions
Forbid them their languages; then further say that
Canadian history really began
when explorers set sail out of Europe and stress
that the nations of leeches who conquered these lands
were the biggest, and bravest, and boldest, and best.
And yet where in your history books is the tale
of the genocide basic to this country's birth?
Of the preachers who lied? And the peoples who died?
How the nation of patriots returned to their earth?
And where does it tell of the starvation hell
where the children were herded,
and raped and converted
And when do we rescue the missing and murdered?
My country 'tis of thy people you're dying

My Country 'tis of Thy People You're Dying

A few of the conquered have somehow survived
Their blood runs the redder though genes have been paled.
From Arctic Inuvik to Niagara Falls
the wounded, the losers, the robbed sing their tale.
From Vancouver Island to the Labrador Sea
the white nation fattened while others grew lean.
Oh the tricked and evicted they know what I mean:
My country 'tis of thy people you're dying.

The past it just crumbled; the future just threatens
Our life blood is shut up in your papers and banks,
And now here you come, with a bill in your hand
and surprise in your eyes, that we're lacking in thanks
for the blessings of civilization you brought us
The lessons you've taught us. The ruin you've wrought us.
Oh see what our trust in O Canada got us.
My country 'tis of thy people you're dying.

Now that the rivers are dumps for your chemicals
Now that the forests are dead like the moon
Now that my life's to be known as your heritage.
Now that even the graves have been robbed.
Now that our own sacred way is your novelty
Hands on our hearts we salute you your victory:
Choke on your true white and scarlet hypocrisy.
Pity your blindness—how you never see

that the eagles of war whose wings lend you glory
are never no more than buzzards & crows:
Push some wrens from their nest;
steal their eggs; change their story.
The mockingbird sings it: It's all that she knows.

"Aw what could I do?" say a powerful few
with a lump in your throat and a tear in your eye:
Can't you see that their poverty's profiting you?
My country 'tis of thy people you're dying.

Reconciliation on Trial
Evaluating What Reconciliation Means in the Context of Aboriginal Justice

David Milward

The past horrors of the Canadian Indian residential schools, and the social legacies they have left behind, are perhaps well enough known in Canadian academic and political circles. Growing awareness of the fallout from residential schools made it at least politically expedient enough for then Prime Minister Stephen Harper to offer the following apology: "Today, we recognize that this policy of assimilation was wrong, has caused great harm and has no place in our country ... The government of Canada sincerely apologizes and asks the forgiveness of the aboriginal peoples of this country for failing them so profoundly. We are sorry."[1] The apology, plus lawsuits,[2] from the survivors of the residential schools, contributed to the formation of the Truth and Reconciliation Commission of Canada (TRC). The TRC released its final report in 2015, which detailed and chronicled the harms inflicted by the residential schools, as well as exploring ways to address the social catastrophe that has been left behind.[3] The very term "reconciliation" presupposes that Aboriginal peoples remain part of Canada, but that the relationship between Aboriginal peoples and non-Aboriginal Canadians needs to change on very fundamental levels.

It is a sad coincidence that the 150th anniversary of the *Constitution Act, 1867*[4] and the release of the final report of the TRC are a mere two years apart, as both events invite profound questions about the place of Aboriginal peoples within the nation-state that is called Canada. And indeed different Aboriginal thinkers have come to different responses to those questions.

Taiaiake Alfred, for example, is of the view that the only satisfactory resolution for Aboriginal peoples is to become their own completely independent polities, separate from Canada.[5] He also views reconciliation absent of a massive restitution of land and economic resources as "an emasculating concept, weak-kneed and easily accepting of half-hearted measures of a notion of justice that does nothing to help Indigenous peoples regain their dignity and strength."[6] At the risk of placing words in someone else's mouth, it may be reasonable to conjecture that Alfred would reject the 150th anniversary as something to be celebrated.

Others have taken more moderate views, including the TRC itself. The final report of the TRC calls for Canada to develop a Royal Proclamation of Reconciliation in consultation and partnership with Aboriginal peoples. This royal proclamation would recognize Aboriginal peoples as "full partners in Confederation," establish a nation-to-nation relationship between Aboriginal peoples and Canada, and would involve the "recognition and integration of Aboriginal laws and legal traditions."[7] John Borrows argues that the depiction of Canada as founded by two legal traditions, common law and civil law, is inaccurate because it fails to recognize Aboriginal legal traditions as a third and equally important legal foundation for the formation of Canada. Giving effect to that recognition also demands that Aboriginal peoples have the freedom to apply their own laws and traditions in addressing their own needs.[8]

One of the key focuses of the TRC's final report, and the one for this chapter, is the well-known problem of Aboriginal over-incarceration. Statistical estimates as of 2011 report that Aboriginals amount to 27 percent of provincial and territorial inmates, and 20 percent of federal inmates.[9] It is not my intention in this chapter to engage with extensive debates about the efficacy of Aboriginal justice initiatives, or feminist concerns about whether such initiatives place vulnerable victims and communities in coercive danger. I have engaged with those concerns elsewhere.[10]

This chapter is predicated on the assumption that Aboriginal peoples having the capacity (and inherent authority) to use their own laws and traditions, particularly those that parallel restorative justice, is necessary to overcome the problem of Aboriginal incarceration. It is possible for reconciliation, as described by Borrows and the TRC, to realize this goal. However, the existing initiatives, including sentencing initiatives and diversionary programs housed within the Canadian justice system, are inadequate, piecemeal initiatives. They fall short of what I and others envision as true reconciliation, a genuine sharing of decision-making power with Aboriginal peoples so that they have real capacity to address the persisting social problems that still stem from colonialism. Thus, my intention is to explore fundamental questions about the extent to which Canada is prepared to depart from the status quo and make serious efforts to address Aboriginal incarceration, and thereby achieve reconciliation through actions and not just hollow words. As for what reconciliation could and should mean, is the subject to which I now turn.

Reconciliation

The mandate of the TRC in part builds on the "Statement of Reconciliation" made by then Minister of Indian Affairs and Northern Development Jane Stewart on January 7, 1998. The statement emphasized that Canada must go beyond mere words and rhetoric, and must work toward addressing the social problems of Aboriginal peoples through concrete actions. The statement also stressed that Canada and Aboriginal peoples must work together in an equitable partnership that involves a genuine sharing of power, and not a paternalistic top-down imposition, in working together to address the problems.[11]

Others have also stressed that reconciliation means a genuine partnership whereby the Canadian government and Aboriginal communities work together as equals in addressing the problems left behind by the residential schools. The Royal Commission on Aboriginal Peoples (RCAP) emphasizes partnership and reciprocity as follows:

> [T]he principle of mutual recognition . . . requires both sides to acknowledge and relate to one another as partners, respecting each other's laws and institutions and co-operating for mutual benefit . . .
>
> From mutual recognition flows mutual respect . . . the quality of courtesy, consideration and esteem extended to people whose languages, cultures and ways differ from our own but who are valued fellow-members of the larger communities to which we all belong . . .
>
> Closely related to mutual respect is the principle of sharing: the giving and receiving of benefits . . .
>
> Ideally, Aboriginal peoples and Canada constitute a partnership in which the partners have a duty to act responsibly both toward one another and also toward the land they share.[12]

Michael Murphy adds:

> [r]econciliation speaks to the past, present, and future of Aboriginal-state relations in Canada. Perhaps nowhere was this message more clearly articulated that in the final report of the Royal Commission

> on Aboriginal Peoples ... [T]he commissioners recommended an honest and open confrontation with the history of colonization, concrete measures to address the contemporary legacy of injustice, and the forging of a new relationship built on the foundations of mutual recognition, respect, and trust.[13]

Brian Rice and Anna Snyder emphasize that true reconciliation means a willingness to engage in meaningful co-operation with Aboriginal peoples, and to share power with them as part of equitable partnership:

> Reconciliation is about healing relationships, building trust, and working out differences ... Reconciliation must meet concerns about both the past and the future. Acknowledgement of the past through truth telling, recognition of interdependence, and desire or necessity for peaceful co-existence in the future are key elements of reconciliation ...
>
> Trust comes, in part, from a general belief in the good intentions of the other and from indications that past behaviour and/or patterns of violence will not be repeated.
>
> In order for reconciliation to occur, the process must reflect the mutual interests of the parties involved. Without power-sharing in decision-making, a constructive outcome from the reconciliation process is unlikely. A destructive outcome results from one party imposing decisions made unilaterally with little or no consideration for the interests and needs of the other party.[14]

David MacDonald suggests that reconciliation includes a genuine sharing of power and decision-making with Aboriginal peoples; not only is the space for Aboriginal processes and institutions increased, but Canadian institutions themselves need to be fundamentally altered in a process he calls "syncretic democracy."[15]

Call to Action number 30 of the TRC Final Report calls upon the Federal Government to commit to eliminating Aboriginal over-incarceration over the next decade, and during that time period, to produce annual reports that "monitor and evaluate progress in doing so."[16] It is evident that what initiatives Canada has in place so far to address the problem of over-incarceration fall well short of any sort of partnership that involves an equitable sharing of power.

Aboriginal Justice Accommodations

By way of overview of contemporary accommodations of Aboriginal justice perspectives within the Canadian justice system, I begin with the sentencing circle. This process involves the offender, the victim(s), the extended family of the offender, as well as interested members of the community assembled together in a circular seating arrangement. Justice personnel, such as lawyers, probation officers, the judge, and counselling professionals, will often participate as well. The circle often commences with a smudging ceremony or similar rite. A spiritual symbol, often a feather, is then passed around to one participant at a time. The person holding the sacred object has the opportunity to speak to matters being considered by the circle, and is then passed on to the next person in the circle to do the same. This process continues until a consensus is reached on the appropriate resolution.[17] Examples of communities that have engaged in this practice include the Kwanlin Dün in the Yukon,[18] the Hollow Water community in Manitoba,[19] and the Innu at Sheshashiu and Davis Inlets.[20]

There is no *Criminal Code* provision that authorizes or even mentions the practice of sentencing circles. Whether a judge will allow a sentencing circle as part of the sentencing process is purely a matter of judicial discretion.[21] A judge is neither bound by the recommendations of the circle, and can impose a harsher sentence if he or she concludes that the recommendations provide an unsuitable sentence.[22] Indeed, a trial judge's adoption of the circle's recommendation can be appealed on the grounds that the sentence gives insufficient emphasis to deterrence (for example, by means of incarceration).[23]

Another example of accommodation is diversion. Diversionary programs allow offenders to resolve their cases outside of the court system. The usual first step is that a prosecutor approves an offender for participation in a program based on certain criteria. These include the offence being of minor gravity, the offender having no previous involvement with the program, and when the accused is willing to accept responsibility for the offence. Note that diversionary programs often allow an accused to accept responsibility for an offence without prejudicing his or her right to plead "not guilty" at a later time. The court then typically adjourns the case for a period of months or longer. During this time of adjournment, the offender is required to perform certain tasks or meet certain conditions, with a view toward correcting his or her behaviour. In diversionary programs with an Aboriginal emphasis, these tasks may include attending counselling to address certain types of behaviour, meeting with the victim(s) under appropriate conditions in order to resolve differences, completing the performance of community service hours, participating in cultural activities, and meeting with Elders for spiritual guidance. If an offender successfully completes the required steps, then the prosecutor will typically withdraw the charge on the next court date. If an offender does not complete the requirements, and the prosecutor is unwilling to provide an additional opportunity, the case is returned to the court system.[24] Such diversionary programs are usually confined to minor offences, and cases are subject to approval by Crown prosecutors.[25]

Another key accommodation has been Section 718.2(e) of the *Criminal Code*, which reads in part:

> A court that imposes a sentence shall also take into consideration the following principles: . . .
>
> (e) all available sanctions other than imprisonment that are reasonable in the circumstances should be considered for all offenders, with particular attention to the circumstances of Aboriginal offenders.

In *R v. Gladue*, the Supreme Court stated that this provision was enacted in response to alarming evidence that Aboriginal peoples were incarcerated disproportionately to non-Aboriginal people in Canada.[26] This case led to the creation of Section 718.2(e), and is thus a remedial provision, enacted specifically to oblige the judiciary to reduce incarceration of and seek reasonable alternatives for Aboriginal offenders.[27] Accordingly, the sentencing process and the sentence itself may be crafted "in accordance with the Aboriginal perspective."[28] A judge must take into account the background and systemic factors that bring Aboriginal people into contact with the justice system, such as poverty, substance abuse, and "community fragmentation," when determining a sentence.[29] A judge must also consider the role of these factors in bringing a particular Aboriginal accused before the court.[30] A judge is obligated to obtain that information with the assistance of counsel, through a probation officer's report, or by other means. A judge must also obtain information on community resources and treatment options that may provide alternatives to incarceration.[31]

It may certainly appear that the *Gladue* provision has some potential to address the social problems stemming from colonialism; however, there are very significant limitations involved with *Gladue* itself. Firstly, *Gladue*'s applicability has been limited for the most part to less serious offences. It must be kept in mind that Section 718.2(e) is part of a larger framework of s. 718 of the *Criminal Code*, which sets out the general goals of sentencing. Included within those goals are concepts like victim restitution and rehabilitation, but also goals like deterrence and retribution. The objectives of deterrence and retribution can indeed, and in fact do, work at cross-purposes with *Gladue*.

Lower courts following *Gladue* still demonstrate a clear preference for incarceration sentences, allegedly to give effect to deterrence and retribution. Andrew Walsh and James Ogloff analyzed 691 randomly selected sentencing decisions to determine the effects of s. 718.2(e). They found that Aboriginal status did not have any correlation with receiving either a custodial or non-custodial sentence. The strongest correlates within those same sentencing decisions were instead recognized by sentencing law prior to the passing of s. 718.2(e), with the frequent result that aggravating factors rendered an offence too serious for *Gladue* to justify a non-custodial sentence.[32] Lower courts will customarily enjoy appellate deference when their decisions to use incarceration are appealed as well. As a result, as Kent Roach has noted, appellate courts in a variety of jurisdictions have prioritized the seriousness of the offence, leading to the acceptance of incarceration sentences determined by lower courts, thereby denuding *Gladue* of much of its potential.[33]

The paradoxical result is that many Aboriginal persons who have been deeply damaged and traumatized by colonialism, who are the most in need of *Gladue*'s promise, end up being cut off from the remedial benefits explicitly intended by *Gladue*.[34] In *R v. T(L)*, an Ontario Court of Appeal Justice recognized the futility of calling upon incarceration in sentencing an Aboriginal accused, but nonetheless felt constrained to do so by Canadian sentencing law as follows:

> I have the view that in the fullness of time we will come to realize that we should go back well into the childhood of aboriginal persons who suffer the kind of misfortune this person suffered and determine whether it is appropriate to sentence them in a conventional way. I think that matter needs a great deal of attention. If I did not find myself constrained by authority, I would be seriously tempted to allow this appeal and to provide what I think would be a more enlightened sentence—a sentence that would return this person to his community under supervision where he would receive the kind of supervision and attention he deserves. In the present state of the law however, I do not think that I can say that the learned trial judge erred in failing to give proper consideration to the aboriginal status of the appellant.[35]

The Supreme Court recently attempted to provide a corrective to this trend in its decision, *R v. Ipeelee*, stating that offence bifurcation limiting the applicability of *Gladue* to a small range of less serious offences amounted to "a fundamental misunderstanding and misapplication of both s. 718.2(e) and this Court's decision in *Gladue*."[36] *Ipeelee* reinforces that there is often justification for sentencing Aboriginal offenders differently under s. 718.2(e), and that justification is tied to colonialism itself, of which residential schools were an integral part. Justice LeBel stated, "The overwhelming message emanating from the various reports and commissions on Aboriginal peoples' involvement in the criminal justice system is that current levels of criminality are intimately tied to the legacy of colonialism."[37] Justice LeBel continued:

> To the extent that *Gladue* will lead to different sanctions for Aboriginal offenders, those sanctions will be justified based on their unique circumstances— circumstances which are rationally related to the sentencing process. Courts must ensure that a formalistic approach to parity in sentencing does not undermine the remedial purpose of s. 718.2(e).[38]

Even so, there are parts of *Ipeelee* that may be concerning from an Aboriginal perspective. The Court emphasized that s. 718.2(e) does not amount to a "race-based discount on sentencing."[39] The Court also underscored the ongoing relevance of proportionality and other sentencing objectives that can justify incarceration, stating:

> The fundamental principle of sentencing (i.e., proportionality) is intimately tied to the fundamental purpose of sentencing—the maintenance of a just, peaceful and safe society through the imposition of just sanctions. Whatever weight a judge may wish to accord to the various objectives and other principles listed in the *Code*, the resulting sentence must respect the fundamental principle of proportionality. Proportionality is the *sine qua non* [the essential element] of a just sanction. First, the principle ensures that a sentence reflects the gravity of the offence. This is closely tied to the objective of denunciation. It promotes justice for victims and ensures public confidence in the justice system . . . Second, the principle of proportionality ensures that a sentence does not exceed what is appropriate, given the moral blameworthiness of the offender. In this sense, the principle serves a limiting or restraining function and ensures justice for the offender.

> In the Canadian criminal justice system, a just sanction is one that reflects both perspectives on proportionality and does not elevate one at the expense of the other.[40]

The court further reaffirmed *Gladue*'s statement that the more serious the crime, the more likely that a sentence of incarceration will be appropriate.[41]

There are certainly inadequacies with existing initiatives. Diversionary programs are for the most part limited to lower range offences for which fines, or at most probationary terms, would be assessed. Sentencing circles keep the ultimate decision-making power in the hands of Canadian judges, who can and often do veto circle recommendations based on the demands for deterrence and retribution inherent in Canadian sentencing law. *Gladue* and *Ipeelee* certainly hold out some nominal promise, and yet even those judgments contain commentary that retains a distinct tilt toward deterrence and retribution through incarceration. Two patterns emerge: One, the range of offences to which Aboriginal communities can apply their own laws and methods becomes severely limited. That in turn means Aboriginal communities have no say in addressing problematic behaviours in their communities that are particularly reflective of colonialism and intergenerational trauma, where there is the greatest need. Such behaviours include domestic violence, sexual violence, and many other crimes that stem from mental health issues and substance abuse. The other pattern is that a great deal of decision-making authority is vested not in Aboriginal communities themselves, but in state authorities, such as judges and prosecuting lawyers who will have their own priorities that often fail to take the best interests of Aboriginal communities into account. Undoubtedly, the Tory government under Harper did its part to further exacerbate this already dismal state of affairs for Aboriginal offenders.

Tory Policy

In 2006, in the years preceding the release of the TRC Final Report, the Tory government that came into power made itself clear: Aboriginal social concerns were not its priority. A portentous event is the attempt to address Aboriginal social problems through the Kelowna Accord. After eighteen months of negotiations between the Federal Government—led by former Prime Minister Paul Martin—and Aboriginal leaders, the Accord was finalized in November 2005. It promised $5.1 billion over ten years to address Aboriginal social problems in key areas such as health, education, and poverty.[42] Martin's minority Liberal government was subsequently defeated and replaced by a minority Tory government led by Stephen Harper. Under the original Accord, $600 million would have been spent during the 2006 fiscal year on the Accord's objectives. However, Harper's government, upon assuming power, replaced the Accord with a budgetary allocation of $150 million during 2006, and $300 million during 2007, to address similar objectives.[43] Aboriginal peoples and their leaders have many times since decried this development as bad faith and neglect on the part of the Federal Government.[44]

This trend continued as Parliament, almost at the same time as *Ipeelee*, promoted legal developments that are likely to further denude s. 718.2(e) of much of its remedial potential. Bill C-10[45] received royal assent on March 13, 2012. The legislative scheme has at least two key features relevant to this discussion. One, it relies on mandatory terms of imprisonment for many offences, particularly those of sexual violence and possession or trafficking in narcotics, which judges could add to but not reduce. Second, it also relies on ineligibility for conditional sentences for many offences, such as personal violence offences and several property-based offences. The intention behind the bill is to enhance public safety on the assumption that longer sentences will increase deterrence, and by the separation of offenders from society. Perhaps some of the concerns about Bill C-10 may be alleviated by the stance the Supreme Court demonstrated in *R v. Nur*, where it ruled that three- and five-year mandatory minimums for firearms offences were a violation of Section 12 of the *Canadian Charter of Rights and Freedoms* prohibiting cruel and unusual punishment. The court's reasoning was that mandatory minimum sentences, and the resulting removal of judicial discretion, might result in undeservedly severe punishments in some individual cases.[46] It may be speculative at this point to wonder how far the reasoning in *Nur* can be taken against various components of Bill C-10. Be that as it may, even prior to Bill C-10, there were concerns about the scope or capacity of *Gladue* to provide remedial effect against Aboriginal over-incarceration, which Bill C-10 further accentuates. Mandatory sentences thus deny the availability of a conditional (that is, a more appropriate) sentence for many Aboriginal offenders who are living with the effects of Canada's colonial legacy. Canadian judges thus, even those who may be so inclined, cannot even begin to consider non-custodial alternatives pursuant to *Gladue*.[47] Elizabeth Sheehy adds, "Bill C-10 will effectively repudiate s. 718.2(e) and swell even further our jails with Aboriginal offenders . . . ."[48] Indeed, there are reported cases where mandatory minimums dictated incarceration in cases where a non-custodial sentence would otherwise be in the range of possibility for an Aboriginal accused under *Gladue*.[49] There is also at least one reported case where an Aboriginal accused was unable to obtain a conditional sentence due to the new restrictions under Bill C-10.[50] Although to be fair, the restrictions would be equally operative against non-Aboriginal offenders since s. 718.2(e) embodies a general call for restraint in the use of imprisonment.

During this time, the Tory government doggedly pursued this course, despite the mound of social science evidence showing that lengthier jail terms do not enhance deterrence,[51] and in spite of spiralling costs for the Department of Justice. The annual budget for the federal prison system went from $1.6 billion in the 2005/06 fiscal year to $2.98 billion for 2011/12. Much of this increase can be attributed to the Tory government's measures that included revoking the "2-for-1" credit for interim custody, and amendments to s. 752, which restricted the availability of conditional sentences for serious personal injury offences.[52] Those costs are expected to increase even more with the recent passing of the omnibus crime bill that makes extensive use of mandatory minimum prison terms for many offences. Ontario has estimated its yearly costs for corrections will increase by $1 billion in order to accommodate the increased influx of inmates. Québec has estimated that its yearly costs will increase by $600 million. Ministers of both provinces have publicly indicated that they are not willing to pick up the whole tab.[53] At a time of fiscal restraint, when governments are struggling to ensure that all Canadians receive basic services, these ballooning costs cannot be justified, particularly given the ineffectiveness of incarceration. The fact that mandatory minimum sentences disproportionately affect Aboriginal people makes it obvious that such a course falls well short of any meaningful sense of reconciliation.

Tokenism or Reconciliation?

A frequent criticism made against existent restorative justice programs is that they represent the institutionalization of restorative justice by the state, which in turn leads to half-hearted initiatives that do not truly reflect restorative justice.[54] Similar criticisms have been made against Aboriginal justice initiatives. Chris Andersen argues that contemporary Aboriginal justice initiatives in Canada reflect an effort by the Canadian political hegemony to indirectly regulate Aboriginal offenders and restrict Aboriginal aspirations for greater control over "justice" affecting them, which in substance leaves the status quo intact. What is apparent is that

Aboriginal justice initiatives provide a medium that displays a veneer of community empowerment under the guise of accommodation of cultural difference.

It is, however, the Canadian state that provides the funding for, and exercises ultimate legal authority over, Aboriginal justice initiatives. It is therefore the state that enjoys the unchecked power to set the parameters of justice initiatives. For example, justice initiatives will usually only address less serious offences, for which the conventional justice system would normally resort to community-based sentences (for example, probation or conditional sentences) anyway. The Canadian state thus accommodates Aboriginal justice initiatives, but only to the extent that its own interests happen to converge with those of Aboriginal communities. In the absence of that convergence, such as when Aboriginal communities desire to consider their own approaches to offences as alternatives to incarceration, then the accommodation is revoked.[55] Jesse Sutherland sums this up succinctly: "A successful Aboriginal Justice Strategy must go beyond participatory and indigenised justice processes. Rather, it must support healing and capacity building within First Nations' communities as well as endeavour to decolonize and repair the relationship with the Canadian state."[56] Taiaiake Alfred goes further in his criticism; in his view, surface indigenization leads some Aboriginal participants to believing they are renewing Aboriginal self-determination, when really they end up co-opted by the state apparatus. The status quo is thus perpetuated.[57]

The impacts of the Tory government initiative, however, go further than mere indigenization or co-optation. By insisting on policies that are fundamentally inconsistent with reconciliation, they sustained, and arguably exacerbated, Aboriginal over-incarceration. They have effectively neutered policies that would be far more constructive and help end social problems, most notably the impacts of residential schools. Again, despite substantial and growing empirical evidence that mass incarceration policies are counter-productive, the Tory government continued to pursue these destructive policies. Whether intentional or by oversight, these policies were unsurprisingly pursued without any meaningful consultation with Aboriginal peoples. This falls far short of the Canadian government's ideal to act in genuine partnership with Aboriginal peoples, or to share mutual decision-making power with Aboriginal communities. For former Prime Minister Harper to have provided a verbal apology, only to then pursue counter-productive policies that worsened the problems for Aboriginal peoples, amounts to mere "words" but without any "concrete action."[58] The recent election of a Liberal government has indeed revived the potential to reverse that course, but that is not necessarily a given.

Reconciliation at a Crossroads

It must be noted here that the notion of reconciliation is not without its critics. For some it is not the ideals of reconciliation *per se*, but rather the questions they raise regarding the potential for reconciliation to become a hollow gesture that accomplishes little. For example, some scholars view reconciliation as an effort to relegate colonialism to a past misfortune, and to legitimize the present status quo.[59]

Similarly, Carole Blackburn argues that while reconciliation has the potential to lead to fundamental change, it has thus far amounted to little more than a continuation of colonialism.[60] As Deena Rymhs points out, reconciliation from the state's perspective may not be so much about doing right by those who have been victimized by the state, but rather a cynical, illusory, and very public gesture aimed at restoring legitimacy and confidence in a nation-state that has been exposed for wrongdoing against Aboriginal Peoples.[61] Perhaps the most scathing criticism comes from Alfred, who writes: "The logic of reconciliation as justice is clear: without massive restitution, including land, financial transfers and other forms of assistance to compensate for past harms and continuing injustices committed against our peoples, reconciliation would permanently enshrine colonial injustices and is itself a further injustice."[62]

The previous Tory government certainly provided plenty of justification for such critique; Matthew Dorrell views Harper's Residential Schools Apology as minimizing the extent of harm and injustice done to Aboriginal peoples in the past. Dorrell also reads the apology as not so much an apology for assimilation itself as an objective, but rather how it was carried out in the past. He thus views assimilation as an ongoing state endeavour.[63] Sheryl Lightfoot reinforces Dorrell's critique, while at the same time offering her views on what reconciliation truly requires:

> I argue that official apologies to Indigenous peoples have the potential to play a meaningful role within a larger program of Indigenous-state reconciliation only if such apologies are employed in a way that moves beyond rhetoric and helps reset the relationship between the state and Indigenous peoples away from hierarchical and colonial power relations and toward one grounded in mutual respect. A state apology to Indigenous peoples must meet two criteria in order to be meaningful in this way. It must, first, fully and comprehensively acknowledge the wrongs of the past and/or the present. Second, the state must make a credible commitment to do things differently, to make substantial

changes in its policy behavior [sic], in the future. Any state apology that fails to deliver both of these two elements will not be meaningful in the eyes of Indigenous recipients, regardless of how "authentically" it is delivered by the state . . .[64]

There is perhaps the potential for true reconciliation with a new government, but that remains an open question. Prime Minister Justin Trudeau promised a full implementation of the TRC's 94 Calls to Action shortly after the release of the final report.[65] If the new Liberal government makes good on its promise, then there is hope that a truly equitable partnership is possible when addressing the social problems of Aboriginal people, over-incarceration included. But that is far from a given. Trudeau has apparently reneged on his previous promise to fully implement the United Nations Declaration on the Rights of Indigenous Peoples.[66] It is to be hoped that the new government also does not back out of its promise to implement the recommendations of the Final Report. Canada has compelling human rights and moral imperatives to begin true reconciliation, given the appalling nature of the social traumas inflicted upon Aboriginal peoples throughout colonialism. That, in and of itself, should be sufficient reason for the state to change course. I could, however, add to that an appeal to pragmatic self-interest as well. If the social fallouts continue unaddressed, the long-term costs to mainstream Canada itself may prove quite dire indeed. If that happens, it will fully justify all of the critiques that have been made about reconciliation, Alfred's included.

Conclusion

Reconciliation in its truest sense means Canada and Aboriginal peoples working together in a genuine partnership, in order to overcome the social problems experienced by the latter. That is particularly true when it comes to the problem of Aboriginal over-incarceration. Reconciliation in that context means that Canada must be willing to let go of a significant amount of its power over criminal justice, and concurrently, encourage Aboriginal communities to take on greater decision-making power with respect to crimes committed by their own members. Reconciliation requires more than minimalist accommodations that rarely extend any further than minor offences, for which the Canadian justice system itself would use non-custodial sentences anyway.

Canada has never departed to any significant degree from that status quo, a fact that was exacerbated by the policies of the Tory government, which likely only served to worsen the problem of over-incarceration. This reality may justify critiques that have been made against notional reconciliation, suggesting that government efforts amount to little more than a hollow gesture of empty rhetoric, and that in substance leaves the status quo intact. The new Liberal government now has the opportunity to help realize true reconciliation as it has been idealized, especially given that it has promised to implement the recommendations of the TRC Final Report. However, if it reneges on its promises, then the critiques will continue to be justified and the crisis of Aboriginal over-incarceration will continue unabated.

1. Canadian Broadcasting Corporations Archives (2008), "A long-awaited apology for residential schools": www.cbc.ca/archives/entry/a-long-awaited-apology-for-residential-schools.
2. Blackwater v. Plint, 3 SCR 3 (2005).
3. Truth and Reconciliation Commission of Canada (2015), *Honouring the Truth, Reconciling for the Future*, Winnipeg: Truth and Reconciliation Commission of Canada.
4. *Constitution Act, 1867*, 30 & 31 Victoria, c 3 (UK).
5. Alfred, Taiaiake (2008), *Peace, Power, Righteousness*, London: Oxford University Press.
6. Younging, Gregory, Jonathan Dewar, and Mike DeGagné, eds. (2009), "Restitution is the Real Pathway to Justice for Indigenous Peoples," *Response, Responsibility and Renewal: Canada's Truth and Reconciliation Journey*, Ottawa: Aboriginal Healing Foundation, p. 181.
7. Truth and Reconciliation Commission of Canada, pp. 252-253.
8. Borrows, John (2010), *Canada's Aboriginal Constitution*, Toronto: University of Toronto Press.
9. Dauvergne, Mia (2012), *Adult Correctional Statistics in Canada, 2010-2011*, Ottawa: Statistics Canada, p. 11.
10. Milward, David (2012), *Aboriginal Justice and the Charter: Realizing a Culturally Sensitive Interpretation of Legal Rights*, Vancouver: UBC Press.
11. Schedule N to the *Indian Residential Schools Settlement Agreement* (May 8, 2005).
12. *Ibid*. For further discussion, see Chartrand, Paul, "Towards Justice and Reconciliation: Treaty Recommendations of Canada's Royal Commission on Aboriginal Peoples," *Honour Among Nations?: Treaties and Agreements with Indigenous Peoples*, eds. Marcia Langton, Maureen Tehan, Lisa Palmer, and Kathryn Shain (2004), Carlton: Melbourne University Publishing Ltd., p. 120; Ladner, Kiera L. (2001), "Negotiated Inferiority: The Royal Commission on Aboriginal People's Vision of a Renewed Relationship," 31:1-2 Amer. Rev. Can. Stud., p. 241.
13. Murphy, Michael, "Civilization, Self-Determination, and Reconciliation," *First Nations, First Thoughts: The Impact of Indigenous Thought in Canada*, ed. Annis May Timpson (2009), Vancouver: UBC Press, at 251.
14. Rice, Brian and Anna Snyder (2008), "Reconciliation in the Context of a Settler Society: Healing the Legacy of Colonialism in Canada," *From Truth to Reconciliation: Transforming the Legacy of Residential Schools*, Ottawa: Aboriginal Healing Foundation, pp. 45-46.
15. MacDonald, David (2013), "Reconciliation after Genocide in Canada: Towards a syncretic model of democracy," *AlterNative: An International Journal of Indigenous Peoples*, 9:1, p. 60.

16. Truth and Reconciliation Commission of Canada (2015), *The Legacy*,Winnipeg: Truth and Reconciliation Commission of Canada, p. 234.
17. Wilson, Robin J. Wilson, Bria Huculak, and Andrew McWhinnie (2002), "Restorative Justice Innovations in Canada," 20 Behav Sci & L, p. 363.
18. Stuart, Barry (1997), *Building Community Justice Partnerships: Community Peacemaking Circles*, Ottawa: Department of Justice, Canada.
19. Sivell-Ferri, Christine, et al. (1997), *The Four Circles of Hollow Water Aboriginal Peoples Collection*, Ottawa: Ministry of the Solicitor General.
20. Harrison, Anne, Muriel Meric, and Alan Dickson (1995), *Justice as Healing at Sheshatshit and David Inlet*, Ottawa: Peace Brigades International.
21. R v. Morin, 134 Sask R 120 (CA) (1995).
22. Ibid., para 9.
23. For examples, see R v. Morris, BCAC 235 (2004); R v. HR, 205 AR 226 (Prov Ct) (1997); and R v. Desnomie, Sask. R. (C.A.) (2005).
24. Note that this is often, but not always, the case. There are examples of programs where once a matter is diverted the offender remains accountable only to members of the Indigenous community, and the Crown has no further role. See, for example, Palys, Ted and Winona Victor (2007), "'Getting to a Better Place': Qwi:Qwelstom, the Sto:lo, and Self-Determination" in Law Commission of Canada, ed., *Indigenous Legal Traditions*, Vancouver: UBC Press, p. 12.
25. *Aboriginal Justice Strategy Summative Evaluation: Final Report* (2007), Ottawa: Department of Canada, Evaluation Division.
26. *R v. Gladue*, 1 SCR 688, para 58-65 (1999).
27. Ibid., para 64.
28. Ibid., para 74.
29. Ibid., para 67.
30. Ibid., para 69.
31. Ibid., paras 83-84.
32. Walsh, Andrew and James Ogloff (2008), "Progressive Reforms or Maintaining the Status Quo? An Empirical Evaluation of the Judicial Consideration of Aboriginal Status in Sentencing Decisions," *Canadian Journal of Criminology*, 50:4, p. 491.
33. Roach, Kent (2009), "One Step Forward, Two Steps Back: *Gladue* at Ten and in the Courts of Appeal," *Criminal Law Quarterly*, 54, pp. 503-504.
34. Pelletier, Renee (2001), "The Nullification of Section 718.2(e): Aggravating Aboriginal Over-Representation in Canadian Prisons," *Osgoode Hall Law Journal*, 39, pp. 479-480.
35. R v. T(L), ONCA 2431, para 4 (2008).
36. R v. Ipeelee, 2012 SCC 13, para 63 (2012).
37. Ibid., para 77.
38. Ibid., para 79.
39. Ibid., para 75.
40. Ibid., para 38.
41. Ibid., para 84.
42. Ibbitson, John, "In praise of a flawed Native accord" *Globe and Mail*, November 26, 2005, p. A4.
43. Bailey, Sue, "Tories gut Liberal brokered $5.1 billion in Native funding" *Toronto Star*, May 3, 2006, p. A6.

44. See for example Perkel, Colin, "Fontaine calls on Ottawa to fulfill its responsibility to Aboriginals," *Globe and Mail*, October 13, 2007, p. A7; Auld, Alison and Keith Doucette, "Aboriginal leaders call for more protests, days of action," *Globe and Mail*, July 11, 2007, p. A8; "Ottawa's neglect invites Indian anger," *Toronto Star*, May 20, 2007, p. A16.
45. *Legislative History, Bill C-10: An Act to enact the Justice for Victims of Terrorism Act and to amend the State Immunity Act, the Criminal Code, the Controlled Drugs and Substances Act, the Corrections and Conditional Release Act, the Immigration and Refugee Protections Act and other Acts* (Ottawa: Library of Parliament, 2012), pp. 26-27.
46. R v. Nur, SCC 15 (2015).
47. For similar critiques, see Chartrand, Larry (2001), "Aboriginal Peoples and Mandatory Minimums," *Osgoode Hall Law Journal*, 39, p. 449; Sewrattan, Christopher (2013), "Apples, Oranges and Steel," *University of British Columbia Law Review*, 46, p. 121; Newell, Ryan (2013), "Making Matters Worse: The Safe Streets and Communities Act and the Ongoing Crisis of Aboriginal Incarceration," *Osgoode Hall Law Journal*, 51, p. 199.
48. Sheehy, Elizabeth (2010), "The Discriminatory Effects of Bill C-15's Mandatory Minimum Sentences," Criminal Reports (6th), 70, p. 311.
49. R v. Anderson, 2 SCR 167 (2014); R v. EMQ, BCSC 201 (2015); R v. RS, BCPC 0227 (2014).
50. R v. Arcand, SKPC 12 (2014).
51. Paternoster, Raymond (2010), "How Much Do We Really Know about Criminal Deterrence," *Journal of Criminal Law & Criminology*, 100:3, p. 765.
52. Davis, Jeff, "Prison costs soar 86% in past five years: report," *National Post*, July 18, 2011.
53. Cohen, Tobi, "Tories use majority to pass omnibus crime bill," *National Post*, March 12, 2012.
54. Hudson, Barbara (2007), "The institutionalisation of restorative justice: justice and the ethics of discourse," *Acta Juridica*, p. 56.
55. Andersen, Chris (1993), "Governing Aboriginal Justice in Canada: Constructing responsible individuals and communities through 'tradition,'" *Crime, Law & Social Change*, 31, p. 303. See also Havenmann, Paul (1992), "The Indigenization of Social Control in Canada," *Aboriginal Peoples and Canadian Criminal Justice*, eds. Robert A. Silverman and Marianne O. Neilson, Toronto: Harcourt, Brace & Co., p. 113.
56. Sutherland, Jessie, "Colonialism, Crime and Dispute Resolution: A Critical Analysis of Canada's Aboriginal Justice Strategy" (unpublished).
57. Alfred, Taiaiake (2008), *Peace, Power, Righteousness*, London: Oxford University Press, p. 70.
58. Henderson, Jennifer and Pauline Wakeham (2009), "Colonial Reckoning, National Reconciliation?: Aboriginal Peoples and the Culture of Redress in Canada," *English Studies in Canada* 35:1, p. 1. See also Johnson, Miranda (2011), "Reconciliation, indigeneity, and post-colonial nationhood with settle states," *Postcolonial Studies*, 14:2, p. 187.
59. Corntassel, Jeff (2009), "Indigenous Story-Telling, Truth-telling, and Community Approaches to Reconciliation," *English Studies in Canada*, 35:1, p. 137.
60. Blackburn, Carole (2007), "Producing legitimacy: reconciliation and the negotiation of Aboriginal rights in Canada," *Journal of the Royal Anthropological Institute*, 13, p. 621.
61. Rymhs, Deena (2006), "Appropriating Guilt: Reconciliation in an Aboriginal Canadian Context," *English Studies in Canada*, 32:1, p. 105; see also Wakeham, Pauline (2012), "Reconciling 'Terror': Managing Indigenous Resistance in the Age of Apology," *American Indian Quarterly*, 36:1, p. 1.
62. Alfred, Taiaiake (2005), *Wasáse: Indigenous Pathways of Action and Freedom*, Peterborough: Broadview Press, p. 152.

63. Dorrell, Matthew (2009), "From Reconciliation to Reconciling: Reading What 'We Now Recognize' in the Government of Canada's 2008 Residential Schools Apology," *English Studies in Canada*, 35:1, p. 27.
64. Lightfoot, Sheryl (2015), "Settle State Apologies to Indigenous Peoples: A Normative Framework and Comparative Analysis," *Native American & Indigenous Studies*, 2:1, pp. 15-16.
65. "Statement by Prime Minister on Release of the Final Report of the Truth and Reconciliation Commission," December 15, 2015: www.pm.gc.ca/eng/news/2015/ 12/15/ statement-prime-minister-release-final-report-truth-and-reconciliation-commission
66. McParland, Kelly (2016), "Trudeau's first broken promise to First Nations People is a whopper, but it won't be the last," *National Post*, July 18, 2016.

Got Tolerance?

Felicia Sinclair

For many, Canada's 150th anniversary is a celebration of independence of state and a history of national achievement. Like any other anniversary, it warrants reflecting on the historical events leading up to this milestone. Unfortunately, for Indigenous people who Canada claimed for itself, this 150-year milestone is much more sombre. Now a minority in our mother country, we as the original people of this land have many painful memories when reflecting on the last 150 years. This anniversary represents 150 years of strategic oppressive and coercive policies and actions inflicted upon us as Indigenous peoples. As an Indigenous woman who has resided, studied, laboured, and reproduced in this country, it matters to me that Canada comes to grips with a truer understanding of its past—one that includes Indigenous people.

Too often throughout Canadian history, Indigenous history and perspectives have been omitted. Similar to the campaign of Duncan Campbell Scott, who set out to "Get rid of the Indian problem" during the height of the Indian residential school era, recorders of history omitted Indigenous perspectives from their historical documents, referring very little to the accomplishments of the Indigenous population. If an Indigenous person was referenced, it often highlighted failure or used derogatory terms to describe us. This was done to ensure the narrative of Canadian success and virtue was reinforced. This narrative must change. In the spirit of reconciliation, a review of our history in terms of Canada's relationship with Indigenous people of this land is vital. A fresh look at our history is a powerful tool for reconciliation. It permits a position of understanding that can guide us toward a more unified future for Canada. Moreover, it can thwart the reoccurrence of events that further degrade us as the original landowners of Canada. I am privileged to share a story from an Indigenous perspective that promotes social change, and contributes to laying the groundwork for a more unified Canada.

In 2014, Tenelle Starr, a youth from Star Blanket First Nation, Saskatchewan, received a very special gift for Christmas: a bright pink hoodie with the words "Got land?" on the front, and "Thank an Indian" on the back. The "Got land—Thank an Indian" slogan, created by Jeff Menard, was inspired by the "Got Milk" trademark established by popular advertisements beginning in 1993. More than just a sweatshirt, the gift Starr received had the ability to provoke thought and even encourage education about the origins of our country. Presuming she was able to exercise her fundamental right of expression, she decided to wear that sweater to her school. There couldn't be a more suitable place for this teen to exert her right to freedom of expression than at an institution entrusted to educate our youth. I doubt she was expecting the response that she received.

Unfortunately, Starr was taught a terrible lesson in school that day, one that neither she nor her family was expecting her to have to learn. She was confronted, at the early age of thirteen, with a lesson not in science, mathematics, or literature, but in intolerance.

Starr's schoolmates returned home and recounted to their parents the message on the sweatshirt. The next morning, the school's principal received complaints from parents, claiming that Starr had worn a sweatshirt with a racist message. Balcarres Community School staff soon found themselves fielding complaints regarding the sweatshirt's message. The complaints claimed the slogan on Starr's sweatshirt was racist and offensive. When Starr wore the sweatshirt a second time to school, she was approached by Balcarres Community School staff and asked to either remove the "offensive" and "racist" sweatshirt or turn it inside out so the offensive message could not be seen. Starr told her story to CBC reporters on January 14, 2014. She could not understand how the shirt generated so much controversy, and did not understand why people were so offended by it.

"Got Land? Thank an Indian." These five simple words was all that was required to expose Canadian's unwillingness to consider Indigenous perspectives about their past. By responding with disapproval and censorship, staff and parents perpetuated a distinct silence around the history of dispossession and genocide that our country has steadfastly maintained. They also stifled the voices of Indigenous people, including a young girl who had courageously interrupted a 150-year-old illusion.

Why did students, parents, and staff view this message as racist? Why was their first response to complain, rather than question or investigate the meaning of the message? Why did the school itself not seize this valuable opportunity to educate students and parents about historic and contemporary Canadian-Indigenous relations? The outright refusal to contemplate the message of the sweatshirt and deliberate neglect to educate students is astounding. Here, right in front of them, was an excellent opportunity to educate by informing and addressing ignorance—not only the students within the school but also their parents, and by extension the community. Instead, this small Saskatchewan school missed an opportunity to demonstrate tolerance and promote true education.

Nevertheless, lessons were taught. In asking a young Indigenous girl to silence herself and her point of view, the adults in her life taught Starr that her right to freedom of expression was limited to what was acceptable to her non-Indigenous peers. The clear message was that it is acceptable to muzzle Indigenous perspectives to preserve the comfort of those unwilling to accept the historic role of Aboriginal peoples in the making of the country we today recognize as Canada.

Had Starr accepted the direction of her authority figures at school, and allowed herself to be intimidated into silence, this lesson of intolerance would not be available for me to share. Thankfully, Starr stood up and, with courageous conviction that would make many adults quiver, was not swayed by the misguided lesson forced onto her by the Balcarres staff. She refused to accept the notion that the words on her sweater were offensive or racist. As the result of her decision to speak out, a national conversation was sparked—a heated conversation among Indigenous people from across the nation, ignited by truth to support this young voice.

Conversely, the settlers of a nation built on the blood and land of our ancestors reacted with hate. Indignant anger from the non-Indigenous community was directed toward this young woman. Starr received numerous hate-filled messages and death threats; according to *Winnipeg Free Press* reporter Melissa Martin, there was a "rain of anger that beat down" on Starr. In fear for their safety, the Starr family contacted the RCMP for their protection. The hate-filled response Starr received in many ways reflects the current status of the Canada-Indigenous relationship.

This is a relationship in which gender, age, race, and land has always mattered. This small event involving a hoodie and a young Indigenous woman speaking truth about a history of Indigenous land dispossession mattered. Even more so, since it happened in a community that has directly benefited from Aboriginal dispossession—a public school in a settler Saskatchewan community. Rather than "thanking an Indian," Starr was the one expected to be grateful for all that Canada has provided for her. It is Starr, many suggest, who should be thankful, especially as an "Indian." Like all Canadians, she has free education, can access universal health care, and enjoys the benefits of being part of such an amazing nation that promises freedom to people from so many other countries. In addition, many people hold common sentiments that reflect an ignorant understanding of Indigenous people. Misconceptions regarding additional health benefits, for example, that only "registered" First Nations people of Canada (considered "Indians" under settler law) have for some medical, optical, and dental services, has been a major source of fuel for intolerance exhibited by so many Canadians. It is quickly forgotten that these are treaty rights—not handouts resulting from treaties negotiated between the Crown and certain First Nations people. These so-called benefits reflect only a small portion of the promises made by the Crown, many of which have never been fully honoured by the Crown. Yet, in spite of these less than honourable acts of government, Canadians on the whole continue to benefit from the vast resources of land, water, timber, minerals, and good will of the First Nations who welcomed them.

There exists a profound gap in education regarding our nation's history, which I suggest continues to fuel intolerance like that which was aimed at Starr. I am left to wonder if the school would have had any reaction at all if Starr had shown up to school in a "Straight out of Compton" sweatshirt? I would assume that there would be no objection for an Aboriginal student wearing a sweatshirt claiming that she is from Compton. After all, what could be more offensive than wearing a sweatshirt promoting an extremely vulgar, violent, and sexist rap album from 1988? It seems suspicious that "Got land? Thank an Indian" is more offensive to the school staff and certain students than the multitude of other, far more offensive messages printed onto shirts that students wear to school all the time. The real problem here is that a young Indigenous woman was aware of her place and her ancestors' role in the making of this country, and that she was willing to take this message to her school. The truth, therefore, is what is offensive for many Canadians.

It has been 150 years and yet the relationship between the people of Canada and the First Nations people of this land has been characterized by struggle and conflict. Reflecting on this nation's history from an Indigenous perspective, ask yourself: Am I a Canadian who will continue supporting the social constructs built to stifle the voices of Canada's Indigenous people? Or am I a Canadian who is willing to recognize the cost of this nation's success that has been borne by Aboriginal people and "thank an Indian"?

We have all been encouraged and motivated to think critically about Canada's long history of infringing on the rights of Indigenous peoples rights here in Canada, especially recently. For example, "Got Water? Thank an Indian" was one movement that should have garnered the attention of people in the City of Winnipeg. The aim of this particular slogan was to draw attention to the source of Winnipeg's drinking water. For nearly 100 years, Shoal Lake First Nation, which is located southeast of Manitoba near the Manitoba-Ontario border, has been the source of a reliable and abundant water supply for the city. In building the aqueduct to bring water from Shoal Lake to Winnipeg, engineers created an island of the community, and isolated it from the mainland. Moreover, ironically, this same reserve has no access to its own fresh water supply, and has been under a "boil water advisory" for eighteen years. The slogan again drew attention to Canada's systemic mistreatment of Indigenous people.

Starr's experience and struggle was especially meaningful to me, because that same year I brought into the world my own daughter. The version of Canada that I envision raising my daughter in is not one where she will be told to silence her voice, or to endure stereotypes associated with her nationality. Rather, as my daughter grows, I hope Canada will become a place that respects her unique connection to this land. It is also my hope that my daughter will be taught accurate Canadian history in school, highlighting the crucial contributions that Indigenous people of this land have made.

When looking back on the last 150 years, let's not forget to look to the many elements of Canadian history that are often omitted or glossed over. These segments often exclude the important stories of Indigenous people and their land. Denying the existence of this history is to deny the foundation of Canada. Yet, so much hate still exists toward the original land owners of Canada. Hate is so often generated from not understanding the bigger picture; once a fuller understanding exists, hate can be more easily extinguished. It follows then that the hate-filled response young Tenelle Starr received exhibited not simply a lack of tolerance and understanding, but an embarrassing and tenacious ignorance in the Canadian memory. We dare not allow another generation to miss out on such important history lessons.

Drinking Dispossession
Shoal Lake 40, Winnipeg, and the Making of Canada

Adele Perry

In recognition of the 150 years since the formation of Canada as a particular kind of settler nation-state, I am going to tell a story. It isn't the story of Confederation in 1867, or of the complicated and sometimes violent expansion of Canada westward in the years that followed, though it is bound up with all of that. The story I want to tell is of how Canada used its laws to allow the City of Winnipeg to take land from Anishinaabeg people, and in particular Kekekoziibii or Shoal Lake 40 First Nation, in order to secure a water supply for the city. The critical parts of this story occurred between 1913 and 1919, but the consequences of these events endure to this day. The story of Canada and Shoal Lake 40 First Nation is one among many, but it tells us something about the character of Canadian colonialism, and how it has resourced settler communities at the expense—sometimes the undeniably direct expense—of Indigenous communities.

Shoal Lake sits in the Lake of the Woods watershed, and borders the provinces of Manitoba and Ontario. A cement aqueduct of a little more than 150 kilometres in length makes it possible for Winnipeg to divert its water supply from there. Since Shoal Lake water first flowed in Winnipeg taps in 1919, the city's water supply has been good: abundant, cheap, overwhelmingly secure, and almost always drinkable. Shoal Lake water has kept the city's population relatively healthy, certainly much healthier than the water that the city used to draw from its rivers or, later, artesian wells did. For almost a century, Shoal Lake water has fought our fires, watered our lawns, fuelled our industry, iced our rinks, flushed our toilets, lined the city's coffers, and, of course, quenched our thirst.

At the other end of the aqueduct is Shoal Lake 40. When the aqueduct was built, the land reserved for Shoal Lake 40 was divided into three parts; the main settlement was relocated and rendered an artificial island. It has remained as such.

Shoal Lake 40 has endured what might politely be called a terrible century. As of late 2016, Shoal Lake 40 relies on a precarious and costly barge to come and go during the ice-free months. They have no secure method of travelling to and from the community during break-up in the spring and freeze-up in the fall. Shoal Lake 40 has no reliable system of garbage removal and a failing sewer system. Shoal Lake 40 does not have regular access to emergency services or the mail. Since 1997, Shoal Lake 40 has been on a boil water advisory, unable to access the water that flows in Winnipeg taps, and without the tools to treat the water they are left with. These are not conditions that easily sustain community, and in 2016, more than half of the community's registered members live elsewhere.[1]

The contrast between Winnipeg and Shoal Lake 40 is illustrative and painful. In the 2000s and 2010s, clever, effective, and persistent community activism punctured the almost century of silence and denial that had elided Shoal Lake 40's experience of Canadian modernity. For much of 2015, Shoal Lake 40 was in the national news, the subject of headlines, documentaries, and a crowd-funded campaign. Shoal Lake 40's status as an ironically waterless community became an issue in the federal election, and late in 2015, Justin Trudeau's Liberal Party was elected on a platform that included a federal commitment to funding a road linking Shoal Lake 40 to the Trans-Canada Highway, and to end boil water advisories in Indigenous communities. A year later, the complicated, multi-jurisdictional, and long-fought road that would make a water treatment plant feasible remains in the early stages, its plans fragile.[2]

These circumstances cannot be blamed on the nebulous and often evoked circumstance of "isolation." Shoal Lake 40 is about a two-hour drive from Winnipeg, and falls squarely within any definition of southern Canada. It is close to the Trans-Canada Highway, and nearby some very swanky cottages. That Shoal Lake 40 faces many of the challenges routinely associated with what the mainstream media likes to call "isolated" or "remote" Indigenous communities is a reminder that such conditions are created by history and policy, rather than intransigent geography.

There are many ways that one might tell the story of Canada and Shoal Lake 40. Most importantly, one might tell it from the vantage point of Shoal Lake 40 itself, its people, its land, and their enduring historical knowledge. But that is not the story I am telling here. I am a settler and an academic historian. In this essay, I offer what can be reconstituted through the particular lens of the colonial archive, especially the records created by Canada's Department of Indian Affairs

(DIA). These records are housed in Library and Archives Canada, in Ottawa, collected by the City of Winnipeg, and written by journalists reporting at the time. Unsurprisingly, these records are brittle and self-serving, and tend to tell us much more about the non-Indigenous men who wrote them than anything else. But still, this archive contains material that can help us understand what happened between Canada, Winnipeg, and Shoal Lake 40 in the 1910s.

I hope that putting the focus on settlers and state makes clear where responsibility lies for the colonial violence enacted. What occurred to Shoal Lake 40 between 1913 and 1919, and has been done and not done since, is emblematic of Canada's story. Understanding how Shoal Lake 40 was dispossessed and impoverished in the interests of Winnipeg helps us see Canada's much celebrated economic and social success in a sharp light. Canadian prosperity has been built on Indigenous peoples, lands, and resources. Indigenous peoples have long called these histories out, and, as this book attests, continue to do so. On Canada's 150th birthday, perhaps non-Indigenous people like myself might consider the ways that our lives and communities have thrived in no small part at the expense of Indigenous ones.

Early twentieth-century Winnipeg was in desperate need of a better water supply. The means by which Anishinaabeg, Nehiyawak, and Métis people who lived near the juncture of the Red and Assiniboine Rivers had secured drinking water for generations could not sustain the population that came following Manitoba's difficult entry into Confederation in 1870. In the last decades of the nineteenth and the first of the twentieth century, Winnipeg attempted a number of options to meet its growing needs for water: public ownership, private ownership, river water, and well water. Some of these water supplies imperilled public health, while others were inconvenient or a problem for the kind of population and industrial growth that the leaders of the day most desired.[3]

The idea that water might be brought from Lake of the Woods to Winnipeg found its champion in a man named Thomas Russ Deacon. In 1906, Deacon was elected Winnipeg City Councillor. In 1912, he ran for mayor on a "Shoal Lake water" platform, pledging: "I am in favour of providing at once for the people of Winnipeg an ample and permanent supply of pure soft water, which will forever remove the menace now hanging over Winnipeg of a water famine and the consequent danger of conflagration and sickness."[4] Once mayor, Deacon set about engaging various levels of settler state government. They formed the Greater

Winnipeg Water District (GWWD), a special body that combined five municipalities. Within the space of two years, the GWWD sought and received approval for their plan from the Federal Government, the province of Ontario, the province of Manitoba, and, since Lake of the Woods crossed the Medicine Line that artificially divides Canada and the United States, the International Joint Commission.[5]

Anishinaabeg communities at Shoal Lake received little mention in the voluminous, and often lovingly, detailed commentary about the proposed aqueduct that accompanied these legislative manoeuvres. In 1905, one newspaper commented that the canal would leave "the lake at the Indian reservation."[6] A year later, another declared that there was "practically no habitation with the exception of a few Indians and an odd mining camp and no possibility of contamination from this source."[7] As newspapers wrote more about the aqueduct, they had less and less to say about Indigenous people who lived and had lived there for so long. A reference to an inspection trip mentioned passing "the time between supper and the lake darkness" by visiting "the interesting local exhibit, the Indian burying ground."[8]

The near silence about Indigenous people both reflected and helped to secure the formal dispossession the aqueduct required. Even then, the aqueduct's intake was to be built on what the settler state recognized as Indigenous land, the particular category born of North American settler policy: the Indian reserve. The reserves around Shoal Lake were laid out following the cementing of Treaty 3 in 1873. In 1876, the first *Indian Act* was passed into law, providing the legislative framework that the Federal Government would use to give the GWWD the reserve lands that it wanted in order to solve Winnipeg's water issues.

The dispossession of Shoal Lake 40 in the interests of Winnipeg occurred in a couple of stages. In the fall of 1913, the GWWD's lawyer wrote the DIA and requested permission "to erect a camp and to do the survey work on Indian Reserve No. 40 on Indian Bay at Shoal Lake." Permission was granted, with no evidence of consultation with the First Nation and no requirements for compensation beyond general comments about the GWWD's responsibility for damages.[9] A few months later, Shoal Lake 40 Chief Pete Redsky wrote to the Indian agent, asking: "Has the Greater Winnipeg Water Commission made any arrangement about occupying any part of the reserve or about taking sand, gravel or timber from it?" He then reminded him, "We look to you to care for the interests of the Indians in this matter."[10]

Canada's response was to strip Shoal Lake 40 of their rights to some of the resources that Redsky mentioned. Located at a key juncture in longstanding

Indigenous and fur-trade networks, and amid a mining boom and tourist economy, Shoal Lake 40 was well accustomed to trade, commerce, and wage work. In keeping with this economic practice, Redsky responded to the GWWD's arrival in 1913 by negotiating with the contractor to sell gravel and sand. The Kenora-based Indian agent and his Ottawa superiors intervened, explaining that the First Nation could not sell gravel and sand unless they "surrendered" whatever rights they had to it. Surrender was the legislative process that separated Indigenous people from the little land and resources Canada recognized them as holding. Early in 1914, the DIA conducted a version of their usual surrender process. They gathered together the male band members aged over 21 and a slim majority—eleven out of 21—voted in favour of surrendering their rights to gravel and sand. After that, the Federal Government would possess the rights to those resources and hold whatever proceeds they made off them in trust for Shoal Lake 40.[11]

Surrender was the price that Shoal Lake 40 had to pay to make a living in a cash economy. They were far from alone in losing their lands and resources through this particular process. These were years that witnessed the consolidation of settler control, and increasing regulation and restriction of Indigenous peoples, and surrender was a key means through which this was secured. Between 1896 and 1911, a remarkable 21 percent of lands reserved for First Nations in Alberta, Saskatchewan, and Manitoba were taken through surrender.[12] About half the reserve lands in southern Saskatchewan were lost to surrender between 1896 and 1928.[13]

These figures did not include the over 3,000 acres of land that Shoal Lake 40 would lose in the years between 1914 and 1919. When it became clear that the GWWD sought Shoal Lake 40 reserve land, it seemed like the DIA would follow their general practice and seek a formal surrender arrangement for the land required to build the aqueduct, as well as the canal and dyke, all designed to ensure that it did not deliver murky-looking water to Winnipeg. But the process that would ultimately take the most critical part of Shoal Lake 40's land did not even follow these conventions. In January, Ottawa set some modest limits on the GWWD's continued work on the reserve. The DIA explained that they were "not disposed" to let the GWWD build additional buildings unless more information was provided and a surrender was granted.[14] Duncan Campbell Scott, Deputy Superintendent of the DIA and part-time poet, explained: "I have to request that you will kindly advise the Department fully as to your plans in connection with carrying on operations on this reserve, as you are aware no rights can be granted without the consent of the Indians."[15] Deacon responded with maps and the revealing admission that "We recognize that the Indians are entitled to reasonable compensation for this and we are prepared to pay what the Department would think just."[16]

With those comments, Deacon nodded to the concept of Indigenous title, but made clear that he considered it something the Federal Government could control and value. Indian Agent R.S. McKenzie rightly registered these conversations as a kind of formality, and the granting of Shoal Lake 40 land to the GWWD was, more or less, inevitable. In February 1914, he accessed that the GWWD had already built "two very fine buildings," and that the "whole operation will be on the reserve." "I suppose that sooner or later they will be given the privelage [sic] asked for," he concluded.[17]

This was a classic colonial dance—a privilege requested that could not be refused, a request that could not conceivably be denied. It was a particularly sharp legislative stick that brought the dance to a close. By late February 1914, Ottawa had dropped the language of surrender and explained that Shoal Lake 40's lands would be appropriated through a different, and demonstrably more coercive, instrument within the *Indian Act*: Section 46.[18] Minister of the Interior and Superintendent-General of Indian Affairs Frank Oliver had introduced this as an amendment of the 1906 *Indian Act*, part of a suite of changes helping to expedite the process by which First Nations might be stripped of their lands. Historian Brian Titley explains that Section 46 "gave the department greater powers of coercion," by allowing reserve land to be taken by municipalities or companies for roads, railways, or other "public works" with only the permission of the governor-in-council.[19] These provisions would remain in place until 1951, when the *Indian Act* was revised to remove some of its most heavy-handed, and increasingly embarrassing, powers.[20]

This was a discussion about *how* to take Shoal Lake 40's land, not whether to take it. It occurred not at Shoal Lake, or even Kenora. The discussion was conducted largely on paper, and in person, between settler men in Ottawa and Winnipeg. The DIA's clerk advised Winnipeg's mayor:

> Since the above lands may be acquired under Section 46 of the Indian Act a surrender from the band will not be necessary. The valuation has been placed at $3.00 per acre in addition to a charge of 5 c per cubic yard for the sand and gravel in the pit.[21]

This deal was consolidated and nudged further in Winnipeg's favour when Mayor Deacon travelled to Ottawa early in March. He did so to arrange the complicated financing of the GWWD's aqueduct scheme, which involved the sale of public bonds. Deacon also firmed up the terms under which Winnipeg would take Shoal Lake 40's land. The Toronto daily newspaper the *Globe* reported, "While in Ottawa the Mayor took up the question of securing terminals for the pipeline and the railway in Indian Reserve No. 40, and he reports that very satisfactory arrangements have been made."[22]

The arrangements that were "very satisfactory" for Deacon seem to have been arrived at without any dialogue with the First Nations whose lands were at stake. In Ottawa, officials assured themselves that these plans were supported by the community, explaining: "The Department is pleased to note however, that the members of the Band appear to be quite willing to part with these lands."[23] This comforting assertion was never put to the test, and Canadian policy made sure it didn't need to be. If the DIA's assessment of community interest in a land sale was correct, why didn't they conduct a surrender process as they had the year before, and as they continued to do in so many communities? Section 46 required a significant mobilization of influence, prestige, and connections with officials in Ottawa. The DIA's decision to utilize Section 46, and presumably the GWWD's advocacy for it, should give us serious pause. Among the reasons for using Section 46 is that the GWWD's dyke and canal construction were more or less complete, before "legalities" were finalized.[24] In this sense, the expropriation of land under Section 46 was retroactive.

The biggest hurdle to this dispossession was not Shoal Lake 40's treaty rights, or the presumed protections of the *Indian Act* of their land or resources, but Winnipeg's miserly unwillingness to pay the price that Ottawa unilaterally set. By February 1914, the DIA had arrived at a price: three dollars per acre of land and five cents per cubic yard of sand and gravel, resources the Federal Government possessed the rights to thanks to the surrender process conducted the year before. Deacon expressed considerable indignation that the GWWD would be charged anything for gravel and sand. The mayor wrote that the city was already paying enough, more than was being charged for adjacent Crown lands.[25] Here Deacon made clear exactly how he, and presumably men like him, thought of reserve lands: as more or less equivalent to Crown ones, lands that might be taken by settlers who paid nominal fees, filled out the right paperwork, and lined up in the right office. Deacon's empowered outrage won the day, and Scott sent a letter by special mail confirming their oral agreement: Winnipeg could have the gravel and sand for no additional cost.[26]

At Shoal Lake 40 in 1914, Anishinaabeg men provided manual labour for the GWWD's works. Many families would have moved, and had little choice in the matter, with their reserve lands divided into three parts by the GWWD's aqueduct, canal, and dyke.[27] The community pressed Indian Agent McKenzie for information about what, exactly, was happening to their lands. In July 1914, McKenzie sent their discontent up the bureaucratic food chain, explaining that "the Indians was very much excited about the work of the Greater Winnipeg Water works, and requested me to tell them what right they had to operate on their Reserve, and demanded to know what they were to get for the land taken, and what quantity is taken from them."[28] McKenzie had "not received any Official report on this matter" and requested a survey "so the Indians will know just where they are at."[29] Ottawa replied with a blueprint coloured in to show the extent of the land loss, and a brief recitation of the state's power to dispossess even those lands supposedly reserved for Indians, accompanied by a reflexive and, in this case, clearly empty reiteration of settler benevolence. "The Corporation of the city of Winnipeg has the power to expropriate the lands required, but you may assure the Indians that their rights will be safeguarded by the Department."[30]

In the year that followed the dispossession of about 3,350 acres of Shoal Lake 40's reserve lands would be confirmed, codified, and archived. In December 1914, Winnipeg sent a cheque, and in Ottawa, a law clerk noted that "The Greater Winnipeg Water District has the requisite statutory authority as referred to by Sec. 46 of the Indian Act as amended by S. Ch. 14, 1-2 for taking and using land without the consent of the owner."[31] On the March 3, 1915, the whole deal would be further reviewed by a committee of the Privy Council, and approved by Canada's head of state, "His Royal Highness the Governor General."[32]

At Shoal Lake 40, Chief Pete Redsky responded through the mechanisms available to him. In a December 1918 letter signed with an X and dated from the residential school, Redsky laid out the community's substantial grievances in certain terms: "This is asking the Government for the pay for the Reserve." Redsky went on to explain that the land the GWWD had taken was "the best part of our Reserve." He explained: "The land is very good Farming, Good timber, good hay land. We are now very anxious for 'The district' to pay for our land, and if they are not willing to pay for our land, I think they had better hand it back. I think it is time for you to fix up with us."[33] Redsky threatened to go to Ottawa himself, accompanied by a translator. McKenzie relayed the message: "They are quite dissatisfied with this and he is bound to go down."[34] In response, Ottawa reiterated that the land had been taken under Section 46, that Winnipeg had paid $1,500 for the land covered by water and $1,065 for the land on reserve, and the DIA was holding that amount.[35] Redsky continued to press for answers, and to pledge to lead a delegation to Ottawa. In response, the DIA decided to distribute half of the amount and the interest that had accrued at treaty day. It worked out to fifteen dollars per person.[36]

In 1919, Winnipeg acquired another parcel of Shoal Lake 40's reserve land. Winnipeg explained that they needed to own that land to protect their water supply, and gain control over the sandy beach used by tourists who travelled to Shoal Lake on the excursion trains that helped finance the GWWD's operations. For a dollar round-trip, Winnipeggers could take the GWWD train to Shoal Lake, spend the day at the beach, and monitor the progress of construction. An issue of the *Winnipeg Telegram* published during the 1919 general strike boasted that the trip "will give the citizens a chance to get away from the heat of the city to the cooling breezes of the lake and to let them see the work which has been done to secure the splendid supply of soft water for Winnipeg."[37]

In Ottawa, discussions to again use Section 46 were dropped fairly quickly.[38] John Semmens, Inspector of Indian Agencies for Lake of the Woods, was growing tired of the GWWD's requests. Semmens announced that he was "disposed to make a trip up there to assure myself that nobody's claim is being interfered with under the desired possession of the land asked for," and "at the same time consult the Indians so as to be able to tell the Department what they think about the surrender of the portion specified."[39] When the GWWD replied, the amount of land in question had risen from 20 to "about 32" acres.[40]

Shoal Lake 40's leadership took this as an opportunity to return to their grievances about gravel and sand. They pressed Ottawa about their rights to gravel and sand, and Chief Redsky along with eight other men and two witnesses put their marks to a detailed letter that carefully documented the discussions and promises they recalled.[41] Officials in Winnipeg and Ottawa rejected Redsky's version of events, with Winnipeg mayor R.D. Waugh writing emphatically that the gravel and sand came from "our *own* property, which the Water District bought from the Indians."[42] Redsky continued to advocate, explaining, "We would like to find out about the sand & gravel first," before they would consider the new request.[43]

Winnipeg justified this effort to acquire additional Shoal Lake 40 land as somehow in the community's interests, even an effort to protect the community's reserve rights. Waugh explained that tourists who made use of the GWWD's excursion trains trespassed on Shoal Lake 40's reserve lands and expressed "great interest" in the "small Indian graveyard." If Winnipeg became the owners of that land, they might prevent trespass and put up a fence to "keep the public from disturbing the graves."[44] It was only by selling more land to settler governments that Chief Redsky would be able to protect his peoples' burial area from trespass and violation. In June 1920, a further 32 acres of Shoal Lake 40's lands would be transferred to the GWWD through surrender.[45]

A year later, Shoal Lake 40 people would again find themselves needing to advocate for access to funds kept by the Federal Government in trust. The Indian agent relayed some of Shoal Lake 40's concerns to Ottawa and undermined them at the same time, explaining: "They do not appear to really need the money at the present time."[46] It was as if Indigenous claims could never be about rights, only need, and the state's obligations a kind of optional charity given only grudgingly. It was not until 1928 that Shoal Lake 40 members would receive payment of five dollars per person.[47]

We tend to associate Indigenous land loss with particular moments: when colonizers first arrived, after armed conflict, when states were formed, when territorial treaties were negotiated, or when reserve systems laid out. The case of Shoal Lake 40 and Winnipeg reminds us that this process was more ongoing and diffuse, nestled within Canada's distinctly modern settler regime.

We see here how modern settler colonialism took land, and resources, and land as a conduit to those resources. Between 1913 and 1919, Canada used the mechanisms of the *Indian Act* to take Shoal Lake 40's land, gravel, sand, and water, and then sold it to Winnipeg at a price that Ottawa set. Two of these losses were managed through the surrender process, while another, and the most significant loss, utilized the much heavier hand of Section 46. This was the land that allowed Winnipeg to build the intake for its aqueduct, and deliver the quality of water that urban people expected to sustain their own urban economy, growth, and health.

A sale in which the seller had no choice, and has no power to negotiate the price, might better be described as a theft. What occurred at Shoal Lake 40 between 1913 and 1919 was a particular kind of colonial theft, one guaranteed by colonial policy and law, in the years where the settler state was particularly equipped to monitor Indigenous peoples lives and strip them of some of the very limited and circumscribed rights they had to land and resources. The decision to take over 3,000 acres of Shoal Lake 40's land, trisect the reserve, and leave the community an artificial island was made in Ottawa, and in the primary interests of Winnipeg. Later in the twentieth century, the mechanisms of appropriation changed, and the City of Winnipeg asserted its interests in controlling economic development within Shoal Lake 40's remaining lands[48]. The relative prosperity of Winnipeg was secured through its access to drinkable, cheap, bountiful Shoal Lake water, which in turn directly depended on the unilateral land loss suffered by Shoal Lake 40. Canada is a country built on Indigenous land and Indigenous water.

Acknowledgements:
I would like to thank Shoal Lake 40 First Nation, the Friends of Shoal Lake 40, and Honour the Source, for their support, engagement, and solidarity. The University of Manitoba's Centre for Human Rights Research has provided tangible support for this research and I am also grateful for that. Cuyler Cotton and Myra Tait provided detailed feedback on this essay and it is better for it.

1. Canada, "Registered Population, Shoal Lake No.40," accessed at: www.pse5-esd5.ainc-inac.gc.ca/fnp/Main/Search/FNRegPopulation.aspx?BAND_NUMBER=155&lang=eng
2. See Akin, David, "After Trudeau Visit, Shoal Lake First Nation hopes 100-year wait for Freedom Road near end," *National Post*, September 12, 2016: www.news.nationalpost.com/news/canada/canadian-politics/after-trudeau-visit-shoal-lake-first-nation-hopes-100-year-wait-for-freedom-road-near-end. I explore these histories further in Perry, Adele (2016), *Aqueduct: Colonialism, Resources, and the Histories We Remember*, Winnipeg: ARP Press.
3. The best discussion of this history remains Artibise, Alan (1975), *Winnipeg: A Social History of Urban Growth, 1874-1914*, Montréal: McGill-Queen's University Press.
4. Electoral ticket, "Vote for Deacon: The People's Choice for Mayor," in "Clippings re Mayoralty," Deacon papers. Also, see advertisement in *Winnipeg Free Press*, December 7, 1912. On Deacon, see Bumsted, J.M. (2014), "Thomas Russ Deacon," *Dictionary of Manitoba Biography*, Winnipeg: University of Manitoba Press, 66; "Thomas Russ Deacon," www.mhs.mb.ca/docs/people/deacon_tr.shtml; Shropshire, Lorne, "Mayor Battles Critics," *Winnipeg Real Estate News*, January 7, 1994.
5. See International Joint Commission, *Hearing and Arguments in the Matter of the Application of the Greater Winnipeg Water District for Approval of the Diversion of the Waters of the Lake of the Woods and Shoal Lake for Sanitary and Domestic Purposes* (Washington, Government Printing Office, 1914); and "An Act to Confer Certain Rights and Powers Upon The Greater Winnipeg Water District," found at: www.ijc.org/files/dockets/Docket%207/ Docket%207%20Order%20of%20Approval%201914-01-14.pdf
6. "New Proposition for Water Supply," *Manitoba Free Press*, March 1, 1905.
7. "Water Commission Visits Shoal Lake," *Manitoba Free Press*, September 3, 1906.
8. "Inspection Trip to Shoal Lake," *Manitoba Free Press*, July 27, 1914.
9. Stewart, S. to R.S. McKenzie, 27 October 1913, and Honorable Dr. Roche, Memo, October 28, 1913, Indian Affairs, Library and Archives Canada RG 10, Vol. 3178, File 447, 733-1 and 733-1A. Hereafter RG 10. These files are available online at Library and Archives Canada's website: www.collectionscanada.gc.ca/.

10. Red Sky, Pete [Redsky] to R.S. McKenzie, December 7, 1913, RG 10, Vol. 3178, File 447, 733-1A.
11. McKenzie, R.S., "Report of a Council Meeting held at Shoal Lake on Above Date of the Shoal Lake Band No. 40. Before Indian Agent RS McKenzie and Record all Voting Members, of said band over 21 Years for the purpose of surendring [sic] there [sic] rights to all the sand and gravel on said reserve, to the Department," January 7, 1914, RG 10, Volume 3178, File 447, 733-1.
12. Spaulding, Richard, "Executive Summary"; Martin-McGuire, Peggy, "First Nation Land Surrenders on the Prairies, 1896-1911," (Ottawa, Indian Claims Commission, 1989) ixiii. Also see Carter, Sarah, "'An Infamous Proposal': Prairie Indian Reserve Land and Soldier Settlement after World War 1," *Manitoba History*, Spring/Summer 1999 (37), pp. 9-23.
13. See *Report of the Manitoba Aboriginal Justice Inquiry*, November 1999, Vol. I, Chapter Three, fn 50.
14. McLean, J.D. to R.S. McKenzie, January 26, 1914, RG 10, Vol. 3178, File 447, 733-1.
15. Scott, Duncan Campbell to H. Reynolds, February 3, 1914, RG 10, Vol. 3178, File 447, 733-1.
16. Deacon, Thomas R. to Duncan Campbell Scott, February 26, 1914, RG 10, Vol. 3178, File 447, 733-1.
17. McKenzie, R.S. to J.D. McLean, February 23, 1914, RG 10, Vol. 3178, File 447, 733-1.
18. McLean, J.D. to Thomas R. Deacon, February 26, 1914, RG 10, Vol. 3178, File 447, 733-1.
19. Titley, Brian (1986), *A Narrow Vision: Duncan Campbell Scott and the Administration of Indian Affairs in Canada*, Vancouver: UBC Press, p. 21.
20. Treaties and Historical Research Centre, Indian and Northern Affairs, *The Historical Development of the Indian Act*, Ottawa: 1978, pp. 107-9, 150.
21. McLean, J.D. to Thomas R. Deacon, February 26,1914, RG 10, Vol. 3178, File 447, 733-1.
22. "Arrangements Made to Float Winnipeg Bonds," *Globe*, March 5, 1914.
23. McLean, J.D. to R.S. McKenzie, March 4, 1914, RG 10, Vol. 3178, File 447, 733-1.
24. I am grateful to David Ennis for this important point, and for his assistance with this work.
25. Deacon, Thomas R. to J.D. McLean, March 7, 1914, RG 10, Vol. 3178, File 447, 733-1.
26. Deacon, Thomas R. to Duncan Campbell Scott, March 23, 1914, RG 10, Vol. 3178, File 447, 733-1.
27. See Ennis, David A., "Not All Down Hill From There: The Shoal Lake Aqueduct and the Greater Winnipeg Water District," *Manitoba History*, 75 (Summer 2014), pp. 38-44.
28. McKenzie, R.S. to J.D. McLean, July 20, 1914, RG 10, Vol. 3178, File 447, 733-1
29. Ibid.
30. McLean, J.D. to R.S. McKenzie, July 27, 1914, RG 10, Vol. 3178, File 447, 733-1.
31. McLean, J.D. to J.G. Harvey, December 23, 1914, RG 10, Vol. 3178, File 447, 733-1.
32. Boudreau, Rodolphe, "Certified copy of a Report of the Committee of the Privy Council, approved by His Royal Highness the Governor General on 3rd March, 1915," RG 10 Vol. 3178, File 447, 733-1.
33. Chief Redsky to R.S. McKenzie, December 19, 1918, RG 10 Vol. 3178, File 447, 733-1.
34. McKenzie, R.S. to J.D. Mclean, December 31, 1918, RG 10 Vol. 3178, File 447, 733-1.
35. McLean, J.D. to R.S. McKenzie, January 10, 1919, RG 10, Vol. 3178, File 447, 733-1A; Undated note, RG 10, Vol. 3178, File 447, 733-1A.
36. McLean, J.D. to R.S. McKenzie, April 28, 1919, RG 10, Vol. 3178, File 447, 733-IA.
37. "Shoal Lake Excursion Leaves Here Tomorrow," *Winning Telegram Strike Edition*, June 20, 1919.
38. Bray, S. to Deputy Minister, October 15, 1919, RG 10, Vol. 3178, File 447, 733-1A.
39. Semmens, John to J.D. McLean, December 9, 1919, RG 10, Vol. 3178, File 447, 733-1A.
40. Chase, W.D. to John Semmens, March 6, 1920, RG 10, Vol. 3178, File 447, 733-1A.

41. Oshashenahoo, Bald-head, Cheenah, Nahwahchewapetung, Jim Cheenah, Peter Redsky, Opahshusk, Okeshe Koona to John Semmes, nd [late 1919, early 1920] RG 10, Vol. 3178, File 447, 733-1A.
42. Waugh R.D. to John Semmens, January 3, 1920, RG 10, Vol. 3178, File 447, 733-1A.
43. Redsky, Pete to John Semmens, December 20, 1919, RG 10, Vol. 3178, File 447, 733-1A.
44. Waugh R.D. to John Semmens, June 21, 1919, RG 10, Vol. 3178, File 447, 733-1A.
45. "Vote of Shoal Lake Band No. 40 Taken for The Surrender of a Part of their Reserve to the Department for Sale to the Greater Winnipeg Water District," June 4, 1920.
46. Edwards, Frank to J.D. McLean, May 11, 1921, RG 10, Vol. 3178, File 447, 733-1A.
47. "Red Sky—Summary For Mrs. Young," nd [1934?] RG 10, Vol. 3178, File 447, 733-1A.
48. On this, see Lorraine, Brian, "Shoal Lake 40 Water crisis an ugly reminder of Canadian Colonialism," *Ricochet*, June 22, 2016: www.ricochet.media/en/1239/shoal-lake-40-water-crisis-an-ugly-reminder-of-canadian-colonialism

Refusing Canada

Eric Ritskes

COLONIALISM 150

"I don't want no fucking country . . ."
—DIONNE BRAND[1]

This is a call for us all to refuse the country, the violence of its founding and maintenance, and its profound, ongoing mechanisms of exclusion; this is a call to refuse its false sense of belonging. This image, and the above quote, calls us to upend the national imagination and embrace otherwise possibilities.[2]

The Canada 150 logo is described as a series of diamonds coming together to form the national symbol of the maple leaf.[3] It is intended to be a celebratory logo of belonging and inclusion, to represent the many pieces of a multicultural whole that come together to form Canada.

But, as Rinaldo Walcott reminds us, the oft-celebrated multicultural project of Canada is not a project of belonging; rather it's a project of whiteness that exacerbates the problem of belonging for those who do not subscribe to this normative whiteness.[4]

It is not only a project of profound whiteness (and anti-blackness); it is also a settler colonial project. Canada is an ongoing project of violence that seeks to subdue and destroy Indigenous peoples, cultures, and lands. To celebrate Canada is to celebrate colonial conquest, settlement, and the attendant violence necessary to secure the nation's ongoing legitimatization and normalization.

If the Canadian government wants to make reconciliation a central part of its birthday celebrations[5], doesn't truth need to be a part of the process before we can celebrate reconciliation? And, if we're being truthful, isn't there more than just truth needed before we can celebrate reconciliation?

Instead of allowing Canada to recuperate its image through celebrations of reconciliation and inclusion (a classic counterinsurgency method, as Dean Spade reminds us[6]), truth-telling disrupts the peaceful, multicultural narrative that marginalizes the experiences of those who are subjected to the colonial violence of the state.

A politics of "no fucking country," a politics that upends the nation and its symbols, is a process of truth-telling; it is not merely a rejection of the violence of the state, but a generative stance, the opening of otherwise possibilities. The politics of refusal is not merely reactionary, nor is it foundering for lack of otherwise possibilities. In this image, the logo is flipped and the diamonds no longer symbolize celebration but the sharpness of their edges, a cutting edge that brings clarity. In refusal, we find a tool to aid in crafting the future we are hoping for.

> *"I am not a nation-state, nor do I strive to be one."*
> —LEANNE SIMPSON[7]

There are otherwise worlds being built, otherwise possibilities being breathed and being dreamed into being. There are alternatives to the nation-state. As Leanne Simpson writes, Indigenous nationhood models otherwise worlds, ones that do not rely on violence, that are not enclosures. Indigenous nationhood demonstrates for us a possibility that requires a different sort of embodied relationality and accountability to one another, and to the land on which we live.

So, in refusal of the settler nation-state of Canada we find not only a rejection of the celebration of ongoing colonialism, but an opportunity to support and celebrate the ongoing resistance to it. In refusal, we disrupt the normalization and legitimization of colonial violence and open space for otherwise possibilities to be dreamt and built into being. That is something worth celebrating.

1. Brand, Dionne (1997), *Land to Light On*, Toronto: McClelland & Stewart, p. 48.
2. Crawley, Ashon, "Otherwise Movements," *The New Inquiry*, January 19, 2015: www.thenewinquiry.com/essays/otherwise-movements/
3. Government of Canada, "The Canada 150 Logo," last modified August 01, 2016: www.canada.pch.gc.ca/eng/1469537603125
4. Walcott, Rinaldo (2006), "Land to Light On? Making Reparation in a Time of Transnationality," *Metaphoricity and the Politics of Mobility*, ed. Maria Margaroni and Effie Yiannopoulou, Amsterdam: Rodopi B.V., p. 89.

5. Quinn, Mark, "Reconciliation with Indigenous People to Underscore Canada 150 Celebrations, says Federal Minister," CBC.ca: www.cbc.ca/news/canada/newfoundland-labrador/reconciliation-with-indigenous-people-to-underscore-canada-150-celebrations-says-federal-minister-1.3907062
6. Spade, Dean, "Now Is the Time for 'Nobodies': Dean Spade on Mutual Aid and Resistance in the Trump Era," *Alternet*: www.alternet.org/activism/now-time-nobodies-dean-spade-mutual-aid-and-resistance-trump-era
7. Simpson, Leanne, "I am Not a Nation-State," *NationsRising.org*: www.nationsrising.org/i-am-not-a-nation-state/.

O Canada
"A country cannot be built on a living lie."[1]

James (Sa'ke'j) Youngblood Henderson

As Canadians approach the expensive memorialization and commemoration of the sesquicentennial of federal colonialism in Canada, it is time to reassess the foundations on which Canadians think they are celebrating. Canadians may consider that confederation begins with the confederation of the British colonies into a dominion of responsible government in the *Constitution Act, 1867* (originally the *British North American Act, 1867*). Yet, this belief is a part of a complex colonial myth.[2] It is a manifestation of a lingering complex structure of colonial evasive thinking embodied in institutional fetishism based on systemic denial and avoidance of its relational beginnings with Indigenous peoples and nations. It is a ritualization of the historical denial of the fundamental and integral role alliances and treaties between Indigenous nations and British sovereigns played in generating Canada that needs to be decolonized. It is a narrative that turns away from the actual treaty federalism of the Indigenous nations to focus on branding the nationalism around colonizer and settler narratives and myths.

Most Canadians remain unsettlingly evasive of these core Indigenous relational foundations that surround the commemoration. Most Canadians hold happily to the country's rich heritage, thinking it begins with their colonial roots with the British and French, and are clueless to the absence of the alliance and treaties in the commemoration; others choose to operate without confronting openly the problematic character of their confederation, and the source of their idea of confederation. Most remain unconscious of the betrayal of the dominion to the Indigenous nations and their treaties with the royal family of Great Britain. No extant record of a debate or any other document exists that clearly explains why the founding fathers of the uniting provinces transferred jurisdiction over "Indians" from the provinces to the newly created federal dominion. The 1864

Charlottetown Conference of the provinces makes no mention about Indians. At the later Québec Conference, in October of that same year, at the end of this conference "Indians and Lands reserved for Indians" had been silently included under resolution 29 of "the General Parliament" without any recorded debate or reasons. However, the Select Committee of the UK House of Commons Report in 1837 had established that the purpose behind such imperial delegation of power over Indians and their treaties was to protect them from the local colonial provinces and colonialists.[3]

Section 91(24) of the *Constitution Act, 1867* established the exclusive constitutional responsibilities of the newly formed federal government for "Indians," while all other peoples were the responsibility of the uniting provinces. As part of their constitutional obligations to the imperial sovereign, the federal government in Section 132 of the *Constitution Act, 1867* was delegated authority to carry out the imperial obligations arising under the existing imperial treaties, which included the existing treaties with the Indigenous nations. The power of the federal government, constitutionally speaking, was to administer the existing duties and obligations of treaty nations for the imperial Crown.[4]

The ideological element of the commemoration of confederation conceals the original federation of the Indigenous nation with the British sovereign by treaties as a shared secret. The federal government has kept clandestine the Indigenous treaty foundation of the nation.[5] Successive governments sought to end the nation-to-nation relations in the imperial treaties,[6] refusing to fulfill their treaty obligation by legislation. Rather they sought to terminate and replace the treaties with colonial-styled band institutions that ignored Aboriginal rights, and through a process of forced cognitive assimilation and cultural genocide caused Indians to cease to exist as distinct legal, social, cultural, religious, and racial nations in Canada.[7] In short, they attempted, albeit unsuccessfully, to abolish the constitutional category of Indians.

This mythical construction of Canada in the commemoration by successive federal governments was and remains occupied with discourses dealing with accommodation of the French peoples, immigration and settlement of new peoples characterized as "aliens," generating responsible government, and nation building. These successive federal governments were preoccupied and struggled with the immigrant heritage of the French and English people, gradually moving from an English narrative of the creation of Canada to a mythical and idealized concept of Canada from two founding settler colonialists from Great Britain and France.[8]

narrative: Britain + France (omits Ind. people)

This narrative has been harmful to the Indigenous nations as it conceals the true nature of the original agreements and the failure of federal responsibility to protect them from the resulting outcomes of paternalistic policies while generating false assumptions about the treaty nations, creating divisive myths about the peoples and the poverty they created, and ultimately leading to cultural genocide.[9] Aboriginal peoples understand and have lived the profound and systemic injustice of the federal government toward their knowledge system, heritage, and rights, and have little reason to celebrate their oppression or their oppressors.

An Indigenous version of the jurisgenesis narrative of Canada begins with Indigenous nations entering into ceremonial alliances and negotiations, then written treaties with the generation of compound monarchy and royal families of Great Britain in North America. These hidden and dispossessed alliances and treaties led to the treaty confederation that is the foundation of the concept of Canada. These Indigenous alliances and treaties as part of the imperial law that acknowledged and accommodated the presence of settlers in Indigenous territory, which gradually creates British North America, the United States of America, and Canada within Indigenous sovereignty and territory. The treaty relations are based on an Indigenous concept of empathetic and consensual federation[10] as represented by the structure of the Wabanaki Confederacy, Wendat Confederacy, the Haudenosaunee Confederacy ("People who are building an extended house," more commonly translated as "People of the Longhouse") and its League of Peace, the Seven Fires Confederacy, the Three Fires Confederacy, the Cree Confederacy, the Blackfoot Confederacy, and others. This Indigenous narrative of Canada has never been commemorated or celebrated, but is a deeply inspiring story of Indigenous hospitality and respect for newcomers.

The Indigenous story of Canada begins with the Royal Charter of 1621, and the nation-to-nation relationship begins in 1630 with Mi'kmaw Saqamaq Segipt and family meeting with King Charles I in London, which was reaffirmed in the treaties with King George. In 1621, King James I originally granted a Royal Charter for northwestern Newfoundland in North America to Sir William Alexander of Menstrie, Scotland, who later became Lord William, then 1st Earl of Stirling.[11] On September 29, 1621, Sir William abandoned this Royal Charter for Newfoundland for another Royal Charter for a much larger tract of land north of the St. Croix River, often called by the French "la Cadie" or "Acadie."[12] In 1625, the Royal Charter of 1621 was renewed although Sir William had failed to create a colony in "New Scot Lande." In 1625, Sir William created New Scot Lande's flag, coat of arms,

Indigenous story of Canada

and its own chivalric order that represented the alliance with the Mi'kmaq, which is now Nova Scotia's coat of arms. On February 2, 1628, King Charles I extended the 1621 Charter to include a lordship of Canada, and Lord William became the Viscount of Canada.[13] In the 1628 grant, Canada is described as all lands within 50 leagues of the area drained by the St. Lawrence River and its tributaries, as well as within 50 leagues of a passage leading from that river's source to the Gulf of California,[14] and all lands adjacent to the gulf on the west and south.

The 1628 Charter expands the recognition of Indigenous nations as declared in the 1621 Charter. The 1621 Charter acknowledges that the territory belongs to, was already occupied by, and remains owned by the Suriqui (Mi'kmaw Nation)[15] and by the Etechemini (Wabanaki Confederacy).[16] This territory included what is now called Nova Scotia, New Brunswick, Prince Edward Island, part of Québec, and parts of the states of Maine, New Hampshire, and Vermont. The Mi'kmaw ceremonial 1610 alliance with the Holy See and their baptism has established a ceremonial alliance and friendship with the French king, and the nations of the Wabanaki Confederacy expanded that alliance.[17]

Consistent with the idea of generating another composite monarchy that dominated British aristocratic thought and law at the time,[18] King James I ordered Sir William Alexander in these royal charters to enter into alliances with the nations of the Wabanaki Confederacy:[19]

> It is very important that all our beloved subjects who inhabit the said Province of New Scotland or its borders ... cultivate peace and quiet with the native inhabitants and savage aborigines of these lands, so that they, and others trading there, may safely, pleasantly and quietly hold what they got with great labour and peril.[20]

In addition, the royal charters grant Sir William and his deputies:

> Free and absolute power of arranging and securing the peace, alliance, friendship, mutual conferences, assistance, and intercourse with these savage aborigines and their chiefs, and any other bearing rule or power among them; and of preserving and fostering such relations and treaties as they or their aforesaids shall form with them ...[21]

These prerogative laws in the Charter recognized that the Mi'kmaw Nation and other nations of the Wabanaki Confederacy were territorially sovereign and had their own sovereign governments.

Under the lordship of Canada, Lord William's son, Alexander Junior, met with the "Commanders of the nation, called by them Sagamoes (*Saqmaq*)."[22] Lord William wrote of the resulting Mi'kmaq "alliance" of 1628.[23] He wrote "one of the [Mi'kmaw] cheefe of them, called 'Sagamo Segipt', to come, in the name of the rest."[24] His son Alexander recorded his translated idea of subsequent friendly convention or alliance with Sagamo Segipt in English:

> [S]o that [no] obstacle might remain, the very savages, by their commissioner, willing offring their obedience vnto his Matie; so that his Matie now is bound in honor to maintaine them, both in regard of his subjects that have plated there upon his warrant and of the promises that he made to the Commissioner of the natives that came to him from them.[25]

Thus began the ideas of the honour and duty of the King of Great Britain in his relationship with the Mi'kmaq in Canada.[26]

The Mi'kmaw concept of alliance or treaty is not of obedience but of expanding their kinship with the royal family of Great Britain. This is embodied in their concept of *ankukamewe* or in the plural is *anku'kamkewel*, referring to the notion of many things being brought together, combined, or built upon.[27] The root word *ankukamk* signifies the process of adding to an existing group or collective, thus the treaties are a method of adding families to the allied family. The relationship to the newcomers was an extended confederation. This Indigenous concept was applied to the alliance with the royal families of France, Scotland, and Great Britain suggesting that the Mi'kmaq viewed the kingdoms as joining with the various districts or tribes of the Mi'kmaw nation.

Richard Guthry's 1629 letter from the settlement to his family in Scotland provides a description of the good relations that had been established between the settlers and the Mi'kmaq of the area with the purpose of making a trading post with the Mi'kmaq and Wabanaki.[28] He wrote that the Mi'kmaq were "infinitly loving to there wyves and children, and to one another; feasting when they meet, till all there store be gone so every day serves itselfe."

To affirm the alliance with the Mi'kmaw, in December 1629, King Charles I by a royal letter directed the governor of Plymouth, Sir James Bagg, to bring to the royal court "one of the Commanders of Canada."[29] Governor Bragg was to give every assistance possible to the King's agent, whom he had sent to conduct the "royal party" to court when they arrived in 1630. The Mi'kmaq selected Sagamo Segipt to be "representative of the rest."

British historian Harvey noted that Segipt, his wife, and son, travelling as king, queen, and prince of "Canada",[30] on a ship returned to Britain to pick up supplies for the colony. They arrived in February 1630 and were treated with the "utmost courtesy."[31] From the correspondence of the period, it appears that they evoked much curiosity. They arrived at Plymouth, were entertained at Lord John Poulet's estate in Somersetshire. Much was made of the unnamed Mi'kmaw queen. Lady Christian Poulet is said to have placed "a chain about her neck, with a diamond valued by some at near £20." It was reported that the Mi'kmaq "took all in good part, but for thanks or acknowledgment made no sign or expression at all."[32]

The "king, queen, and prince of New Scotland" travelled by Lord Poulet's coach to London to meet with King Charles I.[33] In February 1630, English historian Thomas Birch and the Rev. Joseph Mead[34] commented on their visit:

> There came last week to London the king, queen, and young prince of New Scotland. This king comes to be our king's religion, and to submit his kingdom to him, and to do his homage for the same, that he may be protected against the French in Canada.[35]

In May of 1630, Mi'kmaw chief Segipt and his family returned home. They were accompanied by more English and Scottish. The Putus traditions of the Mi'kmaw Grand Council acknowledge the trading alliance and meeting with the royal family of England, but are silent on submitting to his kingdom or his religion, or protecting the British from the French. However, the gift of the chain with the diamond to Segipt's wife became an important symbol of the Mi'kmaq relationship and alliance with the Scottish and English kingdoms. The vision of the sun's relations with the diamond affirmed Mi'kmaq traditions in their creation story, and its prismatic radiation of invisible colour affirmed the nature of the transatlantic federation with the royal families. The alliance, meeting, and the chain and diamond formed the Mi'kmaq exemplification of the "covenant chain" of peace and friendship. This symbol became embedded in their symbolic law of the Nation, and an innovation in their decorative weaved baskets and symbolic art.

The Mi'kmaq alliance with the royal families and subjects of Great Britain generated a unique transatlantic system of confederation of Indigenous nations with the imperial king of Great Britain. In British law, the king's alliances and treaties with the Indigenous nations and confederacies were part of the imperial law as well as the mercantile system. These royal alliances established the royal or imperial relationship with the royal families with Canada, which parliament, the chartered companies, colonists, and the colonies had to respect.[36]

In more than 400 treaty conferences between 1613 and 1842, the Wabanaki and Haudenosaunee ambassadors taught the English colonists how to translate the metaphoric concept of alliance or treaty into a political confederation of compound sovereignty. In 1751, after reading a transcript of the 1744 meeting by a Haudenosaunee interpreter, Ben Franklin, arguing for a confederacy of the colonies, mused in a letter to James Parker:

> It would be a very strange Thing, if six Nations of Ignorant Savages should be capable of forming a Scheme for such an Union, and be able to execute it in such a Manner, as that it has subsisted Ages, and appears indissoluble; and yet that a like Union should be impracticable for ten or a Dozen English Colonies, to whom it is more necessary, and must be more advantageous; and who cannot be supposed to want an equal Understanding of their Interests.[37]

However, the innovative concept of a federation of alliance or treaty remained a difficult concept in British thought, which was stalled in the king-subject relationship. It would be called treaty commonwealth, a compact, and treaty federalism. By 1752, Governor Pownall of Massachusetts would comment on the idea of treaty federation with the Wabanaki Confederacy:

> This Modelling [of] the Peoples into various Orders, and Subordinations of Orders, so as to be capable of receiving and communicating any political Motion, and acting under that Direction as a one whole, is what the Romans called by the peculiar word *Imperium*, to express which particular Groups of Ideas, we have no word in English but by adopting the Word Empire. 'Tis by this System only that a People become a political Body; 'tis the Chain, the Bond of Union, by which very vague and independent Particles cohere.[38]

These treaties with Indigenous nations and confederation with the monarchs of Great Britain established the original federation or compound sovereign in North America. They are the foundation of both the United States and Canada. These sacred and inviolate written treaties, under the prerogative power of the monarchy, establish the principles of written constitutionalism and the imperial or royal rule of law that lies at the root and heart of imperial federalism in North

America, generating a stable, predictable, and ordered colonial society. The written treaties serve to reconcile pre-existing Aboriginal sovereignty with assumed Crown sovereignty.[39] These principles were embodied in imperial law, instructions, proclamations, and acts that protected the Indigenous nation and confederation.

I would suggest that the implied federalism principle of the newly created federal and confederating provinces in the *Constitution Act, 1867* originated from the treaties among Indigenous nations and the United Kingdom, as the treaties are part of the constitutional principles of the United Kingdom, which includes the rule of law.[40] However, the imperial confederation of responsible government for the united colonies avoided applying the rule of law to treaties, and successive governments remained silent about the British treaty federation with Indigenous nations that permitted existing British settlements. Although the imperial act vastly expanded the authority of the colonies and created the Federal Government, the consent of treaty nations to the colonial confederation was neither sought by the provinces or the imperial Crown, nor was it given by the treaty nations. Treaty nations were not a partner in responsible government derived from the UK Parliament. They did not consent to the imperial delegation or union, and did not view it as legitimate or consistent with the terms of their imperial treaties. It was an encroachment on the existing treaty relationship. It was not until the patriation of Canada's constitution in the *Canada Act* in 1982 that existing Aboriginal and treaty rights were constitutionally recognized and affirmed as part of the supreme law of Canada.[41] This section did not create these rights, which are part of Indigenous knowledge systems and legal traditions, as well as British law. Instead, it constitutionalized these rights and the guiding principle of the government's responsibility to act in a fiduciary capacity and an honourable way toward these rights, which are a "solemn commitment that must be given meaningful content."[42]

The Canadian idea, as expressed by Prime Minister Pierre Elliot Trudeau in the First Ministers' Conference on Aboriginal Constitutional Matters, was "We in this country do not seek a constitution that is nothing but a paper monument for rights that are buried under a pile of empty words. We seek constitutional provisions that have practical meaning and benefit for the people they concern."[43] He established the imperative need for Canadian governance and political theory to constitutionally accommodate, recognize, and implement the Aboriginal and treaty rights of Aboriginal peoples. The Canadian government turned their attention to transforming Aboriginal rights into modern treaties. Gradually, the Supreme Court of Canada held that the Indigenous treaties with the King and

Queen of Great Britain served to reconcile pre-existing Indigenous sovereignty with assumed Crown sovereignty,[44] and declared that the ignored and denied business of implementing existing treaties was the constitutional responsibility of both the federal and provincial governments.[45]

In reviewing the constitutional history of Canada, Justice Marie Deschamps, in her decision in *Beckman v. Little Salmon/Carmacks First Nation*, stated that the four organizing principles of the Constitution of Canada—constitutionalism and the rule of law, democracy, federalism, and respect for minority rights—are interwoven into three basic constitutional compacts: (1) one between the non-Aboriginal population and Aboriginal peoples with respect to Aboriginal rights and treaties with Aboriginal peoples (Treaties); (2) a "federal compact" between the provinces (Constitution Acts); and (3) one between the Crown and individuals with respect to individuals' fundamental rights and freedoms (Charter).[46] Yet only the federal compact is celebrated, memorialized, and commemorated in Canada.

Based on the court's decisions on the constitutional rights of Aboriginal peoples, and the recommendation of the Royal Commission on Aboriginal peoples,[47] in 2015 Prime Minister Justin Trudeau has stated that "it is time for a renewed, nation-to-nation relationship with Indigenous peoples, one that is based on recognition of rights, respect, co-operation, and partnership."[48] He stated that Aboriginal and treaty rights have to be understood not as inconveniences to the rest of Canada but as sacred obligations. As Justice Ian Binnie stated when he sat on the Supreme Court, the patriated nation of Canada "must include at least the idea that aboriginal and non-aboriginal Canadians together form a sovereign entity with a measure of common purpose and united effort. It is this new entity, as inheritor of the historical attributes of sovereignty, with which existing aboriginal and treaty rights must be reconciled."[49]

As part of this renewed relationship, guided by the spirit and intent of the original treaty relations and inherent rights of a justice-seeking relationship, it is time to celebrate the treaty compacts that established the idea of Canada, rather than only the quirky, living lie of the sesquicentennial of a colonial constitution for settlers. Canada—despite its pretensions, its accomplishments, its potential—owes its existence to treaties with Indigenous nations and confederation with the imperial Crown. It is time to reconcile the intractable gaps in the constitutional narrative and remedy the wrongs in the path toward Canadian nationhood. The constitution has been reformed to reflect this reality; the courts have spoken, now government should act to revise its complicity with colonial myths and systemic injustice. It is time to unite treaty federalism with provincial federalism. The 150th memorial now begun should articulate a vision of the sort of inclusive, cooperative, and altruistic nation that Canada must eventually become in order to achieve and establish the conditions for realizing human wellbeing. It should remind Canadians of the importance of decolonizing Canada as a quest for greater understanding and a deepening vision of the nation they desire to create, even if most Canadians do not conceptualize themselves as colonizers. Patriotic celebration that sustains federal colonization of Indians and denial of imperial treaties are highly problematic.

To assist in changing the consciousness about the meaning of Canada, the federal government should issue a proclamation as part of the 150th anniversary of the formation of the colonial constitution to articulate its plans to assist the Aboriginal peoples of Canada in generating renewed nation-to-nation relations. It should celebrate and invite Aboriginal peoples who do not have treaties into the Canadian federation, but should not coerce them. The proclamation is necessary in order to complete the unfinished work of constitutional reform in Canada, by formally implementing treaty federalism and constitutional reconciliation among Indigenous nations and the federation. This work is crucial to transforming constitutional rights into institutional changes, and generating alternative futures for Canada with clarity and deliberation.

1. Royal Commission on Aboriginal People (1996), *Report of the Royal Commission on Aboriginal Peoples*. Vol. 2: *Restructuring the Relationship*. Ottawa: Canada Communication Group, p. 1.
2. Mahoney, Kathleen, "The roadblock to reconciliation: Canada's origin story is false," *Globe and Mail* October 5, 2016: www.theglobeandmail.com/opinion/the-roadblock-to-reconciliation-canadas-origin-story-is-false/article29951998/
3. Report of the Select Committee on Aborigines, 1837, (UK), Vol. 1, Part II (Imperial Blue Book, 1837 nr VII 412) 26 June 1837, Command Papers. The compendious Report based solely on the testimony of colonial civil servants recommended against local colonial control or trust administration over the Aboriginal peoples to remedy the lack of protection and buses of the colonial governments and to prevent further injustices. It proposed that political authority over the Aboriginal Peoples should be withdrawn either to London or to the Crown's representatives in the colonies, at 77. The Report noted that violations of the imperial treaties by colonial officials because of "A ready pretext for complaint will be found in the ambiguity of the language in which their agreements must be drawn up, and in the superior sagacity which the European will exercise in framing, in interpreting, and in evading them," at 80.
4. For a list of these treaty nations, see Henderson, James Youngblood (2007), *Treaty Rights in the Constitution of Canada*, Toronto: Carswell, pp. 143-259.
5. *Report of the Royal Commission on Aboriginal Peoples*. Vol. 1: *Looking Forward, Looking Back*, pp. 114-122, 228-396; *Report of the Royal Commission on Aboriginal Peoples*. Vol. 3: *Gathering Strength*, pp. 612-623.
6. *Report of the Royal Commission on Aboriginal Peoples*, Vol. 2: *Restructuring the Relationship*, pp. 16-17.

7. Battiste, Marie (1986), "Micmac literacy and cognitive assimilation," *Indian education in Canada: The legacy*, Vol. 1, eds. J. Barman, Y. Hébert, and D. McCaskill, Vancouver: University of British Columbia Press, pp. 23-44; *Report of the Royal Commission on Aboriginal Peoples*. Vol. 1: *Looking Forward, Looking Back*, pp. 162-173; Truth and Reconciliation Commission of Canada (2015), *Honouring the Truth, Reconciling for the Future: Summary of the Final Report of the Truth and Reconciliation Commission of Canada*, Winnipeg: Truth and Reconciliation Commission of Canada, pp. 1-3.
8. See Saul, John Ralston (1988), *Reflections of a Siamese Twin: Canada at the Beginning of the Twenty-first Century*, Toronto: Penguin Canada.
9. *Honouring the Truth, Reconciling for the Future*, pp. 1-3.
10. *Report of the Royal Commission on Aboriginal Peoples.* Vol. 1: *Looking Forward, Looking Back*, pp. 112-114.
11. Insh, George Pratt (1922), *Scottish Colonial Schemes, 1620-1686*. Glasgow: Maclehose, Jackson; Finnan, Mark (1997), *The First Nova Scotian: The Story of Sir William Alexander and His Lost Colony of Charlesfort, Nova Scotia's First English-speaking Settlement*, Halifax, NS: Formac; Laing, David (1867), *Royal letters, Charters, and Tracts, relating to the Colonization of New Scotland*, Edinburgh: Bannatyne Club, reprint Kila: Kessinger Publishing, 2010: www.archive.org/stream/memorialsofearl00rogeuoft/memorialsofearl00rogeuoft_djvu.txt The Scottish Privy Council had acceded to the oral request on August 5, 1621. The Charter was granted at Windsor Castle on September 10, 1621. On September 29, the Charter passed under the Great Seal of Scotland, and Sir William Alexander was appointed hereditary lieutenant of the new colony. See Patterson, G. (1893), "Sir William Alexander and the Scottish Attempt to Colonize Acadia," *Proceedings and Transactions of the Royal Society of Canada* Vol. 19, No. 2, pp. 82-83. See also Slafter, Rev. Edmund F., ed. (1966), *Sir William Alexander and American Colonization*, Vol. 8 & Vol. 8A, reprint, New York: Burt Franklin.
12. The concept of Arcadia as a utopian wilderness was articulated in the English Renaissance of the Elizabethan Age, before colonization. See More, Sir Thomas (1515), *Utopia*, reprint Cambridge: Cambridge University Press, 2002. The image of Arcadia appears in Sir William's epic poem *Doomes-day* Vol. 2 (1637) London: Thomas Harper, pp. 3-379, where he sought to complete Sidney's *Arcadia*.
13. Slafter, 1966, pp. 243, 246.
14. Ibid., pp. 84, 185, 241-242. The Gulf or Bay of California may be referring to the Pacific Ocean. The Gulf or Bay is a body of water that separates the Baja California Peninsula from the Mexican mainland. The name "Gulf of California" predominates on most maps in English today; the name "Sea of Cortes" or *Mar de Cortés* the Spanish.
15. "Souriquois" is a French name for the Mi'kmaq in European literature.
16. As usual, confusion exists around these descriptions; both have been used to refer to the Mi'kmaq.
17. Henderson, James (Sa'ke'j) Youngblood (1997), *Mi'kmaw Concordat*, Halifax: Fernwood; Cronon, William (1983), *Changes in the Land: Indians, Colonists, and the Ecology of New England* Toronto: McGraw-Hill Ryerson, pp. 34-53.
18. Pagden, Anthony (1995) *Lords of All the World: Ideologies of Empire in Spain, Britain and France, c. 1500-c. 1800*, New Haven: Yale University Press, pp. 29-62; Richardson, J.S. (1981), "*Imperium Romanum*: Empire and the Language of Power," *Journal of Roman Studies* 81, pp. 1-9; Folz, Robert (1969), *The Concept of Empire in Western Europe from the Fifth to the Fourteenth Century*, trans. Sheila Ann Ogilvie (1969) London: Edward Arnold; Ullmann, Walter (1949), "The Development of the Medieval Idea of Sovereignty," *English Historical Review* 64, p. 1.

19. Pagden, 1995, p. 84. Compare with Alden T. Vaughan's (1978) article about events in Carolina under its Charter: "Expulsion of the Savages: British Policy and the Massacre of 1622," *William and Mary Quarterly* Vol. 35, No. 1, pp. 35, 57-84.
20. Pagden, 1995, p. 84
21. Slafter, 1966, p. 136-37; Slattery, Brian (1979), *The Land Rights of Indigenous Canadian People*, D.Phil Thesis, Oxford University, p. 106. Slattery notes that these clauses are similar to the French King's 1603 Letters Patent to De Mons. They may be modelled after them.
22. "Reasons Alleged by the Scottish Adventurers For the Holding of Port Royal," (1630), *Royal Letters*, CO 1/5, No. 102, p. 63.
23. Rogers, Charles (2013), *Memorials of the Earl of Serling and the House of Alexander*, London: Forgotten Books, pp. 118-119.
24. "Reasons Alleged by the Scottish Adventurers For the Holding of Port Royal," pp. 63-65; UK Public Record Office, "Calendar of State, Colonial Series, 1574-1660," p. 119. The meaning of the name Segipt, as written by Alexander, is ambiguous, see Harvey, D.C. (1979), "Segipt," *Dictionary of Canadian Biography Online*, Vol. 1: www.biographi.ca/en/bio/segipt_1E.html.
25. Slafter, 1966, p. 66; *Scottish Colonial Schemes*, supra note 11 at 92-93. Emphasis added.
26. This is one of the earliest expressions of the constitutional doctrine of the honour of the Crown toward Aboriginal Peoples of Canada. The obligation of honourable dealing was recognized from the outset by the Crown itself in the *Royal Proclamation* of 1763, reproduced in RSC 1985, App II, No 1. The honour of the Crown has since become a constitutional principle in treaty interpretation, R v. Badger, 1 SCR 771 (1996); R v. Marshall, 3 SCR 456 (1999); and Mikisew Cree First Nation v. Canada (Minister of Canadian Heritage), 3 SCR 388 (2005).
27. See Marshall, Joe B. (2002), "Overview of Mi'kmaw, Maliseet and Passamaquoddy Covenant Chain of Treaty," Presentation at the Assembly of First Nations Conference, "Looking Forward: Treaty Implementation" (unpublished). This term has not been fully translated by the Mi'kmaw Elders. The word *ankukamk* signifies the process of adding to an existing group or collective, thus the treaties are a ritual, rite, or method of adding members to the kin-group. This is similar to the concept of *hunkapi*, the Lakota rite for the making of relatives.
28. "Anonymous Account of New Scotland," (1630), *Hawthornden MSS*, Vol. 4, Edinburgh: National Library of Scotland, p. 149. The colonists were visited shortly after their arrival by "2 savages in a Canou," and a few weeks later by "9 savages in a Shalles [shallop] from S. Johns River with beaver skines and hydes [who] gave the generali a present." These Indians were the Wolastoqey or Maliceet Nations.
29. "To the Governor of the Toun of Plimouth" (nd), *Royal Letters*, p. 52: www.archive.org/stream/cihm_24687/cihm_24687_djvu.txt; "Reasons Alleged," p. 63; Birch, Thomas (1848), *Court and Times of Charles I*, Vol. 1, London: Henry Colburn, p. 602; Birch, *Court and Times of Charles I*, Vol. 2, pp. 53-55, 60, 63.
30. This title is derived from the 1628 royal grant, which made Sir William Alexander the Lord of Canada.
31. Harvey, 1979
32. Letter from Christ College, 12 February 1630, Birch, *Charles I*, vol 2 at 60.
33. Vaughan, Alden T. (2006), *Transatlantic Encounters: American Indians in Britain, 1500-1776*, Cambridge: Cambridge University Press, pp. 100-101.
34. Rev. Mead was a Biblical scholar at Christ College, Cambridge, and author of several learned works. He is better known as a news reporter.
35. Birch, Vol. 1, p. 95. Birch does not discussion any religious issues, only the homage and protection of the king.

36. Pollock, Sir Frederick and Frederic William Maitland (1899), *History of English Law Before the Time of Edward I* Vol. 1, 2nd ed., Cambridge: Cambridge University Press, pp. 486-511; Ullmann, Walter (1944), "The Mediaeval Theory of Legal and Illegal Organizations," *Law Quarterly Review* 60, pp. 285-91; Blackstone, Sir William (1809), *Commentaries on the Law of Britain*, Vol. 1, 15th ed., London: Cadell & Davies pp. 455-73; Hale, Sir M. (1971), *The History of the Common Law of England*, ed. C.M. Gray, Chicago: University of Chicago Press, pp. 17-18; Skinner, Quentin (1978), *The Foundations of Modern Political Thought* Vol. 2, Cambridge, UK: Cambridge University Press, pp. 114-15, 123-34.
37. Printed in "Archibald Kennedy" (1751), *The Importance of Gaining and Preserving the Friendship of the Indians to the British Interest, Considered*, New York: Yale University Library, pp. 27-31.
38. Pownall, Thomas (1752), *Principles of Polity, being the Grounds and Reasons of Civil Empire*, London: Edward Owen, pp. 35-36.
39. Haida Nation v. British Columbia (Minister of Forests), 3 S.C.R. 511 at para. 20 (2004).
40. Preamble, *The Constitution Act, 1867*, 30 & 31 Victoria, c. 3 (UK).
41. Sections 35 and 52(1) of the *Constitution Act, 1982*, being Schedule B to the *Canada Act 1982* (UK), 1982, c. 11; non-derogation of aboriginal and treaty rights clause in section 25 of *Charter of Rights and Freedom*, 1982.
42. R v. Sparrow, 1 S.C.R. 1075, 1108 (1990).
43. Statement by the Prime Minister of Canada the Right Honourable Pierre Elliot Trudeau to Conference of First Ministers on Aboriginal Constitutional Matters, March 8-9, 1984, required by section 37 of the *Constitution Act. 1982*, [now repealed].
44. *Haida Nation*, 2004, at para 20.
45. Grassy Narrows First Nation v. Ontario, 2.C.R. 447 (2014).
46. Beckman v. Little Salmon/Carmacks First Nation, 3 S.C.R. 103 at para 97 (2010).
47. *Report of the Royal Commission on Aboriginal Peoples*. Vol. 1: *Looking Forward, Looking Back*, pp. 582-663.
48. www.pm.gc.ca/eng/minister-indigenous-and-northern-affairs-mandate-letter#sthash. 05wcHSgS.dpuf
49. Mitchell v. MNR 1 S.C.R. 911, para 129 (2001).

It's Not Your Fault

Raven Davis

In this exhibition, Davis combines a short film they produced and a live contemporary dance performance responding to the Canadian Government's disregard of Indigenous lives, specifically those of women, children, and Two Spirit people. At the same time, highlighting coercive protocols have been put in place by Heritage Canada that are intended to protect the Canadian National flag, ultimately disavowing Indigenous sovereignty and overtly exhibiting a lack of, and negligence toward the protection of Indigenous lives.

It's Not Your Fault is a short film highlighting the negligence of media on social platforms that allow racist, violent, non-monitored hate speech online. Its focus is the violence of online comments made toward Indigenous people, and specifically about Indigenous women of Canada, and the negligence of online/social media outlets allowing hate speech. *It's Not Your Fault* is a personal response recorded, edited, and performed by Davis, an Indigenous Two Spirit person who has experienced violence by both Indigenous and non-Indigenous men.

In the short film, Davis uses *manoomin*, a grain also known as "wild rice," which had been a food staple for many Indigenous people in Canada. Throughout the short film, Davis records as they prepare their bundle to pray and help heal from what they've read online, but are unable to complete the ceremony because the abalone prayer shell that they hold fills up with manoomin—symbolically, the lives and struggles of all Davis's relations, extended family, chosen family, women, children, and other Two Spirit people across Canada whose lives have been taken; those who are still suffering and those who have not been able to escape their abusers or violent situations.

Throughout the short film, Davis performs a song with a fringe, leather handled and horn and bean shaker. The "Strong Women's Song," also known as the "Women's Warrior Song," was taught to Davis over 20 years ago by the Ode'min

A response to Raven Davis's movie *It's Not Your Fault*, 2016. PHOTO: SAMSON LEARN

Kwe Singers. It was at that time that they sang with the Ode'min Kwe Singers and Pasiwegiik Drummers at different events and gatherings in Ontario. Davis performed a slightly different version of the song to make it a bit slower, deeper, and more like something a child would hear from one's mother or grandmother, similar to a lullaby or cradle song, to calm a crying child or to prepare them for bed. Davis sang the song in this way to comfort their sadness as it related to what they were reading, and to honour all women, children, and Two Spirit people.

In response to the short film, during the performance and to counteract the hate speech online, visitors to the gallery were invited to participate in writing self-reflective words, wishes, or prayers for the missing and murdered Indigenous women, children, or Two Spirit people, and for those who are still are in abusive relationships or situations. These prayers were written on small pieces of red paper and tied to Davis's regalia with a red ribbon. Davis's dance became a live prayer.

Link to youtube movie: *It's Not Your Fault*: https://youtu.be/yXOHTNFWujQ

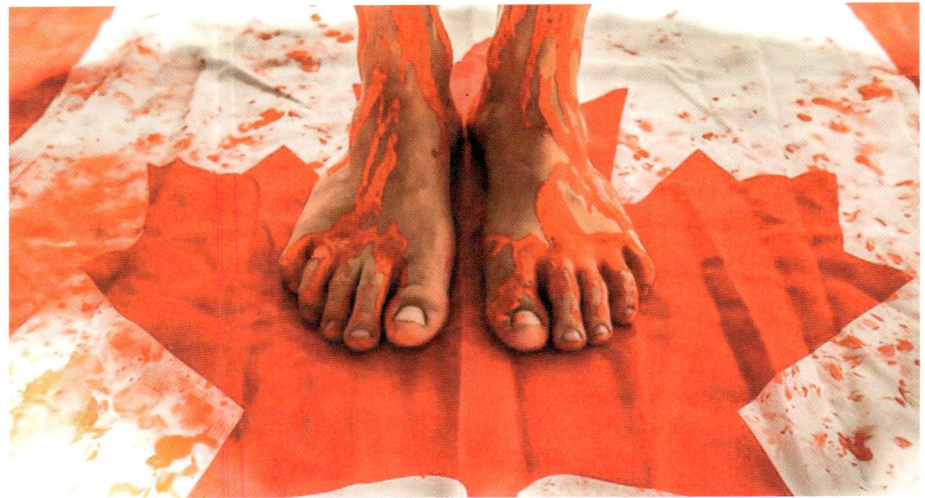

A response to Raven Davis's movie *It's Not Your Fault*, 2016. PHOTO: SAMSON LEARN

Khyber Gallery, Halifax | A response to Raven Davis's movie
It's Not Your Fault, 2016. PHOTO: RAVEN DAVIS

Unfinished Business
Bringing the Métis into Confederation

Janique Dubois and Kelly Saunders[*]

As part of his 2015 electoral promise for "real change," Prime Minister Justin Trudeau pledged to "complete the unfinished work of Confederation," by establishing a renewed nation-to-nation relationship with the Métis in Canada based on trust, respect, and cooperation.[1] Trudeau's commitment represents the latest iteration in a long line of assurances by the Crown to respect the rights of the Métis to land and self-government—promises that remain unfulfilled. The Métis have been down this road before; in 1869 and again in 1982, Canada committed to bringing the Métis into Confederation and respect their inherent rights, only to renege on its obligations.

As Canada celebrates its 150th anniversary, what are we to make of this latest commitment on behalf of the Federal Government? Is Canada finally prepared to live up to the promises it made to the Métis that led to Manitoba's entry into Confederation and the opening up of the Northwest? With these questions in mind, we offer a retrospective of how the constitutional relationship between the Métis Nation and Canada has evolved, assess where it currently stands, and offer insight into what potentially lies ahead, notably in light of recent Supreme Court of Canada rulings on Métis rights, land claims, and the state's fiduciary responsibilities to the Métis. On the basis of these assessments, we conclude that, in the absence of meaningful reconciliation, bringing the Métis into Canadian Confederation will remain "unfinished business."[2]

The Deal of Confederation

The Métis Nation emerged in the context of the fur trade, rising to become an integral economic and political force in the historic Northwest. In the eighteenth and early nineteenth centuries, European and Euro-Canadian men formed alliances with Indigenous societies through marriages *à la façon du pays* (in the custom of the country).³ Successive generations of dual-heritage children intermarried and created kinship networks that—sparked by political action—would lead to the emergence of a new nation, the Métis.⁴ As Darren O'Toole and Chris Andersen argue, the Métis developed a political consciousness as a distinct Indigenous nation through events such as the 1816 *Victoire de la Grenouillière* (Victory at Frog Plain) where they mobilized to protect their right to hunt and trade freely in the Northwest.⁵ It was the commitment to protecting their economic, political, and cultural way of life that led the Métis to discover themselves as *li novel nasyoon*—the new nation.⁶

The biannual buffalo hunts were central to the Métis way of life and informed the development of Métis governance practices. Each fall and spring, heads of families would gather to democratically adopt laws and select leaders to oversee the hunts. The elected chief and council managed the hunting brigades with strict military precision to ensure the safety of the families and the success of the hunt. Beyond providing food for consumption and economic trade, however, the hunts served as touch points in political mobilization and nation building amongst the Métis. Grand events involving thousands of people at a time, the hunts provided opportunities for families throughout the plains to come together in an expression of cultural and national pride. At the end of each hunt, Métis families would return to settlement communities where they continued to live collectively according to the rules and practices of the buffalo hunt.

As a self-governing people, the Métis rejected the notion that a foreign power could make unilateral decisions that affected their way of life without their consent. It should therefore come as no surprise that in 1869, the Métis led a resistance against the supposed "sale" of lands on which they had established settlements by the Hudson's Bay Company to the Canadian state. Upon hearing of the impending sale, the population in the largest trading settlement in the Plains—the Red River Settlement—mobilized to oppose the transaction. Under the leadership of Louis Riel, the population at Red River formed a provisional government through which they would enter into negotiations with the state.

Constituted of elected representatives from the French- and English-speaking parishes in the Settlement, the Métis-led provisional government adopted a List of Rights that outlined the conditions under which the population would agree to join Canada. After Canada's attempts to quell the unrest at Red River proved unsuccessful, delegates of the provisional government were invited to Ottawa to discuss the terms of Manitoba's entry into Confederation. During negotiations in the nation's capital, Prime Minister John A. Macdonald and Minister of Militia and Defence George-Étienne Cartier agreed to many of the provisional government's demands. In addition to agreeing to protect Métis linguistic and religious rights, Canada promised 1.4 million acres of land to Métis children, and control of land already occupied by the Red River Métis in exchange for the province's peaceful entry into Confederation.[7] The agreement reached between Canadian and Métis delegates ensured that Manitoba would retain its independence and establish its own government, which was expected to be responsive to Métis interests as they made up the largest proportion of the local population.

From Founding to Forgotten People

The members of the provisional government in Red River reacted joyously to the news that a deal had been reached with Canada, and promptly ratified the agreement.[8] Meanwhile in Ottawa, Prime Minister Macdonald was facing challenges in garnering parliamentary approval for the deal. While Canada agreed to parts of the agreement negotiated in the *Manitoba Act, 1870*, political pressure to reconcile English and French factions, and ward off incursion by Americans, led Macdonald to renege on his commitments.[9] Significantly, Macdonald refused to give amnesty to those who had participated in the Red River Resistance. Outrage in Ontario over the execution of Thomas Scott, an Orangeman found guilty of treason by the provisional government, had notably turned the tide of public opinion against the Métis. Warned that Canadian troops were arriving at Red River to sanction Métis leaders, Riel and a number of his supporters were forced to flee for their lives.

Subsequent attempts by the Métis to secure rights to land and to self-government were largely ignored by Canada. Refusing to engage in further negotiations with the Métis, Canada asserted its power westward through military force. As Riel writes in his final memoirs, "[t]he Ottawa Government had made with me, in 1870, an agreement not a single clause of which it ever honoured."[10] Métis efforts to resist the imposition of colonial rule led to several confrontations that culminated with their defeat in the 1885 Battle at Batoche. With the threat of further persecution of the Métis, Riel surrendered himself to Canadian authorities. A jury found him guilty of high treason, a crime for which Riel was sentenced to hang.

"Canada's forgotten people"

In the years that followed, the Métis became "Canada's forgotten people."[11] Forced off their lands through ongoing settlement and with no recognized land rights of their own, the Métis scattered throughout western Canada, settling along road allowances and in temporary communities. The estrangement of the Métis from their traditional lands and ways of life, and the destitution, oppression, and marginalization that followed was accelerated by the state's maladministration of land distribution through the scrip process.[12] Calling the history of scrip speculation and devaluation "a sorry chapter in our nation's history," the Supreme Court of Canada noted that the Federal Government's use of scrip was based on fundamentally different assumptions about the nature and origins of its relationship with the Métis.[13] Presented as a measure to fulfill Canada's obligations to the Métis as outlined in the *Manitoba Act, 1870*, scrip was instead used by the Crown to extinguish Métis claims to title.

Through military and political tactics, Canada reneged on the promises that it had made in the *Manitoba Act* to bring the Métis into Confederation. Rather than fulfilling its obligations to respect Métis rights to land and self-government, the Canadian state took control of the Northwest through military force and deceit. It would take almost 100 years before the opportunity arose to revisit the constitutional relationship between the Métis and Canada.

scrip process

1982: A New Constitutional Deal?

Triggered by the threat of Québec's secession, growing discontent in the west and rising Indigenous nationalism, the climate of social and political unrest that arose in Canada in the 1970s would lead to a decade-long search for national unity. At the heart of this process were discussions amongst first ministers around a patriated constitution, an amending formula, and a new Charter of Rights and Freedoms. Originally designed as a means to appease Québec, other groups—including Indigenous peoples—began to press for inclusion in a renewed federation.

For the Métis, this meant revisiting the unfulfilled promises made in 1869. As Métis leader John Morrisseau would testify before the Métis and Non-Status Indian Constitutional Review Commission in 1981, "[w]e can't draw up the rights of a new constitution when our rights entrenched in the Manitoba Act of 1870 are still outstanding."[14] In the tumultuous and high stakes political environment that marked this period, the Métis reminded first ministers of the significant role that the Métis Nation played in unifying the country at the time of Confederation,

Métis want a role → emphasizing the role they played.

and their contribution to the founding of Canada.[15] Through the strategic and persistent efforts of their leaders to impress upon first ministers the unfinished legacy of this history, the Métis succeeded in achieving constitutional recognition as one of three rights-bearing Aboriginal peoples in Canada in Section 35 of the *Constitution Act, 1982*.[16] Marking the explicit inclusion of the Métis within Canada's constitutional framework, this recognition represented a monumental achievement for the Métis.[17]

Within the context of constitutional discussions surrounding patriation, federal and provincial governments committed to Indigenous leaders that Section 35 rights would be negotiated and defined through a series of four conferences. Métis leaders from across the prairies seized the initiative to create a new national body, the Métis National Council, to advocate for Métis rights to self-government and to a land base. Throughout these conferences, which were held from 1983 to 1987, the Métis stood firm in their commitment to secure the rights that were originally pledged to them in 1869. In the end, the parties did not reach agreement on the meaning of Aboriginal rights. The "old and difficult grievances" between the Crown and the Métis that Section 35 was meant to address remained unresolved.[18]

Surviving Canada

While constitutionally recognized as a rights-bearing Aboriginal people, the Métis continued to remain ignored by state governments. The constitutional promise of rights as contained in Section 35 did little to address the exclusion of the Métis from the state's political and legislative framework.[19] To this day, the Métis remain shut out of the Federal Government's land claim resolution process, and are denied access to Métis-specific federal programming.[20] As Catherine Bell argues, the Métis's exclusion is in large part a consequence of jurisdictional disputes between federal and provincial governments, both of whom refuse to negotiate with the Métis or to enact legislation for the purposes of recognizing and implementing Métis Aboriginal rights.[21] In the absence of a political settlement to advance their rights to land and self-government, the Métis have taken it upon themselves to exercise their inherent rights. Through various grassroots initiatives in communities across their homeland, the Métis are finding creative ways to "survive" Canada.

In addition to their continued efforts on the macro-constitutional front, Métis leaders have turned their attention inward. Through a steady process of nation building, capacity development, and institutional renewal, Métis leaders have been steadily building the mechanisms of self-government from the ground up. Over the last decades, the Métis have transformed their political organizations into democratic and representative governments accountable to Métis citizens, while remaining committed to the same principles that informed nineteenth century governance practices (including democracy, kinship, and the rule of law). Today, democratically elected Métis governments from British Columbia to Ontario pass laws, deliver programs and services, generate revenues, and negotiate with private and public actors on behalf of their people. By continuing to strengthen their own systems and structures of governance, and seeking out strategic opportunities to promote their interests, contemporary Métis governments have actively sought to position themselves as full and equal participants in the Canadian federation.[22]

This internal process of nation building has garnered external benefits for the Métis Nation in Canada. No longer invisible, the Métis have emerged as prominent actors in the Canadian federation. By leveraging relationships in the private and non-profit sectors, the Métis have carved out a place for their governments alongside state actors at the negotiation table. In addition to playing a larger role in the informal processes and networks of multilevel governance, Métis governments increasingly participate within the formal mechanisms of intergovernmental relations, as outlined in the Métis Nation Protocol first negotiated between federal and Métis leaders in 2008 (and renewed in 2013).[23] While these incremental shifts have increased the visibility of the Métis in Canada's federal framework, Métis rights to land and self-government still remain unfulfilled.

To advance their political agenda, and to help breathe life into their constitutional rights, the Métis have also turned to the courts. As Métis National Council President Clément Chartier explains, this was a conscious decision given the state's ongoing reluctance to negotiate a just settlement with the Métis on their inherent rights to land and self-government.[24] While Métis leaders state that they would prefer political negotiation over litigation to advance their Section 35 rights, the adoption of this legal strategy has met with a certain degree of success.

Supreme Court rulings affirming the right of the Métis to harvest and to define Métis identity has put pressure on state governments to return to the bargaining table.[25] Of particular import has been the Supreme Court of Canada's decision in *Manitoba Métis Federation v. Canada*, which reignited the hope of a renewed constitutional relationship between Canada and the Métis. Confirming that Canada "did not work diligently to fulfill its constitutional promise to the Métis, as the honour of Crown required,"[26] the Court reiterated that the honour of the

Crown is engaged by Section 35 of the *Constitution Act, 1982*. In the wake of this decision, the Federal Government appointed a Ministerial Special Representative, Thomas Isaac, to map out a process for dialogue on Section 35 rights, and to explore ways to address unresolved Métis land claims. To this end, Isaac put forward seventeen recommendations that aim to bring about reconciliation with Métis people. He concludes that reconciliation must go beyond "platitudes and recognition," and instead be grounded in "practical actions."[27]

Reconciliation through Relationship Building

In 2013, the Supreme Court of Canada declared that "[t]he unfinished business of reconciliation of the Métis people with Canadian sovereignty is a matter of national and constitutional import."[28] This statement follows decades of rulings by the country's highest court outlining how the honour of the Crown requires reconciling the pre-existence of Aboriginal societies with Crown sovereignty.[29] However, as the Ministerial Special Representative on Renewing the Comprehensive Land Claims Policy notes in his 2015 report, "[r]econciliation is more than a legal theory. At a practical level, it is a product of successful relationships."[30]

As part of their comprehensive inquiry into the evolution of the relationship between Indigenous peoples and the state in the early 1990s, commissioners of the Royal Commission on Aboriginal Peoples (RCAP) sought to uncover the foundations of a "fair and honourable relationship." In the introductory remarks of their report, the commissioners explain that, in order to bring about fundamental change in this relationship,

> Canadians need to understand that *Aboriginal peoples are nations*. That is, they are political and cultural groups with values and lifeways distinct from those of other Canadians. They lived as nations—highly centralized, loosely federated, or small and clan-based—for thousands of years before the arrival of Europeans. As nations, they forged trade and military alliances among themselves and with the new arrivals. To this day, Aboriginal people's sense of confidence and well-being as individuals remains tied to the strength of their nations. Only as members of restored nations can they reach their potential in the twenty-first century.[31]

For Métis leaders, reconciliation involves the development of a meaningful nation-to-nation relationship with the state. It is a relationship founded upon historical commitments, but that also serves as the basis through which the contemporary needs and aspirations of Métis citizens can be realized. Reconciliation thus involves moving forward toward self-determination for the Métis Nation in Canada, but it also requires looking back to the original promises that were made in 1869, and again in 1982.

Upon taking office in 2015, Prime Minister Trudeau pledged to "work, on a nation-to-nation basis, with the Métis Nation to advance reconciliation and renew the relationship, based on cooperation, respect for rights, our international obligations, and a commitment to end the status quo."[32] Canada is proposing to bring the Métis into Confederation by building a relationship through which reconciliation can be achieved. However, such an outcome will not occur without real progress on Métis rights to land and self-government. The government's repeated failure to fulfill Métis rights, Riel noted, is a "profanation of a people's trust."[33] Honouring the obligations agreed to almost 150 years ago is a first and necessary step to rebuilding trust and establishing the relationship required to advance reconciliation.

On the brink of Canada's 150th anniversary, what does the future hold for Métis-Canada relations? At a recent meeting between Indigenous leaders and the Prime Minister to advance reconciliation, David Chartrand, Vice-President of the Métis National Council, commended the Federal Government for its positive approach to a renewed government-to-government relationship with the Métis Nation.[34] At the same time, Vice-President Chartrand drew attention to the "systematic and structural discrimination" that continues to exist in Canada's approach to the Métis. While the moment of Canada's sesquicentennial offers the possibility of reconciliation, as the Ministerial Special Representative concluded, it will take more than words to complete the unfinished business of Confederation. In the absence of concrete actions to implement Métis rights to land and self-government, Prime Minister Trudeau's latest overtures will simply be added to the queue of a long list of unfulfilled promises that have become the foundation of Canada's relationship with the Métis Nation.

Yet, if one theme stands out in our country's history, it is the resilience and fortitude of Riel's people. Just as the Métis persevered in the face of Canada's broken commitments in the *Manitoba Act* nearly 150 years ago, history suggests that the Métis Nation will continue to not only survive Canada in the generations to come, but indeed thrive. As Riel himself disclosed in the weeks following his trial and sentencing for high treason, "deeds are not accomplished in a few days, or in a few hours. A century is only a spoke in the wheel of everlasting time."[35]

1. "Métis National Council," Liberal Party of Canada, September 21, 2015: www.metisnation.ca/wp-content/uploads/2015/09/Liberal-Party-Response-Sept-21-2015-.pdf.
2. This phrase is used by the Supreme Court of Canada in Manitoba Métis Federation Inc. v. Canada (Attorney General), SCC 14, 1 S.C.R. 623 at para 140 (2013). It is also taken up by the Ministerial Special Representative, Tom Isaac, in his 2015 report "A Matter of National and Constitutional Import: Report of the Minister's Special Representative on Reconciliation with Métis: Section 35 Métis Rights and the *Manitoba Métis Federation* Decision," June 14, 2016: www.aadnc-aandc.gc.ca/eng/1467641790303/1467641835266.
3. Kirk, Sylvia Van (1983), *Many Tender Ties: Women in Fur-Trade Society, 1670-1870*, Norman: University of Oklahoma Press, p. 4.
4. St-Onge, Nicole and Carolyn Podruchny (2012), "Scuttling along a Spider's Web: Mobility and Kinship in Métis Ethnogenesis," *Contours of a People: Métis Family, Mobility, and History*, ed. Nicole St-Onge, Carolyn Podruchny, and Brenda Macdougall, Norman: University of Oklahoma Press, p. 61.
5. For an events-based discussion of Métis peoplehood, see Andersen, Chris (2014), *"Métis" Race, Recognition, and the Struggle for Indigenous Peoplehood*, Vancouver: UBC Press, pp. 109-32. For a discussion of Métis political consciousness, see O'Toole, Darren (2013), "From Entity to Identity to Nation," *Métis in Canada: History, Identity, Law and Politics*, eds. Chris Adams, S. Gregg Dahl, and Ian Peach, Edmonton: University of Alberta Press, pp. 143-203.
6. Stanley, George F.G. (1972), *Manitoba 1870: A Métis Achievement*, Winnipeg: University of Winnipeg Press, p. 10; see also Arthur S. Morton (1978 [1939]), "The New Nation, The Métis," *The Other Natives: The-Les Métis*, vol. 1, 1700-1885, eds. Antoine S. Lussier and D. Bruce Sealy, Winnipeg: Manitoba Métis Federation Press and Éditions Bois-Brûlés; Dickason, Olive Patricia (1985), "From 'One Nation' in the Northeast to 'New Nation' in the Northwest: A Look at the Emergence of the Métis," *The New Peoples: Being and Becoming Métis in North America*, eds. Jacqueline Peterson and Jennifer S.H. Brown, Winnipeg: University of Manitoba Press.
7. Sprague, D.N. (1988), *Canada and the Métis, 1869-1885*, Waterloo: Wilfrid Laurier University Press, p. 105.
8. Stanley, George F.G. (1963), *Louis Riel*, Toronto: The Ryerson Press, pp. 148-49.
9. See Sprague, 1988, pp. 55-64.
10. Quoted in de Trémaudan, A.-H. (1982), *Hold High Your Heads: History of the Métis Nation in Western Canada*, trans. Elizabeth Maguet, Winnipeg: Pemmican Publications, p. 208.
11. Sealy, D. Bruce and Antoine S. Lussier (1975), *The Métis: Canada's Forgotten People*, Winnipeg: Manitoba Métis Federation Press.
12. Scrip was a voucher redeemable for land that could be sold for cash.
13. R. v. Blais 2 S.C.R. at para 34, 25 (2003).
14. John Morrisseau, quoted in: www.metisnation.ca/index.php/who-are-the-metis/order-of-the-metis-nation/john-morrisseau.
15. Daniels, Harry W. (1979), *We are the New Nation: the Métis and National Native Policy*, Ottawa: Native Council of Canada, p. 4; Belcourt, Tony (2013), "For the Record ... On Métis Identity and Citizenship within the Métis Nation," *Aboriginal Policy Studies* 2(2), pp. 128-41.
16. Dubois, Janique and Kelly Saunders (2017), "Explaining the Resurgence of Métis Rights: Making the Most of 'Windows of Opportunity,'" *Canadian Public Administration* 60(1).
17. Weinstein, John (2007), *Quiet Revolution West: The Rebirth of Métis Nationalism*, Calgary: Fifth House Ltd., p. 45.
18. Teillet, Jean (2004), "Old and Difficult Grievances: Examining the Relationship between the Métis and the Crown," *Supreme Court Law Review* 24, Article 12, pp. 291-323.

19. Even after 1982, the Métis continued to be sidelined from federal policy channels. The ministry primarily responsible for Canada's other Aboriginal groups, at the time called the Ministry of Indian and Northern Affairs, explicitly excluded the Métis. To address this situation, Canada created the Office of the Federal Interlocutor in 1985 through which the Métis could indirectly speak to the federal minister responsible for other Aboriginal groups. This changed to some extent with the renaming of the ministry to the Department of Aboriginal and Northern Development in 2011, which was again renamed in 2015 to the Department of Indigenous and Northern Affairs. For a discussion of Métis exclusion, see Bell, Catherine (2015), "*R v. Daniels*: Jurisdiction and Government Obligations to Non-Status Indians," *Aboriginal Multilevel Governance. Canada: The State of the Federation 2013*, eds. Martin Papillon and André Juneau, Kingston: Queen's-McGill University Press, pp. 215-33.
20. With the exception of the Métis north of 60, see Eyford, Douglas R., "*A New Direction: Advancing Aboriginal and Treaty Rights*," February 20, 2015: www.aadnc-aandc.gc.ca/eng/1426169199009/1426169236218.
21. In a seminal 2016 decision, the Supreme Court of Canada ruled that the responsibility to enact such legislation lies with the Federal Government insofar as the Métis are included within the meaning of "Indians" in section 91(24) of the *Constitution Act* of 1867. At the time of writing, the Federal Government has yet to adopt Métis-specific legislation.
22. Dubois, Janique and Kelly Saunders (2013), "'Just Do It!': Carving Out a Space for the Métis in Canadian Federalism," *Canadian Journal of Political Science* 46 (1), pp. 187-214.
23. Dubois, Janique (2015), "Federal-Provincial-Métis Relations: Building Multilevel Governance from the Bottom Up," *Canada: State of the Federation 2013. Aboriginal Multilevel Governance*, eds. Martin Papillon and André Juneau, Kingston: McGill-Queen's University Press, pp. 189-214.
24. Interview with Clement Chartier, March 21, 2013, Vancouver BC.
25. Notably, Alberta (Aboriginal Affairs and Northern Development) v. Cunningham, SCC 37, 2 S.C.R. 670 (2011); and R. v. Powley, 2 S.C.R. 207, SCC 43 (2003).
26. *Manitoba Métis Federation Inc.*, SCC 14, 1 S.C.R. 623 at para 150, 69-70.
27. Isaac, Thomas, "A Matter of National and Constitutional Import: Report of the Minister's Special Representative on Reconciliation with Métis: Section 35 Métis Rights and the Manitoba Métis Federation Decision," June 14, 2016, p. 3: www.aadnc-aandc.gc.ca/eng/1467641790303/1467641835266.
28. Supreme Court of Canada, *Manitoba Métis Federation Inc.*, SCC 14, 1 S.C.R. 623 at para 140.
29. This was marked by R. v. Van der Peet, 2 S.C.R. 507 (1996).
30. Eyford, p. 35: www.aadnc-aandc.gc.ca/eng/1426169199009/1426169236218.
31. Canada (1996), *People to People, Nation to Nation: Highlights from the Report of the Royal Commission on Aboriginal Peoples*, Ottawa: Royal Commission on Aboriginal Peoples, pp. x-xi.
32. "Minister of Indigenous and Northern Affairs Mandate Letter": www.pm.gc.ca/eng/minister-indigenous-and-northern-affairs-mandate-letter.
33. Quoted in de Trémaudan, 1982, p. 209.
34. Métis National Council, "PM and Indigenous Leaders Meet to Advance Reconciliation," December 15, 2016: www.metisnation.ca/index.php/news/pm-and-indigenous-leaders-meet-to-advance-reconciliation.
35. Quoted in the *Montreal Weekly Star* (August, 22 1885), and *War in the West: Voices of the 1885 Rebellion* (1985) by Wiebe, Rudy Henry and Bob Beal, Toronto: McClelland and Stewart, p. 2.

By Any Means Necessary
Canada 150—No Reason To Celebrate as an Onkwehón:we Peoples

Ellen Gabriel

> "We declare our right on this earth … to be a human being, to be respected as a human being, to be given the rights of a human being in this society, on this earth, in this day, which we intend to bring into existence by any means necessary."
>
> "Our objective is complete freedom, justice and equality by any means necessary."
>
> —MALCOLM X

Let me begin by saying that I love the people of Canada—its culture of entertainment, its music and film industry. Canada is a beacon of hope for so many disenfranchised people from all over the world. It is a great country to live in, but it is not perfect … far from it, especially if you are an Indigenous person still under the mallet of colonialism. It is the political landscape that I find morally reprehensible, with all its constructs of colonialism and assimilation, which began centuries ago but are still forced upon Indigenous peoples in Canada today.

As Malcolm X stated: "Our objective is complete freedom, justice and equality by any means necessary," which, as I embrace this statement, is not one that evokes violence, nor hate, but is an opportunity to educate all Canadians on their own history. It is a means by which to rid our lives of the colonial praxis that governs the relationships between Onkwehón:we peoples and nations and the Canadian state.

As an activist for Indigenous human rights and environmental rights since 1990, I have seen positive changes in the mindset of the people of Canada. I've also seen a change in Indigenous peoples, in how they understand that so much of their self-hatred is rooted in the education system of Canada: the Indian Residential

School system. I have met many Canadians and Québécois who are shocked and ashamed of the settler history of Canada. The pain of colonialism is not only carried by Indigenous peoples, but is also a burden for those settlers with compassion, those with love and respect in their hearts and minds. These are the ones who seek justice and truth, and want the experiences and realties of Onkwehón:we peoples of the Americas to be known and owned by all Canadians.

As an Indigenous person, I have also seen the powerful energy of Canadians and Québécois rigidly tethered to the colonial constructs of colonialism. The challenge of reconciliation remains even more poignant when I witness certain Indigenous peoples, those "moderate Indians" whose minds are shackled to insidiously disguised forms of assimilation and colonial constructs. It is these "moderates" who cannot or will not see the truth about what has hindered our efforts toward achieving wellbeing in our communities. Too often the views of the moderates resemble the colonizers' goal: eradicating the identity of Indigenous peoples, and leaving little common ground upon which we can work together as Indigenous peoples. Divide and conquer is the formula for success for the colonizer, who feigns interest in the wellbeing of Indigenous peoples but quickly resorts to the use of force against those who defend their rights to their lands, and who demand self-determination.

The community I come from, Kanehsatà:ke, has fought for three centuries against the land dispossession and hatred of the colonizers, which exploded into one of Canada's most grievous and historic land and human rights violations of recent times. Today, we are still no further along in finding a solution to the long-standing historical dispute of 1721, and our land remains vulnerable to further dispossession. We remain in conflict with colonizers who continue to rely on Canadian law, claiming our land as Crown land, in complete defiance of what the Royal Proclamation of 1763 is purported—even in Canada's highest law, the Constitution—to protect.

Consequently, we continue the multi-generational struggle against land dispossession. Canada's refusal to denounce their doctrines of assumed superiority, such as the Doctrine of Discovery, continues to act as the foundation of Canada's assumed sovereignty. Canada claims it never followed the Doctrine of Discovery and terra nullius—literally meaning empty land—but the principles of discounting the humanity of Indigenous peoples remains foundational. These doctrines of superiority have been condemned by the United Nations, repudiated in other commonwealth law, and are mentioned in the preambular paragraphs of the United Nations Declaration on the Rights of Indigenous Peoples (UNDRIP).

Even with the force of international opinion against them, Canada hasn't stopped the imperial machine. The colonizer's approach for perpetuating land dispossession remains implemented through coercive community funding agreements, disempowering processes, and mechanisms like land claims and modern-day treaties. Indigenous peoples must still prove their rights of occupancy on their own land by complex tests set out by the Canadian court, simply in order to get to the negotiating table. Even then, Canada takes huge advantage for itself, by negotiating within a process containing a grossly lop-sided power differential.

Radicals—or, as I see them, defenders of the land, who stand up for the land—continue to be ostracized through whisper campaigns, and consequently criminalized for defending our rights, even our basic human rights. As defenders, we continue to be the "other" who, at the whim of the authorities and ill-informed politicians, have it decided for us whether we are worthy of justice, self-determination, land, or even keeping our languages alive. While Canada continues to define and confine our identities as Indigenous peoples, we continue to lose our fluent first language speakers and traditional knowledge holders. These are the very people who grew up in poverty while Canada became a wealthy nation, yet remained kind and open to settlers. These are the "radicals" Canada fears.

It is fear that compels Canada to continue to interfere with the rights of Indigenous peoples to self-determination, by trying to persuade us that they alone can define us. Why? Perhaps it is because Indian status—as set out in the *Indian Act*—connects us to certain so-called economic perks, which seemingly put us at an advantage over the average Canadian. Surely they must know that these so-called rights or perks are virtually worthless, especially considering that the majority of Indigenous peoples remain among the poorest of society. With all of our perks, what can explain our communities having the highest suicide rates in spite of the fastest growing youth population? Is it our riches that cause the violence, hopelessness, and loss of any sense of worth? The Canadian state seeks to control Indigenous peoples in every aspect of our lives. Our hope is that the youth will be the agents of change to reset the relationship with the colonial state. Movements like Idle No More and anti-pipeline protests have shown us that Indigenous youth are picking up the gauntlet of the struggle against colonialism and assimilation.

Settlers whose eyes have opened up to the not-so-invisible class system of the Americas have now joined those who have remained dedicated to the teachings of our ancestors, who desire to leave a legacy for future generations in caring for the land and the environment. Ours is a system that sadly continues to oppress us all, Indigenous and settler alike. Like a film covering our eyes, the government propaganda machine continues to place emphasis on jobs, energy (at the expense of pillaging the land), and a "strong" (read: white) economy, and unless you can get on the "let's make money bandwagon," then you are an enemy of the state, and deserving to be poor and disenfranchised.

While I realize that 2017 marks Canada's 150 anniversary, and that some Indigenous peoples will join in the celebration, I think of how little has changed in our realities. The Canadian government still controls every part of our lives, our history is still not being told in an honest manner, and Indigenous peoples are still being criminalized for insisting on justice. As Indigenous peoples, we have not even been allowed to grieve properly for all the losses we have experienced. I await the day when I will witness Canadians—not just their governments—actually accepting responsibility for the harms colonization has caused Indigenous peoples, beyond the many harms of the Indian Residential Schools system. All of it. Canadians must understand the impact on us of the loss of our languages, our hardships in trying to rebuild our nations' traditional governance, cultures, lands, and resources. Fear, greed, and a heartless disregard for the family units of Indigenous peoples have brought us to the point where I don't think our ancestors would recognize who we are today or the land they so lovingly used. This is what Canadians must come to understand—not just with their heads, but also with their hearts.

This can only happen once Canada becomes unshackled from the economic reasons it remains tethered to its perpetuation of the oppression of Indigenous peoples. Until Canada actually partakes in true reconciliation through the restitution of our lands, languages, and other pillars of our identity, I will remain in the corner, looking out at Canada and the great potential it has for compassion and respect for the human rights of Indigenous peoples.

Skén:nen Shenontenionhe'k—let peace be in your minds.

Canada's Three Sovereignties and the Hope of Indigenous-Led Populism

Jobb Arnold

Introduction

Canada has always been and continues to be shaped by European forms of sovereign violence. Sovereign boundaries that have been created and maintained through police and military violence deployed at borders, in prisons, and on the frontlines of both urban and land-based struggles. This violence is ostensibly legitimated and practically facilitated by the sovereign power that grants agents of the state the authority to use violence to ensure that Canada's national interests are protected and its expansionist objectives continue to be met. Sometimes, the assertion of sovereign violence itself is the only objective. This particularly European idea of state sovereignty (that is, the Crown) relies on the singular capacity to suspend individual legal rights and unleash violence against anyone perceived to threaten the state's preservation.[1]

Sovereign violence in Canadian society impacts the lives of different groups of people in very different ways. For example, the state's capacity for violence makes some people feel more secure, because they think it will only be used to protect their rights and privileges. For many Indigenous and non-status migrant peoples, sovereign violence has always been the threatening and brutal force behind ongoing processes of colonization and forcible displacement from ancestral lands and all manner of exploitation. By conflating the Canadian state's preservation with an extractivist idea of "national interest," sovereign violence has become a tool to ensure unfettered access to land-based resources.

Canadian sovereignty is troubling, but it is also in trouble. The violence that sustains Canada's current "national interest" is deeply contested. Amidst the ongoing global upheaval of power, there are unprecedented opportunities to re-articulate Canada's national interest in ways that deprive systemic violence of its legitimacy, as well as its capacity to function. These positional struggles manifest as frontline battles, sites of physical contestation where the legitimate role and capacity of state sovereign violence is laid bare. In what follows, I identify and distinguish between the global, national, and regional forces that are defining what Canada will become.

In Canada today, there are three realms of sovereign force, which I will simplify as: 1) Canadian nation-state sovereignty, 2) global corporate sovereignty, and 3) Indigenous sovereignty. The overlap and jurisdictional uncertainty that characterizes these sovereign relations demonstrates that the balance of sovereign power is always in a state of flux. There are moments in the history of nations when the balance of sovereign power can be redistributed, the flows of violence disrupted, and political boundaries shifted.

During such moments of contestation, these sovereign forces come into direct and visible conflict with each other. Such encounters are often characterized by the emergence of clear antagonisms between groups of people (often a popular movement facing off against state agents such as the police) that are separated by intense emotional edges backed by different formations of mobilized sovereign power. These are the frontlines. Social media tools and mobile devices have become a powerful force in articulating these frontlines and providing organizational platforms for mobilizing affinity-based alliances.[2] It is against these antagonistic edges that competing sovereign forces mobilize their human, financial, and legal capacities to redefine relations of power by diminishing, deflecting, or even destroying the coherence and capacity of competing formations. In such scenarios, the relative legitimacy and power of these forces are in direct contest without a preordained outcome (as much as politicians and big business hate to admit it). As the balance of sovereign power is altered, what seemed inevitable can become impossible, and what was unimaginable can suddenly become possible.

For shifts in the balance of power to be realized, tangible gains can be made through direct, productive conflict on the frontlines. Holding hard-won new ground against instant recapture requires different strategies. An example of one strategy can be found in international legal frameworks such as the United Nations Declaration on the Rights of Indigenous Peoples (UNDRIP), which provides a framework drafted by Indigenous peoples and grounded in legal principles that can help to express and stabilize new relations of power based on international legal norms.

To put it another way, ground can be gained when emotionally charged, popular momentum is mobilized to assert sovereign control over specific lands and territories. The difference is that by and large, corporate sovereignty is mobilized toward extraction, while Indigenous sovereignty is asserted as a means of protection. If frontline actions are able to assert sufficient force and popular momentum, legal formulations can be used to establish and maintain the legitimacy of the changed relations. Legal mechanisms, in this sense, are envisioned as a way of holding a political line on the threshold of political antagonism, between extraction and protection, life and death. As the sole arbiter of legitimate sovereign violence, the Canadian state cannot remain neutral in this conflict. The frontlines are emerging everywhere.

Canadian State Sovereignty: Violence and States of Exception

The European predecessors of the Canadian nation-state established their exceptional territorial claims over the lands and peoples of Turtle Island through false doctrines of discovery and violent processes of exploitative colonization. One hundred and fifty years after Canada's Confederation, the nation-state's colonial processes continue to operate with the backing of violent force.[3] Having established itself through an acute period of founding violence, the Canadian state can now focus its use of violence on preserving itself and expanding its control.[4]

In the post-9/11 world, Canada, like many other western nations, increasingly exercises its sovereign violence selectively through the imposition of "states of exception." States of exception occur when the executive power of the state is used to suspend normal laws (including ones that ensure due process, privacy, and protection for citizens), implementing in their place a "state of emergency" justified in the name of so-called "reasons of national security."[5] When a particular person or group of people is subjected to the violent power of the state under such emergency laws, they are effectively outside of the law, meaning their citizenship rights, even their human rights, do not apply.[6] What is most disturbing about this type of sovereign power is that the potential use of violence is virtually unlimited and unaccountable.[7] Examples of sovereign states of exception are clearly demonstrated by the United States proliferation of "black sites" of indefinite detention and torture, such as the military prison at Guantanamo Bay, as well as unprecedented programs of mass surveillance and the extrajudicial assassination of American citizens.[8,9]

The Canadian state has been a leader at extending the logic of states of exception to massive industrial projects like the Athabasca Tar Sands developments, creating large-scale "national sacrifice areas."[10] Sacrifice zones are states of exception imposed upon the land, stripping it of all rights, and exposing it to unlimited and unaccountable violence. Like sites of indefinite detention, there are virtually no legal restrictions governing what can permissibly be done to lands designated as sacrifice zones.

Paranoid governmental decisions follow the logic of emergency law, and reflect the inherent instability between rulers and the ruled. Governments get scared when people resist the smooth functioning of the profitable colonial processes they rely upon for revenues. A large number of politicians across the political spectrum in Canada (save perhaps for the Green Party) are unable to imagine how the state apparatus could run without oil. The result of such dull imaginations is that the fear of oil-revenue disruption has become an existential threat for many politicians, a true state of emergency to be avoided at all costs. It is a strange existentialism that relies on the industrialized production of a substance as globally destructive as oil to allay its anxiety. Of course, this contradiction could be addressed significantly by de-coupling the state from the reckless imperatives of colonial capitalism to create immense wealth for a few, and true existential precarity for everyone else, especially the marginalized.

Rather than addressing the conditions that create truly fearful ecological uncertainty and senseless economic precarity, the Canadian state continues to cower in front of its economic puppet masters, providing subsidies and support to industrial extraction rather than taking a principled stand.[11] As a result of this national dogma, scientifically grounded fears remain unaddressed, while state propaganda projects its anxieties onto dissenters who are labelled "extremists," "enemies," or even "terrorists."

States of exception are intended to give the state sweeping powers so that it can adequately respond to actually existing states of emergency. This is the logic that legitimizes exceptional tactics to thwart terrorism. In Canada, exceptional measures meant for terrorists and extremists have been used to institutionalize the ongoing criminalization of Indigenous peoples. The Canadian state is ready to use emergency laws to deal with Indigenous land defenders and water protectors, while it simultaneously supports the industries that are worsening climate change, which actually is the defining global emergency of our time. The attitudes and actions of senior politicians demonstrate this position clearly. For example, after the Liberal government approved Kinder Morgan's $6.8 billion dollar Trans Mountain Pipeline, Canadian Minister of Natural Resources Jim Carr responded to concerns about widespread opposition to the environmentally disastrous project by saying, "If people choose for their own reasons not to be peaceful, then the government of Canada, through its defense forces, through its police forces, will ensure that people will be kept safe."[12]

The Canadian state has consistently demonstrated that it is willing to use its sovereign violence to ensure that, when it comes to control over the land, the balance of power remains decisively in favour of corporate industrial interests. Such a position is in direct opposition to Indigenous peoples right to say "no" to the Canadian state when it comes to projects that directly affect their lands, lives, and cultures. The construction of this fundamental antagonism currently entails that 1) colonial-capitalist imperatives determine what is in "the national interest," and 2) the Canadian state's deployment of the logic of "national security" to justify the use of sovereign violence and criminalization against opposition to such destructive fabrications of Canadian national interest.

Canadian National Interest

Minister Carr's readiness to use militaristic violence as a means of suppressing communities struggling to protect and preserve the land from destructive industry is sadly not an aberration in Canadian policy. Rather, the state's right to deploy sovereign violence is in keeping with the logic of colonial capitalism, and has thoroughly infected all the major political parties. Take for instance Carr's predecessor, former Conservative Minister of Natural Resources Joe Oliver, who said in an open letter to the *Globe and Mail* regarding tar sands pipeline expansion:

> Unfortunately, there are environmental and other radical groups that would seek to block this opportunity to diversify our trade. Their goal is to stop any major project no matter what the cost to Canadian families in lost jobs and economic growth ... We believe reviews for major projects can be accomplished in a quicker and more streamlined fashion ... It is an urgent matter of Canada's national interest.[13]

While the 2015 federal election brought in a new majority Liberal government, it did not change the Canadian state's commitment to reckless exploitation of natural resources, despite the obvious and ongoing ecological harms. The Liberal expansion of tar sands operations and approval of major new pipeline infrastructure guarantees that Canada will not meet the commitments it made at the Paris Climate summit shortly after the Liberals took power. Despite the

Liberal rhetoric of progressive change, in practice mass industrial resource extraction remains safeguarded and supported by their unquestioned assumption that such destructive projects are in fact in Canada's national interest.

The Liberal government has followed the status quo set by previous governments, using state sovereignty to push through projects that are directly responsible for "dispossess[ing] [Indigenous peoples] of their lands, territories and resources, thus preventing them from exercising, in particular, their right to development in accordance with their own needs and interests."[14] The structure of Canadian state sovereignty is more primary than the specific ideological content of the different political parties. It will not take "no" for an answer.

As Liberal Minister of Natural Resources Jim Carr has affirmed, ensuring that industrial resource projects proceed is "at the heart of my mandate letter from the Prime Minister."[15] Rather than seeking to establish a form of Free Prior Informed Consent that would constitute nation-to-nation engagement with Indigenous communities, Carr continues to assert the Canadian state's sovereign right to relegate Indigenous involvement to an ineffectual position limited to "consultation and accommodation." Canada uses sovereign violence to assert its colonial-capitalist national interests, and to exclude large segments of the population opposed to such a systematically unjust and unsustainable agenda. By wilfully promoting an extractivist framing of Canada's national interest, the Liberals are calcifying a deep political antagonism. Canadian citizens, especially Indigenous peoples, are finding themselves being forced into the absurd position where protecting the basic ecological underpinnings of our collective existence means taking the risk of being labelled as terrorists and subjected to the exclusionary powers of state sovereignty, including all forms of violence up to and including death.[16]

Canadian National Security

Because the Canadian national interest is tied to the corporate colonial agenda of resource extraction, those who actively oppose this agenda often get framed as radical, extreme, or even terroristic. The rhetoric of national interest is intended to delegitimize even the most scientifically based counter-narratives, and to minimize widespread popular support for fundamental Indigenous rights and a swift transition to widespread renewable energy alternatives. Recent surveys suggest that the vast majority of Canadian citizens believe that climate change is a threat to Canada's economic future, and favour decisive action to reduce emissions from burning fossil fuels such as coal, oil, and natural gas.[17]

The Canadian state's colonial-capitalist agenda is protected by the police, army, private security contractors, and other private specialists as a matter of national security. As Eli Sopow, Director of Research & Analysis for the Royal Canadian Mounted Police (RCMP), explains, "Modern police forces were created to protect political systems from anarchy and to maintain social order and control for the needs of industrialized capitalism ... What has changed over time is the strategy and tactics of protest policing, not the intended outcomes."[18] What Sopow designates here as "anarchy" is in fact a broad condemnation of any force that challenges state sovereignty as formulated by the Canadian neoliberal political system.[19]

Ironically, the type of social breakdown Sopow evokes will not come from groups that reject hierarchical oppressions in society (so-called anarchists), but rather from the deepening crises of ecological collapse, displacement, and food insecurity caused by the worsening climate change that is being caused by the very systems his organization is charged with protecting. By way of contrast, traditional Indigenous governance structures are neither hierarchical in a statist sense, nor are they anarchic in the sense that Sopow implies. The main difference is that the intended outcomes of Indigenous systems—healthy peoples and lands—are increasingly in a life-and-death struggle against the colonial-capitalist state's drive toward greater and greater profit, no matter what the consequences to peoples and lands.

The RCMP's commitment to serving the state by protecting the "needs of industrialized capitalism," is demonstrated by its ongoing surveillance of Indigenous-led opponents to specific industrial resource developments. For instance, documents released from the RCMP's 2015 SITKA project reveal extensive police surveillance that focused on Indigenous land protectors and water defenders. The actual surveillance collected through the SITKA project itself indicates that Indigenous-led actions are mostly peaceful, last-ditch attempts to protect sacred areas and threatened ecosystems from imminent violation or destruction. Despite their own findings that Indigenous-led actions are defensive reactions and entail low levels of threat, the RCMP chooses to frame these actions in terms of "Serious criminality associated to large public order events with national implication."[20]

In reality, Canada's resource-based, national interest narrative, and its attendant security apparatus, are a way to guard against and manage the enormous force of the people power that is now amassing against the political antagonism the state has created. Indigenous-led opposition to industrial extraction is emerging and taking shape through political alignments, based on shared values and practices that are emotionally charged and motivated by the existential threat posed by industrialism and the faith that something better is possible. The fight over land is being starkly revealed for what it is: a struggle between the forces of life and the forces of death.

The depth of this land-based antagonism is underscored by the fact that the Canadian government continues to literally re-write the law to legitimize the extractivist agenda and criminalize its opposition. When the Conservative government passed Bill C-51, the so-called *Anti-Terrorism Act*, in 2015, it defined terrorism as any action that "undermines the sovereignty, security or territorial integrity of Canada," including but not limited to "interference with critical infrastructure."[21] Unsurprisingly, *critical infrastructure* under the Canadian Ministry of Public Safety's national strategy includes the oil and gas pipelines and their land-based sources.[22] The Canadian political system is legally engineered so that Indigenous-led land defence, even on Indigenous territories, and even in order to prevent imminent harm being done to the broader public and global interests, can be labelled and prosecuted as terrorism.

Global Corporate Sovereignty

In its current form, Canadian sovereignty functions to ensure the balance of power is tilted in favour of a smooth functioning neoliberal colonial capitalism.[23] State violence is justified in order to protect Canada's national interest, which, in its current framing, has become indistinguishable from the industrial-corporate agenda, particularly that of industrial resource extraction. As a colonial state, Canada has always had recourse to violence when it needed to displace Indigenous peoples from their lands, so that private settler interests could benefit. Today, because of the transnational nature of neoliberal capitalism, the powerful interests behind Canada's national interest are largely organized under the banners of multinational corporations. The collective influence of these corporate bodies has increased to such an extent that they have established, and have begun using, international legal mechanisms to assert a form of supra-state sovereignty, extending their influence further into the realms of nation-state and Indigenous jurisdictions.

The capitalist need for constant growth translates into continuous corporate demands for greater access to valuable natural resources and fewer government regulations, slowing down moneymaking activities.[24] Corporations can afford to continuously pressure the state to use its sovereign force (the police, army, border, prisons, etc.), to remove any barriers standing in the way of their extractive activities and the ability to get these resource products to markets. What corporations want, and to some extent have established, is a form of supra-national global corporate sovereignty. By influencing the state from the outside, corporations benefit from being part of the national interest, but with little or no accountability to the state or the people of the nation.

The role of global corporate sovereignty is at play at the level of international trade deals, through provisions that allow the rights of corporations to trump state sovereignty called Investor-State Dispute Settlement (ISDS) tribunals. ISDSs are international trade litigation tribunals made up of corporate lawyers with the power to decide on the *fair* balance between the interests of countries and corporations. For example, if Canadian environmental protection laws were to prevent a large-scale mining project from going ahead (because it would cause too much ecological damage or displace Indigenous peoples), an ISDS tribunal could rule that these laws "unfairly" hurt the corporation's international investment treaty right to make money. The mining company could then sue Canadian taxpayers for lost profits.

This is not an abstract example. The Canadian mining company OceanaGold recently sued the nation of El Salvador for lost future profits, because elected politicians revoked the firm's license due to the fact the mine was causing extreme harm to the natural environment and the local people. In Canada, US firm Bilcon secured an ISDS victory last year, when a NAFTA ISDS tribunal found a government environmental assessment process had violated the mining company's guarantee to minimum standards of treatment.[25] Bilcon now wants Canada to pay $300 million US in compensation.

International trade lawyer Luis Prado puts the situation this way: "The ultimate question in the case [of ISDS] is whether a foreign investor can force a government to change its laws to please the investor as opposed to the investor complying with the laws they find in the country."[26] Whether the current neoliberal system of states will continue to prevail or is gradually replaced by protectionist forms of nationalist right wing authoritarian capitalism remains to be seen.[27] What is clear is that corporate sovereignty, in different guises, will continue to exert as much force as possible to bend national legal systems to suit its greedy, destructive interests. As global corporations continue to flex their supra-national sovereign muscle through ISDSs, this will create even stronger incentives for states to serve the interests of their corporate masters over anything and anyone else. Given the extent to which the Canadian state already protects corporate interests, it is concerning to imagine the ways that corporate sovereign violence might be used to enforce legally binding arbitration outcomes.

Colonial capitalism has created a twisted, perverse, and violent frame of reference, which must be reckoned with. Rather than taking the necessary action to avert disaster and transition to ecologically resilient communities, the Canadian state has actively used its power to contribute to more uncertainty and injustice, both at home and abroad. Elite corporations exert a great deal of influence over the legislative framing of Canada's national interest, while grassroots movements opposed to ecological destruction and destabilizing climate change have been downplayed as either fringe players or radical terrorists. Sovereign Indigenous peoples living on Turtle Island have been fighting back against the imposition of arbitrary colonial boundaries and violence that only serve the interests of selfish exploiters. After centuries of genocidal colonial processes, Indigenous peoples are again becoming an uncontested force, both demographically and politically.[28] Despite facing ongoing oppression at the hands of the colonial state policies, Indigenous peoples are attaining an unprecedented degree of political and social force in Canada. The growing cultural and political momentum in Indigenous communities has been amplified by an increasingly large segment of settler-allies. Being an ally entails that individuals with white privilege not only recognize the injustices faced by Indigenous peoples, but proactively use their privilege to support Indigenous-led politics in material ways. In terms of the political antagonism described above, Indigenous-led movements occupy a unique position at a critical juncture in Canadian history. In a world suffering from crises of political legitimacy and environmental collapse, Indigenous peoples are in a unique position to articulate an ecologically sane version of Canada's national interest, backed by a reformulated balance of sovereign power.

Dimensions of Indigenous Sovereignty in Canada

Inherent forms of Indigenous sovereign power are unlike either Canadian or corporate sovereignty. When seeking alternatives to colonial capitalist forms of control, Taiaiake Alfred warns that "there is a real danger in the assumption that [European state] sovereignty is the appropriate model for indigenous government."[29] In Canada, Indigenous peoples ostensibly have the right of self-determination, including jurisdiction over traditional political, legal, economic, social, and cultural systems. However, under the *Indian Act*, these rights remain fundamentally constrained by Euro-Canadian sovereignty.[30] Although Aboriginal rights are recognized under Section 35 of the *Constitution Act, 1982*, the application of these rights has been piecemeal at best. It is important to note that, even within the Eurocentric Canadian legal system, being Indigenous to the land is recognized as a basis for a functional self-determination. Take for instance the Supreme Court of Canada's ruling recognizing Aboriginal land title in *Tsilhqot'in v. British Columbia*, a kind of powerful pseudo-sovereignty that recognizes unique Indigenous jurisdiction but ultimately remains subordinate to the British Crown. The 2014 ruling established that,

> Occupation sufficient to ground Aboriginal title is not confined to specific sites of settlement but extends to tracts of land that were regularly used for hunting, fishing or otherwise exploiting resources and over which the group exercised effective control at the time of assertion of European sovereignty.[31]

It is significant that the highest courts of the colonized lands recognize the legitimate and functional Indigenous control of substantial tracts of un-ceded and un-surrendered land. Indigenous peoples control does not come from anarchic occupation, but is guided by interdependent governance structures that were, and continue to be, based on the formation and preservation of long-standing relationships with ancestral lands.[32] Maintaining balance is a foundation for preserving a legitimate legal system. There are many Indigenous nations on Turtle Island, each with different laws, customs, and perspectives on how to honour human interdependence with broader ecosystemic life. Such land-based values systems are often in fundamental opposition to the destructive economic efficiency of the mass-industrial extraction methods of colonial capitalism.

The Sovereign Force of Indigenous-Led Change in Canada

The Canadian state needs to be changed, and changed utterly. This will require the reformulation of sovereign relations of force, and specifically, a shifting of the parameters governing the state's potential and actual capacity for violence. The balance of sovereign power in Canada can be significantly shifted by ensuring that Indigenous peoples assert more influence, and have greater sovereign force, than corporations when it comes to defining and deciding what constitutes the public interest, and what warrants the legitimate use of sovereign violence.

Changing relations of power will be an unsettling process for many Canadians. Change will not happen if it is limited to political platforms and reforms premised on the good intentions of settler agents of the state. Indigenous peoples must be the ones to set the terms of engagement in ways that include traditional land-based governance principles as well the capacity for political diplomacy and innovative approaches to economics.[33] Indigenous sovereignty draws on the inherent legitimacy that comes from relationships between diverse communities grounded in land-based governance and ethics, independent of state recognition.[34] Increasingly, Indigenous-led movements, coordinated through online means, have the capacity to articulate, mobilize, and assert the types of massive collective force needed to shift the balance of sovereign forces and significantly realign power relations. Indigenous-led movements *should not* mean that Indigenous peoples are left alone, taking risks, and facing the threat of state violence on the frontlines.[35]

Changing the relationships between Canada's three sovereign forces will require shifting the boundaries of political antagonism at the points where they are implemented and protected by violence. The Canadian state sanctions the use of violent police force against Indigenous peoples opposed to corporate industrial projects and infrastructure that threaten their existence. Such actions demonstrate the extent to which Canada has been hijacked by the priorities of corporate colonial capitalism. What if the Canadian state used its sovereign violence to enforce a broader, interdependent conception of the public interest? What if Canada recognized its true "critical infrastructure" to be the complex ecosystems, rivers, forests, marshes, and plains that sustain life, rather than pipelines and logging roads that jeopardize these systems?[36] What if law enforcement re-assessed what constitutes real terrorism in Canada, based on holistic threat assessments that included climate change? The Canadian state has provided no satisfactory answers to these questions, and the more such questions are asked only serves to further expose the disproportionate and illegitimate influence that corporate agendas continue to exert on Canada's sovereign balance of power.

Sovereignty, whichever way you cut it, is still largely a matter of what "we the people" feel we are able to do, and our willingness, determination, and capacity to do it. In a climate of great uncertainty, there is a coalescence of forces in Canada that have the collective strength to push for real transformation. Indigenous-led resurgence is providing a grounded alternative to the disaster of corporate governance, as a means of shaping local, national, and international politics.[37] Young leaders are breathing life into the fires of old teachings, and they are mobilizing others.

The Need for an Indigenous-Led Populism

As Canada celebrates and mourns 150 years of Confederation, we are at a critical and perhaps unprecedented historical juncture not only for the country, but also for the entire planet. The gulf between the rich and the poor is now oceanic. Climate change, caused by industrial activities like the tar sands, is destroying global ecosystems and causing extreme weather that disproportionately impacts the most marginalized among us. Refugees are forced to flee their homes because of food scarcity and wars over oil. Tens of thousands of displaced people are left to die at the borders of the very countries that have benefitted from wealth stolen from the lands they came from. The status quo is not acceptable. This generation has a profound responsibility to shift the current balance of power in order to preserve the very habitability of the planet and the potential lives of future generations. This cannot be accomplished by sacrificing marginalized people. Transition must be a process toward energy justice, in which the day-to-day means are congruent with the desired ends.

There is a great deal of social momentum in Canada that has the potential to develop into an inclusive, populist politics that supports the meaningful implementation of Indigenous sovereignty. Populism is often, and rightly, associated with right wing politics the likes of Brexit, Trump, and Le Pen. The structure of populist political movements is, however, more important than the particular content that make up popular ideologies. Alongside the surge of effective right wing populist organizing there is also large-scale leftist populist successes including Greece's anti-austerity Syriza party, the Spanish *Indignados* movement, and mass support for Bernie Sanders. This is not to mention the successes of Indigenous-led autonomous movements in Latin America, which also have distinctly land-based populist strategies.[38]

The Internet and new uses of social media have contributed to this extremely powerful moment for populist politics. News bubbles, created by targeted marketing algorithms, have become a major force in framing political antagonism, aligning large groups of people behind shared ideas and mobilizing enormous emotional force to support these social formations.[39] For example, phases of the

Standing Rock Sioux tribe's battle to protect their water from pipeline expansion across their territory engaged millions of people around the world and mobilized tens of thousands of people on the ground. So while the mainstream media continues to play an extremely important role in how encounters with state forces are characterized, it's clearly no longer the only show in town. Critically, Indigenous-led movements have the capacity to articulate social demands that exist outside of the right-left Eurocentric governance structure in Canada. Popular demands framed by Indigenous perspectives could significantly mitigate the influence on extremist white supremacist tendencies that provide core support for Canada's colonial-capitalist project.

Effective populism includes a clearly stated demand that has powerful emotional resonance and is inclusive, while remaining open-ended enough to accommodate a major alliance of groups. The World Social Forum's slogan "Another World is Possible" and Trump's "Make America Great Again" are clear examples of populist demands. Such broad slogans must encompass the core demands of multiple and diverse struggles being waged by equally diverse peoples. Once these diverse groups are mobilized in large numbers, further political alignment can take place through the feeling of a common purpose. Such effective alignments are central to creating the type of powerful unity that can win substantive gains on the ground, without homogenizing individual identities and issues. By remaining undefined by a clearly specified (and hence rigidified) doctrine, platform, or policy, populism remains flexibly able to incorporate an extremely broad sub-set of perspectives from groups that identify the specificities of their own struggle in the collective aims of the movement.

This is not to suggest that all populism is without an ethical core or imperative principles.

While appearing in some senses so broad as to be *empty* or value-neutral, populism creates space and a temporary discursive structure that can lead to potentially unprecedented *fullness*.[40] In populist politics, individuals can identify themselves with the very essence of the political project, and can clearly identify the fundamental antagonism against which they are struggling. Take for example the hundreds of different Indigenous nations on Turtle Island; each have different demands based on vastly different lived experiences and land-based contexts. Rather than trying to address these specific demands one by one, an Indigenous-led populism would assert a demand that responds to an emotional core for all of them. At Standing Rock, this emotional core demand was "Mni Wiconi—Water is Life." As Ernesto Laclau has put it "Populism is, quite simply, a way of constructing the political."[41]

What is unique about the prospect of Indigenous-led populism is that it fundamentally decentres western political thinking, re-grounding it in the sovereign power of the land. The powerful emotional core of such land-based politics goes beyond identity, class, or gender politics, distilling the antagonism in terms of the basic human need for clean water and land. While fighting against injustice is a powerful motivation for many, people mobilize on the frontlines because they emotionally recognize that they are doing something urgent and bigger than themselves. Political momentum is generated by the intensity of individuals who recognize that what they are fighting for is a matter of life and death, and in many ways one of good versus evil. During circumstances when feelings meld into collective action, the capacity for action is increased and the balance of power can be shifted.[42]

Reframe for Inevitable Transition: Mobilize, Organize, Change

We are living through a period of momentous historical transition, defined by both uncertainty as well as opportunity. The realities of climate change, population growth, and right wing governance have created a volatile mixture of fear, greed, and violence. An Indigenous-led populism in Canada would have the capacity to influence the inevitable processes involved in complex systems changes, by shifting the balance of power away from colonial capitalism toward Indigenous governance models that address historical injustices while being ecologically sustainable. This would be a significant shifting of the narrative of Canadian national interest, away from the exploitation of non-renewable land-based resources, toward values and practices of interdependence. Shifting toward locally based objectives, such as food sovereignty and renewables, creates resilient communities, while taking the necessary steps toward global climate justice. Such transitions would also create many new jobs focused on developing and implementing the nuts and bolts of widespread social transition to renewable energy, and providing food. These aims are simple but profound. Mass participation is growing, and practical strategies for implementing concrete changes exist. This process includes changing the stories we, as Canadians, tell ourselves about who we are and what is at stake in relation to the history of colonization and a future of climate change. New ways forward have been outlined in public documents such as the Leap Manifesto, which continues to grow as broad popular momentum finds collective expressions.[43]

Within Canada, there are already robust legal frameworks that would allow for the translation of popular political force into Indigenous-led forms of governance. Take for example UNDRIP, the most fully developed legal mechanism of this type, adopted by the UN in 2007, and drafted by an international coalition of Indigenous legal experts over a period of two decades. UNDRIP provides an international legal instrument that, if adopted and implemented at the level of the Canadian Constitution, could enact Indigenous sovereign control at a level equal to that of Canadian State sovereignty. Such a constitutional amendment would establish the practical sovereign conditions needed for an actual nation-to-nation arrangement, first established in the Royal Proclamation of 1763, the subsequent Treaty of Niagara in 1764, and other treaties.

The Trudeau Liberal government has deployed the rhetoric of embracing UNDRIP, but in practice has carefully worded its endorsements in ways that avoid UNDRIP's potential implications for affecting constitutional change. Such provisions for a meaningful implementation of UNDRIP exist and have been championed by Indigenous jurist and member of Parliament Romeo Saganash in his private member's Bill C-262, entitled *United Nations Declaration on the Rights of Indigenous Peoples Act*.[44] Such a legislative move would be a substantial legal shift toward enshrining the sovereign force of Indigenous peoples in practical terms. For example, UNDRIP would ensure that Free Prior Informed consent had the force of law, giving Indigenous nations meaningful veto powers with regards to whether or not industrial developments proceed on their territories.

Rather than using its sovereign exception to legitimize ecological sacrifice zones and criminalize land defenders and water protectors, Canada could fully adopt and implement UNDRIP, reorienting its state sovereign power through an internationally recognized legal framework. This would be a powerful move, and would help to facilitate a popular shift in direction toward sustainable social, political, economic, and ecological horizons. Sovereign Indigenous governance entails the possibility of absolute veto power over land use. This would also be moving toward restorative justice and realizing reparations. UNDRIP provides a framework that would benefit both settler and newcomer Canadians, by helping to build meaningful forms of social and ecological resilience. The synthesis of land-based ways of knowing and international legal conventions in UNDRIP would be a gift for all non-Indigenous Canadians.

In the midst of unprecedented global uncertainty, UNDRIP would provide all Canadians with a practical, legally grounded basis from which to establish forms of governance, framed in terms of interdependence rather than individualist greed. Just as the early Canadian settler communities would not have survived without the help and guidance of Indigenous peoples, in the future this is no less true. Indigenous scholars and activists such as Glen Coulthard, Harsha Walia, Leanne Simpson, Cindy Blackstock, Taiaiake Alfred, Arthur Manuel, Sarah Hunt, Brian Rice, Pam Palmater, and many others, have collectively provided Canadians with excellent guidance in terms of how to practically shift our day-to-day values and practices in ways that strengthen the collective whole.[45]

Shifting away from colonial capitalism, toward Indigenous-led sovereignty, hinges on collectively rearticulating Canadian identity. Many Canadians identify with the natural environment, human rights, and, increasingly, thanks in part to the work of Murray Sinclair and the Truth and Reconciliation Commission (TRC), with Indigenous rights. The TRC, like UNDRIP, provides a historical opportunity, along with a clear framework, for catalyzing substantive change in regards to the sovereign force underlying Canadian governance systems.[46] Implementing the framework changes would go a long way toward providing individuals with a legitimate opportunity to turn impoverished systems into the grounds for good lives, what Anishinabek writer Leanne Simpson translates as processes of *mino bimaadiziwin*.[47]

Shifting the balance of Canadian sovereign power away from facilitating the supra-national sovereignty of corporate ISDS tribunals, toward an Indigenous sovereignty framed by the internationally recognized principles of UNDRIP, is possible. Such a change would mean that Canada's national interest could no longer be tethered to the reckless and short-sighted priorities of corporate agendas, which benefit global elites at the expense of local Indigenous and environmental rights. Bringing about such a shift requires strategic planning that anticipates conflict and understands the nature of the current political antagonism. Corporations wield a huge amount of power in our society, which has effectively been used to shape the institutions of government. Decades of social movement experience make it abundantly clear that the corporate-state alliance will not easily be separated. As Gustavo Esteva observes, "Returning policy and ethics back to the center of social life can only be done in the midst of real, lived entities, such as the community.

Attempting to do this at the scale of abstract entities, such as the multinational organization or the nation-state, is impossible and counter-productive ... The case of peace and violence illustrates the nature of the problem."[48]

Despite the potentially meaningful legal frameworks outlined in UNDRIP, sovereign violence continues to be used to enforce the agenda of destructive neoliberal industrialism. Rather than implementing socially responsible, Indigenous-led, land-based responses that can sustain interdependent ecological life systems, the government is sticking to a suicidal status quo. Changes need to be implemented immediately, and this will lead to a necessary confrontation between life-sustaining and life-destroying processes. This confrontation will continue to be the defining antagonism in Canada's future.

Matters of Life and Death: Articulating Populist Objectives as Canada's National Interest

Canada as a nation-state stands at a historic juncture, a forking path. Shifting the balance of state power from corporate to Indigenous-led priorities would have enormous benefits in every area the current Canadian state claims are its highest priorities. Humans are subject to the immutable laws of land-based interdependence and we can no longer avoid the fact that our future will be one of extreme weather, climate refugees, and conflict over scarce resources.[49] The ability for Canada to adapt as a nation requires the state to reject its corporatist interest and take decisive action to stop facilitating the ecological death spiral that is accelerated by the cynical aims of late-stage capitalism.

Taking such actions would be a means of responding to ecological threats that pose tremendous risks to national security. Security challenges related to climate change already pose the greatest challenges to the preservation of state sovereignty and functional borders. For example, in his 2016 Worldwide Threat Assessment of the US Intelligence Community, given to the American Senate's Armed Services Committee, Director of American National Intelligence James Clapper identified "Extreme weather, climate change, environmental degradation, rising demand for food and water, poor policy decisions and inadequate infrastructure" as primary threats to national security.[50]

Ecological destruction and climate change pose an existential threat, most acutely for Indigenous and marginalized peoples. The creation of environmental sacrifice zones simultaneously creates criminals out of threatened communities that fight against them as a means of preserving fundamental ways of being and elemental sources of life.[51] There are frameworks in place for undertaking the needed action, including UNDRIP and the TRC as discussed above, not to mention the Paris Climate Summit targets for cutting carbon emissions. The problems are clear, the solutions are available, and people are desperate for change. However, rather than taking the necessary steps, the current neoliberal Canadian state has been actively complicit in facilitating massive industrial projects that exacerbate climate change, facilitating the ongoing processes of Indigenous genocide.[52]

Amassing Popular Sovereign Force on the Frontlines

Canada continues to use sovereign state violence to empower corporate industrialism and dominate Indigenous-led land defenders and water protectors through criminalization and intimidation. The frontlines of these struggles are manifesting as open physical conflicts between Indigenous-led movements opposed to ecocide, and state backed corporations propelling it. Indigenous peoples continue to assert their sovereign jurisdiction through their sustained presence on the land, and the revitalization of ceremony and language. When needed, they have demonstrated the capacity to effectively use direct action to stop corporate violence against their lands and peoples.

State sovereign violence does not have to be used to back up the rights of multinational industrial corporations that dispossess Indigenous people while destroying the planet. To continue to do so is to wilfully perpetrate violence against the very people who are supposed to give sovereign power its force. An Indigenous-led populist force, backed up by millions of other Canadians, has the capacity to stop industrial projects on the ground. There is immense, latent power in Canadian society, stifled by the inertia of an over mythologized narrative of passivity. Climate change and Indigenous resurgence have begun to awaken the potential of a truly active citizenry that wields a profoundly emotional force. Even a small fraction of this force, mobilized in direct action at local sites and at critical moments, could effectively overwhelm both state and corporate sovereign forces. What will determine the lasting impact of these engagements is whether or not populist movements are able to establish the legitimacy of these forceful assertions through widespread popular endorsements. When the frontlines give way and new formations of sovereign power begin to take shape, these gains need to be practically sustained through the financial backing and social-political buffering of mainstream Canadians.

The frontlines of active struggle against ecocide and genocide are many and mobile, with Indigenous-led opposition fighting industrial projects on numerous fronts such as Unist'ot'en Camp, Grassy Narrows, West Moberly First Nation, Elsipogtog, and Muskrat Falls, not to mention the vast numerous Indigenous territories threatened by major pipeline projects being pushed by companies such as Kinder Morgan, Husky, TransCanada, and Enbridge.

Pushing on the frontlines of a sovereign antagonism will necessarily be conflictual. Mass mobilization will be needed, its primary strength being its connection to forces of life that find expression through the incredible capacity for human emotions to continually make and unmake "the boundaries of the political."[53] Canadian identities need to make spaces that can be filled and transformed by the emotional force and powerful knowledge of the Indigenous peoples of Turtle Island. Indigenous-led populism is perhaps Canada's best opportunity to fundamentally re-structure power relations, stop historical injustices, and respond to the imminent threat of climate change.

The legitimacy of Canadian sovereign force needs to be re-constituted in a way that disentangles the country's national interest from the colonial-capitalist agenda. Alternative frameworks already exist, but their implementation requires that this political antagonism be engaged through mass mobilization on the frontlines to assert the jurisdiction of specific peoples on specific lands. Emergent forms of Indigenous-led populism that combine successful use of social media have the capacity to become a puncturing force, orchestrating events that can exert pressure at the levels of national and international governance, forcing colonial-capitalist systems to shift their agendas in accordance with the will of a mobilized and powerful people. Such populist mobilizations have proven themselves a major political force in our highly networked, socially uncertain, and ecologically precarious times.

The prospect of a uniquely Canadian, Indigenous-led populism has the potential to demand that the Canadian state fundamentally reframe its natural interest, away from corporate greed, in favour of supporting ecological resilience based on Indigenous leadership. Concerted populist demands driven by emotional intensities that reflect the existential stakes of the crises being faced have the capacity to bring about large-scale shifts in the balance of sovereign power in Canada. The ongoing Indigenous cultural resurgence in Canada is laying the groundwork for Indigenous-led populism. Frontline struggles will inevitably occur, but these should be seen as forms of productive conflict, which are part of an ongoing process of decolonizing Canada through the redistribution of sovereign force into more sustainable formations. As these shifts begin to take place, spaces will open-up in which the overly broad populist demands can be disaggregated to meet the needs of particular groups, empowering local-level formations.[54]

What shape these political alternatives will take remains to be seen, but local-level Indigenous governance, rooted in interdependent relationships, will certainly be central in many areas.[55] Whatever alternatives emerge as a result of pushing for Indigenous-led populist change, it is crucial that these changes empower people most directly impacted by the destructive effects of capitalism, be it through climate change displacement, colonial dispossession, or endemic poverty. The goodness of any alternative needs to consider how it impacts the practical day-to-day situation of our society's most vulnerable people, who are often the least culpable for the current crises.

There are grave risks involved in rising populist fervour. Any such movements are susceptible to charismatic and authoritarian leaders who are quick to categorize and scapegoat the "other."[56] Politics based on notions of purity can likewise undermine the capacity of movements to grow.[57] Our capacity to mitigate and adapt to climate change will be a major determinant of the type of social, ecological, and political relations we want to leave for the generations to come. Space for diversity is an essential part of fostering a collective resilience needed to withstand and thrive amidst the coming social and ecological transitions.

1. Agamben, Giorgio (1998), *Homo Sacer: Sovereign power and bare life*, trans., Daniel Heller-Roazen, Stanford: Stanford University Press.
2. The role of social media in mobilizing large scale demonstrations that are perceived as being "anti-state" or "violent" are particular prone to surveillance and manipulation through infiltration and other subversive acts on the part of the state or corporate actors. Recognizing and building alternative organizing methods is a key part of building resilient movements that are not solely dependant on a single method.
3. Rifkin, Mark (2009), "Indigenizing Agamben: Rethinking Sovereignty in Light of the 'Peculiar' Status of Native Peoples," *Cultural Critique* 73, pp. 88-124.
4. Benjamin, Walter (1968), "Critique of violence," in *Reflections: Essays, aphorisms, autobiographical writings*, trans., Edmund Jephcott, New York: Harcourt Brace, pp. 277-300.
5. Agamben, Giorgio (2015), "From the state of law to the security state: Giorgio Agamben on the state of emergency in France," trans. Julius Gavroche, *Autonomies*, December 18, 2015: www.autonomies.org/it/2015/12/from-the-state-of-law-to-the-security-state-giorgio-agamben-on-the-state-of-emergency-in-france/
6. Agamben, 1998.
7. Canada has implemented Security Certificates in order to conduct secretive trials of non-status newcomers living in Canada who are perceived to be a threat to state security. Such was the case of the so-called "Secret Trial Five.": www.theglobeandmail.com/arts/film/the-secret-trial-5-explores-story-of-five-men-held-without-trial-in-canada/article18213494/

8. Butler, Judith (2004), "Indefinite detention," *Precarious Life: The powers of mourning and violence*, London: Verso, pp. 50-101.
9. Lerner, Steve (2010), *Sacrifice zones: The front lines of toxic chemical exposure in the United States* Cambridge: MIT Press.
10. I would like to thank the *Affect Project* (affectproject.ca) at the University of Manitoba for the support of a postdoctoral fellowship in Affect Studies that made this research possible, especially Arlene Young, Brenda Austin-Smith, and Jason Leboe-McGowan.
11. Milman, Oliver, "Canada gives $3.3bn subsidies to fossil fuel producers despite climate pledge," *The Guardian* November 15, 2016: www.theguardian.com/world/2016/nov/15/climate-change-canada-fossil-fuel-subsidies-carbon-trudeau
12. Maloney, Ryan, "Jim Carr's Remarks About Using Military At Kinder Morgan Protests Were 'Reckless': NDP," *Huffington Post Canada* February 12, 2016: www.huffingtonpost.ca/2016/12/02/jim-carr-military-kinder-morgan-ndp_n_13375946.html.
13. Oliver, Joe, "An open letter from Natural Resources Minister Joe Oliver," *Globe and Mail*, January 9, 2012: www.theglobeandmail.com/news/politics/an-open-letter-from-natural-resources-minister-joe-oliver/article4085663/
14. www.un.org/esa/socdev/unpfii/documents/DRIPS_en.pdf
15. www.un.org/esa/socdev/unpfii/documents/DRIPS_en.pdf
16. Mbembe, Achile (2003), "Necropolitics," *Public Culture* Vol. 15 No. 1, p. 11–40.
17. www.cleanenergycanada.org/wp-content/uploads/2016/09/Clean-Energy-Canada-Nanos-Climate-Policy-Polling-Report-Oct-2016.pdf
18. Sopow, Eli (2008), *The age of outrage: The role of emotional and organizational factors on protest policing and political opportunity frames*, Saarbrucken: VDM Verlag, p. 111.
19. For a discussion of the diverse formations that compromise contemporary forms of anarchism see, Day, Richard J. F. (2005), *Gramsci is Dead: Anarchist Currents in the Newest Social Movements*. Toronto: Between the Lines Press.
20. www.warriorpublications.wordpress.com/2016/11/08/the-rcmps-project-sitka-full-pdf-document/
21. www.parl.gc.ca/HousePublications/Publication.aspx?DocId=8056977&File=35
22. www.publicsafety.gc.ca/cnt/rsrcs/pblctns/srtg-crtcl-nfrstrctr/index-eng.aspx
23. For an overview of neoliberal processes see Harvey, David (2005), *A brief introduction to neoliberalism*, Oxford: Oxford University Press.
24. Ibid.
25. Provost, Claire and Matt Kennard, "The obscure legal systems lets corporations sue countries," *Guardian*, June 10, 2015: www.theguardian.com/business/2015/jun/10/obscure-legal-system-lets-corportations-sue-states-ttip-icsid
26. Ibid.
27. On some examples of existing authoritarian capitalist regimes, see Zizek, Slavoj (2008), *In defense of lost causes*, London: Verso, pp. 360-374.
28. Woolford, Andrew, Jeff Benvenuto, and Alexander Hinton, eds. (2014), *Colonial Genocide in Indigenous North America*, Durham: Duke University Press.
29. Alfred, Taiaiake (1999), *Peace, power and righteousness*, Oxford: Oxford University Press, p. 79.
30. www.laws-lois.justice.gc.ca/eng/acts/i-5/page-1.html#h-4.
31. Tsilhqot'in Nation v. British Columbia, SCC 44, 2 S.C. R. 256, para. 260 (2014): http://scc-csc.lexum.com/scc-csc/scc-csc/en/14246/1/document.do
32. Alfred, Taiaiake (2005), *Wasáse: Indigenous Pathways of Action and Freedom*, Peterborough: Broadview Press.

33. Leaders such as Art Manuel have powerfully expressed the capacity that already exists for Indigenous Peoples to develop solutions that address many of the complexities involved in transforming contemporary Canada. See Manuel, Arthur and Ronald M. Derrickson (2015), "Unsettling Canada: A national wake up call," Toronto: Between the Lines Press.
34. Coulthard, Glenn (2014), *Red Skins, White Mask: Rejecting the colonial politics of recognition*, Minneapolis: University of Minnesota Press.
35. Walia, Harsha (2013), *Undoing Border Imperialism*, Oakland: AK Press.
36. I owe this understanding of "critical infrastructure" to comments made by Freda Huson, spokesperson for the Unis'tot'en camp on Wet'suwet'en territories.
37. Kino-nda-niimi Collective, ed. (2014), *The winter we danced: Voices from the past, the future, and the Idle No More movement*, Winnipeg: ARP Books.
38. Luisetti, Federico, John Pickles, and Wilson Kaiser, eds. (2015), *The anomie of the earth: Philosophy, politics and autonomy in Europe and the America*, Durham: Duke University Press.
39. Ahmed, Sarah (2004), "Affective economies," *Social Text* Vol. 51: pp. 117-139.
40. Laclau, Ernesto (2005), *On populist reason*, Verso: London.
41. Ibid., p. xi.
42. Gould, Deborah B. (2009), *Moving politics: Emotion and ACT UP's fight against AIDS*, Chicago: University of Chicago Press.
43. www.leapmanifesto.org/en/the-leap-manifesto/
44. www.parl.gc.ca/HousePublications/Publication.aspx?DocId=8210051
45. Coulthard, 2014; Walia, 2013; Alfred, Taiaiake (2014), "The Akwesasne cultural restoration program: A Mohawk approach to land-based education." *Decolonization: Indigeneity, Education & Society* Vol. 3, No. 3, pp. 134-144; Simpson, Leanne Betasamosake (2014), "Land as pedagogy: Nishnaabeg intelligence and rebellious transformation," *Decolonization: Indigeneity, Education & Society*, Vol. 3, No. 3, pp. 1-25; Hunt, Sarah (2014), "Ontologies of Indigeneity: the politics of embodying a concept," *Cultural Geographies*, Vol. 21 No.1, pp. 27–32; Rice, Brian (2013), *The Rotinonshonni: A Traditional Iroquoian History Through the Eyes of the Teharonhia:Wako and Sawiskea*, Syracuse: Syracuse University Press; Palmater, Pamela (2015), *Indigenous Nationhood: Empowering grass roots citizens*, Halifax: Fernwood Publishing.
46. It is no coincidence that one of the TRC's recommendations, as well the 43rd and 44th Calls to Action, refer to fully adopting and implementing UNDRIP.
47. Simpson, Leanne (2011), *Dancing on Our Turtle's Back: Stories of Nishnaabeg Re-Creation, Resurgence and a New Emergence*, Winnipeg: ARP Books.
48. Esteva, Gustavo (2015), "Enclosing the enclosers: Autonomous experience from the grassroots beyond development, globalization and postmodernity," *The anomie of the earth: Philosophy, politics and autonomy in Europe and the America*, ed. Federico Luisetti, John Pickles, and Wilson Kaier, Durham: Duke University Press: pp. 71-92.
49. Welzer, Harald (2012), *Climate wars: Why people will be killed in the 21st century*. London: Polity Press.
50. www.dni.gov/index.php/newsroom/testimonies/217-congressional-testimonies-2016/1314-dni-clapper-opening-statement-on-the-worldwide-threat-assessment-before-the-senate-armed-services-committee-2016
51. Woolford, Andrew (2009) "Ontological Destruction: Genocide and Canadian Aboriginal Peoples," *Genocide Studies and Prevention*, Vol. 4, No. 1, pp. 81-97.
52. Huseman, Jennifer and Damian Short (2012), "'A slow industrial genocide': Tar Sands and the Indigenous peoples of northern Alberta," *The International Journal of Human Rights*, Vol.16, No.1, pp. 216-237.

53. Gould, 2009, p. 4.
54. See Bookchin, Murray (2015), "Libertarian municipalism: A politics of direct democracy," *The next revolution: Popular assemblies and the promise of direct democracy*, eds. Debbie Bookchin and Blair Taylor, New York: Verso, pp. 83-97.
55. Simpson, 2011.
56. Erich Fromm's insights seem highly relevant today. Fromm, Erich (1941), *Escape from freedom*, New York: Henry Holt and Company.
57. Shotwell, Alexis (2016), *Against Purity: Living Ethically in Compromised Times*, Minneapolis: University of Minnesota Press.

Magic Anniversary Syndrome

Ravi de Costa

> We need to recognize that ours was a nation forged without the meaningful participation of Aboriginal Peoples.
>
> That this unlikely country has endured for a century and a half is cause for celebration. But at the same time, this commemoration stands as a reminder that much work remains. One hundred fifty years on, we've yet to complete the unfinished business of Confederation. … If the federal government sets priorities and devises solutions without the input of Aboriginal communities, those solutions will fail..[1]
>
> The Commission believes that, as Canada's 150th anniversary approaches in 2017, national reconciliation is the most suitable framework to guide commemoration of this significant historical benchmark in Canada's history. This intended celebration can be an opportunity for Canadians to take stock of the past, celebrating the country's accomplishments without shirking responsibility for its failures. Fostering more inclusive public discourse about the past through a reconciliation lens would open up new and exciting possibilities for a future in which Aboriginal peoples take their rightful place in Canada's history as founding nations who have strong and unique contributions to make to this country.[2]

All enduring human societies develop a collective relationship to time, a mix of reminiscences and arguments about responsibility in the present and future aspirations.[3] As Charles Turner observes, "if there is a politics of time, it is because the temporal logic of one type of collectivity may be imposed upon the life of another."[4]

Among the settler-colonial nations, the politics of national time is reproduced perennially, as many in dominant cultures and institutions seize on national anniversaries as moments to discuss, lament, or celebrate the quality of the relationships between settler and Indigenous nations. The language of nation to nation is not one that is typically used in these moments, however. The underlying framework of Justin Trudeau's remarks to the Assembly of First Nations in 2015 is a rhetoric that seeks completion of the postcolonial nation, not an attempt to take seriously the idea that many nations continue to be colonized within the territories that now make up Canada. No doubt, others in this volume will take up the implications of this, as well as the problem that Canada Day not only excludes much older Indigenous histories and forms of relationship, but that it recalls events at the beginning of the high point of colonial interventions into Indigenous life.

However, let us conjure here with the idea of a sesquicentenary. A self-aggrandizing way of saying "150th anniversary," there's no denying that 150 just sounds so much more significant than 143, or perhaps even, 157. It is certainly the case that mainstream politicians, institutions, and dominant cultures seem to pay more attention when the anniversary is divisible by ten or 25, just as many of us do with our own birthdays. Where nations are concerned, the assumption is that these anniversaries have some kind of magic power that others just can't muster. They command a level of attention, or of perceived achievement that in turn provides a political opportunity. Somehow—we seem to be saying—the very system for the calibration of time contains within it social and cultural resources for change.

Rather than drag the reader into the realms of numerology, it may be more revealing to look at other settler-colonial nations' experiences of how such centennials, sesquicentennials, and bicentennials have played out, and what they indicate about the actual qualities of Indigenous-settler relations. The co-optation of Indigenous peoples into these state-led celebrations, as well as movements to resist and disrupt them, punctuate the history of settler-colonial relations.

I will consider the case of Australia at some length, as it more closely reproduces the nationalist interactions of the Canadian settler state with Indigenous peoples than any other. However, it is worth considering briefly Aotearoa New Zealand, where the national day of celebration—Waitangi Day—commemorates the constitutional agreement between the British Crown and a number of Māori chiefs on February 6, 1840 (more chiefs signed the treaty later). The origins of this national celebration, being based on an agreement between the Crown and Indigenous nations, are distinctive in the settler-colonial experience.[5]

Māori people felt that the commitments set out in the treaty, in particular about their land rights, were being ignored during the rest of the nineteenth and much of the twentieth century. Commemorations of the day of signing were not significant until the 1930s. However, an earlier spatial division had taken place during the 1870s, which began to mark the meaning of the event and subsequent celebrations. The treaty had been signed at the house and grounds of the then British Resident at Waitangi on the North Island. However, Māori leaders began gathering regularly on the nearby Ngapuhi tribe's land, the Te Tii Waitangi *marae* (meeting grounds), and this latter location became a key site for discussion and political organizing amongst Māori.

When the anniversary was first observed officially, in 1934, this division marked the celebrations, with 10,000 Māori gathering at Te Tii, while the Crown hosted official events such as flag-raising ceremonies at the Treaty Grounds. It is a distinction that continues to play out in contemporary life, now enabling an often fruitfully contradictory performance of nationality each year, with multiple Māori and *pakeha* positions being taken. Patrick McAllister discuses this insightfully:

> The spatial dimensions of the commemoration of the Treaty form a symbolic structure and perform a significant meta-communicative function, for they show that the "landscape of nationhood" is symbolically bifurcated ... there are two aesthetics of nation at Waitangi, one at Te Tii, one at the Treaty Grounds—each associated with their own cultural spaces, artifacts, styles of meeting, songs and oratory ... However the messages conveyed are not fixed and vary from year to year ... the two venues are not only structurally opposed but also complementary and linked in a variety of ways.[6]

Since the 1970s, Māori began more systematically and decisively campaigning for the spirit of the Treaty to be honoured, and Waitangi Day became intensely conflictual. State and pakeha political leaders have often declined to participate, while Māori activists used the Day as an opportunity to press their grievances.[7] There is now a complex duality to Waitangi Day as a kind of national memory-event, which obliges people annually to return to fundamental questions about history, justice, and identity in Aotearoa New Zealand.

By contrast, Australia has multiple dates that give rise to what might be called "magic anniversaries": January 26, 1788; January 1, 1901; and May 27, 1967. January 26 recalls the arrival of the eleven ships of the First Fleet. These contained British colonists (mainly convicts transported from the overcrowded gaols of Georgian England). Their arrival led to the founding of the first colony of New South Wales, by Captain Arthur Phillip, who planted a British flag at Sydney Cove.[8] January 1, 1901 was the date of Federation in Australia, as July 1, 1867 was of Canadian Confederation. May 27, 1967 was the date of a national referendum that offered two changes of limited material significance, but symbolic importance for Aboriginal Australians. It has come to be remembered by many as nationally momentous, possibly because it offers some resonances of Waitangi Day in that it was seemingly a moment of converging interests between settlers and Indigenous peoples. However, as we shall see, its memory is weighed down with multiple conflicting interpretations. I treat the anniversaries of these events in chronological order.

On the celebration of 50 years of British colonization, the 1838 Jubilee, a Sydney newspaper reported on the official regatta that was organized to dignify the celebration, "numerous crowds of gaily attired people, attended by servants and porters . . . bearing the supplies for the day's refreshments . . . wending their way towards the water's edge." No mention is made in the official history, and the news reports mention neither the presence of Indigenous peoples nor their thoughts about the event.[9] However, in a recent official history of Australia Day, Elizabeth Kwan described the strongly racist discourse of colonial Sydney in 1838, where there was now "a sharp contrast between the 'untutored savage' and 'industrious and civilised man.'"[10]

Originally known as Foundation Day, the valence of January 26 ebbed and flowed in the nineteenth century, being seen early on as a New South Wales event, rather than a national one: it emphasized both its status as the first British colony in Australia as well as its history as a convict settlement, which some of the other colonies resented. Other days had pre-eminence at different points in the period up until Federation, and other colonies held their own days of celebration.[11]

However, by 1888, the centennial of British colonization coincided with the ubiquity of thinking about the inevitable disappearance of Indigenous peoples. One historian, writing of the events in Sydney and Melbourne held to celebrate the centennial, noted that, unlike in the US where Native Americans were still perceived as a threatening "other," Indigenous Australians at the time of the centennial in 1888 were not perceived as a threat to the burgeoning national identity. In fact, Australians had begun to see Indigenous peoples purely as cultural curiosities, and this trope marked the centennial celebrations with an "Aboriginal Troup" who had been hired to perform a corroboree,[12] and advertised as an "Historic Relic of a race now rapidly being civilized into oblivion." An exhibition in Melbourne in August that year included Indigenous weapons that had been made by "Aboriginal natives in gaol."[13] The then Premier of NSW, Sir Henry Parkes, "when asked what was being planned for the Aborigines . . . retorted, 'And remind them that we have robbed them?'"[14]

As I noted above, 1901 is to Australia as 1867 is to Canada: an inter-provincial agreement to create a federal nation-state. The Constitution that was enshrined in 1901 contained two references to Indigenous peoples: first, it held that "in reckoning the numbers of people . . . Aboriginal natives shall not be counted." It also provided that the national government, the "Commonwealth," would *not* have legislative authority over Aboriginal peoples and issues. That is, precisely the inverse of the Canadian experience (this was altered in 1967—see below). Until 2001, Federation did not have much importance as a national event, the anniversary of which could be useful in some way.

By contrast, 1938 is remembered both as the high point of an un-self-conscious, colonial racism, as well as a critical moment in Indigenous activism. One hundred and fifty years years after British colonization, official re-enactment was very much still in vogue, with a flotilla of boats leading to the symbolic re-arrival of Phillip and his flag. Twenty-six Aboriginal people were brought from Menindee and Brewarrina in the far west of NSW, to serve as reminders of a more authentic Indigeneity. They were housed in the stables of a nearby police station during the events.[15]

Much more significant was the Day of Mourning protest, called by Aboriginal activists and community leaders. This had its origins in the activism and political thinking of the Aboriginal leader William Cooper and experiences he'd had on Australia Day in 1937.[16] The thrust of the Day of Mourning and subsequent campaigning was equality and freedom from discrimination, particularly in the area of labour, and against the draconian "protection regimes" under which Aboriginal people were regulated in each state. The day comprised a conference to which "Aborigines and persons of Aboriginal blood only" were invited, and about 100 people attended.[17] The conference centred on a resolution that was debated and passed unanimously:

> We, representing THE ABORIGINES OF AUSTRALIA, assembled in Conference at the Australian Hall, Sydney, on the 26th day of January, 1938, this being the 150th anniversary of the whitemen's seizure of our country, HEREBY MAKE PROTEST against the callous treatment of our people by the whitemen during the past 150 years, AND WE APPEAL

> to the Australian Nation of today to make new laws for the education and care of Aborigines, and we ask for a new policy which will raise our people to FULL CITIZEN STATUS and EQUALITY WITHIN THE COMMUNITY.

The year 1967 marked the moment when the nation as a whole considered the idea of equality for Aboriginal Peoples. The constitutional referendum in May that year did two things: it enabled the counting of Aboriginal people for the purpose of determining the population, and hence the number of parliamentarians there should be (they had been excluded in the 1901 constitution in Section 127); and secondly, it extended legislative authority, enabling the Commonwealth Parliament, as well as state parliaments, to pass laws pertaining to Aboriginal people (in 1901, states had been given that power exclusively in Section 51). However, it has subsequently been remembered as having done something much greater. Pro-referendum campaigners, both at the time and subsequently, have characterized the change as granting citizenship rights to Aboriginal people, or extending the franchise. The fact that it was so overwhelmingly passed (by almost 91 percent of voters), in a society that rarely amends its constitution, has given rise to a heavy imaginative loading of the event.[18] It is, as we will see, now the preferred anniversary for mainstream political actors seeking to invigorate Indigenous-settler relations in some way.

Australia Day continued to be a site of contestation, and in 1972 came a pivotal moment. Indigenous activists stole the nationalist agenda and turned it on its head, setting up the Aboriginal Tent Embassy directly in front of Parliament House in the national capital, in response to the Commonwealth government denying Aboriginal land rights. The event still included claims to equality and civil rights, but in the face of their exclusion from the nation-state, this was a decisive statement of Aboriginal difference and identity, and Indigenous rights.[19] The Embassy grew and garnered national and international attention before police violently ended the protest after six months. It was reconstructed numerous times in the years afterwards, remains an important site for Aboriginal gatherings and protests, and in 1995, it was listed on the Register of the National Estate.[20]

In 1992, the first Survival Day events were held in Sydney. An attempt to reconfigure Australia Day had happened around a key event in 1988. Aboriginal nations from central Australia had presented then Prime Minister Bob Hawke with the Barunga Statement in 1987. This document insisted on recognition and protection of Aboriginal cultural rights, self-determination and control of lands, compensation for loss of lands, and negotiation of a "Treaty or Compact recognising our prior ownership, continued occupation and sovereignty."[21] Hawke promised to respond by beginning national treaty negotiations, but his failure to do so led to the Treaty '88 campaign. This campaign became a key site for embarrassing the national government, leading up to the celebration of Australia's bicentennial in 1988.[22]

The organizers of the bicentennial—perhaps conscious of Ernest Renan's dictum that forgetting is about as important as remembering when it comes to nations[23]—were anxious that the supremacist traditions of national celebration be left behind, leaving space for a new multicultural and postcolonial framing. Bennett observed, "the bicentennial conception of the nation was one that included, or desperately sought to include, Australia's Aboriginal people."[24] It was widely noted that the official organizers of the bicentenary tried to downplay memory of the founding moment greatly, "to strip the event of its historical elements," realizing these would be a lightning rod for protests.[25] However, decades of disappointment and broken promises meant that Aboriginal people were not going to allow this strategy to succeed. Moreover, this forced forgetting sought by the organizing authorities was overwhelmed by private activities: re-enactments organized by groups of citizens and sponsored by banks, radio stations, and other interests, included an eight-month voyage of vintage ships, which sailed from the UK in 1987, re-enacting the entire voyage of the First Fleet and arriving in Sydney Harbour on the morning of January 26, 1988, just as Prince Charles gave a speech on the steps of the Sydney Opera House.

Simultaneously, some of the biggest protests in Australia since the Vietnam War were taking place. Early in the day, about 2,000 activists and supporters marched from the largely Aboriginal community of Redfern in Sydney's inner city, to a tent embassy that had been erected at Mrs. Macquarie's Chair, opposite the Opera House, to protest the anniversary and draw attention to issues of Aboriginal land rights and black deaths in custody, amongst others. During the afternoon, tens of thousands of people from many backgrounds converged a few steps up the hill in Sydney's Hyde Park, to hear Aboriginal activists speak about an alternative vision of race relations in Australia.[26] Meanwhile on the south coast of England, Aboriginal activist Burnum Burnum took possession of the British Isles for Aboriginal people by planting the Aboriginal flag in the White Cliffs of Dover.[27]

It might be argued that 1988 prepared the ground for the "History Wars" that consumed Australian public discourse during the 1990s.[28] The conflicting interpretations of the anniversary made plain the incommensurable positions on whether Australia was a good country or not. These would play out around several developments through that decade that were significant in our story of anniversaries.

At the beginning of the 1990s, the Labor government sought to cover up its failure to embark on treaty negotiations by commencing a national process of "reconciliation." Then Minister for Aboriginal Affairs Robert Tickner recalled that, "the proposal for a treaty was soon put into the too hard basket by the government until this and the associated issues were addressed through the strategic advancement of the reconciliation process."[29] This had been one of the many recommendations of the Royal Commission into Aboriginal Deaths in Custody.[30]

The government established a Council for Aboriginal Reconciliation (CAR), a panel of distinguished Indigenous and non-Indigenous leaders from various sectors, which would conduct public advocacy, education, and promotion of "reconciliation": it was hortatory, had limited power, and would need to complete the work of national reconciliation in time for a national anniversary. Tickner noted that the CAR had been "carefully framed to achieve continuing cross-party commitment to the process of reconciliation through to the centenary of Federation in 2001."[31] Not a few Indigenous leaders called it a sell-out.

As 2001 approached, two unfolding processes intersected with the process of reconciliation. The first was the ruling of the High Court of Australia in *Mabo v. Queensland*, on June 3, 1992.[32] Like with *Calder v. British Columbia* in Canada's Supreme Court in 1973, this case determined that Aboriginal title continued in Australian law. Uncertainty attended it at first, but within a few years, "native title," as it is known, became the most divisive issue in Australian public policy. As the process of reconciliation was underway, the Human Rights and Equal Opportunities Commission was conducting an inquiry into the forcible removal of Aboriginal children from their families and communities, which became known as the Stolen Generations. When it produced its final report to coincide with the 30th anniversary of the 1967 referendum, any memory of national unity was quickly forgotten. Indigenous peoples rightly asked for apologies and compensation; Conservative politicians and commentators attacked virulently the Inquiry and its findings. It was and remains common in Australia to hear arguments that the removal of children was done for their own good. Chief among the grievances of the right is the implication that the nation was in fundamental ways unjust.

Both these substantive issues of Indigenous and human rights generated such opposition that the very meaning of reconciliation became contested. At the time of the centenary of Federation in 2001, under the Conservative Federal Government, reconciliation itself had become split in much public discourse, with a dubious distinction between "practical reconciliation" and other "symbolic" forms, including apologies; dismissed as impractical were any substantive measures such as a treaty, which had definitely been contemplated at the outset of the reconciliation process.[33]

The 2007 federal election saw a promise by the outgoing Liberal PM John Howard, to hold a constitutional referendum "recognising" Indigenous Australians; then opposition leader Kevin Rudd agreed, committing his party to such a referendum. Rudd's Labor successor as PM, Julia Gillard, actually began the formal process, appointing an Expert Panel in 2010 to conduct extensive consultations with Aboriginal and Torres Strait Islander communities and non-Indigenous people, and present a proposal for constitutional reform.[34]

Very quickly though, voices from across the political spectrum seized upon 2017—the 50th anniversary of the 1967 referendum—as a significant opportunity for a new referendum that would recognise Indigenous peoples in some positive ways in the Australian constitution. The eminent Aboriginal leader Pat Dodson opined that "Perhaps the vote should be held on or near the anniversary of the 1967 referendum—May 27—so as to advance the demand of that earlier generation 'for a just relationship between our peoples' to its next logical step—a proper recognition of the indigenous people of Australia as the First Peoples, and acknowledgement of our culture, our languages and our economies within the constitutional firmament."[35] The sometime PM Tony Abbott concurred: "I hope that it might happen on the 50th anniversary of the 1967 referendum, May 27, 2017. That would be a richly symbolic time to complete our constitution."[36]

At the time of writing, the prospects of a constitutional recognition referendum in 2017 appear remote. Many people—including most problematically Indigenous peoples—do not see it as a way to advance their varied goals. Probably the only thing that appears to sustain its advocates is the realization that they might have to wait another ten or 25 years for another such an opportunity. However, the state governments in both Victoria and South Australia have opened up dialogues with Indigenous peoples about the possibility of negotiating treaties. It is too early to know what the substance of these will be, or whether they will be obliged to work to arbitrary timelines, based on how we might be feeling as we reach significant anniversaries.

Magic Anniversary syndrome invokes historic passages of time and hopes to sweep us up in it, usually to celebrate banal forms of nationalism or to engage in mild forms of progressivism. These events are usually only important for Indigenous peoples as moments for untimely embarrassment of the colonial nation-state and their own self-assertion, but they are significant nonetheless. It seems politicians rarely miss an opportunity to conflate these national anniversaries with milestones of achievement in other areas, or sometimes to invoke them as a way to build enthusiasm for the latest state intervention into Indigenous life, or proposal for a new relationship.

As Canada reaches another national milestone, Indigenous peoples here have an important canvas on which to distinguish their own aspirations from those of the colonial nation-state. They will do so with great creativity, to cut through the forced forgetting and false unities of the official celebrations. Indigenous resistance is inherent to Canada as it is and remains, 150 years after its creation.

1. Justin Trudeau's remarks at the Assembly of First Nations 36th Annual General Assembly on Tuesday, July 7, 2015: www.liberal.ca/justin-trudeau-at-assembly-of-first-nations-36th-annual-general-assembly/
2. Truth and Reconciliation Commission of Canada (2015), "Canada's Residential Schools: Reconciliation," *The Final Report of the Truth and Reconciliation Commission of Canada*, Vol. 6, p. 137, online: www.myrobust.com/websites/trcinstitution/File/Reports/Volume_6_Reconciliation_English_Web.pdf.
3. Turner, Charles (2006), "Nation and commemoration," *The SAGE Handbook of Nations and Nationalism*, eds. Delanty, Gerard, and Krishan Kumar, Thousand Oaks: SAGE, p. 205.
4. Ibid.
5. My discussion draws heavily on Fleras, Augie and Paul Spoonley (1999), *Recalling Aotearoa : Indigenous Politics and Ethnic Relations in New Zealand*, Oxford: Oxford University Press; and McAllister, P.A. (2012), *National Days and the Politics of Indigenous and Local Identities in Australia and New Zealand*, Durham: Carolina Academic Press.
6. McAllister, P.A. (2012), *National Days and the Politics of Indigenous and Local Identities in Australia and New Zealand*, Durham: Carolina Academic Press, p. 45.
7. Ibid., pp. 29-40.
8. Its original name is reported to be, variously, War-ran, Weé-rong, Warrane, or Warrang. Australian Museum, *Place Names Chart*: www.australianmuseum.net.au/place-names-chart.
9. Australia Day, the Jubilee, 1838: www.australiaday.org.au/australia-day/history/1838-the-jubilee/; "Domestic Intelligence," *Sydney Herald* (NSW: 1831-1842), January 29, 1838, p. 2: nla.gov.au/nla.news-article12863098.
10. Kwan, Elizabeth (2007), "1838-The Jubilee,": www.australiaday.org.au/australia-day/history/
11. Pearson, Warren and Grant O'Neill (2009), "Australia Day: A Day for All Australians?" *National Days: Constructing and Mobilising National Identity*, eds. David McCrone and Gayle McCrone McPherson, London: Palgrave Macmillan, p. 73-88.
12. A "corroboree" is a ceremonial dance or social gathering, the term derived from the language of the Darug nation, the traditional owners of the Sydney region.

13. Spillman, Lynette P. (1997), *Nation and Commemoration: Creating National Identities in the United States and Australia*, Cambridge: Cambridge University Press, p. 54.
14. Cited in Pearson, Warren and Grant O'Neill (2009), "Australia Day: A Day for All Australians?" *National Days: Constructing and Mobilising National Identity*, eds. David McCrone and Gayle McCrone McPherson, London: Palgrave Macmillan, p. 80.
15. Kwan, 2007.
16. Attwood, Bain (2003), *Rights for Aborigines*, Crows Nest NSW: Allen and Unwin, pp. 54-74.
17. Australia Abo Call, no. 1, April 1938. "Our historic Day of Mourning and Protest. Aborigines Conference. Held at Australian Hall, Sydney, January 26, 1938. Report of Proceedings." Reprinted in Attwood, Bain and Andrew Markus (1999), *The Struggle for Aboriginal Rights, a Documentary History*, Crows Nest, NSW: Allen & Unwin, pp. 86-89.
18. Attwood, Bain, Andrew Markus, Dale Edwards, Kath Schilling, and Australian Institute of Aboriginal and Torres Strait Islander Studies (1997), *The 1967 Referendum, Or, When Aborigines Didn't Get the Vote*, Canberra: Aboriginal Studies Press.
19. Schaap, Andrew, Gary Foley, and Edwina Howell, eds. (2014), *The Aboriginal Tent Embassy: Sovereignty, Black Power, Land Rights and the State*, London: Routledge.
20. Australia. Department of Environment and Energy. Australian Heritage Database: www.environment.gov.au/cgi-bin/ahdb/search.pl?mode=place_detail;place_id=18843
21. Central and Northern Land Councils, *The Barunga Statement*, June 12, 1988. Reproduced in RE Tickner (2001), *Taking a stand: Land rights to reconciliation*, Crows Nest: Allen & Unwin, pp. 40-41.
22. Treaty '88 Campaign (1988) Aboriginal sovereignty—never ceded. *Australian Historical Studies* 91, pp. 1-2.
23. Turner, 2006, p. 206.
24. Bennett, Tony (1992), "Introduction: National Times", *Celebrating the Nation: A critical study of Australia's Bicentenary*, Bennett et al., eds., Sydney: Allen & Unwin, pp. xiii-xviii.
25. Frost, W. and J. Laing (2013), *Commemorative Events: Memory, Identities, Conflict*, London: Routledge, p 10. See also Spillman, Lynette P. (1997), *Nation and Commemoration: Creating National Identities in the United States and Australia*, Cambridge: Cambridge University Press, pp. 114-115.
26. *Herald Sun* (Melbourne) "Black power on the march," January 27, 1988. Reprinted in Attwood, Bain and Andrew Markus (1999), *The Struggle for Aboriginal Rights, a Documentary History*, Crows Nest: Allen & Unwin, pp. 315-6.
27. Norst, Marlene J. (1999), *Burnum Burnum: A Warrior for Peace*, East Roseville: Kangaroo Press, pp. 130-135.
28. Macintyre, S. and Anna Clark (2003), *The History Wars*. Melbourne: Melbourne University Press, p. 118.
29. Tickner, R.E. (2001), *Taking a stand: Land rights to reconciliation*, Crows Nest: Allen & Unwin, p. 26.
30. RCADC, *National Report Volume 5*, Part G: "The Process of Reconciliation,": www.austlii.edu.au/au/other/IndigLRes/rciadic/national/vol5/
31. Tickner, 2001, p. 30.
32. Mabo and Others v Queensland (No 2), HCA 23 (1992).
33. de Costa, Ravi (2002), *New Relationships, Old Certainties: Australia's Reconciliation and the Treaty-Process in British Columbia*, PhD Thesis, Melbourne: Swinburne University of Technology, pp. 27-90.

34. The definition of "Indigenous recognition," and people's aspirations for it, of course vary widely: some see it as little more than a moving piece of prose to preface important constitutional clauses about the salary of the governor general and the procedures for filling casual vacancies in the Senate; others think it might be a way to entrench racial discrimination principles and even begin to form a bill of rights.
35. Dodson, Patrick, "Genuine attempt to write First Peoples into nation's contract," *Sydney Morning Herald*, November 15, 2010: www.smh.com.au/federal-politics/politicalopinion/genuine-attempt-to-write-first-peoples-into-nations-contract-20101114-17sm8.html
36. The Prime Minister the Hon. Tony Abbott MP, Speech to RECOGNISE, December 11, 2014: www.pm.gov.au/media/2014-12-11/address-recognise-inaugural-gala-dinner-sydney-0

CANADA PROBLEM

Robert Jago

We Indigenous peoples have a problem. For the last century, it's been presented as "the Indian Problem." The definition has changed, from it being a problem of our continued existence to a group of social problems that come with our continued existence as separate peoples. But regardless of the description that the non-Natives of the era force upon us, the core of the Indian Problem is that we reject what white people value, and in this country, that's "Canadianness."

Our rejection of Canadianness and refusal to be absorbed into their society has consequences, and those are the social problems we see bundled together, described now as the Indian Problem: unfair policing, murderous child welfare systems, unequal healthcare and education, and colonial exploitation of our resources.

Generations of Indigenous leaders have fought to claim rights and fair treatment while accepting the premise of the Indian Problem. Those rights and that fair treatment begin with us accepting, piece by piece, Canadianness.

But the Indian Problem isn't *our* problem; we don't need to be more Canadian. Our problem is "the Canadian Problem." And put in absolutely basic terms, that problem is numbers. They have them and we don't.

It's not about ideology or vision; it's about math. These nomads outnumber us by sixteen-to-one. Every problem we face is an effect of their superior numbers.

By weight of numbers, we are denied our democratic rights. With their majority, their control over our lands and resources seems natural and is granted democratic cover. With their pursuit of the greatest good for the greatest number, so-called democracy ensures this works against us. The greatest good is always their good; the greatest number is, by definition, them. Our lesser goods are compromised away.

Understanding what the Canadian Problem is makes it all the more important to reject Canadianness. The embracing of Canadian identity above our own deprives us of numbers. Through one private compromise after another, we lose our people—one by one the Canadian Problem gets worse.

Before we go on, what exactly is a Canadian? For me (and take notes, Kellie Leitch), it's this: democracy, inclusion, and love of nature. At the very least, a Canadian is a democrat, and they follow the rules created by their democratic institutions. Canadians welcome people to become part of their country, and to share their values and their identity. Canadians define their character by their proximity to nature and by their love of the outdoors.

But these are democrats who keep a permanent minority in limbo. They treat our defiance as something like a hunger strike. They're not going to let us starve; for our own good, they're going to keep us going 'til we give in and accept their "help."

They argue that this democracy has space for Indigenous people. While Canadians might believe in majority rule, they also believe minority rights means accepting that their side makes all the rules, and that our side is at most given tools to defend our rights against their own excesses. But how do we fix our problems and advance in our national life if all we can do is hold back a tide of foreign law?

Solving this problem of numbers and providing outsized influence is not alien to Canadians. Note the size of rural versus urban ridings, or the size of PEI's contingent in the Senate. Canadian democracy bends the rules for predominantly white minorities, but not for us. They ensure white minorities can't be overrun or kept out of decision-making. But for us, the Canadians discover "higher principles" of so-called democratic equality.

If we Indigenous peoples lived in a real democracy, we'd spend our time convincing members of our nations to vote for solutions to our problems. Instead, our time is actually spent lobbying politicians someone else voted for to do something their constituents don't care about. Even to the most progressive of our non-Native supporters, we're just an "issue"—one to be weighed against other issues like clean water, carbon taxes, same-sex marriage, one trade agreement or another, "Indian stuff," CBC funding . . .

But we are not an issue; we are nations. And compromise on that fact is impossible. Canada can't be a democracy for us.

Joseph Boyden likes to say there are three solitudes in this country—not just French-English, but French-English-Indigenous. However, "solitudes" means that we're each living a national life, disconnected and unaware of the other solitudes. Which is true for Québec. But for Indigenous people, it's impossible for us to live our lives unaware of and unaffected by what white people want.

And for the record, we aren't three solitudes; we are three broadly drawn communities: English Canada, French Canada, and 600 variations on the Indigenous nations of Canada.

Canada can't be a democracy, because one of these three solitudes so vastly outnumbers the others. Of the three founding "nations," our current constitution was written and passed by one of them alone. We live in a country unfairly dominated and run in the sole interests of that single nation—English Canada.

Canada can't continue being run as the private estate of the English Canadian elite. Canada by right is a "communal" state. A communal state is one in which each community governs itself internally by its own rules and comes together at a country-wide "national" level, each with reserved positions in the communal administration, each with a veto.

In a communal state, 1.4 million Indigenous people would have an equal say in the running of Canada. Not equal to 1.4 million Ontarians, but equal to all of English Canada, all of French Canada.

Indigenous people have long been kept outside of Canadian society. Then, confined to the reserve, we were brought in one by one. With the rights era, we formed groups that tried to mediate our entry into Canadian society. Each of these small steps brought us further out from the darkest days of colonial oppression.

The natural next step in our development as nations is for us to finally reject the paradigm of the Indian Problem, confront the Canadian Problem directly, and work toward forming a union of equals with Canada. Not a union of equals with Canadians—democracy prevents that—but a union of equals with Canada.

This might sound impossible, but how many of Québec's demands sounded impossible before they were granted? We need to learn from the Québec model of crisis diplomacy and take it to heart. Each referendum, each riot, strike, threat, moved Québec's national interests forward.

Granted, unlike us, Québec isn't hobbled by a weak accommodationist leadership with no true love of nation. Our Indigenous leaders have the national vision and spirit of a small town chamber of commerce. In order for us to advance into the crisis era, which must precede our ultimate success, we need to get rid of this "leadership" we are currently burdened with. We need people who have a national vision, and who will do anything to instigate a crisis that will move us forward.

English Canada feared the loss of Québec because they can't resist the pull of America without them. They didn't cave to Québec for love of Québec culture, or the Québec people. They needed them. A means to an end. Our current leaders want to make friends, want English Canadians to like us. That's why they always restrain their people. But we don't need Canadians to like us. We need them to fear us, and fear not giving in to us, and understand that their country cannot function without our consent.

We Natives live with the Canada Problem, and we Natives can only solve that problem ourselves. Democracy won't help us, rights won't help us—and lord knows the fairy tale called the "rule of law" will not help us. We need to be harder on our leaders until they grow a spine. And we need to get rid of those fake leaders who will sell us out.

The Canada Problem is a problem of numbers. With their numbers, they steal our democracy, lay claim to our lands and resources, and ignore our needs. With their numbers, Canadians force their way of life on us—a way of life made up of democracy, inclusiveness, and love of nature.

The Canadian idea of inclusiveness is one of their proudest accomplishments. Think of Justin Trudeau as he greeted the Syrian refugees shortly after his election: "Tonight they step off the plane as refugees. But they walk out of this terminal as permanent residents of Canada with social insurance numbers, with health cards and with an opportunity to become full Canadians." Trudeau went on to define Canadian as people with "a shared set of values, aspirations, hopes and dreams." Undoubtedly, a Syrian could share those values easier than I could, than my community could. Because those are the values of rootlessness, of refuge, of the quiet, nomadic life. They aren't Indigenous values.

To a Canadian, Indigenous values are wrong. To be Indigenous is to be defined by your background, not in spite of it. Our great-great-grandparents lived free, citizens of 10,000-year-old cultures that developed unique ways to live and to know God. Our great-grandparents survived an apocalypse, saw the whole world fall around them, and they made it through and rebuilt. That we're here now shows that that earlier generation was one of the greatest in the history of humanity.

Our grandparents suffered through the darkest days of our oppression, virtual prisoners on their reserves. Our parents fought for our rights, became the first generation of Native professionals, rebuilt faith and family life. The work of those people in this country—that defines me more than a health card or an insurance number. It brings with it an obligation to carry the torch for the next generation, and to make all this work have value. To the Canadian though, this is "old country garbage" that should be cast aside to make way for Canadianness.

Canada can give you a lot. It gives that freely to some of the neediest and most deserving people from around the world. The price, though, is to sacrifice a part of your identity, your sense of belonging and duty to your ancestors. Our rooted Indigenous identities are destructive and antithetical to what it means to be Canadian. To be Indigenous is to be based on ancestry, land, and struggle. All alien to these foreigners who rule us.

The Canadian concept of inclusiveness is exclusive of First Nations people and is a threat to us. You all know Jay's Treaty. It gives Canadian First Nations people access to the United States, but denies American First Nations people the reverse. In Canada, a nation with a quarter million immigrants a year, the only wall they put up is against our people.

Canada's inclusiveness ends where rooted identity begins. Rootless, drifters come in and share our Canadian values. Share our blood and land? Stay out. Inclusiveness is about the desire to vanish. To melt away, turn off that sense of obligation, and live only for yourself and your children.

You know, we could do it, too: be included, be multicultural, give up our lands, vanish, and take equal services. Every problem could be solved if we gave up our "hunger strike," and took on their values and became Canadians.

But in the ruins of our villages, with dead all around, on the same land my family lives on now, someone thought of me. And, today, I think of them. They kept on because of their obligation to me, and I trade the easy out for my obligation to them.

These people who come to Canada to share in Canadian values? They're as anomalous as the Canadians themselves. The majority of the Irish, the Jamaicans, the Chinese, feel the same pull we do. The love of homeland. They stayed put. Inclusiveness excludes our way of being. And inclusiveness both undermines our identities and worsens the numbers problem, the Canadian Problem, more every year.

Lastly we come to Canada's professed love of nature and the outdoors.

The definitive Canadian statement on Canada's connection to our lands is the Glenn Gould radio documentary, *The Idea of North*. In it, the pianist Gould interviews people from across the North about their love of the region, their concept of it. And in that documentary, Gould does not speak to a single Indigenous person. Instead, we hear a literal justification of colonialism, a treatment of the lands as an ahistorical terra nullius.

The Idea of North is the idea of Canada. It's the joke that a Canadian is someone that knows how to make love in a canoe. It's the dream of our land, empty and open for exploration and adventure. Our land, cleansed of us.

Look at how official Canada portrays their country, our land. Look at the PR for Canada's 150th birthday celebrations—all the smiling faces are theirs, having fun, in land unsullied by us. Look at the Canadian tourism agency's hundreds of trip ideas for Canada 150. Where they live, the experiences are about culture; where we live, the experiences are about a wild, untouched land—our cultures made invisible.

The one thing that wrecks a Canadian's love of the outdoors is to tramp through it in their expensive clothes with all their gear, and to find us packed in, ten at a time, in our hovels, drinking brown water. We wreck nature.

They want us to leave our remote communities—but never tell the same to their exploitative corporations. They want to disperse us and destroy our democratic potential, undermine our legitimate claim to our resources. And by weight of their numbers, they have the power to force their vision of the North, of nature, on us.

Their love of the land that we need to survive is a threat to us. We need to put roads through their perfect wilderness. We need to expand our towns and build more homes in that wilderness; some of us want greater resource extraction. We will protect the land better than they will, undoubtedly, but not for extreme biking, canoeing, and hiking. We will protect the land for our use.

On my mother's home reserve, we share an island with non-natives. Half is park, half is our reserve. We have to put barricades up on our roads and have security present to keep the non-natives from going through our yards. Their numbers make them feel entitled to take in every park and play area and wilderness. Even when we build one specifically for them, they want ours, too. This past summer there were a half-dozen squatters. One group plugged their RV into my brother's home. Didn't ask him. His house was next to some trees, so why not?

And they hate it when we build homes there, cut down more of the island for our growing population. For them, the Natives are intruding on the park; for us, the park is an intrusion on our island. We develop these areas for living. They covet them for fun.

This conflict between our homelands and their untouched playgrounds are too many to count. Where we do succeed in defending our lands, they see it as us usurping their right to access the outdoors. When Indigenous people fought and died to reclaim land at Ipperwash, Ontario, the local paper headlined their victory: "Ipperwash: Paradise lost, probably never to return." Their paradise, lost to us. Whenever you see one of these stories in the Canadian press, pay attention to who is and who isn't the public—who has a right to the outdoors.

Far from being a wilderness, the nature we love is a haunted place. Our nature is full of stories and legends that give meaning to the mountains and rivers.

Our nature isn't there to be conquered; it is to be lived in. When we must take resources from our lands, only we know their real value, and only we are entrusted with the right to make the compromises necessary to draw wealth from this land.

This land that they call wild has a name and is alive in the stories of our elders, stories that have been with us since before these nomads came, and will still be here after Canada itself has been long forgotten.

When Canada presents itself as an untouched wilderness, they expose their desire to silence our storytellers; to erase the names of things, to take from us. Their love of nature is predicated on a desire to erase us.

The Canada Problem can be solved. But to begin to solve it, you have to begin to understand it. First is to understand that within each of their highest ideals is a lure to separate us from our Indigenous identities, and a method for exacerbating the problem. Next we need an eye on the solution, which is a communal state where our nations are truly partners with Canada and Québec. Lastly, we must get rid of this leadership that is holding us back and embrace those Indigenous leaders who have a national vision, and who have the bravery to move us into the crisis era, and set the stage for our ultimate victory.

1. http://www.cbc.ca/news/canada/toronto/syrian-refugees-justin-trudeau-remarks-1.3360401

Building Relations
Confederation Treaties and Settler Obligations Today[1]

Michael Asch

Introduction

The 150th anniversary of Canadian Confederation presents a moment for celebration, but even more for us to address what might be called the unfinished business we have inherited. In this category, I cannot imagine any matter more profound, at least for those of us who are un-problematically linked to the history of British colonization, than the political relationship between Indigenous peoples on whose lands Confederation was founded and the settler state that resulted from it. This paper presents a reflection on that history, but with an eye in particular to the untold story of the early post-Confederation period, and from it to some thoughts on how we move on from here. In other words, it offers a possible way to push toward a just political relationship that traces to Confederation's birth—a time, as my research is beginning to make clear, when there was a glimpse of a possible way to build a relationship that offered hope this country would be grounded in a set of principles that could have produced the just relationship that so many of us now seek. It is my hope that returning to the principles certain leading figures in the Dominion espoused at that time (but were soon snuffed out and are now largely forgotten) offers us food for thought on taking a next step in building that relationship should Indigenous peoples be prepared to offer us this chance, despite what has transpired in the past century and a half.

To set the context, let me briefly recapitulate the story we tell ourselves of the political history of our country and the place of our relations with Indigenous peoples within it, for, as I hope you will agree, it offers a good reflection of the distance we still need to travel even to begin the journey of which I write.

The Standard Narrative of Canadian Political History

In the standard narrative of Canada's history, as reflected in such key introductory texts, treaties with Indigenous peoples play an insignificant role.[2] Rather, it revolves around this country's step-by-step movement from a colony to an independent nation-state. Central to that story is Confederation, the moment when Canada gained full rights to internal self-determination, and the governance structure *that*, by and large, has remained in place from its inception in 1867 until today, some 150 years later.

Treaties and treaty-making with Indigenous peoples, to the extent that they emerge within the history, rate particular mention only in the period immediately after Confederation, and then only in the West, where they are depicted as one of the events (the building of the transcontinental railway and the entry of British Columbia into Confederation being two significant others) that resulted in Canada's present territorial shape and governance arrangements; and here the standard narrative portrays treaty-making as the manner in which Canada cleared the land for settlement—peacefully and inexpensively, it is said, when compared to the violent acts that made the country to our south a transcontinental polity.[3]

And then treaties disappear from the story, notwithstanding that from 1899 until 1922 (which represents the end of treaty-making until the so-called "modern treaties" were first negotiated in the 1970s), treaties covering a large portion of what is now Canada, including much of the North, were negotiated. Instead, attention is drawn to policies (such as residential schools) imposed by governments, and on the deleterious effects of these policies on Indigenous peoples.

Now, I am not objecting to this depiction. It *is* important to the telling of the story of a country such as this one to recount our path to full independence from Great Britain; and it is *essential* that we bring to consciousness the horrors that our policies created (and still create) for Indigenous peoples. Rather, my objection is that this narrative pushes to the side a central aspect of this story: how we have acted to forge a relationship (no matter how poorly) with those on whose lands we settled. For it is *at least* as important to tell the story of the relations we are building with those we met when we first arrived in the place we chose to stay as it is those living in the place we left for all time.

The problem is not merely setting the record straight, for as I have come to understand, there is much we can learn from our past as to how to develop the just relationship we now say we seek. In that regard, the agreements we made in

need to focus on treaties

treaties at the birth of Confederation can play a significant role in laying out a direction to take now, a century and a half later. And there is one more reason for us to place focus on these and other treaties: unless you believe that we had a right to settle on these lands without the permission of Indigenous peoples, the bedrock on which Confederation rests is the agreements that we reached with them, for that is the only means by which we could legitimately settle on these lands. For these reasons, I will ultimately discuss the terms of certain treaties made at the time of Confederation. However, first I need to recount a bit of the history that leads up to these negotiations.

Settling on Other's Lands: Western Understandings

To our way of thinking, it is wrong to go onto other peoples' land without their permission. Of course we have done it over and over again (as with conquest), but deep down we still know that taking lands that belong to others is just not right. At the same time, to our way of thinking (and here I mean political thought that traces back at least to the 1648 Treaty of Westphalia), each territory rightfully comes under the political authority of a sovereign—a "boss of the land," if you will.[4] This means that, unless everyone stays in one place in perpetuity, moving onto lands that belong to another can bring up the question as to who is the boss of that land. And that is a devil for us to sort out. But how we do so is not this paper's focus, except to say this: ideologically speaking, Canada today justifies its sovereignty and jurisdiction largely by imagining that this territory was not occupied by people whose political authority required our recognition, and that therefore we could rightfully assert sovereignty over it as though it were an empty land, notwithstanding that people were already here, living in political societies when we first arrived. It is a matter to which I will return in my conclusion.

Historically in addition to this position, those trained in Western political thought have advanced at least two other positions regarding the right way to deal with arriving on lands belonging to others. One is to conclude that we have no right to settle on them under any circumstances (except perhaps as immigrants into their polities). Many prominent figures, from what I have read, appeared in full support of that view. As Johann Herder wrote in 1784:

> Even when the natives are reasonably well treated by the European, they feel cheated, and can scarcely conceal their hatred. "You have

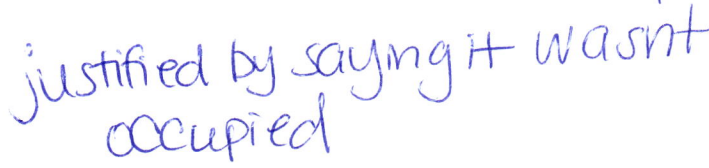

justified by saying it wasn't occupied

no business here, for this land is ours," is a thought they cannot suppress. Hence the "treachery" of all the so-called savages ... To us this seems horrible; and so it is, no doubt. Yet it was the European who first induced them to this monstrous deed. Why did they come to their country? Why did they enter it as despots, arbitrarily practicing violence and extortion?[5]

The other position is that settlement on lands that belong to others can only be legitimate if done with the permission of those already living on those lands; that is, by agreement or, in other words, by treaty. This position also has a long history, as is reflected in the terms of the Royal Proclamation of 1763 (as confirmed in the Treaty of Niagara of 1764) where it states that:

> And whereas it is just and reasonable, and essential to our Interest, and the Security of our Colonies, that the several Nations or Tribes of Indians with whom We are connected, and who live under our Protection, should not be molested or disturbed in the Possession of such Parts of Our Dominions and Territories as, not having been ceded to or purchased by Us, are reserved to them or any of them, as their Hunting Grounds.[6]

And that:

> We do, with the Advice of our Privy Council strictly enjoin and require, that no private Person do presume to make any purchase from the said Indians of any Lands reserved to the said Indians, within those parts of our Colonies where, We have thought proper to allow Settlement: but that, if at any Time any of the Said Indians should be inclined to dispose of the said Lands, the same shall be Purchased only for Us, in our Name, at some public Meeting or Assembly of the said Indians, to be held for that Purpose by the Governor or Commander in Chief of our Colony respectively within which they shall lie ...[7]

In other words, we recognize here that a treaty granting us permission is required before we settle on these lands. Of course this formulation begs the question of whether we can presume that we acquired sovereignty in these lands without the consent of those already living on them. However, what is important to note is that in this way of thinking, even when we assert we have sovereignty, we take the position that we still have no authority to settle on their lands without first gaining their express permission.

Following from this understanding, Canada negotiated seven treaties with Indigenous peoples in the West in the first decade of Confederation—that is, between 1871 and 1877. The question is: What were the terms on which this permission was granted? To that end, I will focus on what was negotiated in two of them; Treaty 4, which covered lands now included in southern Saskatchewan and parts of Manitoba and Alberta; and Treaty 6, which covered Central Saskatchewan and Alberta. I do so because there is good information with respect to both on what actually transpired, including transcriptions of the events as recorded by the Crown. It is information I have found very helpful in ferreting out what these terms were—a matter for which there is a sharp difference of opinion; a matter to which I now turn.

On Treaty Interpretation

Speaking generally, there are two dominant ways of determining the terms on which our settlement was permitted. The first, consistently maintained by Canadian governments, asserts that the text of the agreements spells out these terms in their totality. Sometimes dubbed the "literal" or "textual" interpretation, this approach leaves the impression that these treaties were contracts. Contracts in which, in return for ceding all rights to their lands, the Indigenous parties received very specific and in general one-time benefits such as a specific number of tools for taking up agriculture, as well as reserve lands of fixed size along with certain ongoing rights, such as the ability to hunt on lands not taken up by settlement. Indigenous parties espouse the other view—often described as based on "spirit and intent"—virtually universally. It describes these treaties as establishing an enduring relationship based on sharing the land, which includes the Crown's agreement to ensure that Indigenous peoples would benefit from the process; and one in which, at the very least, Indigenous parties would retain their political autonomy.

Accounting for this strong divergence of views has been a preoccupation of scholarship on treaties, which I do not intend to revisit here. Suffice it to say that, as I describe in detail in *On Being Here to Stay*,[8] I have found the transcriptions of events as recorded by the Crown—and memorialized in the book *The Treaties with the Indians of Canada*, authored by Alexander Morris, Chief Commissioner for treaties 3 through 6—most helpful in navigating the differences.[9] And as I have discussed in *On Being Here to Stay*, the evidence they provide offers substantiation that the position advanced by Indigenous parties more accurately depicts the terms of the agreement as negotiated than does the written text.

Terms of Treaties Made at Confederation as illustrated in Treaties 4 and 6

With that in mind, I will now turn to the terms of the agreement as reflected in what is reported in the transcriptions. Due to space constraints, I will limit my discussion to an aspect of each of two key issues raised in negotiations of treaties 4 and 6. The first pertains to the scope of the specific promises made by the Crown regarding its commitments with respect to agriculture.

The position of the Canadian governments relies on the text. And here the promises respecting agriculture are spelled out in detail. Here are the terms in Treaty 4:

> two hoes, one spade, one scythe and one axe for every family so actually cultivating, and enough seed wheat, barley, oats and potatoes to plant such land as they have broken up; also one plough and two harrows for every ten families so cultivating as aforesaid, and also to each Chief for the use of his band as aforesaid, one yoke of oxen, one bull, four cows, a chest of ordinary carpenter's tools, five hand saws, five augers, one cross-cut saw, one pit-saw, the necessary files and one grindstone, all the aforesaid articles to be given, once for all, for the encouragement of the practice of agriculture among the Indians."[10]

This, they say, represents the full extent of the agreement.

In contrast, the Indigenous parties assert that the agreement established an ongoing relationship that went well beyond what was contained in the text. Thus, Elder Danny Musqua states: "we agreed to a relationship, a perpetual land use agreement between (ourselves) and (the Crown) in Treaty 4, that (settlers) would harvest the land for the purposes of agriculture, sow crops and we, along with that, (would learn agricultural skills); they would give us the technology to also do that ourselves."[11] Similarly, it is reported in the *Saskatchewan Indian* for February/March 1986 that: while "farming implements and supplies were to be provided as an initial outlay," the Treaty stipulated that more generally, "the government was to provide assistance to advance the Indian in farming or stock-raising or other work."[12]

The transcripts support the Indigenous point of view. On the one hand, to take Treaty 4 as the example, Alexander Morris laid out the tangible benefits offered as they appear in the text. That is, as well as other provisions, he specifically mentions on the fourth day that:

> When you are ready to plant seed the Queen's men will lay off Reserves so as to give a square mile to every family of five persons, and on commencing to farm the Queen will give to every family cultivating the soil two hoes, one spade, one scythe for cutting the grain, one axe and plough, enough of seed wheat, barley, oats and potatoes to plant the land they get ready.[13]

However, he did not stop there. Just before mentioning those specifics he made the following blanket promise, which indicates that it is more than merely the one-time provision of implements:

> I know that there are some red men as well as white men who think only of today and never think of to-morrow. The Queen has to think of what will come long after to-day. Therefore, the promises we have to make to you are not for to-day only but for to-morrow, not only for you but for your children born and unborn, and the promises we make will be carried out as long as the sun shines above and the water flows in the ocean.[14]

More explicitly, elsewhere Commissioner Morris explains that: "What the Queen and her Councillors would like is this, she would like you to learn something of the cunning of the white man. When fish are scarce and the buffalo are not plentiful she would like to help you to put something in the land."[15] He continues with these words, which I think it is fair to say represent a commitment that stands long after the obligations written into Treaty 4 have been discharged: "I will pass away and you will pass away. I will go where my fathers have gone and you also, but after me and after you will come our children. The Queen cares for you and for your children, and she cares for the children that are yet to be born."[16]

Furthermore, as Morris states explicitly in Treaty 6, the intent of these benefits is not to force them out of their way of life, but to offer them an alternative means of making a living, for he says: "What I have offered does not take away your living, you will have it then as you have it now, and what I offer is on top of it. This I can tell you, the Queen's Government will always take a deep interest in your living."[17]

From this, it is fair to conclude that, notwithstanding what is found in the text, the agreement, as the Indigenous parties recount, is that in return for permitting settlement on Indigenous lands, the Crown offered open-ended support for the development of agricultural practices even when this was undertaken only to supplement hunting activities. Furthermore, as phrases like "on top of" and "a deep interest in your living" offer, it seems clear that, far from presuming that Canada gained permission to undertake activities (such as massive oil and gas development as in the tar sands) that would undermine the opportunities of Indigenous peoples in pursuing their economic activities without their consent, the treaties committed it to encourage the kind of economic development that would benefit them.

The second matter I will raise concerns the political status of Indigenous peoples after treaties are negotiated. Canadian governments act as though the treaties provide (or at the least confirm) that the Indigenous parties come under the sovereignty and jurisdiction of Canada. And, at least to the contemporary mind schooled in Western thought, the text supports this claim. Again using Treaty 4 as an example:

> The Cree and Saulteaux Tribes of Indians, and all other the Indians inhabiting the district hereinafter described and defined, do hereby cede, release, surrender and yield up to the Government of the Dominion of Canada, for Her Majesty the Queen, and Her successors forever, all their rights, titles and privileges whatsoever.[18]

At the same time, notwithstanding this text and the signatures of their leaders, Indigenous parties unequivocally reject that this is what transpired. As Elder Kay Thompson says, they "didn't give the land, they didn't say, we give you this land. They just gave permission to use the land."[19] Or, as the article in the *Saskatchewan Indian* cited above:

> 1. The Indian nations retained Sovereignty over their people, lands, and resources, subject to some shared jurisdiction with the appropriate Government bodies on the lands known as occupied Crown lands. This is the foundation of Indian Government.[20]

The question is whether the transcription can shed light on determining which view more accurately reflects the agreement. Here the evidence is less clear. The only thing we know for sure is that there is no record of the matter of cession being introduced by the Crown during negotiations (except perhaps when Commissioner Morris read out the treaty terms in full—but there is no record of what he said at that time). At the same time, the transcriptions offer good evidence that Morris represented the treaties as establishing a partnership based on sharing rather than a deal based on Indigenous peoples surrender of political autonomy. Thus, he explains to the Indigenous leadership:

> We have two nations here. We have the Crees, who were here first, and we have the Ojibbeways (Saulteaux), who came from our country not many suns ago. We find them here; we won't say they stole the land, and the stones and the trees; no, but we will say this, that we believe their brothers, the Crees, said to them when they came in here: "The land is wide, it is wide, it is big enough for us both; let us live here like brothers," and that is what you say; and that is what you say, as you told us on Saturday, as to the Half-Breeds I see around. You say you are one with them; now we all want to be one."[21]

Further, the transcriptions confirm the assertions of the Indigenous party that they did not actively agree to the cession. Therefore, it appears that when read from a contemporary point of view, there was complete disagreement between the parties on this matter with the Crown presuming (based on the written text) that at the very least the treaties confirmed the blanket authority of Canada respecting sovereignty and jurisdiction, and the transcripts confirming the Indigenous assertion that these were not transferred by consent.

At the same time, this does not mean that Morris made the same assumption. The matter is more complicated than that. For my preliminary research indicates that Morris and his contemporaries conceived of sovereignty and jurisdiction within the British Empire through a slightly different lens than we do today. And as I will indicate below, when viewed through that lens the views of the parties come closer to consonance.

On Morris's View of Sovereignty and Jurisdiction

In contemporary Western-based thinking, sovereignty and jurisdiction are the inseparable conditions that define a self-determining polity. While this may have been the case in many respects in the nineteenth century, this was not the case when it came to polities within the British Empire. Let me start with sovereignty.

While Confederation conveyed the right of self-governance, the fact is that it did not grant Canada the kind of sovereignty associated with an independent state.

That Alexander Morris saw Canada in the same way is laid out explicitly in the following passage of a speech he made as a Member of Parliament, on behalf of those advocating for Confederation:

> We have either to rise into strength and wealth and power by means of this union, *under the sheltering protection of Britain*, or we must be absorbed by the great power beside us . . .[22]
>
> We will have the pride to belong to a great country still attached to the Crown of Great Britain, in which, notwithstanding, we shall have entire freedom of action and the blessing of responsible self-government.[23]

In contrast to our understanding today, at the time of Confederation, within the British Empire, sovereignty and jurisdiction were separable matters, and while Canada gained jurisdiction over our own affairs (the blessing of responsible self-government), Britain retained sovereignty. In this sense, to come under the sovereignty of Britain was in effect to join an alliance (sheltering protection) with the most potent power on Earth at that time.

Given this context, I think it fair to suggest that the commissioner assumed that the matter of sovereignty did not need discussing as the Indigenous parties were already under the sheltering protection of the Queen—a position I imagine Morris could have believed the Indigenous parties would not find objectionable, given that, like Canada, they faced invasion from the United States, which at that time was waging a war of extermination against Indigenous peoples south of Canada's border. Furthermore, Morris makes it clear that the sovereign status he projects on Indigenous peoples is equivalent to that which he assigns to Canada, for he says that, like Indigenous peoples, Canadians are equally "children of the Queen" (that is, coming under her sheltering protection). While this position does not dovetail with the firm truth that Indigenous peoples did not surrender sovereignty, I think it fair to say that imagining the assertion of sovereignty over Indigenous peoples as meaning being a member of a military alliance led by the most powerful force in the world, rather than as an act of subordination to the Queen, is more consonant with it.

Similarly, when viewed through the contemporary lens, to have jurisdiction is to assert final authority within a recognized nation-state. Therefore, Canada did not obtain jurisdiction in 1867. Rather, as Morris makes clear, Confederation

part of alliance, not act of subordination

gave Canada self-governance rights, at least for some matters (foreign policy for one), while Britain retained jurisdiction. Indeed, Canada did not gain jurisdiction over all of its affairs until the passage of the Statute of Westminster in 1931. And in fact until Patriation in 1982, Britain retained jurisdiction in Canada (albeit with our consent), at least in the sense that ratification of constitutional amendments required confirmation by legislation of the British Parliament.

The question then is to what extent did Morris assume that either through treaty or by fiat Indigenous peoples had come under the complete jurisdiction of the Dominion government. This, again, is complicated to untangle. It is possible to imagine that he did. At the same time, there is evidence to the contrary. First, it must be agreed that the Royal Proclamation of 1763 recognized Indigenous jurisdiction with respect to the final authority to block settlement on their lands without their agreement; a position affirmed contemporaneously even in British Columbia by Canada's third post-Confederation Governor General, Lord Dufferin, when he said in 1877 that: "In Canada, no Government, whether provincial or central, has failed to acknowledge that the original title to the land existed in the Indian tribes and the communities that hunted or wandered over them (and that) ... not until (we negotiate treaties) do we consider that we are entitled to deal with a single acre."[24] Hence, it is reasonable to conclude that Morris among many others understood that treaty negotiations affirmed Indigenous jurisdiction regarding the granting of permission to settle, and that the treaties specified the terms on which that permission would be given.

But what of other aspects of jurisdiction? On this point I have only completed initial research. First, there is evidence to conclude that, at the very least, there were government leaders who took the view that the ultimate relationship with Indigenous peoples was with the Crown, not the government, even after Confederation. This was asserted specifically by Lord Dufferin in the speech cited above: "You must remember that the Indian population is not represented in Parliament, and, consequently, that the Governor-General [who was responsible to the Colonial Office in Britain] is bound to watch over their welfare and especial solicitude."[25] Thus it is reasonable to conclude that, in the mind of the Governor General and those who shared his view, Indigenous peoples had a direct political relationship with the Crown that, when invoked, could supersede any laws and policies of the Dominion government.

There is also evidence that Indigenous peoples were understood to retain internal self-governance. Thus, for example, in the 1876 debate on the *Indian Act*, John Christian Schultz, member for the (now defunct) riding of Lisgar, argued when speaking of the Indigenous peoples of the region that "The Indians are everywhere so attached to their tribal system that they will not abandon it, and some way should be found of leading them to civilization and independence without trenching on this, their most cherished institution."²⁶

Finally, a view supporting internal self-governance is also found in the philosophical orientation of settlers, like Morris, to the kind of political relationship with Indigenous peoples they conceptualized for the Dominion. It is true that, like most of their contemporaries, this group (that included people who held views like the one expressed by Schultz) imagined assimilation (and enfranchisement) to be the ultimate goal. However, in contrast to those who presumed that Indigenous peoples were too backward or recalcitrant to achieve this on their own, this position held that Indigenous peoples are fully rational beings and thus are perfectly capable of voluntarily making the transition once they understood the (ethnocentrically imagined) inherent superiority of Western ways (a view that still dominates such aspects of Western thought as development theory). To them, all that was required was some assistance, encouragement, and most of all leading, setting an example through their own virtuous behaviour. Thus, for example, the Aborigines' Protection Society (a leading proponent of this view) argued in 1840 that:

> to help, and not to oppress, should be our object;—so as to cultivate and promote that mutual dependence and reciprocal good-will, which should make them view us as brothers and patrons, and not as intruders or hard task-masters;—and which by arousing and enlisting their sympathies, would infallibly lead them to be moral, intelligent, peaceful, and happy,—attached friends, and faithful allies.²⁷

Along with this view, it was often argued that Indigenous peoples ought to retain a degree of self-governing authority.²⁸ Proponents of the other approach (the one with which we are familiar) insisted that the way forward required forcibly severing them from their "primitive" ways, and especially from their "tribal institutions" of self-governance. Therefore, consistent with that reading, Morris would not have understood the cession clause as completely transferring governance authority from Indigenous peoples to the Dominion government. However, the extent to which that authority was retained in his mind remains unclear.

In short, my preliminary research indicates that at the least Morris and Dufferin held the position that Indigenous peoples retained some degree of self-governing authority even after the treaties were negotiated, and maintained a degree of autonomy from the authority of Parliament. While this does not dovetail with the Indigenous understanding that jurisdiction was never surrendered by consent (a position that my research confirms), nonetheless as a practical matter, as with sovereignty, I believe that there was sufficient overlap between them that a working relationship between the parties on governance could have developed had this route been taken. But that is not what happened.

Treaty Implementation

My research indicates that the 20 years between Confederation and roughly 1887 was a time of contestation between powerful and influential advocates for both points of view. In the decade after Confederation, advocates for a policy based on the understanding that Indigenous peoples were intelligent beings, capable of making rational decisions, and the belief that treaties formed a partnership in which Canada would provide ongoing assistance included figures such as Conservative Member of Parliament Alexander Morris, a Cabinet Minister in the government of Sir John A. Macdonald, leading advocate for Confederation, and eventual lieutenant governor of Manitoba; and Lord Dufferin, Canada's third post-Confederation Governor General. To them, inducing change in Indigenous ways, such as by providing schools and teachers for those who sought a Western education, was not in question, but it was based on the understanding that attendance would be a matter of choice—one that, they were nonetheless convinced, Indigenous peoples would soon make given the presumptively indisputable superiority of Western ways, and therefore the desirability of assimilation.

The other position was advanced at that time by figures no less prominent than our first prime minister, Sir John A. Macdonald. For them, Indigenous peoples were incapable of or unwilling to make the necessary transition without the disciplining authority of government to prod them along. To them, regardless of what was said during negotiations, the text of the treaties provided further legal justification for taking full control over their lives and their lands. In harmony with this view, in 1883, Macdonald, using education as his example, argued in language justifying the establishment of residential schools that:

> When the school is on the reserve the child lives with its parents, who are savages; he is surrounded by savages, and though he may learn to read and write his habits, and training mode of thought are Indian. He

is simply a savage who can read and write. It has been strongly pressed on myself, as the head of the Department, that Indian children should be withdrawn as much as possible from the parental influence, and the only way to do that would be to put them in central training industrial schools where they will acquire the habits and modes of thought of white men.[29]

These stark policy differences played out in the manner in which the numbered treaties were implemented. According to a recent biography, in the early years, as Lieutenant Governor of Manitoba and chief commissioner for the Crown in treaty-making, Alexander Morris, was able to play a significant role in this process.[30] At that time, he not only advocated strongly for government to fulfill the promises *as written* down, quickly and fully, but more importantly he encouraged building "a relationship of mutual trust and reciprocity."[31] However, he was faced from the outset with opposition from advocates of the opposing position from the highest levels of the department officially responsible for implementation.[32]

As a result, "by late 1876 the Department of the Interior had more or less abandoned the intent and spirit of the treaties, taking control of treaty implementation policy and paying no heed to the concerns of First Nations."[33] Morris's influence on implementation ended in 1878 with the end of his term as Manitoba's Lieutenant Governor, and the appointment the following year of Edgar Dewdney, a strong opponent of implementation, as the all-powerful Commissioner of Indian Affairs and Lieutenant Governor of the North-West Territories. As Talbot reports, "with the explicit support of the Macdonald government, Dewdney abandoned treaties and set in motion a policy he called 'sheer compulsion,'" thereby setting in place the policy direction on which future relations with Indigenous peoples in Canada would be grounded.[34]

However, what I am arguing is that there was a brief but crucial period in the decade after Confederation when there were leading figures who advocated for a different approach to relations with Indigenous peoples; an approach that, while not perfect, I think it is fair to say would have offered the beginnings for a much more nuanced and fulfilling relationship with Indigenous peoples than the path we took. But that is not the path we took; and we know the horrors it brought, of which the residential school system is but one example.

Implications for Future Action

Still, I think it important to bring the "path not taken" at Confederation to mind now, 150 years later, for the following reasons. First, it reminds us that the incredibly destructive approach we have taken in our relations with Indigenous peoples was one we chose and not one dictated, as we often like to believe, by the values we held at that time. Yes, Sir John A. Macdonald was a product of his times, but so was Alexander Morris. Second, it delegitimizes the arrogant story our generation tells itself that, while we may not be all that good in our relations with Indigenous peoples, we are at least far better than were our forebears. In fact, this more contextualized reading of our history shows that, virtually from the outset, those who colonized this place were divided over the question of whether the lands were empty and there for our taking, or whether we recognized that they were already occupied by people living in societies and thus we were required by our own belief system to gain their permission before moving on them. The trouble has been that those who held that latter position have never gained ascendency. That is our task today. Finally, I think an awareness that there were those, like Morris, who offered us a different path at the moment of Confederation grounds the just relationship we seek in a long history of struggle. That, I think, only gives us encouragement to press on.

But I don't want to take my enthusiasm too far. I am well aware that Morris's vision of that future is not one I (and most of us) can embrace today. When Morris proposed that we were here to share the land, not take it over, he assumed that sharing the lands ultimately meant living together as individual citizens of Canada. But, if nothing else, we know that virtually all Indigenous peoples have made it clear that this is not a goal they share (nor to be frank is it one many of us would favour). Rather, the end result, as far as I understand, is for peoples who share different ways, living in relation on lands they share; and that, as I said in the introduction, is a much more difficult thing for the Western-trained mind to understand much less put into practice,[35] for we believe, fiercely, that political relations only work when one party is "boss of the land."

But that does not mean that we are unable to take steps in that direction; and taking one is what I propose we do now. In this regard I am convinced that Morris's understandings of the shared agreement can be of great assistance. In my reading, Morris articulates what he means by the "spirit and intent" of the treaties in a number of places during the negotiations of treaties 4 and 6. Of these, let

[Handwritten annotation at top: Morris't as providing guidance for how to proceed]

me choose two I believe offer us good guidance on a way for us to proceed. The first comes from Treaty 4. Here Commissioner Morris and the Indigenous leadership agree on treaties establishing a relationship between the parties governed by a principle they both describe as acting with "kindness" toward each other.

The notion is introduced first by a spokesperson for the Indigenous parties named "the Gambler" on the fourth day of negotiations. He says:

> Look at these children that are sitting around here and also at the tents, who are just the image of my kindness. There are different kinds of grass growing here that is just like those sitting around here. There is no difference. Even from the American land they are here, but we love them all the same, and when the white skin comes here from far away I love him all the same. I am telling you what our love and kindness is. This is what I did when the white man came . . .[36]

It is brought up again, first by Kanooses, another spokesperson for the Indigenous party, at the end of negotiations on the sixth day, as a means to clarify the "spirit and intent" of the treaty as a whole. It begins with his asking for this assurance:

> KAN-OO-SES: Is it true you are bringing the Queen's kindness? Is it true you are bringing the Queen's messenger's kindness? Is it true you are going to give the different bands the Queen's kindness? Is it true that you are bringing the Queen's hand? Is it true you are bringing the Queen's power?
>
> MORRIS: Yes, to those who are here and those who are absent, such as she has given us.
>
> KAN-OO-SES: Is it true that my child will not be troubled for what you are bringing him?
>
> MORRIS: The Queen's power will be around him.[37]

To act with kindness, which following from the Oxford Dictionary definition I take to mean "having a gentle, sympathetic, or benevolent nature; ready to assist, or show consideration for, others," offers good guidance as to the general orientation treaties instruct us to take in our dealings with Indigenous peoples. And, as the remarks of the Gambler indicate, it is a way of relating Indigenous peoples intended to practice in their relations with us.

The second promise I offer precisely articulates one aspect of what acting with kindness means. It is found in what is called the "famine provision" in Treaty 6. The commissioner agreed to insert this provision after a lengthy exchange between the parties during the negotiations. The concern that gave rise to it was first expressed in an 1871 letter from the Indigenous leadership requesting that any treaty negotiated "make provision for us against years of starvation, we have had great starvation this past winter, and the small-pox took away many of our people . . ."[38] When the matter was first raised during Treaty 6 negotiations, Morris's initial response *was* negative. In the first place, he believed that the clause was unnecessary, for "I know that the sympathy of the Queen, and her assistance, would be given you in any unforeseen circumstances. You must trust to her generosity."[39] In other words, she will act with kindness, as was described in Treaty 4.

Additionally, Morris raised fear that the Indigenous parties would rely on such a provision to avoid taking personal responsibility for their own welfare. To this, Chief Mis-tah-wah-sis responded:

> It is well known that if we had plenty to live on from our gardens we would not still insist on getting more provision, but it is in case of any extremity, and from the ignorance of the Indian in commencing to settle that we thus speak; we are as yet in the dark; this is not a trivial matter for us.
>
> We were glad to hear what the Governor was saying to us and we understood it, but we are not understood, we do not mean to ask for food for every day but only when we commence and in case of famine or calamity.[40]

The Beardy, another spokesperson, added "When I am utterly unable to help myself I want to receive assistance," before continuing in the spirit of a partnership based on kindness with, "I will render all the assistance I can to my brother in taking care of the country."[41]

These arguments persuaded Commissioner Morris. Consequently, he added the following clause to the text of the treaty he was given by the Dominion government on behalf of the Queen:

> That in the event hereafter of the Indians comprised within this treaty being overtaken by any pestilence, or by a general famine, the Queen, on being satisfied and certified thereof by Her Indian Agent or Agents, will grant to the Indians assistance of such character and to such extent

as Her Chief Superintendent of Indian Affairs shall deem necessary and sufficient to relieve the Indians from the calamity that shall have befallen them.[42]

The specific language of this clause clearly presumes that we are better judges of what constitutes a true crisis than are the Indigenous parties, and as such reflects attitudes commonly espoused by those schooled in the developmental logic of nineteenth-century evolutionism. But these terms do not reflect the "spirit and intent" of that provision, as Morris expressed it during negotiations. Specifically, these are the words he used to describe this provision to our Indigenous partners: "In a national famine or general sickness, not what happens in every day life, but if a great blow comes on the Indians they would not be allowed to die like dogs."[43] And that, it seems to me, gives us a purchase on which to reflect on how to shape one dimension of our promise to act with kindness should Indigenous peoples be prepared to give us that chance. Here is what I mean.

In my reading, this promise Morris describes offers the minimum conditions for acting with kindness. It says that we will not treat Indigenous peoples like dogs should they face a great blow, much less visit great blows on them ourselves! But, as exemplified by forced enrolment in residential schools and the imposition of developments that poison their lands, our policies have done just that; and, while I hesitate to put it in these terms, isn't treating Indigenous polities as subordinates rather than those with the right to make decisions for themselves precisely treating them "like dogs" and not people?

In short, to treat with kindness means treating Indigenous peoples as partners (indeed senior to us in at least some respects)[44] rather than as adversaries or subordinates; that we work with our partners to ensure that our actions never again cause them any great blows, and remediate the harms caused by those blows we have already visited on them. In other words, by fulfilling the terms of the famine provision alone we can not only change specific policies, but more crucially change the overall tone of the relationship between Indigenous peoples and Canada. And would that not be a fitting undertaking for us to propose to our partners as a first step in building the kind of relationship some of our leaders imagined at the time of Confederation, in the hopes that they will be willing to work with us now some 150 years later?

Conclusion

Indigenous peoples have the full measure of sovereignty and jurisdiction everywhere in Canada that they held prior to European colonization.[45] To reconcile our presence on these lands, with values profoundly held by those who insist that to be here, to stay legitimately, derives from the permission we were given through treaties to settle here, our ultimate goal must be to establish a political relationship that embraces this fact. At the same time, we know that we will not readily relinquish the authority we usurped, regardless of the merits of the arguments I, and so many others, have made. Therefore the question is: How, given this reality, can we ever move forward?

In this regard, we have a choice to make. On the one hand, we can say it is not possible, and continue to use the power we have to impose our will on the peoples on whose lands we have settled. On the other, we can insist that we use the authority we will not yet relinquish to always act in accordance with concern for the wellbeing of those on whose lands we have settled as these are set out in the promises we made in treaties 4 and 6. That is the position I advocate, first because it is a sure way to guarantee that we begin to learn what it means to live together on these lands. But to me, there is a second compelling reason. I realize that, given the power we now have and the way in which we understand political relations, establishing the kind of partnership envisioned in the treaties, even when we have the best of intentions, will be an arduous journey. I do not think there is any chance we will get there in one great leap forward. In my view, fulfilling fully the promises spelled out in these treaties is to take a first step in that direction. Taking it will teach us what it means to act with kindness, and thus will ground us in the understanding I have come to see as foundational if we are to be successful in building the kind of partnership to which we committed ourselves when we first gained permission to be here to stay at the foundational moment of Confederation.

1. I would like to thank Joshua Hazelbower for his assistance in this paper, and particularly for finding the words of John Christian Schultz in the course of the research he is undertaking for his nearly completed, important thesis that includes analysis of the positions taken by various parliamentarians during the debate on the 1876 *Indian Act*.
2. For example, see Blake, Raymond, Jeffrey Keshen, Norman Knowles, and Barbara Messamore (2011), *Narrating a Nation: Canadian History Post-Confederation*, Toronto: McGraw-Hill Ryerson; Finkel, Alvin and Margaret Conrad (2002), *History of the Canadian Peoples, Vol. 2: 1867 to the Present*, 3rd edition, Toronto: Addison Wesley Longman; Francis, R. Douglas, Richard Jones, and Donald B. Smith (2004), *Destinies: Canadian History Since Confederation*,

        5th edition, Scarborough: Thomson Nelson; Granatstein, J. L., Irving M. Abella, T. W. Acheson, David J. Bercuson, R. Craig Brown, and H. Blair Neatby (1990), *Nation: Canada Since Confederation*, Toronto: McGraw-Hill Ryerson.
3. Miller, J.R. (2009), *Compact, Contract, Covenant: Aboriginal Treaty-Making in Canada*, Toronto: University of Toronto Press, p. 210.
4. Asch, Michael (2014), *On Being Here to Stay: Treaties and Aboriginal Rights in Canada*, Toronto: University of Toronto Press.
5. Barnard, Frederick M. (1965), *Herder's social and political thought: From Enlightenment to nationalism*. Oxford: Clarendon, p. 286f.
6. "The Royal Proclamation—October 7, 1763" (1763), Accessed from the Lillian Goldman Law Library, Yale University: www.avalon.law.yale.edu/18th_century/proc1763.asp
7. "The Royal Proclamation—October 7, 1763."
8. Asch, 2014.
9. Morris, Alexander (1880), *The treaties of Canada with the Indians of Manitoba and the North-West Territories, including the negotiations on which they were based, and other information relating thereto*, Toronto: Belfords, Clarke and Co.
10. Treaty 4 (1874). *Treaty No. 4. Between Her Majesty the Queen and The Cree and Saulteaux Tribes of Indians at Qu'Appelle and Fort Elice*: www.aadnc-aandc.gc.ca/eng/1100100028689/1100100028690
11. Cardinal, Harold and Walter Hildebrandt (2000), *Treaty elders of Saskatchewan: Our dream is that our peoples will one day be clearly recognized as nations*, Calgary: University of Calgary Press, p. 66.
12. "Indian Government and the Treaties" (1986), *Saskatchewan Indian*, p. 9.
13. Morris, 1980, p. 96.
14. Ibid., Emphasis mine.
15. Ibid., p. 92.
16. Ibid.
17. Ibid., p. 211.
18. *Treaty No. 4. Between Her Majesty the Queen and The Cree and Saulteaux Tribes of Indians at Qu'Appelle and Fort Elice*.
19. Elder Kay Thompson, as cited in Cardinal and Hildebrandt, *Treaty elders of Saskatchewan: Our dream is that our peoples will one day be clearly recognized as nations*, p. 62f.
20. "Indian Government and the Treaties," p. 9.
21. Morris, 1980, p. 108.
22. "Halsbury's Laws of England" (2009), *Halsbury's Laws of England*, 5th ed., London: LexisNexis, p. 504 Emphasis mine.
23. Talbot, Robert J. (2009), *Negotiating the numbered treaties: An intellectual and political biography of Alexander Morris*. Saskatoon: Purich Publishing Limited, p. 47f.
24. Earl of Dufferin (1882). *Speeches and Addresses of the Right Honourable Frederick Temple Hamilton, Earl of Dufferin*, Edited by Henry Milton, London: John Murray, p. 210.
25. Ibid., p. 209.
26. Burgess, A.M., ed. (1876), *Debates of the House of Commons of the Dominion of Canada*, Ottawa: Maclean, Roger and Company, p. 1039.
27. Aborigines Protection Society (1840). *Outline of a System of Legislation for the Securing of Protection to the Aboriginal Inhabitants of all Countries Colonized by Great Britain: Extending to the Political and Social Rights, Ameliorating their Condition, and Promoting their Civilization*. London: John Murray, etc., p. 9 www.eco.canadiana.ca/view/oocihm.47266/3?r=0&s=1

28. Ibid., p. 16f.
29. "Residential Schools in Canada: Education Guide" (ND), *Historica Canada*: hwww.historicacanada.ca/sites/default/files/PDF/ResidentialSchools_English.pdf
30. Talbot, 2009.
31. Ibid., p. 143.
32. Ibid., p. 147.
33. Ibid., p. 149.
34. Ibid., p. 160.
35. For a detailed discussion on this matter see Asch, 2014, pp. 100-133.
36. Morris, 1980, p.100.
37. Ibid., pp. 117-118.
38. Ibid., p. 171.
39. Ibid., p. 211.
40. Ibid., p. 213.
41. Ibid., p. 227.
42. Treaty 6 (1876). *Treaty No 6 between Her Majesty the Queen and the Plain and Wood Cree Indians and Other Tribes of Indians at Fort Carlton, Fort Pitt and Battle Rive with Adhesions*: www.aadnc-aandc.gc.ca/eng/1100100028710/1100100028783
43. Morris, 1980, p. 228.
44. What I mean is that we are the junior partners on this land and need to learn from those who were already here what are the ways to live in harmony with each other and with creation in this place. See Asch, 2014.
45. Asch, 2014, pp. 111-114.

Let's Talk Treaty

Rob Houle

[handwritten annotation: usually ~~always~~ think of negotiation over war as a positive thing, but not always the case.]

Adapted from a series of tweets published by @NehiyawRob (Rob Houle) during his hosting of the handle @IndigenousXca from January 5 to 12, 2017.

Let's talk Treaty. Why do we have Treaty? Treaty process. How do we use Treaty? What are our obligations? What about those without Treaty?

We have Treaty because the Crown is not a legitimate titleholder to the territories within Turtle Island. Guided by Doctrine of Discovery . . .

. . . and other papal bulls, the Crown and Church worked in unison to try and occupy, settle, and control the known world. Rather than engage in . . .

. . . all-out warfare, the Crown decided it best to negotiate Treaty. And as with most things Indigenous related, Treaty can be seen in both good and bad light. In the beginning of Treaty process, which some have argued began with the Royal Proclamation 1763 and Treaty of Niagara in 1764 . . .

. . . which again, ignores the many inter-tribal treaties that existed prior to contact, a framework was created for the ongoing relationship between . . .

. . . Indigenous and non-Indigenous peoples on Turtle Island. These agreements, oral, written, and spiritual in nature, outlined obligations on both sides.

This process included trade, intermarriage, exchange of items, mutual benefit, and in the end, the protection and maintenance of resources.

When examining the process, we must pay special attention to the engagements utilized. And how the crown manipulated our beliefs and relations.

With the fur trade beginning close to 200 years prior to Crown/Indigenous Treaty, a process of trading and engaging had been established.

So when you mirror to the Treaty process, you can see why concessions like jacket exchange, medal provision, and ceremony were utilized by . . .

. . . the crown and Indigenous people. Elders and oral history tell of the early days, traders on behalf of Hudson's Bay would often leave their officers coat . . .

. . . with trade partners as a reminder of the exchange, and recognize future traders that may arrive in the area. This became a common practice . . .

. . . during Treaty deliberations, and there was constant reference and announcement of the Queen and her promises/obligations to her "subjects."

Given the importance of women in our often matriarchal traditional governance structures, coupled with maintaining ongoing trading practices . . .

. . . those discussing, which @LawladyINM hilites did not contain women leaders, hence no real right to negotiate, had every reason to trust the . . .

. . . process and the promises. However, we now know, that the honour of the crown was nonexistent at the time of Treaty, and this is clear when . . .

. . . during negotiations for Treaty No. 6, they were passing the *Indian Act* in Ottawa. This led to hesitancy from leaders like MistahiMaskwa . . .

. . . who understood that if we were to sign Treaty, it would tie us to our partners, and leave the door open for us to be led around with a rope.

Thankfully, in true colonial fashion, and the need to document everything, the crown and commissioners recorded much of the deliberations.

Combined with oral history, it helps to outline and clarify what the true process was like, and how the obligations are still unfulfilled.

With that stated, the title to the lands in Canada is still illegitimate, and the government is still not a shareholder. Hence our bond to . . .

. . . the Crown. The repatriation of the constitution was all for show. But that does not mean the story is over. By thinking of Treaty in these . . .

~~repatriation as all for show.~~

... terms, it helps to shed light on what the intention of bills like C-51 and C-45 were intended to do. Conspiracy theorists could argue, it was ...

... an attempt to criminalize Indigenous people and our connection to the Earth, in order for us to break our obligations under Treaty, which as you will ...

... recall was to openly share the resources and to keep the peace. Once we begin to alter that arrangement, the Crown could take action on Treaty.

So as stated earlier, a good and bad situation. And for the record, Status is NOT Treaty. *Indian Act* and status are colonial interpretations ...

... of Treaty, and not the true obligations outlined with the Crown. What does this mean for those who do not have Treaty. They are still Treaty ...

... people, just in a grey area where one could argue they retain their Indigenous rights recognized by ...

... Royal Proclamation, 1763, and since time immemorial ...

... that proclamation protected and required consultation with all in Indian territory. We have seen recent court rulings point to this type of understanding.

For the record, we did not cede release and surrender anything. It was not ours to surrender, as the creator is the sole owner of the lands ... *not theirs to surrender → Creator*

... for which we are merely stewards whom he/she gifted access to while we reside in this physical plane.

How do we use Treaty? Well first we have to know what the Treaty says, and how our oral history interprets the arrangement.

Additionally, scholars like @adamgaudry are helping to reframe the notion of Treaty with the interpretation that the *Manitoba Act, 1870* ...

... was a Treaty with the Métis as it was negotiated, and included the transfer of lands and resources in a nation-to-nation fashion.

It is important for us to actually read the Treaty. When this takes place we learn each was different, and how to trace the rights we experience ...

Status = colonial creation

... back to said Treaty. For instance, this whole carbon tax BS. Why don't we pay the carbon tax on reserve? Well you can look to Treaty 8 as an example.

We assured them that the Treaty would not lead to any forced interference with their mode of life [or] imposition of any tax.

That excerpt is from the Treaty 8 commissioner report. Then we have things like health, education, destitution, pestilence, and other obligations.

So how do we use them? Well you use them. And push the limits of the definition, and how the Crown interprets. We must remind them of what . . .

. . . they agreed to and how we have been upholding our end of the relationship this whole time. Patiently waiting. Some leaders are there now.

But much work is needed on both sides of the table. Even some of our own leaders do not see this reality, and get caught up in *Indian Act*.

Let's not get caught up in #Canada150 or adding a + to it. There is no Canada in 1866, so adding a + is meaningless. Just respect our arrangement.

Those that existed before you arrived, respect our governance processes, our economics, our social, then we will have something to celebrate.

Treaty is not the end all be all. It serves as a bookmark in this long story, a framework for a relationship, a reminder of what came before/after.

And at the end of the day, a spiritual covenant between peoples to share our being with each other, and to make each other better. Not a monopoly . . .

. . . with all that. Let's start talking more about Treaty while remembering what came before Treaty. Each interpretation is important and required to . . .

. . . keep the conversation going. If I have missed anything or need correction, please provide. I am no expert, never have been, never will be.

As there are eleven numbered, peace/friendship, douglas, robinson/huron, modern and intertribal, that makes for a lot of reading and interpretation.

I continue to read them over. And try to learn more about things like wampum covenants. It is important to know these things. I used to work . . .

Wampum covenants

. . . for a Treaty organization. I wrote many brief notes with a Treaty focus, but again, the colonized mentality would not allow me to progress. Questions . . .

. . . started about whether only members of the Treaty area should work for the organization. Me being . . .

. . . T8, odd man out. So went to work for the man . . . but . . .

They are good people that allow me to focus on Treaty, 'cause the city chief sees Treaty as just as important, and knows that we are all Treaty people.

This message is starting to be taken nationally for the other moniyaw leaders that sit on similar committees and whatnot. But still more must . . .

. . . be done. There was talk of a Treaty commission in Alberta. However, we could never agree on the mandate. Some wanted education, the government wanted . . .

. . . an education focus. We knew this would limit the scope, so we pushed for a Treaty watchdog. To hold the then Conservative/PC government accountable to Treaty.

But alas it was not meant to be. So I continue to try and educate, and push for Treaty consideration in my new role. But we must be vigilant.

True reconciliation is a full enactment of Treaty for those that have it, and for those that don't it is a full consideration of their Indigenous rights . . .

. . . before encroaching on them in the name of "progress." It is much more than what we are seeing today, so we must push for more to be done.

> push for treaty consideration
> full enactment of treaty
> full consideration of indigenous rights

The Natives Are Restless
Indigenous Epistemic Disobedience and Thinking Ourselves Free

Hayden King and Erica Violet Lee[1]

> "Niya oma nêhiyaw, keyapihc oma etahkweyak, moya atoya nime-schikohnanahk."
>
> —SYLVIA MCADAM[2]

In September 2016, a few months before Canada's most auspicious birthday, we sat together on a panel at St. Thomas More College in Saskatoon, Saskatchewan, discussing the English philosopher Thomas More's text, *Utopia*.

The day before, we made the three-hour drive from the city to Mistahi Sipiy (Big River), just past the tree line where the prairie turns into the boreal. Here, Sylvia McAdam Saysewahum—Nēhiyaw writer and lawyer—has set up camp to defend her family's hunting grounds from clear-cut logging. She showed us the destruction: acres of forest home removed in the name of Saskatchewan industry and Canadian progress. She showed us the graves of her ancestors, including both great leaders and small children who died of disease inside and outside of residential schools. Beside the gravesites, mere metres away, settlers have built houses, as if entirely unaware or simply unfazed by their proximity to and participation in this cruel history. During our walk and into the night, we talked about Nēhiyaw and Anishinaabe philosophical concepts, piecing together our ancestral languages. We talked about whiteness and about vulnerability. Later, bundled up in sweaters smelling of campfire smoke, we took the road south with Sylvia and Mistahi Sipiy in our hearts, wondering how to describe the extraordinary *sakihiwawin* (love in resistant action) and how to make the transition between the devastation of the world we were departing into the space we were about to enter. And finally, how could we possibly squeeze our experiences in Mistahi Sipiy, as Indigenous peoples with threatened lives and uncertain liberation, into the utopian vision of an English philosopher, or the Eurocentric canon of philosophy.

The conference on More was a 500-year celebration on the publication of the classic text *Utopia*, about a fictional new country where settlers displace or assimilate the original inhabitants and build a perfect society.[3] It brought together scholars devoted to the work. More was venerated as a visionary and a radical, and his ideas were considered and reconsidered over the course of two days. But we, like Karl Hardy,[4] could not help but notice that More was writing as imperialism was reaching across the ocean to lands full of new possibilities for Spain, France, and eventually England. In conversation, we argued that *Utopia* is a colonial project of settlement dependent on the obliteration of Indigenous bodies and Indigenous thought. We examined the significance of More's brief remark—one sentence in the entire text—that the nation of Utopia rests upon land that had "previously been called Abraxa" (the first inhabitants now entirely assimilated into the utopian state).[5] As in More's text and the 500 years of settler colonization that would follow, Indigenous people are only redeemable if we are assimilated and out of the way.

Abstracting this point, there is no real hope, within the framework of Euro-Canadian progress, that we can exist on Indigenous lands *as* Indigenous. We have considered these processes as academics, but as living, breathing, Nēhiyaw and Anishinaabe people, we saw this reality with our eyes that morning, just as we have seen many times before. Our white settler co-panellists listened respectfully but stayed on the periphery of the theme, despite our repeated prompts to imagine otherwise. When the audience—comprised of Thomas More scholars long tenured in spaces engaged only with like-minded thinkers—had an opportunity to comment, they made clear their disapproval, demonstrating an inability to engage with our philosophies. We suspect their agitation was caused by the audacity of two Indigenous thinkers (junior academics in their eyes, with little expertise on More) challenging their claim of "utopia" as a universally progressive and desirable project. But it is precisely in our disobedient pursuit of worlds beyond a Canadian utopia—our insistent returning-to-the-land physically, intellectually—that shatters the settler myths that: 1) we are extinct, 2) we are objects without memory or kin, or 3) we are assimilation-ready into the state's vision of reconciliation.

But we have been hanging around the fort for a while, contorting ourselves into institutions and places like St. Thomas More College. This is but one of many stories. While technically members of the academy, we also exist in a borderland where hostility, racism, and the rejection of our knowledges still defines the centre. And so we grow extra layers on our already dark and thick skin, wondering when and where (if ever) our philosophies will find a genuine space in the academy. We wonder if aiming for this "inclusion" of Indigenous thought in Canadian institutions is even useful in the interim, or possible in the long term, or if it is simply the old trap of respectability politics. In Canada's short 150 years of existence, this is not a unique or new experience. Our ancestors worked then as now to convince settlers of our humanity and dignity. While we acknowledge their efforts in shifting the discourse by strategic degrees over the years, and the work of our cousins and peers—activists and academics today who do the same—we think Canadians are scarcely more capable of understanding what we have to say on Canada's 150th birthday than they were in 1867. As activists within the academy, one terrain of our struggle is the university. Here, Indigenous students and faculty are quickly consumed by efforts to *redeem* settler colonialism; redemption, as Eve Tuck and Wayne Yang argue, is the aim of all settler reconciliatory projects.[6] And so, the colonial consumption of Indigeneity restrains our existence, and limits it to performance and tokenism.

Challenging the Canon: 150 Years of Erasure

As Indigenous people on these lands who seek intellectual communities, an obvious path is through Canadian institutions. Certainly there are non-institutional Indigenous intellectual spaces, and we can thrive there, to varying degrees. Though a difficult task when those spaces are impoverished reserves, militarized inner cities, or forests logged into the ground. *Our places* are places made deliberately hostile and unliveable through the violence of colonialism. So there are few opportunities where we can be vulnerable on our own terms, and think for ourselves and for our communities. Many of us then find ourselves in the academy. This spatial form of erasure foregrounds another, which is the focus here: the unwillingness of these institutions to honour the original knowledges of this land and its peoples, a wilful ignorance of the ways in which Canada has consistently denied acknowledgment of our ability to think and develop systems of knowledge in a university context. There is a type of Indigenous "knowledge" solicited and supported by Canadian universities: what is often referred to as *wisdom*.[7] "Wisdom" is an essentialist form of knowledge extracted from our bones without regard for its knower, the ancestors, and the modern community who claim the knower as kin, or without acknowledgment of the knower's relationship to ongoing settler colonization. In other words, wisdom in such a context is disembodied, detached, and a safe-for-settlers dilution/reduction of Indigenous knowledge, void of relationships and obligation. Finally, importantly, this is antithetical to the thought Indigenous academics are striving to cultivate.

Indigenous Studies departments—to varying degrees—have been the manifestation of earnest attempts to create hospitable spaces for critical Indigenous thought. Indeed, Indigenous Studies departments can be a well of self-determination on campus. And yet they are frequently reduced to the study *of* Indigenous peoples. And generally, Indigenous Studies departments are placed in some corner of a university building basement, marginalized. They face institutional pushback, underfunding, and are home to overworked Native faculty. As Rauna Kuokkanen writes, in the view of the accommodating universities, these programs are simply holding spaces until the civilization process unfolds. The training grounds for integration into the *real* university.[8] In the era of reconciliation and big birthdays, a key difference from that recent past may be our apparently elevated status. Out of the basement and perhaps into our own building, with some Douglas Cardinal facsimile, and a smudge room (just a room, though, because we still get yelled at if we smudge anywhere else on campus. Thus, our own smudgy reserve. Like Vanessa Watts, we wonder if this "use [or misuse] of ceremony subscribes to the ever-emerging politics of adaptability where we, as Indigenous peoples, are aiding in the design of a space of dispossession?"[9]). In these renovated settings, if students are lucky, their tour guides on this Indigenized educational journey will actually be Indigenous themselves with a modicum of Indigenous pedagogy. Too often we are unlucky. Indeed, in our experiences, it is the case that we are not considered to be the best keepers of our own knowledges, the best storytellers of our own experiences, the best voices for our own communities. This extends beyond teaching, of course, and into research and intellectual thought, generally.

Today in Treaty 6 territory, for instance, the work of 500-years-dead English philosophers is often considered more legitimate, more thoughtful, and somehow, more timely to study than say, Sylvia McAdam Saysewahum's 2015 book, *Nationhood Interrupted: Revitalizing Nēhiyaw Legal Systems*. Indigenous philosophies of resistance, of which there are many (oral and textual alike), are erased from the academic landscape—part and parcel of the ongoing attempts to remove our bodies from this land. Returning to our experience at St. Thomas More College, or the experience of any Dene or Innu student in a classroom challenging their non-Native professor, or any Mohawk or Ojibwe elder calling out settler politicians, or any Métis or Wet'sewet'en youth standing up to racism; we are perceived as unreasonable, considered as angry. How far are we today, really, from our non-Native peers, wondering if we are capable of abstract thought. Related to this discussion, we ask who leads the Canadian conversation on our 150 years together, and importantly, who is actually listening? Where does it take place on Indigenous terms—in the public square? Newspapers, television, and radio? If these are genuine sites of engagement, we as public thinkers see it rarely. And these experiences call into question the hegemonic claims of Canada at 150 years as unified, respectful, and glorious.

Performing Reconciliation: 150 Years of Tokenism and Indigenous Labour

In Canada's 149th year, the Truth and Reconciliation Commission (TRC) released its final report with 94 Calls to Action. In the wake of the TRC's work, it seems more than any other institution in this country, colleges and universities have taken up the cause. Discussions range from mandatory Indigenous content courses, reconciliation workshops for staff, and a thousand committees on "Indigenizing the academy" (to which we both belong, in situations when we believe our presence is more productive than our absence). Often, the administrators who lead many of these initiatives seek a specific kind of performance of Indigeneity in the academy: one that requires the labour of the community, which ultimately devours much of the energy for genuine transformative change. In the era of reconciliation, the agenda for Indigenous education on campus, it seems to us, has been co-opted. It is true that most Canadians come to the table with a deficit of even the most basic, fundamental knowledge of Indigenous peoples, settler history, or even how to relate to Indigenous people (especially thinkers) as subjects. And this requires remedy. Yet, for those of us who join the academy and become informants for their benefit, we are constantly asked to provide intellectual and emotional labour to settlers. Perhaps an obligation for being tolerated in these spaces. Perhaps the sacrifice for making change? But the labour can be intensive, exhausting, and often oppressive. Indigenous academics are often forced to stall the development of their own work of revitalizing and re-articulating Indigenous philosophy. This frames the reconciliation relationship as fundamentally unbalanced and, if there is no resulting transformation, simply extractive.

As Indigenous thinkers increasingly reject this asymmetrical relationship, the reaction tends to be confusion and frustration that we aren't performing as expected. This is particularly so for those of us who are young, queer, women, Two Spirit, or gender nonconforming, who defy multiple expectations of submission to these demands. This parallels the reconciliation discourse in Canada generally. We refuse to be the good-natured good Indians, and in refusing, a threshold of acceptable Indigeneity appears and the aforementioned excusal of our concerns defines the relationship. And so in some cases, institutional spaces will simply circumvent any potential resistance. Last year, for instance, Hayden was invited to the High Table at Massey College, honouring Indigenous peoples in the arts. A handful of sharp, critical Indigenous academics and artists were also invited, none of who spoke or were invited to speak. A band council chief did recite some poetry from his high school days, and then the Master of the college regaled us with Vincent Massey's contribution to reconciliation. He told a story about Massey's encounter with a West Coast artist struggling against the *Indian Act*. So jarring was the artist's story of oppression that Massey went on to single-handedly reform the *Indian Act* in 1951. The story was untrue, of course, and erased the activism of mothers of residential school students and World War II vets, and all the other Indigenous leaders who forced change. It seemed an attempt by the college to *redeem* itself. In retrospect, the event may even have been organized around this myth, and any genuine honouring of Indigenous people in the arts was subsidiary. Their case for redemption was reinforced by the Indigenous scholars sitting beside the Master, silent.

> *I am in a university classroom, an English professor corrects my spoken English in front of the class. I say, "really good." He says, "you mean, really well, don't you?" I glare at him and say emphatically, "No, I mean really good."*
> —MARILYN DUMONT, *A Really Good Brown Girl*[10]

As an undergraduate student, Erica co-developed and co-taught an Indigenous philosophy class at St. Thomas More College in 2013 with her faculty mentor, a settler philosophy professor. That the college, the faculty, and the university permitted an undergraduate student to co-facilitate such a project appeared, on the surface, innovative. Recognizing the limits of even our combined knowledges, as a settler professor and an Indigenous undergraduate student, we nonetheless created a roster of guest speakers—legal scholars, elders, anti-racist and anti-colonial theorists—as well as scheduled class trips to land-based education sites.

The Department of Indigenous Studies had a crucial role in overseeing the development and execution of the course. But despite our efforts, intention, or innovation, the experience was still problematic. First, it arose from the lack of any Indigenous faculty in the college to develop and teach the course. The cost of a third-year undergraduate hourly rate was a cheaper and disempowered alternative to an actual Indigenous hire. Second, there was a departmental unwillingness to allow an Indigenous scholar from another faculty to teach the course if their degree was not in the discipline of philosophy (a clear double standard). This is colonial logic that upholds the whiteness of philosophy as a discipline, serving to dispossess Indigenous students from classrooms, dispossess Indigenous thought from the realm of "legitimate knowledge," and ultimately, continue the dispossession of Indigenous peoples from our lands through the same terra nullius erasures we have contested for centuries. Even the most well-intentioned attempts to integrate Indigenous knowledge and people into the existing structure of Canadian universities may still result in the exploitation of Indigenous labour, and more often than not, the tokenization of Indigenous students.

Surviving the Academy: 150 Years of Spaces Not Meant For Us

Making it in the doors of a Canadian university as an Indigenous student is still the exception, becoming a faculty member even rarer. And so we must be both exceptional and lucky against odds to endure to this point. The narrative of exceptional Indigenous students relies on the racist belief that Indigenous people are underrepresented in the education system because of our own lack of intelligence; that most of us are just not smart or hardworking enough instead of the reality that most of us are deliberately, systematically denied the opportunity for higher education. Once Indigenous people are inside university walls, we endure racist curricula, unsafe classrooms, assumptions of incompetence from our peers, professors, and colleagues; all of this along with the poverty and precarity that comes as the price of surviving ongoing dispossession. Native students are rarely allowed to just be students. Even as undergraduates, our time is spent and our energy is exhausted on correcting the ignorance of peers and teachers alike. For example, white faculty and administrators often approach Indigenous students with questions about indigenization. Surely, more than one white professor has come to tears upon hearing that their idea of painting feathers and an *Inuksuk* on university walls is not enough to make Indigenous students feel "welcome."

Our unpaid and underpaid labour is extracted for the benefit of Canadian universities as an extension of the extractive Canadian state. As young Indigenous thinkers in the era of "reconciliation," we are in high demand for these educational institutions—well, some of us. Following the line of beautifully disruptive questioning developed by philosopher Kristie Dotson,[11] what do settler institutions have to offer Indigenous thinkers? What does Canadian academic philosophy have to offer Indigenous students? What do Canadian universities have to offer Indigenous thinkers beyond tokenism? What could Canada possibly have to offer Indigenous nations? These questions are the standard upon which we should operate, not "what can Indigenous students and faculty do for Canadian universities?" Canada has reparations to give for the disruption of Indigenous worlds and the attempted removal of Indigenous citizens from our systems of thought.

Sometimes we are brought into these spaces by well-meaning (or not) settlers who want to include Indigenous voices, perspectives, and presence in their conferences and events. Sometimes we have to fight to enter a space in the first place, ever aware of the battles of Indigenous faculty and students who came before. But it is an overwhelming amount of labour required to participate—a fact misapprehended by white Canadians by virtue of the fact that these spaces are made specifically for them. Places that rarely allow us to speak our languages, include land-based knowledges, or engage with us in ways that are intellectually rewarding. Here, we are limited to response, reaction, defence, or silence. And so, our participation is reduced from Indigenous peoples to Indigenous bodies. We are seat fillers, tokens, empty, brown husks used to fill a diversity quota, or consent-givers on behalf of nations that do not claim us. As Indigenous thinkers, we must learn at a young age how to operate within a Canadian worldview, because it is required of us as part of our survival in an occupied settler state. We are tired of being reduced to consumable tragedy porn for settlers, or the smiling symbols of Canadian redemption. As this country turns 150, and our institutional homes turn 75, or 90, or 120, or whatever, we are here to say there is no redemption.

Nehiyawnishinaabe Refusal

The discussion here is from *our* experiences. In situating our stories as knowledge valid before and far beyond the narrative of Canada, we create space for Indigenous thought as the fundamental philosophies of this land. For far too long, even beyond the century-and-a-half that Canada claims as its own, we have been told our lived experiences are irrelevant and unsound. As was the case on that fall morning in Saskatoon, as Nēhiyaw/Anishinaabe academics, our interpretations are challenged, our critiques excused as misreadings, our thoughts and bodies preferred at the university as submissive performers. While Canada celebrates its own, fledgling birthday, it rejects our ancient and futuristic Anishinaabe/Nēhiyaw philosophies as folkloric, quaint, or simply untrue. And while the relationship we describe here is specific to the academy, it extends to Canadian society. The extravagant 150th birthday celebration and reconciliatory trends are complimentary, merging into Canada's redemption. But we see the strategy and we refuse to be conciliatory tokens. Our presence, despite its attempted erasure, cannot be named as consent. No, our refusal at the various sites of settler colonialism in this country is multifaceted, constant, and enduring. This includes—and will continue to include—the academy. Indigenous thought is alive in our mourning, in our remembrance of events that Canada would rather we forget, and in the playful moments of vulnerability we claim for ourselves while gathered around the campfire. Indigenous thought is alive in the return of our bodies to the lands, languages, and intellectual traditions that nourish us, and in the pursuit of futures beyond walls that have never been able to contain us. Indigenous thought is alive, whether or not it is recognized by Canada. It is alive in spite of Canada. We are alive in spite of Canada.

Anishinaabe N'daaw, Anishinaabe enendang pane aabideg gida'bimaadiziimigad.

1. Gchi-miigwech to Myrtle Jamieson for help with Anishinaabemowin translation.
2. McAdam, Sylvia (2015), *Nationhood Interrupted: Revitalizing Nehiyaw Legal Systems*, Saskatoon: Purich Publishing.
3. More, Thomas (2016), *Utopia*, London: Verso.
4. Hardy, Karl (2012), "Unsettling Hope: Settler-Colonialism and Utopianism," *Spaces of Utopia: An Electronic Journal* 2, no. 1, pp. 123-136.
5. More, 2016, p. 62.
6. Tuck, Eve and K. Wayne Yang (2012), "Decolonization is Not a Metaphor," *Decolonization: Indigeneity, Education & Society* 1, no. 1.
7. Mignolo, Walter (2015), "Yes, We Can," *Can Non-Europeans Think?* Hamid Dabashi, ed. London: Zed Books.
8. Kuokkanen, Rauna (2007), *Reshaping the University: Responsibility, Indigenous Epistemes and the Logic of the Gift*. Vancouver: UBC Press.
9. Watts, Vanessa (2016), "Smudge This: Assimilation, State-Favoured Communities And The Denial Of Indigenous Spiritual Lives," *International Journal of Child, Youth and Family Studies* 7, no. 1, p. 164.
10. Dumont, Marilyn (1996), *A Really Good Brown Girl*, London: Brick Books.
11. Dotson, Kristie (2012), "How Is This Paper Philosophy?" *Comparative Philosophy Volume 3*, no. 1, pp. 3-29.

Letter to the Minister

Kurtis Schmitz

January 11th, 2017

Dear Minister Bennett,

I do not know if you have the capacity to respond to this message. I will try to send it through various means of communication, in hopes that you hear my voice. As a Caucasian-male with a privileged education, I try to be careful of how I use my voice. Too often in this nation, men with similar backgrounds to mine have used their voices to speak over others, and belittle the ideas and notions of those who did not have the fortune of my background, or ethnicity. But today I hope that my voice is heard not for my own benefit but for that of my students. As I write, Canadians all over the country are preparing to celebrate 150 years as a nation, but should we not be reflecting on how far we still have to come?

My name is Kurtis Schmitz, and I am a secondary teacher at Aglace Chapman Education Centre, a school located some 500 km northwest of Thunder Bay. I write to you today because my community and its neighbouring community are in crisis. Two young girls, both only twelve years old, have passed away by means of their own hand. Unfortunately, this is not an uncommon occurrence in northern communities like ours, and has been a news bulletin on the front page of CBC Indigenous far too many times.

I am aware of your political career, and the good things you have done and said for First Nations in Ontario, for the Indigenous Peoples of Canada, and for equal education. With this knowledge, I write to you as a teacher fighting for the future of his students. When I look at my students, I see not only who they are today but also the potential of who they may someday be. Whether they choose to be doctors, nurses, trades people, construction workers, teachers, or lawyers, I see into the future when I look in their eyes. This Monday morning, however, I stood in front of my class and expected to see that hope for the future and contempt for homework that I usually see. But I didn't see it. It was as if a dense fog had rolled in, and my capacity to see their futures was hidden. A room that is usually filled with laughter, and the conversations of weekend exploits had fallen silent. When I looked at their faces, I could not find that hope. The news of loss spreads quickly in a small community; it takes only a few hours, even just minutes for every community member to hear of stories like these. It was not long before I heard about the tragedy that had unfolded the previous day; by the time I could muster a response to the situation, the worst possible scenario struck: another child had taken her life. In the North, in terrible times like these, the school can be a haven for the students, a safe place that will not judge you for your grief, or force you to keep a stiff upper lip. It is a communal space to come together, to be consoled, and if need be, to talk to a trained professional, teacher, or friend. But often a trained counsellor is not available, as they can only come once every six weeks to my school. So it is up to friends, family, and teachers to advise our students, on top of our regular jobs and responsibilities.

These proud communities are devastated by these losses of innocent life, and are looking for some reason for this tragedy, and maybe for someone to blame. But instead of looking at themselves, or each other, I think they should be looking south. That blame falls on everyone in this nation's shoulders. That blame belongs to all Canadians, including those who sit in the seats around you, Minister Bennett. It is they who actively decide to give my school and my students less funding than any other provincial school system in Canada. They decide that my students, their lives, and their futures are not worth the same amount as students in the public school system. They decide that because my students were not born in Ottawa, Vancouver, or Montréal, they do not deserve to be heard or listened to. How many young boys and girls must we lose before your colleagues in the House of Commons realize that reacting to tragedy is not a sustainable practice? We must get out in front of these issues; we must ensure that all schools in the North are staffed with certified mental health professionals, and not just for the weeks after a tragedy but in the dark hours before these desperate acts.

I teach a Canadian History course to grade nine and ten students, and in the last few weeks we have been covering civil rights movements in Canada and the US, following the footsteps of Martin Luther King Jr., Viola Desmond, Chief Dan George, and Elijah Harper. How do I explain to my students that the fight for equal rights has not yet been won? How do I explain to them that they have inherited a fight that they might not ever win in their lifetimes? That they are not considered worthy of the same treatment of sons and daughters to the south?

I ask you, Minister Bennett, I beseech you to continue speaking out. Do not rest! You have been put into a position of privilege, you must use that position to save not just my students but every young man and woman who loses a friend due to the apathy of a country more than willing to overlook them. I want my students to know that there are people who care about their futures; I want them to know that they are not alone on a fly-in reserve in Northern Ontario. I want you to tell Mr. Trudeau that sunny ways should not be reserved for a select group of Canadians. That the sun still shines in the North, though on days like today it is hard to feel its warmth. I need you to put the hope back into my students' eyes; I need you to put the hope back in their teacher's eyes.

Thank you for reading this,
Kurtis Schmitz

Encountering Memories on the Restigouche River

Fred Metallic and Amy Chamberlin

A man stood at the foot of the Hill surrounded by families with children bustled into snowsuits, couples holding hands, and a few older ones. He edged his way closer to the front, walking past line-ups of people eager for free hot chocolate and beaver tails, and found a place to watch the Show of Lights projected against Parliament's gothic structure. Images turned into stories on the stones, he snapped pictures: wolf chasing rabbit, bear, dreamcatcher, and stars. The final picture posed for a moment longer than the others—150, and Canada's red-and-white flag fluttered proudly on the building. "Looks like the party's started," he said. The images slipped off the stones. He shrugged his hands into his black leather jacket, and headed for home.

In July of 2017, Canada will "celebrate" its 150th anniversary of Confederation. As the editors of this text have noted, for many Indigenous peoples and their allies, the commemoration also marks loss, mourning, and continued colonization. We wrote this article as a way to talk about loss and absences, and also to celebrate the continued existence of Indigenous peoples.[1]

This article (or story) is from the seventh district of Gespe'gewa'gi, Mi'gma'gi. The territory of the Mi'gmaq includes the island of Newfoundland, Nova Scotia, Prince Edward Island, much of New Brunswick and the Gaspé, and part of northeastern Maine, as well as the rivers, tributaries, and waterways.[2] More particularly, we have followed stories about the Restigouche River, a central waterway in Gespe'gewa'gi. We followed the river to better understand how stories from a particular place, over a long period of time, function as a type of witnessing to encounters between Indigenous peoples and settler colonials; from stories we learn about loss, memory, and resurgence.[3]

In Gespe'gewa'gi, there is a mountain near the Restigouche River. Some say the mountain was formed in the shape of a beaver, but most people just call it Sugarloaf. The trail marking the path to the top is well-worn, and from there the view of the region is impressive: Appalachian mountain range, boreal forest, Gaspé beyond, and the Restigouche River, with its salt and fresh water tides, and its tributaries, running through it all.

They met, by chance, at the summit of Sugarloaf. Both men were sitting on the rocks, resting and looking out at the view. They nodded at each other, silent assessments, taking each other in. They could be foils—one with his long, dark braid (thinning slightly), high cheeks, a black T-shirt with four "Indian men" poised on the front, and the words "Original Founding Fathers" scrolled beneath. The other beside him—short, sandy hair (receding), pale face, comfortable hiker shorts, a blue shirt tucked in, with a leather belt cinching it all together.

The one with the sandy hair was flying a drone. The tiny machine hovered above, snapping pictures of the newly planted Canadian flag, of the bronze-coloured commemorative plaque fixed to the metal guardrail. The plaque declared: Battle of the Restigouche "sealed the destiny" between two powers competing for control over territory. A succinct statement commemorating the Battle of 1760, and solidifying official memories of what took place on the Restigouche River below.

The Battle of 1760 is a fragment from the Seven Years' War fought amongst powers seeking to secure transatlantic trade in North America. The strand is part of the narrative that carries the sounds of Canada's mythic birth from two imperial powers battling it out. The battle has been imagined into a national historic site visited in the summer months by those touring the Gaspé Peninsula. The old "contest of empires" storyline is fading somewhat. But there are still omissions, gaps, and long-held silences in Canada's (official) narratives about settler colonial and Indigenous relations. Encounters such as the battle are still being interpreted through reference to British and French documentation. Too often dismissed in the representation of events are the Mi'gmaq perspectives.

The two men struck up a conversation. Above them, the drone whirled (snap, snap, snapping pictures).

The public representations of the battle most often focus on the arrival of the French fleet to the Restigouche.[4] After several weeks of sailing for the colony, the merchant ships (carrying munitions and provisions) changed their course, seeking refuge from the British in the Chaleur Bay. This was not the planned route to Québec, nor was this in compliance with orders for an alternative path. Instead, the captains searched for safety in territory inhabited by "*les sauvages*." The ships ventured into the Restigouche; captains sought reprieve in a type of wilderness dotted by islands of (so called) civility beginning to take root in the footprints of missionaries, recently arrived/deported Acadians, and military batteries.[5]

The sandy-haired man was a reporter. "Originally from the area," he said. He wanted to make a historical documentary. He seemed well informed: John Reid, William Wicken, Daniel Paul, and Olive Dickason. The conversation between the men rolled along.

The Battle of 1760 was hardly important!" the sandy-haired man said. "It was just a rump. The Battle of the Plains of Abraham set the fate of New France!"

For the Mi'gmaq, the Battle of Restigouche was significant for reasons other than the fall of New France. A few weeks following the battle, British troops arrived to secure the terms of capitulation with the French, and to ensure peace with the Mi'gmaq.[6] In the written records, there is a short and succinct account of what transpired "sometime between October 20 and November 5, 1760"; the correspondence affirms that: "near to Ristigoush there is a village, with about one Hundred Mick Mack Indians; the heads of whom I made peace with by burying the Hatchet, giving them a few Blankets, & a little Provisions."[7]

British military officials and Mi'gmaq placed a hatchet in the territory, to solidify an agreement of peace and friendship.

But, the hatchet wouldn't stay put! Sometimes, looking out, that's all you can see. Other times, the hatchet gets so small it is tiny like a gift shop trinket. It's a tricky shifting; it is a restlessness that cuts things up (nets, trust, roads, funding).

The talks along the Restigouche River were more than mere formality or a show of military presence. For Mi'gmaq of Gespe'gewa'gi these talks are linked with the broader Peace and Friendship treaty process that was taking place in other parts of Mi'gma'gi at that time.[8]

treaties

In Mi'gmaw, treaties are referred to as *ungugamge'wel*, which means: "adding to an existing group or collectivity."[9] The treaties, for Mi'gmaq, were not intended to take away from their ways of living; rather peace and friendship were intended to serve as a type of co-existence. As expressed by Mi'gmaq knowledge holders, co-existence is not about living in a separate manner on territory. Rather, from within Mi'gmaq tradition, *a'tugwaqanigtug* (located in story), language speakers use the phrase *Amuj pa na na'talmawqatmu'ti'gw*, which directs us to find ways to live together with our differences, in the same space.[10] *Amuj pa na'* (we have to); *na'tal* (somehow); *maw* (together); *qatm* (live in a place) *'ti'gw*, (inclusive, all of us). The single term, *mawgatmu'ti'gw*, reflects a worldview animated by "interdependent relationships," and relations with each other and with place.[11]

interdependence

But the path that followed early treaty relations was not in keeping with *ungugamge'wel*, nor did the subsequent path foster *mawgatmu'ti'gw*. What followed the early treaty making relations has been well critiqued: treaties were dismissed, ways of coming together and relating were outlawed, and silences were imposed by Confederation, with its many colonial tools of assimilationist policies including successive waves of the *Indian Act*. Under Canada's legislative authority over "Indians and lands reserved for Indians," peace and friendship faltered and seemed to disappear within Canada's civilizing project.

treaties dismissed

The sun dropped behind the mountains. The light changed, the stories heated up.

In Mi'gmaq territory, similar to other places across Canada, there are ongoing questions, tensions, and (mis)understandings about ownership, rights, and responsibilities. Questions about "white lands" and "Indigenous lands" continue to hover around, within and between conversations, negotiations, and disputes. Crises and disputes continue to line up: the Salmon War (1981), the Listuguj Logging Blockade (1998), Oka Crisis (1990), Ipperwash Crisis (1995), Burnt Church Crisis (2000), and the Elsipogtog Anti-Fracking Blockade (2014).

When climbing Sugarloaf, just before reaching the summit, there is a rhythmic sound that you hear, before you see, the Canadian flag flying—red and white colours hit the air.

In the community, that's what many people remember about that day in 1981: a steady sound of helicopters, followed by their arrival. (The man with the braid was speaking.) Over 500 armed men, riot police, and game wardens descended on the First Nation community of Listuguj on June 11, and then a second raid on June 20, 1981.

The salmon war of 1981, the Incident at Restigouche, or—simply—the raids: these are a few of the names, or labels, used to refer to the violent encounters between Mi'gmaq and state authorities in their struggle over resources from the river.[12] However, names and naming is not a neutral process. Labelling may "reduce the complexity," "depoliticize," and act as way to "sanitize" incomprehensible acts of violence.[13] Stories told about violent encounters push beyond neat and tidy labels. Memories, brought to the surface with story, images, and metaphors may help to speak about "experiences for which there are no words in language."[14] Stories about lived experiences of violence may act as witness reflecting the ambiguity, the silences, and the complexity of loss, of trauma, and of ongoing colonialism.

In the moment when the tide shifts there is a stillness that you feel with your body. The wind picks up and hands snap into action. Some of the written records capture the moment when riot police and game wardens "stormed the reserve, seizing and destroying Indian fishing nets and violently arresting a dozen band members, minors among them."[15] Memories of violence seep into skin, edge our voices.

The rocks pressed into their bodies. Yet, the two strangers who met by chance leaned into the story, (almost) like friends.

"I was nineteen years old when the Raids happened. What I remember most was my father handing me the keys to the car, an old black Chevrolet, and telling me: 'If anything happens, open the trunk.' *(I looked at my father.)* 'Don't worry,' he said, 'they'll know what to do.'"

Memories of the raids, shared through stories, give voice to loss. In the community, there are other storytellers who continue to counter Canada's forgetting of events such as the raids. For instance, Wendell Metallic, the son of Alphonse Metallic, chief of Listuguj at the time of the raids, remembers when the *Sûreté du Québec* officers and game wardens stormed the community[16]. Wendell recalled:

> Pasna na newt gis gigilitatiteg wel migwitem wesgeiwasig'p ula mesgig construction ula highway'igutg, emipi'tawg. Na truck'l eteg'p'n, mesgigal. Mesgig company. Na poqji mawtesgatultieg, ula band office, poqji te'witaqal telex'l igtigel nnueigatil, right across the country, na

te'waqgitasigal, telex'l tujiw. Mesgig wejiagp tujiw, pugwelgp apoqan-
mati mesenmug piluwi'nnu'g aq mst nnueigatil je wegaw postung, na
same evening, nige talatigatitesnug egtu apiji pisgwitatij, maw malju-
wajg tujiw, 18-19 tewajultijig, pisgwitajig office, pugwelg truck'al egun-
mulgul gis gepsugwatesnug entrance nnueigati, gis wa'jemwatesnug, aq
gis mawitasnug pugwelog, nagalasnug wen gesgmnaq pesgwi'tatitigw
aq ugjit pas plamu na.

Transliterated: Once [police] arrived and left I remember well... there
was this construction company by the highway. They had these trucks,
a big company! We then started to gather at the band office. We started
to send off these telex's, to other First Nations, right across the country. What got a lot of help from different First Nations and even in
the States! That same evening we asked ourselves, what are we going
to do if they want to come back in? The young men at the time 18-19
years of age, came to the band office, and said "we have all these trucks,
we can close all the entrance points to the reserve, we can gather and
watch together, we will stop anyone before they get a chance to come
in," all for the salmon.

The violence of the raids marked the community. However, Mi'gmaq have remained determined to "stay on the river" and exercise *melgigno'ti aq assusuti* (power and authority to make decisions) over the salmon fisheries. The struggle to exercise this authority was not easy. From 1981 until 1993, a total of 79 fisheries violation charges were made against Mi'gmaq fishers; however, no one was found guilty. A moment of ambivalence in the national narrative: Aboriginal rights were enshrined in the Constitution, in 1982, while on the ground, Mi'gmaq were crimi-nalized for harvesting resources in their homelands.

In the aftermath of experiences of oppression, such as those that occurred along the Restigouche River, there are also stories that attest to a persistence and steadfast commitment to live in accordance with Indigenous practices, and ways of knowing and being. "Resurgence" has been described as part of our in-dividual and collective responsibilities in response to colonialism; resurgence is about rebuilding and transformation.[17] The concept of survivance describes, in part, our relations with, as opposed to dominating over, the natural world.[18] Similarly, from within Mi'gmaq intelligence, the phrase *aji'gna'sultinej* speaks about movement, about making and creating space, and strengthening oneself.

The prefix *aji* is about movement, action; the root verb *gna'sul* refers to strengthening; and the suffix *tinej* refers to all of us. Aji'gna'sultinej implies directing our actions toward strengthening ourselves, and our relations with others (places, peoples, all beings).

Stories—*a'tugwaqann*—that speak about rebuilding after loss, lend nuance and understanding to aji'gna'sultinej, working for and from within a place of strength. For instance, after the raids, elected and traditional leadership, fishers, and community members deliberately crafted a Mi'gmaq Fishing Law. This law, which still stands today, exists outside the authority of the *Indian Act* and recognizes Mi'gmaq inherent rights to access and to manage resources. For Mi'gmaq, it is a law animated by relations, intimate knowledge of territory, and connections.[19]

In addition to strengthening its ability to govern and manage, the community is also strengthening itself through collective remembering of the raids. For instance, each year, on June 11, the local school and government offices (band administration) are closed; there is a parade in the community, followed by a feast at the community centre; and on that day, fishers put their nets out for a full 24-hour period, rather than the usual night fishing conservation measure.

As well, the community has a commercial fishing enterprise resulting from the landmark 1999 Supreme Court of Canada *R v. Marshall* ruling. In *Marshall*, the courts recognized the validity of the treaties made in the eighteenth century, affirming Mi'gmaq treaty rights to earn a "moderate economic livelihood" from the use of natural resources. There is a vessel in the Listuguj fleet that carries the name *Mi'gwitetm 81*, which means "We Remember 81." And a second community vessel, which was built at the same time, in 2003, carries the name *Ugijt Sma'gnisg*, which means, "for the veterans, the defenders, and warriors."[20] These stories about rebuilding attest to the way Mi'gmaq are responding to colonialism through aji'gna'sultinej.

The men stood up. The one who wanted to make a documentary shifted, ever so slightly, from one foot to the other. "How do we reconcile our history?" he asked, bringing in his drone. "That's not the question," the man with the braid said. "The question is 'How do we witness and remember those events so we strengthen ourselves, and our relations?'" He poured the last bit of water from his bottle onto the rocks. The conversation slipped and lowered itself down into the crevice of the stone on which they sat.

The party is underway for Canada 150. Stories about those things that were taken, along with ways of strengthening, attest to ways of living and being, which have persisted despite Crown intrusions and incursions. In this article, we followed stories about and from the Restigouche River. These stories are not about smoothing out and flattening tangles of violence. Rather, there is a need to pay attention to particular places, to the stories that come from the rivers, the mountains, the hills, and our different ways of connecting, seeing, and being. Encountering memories, we may mourn and speak about loss, and we may also remember and celebrate our ways that strengthen all our relations, *ms't noqmaq*.

1. We thank the editors, as well as Sophie Tamas (Carleton University), for their critical and creative feedback.
2. For a description about how Mi'gmaq understand their relationship with Mi'gma'gi see Sable, Trudy and Bernie Francis (2012), *The Language of this Land, Mi'kma'ki*, Sydney: Cape Breton University Press, pp. 16, 21, and 22. There are several Mi'gmaw orthographies, and in this article we use the Listuguj orthography.
3. We draw on ideas about witnessing from Lee Maracle's *Celia's Song* (2014). A theme in this novel is that trauma requires witnesses and ceremonies to restore relations and bring about transformation.
4. www.pc.gc.ca/eng/lhn-nhs/qc/ristigouche/index.aspx
5. Beattie, Judith and Bernard Pothier (1996), *The Battle of the Restigouche*, Ottawa: Parks Canada- Canadian Heritage, p. 11; Macbeath, George B. (1954), *The Story of Restigouche*. Saint John: New Brunswick Museum, p. 8.
6. Gespe'gewa'gi Mi'gmawei Mawiomi (2016), *Nta'tugwaqanminen: Our Story Evolution of the Gespe'gewa'gi Mi'gmaq*, Halifax: Fernwood, p. 98.
7. Doughty, Arthur G., ed. (1916), *The Journal of Captain John Knox: Volume III—Appendix*, Toronto: The Champlain Society, p. 418.
8. Mi'gmawei Mawiomi. 'Ta'n Angugamgewei Gisa'tu'tip Migmewaq Gespe'gewa'gig aq Elege'uti Aqalasie'wei aq ta'n Telnapitoqa'tegeg Ugjit Gepegewei Gpnno'lewuti"/The Treaty Relationship between Mi'gmaq of Gespe'gewa'gig and the British Crown and its Implication for the Province of Quebec," (2009). Listuguj, Québec. Submitted to Government of Canada and Québec. Available online at: www.migmawei.ca. Mi'gmaq perspectives on treaties are explored in Battiste Marie, ed. (2016), *Living Treaties, Narrating Mi'kmaw Treaty Relations*, Sydney: Cape Breton University Press. Still today, the provincial Government of Québec does not recognize that Mi'gmaq, situated in Québec, and have rights stemming from pre-Confederation peace and friendship treaties.
9. *Nta'tugwaqanminen*, p. 97
10. Metallic, Alfred (Gopit) (2010), "Ta'n teligji'tegen 'nnuigtug aq ta'n goqwei wejgu'aqamulti'gw," York University. p. 101
11. Sable and Francis, p. 28.
12. Alanis Obomsawin gave voice to Mi'gmaq experiences of the raid in her film *Incident at Restigouche* (1984); Obomsawin returned to Listuguj in 2003 and recorded encounters from logging dispute in *Our Nationhood*.
13. Tamas, Sophie (2009), "Playing the Survivor: How (and if) women recover from spousal abuse," PhD Dissertation. Carleton University. pp. 129 and 142.

14. Hannah Arendt, quoted in Tamas, Sophie (2011), *Life After Leaving: The Remains of Spousal Abuse*. (city?) Left Coast Press, p. 150.
15. Notzke, Claudia (1994), *Aboriginal Peoples and Natural Resources in Canada*, Toronto: Captus University Publications, p. 64.
16. Testimonials about the raid are taken from an interview with Wendall Metallic, conducted by Fred Metallic in October of 2005 as part of Fred's PhD dissertation research.
17. Simpson, Leanne (2011), *Dancing on our Turtle's Back*, Winnipeg: ARP Books, p. 66.
18. Vizenor, Gerald (2008), "Aesthetics of Survivance: Literary Theory and Practice," *Survivance: Narratives of Native Resistance*, ed. G. Vizenor, Nebraska: University of Nebraska Press, p. 11.
19. National Centre for First Nations Governance (2010), *Making First Nation Law: The Listuguj Mi'gmaq Fishery* [National Centre for First Nations Governance], p. 2; the issue of competing jurisdictions and constitutional orders and ensuing debate over who is responsible for the salmon is explored by Ladner, Kiera (2005), "Up the Creek: Fishing for a New Constitutional Order," *Canadian Journal of Political Science*, 38.4. pp. 923-953.
20. www.listugujfisheries.ca

150 Years and Waiting
Will Canada Become an Honourable Nation?

Kiera L. Ladner

Canada@150 is a celebration of many things. But mainly it is a celebration of those stories that the government and well-meaning Canadians have decided are worthy of celebration—those that tell of a magnificent country from sea to sea to sea; that speak to Canada's history as a welcoming, tolerant, and multicultural nation built on a foundation of "Peace, Order, and Good Government"; that avoid (and/or apologize for) that which divides the country. While I acknowledge this is the Canada that is best known, this is not the Canada I know, or the Canada that I experience.

While most celebrate, I feel as though I have—to paraphrase Archie Roach— the "sesquicentennial blues."[1] This reflects my general state of unhappiness caused by my inability to escape that which I see as the Canadian problem. As such, Canada seems broken and not worthy of celebration. But it could be. Things could be different.

As Chief Justice of the Supreme Court Antonio Lamer stated, "let us face it, we are all here to stay."[2] But the fact that we are all here and all here to stay is not itself worthy of celebration. If we are to have something to celebrate—next year, five years from now, 100 years from now—then we must find a way to live together, as individuals and as nations, in a mutually beneficial and mutually agreeable manner. The question is: How do we do this?

In an episode of the *Vinyl Café* on May 23, 2015, broadcast from Prince George, Stuart McLean spoke of celebrating the town's 100th birthday against a backdrop of colonialism.

> As we look back on the last 100 years, I would also like to think that our Canadian story has, nevertheless, been one of slow—painfully

slow, inexcusably and unbearably slow—but slow as it is, movement nonetheless from solitude to community. And with that from injustice to justice.

Yes, we have stumbled, but in our stumbling ways I would like to think that we are stumbling towards the light.

And one hopes that with Prime Minister Harper's apology to the First Nations for the horrors of the residential schools that we are inching towards the long overdue dialogue when we Europeans will shut up and listen for the wisdom of the people who have lived on this land for so much longer than us . . .

We must remember, as we head off towards the next century, that the loudest voices are not necessarily the wisest.

And so, I would say today as we toast the last 100 years, our toast should contain a certain humility. A modest acknowledgement of our stumbles and our quiet determination to try harder, to listen carefully, to be thoughtful of new ways, to be sure that we are on the right side of history.[3]

Being on the right side of history requires understanding that an apology is not reconciliation, but rather is just the beginning. For Canada to be the mythologized nation it aspires to be, Canadians and Indigenous nations must renew and rebuild their relationship, and come to a mutually agreeable and mutually beneficial understanding of what it means to be Treaty people. It requires Canada to become an honourable nation.

We Are All Treaty Peoples

"We are all Treaty people." For several years now, this catchy slogan has been seen on billboards and buses in the Prairie provinces. Increasingly these words are being spoken in legislatures, universities, and at sporting events across the country as dignitaries read a statement acknowledging treaty, the Indigenous nation's territory on whose land they stand, and reminding those in attendance that we are all Treaty people. These words of acknowledgement might encourage many of those in attendance or watching at home to ponder momentarily, and these "moments of reconciliation" might even entice some to learn more. Still, these statements of acknowledgement are often criticized as they are read without a thought for what it means to live on someone else's land, without an understanding of Treaty, without intent to live as Treaty people, and without intent to implement Treaty. In a recent discussion with Myra Tait, I was reminded that those same people stand for the singing of *O Canada* and usually fail to see the contradiction in those gestures; at one moment calling for reconciliation of nations through a recognition of territory and Treaty whilst the next moment declaring that Canada itself is "native," and that it is a country or a people in its native land. Thus, reading these statements of acknowledgement is not an act of reconciliation and they do not create moments of reconciliation. A meaningful and transformative reconciliation can only be achieved through a reckoning of what it means to live respectfully in another person's home, and by renewing the spirit and the intent of treaties (where treaties exist).

Despite the slogan, we are *not* all Treaty peoples. Treaties do not exist in much of Canada—this despite a so-called modern treaty process where negotiations take ten to 20 years and result in 400-page legal agreements that are barely readable and hard to enforce (without further lining the pockets of an entire industry and a huge bureaucracy). Further, in those areas where treaties exist, it is necessary to understand that there are hundreds of treaties and that all treaties are not the same.

I come from Treaty 6 (1876). As I have been taught, Treaty 6 defines the relationship between, as well as the responsibilities and rights of, the signatory nations (Nēhiyaw (Cree) and Canada). In accordance with oral and written history, Treaty 6 is said to have provided the Queen's people with four Treaty rights: the right to live in *shared* Cree/Nēhiyaw territory (reserves were to be exclusively Nēhiyaw lands, the rest was to be shared); the right to farm in the shared territory (to use the land to the depth of one plough-blade) and to put up fences (the use of lumber/trees was permitted only when consent was granted by Nēhiyaw and a negotiated payment was received); the right to live without molestation (the idea of peace and good order between nations); and the right of settlers to govern themselves in Nēhiyaw/shared territory (more correctly, this should be understood as the right of the Queen to look after and govern her peoples, and that Nēhiyaw would not be expected to look after or govern the alien nation).[4] In exchange, Nēhiyaw would retain sovereignty, culturally and spiritually significant lands as well as other land allotments for their exclusive use, and the ability to access, use, and share responsibility for the lands that were shared. Beyond this, the Queen's representative made many promises which were to last as long as the sun shines, the grass grows, and the rivers run; these include: assistance in times of pestilence and starvation, education, healthcare (the medicine chest clause), five dollars per year, assistance in developing a new way of life (agriculture), and guns and ammunition.[5]

Despite the fact that the treaties were negotiated by representatives of the Crown (both prior to and post-confederation), and that these representatives typically and explicitly (as in the case of Treaty 6) acknowledged that these treaties do not diminish or cede Indigenous sovereignty, we now know otherwise. Settler colonialism has but one primary objective: Indigenous dispossession, or the acquisition of Indigenous lands and resources for the settlement and benefit of the alien nation. Despite treaty promises to respect and, possibly even protect, the sovereignty (and thus, the legal and political orders or traditions) of nations such as the Nēhiyaw, the reality is that the sovereignty of the Crown over all lands and peoples claimed by Canada is assumed and never questioned. Or at least never questioned by state actors. For example, the courts have demonstrated their unwillingness to question the assumption of Crown sovereignty and the presumed destruction of Indigenous sovereignties.

Not only did Canada run roughshod over Indigenous lands, acting as if it was the legitimate sovereign owner and authority, Canada eradicated Indigenous peoples from their homelands and attempted to destroy and dismember Indigenous nations. Though the treaties, from a Nēhiyaw perspective, afforded certain rights and protection to Indigenous peoples in their territories (shared and exclusive), their languages, political and legal orders, health and welfare, and their economic prosperity, in hindsight we know that Canada intended something very different. In 1876, while the Crown's representatives were negotiating Treaty 6, its government was consolidating existing pre-Confederation legislation into the *Indian Act*. Simply stated, the purpose of this legislation was (and still is) to "protect, civilize, and assimilate" any Indigenous peoples that survived colonization into the—formerly alien but now seemingly native—Canadian nation.[6] It is through this legislation that Canada (in association with the Catholic, Methodist (United), and Anglican Churches) established residential schools and pursued its genocidal policies.

Despite the fact that treaties seem to have been little more than a land grab and a means of securing peace with Indigenous peoples to enable "settlement" without the "frontier wars" that plagued the US, there is no doubt that Canada did agree to something much more. Perhaps the sesquicentennial is an opportunity for Canada to reconcile itself with its past and to recreate itself as the nation that many Canadians envision it to be. This is a big ask—but perhaps the time is right for Canada to reconcile itself with the treaties and its history as a nation on stolen lands. The treaties offer a promise and a great potential for renewal of Canadian and Indigenous nations, and for a meaningful, transformative, and political reconciliation. Many would argue that they are the only way forward as there is no possibility for reconciliation without addressing the complex issues of mutual benefit, mutual responsibility, and mutual sovereignty. Despite the fact that treaty implementation is a road less travelled, the evidence is clear and there is a moral imperative to do so. Further, as the move to address treaty issues in New Zealand attests, dealing with the spirit and intent of treaties and there implementation is likely to be of benefit to both Indigenous and non-Indigenous.

The Roadmap: Canada's Constitutional Guidelines

The sesquicentennial marks the anniversary of the *British North America Act, 1867* (also known as the *Constitution Act, 1867*). Not all of Canada's Constitution is 150 years old. Canada's Constitution has been the subject of numerous amendments, judicial interpretations, and great national debates—most of which failed to achieve any significant constitutional renewal. In the 1970s, '80s, and '90s, Canada was engaged in great constitutional debates over Québec, the future of the country and its institutions, and possibilities for its renewal (such as through the creation of the *Canadian Charter of Rights and Freedoms*).

Much like the discussions that led to Confederation, constitutional discussions were primarily an elite-driven process. That said, non-state actors were able to challenge this process and force their way into these discussions, or at the very least get their issues onto the constitutional table. Fearing the impact that Prime Minister Pierre Trudeau's Canadian Charter of Rights and Freedoms could have on Indigenous rights, as well as their legal and political orders, and seeing an opportunity to have their rights as Indigenous peoples and/or under treaty protected in the Constitution, Indigenous peoples took to the streets. They used a myriad of ways to raise their issues, to demand that these issues be dealt with, and to demand a seat at the table. These included pursuing legal challenges in several Canadian jurisdictions and the United Kingdom, lobbying, demonstrating on Parliament Hill, and engaging in international protests.[7] In the end, these efforts did result in the constitutionalization of Indigenous rights within Canada.

However, despite everything that was done to educate non-Indigenous leaders about Indigenous issues, and to get stronger protections for Indigenous rights in the Constitution, most Indigenous leaders viewed the *Constitution Act, 1982* as a failure. In fact, it was opposed by all major Indigenous organizations (the only exception was the Métis Association of Alberta), and many are still critical for its supposed domestification of Indigenous rights and responsibilities.[8] Nevertheless, the Canadian Constitution does afford protection and recognition to existing Aboriginal and treaty rights in Sections 25 and 35.[9]

More limited than desired, Section 35 only recognizes and affirms existing Aboriginal and treaty rights arguably as *sui generis* rights, originating within Indigenous nations and/or the agreements between Indigenous nations and settler society, while Section 25 affords these rights further protection from the Charter. As James (Sákéj) Youngblood Henderson, Marjorie Benson, and Isobel Findlay argue, "the spirit and the intent of section 35(1), then, should be interpreted as 'recognizing and affirming' Aboriginal legal orders, laws, and jurisdictions unfolded through Aboriginal and treaty rights."[10] In essence, this is an argument of treaty federalism or treaty constitutionalism.[11] Simply put, treaty constitutionalism refers to the idea that Section 35 offers protection to Indigenous legal and political orders (often described as constitutional orders). These Indigenous constitutional orders are themselves encrypted as Aboriginal and treaty rights, and therefore provided constitutional recognition.[12]

The ability to exercise these legal and political orders, or to exercise an Indigenous nation's sovereignty and/or jurisdiction within its territory, is protected (really recognized and affirmed) in Canada's Constitution. Further, given the constitutionally protected promises of Canada's non-interference with Indigenous sovereignty in treaties such as Treaty 6, it would follow that Indigenous nations have a legitimate claim to a sphere of jurisdiction that is independent of federal and provincial jurisdictions. Thus, to follow this argument to its logical end, Section 35 and the Indigenous legal and political orders it recognizes, affirms and protects, and Aboriginal and treaty rights should therefore be read as parallel to federal and provincial jurisdictions as outlined in the *Constitution Act, 1867*. That is to suggest that while Section 91(12) establishes that the Federal Government has jurisdiction over sea coasts and inland fisheries, Section 35 recognizes a parallel or Indigenous jurisdiction over fisheries in cases such as that of the Mi'kmaw, given that their treaty with the Crown never infringed on Mi'kmaw fishing rights or Mi'kmaw jurisdiction over its fishery.[13] Viewed in this way, Section 35 recognizes and affirms Indigenous jurisdictions that were protected by treaty as either a exclusive jurisdiction similar to those defined under Sections 91 and 92 as federal and provincial jurisdictions, or as a concurrent or shared federal/provincial jurisdiction similar to those established in Sections 93-95 of the *Constitution Act, 1867* (for example, agriculture).

Not surprisingly, given Canada's unwillingness to live up to even the simplest of treaty promises (land entitlement, health care, and support for building a new prosperity/livelihood post-buffalo), the courts have charted their own path and have interpreted Section 35 extremely narrowly.[14] As Brain Slattery suggests, as a "static [Canadian] constitutional order," Section 35 is being defined by the courts in accordance with the "dominant viewpoint" that contends:

> the Crown's acquisition of sovereignty over indigenous peoples and their territories gave rise to Aboriginal rights in the Common law of Canada. These rights continue to exist in their original form unless or until extinguished by legislation, voluntary surrender or other valid process. As legal rights, Aboriginal rights are cognizable and enforceable in Canadian courts. However, Aboriginal peoples have to prove the existence of these rights on a case-by-case basis in order to gain judicial protection.[15]

In large part, this has led to a criminalization of Indigenous people who are simply exercising their Aboriginal and treaty rights. Such was the case for those individuals involved in the Van der Peet trilogy of Aboriginal rights cases, who faced criminal charges for "illegally selling" fish, despite the fact that people from west coast nations such as the Sto:lo have no treaties limiting their rights, and have always engaged in trading and/or selling fish and other products (this economy existed prior to colonization).[16] Similarly, Donald Marshall Jr. was forced to pursue a treaty rights case after being charged for fishing and selling eels illegally (without a license) despite the terms of the 1725 treaty with the British in which the Mi'kmaw clearly did not "cede" their right to fish or limit their responsibility for (jurisdiction) the fishery.[17]

From the very outset, the courts have used their powers to reinforce colonialism and thus, the assumption of Crown sovereignty. The Court has been fixated on asserting Canadian sovereignty while denying Indigenous sovereignty, and in so doing have provided interpretive principles that deny the transformative potential of Section 35. In *R v. Sparrow* the Supreme Court created an interpretive test that allows governments to infringe on Section 35 rights if done for "a valid legislative objective" (essentially suggesting that a government could do as it pleases so long as they justify it).[18] In the Van der Peet trilogy, the Court further limits Aboriginal rights to include only those that are deemed to be "integral to a distinctive culture" and to have been practiced since contact (the idea of "permafrost rights").[19]

As Kiera Ladner and Caroline Dick suggest, "with the *Van der Peet* decision, the court took Indigenous rights jurisprudence down a new and regrettable path, choosing to embrace a cultural justification for Aboriginal rights."[20] This is because, in reframing the court's conceptualization of Aboriginal rights, Chief Justice Lamer states:

> In my view, the doctrine of Aboriginal rights exists, and is recognized and affirmed by s. 35(1), because of one simple fact: when Europeans arrived in North America, Aboriginal peoples *were already here*, living in communities on the land, and participating in distinctive cultures, as they had done for centuries . . .[21]
>
> [Therefore] the test for identifying the Aboriginal rights recognized and affirmed by s. 35(1) must be directed at . . . identifying the practices, traditions and customs central to the Aboriginal societies that existed in North America prior to contact with the Europeans.[22]

While this interpretation of Section 35 is exceedingly problematic for numerous reasons,[23] what is important for the purposes of this paper is that the Supreme Court attempts to reinforce Canadian sovereignty and its claim that subsumed sovereignty is unquestionable. It does so by stating that that the purpose of recognizing and affirming Aboriginal (and treaty) rights in Section 35(1) of the *Constitution Act, 1982*, was to "achieve a reconciliation of the pre-existence of Aboriginal societies with the sovereignty of the Crown."[24]

As Russel Barsh and James (sákéj) Youngblood Henderson explain, this reconstruction of the purpose of Section 35(1) as reconciliation is "a doctrine plucked from thin air."[25] Beyond this, it is a thoroughly problematic doctrine, which is demonstrative of "The manner in which the Supreme Court obfuscates and denies First Nations their rights and the opportunity to re-establish their own constitutional orders (as well as the ability to realize the nation-to-nation relationship agreed upon)."[26] This is so because the courts have attempted to undermine claims of Indigenous sovereignty, by suggesting that culturally grounded Aboriginal rights claims have already been reconciled with the sovereignty of the state and have, thus, fortified the ultimate sovereignty of the Crown. Worse yet, the Supreme Court has further fortified Crown sovereignty (not that this was needed) by advancing the position that Canadian sovereignty is immutable, and that any possible remnant of Indigenous sovereignty was either subordinated or merged with Canadian sovereignty.[27]

Ten years prior to Canada's last big birthday (125), Canada entered an age of constitutional supremacy and postcolonial potential with the creation of the *Constitution Act, 1982*. Since this time, the courts have had the ability (and the duty) to understand Sections 25 and 35 as having encrypted Indigenous legal and political orders within the Canadian Constitution—affording them both constitutional recognition (Section 35) and a constitutional shield (Section 25) to protect them from any further infringement or derogation. But the courts have not heeded this challenge. The courts have failed to use Section 25 and they have failed to interpret Section 35 in a manner that accommodates Indigenous understandings of treaties and Aboriginal rights. While the courts have managed to peel back its colonial mentality in Aboriginal title cases, enough to question the assumption of absolute Crown ownership, in other instances it has created new law and plucked legal reasoning and interpretive principles out of thin air in an attempt to further entrench Crown sovereignty and deny the spirit and intent of treaties such as Treaty 6.

It is without question that the logics of Anglo settler colonialism that are being upheld by the courts need to be challenged. As John Borrows reminds,

> If the assertion of European sovereignty did not extinguish Aboriginal title, neither did it extinguish Aboriginal jurisdiction and authority over such lands. The same continuity of social organization that enabled Aboriginal people to establish title should also undergird the recognition of Aboriginal governance in subsection 35(1) of the *Constitution Act, 1982*.
>
> So-called underlying Crown title is a fiction . . . More work is necessary to expunge all discriminatory vestiges of underlying Crown title that have submerged Indigenous sovereignty. Until that day occurs, Canada remains a deeply colonial state based on the vilest of discriminatory tenets.[28]

The Bones We Are Thrown

The *Constitution Act, 1982* should have charted a new path to decolonization. But the mere thought that the Constitution could even be used for decolonization is extremely questionable. Instead, the courts have used Section 35 for the reification of settler colonial logics. But is it without potential? Or, can we make something out of the bones that have been thrown?

I have a deep-seated problem with reconciliation as it is commonly understood post-Truth and Reconciliation Commission and in conjunction with Canada@150. Understanding reconciliation as something that is achieved through education, or with an apology, or through a corporation's hosting of a cultural awareness training day, or through the utterance of words welcoming folks at a hockey game to someone else's territory, is dangerous. Reconciliation is not a great big hug. For reconciliation to be meaningful it needs to be transformative. It needs to transform the relationship that exists between treaty nations. It needs to transform the day-to-day lives of Indigenous peoples. It needs to give meaning to the reconciliation that was negotiated in the treaties whereby nations agreed to live together in a shared territory with mutual respect and mutual benefit. It requires settler society to acknowledge and accept some really uncomfortable truths about how they acquired their privileges. It requires settler society to cede the privilege it has denied Indigenous peoples.

Although I have problems with reconciliation as it is typically understood by Canadians, it nevertheless holds incredible potential. This is because Section 35 reconciled Aboriginal constitutional orders with the Canadian constitutional order (and its claims of sovereignty) by placing Indigenous constitutional orders within the framework of constitutional supremacy.[29] It is as Henderson, Benson, and Findlay suggest:

> The *Constitution Act, 1982* has reconciled Aboriginal peoples with constitutional supremacy, the structural division of the imperial sovereignty. It vests their constitutional rights in the constitution of Canada, which is different than the Lamer Court's interpretation of constitutional rights reconciliation of Aboriginal peoples with the sovereignty of the Crown. While treaty relationships still remain vested with the imperial Crown, the treaty and Aboriginal rights are now vested in the Aboriginal peoples of Canada. The constitution of Canada replaces the indivisible sovereignty.[30]

Thus, viewed as an interpretive principle, reconciliation could help realize both the Indigenous understanding of Section 35 and the implementation of treaty constitutionalism. It holds this potential, however, only if we can escape the colonial mentality that upholds the sovereignty of the Crown and its understanding of colonization tantamount to conquest, for these are but "Canadian tales" and neither reflect Canadian history nor assist Canada in realizing its postcolonial potential. That is to say, reconciliation holds potential only if the Court-spun Canadian fantasy of reconciliation known as merging the remnants of Indigenous sovereignty under the sovereignty of the Crown is understood for what it is: a myth or a fantasy of a "master race."[31]

The same holds true for another other one of the Court's interpretive principles—the honour of the Crown. Briefly, the idea of the "honour of the Crown" was discussed in the 1990 *Sparrow* decision, wherein the Court "held that the constitutional affirmation of Aboriginal rights should be interpreted in the light of the fundamental principle of the honour of the Crown."[32] The idea of the honour of the Crown appears again in the 2004 *Haida Nation v. British Columbia* decision, when Chief Justice McLachlin stated:

> The government's duty to consult with Aboriginal peoples and accommodate their interests is grounded in the honour of the Crown, which must be understood generously. While the asserted but unproven Aboriginal rights and title are insufficiently specific for the honour of the Crown to mandate that the Crown act as a fiduciary, the Crown, acting honourably, cannot cavalierly run roughshod over Aboriginal interests where claims affecting these interests are being seriously pursued in the process of treaty negotiations and proof . . .
>
> The controlling question in all situations is what is required to maintain the honour of the Crown and to effect reconciliation between the Crown and Aboriginal people with respect to the interests at stake. The effect of good faith consultation may reveal a duty to accommodate.[33]

For Slattery, the Supreme Court's decisions pertaining to the Crown's "Duty to Consult" with First Nations (the *Haida Nation* and *Taku River* and *Mikisew* decisions), ushered in the new paradigm characterized by a "generative constitutional order," which obligates Canadian governments to engage in consultation (even in cases where an Aboriginal or treaty right have yet to be "established"), to manage conflict in their relationship with Indigenous peoples, and to work toward reconciliation.[34]

Though Slattery claims that these decisions overcame the assertions of Canadian sovereignty that have plagued the Supreme Court's interpretation of Sections 25 and 35, Slattery's line of argument is not convincing. In *Haida*, Chief Justice McLachlin states, "Treaties serve to reconcile pre-existing Aboriginal sovereignty with assumed Crown sovereignty," and suggests "sovereignty claims [will be] reconciled through the process of honourable negotiation."[35] Just because the court is careful in its framing of Crown sovereignty as *de facto* (factual control—legitimate or otherwise), rather than *de jure* (resulting from a legitimate assertion) as Slattery has argued, does not mean that the Court has successfully overcome its own inability to question Canadian sovereignty or recognize the constitutionality of continued Indigenous sovereignties.

The presumption of sovereignty and exclusive jurisdiction has been challenged in Canadian law,[36] and in legal and constitutional scholarship.[37] As Patrick Macklem explains:

> How is it that the settling nations were able to make claims of sovereignty over these people, claims that form the historical backdrop to contemporary assertions of Canadian sovereignty over Canada's First Nations? In the debates surrounding Confederation, there was no discussion whatsoever about the propriety of asserting Canadian sovereignty over Canada's indigenous population. Sovereignty was assumed, and its assumption is basic to the Canadian legal imagination. Aboriginal peoples in Canada are currently imagined in law to be Canadian subjects, or Canadian citizens. Parliament is imagined to possess the ultimate law making authority over all its citizens. A fundamental assumption underpinning the law governing Native people is that Parliament has the authority to pass laws governing Native people without their consent.[38]

Clearly, the exercise of unfettered power is anything but honourable. Notwithstanding the limitations caused by the problematic construction of sovereignty, the demands of the honour of the Crown, along with the necessity of reconciliation, may provide Indigenous peoples and Indigenous understandings of the Constitution(s) a glimmer of hope and opportunity. This opportunity is likely more comparable to a finger hold on a cliff face rather than Slattery's paradigm shift, but it is an opportunity nonetheless. As such, and as Peter Russell has remarked on several occasions, you make the most of every possible opportunity, and when the court throws you a bone you harvest the marrow and use everything they give you.[39] This leads me to ask: What do we do with these bones?

If we take reconciliation and the honour of the Crown as interpretive frameworks and guiding principles, it is possible to begin the process of addressing treaty implementation. The treaties initially served to reconcile jurisdictional responsibilities of Indigenous nations and the settler society, and arguably provided the Crown with recognition of its derivative sovereignty. Derivative sovereignty, such that its authority and ability to govern in another's territory was in essence derived from both its claim of dominion over its own subjects and the delegation of such responsibilities by Indigenous nations, as established through treaty or de facto recognition. Viewed in this light, reconciliation is essentially an interpretive framework for the implementation of treaty constitutionalism, such that it instructs both the court and the government to further engage in political reconciliation, and thus implementation without the limitations imposed by the standard interpretation of Section 35 or the defense of absolute Canadian sovereignty (de facto or de jure).

The Court has instructed that the doctrine of the honour of the Crown is the underlying principle in the relationship between the Crown and constitutional rights of Indigenous peoples in Canada. As Henderson states:

> The purpose of this doctrine is a constitutional therapy for the ill of colonization on Aboriginal peoples, striving to include Aboriginal peoples in Canadian governance and to moderate historical disadvantage and exclusion ... It creates a method for the courts to identify and to resolve the unstable relation between assumptions about governmental power and their policy and practices and constitutional rights of Aboriginal peoples. It allows for an imaginative and noble effort to construct and reconstruct power into honourable governance.[40]

The courts have said that Canadian governments are responsible for upholding the honour of the Crown in their relationships with Indigenous peoples within Canada. This need goes far beyond fiduciary obligations or a responsibility to consult with Indigenous peoples. Upholding the honour of the Crown or governing honourably is required to manage the treaty relationship between Indigenous nations and the settler state. As an interpretive principle or guideline for understanding and implementing Sections 25 and 35 of the *Constitution Act, 1982*, honour of the Crown obligates governments to act with honour and integrity when engaging in reconciliation, and providing for the renewal of Indigenous constitutional orders, which were encrypted as Aboriginal and treaty rights in 1982.[41]

Further, understanding that the purpose of Section 35 is reconciliation requires the reconciliation of Canadian federalism and its jurisdictional claims (Sections 91-95 of the *Canada Act, 1867*) with Indigenous constitutional orders and their jurisdictional claims as encrypted in Section 35 within the rubric of constitutional supremacy. Reconciliation is essentially an interpretive framework for the implementation of treaty constitutionalism such that it instructs both the court and the government to further engage in political reconciliation and thus implementation without the limitations imposed by the standard interpretation of Section 35 or the defense of absolute Canadian sovereignty (de facto or de jure).

This means that federalism must operate constitutionally; it cannot be assumed that all jurisdictions are already occupied by federal and provincial governments, or that Sections 91-95 leave no room for Indigenous governments other than as responsibilities delegated through negotiation.[42] Looking beyond this standard interpretation and acknowledging that Section 35 reconciles competing sovereignties means that upholding the honour of the Crown requires Canadian governments to facilitate the renewal of these constitutional orders as co-autonomous jurisdictions (not subordinate *Indian Act* "governments").

To put it another way, as part of a constitutional dialogue, reconciliation and the honour of the Crown do not integrate Indigenous governments into Canadian federalism, but instead acknowledge Indigenous sovereignty as recognized, protected, and reconciled under the Canadian Constitution, and other governments as having the responsibility of upholding the honour of the Crown in their relationships with the treaty order. Simply put, Canadians and their governments must make jurisdictional space for Indigenous nations.

The problem is that this takes political will. Perhaps Canadians, their government, and their courts will somehow discover that political will while celebrating Canada@150. Or perhaps it is simply time to become the nation that Canadians aspire to be.

1. Archie Roach is an Aboriginal singer-songwriter from Australia whose music raised the voice (and explained the blues) of Indigenous peoples during Australia's bicentennial in 1988. Roach, Archie (2009) "Bi-Centenial Blues," *Music Deli Presents Archie Roach—1988*, Sydney Australia: ABC Music.

2. Delgamuukw v British Columbia, 3 SCR 1010 (1997).
3. McLean, Stuart, "The Roundabout," *The Vinyl Café*, CBC Radio, May 23, 2015: www.cbc.ca/news/canada/british-columbia/in-one-of-his-final-performances-stuart-mclean-spoke-about-canada-s-treatment-of-indigenous-people-1.3984918
4. Johnson, Harold (2007), *Two Families: Treaties and Government*, Saskatoon: Purich Publishing; Epp, Roger (2008), *We Are All Treaty People*, Edmonton: University of Alberta Press; Asch, Michael (2014), *On Being Here to Stay*, Toronto: University of Toronto Press; Cardinal, Harold and Walter Hildebrandt (2000), *Treaty Elders of Saskatchewan: Our Dream Is That Our Peoples Will One Day Be Clearly Recognized as Nations*, Calgary: University of Calgary Press.
5. Ibid.
6. Tobias, John L. (1991), "Protection, Civilization & Assimilation," in *Sweet Promises*, ed. J.R. Miller, Toronto: University of Toronto Press, pp. 127-144; Eberts, Mary (2014), "Victoria's Secret: How to Make a Population of Prey," *Indivisible: Indigenous Human Rights*, ed. Joyce Green, Halifax: Fernwood Publishing, pp. 144-165.
7. See Ladner, Kiera L. (2003),"Rethinking the Past, Present and Future of Aboriginal Governance," *Reinventing Canada*, ed. J. Brodie and L. Trimble, Toronto: Prentice Hall, for a discussion of this history.
8. Ladner, Kiera L. and Michael McCrossan (2008), "The Road Not Taken: Aboriginal Rights after the Re-Imagining of the Canadian Constitutional Order," *Contested Constitutionalism: Reflections on the Canadian Charter of Rights and Freedoms*, eds. James B. Kelly and Christopher P. Manfredi, Vancouver: UBC Press, pp. 263, 267.
9. See Sections 25 and 35 of the *Constitution Act, 1982*.
10. Henderson, James (Sakej) Youngblood, Marjorie L. Benson, and Isobel M. Findlay (2000), *Aboriginal tenure in the constitution of Canada*, Scarborough: Carswell, pp. 432-434.
11. Henderson, James (sákéj) Youngblood (1995), "First Nations Legal Inheritances in Canada: the Mikmaq Model," 23(1), *Manitoba Law Review*.
12. Ladner and McCrossan, 2008.
13. Ladner, Kiera L. (2005), "Up the Creek: Fishing for a New Constitutional Order," *Canadian Journal of Political Science* 38, no. 4: 923-53 R v. Marshall (no 1 & 2). 1999. 3 S.C.R. 456 & 533.
14. Henderson et al., *Aboriginal tenure in the constitution of Canada*, pp. 432-434; Macklem, Patrick (2001), *Indigenous Difference and the Constitution of Canada*, Toronto: University of Toronto Press; Barsh, Russell Lawrence and James Youngblood Henderson (1982), "Aboriginal Rights, Treaty Rights, and Human Rights: Indian Tribes and 'Constitutional Renewal'" *Journal of Canadian Studies* 17, p. 59; Turpel, Mary Ellen, "Aboriginal Peoples and the Canadian Charter of Rights and Freedoms," *First Voices: An Aboriginal Women's Reader*, eds. P. Monture and P. McGuire, Toronto: Innana Publications, pp. 358-373; See also Barsh, Russell and James Sakej Henderson (1997), "The Supreme Court's Van der Peet Trilogy: Naive Imperialism and Ropes of Sand," *McGill Law Journal* 42, p. 993; Murphy, Michael (2001), "Culture and the Courts: A New Direction in Canadian Jurisprudence on Aboriginal Rights," *Canadian Journal of Political Science* 34, p. 109.
15. Slatterly, Brian (2005), "Aboriginal Rights and the Honour of the Crown," *Supreme Court Law Review* 29, p. 434.
16. R v. Van der Peet, 2 SCR 507 (1996); R v. NTC Smokehouse Ltd., 2 SCR 672 (1996); R v. Gladstone, 2 SCR 723 (1996).
17. R v. Marshall (No 1), 3 SCR 456 (1999); R v. Marshall (No 2), 3 SCR 533 (1999).
18. R v. Sparrow, 1 SCR 1075 (1990).

19. R v. Pamajewon, 2 SCR 821 (1996); See Borrows, John (1997), "Frozen Rights in Canada: Constitutional Interpretation and the Trickster," *American Indian Law Review* 22 (1), pp. 37-64.
20. Ladner, Kiera L. and Caroline Dick (2008), "Out of the Fires of Hell: Globalization as a Solution to Globalization—An Indigenous Perspective," *Canadian Journal of Law and Society* 23, p. 63.
21. *Van der Peet*, para 30.
22. Ibid., para 44.
23. See Ladner and Dick, 2008, p. 71; See Michaelsen, R.S. (1991), "Law and the Limits of Liberty," *Handbook of American Indian Religious Freedom*, ed. by C. Vecsey, New York: Crossroad, p. 116, as cited in Barsh and Henderson, 1997, p. 1000; See Tully, James (1995), *Strange Multiplicity: Constitutionalism in an Age of Diversity*, Cambridge: Cambridge University Press, as cited in Murphy, 2001, p. 117.
24. *Van der Peet*, para 31.
25. See Michaelsen, 1991, p. 116, as cited in Barsh and Henderson, 1997, p. 1000.
26. Ladner, Kiera (2009), "Take 35: Reconciling Constitutional Orders" *First Nations First Thoughts*, ed. Annis May Timpson, Vancouver: UBC Press, p. 285.
27. For a discussion of sovereignty and the manner in which the courts have dealt with it, see Ladner and McCrosssan, 2008, p. 278-280, or Borrows, John (2015), "The Durability of Terra Nullius: Tsilhqot'in Nation v. British Columbia," *UBC LAW Review*, 48(3), 701-742; see also Mitchell v. MNR, 1 SCR 911, para. 125 (2001); Tsilhqot'in Nation v. British Columbia, SCC 44 (2014); Grassy Narrows First Nation v. Ontario (Natural Resources), 2 SCR 447 (2014).
28. Borrows, 2015, p. 742.
29. Ladner, 2009, p. 288.
30. Henderson, Benson, and Findlay, *Aboriginal tenure in the constitution of Canada*, pp. 433-434.
31. Churchill, Ward (2001), *Fantasies of the Master Race: Literature, Cinema, and the Colonization of the American Indians*, San Francisco: City Light Publishers.
32. Slatterly, 2005, p. 433; see also *Sparrow*, 1 SCR 1075, para 4-5. Please note, "Honour of the Crown" was used in this context in Calder v. British Columbia (AG) SCR 313 (1973), although it appeared as early as 1909 in Province of Ontario v. Dominion of Canada 42 SCR 1 (1909).
33. Haida Nation v. British Columbia (Minister of Forests) 3 SCR 511, para 5-6 (2004).
34. Slatterly, 2005 p. 436; Mikisew Cree First Nation v. Canada (Minister of Canadian Heritage), SCC 69 at para 50 (2005).
35. *Haida Nation* 3 SCR 511, para 20.
36. Mitchell v. MNR, 1 SCR 911 (2001); R v. Pamajewon, 2 SCR 821 (1996).
37. Henderson, James (Sakej) Youngblood (1995), "First Nations Legal Inheritances in Canada: the Mikmaq Model," *Manitoba Law Review* 23, p. 1.
38. Macklem, Patrick (1993), "Ethnonationalism, Aboriginal Identities, and the Law," in *Ethnicity and Aboriginality: Case Studies in Ethnonationalism*, ed. Michael D. Levin. Toronto: University of Toronto Press, p. 18.
39. Peter Russell, personal correspondence.
40. Henderson, James (sákéj) Youngblood (2009), "Dialogical Governance: A Mechanism of Constitutional Governance," *Saskatchewan Law Review*, 72(1), p. 47.
41. Ibid. Also see: Ladner and McCrossan, 2008.
42. Jhappan, Radha (1995), "The Federal-Provincial Power-grid and Aboriginal Self-Government," *New Trends in Canadian Federalism*, eds. Francois Rocher and Miriam Smith, Peterborough: Broadview Press.

WE WILL HELP EACH OTHER BE GREAT AND GOOD

Louise Mandell

The Dark Times

I first heard the land question in 1977. I was hired by the late and great Grand Chief George Manuel to represent the Union of BC Indian Chiefs (UBCIC) before the West Coast Oil Ports Inquiry. Oil companies were competing for the winning proposal to build a port to service the traffic of oil by tankers. The late Godfrey Kelly, a Haida elder, was testifying on a panel about the risks. I recall him speaking in such a loving way about the Haida, who, he said, are the most fortunate people on Earth because of the wealth of seafood that they harvest year-round at their doorstep on Haida Gwaii. He mentioned each species of fish, how they are prepared and preserved, and he gave the Haida names of bays and inlets, which sounded like music to me. Then he politely raised the land question. In my memory, I heard it said in a number of ways: "Where's the government's bill of sale? Where is the government's authority to put the fish at risk, when the Haida never surrendered our land?"

One way that the land question sounds, or perhaps the voice of the land question at its deepest is: How did Canada's laws come to cover Indigenous territories when our own laws already lived there?

This was a question waiting to find me. I was born in 1947, into a Toronto-based Jewish family—the first post-holocaust generation. The accident/miracle of my birth prepared me for what was in store. As a young girl, I was drawn to Holocaust stories like a moth to light. How was it possible that six million Jewish people and other victims, including Poles, Romas, Soviet prisoners of war, gays and lesbians, Catholic priests and Christian pastors, Jehovah's Witnesses, handicapped and mentally challenged people, gypsies, courageous resistors—how could all these people be murdered, with such meticulous premeditation, apparently done under cover of law? I grew up knowing a powerful law. We needed to hide this law. I knew without being told that it was not safe to tell a stranger that I was Jewish. I should say I'm Canadian. I never heard my parents tell anyone we were Jewish.

I went to law school. I wanted to know justice. I wanted to reveal, to stand up, to speak up, to protect, and to correct. I was a legal thinker with a finely tuned mistrust of the law. I knew that laws are not neutral. I was open to seeing disguised racism and prejudice in the law, or its application. I was open to seeing how well-meaning people and governments could be guilty not because they violated laws, but for following laws that should never have been made in the first place. And I knew to look for ancient laws and ways of knowing, which are hidden for protection.

I found myself on a road with Indigenous people who included me in their journey. My Indigenous friends and family had travelled a long time before I joined them. I read elegant letters and petitions to the Queen and heads of government written by their ancestors dating back to the turn of the century. Here is just a portion of what the chiefs had to say in the 1910 Memorial, which was presented by the Interior Tribes of British Columbia to Premier Sir Wilfrid Laurier:

> The "real whites" we found were good people. We could depend on their word, and we trusted and respected them. They did not interfere with us; not attempt to break up our tribal organizations, laws, customs. They did not try to force their conceptions of things on us to our harm. Nor did they stop us from catching fish, hunting, etc. They never tried to steal or appropriate our country, nor take our food and life from us. They acknowledged our ownership of the country, and treated our chiefs as men . . . They had made themselves (as it were) our guests. We treated them as such, and then waited to see what they would do . . .
>
> With us when a person enters our house he becomes our guest, and we must treat him hospitably as long as he shows no hostile intentions. At the same time we expect him to return to us equal treatment for what he receives.
>
> Some of our Chiefs said, "These people wish to be partners with us in our country. We must, therefore, be the same as brothers to them,

and live as one family. We will share equally in everything half and half in land, water and timber, etc. What is ours will be theirs, and what is theirs will be ours. We will help each other to be great and good."[1]

Then, the chiefs recounted their dispossession, denial of their ancient laws, disrespect for their legal orders, and "demanded that our land question be settled by the governments concluding Treaty with them." They said: "As long as what we consider justice is withheld from us, so long will dissatisfaction and unrest exist among us we will continue to struggle to better ourselves."[2]

Now their demand for a treaty was a simple request that Crown governments follow their own law. The law governing the British colonizers was international law, which became part of the common law first formally expressed in the Royal Proclamation of 1763, requiring Crown government to recognize the laws and occupation of Indigenous peoples to their territories as legal rights, and then the incremental perfection of Crown sovereignty through treaty. In central Canada, these principles were formed in consultation with Indigenous peoples through inter-societal negotiations.[3] The Treaty of Niagara (1764) and other agreements had woven relationships of peace, friendship, and respect into the Canadian constitutional fabric.[4] The Imperial Crown pledged itself to honour these agreements for as long as the sun shines, the rivers flow, and the grass grows.[5]

This foundational law governing the relationships between the newcomers and Indigenous peoples also found expression in the Canadian Constitution. The *British North American Act, 1867* assigned to the Federal Government under Section 91(24) exclusive legislative jurisdiction over "Indians and lands reserved for Indians," vesting authority in Canada "to safeguard one of the most central of Native interests—their interest in their lands."[6] Section 109 makes provincial title and its benefits subject to Aboriginal title.[7]

In an 1888 decision of the Privy Council, *St. Catharine's Milling and Lumber Co. v. The Queen*, relying on s. 109, the Court held that the "lands, mines, minerals and royalties" become available to provinces as a source of revenue only when Aboriginal title has been dealt with by treaty. It follows that if Aboriginal title has not been dealt with, such lands and resources are not available to the province as a source of revenue.[8]

So much for the law. This law was ignored in BC and then forgotten. The few treaties which were concluded in the pre-Confederation period on Vancouver Island, these too were ignored and then forgotten. It was not until 1964, when a pre-Confederation treaty was raised as a defense in a hunting charge, that the Court ordered the Crown back into the treaty relationship.[9]

The rule of law was not upheld when it came to Crown dealings with Indigenous peoples because of greed, ignorance, and prejudice. Joseph Trutch served as chief commissioner of lands and works before the Terms of Union, and became the first lieutenant governor of BC. He articulated the policy of denial and dispossession, which would become the blueprint for Indigenous/Crown relationships in BC for over a century.

> The Indians really have no right to the lands they claim, nor are they of any actual value or utility to them; and I cannot see why they should either retain these lands to the prejudice of the general interests of the Colony, or be allowed to make a market of them to Government or to individuals.[10]

Canada's founding myths were riddled with racism. In a paper I prepared for the 40th Anniversary of the UBCIC,[11] I described this phenomenon as "The Ghost"—the thing from the past that is troubling the present; that continues to cause a disturbance and subvert the goals of Indigenous peoples, and all of Canada, as long as it is being fed.

> Most Ghosts begin their sojourn in fine fettle. This Ghost was a stowaway in the enterprise of European colonial imperialism. It landed in the newly claimed British Columbia with the first settlers. The Ghost created the kind of thing that a Ghost is really good at building: Illusions. The first illusion: By planting the flag, the Crown claimed complete ownership and jurisdiction over everything.
>
> The Ghost then began to spread lies about the Indigenous peoples who had stewarded the land beautifully and successfully for generations and centuries. As with all good lies, they came with many alternative fallbacks. The Ghost's mantra is denial and its favourite illusion is *terra nullius*: The land was unoccupied; or, if occupied, it was by people who were not really civilized; or, if civilized, they did not have concepts of land ownership; they did not have real laws; or, if they did have laws or rights, they were all extinguished; or, if not extinguished, the land they used was just small, spotty, postage-sized parcels (just the size of reserves, actually). And the Ghost was a boaster. The

Crown represented a superior race of people with a real government which made real laws and had real state power. The Ghost whispered: "First Nations are primitive—without laws. The Crown is superior— worthy of the greatest respect and absolute deference."

There were, however, other voices that softened and ameliorated the hubris and manifest destiny extolled by the stowaway. The Queen would not take the land and then just turn her back on the Indigenous people. No, the Crown would bring great benefits to the natives, the Ghost proclaims. The Crown was committed to bringing civilization to these less evolved and less fortunate races. The benevolent goal of assimilation would take time. Meanwhile, the Crown would watch over her Indians and protect them. They were better off living on Indian reserves, but the children should be separated from the regressive influence of their native communities, put in residential schools where they would be suitably educated. Until the natives were fully civilized, they could continue their hunting, gathering and fishing for food; as long as the Crown did not need the land and resources for development. The Crown would let them. The Crown was honourable.[12]

The Crown's weapon for dispossession was Crown law, and the target was the "Indian race." Many academics in the world today argue that there is no such thing as race, genetically speaking.[13] The Indian race is a social construction forced on Indigenous peoples by those who wanted to take their land and then have them disappear.[14]

Colonial legislation declared that the lands in BC, and the mines and minerals, belong to the Crown in fee. The province then developed the legislative machinery to alienate unceded lands and resources without treaty—without consultation, agreement, or compensation; without respect. Initially, the Federal Government rose to dispute the province's claim and Canada went so far as to disallow British Columbia's *Crown Lands Act, 1874* because it dealt with lands assumed to be the absolute property of the province. The Federal Government appears to have agreed that this was a dubious assumption given that Aboriginal title was likely "an interest other than that of the province" under s. 109.[15]

But ultimately, the province and the Federal Governments aligned in a common racist policy and purpose. The land and resources were not seen as territories that were governed and managed by Indigenous peoples, but as "raw materials" outside any legal structure, in a wilderness of inexhaustible natural resources without ecological limits. Real time, they say, began when the settlers rescued the land from disorder and brought civilization to the savages. The theft equation was turned around. Instead of the appearance of the newcomers benefiting from the lands and resources they had wrestled from Indigenous peoples, the idea was presented as a presumed exchange of benefits.

The Federal Government pursued assimilation goals, under successive *Indian Acts*. Meagre reserves were established for the Indigenous peoples who by a miracle survived introduced diseases. Indigenous laws and legal orders were outlawed—there was a prohibition against the potlatch, against the sun dance. Cultural destruction was legalized. Ceremonial regalia were confiscated. Indigenous People could not leave the reserves without a permit. Many elders today recall a time when they could not congregate unless reading a bible or singing hymns. Access to justice was foreclosed. The *Indian Act* made it illegal to raise money to go to court to fight the land question, or for lawyers to assist. This legal barrier remained in place for the next quarter of a century.[16] Eventually residential schools carried out this policy of cultural eradication.

The Truth and Reconciliation Report (TRC) stated simply: "The Canadian Government pursued this policy of cultural genocide because it wished to divest itself of its legal and financial obligations to Aboriginal People and gain control over their land and resources."[17]

Indigenous Law: Let There be Light

It is impossible to speak of this history without taking account of the intense spirituality that underlies resistance by Indigenous peoples, which is a powerful force of persistence—to stand up for what is not right, and to stand up their laws and legal orders.

Over time I started to see contours of Indigenous laws and legal orders I had no idea existed—we expect a parallel universe between legal orders. I didn't recognize Indigenous laws and legal orders initially because they were so unlike western legal traditions. But even though they are not always called laws, what I witnessed is certainly law. Law is rule-directed behaviour toward others, involving legal norms; an expression of values and principles that hold permanence and universality, capable of being applied to new circumstances that arise. Indigenous legal orders emerge from worldviews that deny the dominion of humans over the *worldviews*

Earth, and of one human over another. These legal orders include the Creator, supernatural beings, helpers and healers, ancestors and decedents, and a culture transmitting orally across generations embodying principles to live by giving rise to rights and responsibilities.

Indigenous legal traditions connect to the essential aliveness that courses through the universe, uniting us with that creative power that lives on the Earth, inside the Earth, in the fish, the animals, birds and insects, the stones, the trees— in each of us. In this social arena, ethics are guided by fundamental principles to be deeply respectful of the recognition that the other is important and has value; that everyone has value and something to give to society, that the different gives something to the whole, that the smallest ant can be our teacher. We are reminded of the way we can live in balance with each other and all living things. Every living thing has as much right to live on Earth as humans.

Indigenous laws contain layers of cultural knowledge, which in part come from and are shaped by observations, deliberations, and knowledge of the natural world and its cycles. Human activity is embedded in a larger world, and draws analogies from the natural world to regulate behaviour.

Laws flow from worldviews that are culturally informed. All legal traditions are culturally informed.

> [L]aw is one of the ways we govern ourselves. It is law that enables large groups of people to collectively manage themselves. Law is a process, not a thing, and it is something that people actually do. Since our legal orders and law are entirely created within our cultures, it can be difficult to see and understand law in other cultures. In other words, law is societally bound.[18]

There are as many distinct and diverse Indigenous legal traditions as there are distinct and diverse Indigenous nations. Prior to the arrival of settlers, Indigenous nations held and developed sophisticated laws to govern their territories, manage relationships, organize behaviour, and resolve disputes.

Aboriginal peoples were the earliest practitioners of law in Canada. Living in communities and nations across the land, they developed norms and practices to govern their social interaction, regulate trade, resolve disputes and govern the relationships between different nations. The diverse traditions of different Aboriginal peoples grew into highly developed systems of law that guided Aboriginal societies for centuries in the governance of community, the environment and relationships between people. Passed down through the generations in stories, songs, ceremonies and practices, these legal traditions reflect the unique experiences of different Aboriginal peoples and communities, embodying the values and beliefs and resonating with their cultures.[19]

Delgamuukw v. British Columbia[20] was a leading case testing (and affirming) the existence of Aboriginal title, including Indigenous laws. In the opening statement on behalf of the Hereditary Chiefs, Chiefs Gisday Wa and Delgamuukw put it this way:

> For us, the ownership of territory is a marriage of the Chief and the land. Each Chief has an ancestor who encountered and acknowledged the life of the land. From such encounters came power. The land, the plants, the animals and the people all have spirit-they all must be shown respect. That is the basis of our law.
>
> The Chief is responsible for ensuring that all the people in his House respect the spirit in the land and in all living things... My power is carried in my House histories, songs, dances and crests. It is recreated at the Feast when the histories are told, the songs and dances performed and the crests displayed. With the wealth that comes from the respectful use of the territory, the House feeds the name of the Chief in the feast hall. In this way the Chief, the territory, and the Feast become one. By following the law, the power flows from the land to the people through the Chief, by using the wealth of its territory.[21]

The land is the culture. The chiefs on behalf of the houses use the land for strengthening their relationships. The histories, songs, crests, even food gathered from the land encode the laws and are authority for present and future actions.

Indigenous laws occupy the land with love. Listen to how Chief Wayne Morris described Saanich law in practice, in his testimony in a leading case involving pre-Confederation treaties on Vancouver Island:

> [A practice that] is looked at as real sacred, and if we chop a cedar tree down or cut a cedar tree down, we thank them for the use of the tree itself, and thank them for that use and then for what they're going to do for us. The deer or the elk, or whatever we're hunting for, we than[k]

> the Creator for the meat ... it's going to be a medicine for our people, our families, our ancestors gone before us ...
>
> Our way of life, discipline, respect, all of that that ... came from ... the teachings that my parents and my grandparents, what they gave to me. What they gave to me was something that I look at as an unwritten treasure because none of our teachings are written, they're all—they're all from the heart.[22]

"All my relations"—I have heard these words spoken countless times: closing meetings, closing speeches, closing prayers. Those words create a relationship with other people, with animals, with the land. To have health it is necessary to keep all these relations in mind. We are all connected and interconnected.

Indigenous laws are the law of this land.

Constitutional Renewal: Coming Out of the Shadows

The date is 1980. UBCIC is awakening to the news around the patriation of the Constitution.[23] I am in the office of Grand Chief George Manuel, then President of UBCIC and the World Council of Indigenous Peoples. He has a brown paper envelope, which he opens. It is obvious that we should not have this document in our possession. It is a confidential briefing to the Federal Cabinet, without identified authorship.

> There is likely to be a major effort by Canada's Native Peoples to win national and international support (especially at Westminster) for their stand against patriation. If the Native Peoples press forward with their plans and if they succeed in gaining support and sympathy abroad, Canada's image will suffer considerably. Because Canada's Native Peoples live, as a rule, in conditions which are very different from those of most other Canadians, as sample statistics set out below attest, there would be serious questions asked about whether the Native Peoples enjoy basic rights in Canada:
>
> a. Indians have a life expectancy ten years less than the Canadian average;
>
> b. Indians experience violent deaths at more than three times the national average;
>
> c. approximately 60% of Indians in Canada receive social assistance;

d. only 32% of working-age Indians are employed;
e. less than 50% of Indian homes are properly serviced;
f. in Canada as a whole, the prison population is about 9% Native, yet Native Peoples make up only 3% of Canada's population. In 1977, there were 280 Indians in jail per 100,000 population, compared to 40, the national average.

Native leaders realize that entrenching their rights will be enormously difficult after patriation, especially since a majority of the provinces would have to agree to changes which might benefit Native Peoples at the expense of the provincial power. They therefore demand an entrenchment of Native rights before patriation.[24]

George sounded the alarm. Prime Minister Trudeau's proposal for constitutional change, he said, is "beyond consultation, beyond administrative battles with government, beyond petty politics. It is hitting at the roots—the very existence of the Indian Nations." The White Paper policy (1969) remained a threat. George feared that assimilation would be completed by Crown governments acting together, eliminating constitutional protections for Indigenous peoples, and subjecting treaties to Canada dominance without consent of the Indigenous treaty partners. In spite of Canada's colonial conduct, the BNA Act, and the treaties gave Indigenous peoples a toe hold to achieving a better future based on recognition of their title and rights, laws and legal orders.

Over 100 chiefs at a UBCIC assembly in November 1980 stated their position on the proposed constitutional reform:

> Indian Nations in Canada were never conquered. European traders, and in later years, settlers, were made welcome in the land and environment that was alien to them. Throughout years of European settlement and expansion, Indian nations sought a mutual accommodation, one that would permit a bountiful land to be shared to the benefit of all . . .
>
> Indian Nations understand the constitution to be a pact among founding peoples, among which we include ourselves. We understand our special constitutional relationship with the federal government to be in the nature of a partnership with the federative system, which was intended to permit us to survive and prosper as Indian Nations, while contributing to Canada's total development.[25]

Indigenous peoples across Canada got on track to oppose the patriation of the Constitution. The Constitution Express left the station in December 1980, rolling across the country, picking up support and supporters, making headlines day after day. The train arrived in Ottawa, and leaders then headed to the United Nations in New York, to European cities and to London. The message all along the way was that Britain should not accede to Canada's request to patriate the Constitution without their consent and participation in constitutional renewal. Canada, they said, included Indigenous nations who were not consulted and did not consent.

These strong voices created a wave of political momentum. A provision recognizing Aboriginal and treaty rights was inserted, taken out, and, responding to public outcry, was then amended and reinserted in the Canada Bill, which was sent to Westminster.

The debate about the *Canada Act* in Britain was a debate like no other in Canada's history. When the BNA Act was passed in 1867, the debates were silent about Indigenous peoples. Likewise, there was silence through each of the fourteen times, up until 1975, when amendments to the BNA Act were debated in Westminster. But when the *Canada Act* was debated, 27 of the 30 hours used to debate the *Canada Act*, in both houses, dealt with Indigenous peoples in Canada. MP David Ennals summed up what all this was about:

> The Indians are not asking for material assistance from us or for money. They are asking us to ensure, as we promised, that their constitutional status is protected in the renewed Canadian Federation. They have asked us for the constitutional tools to enable them to develop their own nationhood, their own forms of self-government and to preserve their traditions.[26]

Our Interconnected Legal Journey

I had the privilege to litigate the land question, which is a quest to make space for the reassertion of Indigenous laws in a landscape where these laws were deliberately erased. This litigation primarily centred around the interpretation of rights guaranteed by Section 35, and constitutional obligations that are the other side of the coin. It was in the context of this litigation that I finally heard the Crown governments' answer to the land question. I can describe the force that defiled the rule of law, that smothered Indigenous laws and silenced them. This force was spelled out in Crown governments' defences in litigation where Aboriginal title and rights, and treaty rights were placed before a court, seeking remedies. The force went under the name of extinguishment. Extinguishment is a rash assertion of Crown sovereignty.

Section 35 of the *Constitution Act* reads: "Existing aboriginal and treaty rights of the aboriginal peoples of Canada are hereby recognized and affirmed."[27] When this wording was agreed to, premiers and their advisors were confident that the word "existing" meant "extinguished."[28]

R. v. Sparrow[29] was the first case that went to the Supreme Court of Canada (SCC) interpreting Section 35. Crown governments argued that s. 35 was an empty box; that Indigenous peoples have no constitutional rights until a Court determination, or an agreement concluded with the Crown. The Court disagreed, and held that "existing" means the opposite. It means, "unextinguished," and that the constitution holds the promise of recognition and reconciliation.

The legal debate then turned to whether Aboriginal title has been extinguished in BC. The racist founding myths translated into legal doctrines: the doctrine of discovery and terra nullius. The doctrine of terra nullius is premised on the false inferiority of Indigenous peoples being without real laws. The doctrine of discovery is premised on the false superiority of Crown governments and dominance of Crown laws.

These legal doctrines were supported by the racial stereotyping of Indigenous peoples. I am sensitive to stereotyping. The Holocaust did not begin in the gas chambers; it began with the racial stereotyping of Jewish people, who were said to be less than fully human—even children were taken by cattle car to slaughter. For Indigenous peoples, the stereotype was of an Indian race without laws; a race of people on the low rung of a fictitious ladder of social Darwinism's ascension to civilization. The projected message to Indigenous peoples, which strikes at the heart, is: You have no laws. You need to be changed. You are not good enough as you are.

I go into some detail now to reveal the extinguishment arguments the Crown advanced in all of their declining alternatives, and the stereotypes that silenced Indigenous laws. These ideas are systemic and are embedded in Crown law. Law cannot be separated from or understood apart from the culture. Canada's colonizing cultures carry these cultural ghosts in all their legal forms. They continue to haunt our law, as courts, parliaments, and legislatures reproducing troubling stereotypes about Indigenous peoples in their modern processes and decisions. Each of these fearful manifestations must be brought into the light to be eradicated.

I begin this litigation story with the ending. The startling reality is that, after over 40 years of litigation, the Crown failed to come up with one legal defense for the decades of denial, dispossession, and misery. All Crown extinguishment arguments were rejected by the SCC.

In *Delgamuukw*[30] the Hereditary Chiefs were deliberate in how they framed the case. The chiefs were prepared to bring to court evidence of their laws and legal orders, songs, crests, oral histories, their stewardship and occupation of the land, and they challenged Crown governments to prove the legal basis upon which the Crown claimed complete title and exclusive jurisdiction over their territories in the absence of treaty.

Extinguishment arguments, which the Crown governments raised in the *Calder v. British Columbia*[31], were re-argued in *Delgamuukw*, and new extinguishment arguments came forward.

1. The Settled Colony Theory

The Crown argued that, at the time of the assertion of Crown sovereignty, the land was unoccupied. Not literally, but "Indians," as they were called, were deemed too low on the scale of social organization to have effective control of their territories. The stereotypes included that Indigenous peoples law-making powers were extremely limited. They lived more by custom and tradition than by the rule of law (ironically). Their societies were portrayed as primitive, without concepts of land ownership. They did not have laws that were cognizable at common law.[32]

Their ancestral homelands were terra nullius—empty land, empty of its real owners, of Indigenous laws, culture, oral traditions, ways of learning, knowing, and teaching.

2. The Theory of Crown Supremacy

The Crown argued that Indigenous laws and ancestral title to all of BC were extinguished by operation of the Crown's laws—by regulations; by implication; by the setting up of the machinery for the Crown to grant interests in land and resources to settlers; by creating Indian reserves; by effect, when the Crown granted tenures inconsistent with the continuation of Aboriginal title. The theory goes that Crown laws are dominant, superior, and parliament is supreme. This is a story based on parliament's presumed authority, and the assumed power to override Aboriginal title and rights, Indigenous laws and legal orders, even the terms of treaties, solemnly agreed to last as long as the river flows.

Crown stereotyping of Indigenous peoples wove through cross-examination of witnesses and final arguments. The law arrived with the first colonial legislature and governors—that warfare, disease, scarcity and inter-tribal conflict constantly altered the living arrangements of Indians, but the arrival of the Europeans and their association with western sovereignty broke up the low-level social order and gave Indians the evolutionary advantages of the Western experience. It was manifest destiny for Western societies to bring literacy, technology, opportunities, democracy, economy, and Christianity to less civilized peoples to promote their civilization.

These arguments were all rejected by the SCC in *Delgamuukw*. The Court went back to the basics. As a matter of highest constitutional principle, the SCC held that Aboriginal title has not been extinguished in BC. Aboriginal title is a communal right to land, with jurisdictional and economic components.

In *Delgamuukw*, the Court issued a lengthy judgment that provided a reasoned framework for reconciliation based on title recognition and the implementation of Indigenous laws. But, because of a pleadings defect, the Court did not grant the remedy sought, which was a declaration of Aboriginal title.

i. Extinguishment by Litigation

Ghost-like, the Court's voice often roars as a whisper across the legal landscape. We know it is there, and saying something significant, but it can be difficult to detect its existence in the material realm. The Crown reinvented extinguishment in a new argument that was litigated in the *Tsilhqot'in Nation v. British Columbia* case[33]. The new extinguishment argument was a weave of a different sort. Like an invisible mantle, the Crown clothed itself in robes that deceive, hide, and trick us about the truth of its character. Just like a ghost.

The Crown argued that Indigenous laws and Aboriginal title only exist over small spots on the landscape. Indigenous peoples must prove their title; Crown sovereignty is presumed. If Indigenous peoples fail to prove occupation (which, under the theory, can only ever be small spots on their territories), the effect is that the land becomes, by law, the absolute property of the Crown. The ghost causes the courts to extinguish title when legislative or executive acts fail to accomplish this same purpose.

The stereotype traps Indigenous people with no nationhood in a false sense of isolation. Their laws are not territorial. Peoples who share the same language, laws, customs, and traditions, and historically the same territory, exist politically only as Indian bands, not nations, living on small parcels of land, segregated and separated from each other and other areas of their territory.

The Crown's extinguishment argument was adopted by the BC Court of Appeal in *Tsilhqot'in*,[34] but rejected by the SCC in one sentence: "There is no suggestion in the jurisprudence or scholarship that Aboriginal title is confined to specific village sites or farms," and the Court rejected governments' arguments that a territorial claim of Aboriginal title is legally untenable. The SCC declared Aboriginal title over a large portion of Tsilhqot'in territory.[35]

ii. Extinguishment by Treaty

The issue came before the Court in *Chartrand v. British Columbia*.[36] Relying on the written text of a pre-Confederation "Douglas Treaty," which states that the Kwakiutl surrendered their land, the Crown argued that the Kwakiutl (and by extension, other Douglas Treaty nations) extinguished title to their territory in exchange for hunting and fishing privileges exercisable at the goodwill of the Crown, for the setting aside of reserve lands, and for blankets and a small amount of cash.[37]

The written text of the treaty was drafted by the Crown with no evidence whatsoever that it was ever translated for, let alone accepted by, the Kwakiutl. The treaty was never implemented; it was ignored. The Kwakiutl were decimated by disease. The lands reserved under treaty have to this day not been surveyed as required by the written text of the treaty. What has been survived for the Kwakiutl is a mere 0.2 acres per person compared to an average of 33.02 acres across Canada.[38]

All this is background to the decisions made by the minister of forests in 2007, which were judicially reviewed in the *Chartrand* case. The province granted approval to Western Forest Products Ltd. to remove over 14,000 hectares of private forest lands from a tree farm licence, amounting to about 8 percent of Kwakiutl territory, and to approving a forest stewardship plan enabling the company to manage about 50 percent of Kwakiutl territory for the company's forestry purposes, all over the objections of the Kwakiutl. The province's position was that the treaty extinguished Aboriginal title.[39]

The Kwakiutl Nation is stereotyped as being unsophisticated and stupidly naïve. Why would any nation surrender all of their territory in exchange for harvesting rights, which they were in control of at the time of the treaty under their own laws, in order for these rights to be regulated under Crown laws? Why would any nation want reserve lands comprising a fraction of their territory for villages that were then firmly in their possession? What was it about those dull, wool Hudson's Bay blankets that the Kwakiutl wanted, when they had their own beautiful button blankets? The Court agreed that the Kwakiutl raised a *prima facie* case that they did not intend to extinguish title to their territory by agreeing to the treaty, and found that consultation about the decisions, based on the Crown assuming extinguishment, was flawed.[40]

The SCC has rejected all Crown extinguishment arguments based on doctrines of superiority or inferiority. The Court said: "The doctrine of *terra nullius* (that no one owned the land prior to European assertion of sovereignty) never applied in Canada, as confirmed by the *Royal Proclamation* of 1763."[41] The purpose of s. 35(1) "is to foster the ultimate reconciliation of prior Aboriginal occupation with *de facto* Crown sovereignty."[42] The existing status quo is illegal.

Reclaiming our Country's Strength: The Golden Thread

We stand in the middle of a transition where we cannot remain standing. Something new has entered our hearts as a country. It is in our blood. We could easily be made to believe that nothing has happened, and yet we have changed, as a house changes when a guest has entered.

After more than 20 years of discussion and negotiation, the United Nations Declaration on the Rights of Indigenous Peoples (UNDRIP) was adopted and endorsed by Canada. UNDRIP is the most comprehensive, universal international human rights instrument providing a human rights framework for justice for the specific historical, cultural, and social circumstances of Indigenous peoples. Racial stereotyping is firmly rejected. The principles of Free Prior Informed Consent, and the right to self-determination are fundamental to this human rights framework.[43]

As a country, we laid our sorrows and burdens next to each other before the TRC, which resulted in recommendations that address this question: How do we heal a national wound that has caused such a spiritual rupture? Every citizen has been assigned decolonizing work to do. Schools and Universities have accepted the challenges of re-education, since schools contributed to the problem in the first place. Great new stories are emerging—new partnerships, innovations, and opportunities—new relationships. Canada committed to implementing the TRC recommendations, including UNDRIP, as a step in remediating the cascade of misery and trauma resulting from an illegal colonial history.[44]

Turning and returning, the SCC went back to the law governing Canada's beginnings, recognizing and confirming Indigenous laws and legal orders as the golden thread of the common law. The Court held that Indigenous laws are inherent collective rights, which pre-existed and survived the assertion of Crown sovereignty. These laws and legal orders have never been extinguished and find expression today in the Constitution. The oldest roots of the living tree of Confederation, these ancient laws survived colonization and must be heard when decisions are made about how the land and resources are used and managed.

What we have learned from Indigenous people who spoke to the highest Court, and what has emerged from the SCC, is that there is room for more than one. Our country is an amalgam of diversity. Our strength is unity in our diversity. We are a multi-juridical order. This is legal pluralism—different cultural narratives, worldviews, titles, and jurisdictions co-existing and operating on the same landscape. This is not one order creating space for another, nor is it one order adopting elements of another, but rather the recognition of plurality of orders, and the need to create mechanisms for their healthy, harmonious interaction.

The constitutional imperative is reconciliation. But what does reconciliation mean for Indigenous laws and legal orders?

Hannah Arendt, a Jewish intellectual who witnessed the Eichmann trial, observed that justice can falter here, as anywhere. But she asks: Can we have confidence that it ultimately will prevail? She asks this question in the context of observing collective rights and collective wrongs, where Jewish people were targeted because they were Jewish. The same can be said for Indigenous peoples who were targeted because they were Indigenous. In both cases, what happened to them was radical evil. Indigenous peoples were thought to be without laws. They were trucked to residential schools to take the Indian out of the child, to make way for their assimilation and civilization. Arendt argues reconciliation cannot be found in a legal solution. Reconciliation, in this context, demands a political reconstitution; a public acknowledgment of the evil done; reparations and amends made; a rejection of the world as it is; a revolutionary break, and then a new beginning on different collective terms. This involves all of us who share this history, the land and the future.

Reconciliation is a verb—speaking, listening, hearing, learning, loving, changing, and healing. These are the powerful forces that change the world. Dreaming, making amends, grieving, imagining—taking off our masks. These are the forces capable of making a revolutionary break and a new beginning on different collective terms. Reconciliation is about coming to terms with reality and history, and affirming one's belonging to this reality as one who acts in it.

It's time to exorcize the ghost and tear its invisible garb. We have an alternative. We can array this country with more viable, golden threads, pulled from Indigenous sources, deeply woven throughout the fabric of our law.

Canada's Constitution is cooperative federalism, comprised of three, not two, orders of government: federal, provincial, and Indigenous. Canadian law is only one system of authority. Another source of authority is found within Indigenous legal systems. Indigenous sovereignty existed before contact, and this order of government stands on its own. Its powers do not derive from the Constitution.

Indigenous peoples implementing Indigenous laws are the conditions for bringing about reconciliation. Human rights are the ground that will rebuild Canada and will lead to reconciliation. Crown recognition is not required to possess land and resources, and exercise governmental law-making authority. These powers already exist within Indigenous communities and nations. Section 35 cannot revitalize Indigenous laws until self-determination informs the approach.

With the help of Indigenous laws, we can all take care of this beautiful land we share. The Earth speaks its symptoms to us. We are causing climate change. This geological age we are blessed to live in, beginning about 50,000 years ago, could last another 50,000 years or so, but we are putting too much carbon, heat trapping gasses into the air. The National Climate Assessment, written by top US scientists, recently released its report concluding that global warming is already having widespread effects across the US, causing droughts and wildfires, worsening hurricanes, and flooding coastal areas. We must de-carbonize. We perish, or we live together.

We cannot do what is necessary for Mother Earth with righteous rage, guilt, anger, fear, or fighting, because none of these emotions has enough power to move people to do what is necessary for the planet. The one emotion that makes us as generous and irrational as we need to be is love. The love I speak of is contained in Indigenous laws. I have spent my legal life, working in the company of people who love their territories, who lovingly named each bay and inlet, mountain and meadow. Love is remembering our place in the story of Creation. The Indigenous stories take us back to a remembering, all the way back to our origins, to when the gods first shaped humans out of clay, to when animals spoke with people, to when the sky and water were without form, and all was shaped by such words as "let there be light."[45] These legal orders embrace a belief system and sense of connectedness—an ancient consciousness, intense and holy, honouring the spark of the divine inside all life. These legal orders are engulfed in ceremony, remembering that all things are connected—that humankind is not separate from nature; that there are natural laws beyond human laws, and ways above ours that must be honoured and respected. These legal orders embody principles to live by: respect, reciprocity, harmony, and humility.

These legal orders carry wisdom about going beyond the racism of the colonial experience to reconciliation. In the 1910 memorial presented by the Interior Tribes to Sir Wilfrid Laurier, these ancestors saw the newcomers as partners—part of their family. This vision derives from their legal orders related to bringing resolution and peace by making opposing sides close kin—extending the love and concern for those you have wronged, or who have wronged you, recognizing relatedness instead of "us" and "them."

The journey of Indigenous peoples has led us back home to be better guests in the territories of Indigenous nations and on Mother Earth.

Stories are the crux of healing and at the heart of every ceremony. We cannot erase the past, but we can change the future by the stories we tell. We need new stories that are relevant to the love of the land—a new narrative that would imagine another way.[46]

So I will end by telling this story, which begins like this. As we approach Canada's 150th anniversary, Indigenous laws and legal orders are welcomed back on the Canadian landscape. We are fortunate to have these laws in these dangerous and challenging times. A constitutional conference is underway—the unfinished business of Confederation. Crown and Indigenous governments are developing new processes and agreements giving effect to Free Prior Informed consent, effective shared decision-making, and revenue- and benefit-sharing arrangements. Process certainty for proposed new development is fast becoming a reality.

New dispute resolution mechanisms are transforming an adversarial democracy into relationships based on a mutual recognition of each other's nationhood, and a respectful affirmation of obligations. The country is decarbonizing and decolonizing.

Indigenous laws and legal orders, with their sacred connections and transmuted ancient consciousness, have jurisdictional space to grow and deepen. The story is about Canada, and it is inspiring.

1. Chiefs of the Shuswap, Okanagan and Couteau Tribes, 1910 Memorial to Sir Wilfrid Laurier, Premier of the Dominion of Canada, from the Chiefs of the Shuswap, Okanagan, and Couteau Tribes of British Columbia. Kamloops, August 25, 1910. Archives of Canada, Laurier Papers, Series A Correspondence, July 22-August 30, 1910. MG 26-G, Vol. 641, 174,070-174,077.

2. Ibid.
3. Dennis, Matthew (1993), *Cultivating a Landscape of Peace: Iroquois-European Encounters in Seventeenth-Century America*, Ithaca: Cornell Press; Dowd, Gregory Evans (2002), *War under Heaven: Pontiac, the Indian Nations, and the British Empire*, Baltimore: John Hopkins University Press : Downes, Randolph C. (1940), *Council Fires on the Upper Ohio: A Narrative of Indian Affairs in the Upper Ohio Valley until 1795*, Pittsburgh: University of Pittsburgh Press; Havard, Gilles (2001), *The Great Peace of Montreal of 1701: French-Native Diplomacy in the Seventeenth Century*, trans. Phyllis Aronoff and Howard Scott, Montréal: McGill-Queens University Press; Hinderaker, Eric (1997), *Elusive Empires: Constructing Colonialism in the Ohio Valley, 1673-1800*, Cambridge: Cambridge University Press; Jacobs, Wilbur R. (1966) *Wilderness Politics and Indian Gifts: The Northern Colonial Frontier, 1748-1763*, Lincoln: University of Nebraska Press; Jennings, Francis (1984), *The Ambiguous Iroquois Empire: The Covenant Chain Confederation of Indian Tribes with English Colonies from Its Beginnings to the Lancaster Treaty of 1744*, New York: W. Norton & Co.; Jennings, Francis (1988), *Empire of Fortune: Crowns, Colonies and Tribes in the Seven Years' War in America*, New York: Penguin Books; Jennings, Francis, et al., eds. (1985), *The History and Culture of Iroquois Diplomacy: An Interdisciplinary Guide to the Treaties of the Six Nations and Their League*, Syracuse: Syracuse University Press Jones, Dorothy V. (1982), *License for Empire: Colonialism by Treaty in Early America*, Chicago: University of Chicago Press; Merrell, James H. (1999), *Into the American Woods: Negotiators on the Pennsylvania Frontier*, New York: W W Norton & Co.; MacLeod, D. Peter (1996), *The Canadian Iroquois and the Seven Years' War*, Toronto: University of Toronto Press; Merritt, Jane T. (2003), *At the Crossroads: Indians and Empires on a Mid-Atlantic Frontier, 1700–1763*, Chapel Hill: University of North Carolina Press; Nelson, Larry L. (1999), *A Man of Distinction among Them: Alexander McKee and British-Indian Affairs along the Ohio Country Frontier, 1754-1799*, Kent:Kent State University Press; Nester, William R. (2000), *"Haughty Conquerors": Amherst and the Great Indian Uprising of 1763*, Westport: Praeger; Shannon, Timothy J. (2000) *Indians and Colonists at the Crossroads of Empire: The Albany Congress of 1754*, Ithaca: Cornell University Press; Snapp, J. Russell (1996), *John Stuart and the Struggle for Empire on the Southern Frontier*, Baton Rouge: Louisiana State University Press.
4. Borrows, John (1994), "Constitutional Law From A First Nations Perspective: Self Government and the Royal Proclamation," 28 *U.B.C. L. Rev.* 1
5. For an example of treaty-making on the Canadian Prairies see Ray, Arthur, J.R. Miller, and Frank Tough (2000), *Bounty and Benevolence: A History of Saskatchewan Treaties*, Montréal: McGill-Queen's University Press.
6. Delgamuukw v. British Columbia, 3 SCR 1010, 1997 CanLII 302, para 176 (1997).
7. *Constitution Act, 1867* (UK), 30 & 31 Vict., c. 3, ss. 91(24), 109, reprinted in RSC 1985, App II, No. 5
8. St. Catherine's Milling and Lumber Co. v. The Queen, 14 App. Cas. 46 (P.C.) (1888).
9. R. v. White and Bob, 50 DLR (2d) 613 (BCCA), aff'd (1965), 52 DLR (2d) 481 (SCC) (1964).
10. Trutch, Joseph W., "Report of the Chief Commissioner of Lands and Works to the Acting Colonial Secretary on the Lower Fraser River Indian Reserves, dated August 28, 1867," as reproduced in: British Columbia, Legislative Assembly, "Papers connected with the Indian Land Question: 1850-1875," at p. 42.
11. Mandell, Louise Q.C., "The Ghost Walks the Walk: The Illusive Recognition and Reconciliation Legislation, prepared for the 40th Anniversary of the Union of B.C. Indian Chiefs ('UBCIC'), In Gratitude for the Honour of Representing UBCIC for 32 of the 40 Years," October, 2009.

12. Ibid pp. 3-4. Also see: Mandell, Louise (2009), "the Ghost," *Aboriginal Law since Delgamuukw*, Maria Morellato, ed., Aurora: Canada Law Book, pp. 55-85,
13. For information and discussion, see the Social Science Research Council website, What is Race at: www.raceandgenomics.ssrc.org/ (accessed December 27, 2010); Graves, Joseph (2005), *The Race Myth: Why We Pretend Race Exists in America*, New York: Penguin; Lieberman, Leonard, Rodney C. Kirk, and Alice Littlefield (2003), "Perishing Paradigm: Race—1931-99," *American Anthropologist* 105; Whitmarch, Ian and David Jones, eds. (2010), *What's the Use of Race?: Modern Governance and the Biology of Difference*, Cambridge: MIT Press. For a contrary view, see Sarich, Vincent and Frank Miele (2004), *Race: The Reality of Human Differences*, Boulder: Westview Press.
14. For a discussion of policies of assimilation within the *Indian Act*, see Tobias, John (1991), "Protection, Civilization and Assimilation: An Outline History of Canada's Indian Policy," *Sweet Promises: A Reader on Indian-White Relations in Canada*, James Miller, ed., Toronto: University of Toronto Press, p. 127; Brownlie, Robert (2003), *A Fatherly Eye: Indian Agents, Government Power and Aboriginal Resistance in Ontario, 1918-1939*, Toronto: University of Toronto Press; Armitage, Andrew (1995), *Comparing the Policy of Aboriginal Assimilation: Australia, Canada, and New Zealand*, Vancouver: UBC Press.
15. Foster, Hamar (1988), "How not to draft Legislation: Indian Land Claims, Government Intransigence, and how Premier Walkem nearly sold the farm in 1874," 46 The *Advocate* 411, pp. 414-415.
16. *Indian Act* R.S.C. 1927, c. 98, s. 141.
17. Truth and Reconciliation Commission of Canada (2015), *Honouring the Truth, Reconciling for the Future: Summary of the Final Report of the Truth and Reconciliation Commission of Canada*, Winnipeg: Truth and Reconciliation Commission of Canada.
18. Napoleon, Val (2012), "Thinking About Indigenous Legal Orders," *Dialogues on Human Rights and Legal Pluralism*, eds. R. Provost and C. Sheppard, New York: Springer, pp. 3-4 ("Thinking About Indigenous Legal Orders").
19. Borrows, John (2006), "Justice Within: Indigenous Legal Traditions," Ottawa: Law Commission of Canada, p. 1 ("*Justice Within*").
20. Delgamuukw v. British Columbia, 3 SCR 1010 (1997).
21. Gisday Wa and Delgam Uukw The Spirit in the Land: The Opening Statement of the Gitksan and Wet'suwet'en Hereditary Chiefs in the Supreme Court of British Columbia, 1987-1990. Gabriola, B.C.: Reflections. (1992)
22. R. v. Morris, 2 SCR 915 (2006).
23. Mandell, Louise and Leslie Hall Pinder, (2015) "Beyond Tracking Justice: The Constitution Express to Section 35" in Louis Harder and Steve Patten (eds) *Patriation And Its Consequences*, Vancouver: UBC Press, p. 181.
24. Ibid.
25. Mandell, Louise (1984), "The Union of British Columbia Indian Chiefs Fights Patriation," *Socialist Studies: A Canadian Annual* 2, pp. 164-95
26. Mandell & Pinder, 2015, p. 196
27. *Constitution Act*, s. 35, being Schedule B to the *Canada Act* 1982 (UK), 1982, c. 11.
28. Mandell & Pinder, 2015, p. 197
29. R. v. Sparrow, 1 SCR 1075 (1990).
30. Delgamuukw v. British Columbia, 3 SCR 1010 (1997).
31. Calder v. British Columbia (Attorney General), SCR 313 (1973).

32. Courts have cautioned against regarding Indigenous Peoples being characterized as lower on the scale of social organization, see Amodu Tijani v. Secretary, Southern Nigeria, 2 AC 399 at 402-4 (JCPC) (1921).
33. Tsilhqot'in Nation v. British Columbia, SCC 44 (2014).
34. Roger William et al. v. Her Majesty the Queen in Right of British Columbia et al., BCCA 285 (2012).
35. *Tsilhqot'in Nation*, SCC 44.
36. *Chartrand v. British Columbia* (Forests, Lands and Natural Resource Operations), BCCA 345 (2015).
37. Ibid at para 1.
38. *Chartrand v. The District Manager*, BCSC 1068 at para 29 (2013).
39. Ibid; *Chartrand*, 2015 at para 10-20.
40. *Chartrand*, 2013; *Chartrand*, 2015.
41. *Tsilhqot'in Nation*, SCC 44 at para 69 [underline added].
42. *Taku River Tlingit First Nation v. British Columbia* (Project Assessment Director), SCC 74 at para 42 ("*Taku River*") (2004).
43. *Expert Mechanism Report* at para 20. Also see: *United Nations Declaration on the Rights of Indigenous Peoples*, G.A. Res. 61/295, UNGAOR, 61st Sess. Supp. No. 49, UN Doc A/RES/61/295 (2007).
44. Truth and Reconciliation Commission of Canada (2015), *Honouring the Truth, Reconciling for the Future: Summary of the Final Report of the Truth and Reconciliation Commission of Canada*, Winnipeg: Truth and Reconciliation Commission of Canada.
45. Hogan, Linda (1995), *Dwelling: A Spiritual History of the Living World*, New York: Simon and Schuster.
46. The need to tell new stories was presented by Terri-Lynn Williams-Davidson while delivering her paper "Weaving Together Our Future: The Interaction of Haida Laws to Achieve Respectful Co-Existence," at the Indigenous Legal Orders Continuing Legal Education Conference, Vancouver, BC, November 15-16, 2012; and at the Vancouver Coastal Health, Our Stories: Demonstrating Change through Storytelling Conference, Vancouver, BC, April 2007.

The Case of Invisible Racism & Disappearing Patriarchy

Helen Knott

Okay, by now ya'll have probably heard a variation of these following comments and/or arguments on any kind of topic that focuses on Indigenous issues:

"I'm sick of this. We all have equal opportunity and we need to learn to move forward together AS equals. We can't do that while everyone is focused on differences and stuck in the past. It's 2016 . . ."

"Why only women?? Why is there no focus on Native men? I'd be on board if it talked about that, too, but not when it only focuses on Native women."

And the infamous . . .

"All lives matter"

When it comes to most of the first and the last of these arguments, I just want to say that I want to believe it. I can repeat them to myself as if they are mantras or incantations, attempting to summon them for the future generations, for the young one's growing up right now, but it will not undo the stark realities in which we exist. Heck, I even hate using to word "race" because race is a social construct and not real—BUT until we get rid of racism and prejudice built on "racial differences," I can't stop using the word. I refuse to stop using it until societal and political systems no longer tolerate and perpetuate racism.

"Oh sh*t, there they go again with that Indian pity party. Like THEIR whole lives are struggle . . ." Bi***, please.

Nobody likes living with the struggles that come with being Indigenous, especially if there is a legacy of trauma and dispossession that comes with it. Everybody wants to be an Indian and experience the privileges (*yes, honey, let's be clear, there are privileges, too!*) of our culture, spirituality, and strength, but no one wants to be an Indian when it's really time to be an Indian. Most don't want to commit to rolling their sleeves up and doing the necessary healing and revolutionary work for the collective, and dismantling the oppression that comes with being an Indian. We LIVE that reality and see these "theories" of privilege, power, and oppression play out in our real lives, whether we have learned to call a spade a spade or not. Even those that have "made it to the other side" will often continue to advocate for change because they know full well the existence of racist authorities, of stereotyping leading to sexual violence, and of outright prejudice when dealing with everyday structures (banks, landlords, store owners, restaurant patrons, etc.).

If I could go on with my life and NOT have to talk about this stuff I would be good and happy. Lord, lead me to Utopia where people truly do not see in colour and people aren't oppressed and I'll write about happy sh*t and maybe pop off on some science fiction fantasy writing. We do this work out of necessity. Our voices are the indicator that change needs to happen.

We understand how legacies of colonial violence that have been predicated on racism and sexism have influenced the present-day issues contributing to the Missing and Murdered Indigenous Women epidemic. Yes, I know and we know that our brothers have been suffering, too, and YES, they need to have the issues that affect them, and us as a collective, resolved. Focusing on an issue uniquely experienced by Indigenous women is meant to highlight an issue that otherwise wouldn't be (and still struggles to be) understood for what it is without a specific lens. It has nothing to do with downplaying the pain or space our brothers or white women arise from, but it has EVERYTHING to do with bringing to light and dismantling the spaces and things that perpetuate these specific oppressions.

The comment "once Indigenous men are included then I'd be on board with this issue" really irritated me, as it was a real comment posted on a video where I spoke about the connection between violence against Indigenous women and violence against Indigenous lands. It was almost as if we haven't been living in a society moulded by the power of patriarchy alongside racism.

Although we do have pretty slogans as Indigenous people, like "Women are Sacred," or "Women are the hearts of our Nations," these are not always being followed or enacted. Women are not always being treated as sacred. Women are not always valued. Hell, I'm only 29 and I can still feel the sting of the National Indian Brotherhood collectively fighting against Indigenous women affected by Bill C-31 getting their status back. Present day, we have men in leadership positions that commit sexist acts and make comments aimed at "putting women in their place" that are allowed to continue unchecked because they "do the work of the people." So yes, honey, we are definitely going to have to raise issues separately because this is real, and UNLESS we get real about the presence of this within our own communities and organizations we ain't ever going to get anywhere. I understand the hesitancy to do so, as many within white society will utilize this acknowledgement to point the finger at us and state they never had a hand in it. Well guess what? That sh*t doesn't fly either because there is still a lot of culpability in racist and sexist institutions, biased media, and governments whose inaction makes them accessories. So yes ... Our Women. Indigenous Women's issues. Native Women's lives matter. MMIW. Violence Against Indigenous Lands and Indigenous Women.

I'm not a separatist or some folklore bra-burning feminist. I'm a goddamned realist.

Anyways, going back to invisible racism, this fellow named Pellow (see what I did there) is a professor at a university in the United States of America, and has done a lot of work surrounding the study of environmental racism and how it manifests/persists, etc. He and a group of other academics wrote the following in a paper: "Even though overtly racist attitudes and actions may be a thing of the past in public policy circles, current decisions that may seem racially neutral on their face may nevertheless have discriminatory outcomes, because of past discriminatory actions."[1]

There is so much in these few sentences that speaks to where we are as a society today. Nobody out there in power is outright saying, "screw all these Indians and their rights"; some may actually think it, and some may be against discrimination entirely, but the systems that govern are built on a foundation that exists because of racist and sexist legislation and notions. The tree ain't a new tree if its roots are still located in the dirt that helped it grow.

The refusal to acknowledge the present-day racism and oppression is the same denial that allows for it to perpetuate and continue. If you can't see something or name it then you can't change it, and who benefits from that? People at the top with the most privileges and power, while the people at the bottom continue to suffer from the blindness of a society that does not want to roll up its sleeves and get real. I'm sorry but I'm not sorry for calling a spade a spade, because I know people who live with the ramifications of the continued colonial project, exploitation of our lands, and women and/or racist systemic actions. I think the time is over when the oppressed need to apologize for the discomfort of those benefitting from colonial legacies in neo-colonial times.

When it comes to the "all lives matter" cry, I pose these questions: If "racism" and "privilege" cease to be issues, and stop being acknowledged within larger society, has it really stopped existing because some girl on twitter decided it has? #alllivesmatter #getoverit Or has it just shape-shifted and become more subtle, more acceptable, but all the while remaining palpable in the lives of the silently oppressed? Does the invisibility of racism and privilege then become a matter of convenience for white folk? Is the new battlefield now one where we have to prove that racism and inequality DO exist by measures and methods valid to white society, which needs quantitative measures of everything? (Rhetorical question on that last one, haha, it's YES).

The current system of denial and complacency is what people know. It offers comfortable familiarity. Change is scary. Action and change on matters such as these also includes being hated, disliked, and lashed out against because other people fear what poses threats to what they know and hold dear. The illusion of an equal society of equal opportunity will often be defended with, quite ironically, racism and prejudice. However, if we do not face these items head on because they are "uncomfortable," then we leave them for our children to inherit. And I don't know about you, but I've been taught that I should leave the world a better place than when I came into it.

#racismisreal #talkabouttruth #keeppushingforchange #smashpatriarchy #150issuesignored

1. Mohai, P., D. Pellow, and T. Roberts (2009), "Environmental Justice," *The Annual Review of Environment and Resources*, 34, pp. 405-430.

Adopting and Implementing the United Nations Declaration on the Rights of Indigenous Peoples
Canada's Existential Crisis

Sheryl R. Lightfoot

JUNE 2, 2015: Canada, known the world over as a bastion of democracy and human rights, was told, in no uncertain terms, that it had committed "cultural genocide" against Indigenous peoples, and must change its ways in order to achieve reconciliation. Canada was called upon to reform its governing institutions. Canada was told to alter how it relates to Indigenous peoples in law and practice. Canada was asked to abandon its system of hierarchical, racist, paternalistic, colonial control over Indigenous peoples, and form a new relationship with Indigenous peoples, grounded in mutual respect. Canada was challenged to own up to a great stain on its shiny international reputation and self-image, and explore how to live and act in an entirely new way. Canada was directed, by its own Truth and Reconciliation Commission (TRC), to adopt and implement the United Nations Declaration on the Rights of Indigenous Peoples (UNDRIP).

Yet, Canada is loath to change. Canada wants to talk about Indigenous rights and make gestures toward accepting the Declaration, all the while continuing to resist the fundamental structural changes that are necessary to adopt and implement it. This internal struggle has brought Canada to an important and difficult crossroads. For, as Canada approaches its 150th birthday, pressures are mounting to adopt and implement the Declaration while, at the same time, Canada's venerable methods of ducking and dodging questions about Indigenous rights are not only continuing but are becoming increasingly obvious to the rest of the world—and highly problematic for the Canadian reconciliation project. Simply put, reconciliation must mean more than rhetoric. Fundamental legal and structural change is required, and Canada cannot credibly proclaim its intention to shift to a new relationship with Indigenous peoples while continuing to hold tight to all the legal and governance systems that have enabled cultural genocide over the past century and a half. This is Canada's existential crisis moment.

What is the United Nations Declaration on the Rights of Indigenous Peoples?[1]

The United Nations Declaration on the Rights of Indigenous Peoples, which passed the United Nations General Assembly on September 13, 2007, represents a global consensus on the minimum standard ("the floor") for Indigenous peoples rights that all states are obligated to recognize, protect, and uphold.

The Declaration emphasizes the peoplehood of Indigenous peoples, including their right to exist, to maintain and strengthen their cultures, and to protect and enhance their own traditions and institutions. As a human rights declaration, it prohibits state discrimination against Indigenous peoples, while also recognizing their collective right to remain distinct from their surrounding societies, to pursue their own visions of development, and to promote their full and effective participation in decision-making processes on issues that impact them.

As a human rights declaration, and not an international treaty or convention, UNDRIP is technically not legally binding under either international or domestic law. However, it does join other important human rights declarations, such as the 1948 Universal Declaration of Human Rights, in articulating a global standard that states are morally and politically obligated to respect and promote. The text of UNDRIP was negotiated and drafted by states and Indigenous groups over the course of several decades, but the final text was decided on by states alone. As with all General Assembly resolutions, only states could vote on the floor of the General Assembly, and state commitments to it, votes against it, or endorsements of it, were entirely voluntary. As stated by the United Nations Permanent Forum on Indigenous Issues (UNPFII), all human rights declarations are "generally not legally binding; however, they represent the dynamic development of international legal norms and reflect the commitment of states to move in certain directions, abiding by certain principles."[2] According to a UN press release, UNDRIP represents "a major step forward towards the promotion and protection of human rights and fundamental freedoms for all ... [through] ... the General Assembly's important role in setting international standards."[3] In a separate press release, the first

UN Special Rapporteur on Indigenous issues, Rodolfo Stavenhagen, also highlighted the significance of adding Indigenous peoples rights to the international human rights consensus when he stated, "the Declaration reflects a growing international consensus concerning the rights of indigenous peoples."[4] Furthermore, as former United Nations Special Rapporteur on the Rights of Indigenous Peoples, Dr. James Anaya has stated, it is not the technical legal significance of the document that should be the focus, but rather its normative legitimacy:

> [W]hatever its legal significance, the Declaration has a significant normative weight grounded in its high degree of legitimacy. This legitimacy is a function of not only the fact that it has been formally endorsed by an overwhelming majority of UN Member States, but also the fact that it is the product of years of advocacy and struggle by indigenous peoples themselves.[5]

Since normative change in international human rights can be expected to eventually alter human rights practices by states,[6] it is important to understand what implementation of UNDRIP actually means. As Victoria Tauli-Corpuz, former chairperson of the UNPFII and current UN Special Rapporteur on the Rights of Indigenous Peoples, described, "the Declaration will become the major foundation and reference [for UN agencies, but will also serve] as the main framework to guide States."[7] Tauli-Corpuz also noted that UNDRIP is intended to serve as a "key instrument and tool for raising awareness on and monitoring progress of indigenous peoples' situations and the protection, respect and fulfilment of indigenous peoples' rights."[8]

As a standard-setting tool, the 46 articles of UNDRIP are intended to guide state action toward relationships with Indigenous Peoples; they are based on justice and also to serve as a framework for mutual recognition and respect. Because of the comprehensiveness of the articles, many states have expressed confusion and/or misgivings about how they are expected to implement UNDRIP in practice. Former UN Special Rapporteur Dr. James Anaya has offered the following concrete suggestions for initial steps toward implementation:

> First, State officials, as well as indigenous leaders, should receive training on the Declaration and the related international instruments, and on practical measure [sic] to implement the Declaration . . .
>
> Additionally, States should engage in comprehensive reviews of their existing legislation and administrative programs to identify where

they may be incompatible with the Declaration. This would include a review of all laws and programs touching upon indigenous peoples' rights and interests, including those related to natural resource development, land, education, administration of justice and other areas. On the basis of such review necessary legal and programmatic reforms should be developed and implemented, in consultation with indigenous peoples.

States should be committed to devote significant human and financial resources to the measure required to implement the Declaration. These resources will typically be required for the demarcation or return of indigenous lands, the development of culturally appropriate educational programs, support for indigenous self-governance institutions, and the many other measures contemplated by the Declaration.

The United Nations system and the international community should develop and implement programs to provide technical and financial assistance to States and indigenous peoples to move forward with these and related steps to implement the Declaration, as a matter of utmost priority.[9]

Clearly, these expectations are high for any state, but for the colonial settler-states like Canada, which were originally settled on the basis of dispossession of Indigenous peoples lands, and who have profited for years off of Indigenous resources, these expectations will translate into major changes. In fact, UNDRIP calls on these states to begin a process of resetting the entire framework of their relationship with Indigenous peoples, away from a colonial model and toward an entirely new relationship grounded in mutual respect.[10]

The Harper Government and the UN Declaration on the Rights of Indigenous Peoples

Prime Minister Stephen Harper's resistance to the Declaration was entrenched with his government, which first came to power in January 2006. Even though in the early years of UN working groups on UNDRIP (the 1980s and 1990s) Canada was a strong supporter of Indigenous rights and the draft declaration, by 2006 and 2007—the early Harper years—Canada was reported to have been the most active state lobbyist *against* UNDRIP.[11] In September 2007, when UNDRIP was presented on the floor of the UN General Assembly for a vote, Canada was one of only four countries in the world that issued a "no" vote. Standing steadfastly with Canada was the United States, Australia, and New Zealand. Immediately following passage of UNDRIP by the General Assembly (143 votes in favour),[12] individual states were offered the opportunity to explain their votes. Canada's representative to the United Nations, John McNee, delivered the explanatory statement[13] for Canada's "no" vote.

McNee noted how Canada has long demonstrated its support for the advancement of Indigenous peoples rights, both within Canada and internationally, particularly highlighting Section 35 of the Canadian Constitution, which recognizes existing Aboriginal and treaty rights. In his explanatory statement, McNee first raised Canada's objections to the negotiations behind the Declaration:

> The few modifications presented at the last minute to this Assembly, prepared by a limited number of delegations, do not arise from an open, inclusive or transparent process, and do not address key areas of concern of a number of delegations, including Canada.[14]

Ambassador McNee also noted that Canada rejected UNDRIP's provisions on land rights and natural resources on the grounds that the provisions contained in the Declaration were "overly broad, unclear, and capable of a wide variety of interpretations."[15] McNee further noted that Canada already had a variety of domestic instruments to deal with these issues, and UNDRIP could put "into question matters that have been settled by treaty."[16] According to McNee, Canada could not accept the Declaration's provisions on Free Prior Informed consent (FPIC), which are "unduly restrictive" and would enable the "establishment of a complete veto power over legislative and administrative action for a particular group,"[17] thus creating a situation that would be "fundamentally incompatible with Canada's parliamentary system."[18] It should be noted, however, that Canada's interpretation does not align with that of the Office of the United Nations High Commissioner on Human Rights, which defines FPIC as the requirement of "States to consult and cooperate in good faith with the indigenous peoples concerned through their own representative institutions in order to obtain their free, prior, and informed consent before adopting and implementing legislative or administrative measures that may affect them."[19]

Finally, Ambassador McNee highlighted the aspirational and non-binding nature of UNDRIP as reasons why Canada did not support it. He concluded his remarks: "For clarity, we also underline our understanding that this Declaration is not a binding instrument. It has no legal effect in Canada, and its provisions do not represent customary international law."[20]

Yet, several years later, on November 12, 2010, Canada quietly announced, by way of a statement that suddenly appeared on the website of Indian and Northern Affairs Canada (INAC), an official change in its position on the Declaration to "endorse." This online statement followed a brief announcement by Governor General Michaëlle Jean; in her Speech from the Throne a few months earlier, she announced that Canada was actively reconsidering its position on UNDRIP.

The November 2010 online statement was short—only six paragraphs. It stated that Canada had "formally endorsed the United Nations Declaration on the Rights of Indigenous Peoples in a manner fully consistent with Canada's Constitution and laws,"[21] despite the fact that the document is not "legally binding." Regardless, it said Canada was choosing to support the Declaration "as an important aspirational document [helping Canada take] a significant step forward in strengthening relations with Aboriginal peoples."[22] In a background statement that also appeared on INAC's website, the Harper government indicated that it still had serious concerns about land and resources rights, and FPIC; however, the Harper government was confident that it could endorse the Declaration as long as implementation of Indigenous rights could be interpreted as being in line with existing domestic law and practices. Therefore, even while claiming to endorse the document, the Harper government tightly constrained how it could be interpreted, and refused to allow it to act as a catalyst for fundamental change in Canada, holding tightly to a structural status quo position.

2012-2015: Idle No More to the NDP Victory in Alberta

Sparked by a series of new Harper government parliamentary actions that threatened Indigenous sovereignty and environmental protections, the Idle No More movement of teach-ins, rallies, and protests swept across Canada in late 2012 and early 2013. It brought national and international attention to the Harper government's problematic relationship with Indigenous peoples, including its long-standing opposition to UNDRIP. While Idle No More originally emerged in Saskatchewan as a protest movement against Bill C-45, which involved changes to the *Indian Act*[23] and the *Navigable Waters Protection Act*,[24] and set aside a number of important environmental protections, as well as Aboriginal and treaty rights, the movement quickly grew into a national and international Indigenous rights movement. Activists challenged Canada to move toward a system of government that acted in accordance with UNDRIP, especially the principal of FPIC, as well as protect treaty and Aboriginal rights and title.[25] Even with national and global scrutiny during Idle No More, the Harper government remained steadfast in its resistance to implementing any of the structural changes called for in the UN Declaration.

The first sign of governmental change in its position on UNDRIP popped up unexpectedly in Alberta in May 2015. The New Democratic Party (NDP), led by Rachel Notley, won a surprising electoral victory in the Alberta provincial election, beating the standing Progressive Conservative government—which had been in power for 45 years in Alberta[26]—in an upset victory few saw coming.

One notable element of the NDP party platform was its mention of UNDRIP as a central component of the "Strong Families, Strong Communities, Healthy Environment" theme.[27] In a subsection entitled "A Renewed Partnership with Indigenous Peoples," Section 5.21 explicitly read: "We will implement the 2007 United Nations Declaration on the Rights of Indigenous Peoples and build it into provincial law," a platform position that most certainly played a role in the increased voter turnout among Indigenous peoples in the election and support for the NDP.

By September 2015, however, Premier Notley tempered her official position on UNDRIP. In an interview with APTN, she noted that while her government had been "working furiously" in the months since taking office, implementing the UN Declaration was "not something that was going to happen overnight."[28] She particularly noted the difficulties in implementing UNDRIP's provision on FPIC surrounding natural resources and economic development. Notley stated,

> Quite honestly, we have a province that is very much driven by development and the production of our natural resources. So we're not looking at approaching this in a way that would result in economic development suddenly grinding to a halt subject to free, prior and informed consent. And quite frankly the conversations that I've had with many First Nations leaders is they don't see that that is the consequence of that.

Truth and Reconciliation Commission of Canada

On June 2, 2015, at a press conference in Ottawa, the three commissioners of Canada's TRC, Justice Murray Sinclair, Chief Wilton Littlechild, and Dr. Marie Wilson, announced the release of the TRC *Summary Report: Honouring the Truth*,

Reconciling for the Future.²⁹ This announcement concluded six years of intense and highly emotional work on the part of the TRC, which was created by the Indian Residential Schools Settlement Agreement.³⁰ The TRC was authorized to settle class action legal claims brought forward by residential school survivors. It conducted an extensive study of the century-long, church-run, and government-funded Indian residential schools program in Canada, in order to reveal the truth about the program and its legacy impacts on Indigenous peoples. At the June 2015 press conference, Justice Sinclair, the TRC chief commissioner, said, "The residential school experience is clearly one of the darkest, most troubling chapters in our collective history . . . In the period from Confederation until the decision to close residential schools was taken in this country in 1969,³¹ Canada clearly participated in a period of cultural genocide."³²

The second part of the TRC's mandate was to make recommendations on healing. It focused on how Indigenous individuals and families can heal, but also considered how to reset and renew the broken relationship between Indigenous and non-Indigenous peoples in Canada. Over the course of six years, the TRC held seven national and numerous regional events across Canada, collected tens of thousands of documents, and gathered witness statements from more than 6,000 individuals who had survived their attendance at residential schools. But, as stated in the preface to the TRC's summary report:

> shaming and pointing out wrongdoing were not the purpose of the Commission's mandate. Ultimately, the Commission's focus on truth determination was intended to lay the foundation for the important question of reconciliation. Now that we know about residential schools and their legacy, what do we do about it?³³

The summary report notes that healing the harm done to the relationship between Canada and Indigenous peoples, lasting over a century and a half, will be hard. But, reconciliation, it states, "is about establishing and maintaining a mutually respectful relationship between Aboriginal and non-Aboriginal peoples in this country."³⁴ While finding out the truth of residential schools was important, it was only the initial step in what is to be a very long process. The process of reconciliation will need to involve actions—actions that will fundamentally change behaviour at all levels of government and in all facets of society. Citing the 1996 Report of the Royal Commission on Aboriginal Peoples³⁵ as a lost opportunity for fundamental change, the TRC saw itself as a second chance to fundamentally redesign the relationship between Canada and Indigenous peoples. The TRC therefore included 94 sweeping Calls to Action as part of its report. These 94 recommendations, which were intended to form the blueprint for reconciliation into the future, call upon all layers of government—federal, provincial, territorial, and municipal—to make fundamental changes in policies and programs in order to repair the harm caused by residential schools.

In its 2012 Interim Report[36], the TRC first suggested that UNDRIP could play an important role in any reconciliation project in Canada, and suggested that this avenue be further explored. In the 2015 Summary Report, the TRC stated that it "remain(s) convinced that the *United Nations Declaration* provides the necessary principles, norms, and standards for reconciliation to flourish in twenty-first century Canada."[37] The report goes on to note that an appropriate reconciliation framework would be one where the various legal and political systems of Canada, its educational institutions, religious institutions, corporations, and civil society all operate in ways consistent with the principles of UNDRIP, which provides a guiding framework for the sweeping changes necessary for Canada to work toward respectful relationships between Indigenous and non-Indigenous peoples. As stated near the end of the report:

> Reconciliation calls for federal, provincial, and territorial government action.
>
> Reconciliation calls for national action.
>
> The way we govern ourselves must change.
>
> Laws must change.
>
> Policies and programs must change.
>
> The way we educate our children and ourselves must change.
>
> The way we do business must change.
>
> Thinking must change.
>
> The way we talk to, and about, each other must change.
>
> All Canadians must make a firm and lasting commitment to reconciliation to ensure that Canada is a country where our children and grandchildren can thrive.[38]

The TRC's Summary Report ends with 94 Calls to Action,[39] which are 94 specific recommendations that the TRC views as essential to move toward renewed relationships and, eventually, reconciliation. The 94 Calls to Action are divided into two categories: the first set, numbers 1 through 42, address "Legacy" effects of Indian Residential Schools. These include calling for changes in child welfare, education, language and culture, health and justice, to deal with significant gaps between Indigenous and non-Indigenous peoples, and other various issues that all stem, in one form or another, from policy practices, including the Indian residential schools program. The second set, numbers 43-94, chart a specific pathway toward "Reconciliation." This section begins with, "We call upon federal, provincial, territorial, and municipal governments to fully adopt and implement the *United Nations Declaration on the Rights of Indigenous Peoples* as the framework for reconciliation."[40] The very next Call to Action, number 44, calls for a national action plan and other concrete measures designed to implement UNDRIP. In total, twelve individual Calls to Action referenced the Declaration. Essentially, the TRC recommended that Canada's pathway to reconciliation should be grounded in the goals and principles of UNDRIP.

Upon its release, Prime Minister Stephen Harper icily received the TRC Summary Report. Justice Sinclair met with the Prime Minister and the Minister of Indigenous and Northern Affairs on the TRC Summary Report and 94 Calls to Action prior to the June 2, 2015 press conference. After that preliminary meeting, Sinclair reported that while the prime minister seemed "open to listening to some of our concerns and inquired about some of our recommendations," the government remained steadfast in its resistance to adoption of UNDRIP.[41]

As part of the TRC settlement agreement, Prime Minister Harper issued an apology on behalf of Canada, in the House of Commons, for the Indian residential schools program. In this apology, he recognized that "the policy of assimilation was wrong, has caused great harm, and has no place in our country."[42] Following the announcement of the 94 Calls to Action, PM Harper refused to consider adoption and implementation of UNDRIP as a framework for reconciliation in Canada. Harper instead preferred to emphasize the apology he had delivered in 2008:

> I addressed these issues some years ago in the House of Commons where I spoke about the devastation caused by a policy of Indian residential schools. This was a policy of forced assimilation that not only destroyed the lives of individuals, but of entire families and societies and it has had long-lasting implications on entire communities in this country. That is why we have moved forward with the apology and why this government has taken multiple actions over the years to improve

the lives of Aboriginal Canadians. We continue to do so. These are concrete steps that are taken.[43]

UNDRIP and the 2015 Federal Election

The UN Declaration on the Rights of Indigenous Peoples became an issue during the 2015 federal election, which was launched in mid-summer, on the heels of the June TRC announcement of 94 Calls to Action. Within weeks of the TRC announcement, Liberal Party leader Justin Trudeau addressed the Assembly of First Nations 36th Annual General Assembly in Montréal. He noted that the TRC and the 94 Calls to Action serve as:

> an especially important conversation to have as we prepare to commemorate the 150th anniversary of Confederation. We need to recognize that ours was a nation forged without the meaningful participation of Aboriginal Peoples . . .
>
> this commemoration stands as a reminder that much work remains. One hundred fifty years on, we've yet to complete the unfinished business of Confederation.[44]

Trudeau continued, stating that there is an "urgent need for a renewed relationship between the federal government and Indigenous peoples in Canada. One built on trust, recognition and respect for rights, and a commitment that the status quo must end." Railing against a paternalistic approach to Indigenous peoples and charging the Harper government with a series of failed Aboriginal policies, Trudeau promised an honourable and renewed nation-to-nation relationship, based on "recognition, rights, respect, co-operation and partnership . . . [and] rooted in the principles of the United Nations Declaration on the Rights of Indigenous Peoples." Later in the address, Trudeau specifically mentioned that the Liberal Party's response to the TRC's 94 recommendations would start with implementation of UNDRIP. The full Liberal Party platform, released shortly thereafter, used the same language.[45]

The NDP announced its Indigenous issues platform at an Assembly of First Nations open forum on First Nations issues.[46] In addition to promises of significant funding increases to First Nations communities for education, the NDP promised to respect treaty rights and inherent Aboriginal rights, "take action on the Truth and Reconciliation Commission's recommendations [and] implement the principles of the UN Declaration on the Rights of Indigenous Peoples."[47]

Fuelled by anger over Harper government policies on Indigenous peoples, including voter suppression legislation and the parliamentary actions that sparked the Idle No More movement in 2012, Indigenous peoples surged to the ballot box during the 2015 federal election, helping Justin Trudeau's Liberal Party win the election. Some Indigenous communities saw voter turnout spike more than 200 percent over the previous election.[48] Even Indigenous individuals who had previously been opposed, in principle, to participating in Canadian federal or provincial elections were so outraged by Harper policies that the mantra "anyone but Harper" brought many of them to the polls for the very first time.[49] Many Indigenous communities reported extremely long lines and some polling stations even ran out of ballots.[50] As one Aboriginal vote turnout organizer stated,

> Harper's intent was to suppress the indigenous vote and that motivated me. It just caught on. I think the excitement of getting rid of the Harper government, showing Harper that his oppression tactics weren't going to work—I think that was a huge motivator for many people who decided to step up.[51]

Likewise, Leah Gazan, Indigenous activist and professor at the University of Winnipeg, noted, Harper "was quite violent with indigenous people through aggressive cuts and aggressive legislation that aimed to silence indigenous people ... [but] as much as he attempted to divide, he really brought people ... together."[52]

Prime Minister Justin Trudeau and UNDRIP

Many Indigenous leaders greeted the election of Justin Trudeau and the Liberal Party with hope, optimism, and high expectations, while others remained cautious, especially given past Liberal Party positions on Indigenous issues, which leaned heavily toward assimilative policies. Initial moves seemed positive. The newly elected Prime Minister Justin Trudeau crafted a cabinet that included two Indigenous members, Jody Wilson-Raybould as Justice Minister, and Hunter Tootoo as Minister of Fisheries and the Canadian Coast Guard. The appointment of Carolyn Bennett, as Minister of Indigenous and Northern affairs, was also seen by many Indigenous leaders as a positive sign.[53]

The mandate letter from the newly elected Prime Minister to Carolyn Bennett, which was made public in November 2015, further fuelled high expectations on Canada's new approach to UNDRIP. The Prime Minister directed that the relationship between Aboriginal peoples and Canada must be renewed on a "nation-to-nation" basis because "No relationship is more important to me and to Canada than the one with Indigenous Peoples." In particular, the Prime Minister wrote,

> I expect you to work with your colleagues and through established legislative, regulatory, and Cabinet processes to deliver on your top priorities: To support the work of reconciliation, and continue the necessary process of truth telling and healing, work with provinces and territories, and with First Nations, the Métis Nation, and Inuit, to implement recommendations of the Truth and Reconciliation Commission, starting with the implementation of the *United Nations Declaration on the Rights of Indigenous Peoples*.[54]

A month later, in December 2015, Prime Minister Justin Trudeau addressed the Assembly of First Nations Special Chiefs Assembly, and announced his five-point plan to reset Canada's relationship with Indigenous peoples: "it is time for a renewed, nation-to-nation relationship with First Nations peoples, one that understands that the constitutionally guaranteed rights of First Nations in Canada are not an inconvenience but rather a sacred obligation."[55] Alongside promising to repeal Harper legislation, launch a national inquiry on missing and murdered Indigenous women and girls, and address education funding issues, Trudeau promised to fully implement the 94 recommendations of the TRC, including adoption and implementation of UNDRIP.

In May 2016, both Justice Minister Wilson-Raybould and Indigenous and Northern Affairs Minister Carolyn Bennett went to New York to address UNPFII. Wilson-Raybould spoke at the opening ceremony with a special statement on Canada's new position on the Declaration, the *Indian Act*, reconciliation, and FPIC. In this statement, she indicated the need for Canada to reform the ways it conducts business with Indigenous peoples, and the central role that UNDRIP should play in that re-ordering and renewal. She said:

> We need to find long-term solutions to decades old problems as we seek to deconstruct our colonial legacy. Important to this work will be implementing the Calls to Action set out in the recent report of the Truth and Reconciliation Commission which considered the legacy of the Indian residential schools.
>
> One of the significant challenges to this work is that, although strengthening the nation-to-nation relationship is the goal, practically

speaking the administration of Indigenous affairs in Canada is not actually organized around Indigenous Nations. For the most part, it is organized around an imposed system of governance. With respect to Indians this is through "bands," which are creatures of federal statute under the *Indian Act*—the *Indian Act* being the antithesis of self-government as an expression of self-determination.

Simply put, we need to move beyond the system of imposed governance...

Tied to the fundamental work of Nation rebuilding and implementing the United Nations Declaration, one of the biggest legal questions we need to unpack is how to implement the concept of "free, prior and informed consent."

The Declaration recognizes that Indigenous peoples have both individual and collective rights. Participation in real decision-making is at the heart of the Declaration's concept of free, prior and informed consent—that Indigenous peoples must be able to participate in making decisions that affect their lives.

The next day, Minister of Indigenous and Northern Affairs Carolyn Bennett addressed the first day of UNPFII deliberations. She stated unequivocally that her purpose in speaking at the forum was to address Canada's position on UNDRIP. She announced that Canada would hereafter be a "full supporter of the Declaration, without qualification."[56] Following loud applause and a standing ovation, she continued, "We intend nothing less than to adopt and implement the declaration,"[57] to which she then added some important qualifying terms—"in accordance with the Canadian Constitution"[58]—the first indication from the new government that their agenda for change in their relationship with Indigenous peoples was actually limited by existing governance structures.

Bennett continued with an explanation of the new government's position. She said, "By adopting and implementing the Declaration, we are excited that we are breathing life into Section 35 [of the Constitution] and recognizing it now as a full box of rights for Indigenous peoples in Canada." Next, she said that the new Canadian government believes that its existing Constitutional obligations already fulfill the principles of UNDRIP, including the important but controversial principle of FPIC. Further, she noted, in an important pivotal shift in the new government's rhetoric, "We see modern treaties and self-government agreements as

[Handwritten at top: Wilson-Raybould vs. Bennett's comments]

the ultimate expression of free, prior and informed consent among partners."[59] In other words, Bennett's statement, in stark contrast to Wilson-Raybould's the day before, indicated that the new government is actually quite satisfied that Canada's existing constitutional, legal, and policy positions are already in line with the principles of UNDRIP, and no fundamental structural change is needed.

Only six weeks later, Justice Minister Wilson-Raybould addressed the Assembly of First Nations at their Annual General Assembly in Niagara Falls to discuss the hard work that lay ahead for Canada and First Nations, to rebuild and transform their relationship into one that better reflects the inherent self-determination of Indigenous peoples.[60] She intended to set out a course of action of "transformative change" that would turn all of the "good words" and "good will" into "meaningful progress." As she did several weeks earlier at the United Nations, Wilson-Raybould took aim at the *Indian Act* as a legacy of colonial administration, and one of the major elements of current governance that is "fundamentally inconsistent with the United Nations Declaration"[61] and require change. Referring to whole-scale adoption of UNDRIP into Canadian law as "unworkable" and a "simplistic approach," she rather urged a cautious, thoughtful, controlled and deliberate "process of transition" to finding alternatives to the *Indian Act*. She said, "the way the UNDRIP will get implemented in Canada will be through a mixture of legislation, policy and action initiated and taken by Indigenous nations themselves." However, she also noted that "ultimately, the UNDRIP will be articulated through the constitutional framework of section 35." In other words, while certain policy changes can be expected to proceed slowly, no fundamental constitutional change is planned, anticipated, or seemingly desirable.

[Handwritten: UNDRIP through the constitution! WHAT!]

Canada's Existential Crisis

As it approaches its 150th birthday, Canada stands at a crossroads with respect to Indigenous rights, caught between competing impulses in an existential crisis of its own making. On the one hand, Canada, especially its newly elected Liberal Party and prime minister, wish to respond to the 94 recommendations of the TRC, and set out on a new course with a renewed relationship with Indigenous peoples based on UNDRIP. On the other hand, Canada recognizes just how wide sweeping such change would ultimately entail. This visionary government has yet to develop any viable national plan to make changes, ultimately because

[Handwritten: Crossroads]

the transformations required by the TRC and UNDRIP will, in short, challenge the very foundations of the Canadian state. Unquestionably, Canada is a nation that was built upon the dispossession of Indigenous lands and colonial rule over Indigenous people. Unsurprisingly, the Canadian state has not yet grappled with how to relate to Indigenous peoples, lands, and resources in a fair, just, and enlightened way. Under UNDRIP, the history of Canadian dispossession of Indigenous peoples can no longer be considered legitimate, and colonial administration, or "rule over" Indigenous peoples by such statues as the *Indian Act*, are no longer viable, and Indigenous self-determination, including FPIC, must be respected on an equal basis with the rights of all other peoples in Canada. The TRC and the Declaration have both called for nothing short of full-scale and fundamental change of all existing systems, beginning with Canada's laws, policies, programs, and full systems of governance.

Truly accepting and respecting Indigenous rights would be a bold form of transformational politics. While many questions remain, and the pragmatic details of implementing Indigenous rights have yet to be worked out, especially on self-determination and FPIC, these changes would ultimately lead to a more peaceful, just, and democratic future. There is no doubt that the cost of implementing Indigenous rights is high, but, in a global atmosphere where Indigenous peoples are increasingly asserting their rights, the costs of NOT implementing Indigenous rights are also extremely high and include such intangibles as Canada continuing to compromise its core values of fairness, equality, and human rights. Adopting and implementing UNDRIP would invariably serve to decrease the level of conflict and potential future conflict between Canada and Indigenous peoples. Moreover, the gains of establishing such a fair and just relationship with Indigenous peoples will accrue to both sides.

Canada stands at a juncture of two diametrically opposed directions. It continues to promise to adopt and implement Indigenous rights, while simultaneously resisting the necessary structural change to do so. One of these impulses must eventually give way to the other. The inconsistencies, incongruities, and the moral double bind are becoming too obvious to ignore, and this pattern of deflection is no longer so easy in the social media world. In order to move forward, Canada must ultimately accept the legal and moral legitimacy of Indigenous rights, and then after conducting a deep internal examination, make the requisite changes to law, policy, and institutions. To continue to perpetually duck and dodge Indigenous rights in favour of continued non-democratic institutions that compromise its core values will inevitably perpetuate conflict with Indigenous peoples. There are no other options. Critics of the current Canadian government have noted its crisis moment, exposing a "troubling gap between Trudeau's lofty talk and his government's actions."[62] Citing the government's "incoherent half-embrace of the United Nations Declaration on the Rights of Indigenous Peoples," a *Toronto Star* editorial noted a dearth of practical difference between the Trudeau and Harper governments, in terms of actual policy and programs, particularly on issues related to natural resource development projects.[63] As Canada approaches its 150th birthday, the time has arrived for it to deal with its existential crisis and choose its ultimate path: status quo or fundamental transformation.

1. Portions of the section were previously published in Lightfoot, Sheryl (2016), *Global Indigenous Politics: A Subtle Revolution*, Abingdon, Oxon: Routledge, pp. 97-98.
2. United Nations Permanent Forum on Indigenous Issues, *Frequently Asked Questions— Declaration on the Rights of Indigenous Peoples*, New York, 2007.
3. United Nations General Assembly, "General Assembly Adopts Declaration on the Rights of Indigenous Peoples," news release, September 13, 2007.
4. United Nations, :Adoption of Declaration on Rights of Indigenous Peoples a Historic Moment for Human Rights, UN Expert Says," September 14, 2007.
5. Anaya, James S., "Statement by James Anaya, Special Rapporteur on the Rights of Indigenous Peoples on the Obligations of States to Implement the Declaration on the Rights of Indigenous Peoples" (speech), United Nations, New York, October 18, 2010.
6. Risse, Thomas, Stephen C. Ropp, and Kathryn Sikkink, eds. (1999), *The Power of Human Rights: International Norms and Domestic Change*, Cambridge: Cambridge University Press.
7. Tauli-Corpuz, Victoria, "Message of Victoria Tauli-Corpuz, Chairperson of the UN Permanent Forum on Indigenous Issues, on the Occasion of the Adoption by the General Assembly of the Declaration on the Rights of Indigenous Peoples" (speech), United Nations, New York, September 13, 2007.
8. Ibid.
9. Anaya, 2010.
10. Lightfoot, Sheryl (2010), "Emerging International Indigenous Rights Norms and 'Over-Compliance' in New Zealand and Canada," *Political Science* (Sage) 62, p. 84.
11. Continuing Legal Education Society of British Columbia (2008), *Aboriginal Law Conference 2008, Paper 2.1: United Nations Declaration on the Rights of Indigenous Peoples*, Vancouver, British Columbia.
12. United Nations General Assembly. *Press Release: General Assembly Adopts Declaration on the Rights of Indigenous Peoples*, September 13, 2007.
13. McNee, John (2007), *Statement by Ambassador McNee to the General Assembly on the Declaration on the Rights of Indigenous Peoples*, 13 September 2007, New York: United Nations.
14. Ibid.
15. Ibid.
16. Ibid.
17. Ibid.

18. Ibid.
19. Office of the High Commissioner on Human Rights (2013), *Information Sheet: Free, Prior and Informed Consent*, Geneva.
20. Ibid.
21. Indian and Northern Affairs Canada, "Canada Endorses the United Nations Declaration on the Rights of Indigenous Peoples," accessed January 10, 2011: www.ainc-inac.gc.ca/ai/mr/nr/s-d2010/23429-eng.asp
22. Ibid.
23. *Indian Act*, RSC 1895, c I-5.
24. *Navigable Waters Protection Act*, RSC, 1985, c N-22 à became: *Navigation Protection Act*, RSC, 1985, c N-22.
25. "Calls for Change," Idle No More, last accessed November 11, 2016: www.idlenomore.ca/calls_for_change
26. "Alberta PCs win historic 12th straight majority," *CTV News*, April 24, 2012, accessed November 11, 2016: www.ctvnews.ca/alberta-pcs-win-historic-12th-straight-majority-1.799835
27. Alberta's New Democratic Party, "Leadership for What Matters," April 2015, accessed November 12, 2016: www.poltext.org/sites/poltext.org/files/plateformes/alberta_ndp_platform_2015.pdf
28. Morin, Brandi, "'It's not something that is going to happen overnight.' Alberta premier asks Indigenous peoples to be patient while government works on promises." *APTN National News*, September 15, 2015, accessed November 12, 2016: www.aptn.ca/news/2015/09/15/its-not-something-that-happens-overnight-alberta-premier-asks-indigenous-peoples-to-be-patient-while-government-works-on-promises/
29. Truth and Reconciliation Commission of Canada (2015), *Honouring the Truth, Reconciling for the Future: Summary of the Final Report of the Truth and Reconciliation Commission of Canada*, Winnipeg: Truth and Reconciliation Commission of Canada, accessed November 1, 2016: http://nctr.ca/assets/reports/Final%20Reports/Executive_Summary_English_Web.pdf
30. Indian Residential Schools Settlement Agreement, May 8, 2006, accessed November 1, 2016: www.residentialschoolsettlement.ca/IRS%20Settlement%20Agreement-%20ENGLISH.pdf
31. Even though the decision to begin closing the schools was made in 1969, the last school did not close until 1996.
32. The Canadian Press, "Commission offers 94 ways to redress 'cultural genocide,'" *Maclean's*, June 2, 2015, accessed November 1, 2016: www.macleans.ca/news/canada/trc-offers-94-ways-to-redress-cultural-genocide/
33. Truth and Reconciliation Commission, 2015, p. vi.
34. Ibid., p. 6.
35. Royal Commission on Aboriginal Peoples (1996), *Report of the Royal Commission on Aboriginal Peoples*, Ottawa, accessed November 1, 2016: www.collectionscanada.gc.ca/webarchives/20071115053257/http://www.ainc-inac.gc.ca/ch/rcap/sg/sgmm_e.html
36. Truth and Reconciliation Commission of Canada (2012), *Truth and Reconciliation Commission: Interim Report*, Winnipeg: Truth and Reconciliation Commission of Canada, accessed November 1, 2016: www.myrobust.com/websites/trcinstitution/File/Interim%20report%20English%20electronic.pdf
37. Truth and Reconciliation Commission, 2015, p. 21.
38. Ibid., pp. 316-317.
39. Ibid., pp. 319-337.
40. Ibid., p. 325.

41. Fedio, Chloe, "Truth and Reconciliation report brings calls for actions, not words," *CBC News*, June 2, 2015, accessed November 1, 2016: www.cbc.ca/news/politics/truth-and-reconciliation-report-brings-calls-for-action-not-words-1.3096863
42. Prime Minister Stephen Harper, *Statement of Apology to former students of Indian Residential Schools*, June 11, 2008, accessed November 1, 2016: www.aadnc-aandc.gc.ca/eng/1100100015644/1100100015649
43. "PM Harper won't implement TRC recommendation on UN Declaration on Indigenous Peoples," *APTN National News*, June 2, 2015, accessed November 1, 2016: www.aptn.ca/news/2015/06/02/pm-harper-wont-implement-trc-recommendation-un-declaration-indigenous-peoples/
44. Trudeau, Justin, "Real Change: Restoring Fairness to Canada's Relationship with Aboriginal Peoples: Justin Trudeau's Remarks at the Assembly of First Nations General Assembly," July 7, 2015, accessed November 24, 2016: www.liberal.ca/justin-trudeau-at-assembly-of-first-nations-36th-annual-general-assembly/
45. Liberal Party, "Real Change," accessed November 24, 2016: www.liberal.ca/realchange/truth-and-reconciliation-2/
46. "NDP government would apply UNDRIP, invest $1.8 million in First Nation education," *APTN National News*, accessed November 24, 2016: www.aptn.ca/news/2015/10/07/ndp-government-would-apply-undrip-invest-1-8-billion-in-first-nation-education/
47. New Democratic Party, "Building the Country of our Dreams: Tom Mulcair's Plan to Bring Change to Ottawa," p. 36.
48. Puxley, Chinta, "Anger at Stephen Harper, disenfranchisement fuelled turnout of Aboriginal voters," *Canadian Press*, October 25, 2015, last accessed November 24, 2016: www.nationalobserver.com/2015/10/25/news/anger-stephen-harper-disenfranchisement-fuelled-turnout-aboriginal-voters
49. Ayers, Tom, "N.S. First Nations Group Suggests Voting for Anyone But Harper," *Herald News*, June 22, 2015, accessed November 25, 2016: www.thechronicleherald.ca/novascotia/1300839-n.s.-first-nations-group-suggests-voting-for-anyone-but-harper
50. Baum, Kathryn Blaze, "On-Reserve Voters Endure Lines and Ballot Issues for Historic Election," *Globe and Mail*, October 20, 2015, accessed November 25, 2016: www.theglobeandmail.com/news/politics/some-first-nations-polling-stations-run-out-of-ballots-amid-high-turnout/article26899907/
51. Puxley, 2015.
52. Ibid.
53. Wilson, Tiar, "Hopeful Indigenous Reaction to Justin Trudeau's Cabinet Picks," *CBC News*, November 4, 2015, accessed November 25, 2016: www.cbc.ca/news/indigenous/aboriginal-leaders-react-cabinet-choices-1.3303972
54. Trudeau, Justin, "Minister of Indigenous and Northern Affairs Mandate Letter," November 13, 2015, accessed November 25, 2016: http://pm.gc.ca/eng/minister-indigenous-and-northern-affairs-mandate-letter
55. Mas, Susana, "Trudeau Lays Out Plan for New Relationship with Indigenous Peoples," *CBC News*, December 8, 2015, accessed November 25, 2016: www.cbc.ca/news/politics/justin-trudeau-afn-indigenous-aboriginal-people-1.3354747
56. Bennett, Carolyn, Minister of Indigenous and Northern Affairs Canada, "Announcement of Canada's Support for the United Nations Declaration on the Rights of Indigenous Peoples," United Nations Permanent Forum on Indigenous Issues, New York, May 10, 2016.
57. Ibid.

58. Ibid.
59. Ibid.
60. Wilson-Raybould, Jody, Minister of Justice and Attorney General, "Address to Assembly of First Nations," Niagara Falls, July 16, 2016.
61. Ibid.
62. "For Indigenous Reconciliation, Words are Not Enough: Editorial," *Toronto Star*, November 25, 2016, accessed November 25, 2016: www.thestar.com/opinion/editorials/2016/11/25/for-indigenous-reconciliation-words-are-not-enough-editorial.html
63. Ibid.

Indigenous People Are Not the "Ghosts of History"

By honouring treaties and the rights they bestow, Canada can go a long way toward restoring pride, respect, and dignity to Indigenous people

Leonard Flett with Nicole Letourneau[1]

Canadian Indigenous people have been described as "ghosts of history, spectres lingering in the background, haunting our legacy." Indigenous people have been ignored to a great extent in Canadian history; yet Canadians are fully aware that Indigenous people were here long before the arrival of the Europeans. Canadians are also generally aware that Indigenous people were mistreated over time. Their lands and culture were stripped away through questionable means leaving generations traumatized.

For many Canadians, ignorance is bliss—it has been easier on the conscience to just ignore this unpleasant chapter in Canadian history and pretend that displacement, oppression, and trauma of Indigenous people never happened.

In the short run, ignoring this history might make it easier for Canadians to have pride in being Canadian. But, in the long run, ignoring this history, rather than facing it head on, has costs. It weighs heavily on the Canadian psyche.

The eclipse of the Indigenous people by the English and French settlers by the time of Confederation has left present-day Canada floundering with its identity—and even affects us on the world stage. Canada's attempts to be a leader on the world stage as a champion of human rights are often ridiculed by its enigmatic treatment of its Indigenous population.

In 2014, a United Nations report showed that, of the bottom 100 communities in Canada on the Community Well-Being Index, 96 were Indigenous communities. In 2015, the Conference Board of Canada ranked 117 health regions in Canada and found that Indigenous communities were at the bottom, mostly affected by social problems affecting health. That's the impact of systematically undervaluing a whole group of people. That's trauma in real life.

But history also shows us how important Indigenous people were to the founding of Canada. Philosopher and writer John Ralston Saul argues that Canadian identity extends beyond the French and English, and actually rests on a triangular foundation that includes Indigenous peoples. Early exploration and settlement by the French and English would not have been possible without the assistance of Indigenous people.

Indigenous people taught the rest how to exist on the land. Indigenous participation in the fur trade enabled the establishment of the first major economic activity in this country.

Solutions and newfound pride in the Canadian identity can be found by looking honestly at, and responding appropriately to, the lessons of history. The social problems facing many Indigenous people because of intergenerational trauma are large. But the Indigenous population is the youngest demographic group in Canada. That means we can support change in a large generation of young people that could cascade forward into generations to come.

If we ignore the problems, the trauma will grow exponentially. If we address the problems, the healing will grow exponentially.

So what are the solutions?

Many come under the reconsideration of treaties. Rather than keep our treaties hidden under a cloak of shame, we should acknowledge and celebrate them with pride, by focusing on and emphasizing their original intent: *an agreement between peoples about the peaceful sharing of lands in exchange for security—security from hunger, security from disease, security from obsolescence.*

In addition, many treaties promised schools on reserves, including the adhesion to Treaty 9, signed by Chief Samson Beardy, my grandfather, on behalf of his people in Northern Ontario in 1929. I do not think he intended that our children be abused in Indian residential schools, nor do I think he intended that our schools be funded at levels lower than schools in non-Indigenous communities.

Recognizing the value of Indigenous people, inherent in the intent of treaties, as agreements between two peoples, will reduce the societal push for assimilation. If you value someone, you don't see a need to assimilate that person. Indigenous people have always resisted being absorbed into the larger society through forced assimilation. Chief Sitting Bull once said, "If the Great Spirit had desired me to be a white man, He would have made me so in the first place."

Indigenous people should not be written off derisively as a stone-age people who couldn't develop the wheel, as opined by Conrad Black and others. In fact, Canada is criss-crossed by numerous rivers and lakes that were in summer traversed by light, efficient, birch bark canoes piloted by Indigenous people, and by voyageurs after the Europeans arrived. In winter, snowshoes and toboggans were the only modes of transport over the deep snow. The wheel was useless during this period.

Valuing Indigenous people also means that we are compelled to help them.

Only a handful of reserves, the lucky few adjacent to mainstream markets, have reached standards equivalent to the rest of society. Canada needs to pay attention to the Shamattawa and Attawapiskat of this country, which are plagued by suicides, drugs, and alcohol, amongst other issues. Forced relocation is not an option, although valuing people by enabling them to relocate if they want to, with government assistance, should be available.

Economic corridors linking isolated communities to the nearest regional centres need to be negotiated—because jobs are lifelines to human purpose. Any new resource developments in these areas must include some ownership by the communities. Most importantly, treaty rights need to be portable, no longer used to restrict and confine Indigenous people within the boundaries of their designated reserves.

These are only starting points. But Indigenous people need to be recognized as a people who once had independence, territory, communities, governance, trade, culture, traditions, and spirituality.

Rather than focusing on the shameful outcomes, recognizing and acting upon the original intentions of treaties will go a long way toward restoring pride, respect, and dignity to Indigenous peoples. We can help Indigenous peoples assume their rightful place as one of the three pillars in Canada's foundation.

Together we can bring Indigenous people out of the shadows—they will cease to be ghosts of history and can assume their rightful place as valued citizens of Canada.

1. This article was based on a keynote speech delivered by Leonard Flett at the Indigenous Healing and Trauma conference in Calgary.

Editors and Contributors

KIERA L. LADNER is an Associate Professor in the Department of Political Studies at the University of Manitoba and the former Canada Research Chair in Indigenous Politics and Governance. She does research on treaties, Indigenous constitutional law & politics (in Canada Australia and New Zealand), Indigenous political thought, federalism, Indigenist methodology, Murdered and Missing Indigenous Women and gender diversity. She is particularly interested in issues of decolonization and resurgence. In 2010 she edited a collection with Leanne Betasamosake Simpson entitled *This is an Honour Song: Twenty Years Since the Blockades* (ARP Books). In 2011 she launched Mamawipawin or the Indigenous Governance and Community Based Research Space at the University of Manitoba. Kiera's current projects include: the comparative constitutional law and Indigenous politics project which she works on with Myra Tait examining Indigenous constitutional visions and state responses in Australia and New Zealand; and, the Digital Archives and Marginalized Communities project with Dr. Shawna Ferris which is a community centred digital archives project consisting of three archives—the Sex Work Database, the Missing and Murdered Indigenous Women Database, and the Post-apology Indian Residential School Database.

MYRA J. TAIT is Anishinaabe, and a member of Berens River First Nation. She holds a law degree from the University of Manitoba, and has just completed her Master in Laws (2017). Myra's LLM thesis considers taxation provisions of the *Indian Act* and their relationship to the implementation of Canada's Numbered Treaties. Myra's work with the Comparative Indigenous Constitutional Politics Project at Mamawipawin has included field research in New Zealand and Australia, to meet with Indigenous community members, lawyers, and academics, and at home, bringing a legal perspective to the project.

Biographies of contributors in this collection can be found on the ARP Books website at www.arpbooks.org.

other nations. This article restricts self-determination for the sake of maintaining settler-state territorial integrity.

8. Corntassel and Bryce, 2012, p. 152.
9. Pitty, Roderic (2015), "Restoring Indigenous Self-Determination Through Relational Autonomy and Transnational Mediation," *Restoring Indigenous Self-Determination: Theoretical and Practical Approaches*, ed. Marc Woons, Bristol: E-International Relations Publishing, p. 68.
10. In May 2016, Indigenous and Northern Affairs Minister Carolyn Bennet boasted of the Canadian government's respect of Indigenous rights, specifically referencing the ongoing modern treaty processes such as the BC Treaty Commission. This statement was made in conjunction with a statement on Canada's commitment to full implementation of UNDRIP, which suggests that Canada views its current commitments as fulfilling UNDRIP, as well as representing true self-determination.
11. De Brito, Alexandra (2001), "Introduction," *The Politics of Memory*. Oxford: Oxford University Press, p. 10.
12. Coulthard, 2014, p. 106.
13. Tuck, Eve and K. Wayne Yang (2012), "Decolonization is Not A Metaphor," *Decolonization: Indigeneity, Education & Society* 1.1.
14. Llewellyn, Jennifer and Daniel Philpot (2014), "Restorative Justice and Reconciliation: Twin Frameworks for Peacebuilding," *Restorative Justice, Reconciliation and Peacebuilding*, eds. Jennifer Llewellyn and Daniel Philpot, Oxford: Oxford University Press, p. 17.
15. Woolford, Andrew (2015), *This Benevolent Experiment: Indigenous Boarding Schools, Genocide, and Redress in Canada and the United States*, Winnipeg: University of Manitoba Press, p. 287.
16. Alfred, Taiaike and Jeff Corntassel (2005), "Being Indigenous: Resurgences against Contemporary Colonialism," *Government and Opposition* 40.4, p. 601.
17. Ibid.
18. Stanton, Kim (2011), "Canada's Truth and Reconciliation Commission: Settling the Past?" *The International Indigenous Policy Journal* 2.3, p. 11.
19. James, Matt (2012), "A Carnival of Truth? Knowledge, Ignorance and the Canadian Truth and Reconciliation Commission," *The International Journal of Transitional Justice* 6, p. 189.
20. Nagy, Rosemary and Emily Gillespie (2015), "Representing Reconciliation: A news frame analysis of media coverage of Indian residential schools," *Transitional Justice Review* 1.3, pp. 36–37.
21. Truth and Reconciliation Commission of Canada (2015), *Canada's Residential Schools: Reconciliation* vol. 6, Montreal: McGill-Queens University Press, p. 255.
22. Lightfoot, Sheryl (2016), *Global Indigenous Politics: A Subtle Revolution*, New York: Routledge Press, pp. 180–181.
23. Truth and Reconciliation Commission of Canada, p. 211.
24. Ibid, p. 219.
25. Corntassel and Bryce, 2012, p. 152.
26. Truth and Reconciliation Commission of Canada, p. 207.
27. Coulthard, 2014, p. 8.
28. Glen Coulthard conceptualizes *grounded normativities* as the "modalities of Indigenous land-connected practices and longstanding experiential knowledge that inform and structure our ethical engagements with the world and our relationships with human and nonhuman others over time."
29. Corntassel, Jeff and Cindy Holder (2008), "Who's Sorry Now? Government Apologies, Truth Commissions, and Indigenous Self-Determination in Australia, Canada, Guatemala and Peru," *Human Rights Review* 9.4, p. 472.

30. Lightfoot, 2016.
31. Stark, Heidi Kiiwetinepinesiik (2010), "Respect, Responsibility, and Renewal: The Foundations of Anishinaabe Treaty Making with the United States and Canada," *American Indian Culture and Research Journal* 34.2.
32. Coburn, Elaine (2015), "Indigenous Resistance and Resurgence," *More Will Sing Their Way To Freedom*, ed. Elaine Coburn, Halifax: Fernwood Publishing.
33. Aguirre, Kelly (2015), "Telling Stories: Idle No More, Indigenous Resurgence and Political Theory," *More Will Sing Their Way To Freedom*, ed. Elaine Coburn, Halifax: Fernwood Publishing, p. 185.
34. Wallace, Rick (2013), *Merging Fires: Grassroots Peacebuilding Between Indigenous and Non-Indigenous Peoples*, Nova Scotia: Fernwood Publishing.
35. Barker, Adam (2010), "From Adversaries to Allies: Forging Respectful Alliances Between Indigenous and Settler Peoples," *Alliances: Re/Envisioning Indigenous-non-Indigenous Relationships*, ed. Lynne Davis Toronto: University of Toronto Press, p. 322.
36. Regan, Paulette (2011), *Unsettling the Settler Within*, Vancouver: University of British Columbia Press.
37. Corntassel, Jeff (2012), "Re-envisioning Resurgence: Indigenous Pathways to Decolonization and Sustainable Self-Determination," *Decolonization: Indigeneity, Education & Society* 1.1, p. 88.
38. Ibid., p. 89.
39. gkisedtanamoogk (2010), "Finding Our Way Despite Modernity," *Alliances: Re/Envisioning Indigenous-non-Indigenous Relationships*, ed. Lynne Davis, Toronto: University of Toronto Press, p. 44.